An Analytical Study of the Yamaka from Abhidhamma, Volume II

The sixth book of Abhidhamma Piṭaka

P. B. Tan

An Analytical Study of the Yamaka from Abhidhamma, Volume II
: The sixth book of Abhidhamma Piṭaka

Copyright © 2018 by P.B. Tan

First Printing: June, 2018

Published by CreateSpace

All Rights Reserved. No part of this book may be reproduced, stored in a retrieval system, or transmitted in the modes of electronic copy, photocopying, reproducing, or used in any manner whatsoever without the prior written permission of the author and publisher except for the use of brief quotations in a book review or scholarly journals.

ISBN: 978-1721628865 (paperback)

DEDICATED TO

all sentient beings,

living and dead.

Table of Contents

Abbreviations used

AN	Aṅguttara-Nikāya
CTS4	Chaṭṭha Saṅgāyana Tipiṭaka 4
Cnd	Cūḷaniddesa
Dhs	Dhammasaṅgaṇi
DN	Dīgha-Nikāya
KN	Khuddaka-Nikāya
Kv	Kathāvatthu
MN	Majjhima-Nikāya
Pug	Puggalapaññatti
PañkA	Pañcappakaraṇa-Aṭṭhakathā
SN	Saṃyutta-Nikāya
Vibh	Vibhaṅga
Vis.M	Visuddhimagga

Preface

This analytical book of the Yamaka, Chapter Six to Ten of Volume II, is based on reference sources from the Yamakapāli text in Chaṭṭha Saṅgāyana Tipiṭaka (CTS 4.0), and from the English translation copy by Ven. Isi Nandamedhā in 2011, with its last chapter translated by Ven. U Kumārābhivaṁsa in 2012. My work in Volume II in general will follow the topical outline and order of the Pāli text, and go along with the English rendering of meanings by Ven. Isi Nandamedhā and Ven. U Kumārābhivaṁsa, so as to be in unison with both the Yamakapāli scripture and the reverent authors. For exceptional cases, I may not be following exactly a word-for-word translation from Pāli text, or may not be concordant with the rendered definitions, but to give additional meanings or a second explanation. It is in order to be more inclusive in explanation in the same context for better understanding. Another reason is because I am undertaking an analytical approach in the study of Yamaka, and endeavour to liven up this indeed a difficult book with a better way for people to study. If I may be right, the unwieldy heftiness and unpopularity of the book of Yamaka is making it another least read Abhidhamma literature after the Dhātukathā.

What is it exactly why so many people are rejecting Abhidhamma literatures as dull and dreary, even as not words of the Buddha? Unlike the teaching in suttas which are discourses told by the Buddha to suit the desires and levels of intellectuality of the different audiences, the Abhidhamma, on the other hand, is concerned with minute detail of well-analysed knowledge of the Suttanta teaching and clarification of philological definitions. Because the use of catechetical dialogues with questions and answers is typical of the Abhidhamma evaluative methods, it is common to see the same question or the same answer keeps repeating in many different places. This is the apparent reason which appears to readers that the Abhidhamma literatures are somehow superfluous, and at the same time, tautologous. For example, in the Dhammasaṅgaṇi, the question '*katame dhammā kusalā*' or 'which are the states that are wholesome?', has been asked 146 times in the various sections but understandably with different answers. In Chapter 6 of the Yamaka, for example, the answer '*vinā assāsapassāsehi cittassa uppādakkhaṇe*' or 'at the arising moment of consciousness without breath-in and breath-out', has been the answer given 35 times but from different questions. Almost all the ten chapters of the Yamaka make use of the same diagnostic technique by pairing of catechisms through a direct and regressive mode of enquiries, building into a core section on the process of origination and cessation of phenomenal states. The process loops through three classifications (individuals, planes, and individuals at planes) in dual groupings of positive and negative formulations of enquiries. There are both affirmative and negative answers provided to each question. In many cases, the same No and Yes answers (or either way) to the questions in the positive formulation, also repeats in the negative formulation of enquiries. Besides, there are also answers which overlap between those dialogues regarding the first classification by 'individuals' and the third classification of 'individuals at planes'. Superfluity and repetition in this sense can not be avoided unless the Abhidhamma literature is not using catechetic method. Let me demonstrate with a simple example. You are now happy with A, but not happy with B; or that you are happy with B, but not happy with A. In other times, you are either happy or unhappy with both of them. Let's talk about also during last year and next year, and the same process with B. The two came up with different reasons. There would certainly be reasons that overlap because of the common sharing of functions and responsibilities, and the way questions are paired and formulated with only affirmative and negative answers. Nonetheless, superfluity and repetition have been reduced to some extent in Chapter 7 which makes use of mixed pairing in the pattern of 1-1. 2-1, 3-1, 4-1, 5-1, 6-1. Whether it is single pairs or mixed pairings, we know that its utter thoroughness is the only sure way to investigate all the discernable elements of certain cognisable phenomena without having any remaining doubt. Nonetheless, those logical iterations and repetitions encompassed in the text can only makes possible the preparation of tables and charts which can be used to demonstrate the complex psycho-physical phenomena and the flow of process sequence in a more organised way, and more comprehensible to some people. The information in the charts, representing summarised questions and answers at scale with measures, will save the readers the trouble and inconvenience of having to flip through the pages all the time in order to refer to similar answers in all different places in any one chapter.

Much in the same purpose as in the theoretical foundation underlying the first five topics being examined in Volume I of the Yamaka (roots, matters and feeling-perception aggregates, twelve bases, eighteen elements, and noble truths), the discussion of the next five topics in Volume II are also built on the framework of theories (material and mental formations, latent proclivities, states of consciousness, *dhammā*, and twenty-two faculties). The book of Yamaka is not to be taken as self-sufficiency for the development and accomplishment of the ultimate goal of the Buddhist teachings. The book of Yamaka forms the sound theoretical underpinning essential for insight meditation (*vipassana*) which encompasses the subject matters of the four applications of mindfulness (*Satipaṭṭhāna*), four supreme efforts (*Cattāro sammappadhānā*), four means to accomplishment (*Iddhipāda*), five faculties (*Pañc' indriyāni*), five powers (*Pañca balāni*), seven factors of enlightenment (*Satta bojjhangā*), and noble eightfold path (*Ariyāṭṭhangikamagga*). These practical aspects of the subjects constitute the thirty-seven requisites of enlightenment referred to as *Bodhipakkhiyadhammā*. The ten chapters of the Yamaka, as well as the book of Dhātukathā, are the perfect supplements to insight practical. The empirical knowledge and personal attestation experienced through daily practices in turn reinforce and bolster the practitioner's understanding and confidence in the theoretical tenets of the classic Abhidhamma literatures. My work in Volume II does not differ from the approach used in the first Volume in terms of its contents layout and the use of graphical presentations, so that the two volumes do not fall out of line incongruously.

Chapter 6 of Volume II deals with the three types of formation (*saṅkhāra*) — bodily formation (*kāyasaṅkhāro*), verbal formation (*vacīsaṅkhāro*), and mental formation (*cittasaṅkhāro*). By following the similar methodology as used in all preceding chapters, Chapter 6 examines the subject by using dichotomised pairs of catechisms, going through the complete iterative loop of enquiries by following the forward (or positive) and opposite (or negative) method of enquiring. This pattern of diagnosing using paired catechisms which run through forward and opposite evaluative logic, is incorporated into three divisions for complete analysis.

The first division makes use of three methods to deal with the clarification of terms with respect to the three formation types — the purification of words (i.e. through clarifying word by word in order to bring them to the pure or original intent of the meanings), ascertaining the root of (*dhamma*) wheel based on aforementioned step of word-by-word clarification, and thirdly, analysing the "pure" formations consequent of the antecedent clarified and cleansed process. The second division uses threefold classifications to examine the processes of arising, cessation, arising-and-cessation of the three types of formation. The third division examines the comprehension (*pariññā*) aspect of individuals with regard to the three formation types.

Chapter 7 examines seven kinds of latent states (*anusayā*) of a person's inclining predisposition. In essence, these seven latencies represent a condensed version of the ten fetters of defilement (*saṃyojanāni*) in which restlessness (*uddhacca*) is subsumed as under ignorance (*avijjā*), desire for the fine-material and immaterial phenomenal existences (*rūparāga* and *arūparāga*) are treated as under lust for existence (*bhavarāga*), and individualistic view of identity and ritual observances (*sakkāyadiṭṭhi* and *sīlabbataparāmāsa*) are taken as within the confines of wrong views (*diṭṭhi*).

Unlike in all the preceding chapters, this chapter does not begin with an extensive recourse to clarifying terms in their "pure" attributes. It only gives seven terse questions and answers on the respective seven latencies as some sort of a brief introduction. The content similarly utilises the forward and opposite dichotomised mode of enquiries to deal with all the possible permutations. However, instead of seeing a one-to-one pairing of catechisms, we will see in this chapter a more complex mix pattern of pairing, from single base to six bases, making up six methods of pairing of enquiries. That is the reason attributed to the lengthiness of this chapter. The core contents are allocated with seven sections, designed to examine latent states experienced by common worldling and the four types of noble persons.

The first two topics deal with latencies lying unmanifest in persons, and types of persons who are unmanifest with the respective states of latencies. The third and fourth topics examine the 'renouncing' and 'comprehending' of latent states by the four types of supramundane Path persons in relation to three kinds of feelings. The topics go to such detail of illustrating types of persons renouncing and comprehending the latent states in its entirety, and those who are instead only renouncing and comprehending a part of the latencies. The fifth and sixth topics examine the outcomes after comprehension and post-renunciation in terms of the elimination of latent states by types of persons, and assessment as to the arising of those latent states. Besides the standard yes and no answers, the analysis elucidates to us a third kind of answers which must be used to explain certain inapplicable situations such that "neither had been eliminated, nor had not been eliminated" should be said, and similarly also in certain situations that "neither is arising, nor is not arising" should be the only answer. The last two topics contain sets of questions and answers respectively, are used to examine nine distinct groups of persons. Essentially, the enquiries are formulated to ascertain types of latent states which will remain as unmanifest, or not remaining as unmanifest in a person, with given information that same person has mentally shifted from an element, and mentally reemerged in other elements.

Chapter 8 describes state of consciousness (*citta*), not in the conventional enumeration of the 89 states of consciousness, but *citta* in its 'pure' form without it in association with other types of mental attributes. It covers three sections in its scrutiny of pure *citta* based on person, *dhamma*, person and *dhamma*. Chapter 8 differs slightly from the preceding chapters in its methodological approach. It conducts analysis based on a prescribed list of persons, and measure for outcomes by referencing to fourteen pairs of time-scale verbal conditions (arise and cease, arise and appear … arising and not cease, etc.). However, the process of enquiries remains the same with a mix use of direct and regressive mode of asking questions.

Chapter 9 on '*dhammā*' adopts the same methodological approach as Chapter 6. All pairs of enquiries are still based on the forward and opposite formulations in the three sections (namely terms clarification, phenomenal process, and comprehension as to meditative development), and the predetermined types of persons under discussion are measured against the three categories of *dhammā* differentiated by the attributes of wholesome (*kusalā*), unwholesome (*akusalā*), and indeterminate (*abyākatā*). Because the Pāli term '*dhamma*' carries various shades such as 'norm, truth, object, state, phenomenon, the law of natural existences', and so on, it is better that I just leave the word *dhamma* as it.

Chapter 10 deals with controlling faculties (*indriyaya*). The same topic is also being taught under Chapter five of the second book of Vibhaṅga. The chapter examines faculties in three sections, namely basic terms and meanings of each of the faculties, detail as to arising, and a time-scale analysis on a predetermined list of six faculties at close of the chapter to ensure our comprehension. Because of the long list of faculties and the excessive amount of permutational iterations that have to be performed with the enquiries, the text provides only catechisms on arising of the faculties. Cessation, arising and cessation with regard to faculties are not dealt with by the scriptural text. For the similar reason of its lengthiness, I will not attempt to work on the missing part on cessation.

P. B. Tan

June, 2018
Kuching

Introduction

The seven treatises of the Abhidhammapiṭaka are written with the same single purpose of helping us to develop the right understanding of the ultimate realities of phenomena manifest through our body and mind, conspicuous in everything that we interact with in our daily lives. From nice to the weirder things that came to your dream the night before, to your responses to news and events that impact you in one way or another for the rest of the day or a series of disputes and performance at work in the community, to taking medicine for your deteriorating ailment just before bed, are intricate miscellany of compositional phenomena all of which closely bound up with the teaching of Abhidhamma. The usefulness of Abhidhamma knowledge to liberate us from living in bondage to the world of desires is comparable to the indispensability of oxygen and water that are to life. We avoid living with harmful levels of polluted air and contaminated water so that we can continue with the goal of a healthy life. Through the knowledge we have gained from the study of Abhidhamma, we avoid repeating the same corrupting causes and immoral acts we have done in the past, and retain persistently our mindful vigilance for wholesome acts of the mind and body in order to pursue a virtuous goal of spiritual bliss.

For those who are learning to comprehend the study of Abhidhamma is exactly the learning of how to deal with the true nature of themselves as who they intrinsically are. What you will not find in the scriptural literatures of the Abhidhamma are things like similes, metaphors, analogies, parables, stanzas, verses, abstract description of the philosophical terms, and summarily explanation of important dogmatic principles. Those are the common things which we often come across in the study of suttas, to which the Abhidhamma literatures provide analysis directly down to minute detail in every conceivable way, leaving no other qualms to the truth-seekers. The study of Abhidhamma philosophy is like exploratory digging in the territorial preserve of suttanta tenets to uncover more discernible and convincible facts as to proclaimed truth, and in order the three characteristics of all existences as to impermanence, suffering, and the void of self (sense of individuality, ego, etc.) can be more intelligibly understood, giving us more confidence in our training for insight and wisdom.

The topics of the ten chapters in the Yamaka are the fundamental theories and principal values of Buddhism which are being dissected according to the abhidhamma methods with emphasis on the focal points of insight meditation — at points of origination and cessation of the mind. Although contents of the Yamaka treatise are still regarded as theoretical in its approach of teaching, all the information contained in it are structured with the purpose to directly complement the application methods of the traditional Theravāda Buddhism. The enormous supply of information and answers in the Yamaka are implicit in all the different places in the Suttapiṭaka, and moreover, much of which are either only described in brief or are not set down clearly in the suttas, but which can only be drawn out through inference by the wise minds. Contrariwise, this book unearths the ten valleys of inestimable troves of knowledge in explicit detail. It analyses and delineates all the discussion points with precise clarity based on the Abhidhamma expositional methods, the information of which are indispensable to the training efficacy of all meditation practitioners. But when we take a holistic approach in discussing the essentials for insight development, the information presented in the Yamaka alone is only supplementary and insufficient by order of priorities. It has to go along with other disciplines and methods of application. No matter in what forms of contemplative training for serenity and concentration, for ascendency to jhānic absorption and gaining higher insight which leads to the manifestation of wisdom, the most fundamental precondition to any participant for this purpose is the need to first lay the groundwork of conforming to moral discipline.

The prerequisite groundwork of disciplinary abidance

The preparatory phase of building up a solid base of morality and ethics is imperative as the foundational cleansing process of the mind for any aspirant of insight meditation. The Vibhaṅga explains in a lot detail regarding a series of preparatory steps to be undertaken pertaining to the development of *jhāna*. It specifies foremostly the engagement and compliance to disciplinary rules as the essential requirement before it is possible for a practitioner to attain the first *jhāna* of meditative absorption. The code of disciplines belonging to the Theravāda tradition stipulates a total of 227 rules to be observed by the monastic monks, and 311 rules for the monastic nuns. For the laities of the general Buddhist orders, it is widely recommended to observe the ten precepts, or minimally binding of the five precepts as the basis for cultivating moral virtues and ethical principles. A practitioner's obligatory undertaking of the code of discipline is fundamentally necessary so that the subtler inner forms of taints and latent factors of proclivities can be kept at bay at all times to prevent them from breaking out into the unwholesome physical and mental actions, causing more harms and damage than to be of any good. As much indispensable as water and sunlight are to the growth of seedling, practising restraints of our senses by adherence to precepts actualises in us the easefulness for keeping with calmness, concentration, and inner peace.

By relentlessly keeping our senses closely guarded from going unbridled on their spontaneity and free will, we are able to safeguard against greed, hatred, absence of guilt-conscience, absence of abashedness, and all those other defilement-causing mental factors from arising which bring about our corrupting states of consciousness, thereby avoiding all forms of immoral and unethical transgression, either done deliberately or unwittingly. By not keeping abstinence from the dispersive influence of external temptations and inner desires, it is impossible for us to experience calmness of mind and the right kind of concentration required for practising insight contemplation. Our minds will be kept constantly disruptive like the restless rippling waters on the pond, instead of keeping it like calm water that we can see clearly through it right to the rocks and plants at the bottom.

When an person is observing little or no precept, undisciplined in his deportment and conduct, but is nevertheless zealous in the passing fad of contemplative training for inner serenity and insight, it will, however, always be a futile effort. The reason is because a constant 'tug-of-war' is working between the underlying latencies of faulty mental factors predominate on one hand and an aim wishful of inner peace and wisdom on the other. The right concentration needed for purification process of the mind can never be obtained under such condition of irreciprocity in which two functioning factors are actively opposing one another, although subliminally unnoticed by the person. In this connection, it can therefore be said that when attempts are made to attain meditative absorption without the practitioner having satisfactorily gone through some degrees of strict moral training, it is not possible that the five hindrances of mental defilement can be strongly inhibited or suppressed especially in the higher stages of contemplation process in fine-material element (sensuous desires, ill-will, sloth and torpor, worry or brooding, and restlessness, and skeptical doubt). Simply illustrating this with an example, how do we comprehensibly make out of a Buddhist lecturer who is well-trained with doctrinal principles of Buddhism and also practices *vipassanabhāvanā*, but who is easily getting angry and scoffed at his pupils every now and then in classes. Continuation of such activities works in contrary to insight development, but acts to strengthen the intensity of the undesirable mental factors and anusayas which causes defilement and distraction from concentration. The defiling factors in turn modify and strengthening each other to emerge stronger than ever before. May be in training session the first *jhāna* holding in place by the five principal factors can somehow be attained, but the concentration of which is one that is typically unstable, weak and falling away quickly, as evanescent as bubbles in a glass. And needless to say about perfecting first *jhāna* and advancing any further beyond just that.

Nirodhasamāpanna and *Saññāvedayitanirodha*

In the Yamaka, the Pāli term of '*nirodhasamāpannānaṃ*', meaning those who are at cessation attainment, appears in many places except for the chapters on roots, aggregates, bases, elements, and latent states of tendencies. In a sense, this term has the same meaning as in another term '*saññāvedayitanirodha*' although the descriptions are different (the rendering as cessation of the feeling aggregate and perception aggregate) and which can be seen in many places in the suttas. The difference with those at cessation-attainment being the aggregate of volitive formation and consciousness are also stilled and do not arise. Thus, to be exact, we say that to those who is endowed with cessation-attainment, the part of mental process which involve the aggregates of four mentalities in whom temporarily do not arise, and the mind-produced matters also temporarily cease. The term *nirodhasamāpannāna* is also synonymous in meaning with another term '*nirodhasamāpatti*' (Kv 6.5: Nirodhasamāpattikathā) which is the same state of meditative attainment which surpasses the four fine-material jhānas and the four immaterial jhānas, and is sometimes referred to as the 9th jhānic attainment. At moment of its attainment, the mind of the practitioner is free from process of the four mentalities, utterly aloof from all worldly desires except for keeping with equanimity, striving for the supramundane stage of a stream-winning path-consciousness. In the phasic contemplation process leading up to the fully absorbed stage of cessation-attainment, particularly, persons like the *Anāgāmi* and *Arahat* who have mastered the eight types of mundane jhānas and had already eradicated the taints of all sensuous desires, ill-will and aversion, wrong views, and skeptical doubt (for the case of an *Arahat* which includes also extermination of the desires for existences of the fine-materiality and immateriality, conceit, restlessness, and ignorance), are capable of alternating effortlessly, in addition to normally successive sequence, among these eight jhānas characterised by the different levels of insight. There are those noble persons who are skillful at either entering upon cessation of aggregates right away without the precedent jhānas, or emerging directly from immaterial jhānas, or in combination with all the eight jhānas. In this regard, an *Arahat* who had gained the spiritual fruition with all defilements completely eradicated and who had previously attained also the mundane jhānas by a sequel to immaterial jhānas, is called a noble person liberated by both ways (*ubhatobhāgavimutto*). An *Arahat* who is liberated by virtue of insight resulting in wisdom without having gone through a sequel of mundane insight meditation up to immaterial jhānas is known as a noble person liberated by wisdom alone (*paññāvimutto*). (Pug 24; AN 9.45: Ubhatobhāgavimutta sutta).

When we compare those at cessation-attainment with persons at the ceasing moment of consciousness or at the death-moment, there are many similar phenomenal events which do not arise in the two situations as you will later find out in this book. By comparison in terms of present moment, we will not see any differences between them. For instance, in those circumstances, the three types of *saṅkhāra* do not arise; the four mental aggregates do not arise; the three truths of suffering, origination of suffering, and path-truth do not arise; neither wholesome nor unwholesome *citta* arises; the wholesome *dhāmma* and unwholesome *dhāmma* do not arise; the faculties of mind, pleasure, displeasure, joy, melancholy, and equanimity do not arise; the five faculties and five powers of faith, effort, mindfulness, concentration, and understanding also do not arise. However, those in possession of cessation-attainment are those who are purified and fit for proceeding with supramundane insight contemplation leading to the manifestation of wisdom and the attainment of spiritual liberation. Events characteristic of those at cessation-attainment according to the exposition in the Yamaka, amongst a diversity of many other different things, are that life faculty in whom does not cease (and of course body heat also does not diminish); thought moments and cittas (and mind faculty) do not cease and will arise again; path-truth will arise and be realised; the feeling of pleasure and joy as are all the undesirable feelings are subdued, and will not arise; equanimity and one-pointedness to hold stronger concentration indispensable to supramundane insight will arise; and notably the five spiritual faculties which result in the five powers will arise. These being the differences.

I pay homage to the Blessed One, the Worthy One, the Fully Enlightened One.

CHAPTER 6

VI. Pairs on Formations
(*Saṅkhārayamaka*)

The term *saṅkhārakkhandho*, translated as 'formation aggregate', has been explained in Chapter 2 regarding the clarification of terms — is distinguished by either material or mental formation, i.e., the four mentalities are referred to as mental formation while matters are sometimes specified as material formation. Although the term *saṅkhāra* carries different shades of meaning (mental concomitants, thing conditioned, formation, etc.), the preferred rendering for use in this chapter is still 'formation'. However, it should be noted that *saṅkhāra* exhibits the 'volitional' effort. Thus, the process of *saṅkhāra* is synecdochically also 'volitive formation'.

Chapter 6 uses the same methodology as in the preceding chapters by examining pairs of enquiries in three main parts. Each enquiry is formulated as a pair of catechisms. The analysis is done by using forward (or positive) and opposite (or negative) dichotomised mode of enquiries. Some of the answers given by the text in this chapter and throughout Volume II are short and terse, and in some cases answers are provided plainly as yes or no. In those circumstances, I shall add on with my own explanations which will be given in parenthesis wherever is considered necessary.

The first part in this chapter uses three methods to deal with the clarification of terms in relation to formations, namely — clarifying word by word, ascertaining the root of wheel based on word-by-word clarification, and analysing pure formations. In the first part, the original text maintains the enumeration of questions (*uddesa*) and the expositions (*niddesa*) in two separate sections, in exactly the same way the five chapters are structured. There is really no special significance by repeating the questions all over again. Superfluous information can be avoided by simply grouping the subjects. As what I have done in previous chapters, I will leave out the set of questions as those information are already included in the exposition section. Thus, I will omit the enumeration of questions from nos. 2 to 7. At the end, tables will be constructed to show how the paired questions are formulated in order that all the permutational orders of enquiries are taken in without having any oversight.

The second part uses threefold classifications — origination, cessation, origination and cessation — to examine process (*pavatti*) regarding the three types of formation. The third part examines the comprehension (*pariññā*) aspect of individuals with regard to these three types of formation.

6.1 Clarification of Terms (*Paṇṇatti*)

1. There are three types of formation — bodily formation (*kāyasaṅkhāro*), verbal formation (*vacīsaṅkhāro*), and mental formation (*cittasaṅkhāro*). Examples of *kāyasaṅkhāro*-based actions are the sequenced inhaling and exhaling exercise (*assāsapassāsā*), etc. [1]; verbal formations are referred to the initial application (or initial thought) and sustained application of thought (*vitakkavicārā*) [2]; mental formation are referred to perception and feeling (*saññā ca vedanā ca*). With the exception of initial application and sustained application (*vitakkavicārā*), feeling, perception, and all those concomitants of consciousness (the remaining 48 cetasikas, i.e. 52 to exclude the cetasikas of *sañña*, *vedanā*, *vitakka*, and *vicārā*) are also known as mental formations [3] . Note that *kāyasaṅkhāro* and *vacīsaṅkhāro* also arise in the mind because both are based on *saṅkhāra*. Mental formation leads to the generation of bodily formation and verbal formation.

6.1.1 Clarifying word by word (*Padasodhana*) [4]

Forward expression (*anuloma*)

8. *i* (a) That which is body, is it bodily formation?
— No (breathing in and out are not body but a process formation of the body).
(b) That which is bodily formation, is it body? — No. (Same as aforesaid)

ii (a) That which is speech, is it verbal formation?
— No (initial thought & sustained application are verbal formations which transform into speech).
(b) That which is verbal formation, is it speech? — No. (Same as aforesaid)

---

1 Bodily formations are confined only to individuals at the sensuous planes, and occur with the arising of 44 kāma-cittas in the sensuous sphere (54 excluding the 5 pairs of sense-door consciousness or *dvi-pañcaviññāṇas*), rebirth-linking citta (*paṭisandhi*) and death-citta (*cuti*). Bodily formations does not occur at the fourth *jhāna*. In this chapter, bodily formation is treated as *saṅkhāra* because it is first generated in the mind, then goes into actions.

2 Why *vitakkavicārā* are verbal formations instead of mental is because it is through initial thought and sustained evaluation about those sense-objects which breaks out into words. It is like the "inner representation" of reasoning and directing verbalisation during meditation. Verbal formations happen to all those individuals except for Non-percipient individuals. *Vitakkavicārā* do not arise with the five pairs of sense-door consciousness. The two are the first two of the five *jhāna* factors which must all be present in first *jhāna* in order the five hindrances (*nīvaraṇā*) can be inhibited, temporarily.

3 Mental formations occur at all the 54 sensuous cittas and happen at all the 4 jhānas. Individuals at the Non-percipience plane do not have mental formations.

4 *Padasodhana* is traditionally interpreted as "cleansing or purication of words". I adopt a synecdochic approach by interpreting it as "clarifying word by word" because that is how Abhidhamma terminologies and philological terms can be studied and restore to their "pure" states or original intent of meanings.

iii (a) That which is consciousness, is it mental formation?
— No (Consciousness refers to the 89 states of consciousness; the latter are the other three mental aggregates excluding *vitakka-cetasika* and *vicārā-cetasika*).
(b) That which is mental formation, is it consciousness? — No (same as above).

Opposite expression (*paccanīka*)

9. *i* (a) That which is not body, is it not bodily formation?
— No. Breathing in and out are not body, but are bodily formation.
— Yes With the exception of body and bodily formation, the remainders (verbal and mental formations) are neither body nor bodily formation.
(b) That which is not bodily formation, is it not body?
— No. Body is not bodily formation but the structural support for inhalation and exhalation.
— Yes. Refer to the answer in 9 *i* (a) above.

ii (a) That which is not speech, is it not verbal formation?
— No. That which is not speech, viz. *vitakka-vicārā*, is verbal formation.
— Yes. With the exception of speech and verbal formation, the remainders (bodily and mental formation) are neither speech nor verbal formation.
(b) That which is not verbal formation, is it not speech?
— No. Speech is not verbal formation but spoken words.
— Yes. Refer to the answer in 9 *ii* (a) above.

iii (a) That which is not consciousness, is it not mental formation?
— No. Feeling, perception, the concomitants of consciousness with the exception of *vitakka-vicārā* coefficients are mental formation which is not consciousness.
— Yes. Except consciousness and mental formation, the remainders (bodily and verbal formation) are neither consciousness nor mental formation.
(b) That which is not mental formation, is it not consciousness?
— No. Consciousness is consciousness aggregate which is not mental formation (the other three mental aggregates except *vitakka*-cetasika and *vicārā*-cetasika).
— Yes. Refer to the answer in 9 *iii* (a) above.

6.1.2 Wheel, based on word-by-word clarification (*Padasodhanamūlacakka*)

Forward expression (*anuloma*)

10. *i* (a) That which is body, is it bodily formation?
— No. (Body is the structural base for breath in and out, are not bodily formation).
(b) That which is formation, is it verbal formation?
— Yes. Verbal formation is both a formation conditioned and verbal formation.
— No. The remainders (bodily formation and mental formation) are also formation, but are not verbal formation.

ii (a) That which is body, is it bodily formation?
— No. Answer is the same as in 10 *i* (a) above.
(b) That which is formation, is it mental formation?
— Yes. Mental formation is both a formation conditioned and mental formation.
— No. The two remainders are also formation, but are not mental formation.

11. *i* (a) That which is speech, is it verbal formation?
— No. (Oral communication is speech but not verbal formation).
(b) That which is formation, is it bodily formation?
— Yes. Bodily formation is both a formation conditioned and bodily formation.
— No. The two remainders are also formation, but are not bodily formation.

ii (a) That which is speech, is it verbal formation?
— No. Answer is the same as in 11 *i* (a) above.
(b) That which is formation, is it mental formation?
— Yes. Mental formation is both a formation conditioned and mental formation.
— No. The two remainders are also formation, but are not mental formation.

12. *i* (a) That which is consciousness, is it mental formation?
— No. (Consciousness, or called consciousness aggregate consisting of the 89 cittas, is not mental formation which are the remaining three mental aggregates excluding *vitakka-cetasika* and *vicārā-cetasika*).
(b) That which is formation, is it bodily formation?
— Yes. Bodily formation is both a formation conditioned and bodily formation.
— No. The two remainders are also formation, but are not bodily formation.

ii (a) That which is consciousness, is it mental formation?
— No. Answer is the same as in 12 *i* (a) above.
(b) That which is formation, is it verbal formation?
— Yes. Verbal formation is both a formation conditioned and verbal formation.
— No. The two remainders are also formation, but are not verbal formation.

Opposite expression (*paccanīka*)

13. *i* (a) That which is not body, is it not bodily formation?
— No. Breathing in and out is not body but bodily formation.
— Yes. With the exception of body and bodily formation, the remainders (verbal and mental formations) are neither body nor bodily formation.
(b) That which is not formation, is it not verbal formation?
— Yes. (Speech is neither formation nor verbal formation).

ii (a) That which is not body, is it not bodily formation?
— The two answers are the same as in 13 *i* (a) above.
(b) That which is not formation, is it not mental formation?

— Yes. (Consciousness is neither formation nor mental formation).

14. *i* (a) That which is not speech, is it not verbal formation?
— No. *Vitakka-vicārā* is not speech, but is verbal formation.
— Yes. With the exception of speech and verbal formation, the remainders (bodily and mental formation) are neither speech nor verbal formation.
(b) That which is not formation, is it not bodily formation?
— Yes. (Body is neither formation nor bodily formation).

ii (a) That which is not speech, is it not verbal formation?
— The two answers are the same as in 14 *i* (a) above.
(b) That which is not formation, is it not mental formation?
— Yes. Same answer as in 13 *i* (b) above.

15. *i* (a) That which is not consciousness, is it not mental formation?
Mental formation is not consciousness, but mental formation.
— No. Feeling, perception, the mental concomitants excluding *vitakka-vicārā* are not consciousness, but are mental formations.
— Yes. With the exception of consciousness and mental formation, remainders (bodily and mental formation) are neither consciousness nor mental formation.
(b) That which is not formation, is it not bodily formation?
— Yes. Same answer as in 14 *i* (b) above.

ii (a) That which is not consciousness, is it not mental formation?
— The two answers are the same as in 15 *i* (a) above.
(b) That which is not formation, is it not verbal formation?
— Yes. (Speech is neither formation nor verbal formation).

6.1.3 Pure Formation
(*Suddhasaṅkhāra*)

Forward expression (*anuloma*)

16. *i* (a) That which is bodily formation, is it verbal formation? — No.
(b) That which is verbal formation, is it bodily formation? — No.

ii (a) That which is bodily formation, is it mental formation? — No.
(b) That which is mental formation, is it bodily formation? — No.

iii (a) That which is verbal formation, is it mental formation? — No.
(b) That which is mental formation, is it verbal formation? — No.

Opposite expression (*paccanīka*)

17. *i* (a) That which is not bodily formation, is it not verbal formation?
— No. *Vitakka* and *vicārā* are not bodily formation, but are verbal formation.
— Yes. Other than bodily formation and verbal formation, the remainders (body, spoken words, consciousness, mental formation) are neither bodily formation nor verbal formation.
(b) That which is not verbal formation, is it not bodily formation?
— No. Inhaling and exhaling are not verbal formation, but are bodily formation.
— Yes. Refer to the answer in 17 *i* (a) above.

ii (a) That which is not bodily formation, is it not mental formation?
— No. Feeling, perception, the mental concomitants excluding *vitakka-vicārā* are not bodily formation, but are mental formation.
— Yes. Other than bodily formation and mental formation, the remainders (body, spoken words, verbal formation, consciousness) are neither bodily formation nor mental formation.
(b) That which is not mental formation, is it not bodily formation?
— No. Inhaling and exhaling are not mental formation, but are bodily formation.
— Yes. Refer to the answer in 17 *ii* (a) above.

18. *i* (a) That which is not verbal formation, is it not mental formation?
— No. Feeling, perception, the mental concomitants excluding *vitakka* and *vicārā* are not verbal formation, but are mental formation.
— Yes. Other than verbal formation and mental formation, the remainders (body, bodily formation, spoken words, consciousness) are neither verbal formation nor mental formation.
(b) That which is not mental formation, is it not verbal formation?
— No. *Vitakka and vicārā* are not mental formation, but are verbal formation.
— Yes. Refer to the answer in 18 *i* (a) above.

Tabulated pairs-sequence of the three methods on 'terms'

In Table 6.1 below, the letter 'n' attached to the series of numerals in the cells relative to the row headers and column headers, denotes the meaning "*not*". For example, '7n', which is the direct mode of enquiring, is to be read as "That which is not body, is it *not* bodily formation?". '8n', which is the reverse mode of enquiring, is to be read as "That which is not bodily formation, is it *not* body?" The remaining, 9n, … 12n are to be interpreted in the same way.

Table 6.1 Pairs-sequence on the 'clarification of words' (*Padasodhana*)

	is it bodily formation?	is it body?	is it verbal formation?	is it speech?	is it mental formation?	is it consciousness?
That which is body,	1					
That which is bodily formation,		2				
That which is speech,			3			
That which is verbal formation,				4		
That which is consciousness,					5	
That which is mental formation,						6
That which is not body,	7n					
That which is not bodily formation,		8n				
That which is not speech,			9n			
That which is not verbal formation,				10n		
That which is not consciousness,					11n	
That which is not mental formation,						12n

In Table 6.2 below, for example the first two pairs of enquiries are designated as sequence 1, 2 and 3, 4, are to be read as "That which is body, is it bodily formation? That which is formation, is it verbal formation?" and the second pair as "That which is body, is it bodily formation? That which is formation, is it mental formation?". The remaining 11 pairs are to be interpreted in the same way.

Table 6.2 Sequence of paired enquiries on the subject of wheel, based on 'clarification of words' (*Padasodhanamūlacakka*)

	is it bodily formation?	is it verbal formation?	is it mental formation?	is it not bodily formation?	is it not verbal formation?	is it not mental formation?
That which is formation,	6, 10,	2, 12,	4, 8,			
That which is body,	1, 3,					
That which is speech,		5, 7,				
That which is consciousness,			9, 11,			
That which is not formation,				18, 22,	14, 24	16, 20,
That which is not body,				13, 15,		
That which is not speech,					17, 19,	
That which is not consciousness,						21, 23,

In Table 6.3 below, for example the first two pairs of enquiries are designated as sequence 1, 2 and 3, 4, are to be read as "That which is bodily formation, is it verbal formation? That which is verbal formation, is it bodily formation?" and the second pair goes as "That which is bodily formation, is it mental formation? That which is mental formation, is it bodily formation?". The remaining 5 pairs of questions are to be interpreted in the same way.

Table 6.3 Pairs-sequence on 'pure formation' (*Suddhasaṅkhāra*)

	is it bodily formation?	is it verbal formation?	is it mental formation?	is it not bodily formation?	is it not verbal formation?	is it not mental formation?
That which is bodily formation,		1	3			
That which is verbal formation,	2		5			
That which is mental formation,	4	6				
That which is not bodily formation,					7	9
That which is not verbal formation,				8		11
That which is not mental formation,				10	12	

6.2 Process (*Pavatti*)

6.2.1 Origination of formations (with charts)

Chart 6.0 Enquiry sequence on the arising of formations

		(Respective enquiries below are dealt with each of the following formation types accordingly)								
		Does it arise / Does it not arise : i) in that individual? ii) at that plane? iii) in that individual at that plane?			Had it arisen / Had it not arisen : i) in that individual? ii) at that plane? iii) in that individual at that plane?			Will it arise / Will it not arise : i) in that individual? ii) at that plane? iii) in that individual at that plane?		
		Bodily formation	Verbal formation	Mental formation	Bodily formation	Verbal formation	Mental formation	Bodily formation	Verbal formation	Mental formation
Bodily formation	arises / does not arise : i) in this individual. ii) at this plane. iii) in this individual at this plane.		1a	2a		10a	11a		13a	14a
Verbal formation		1b		3a			12a			15a
Mental formation		2b*i*	3b							
Bodily formation	had arisen/ had not arisen i) in this individual. ii) at this plane. iii) in this individual at this plane.					4a	5a		16a	17a
Verbal formation		10b			4b		6a			18a
Mental formation		11b	12b		5b	6b*i*				
Bodily formation	will arise / will not arise : i) in this individual. ii) at this plane. iii) in this individual at this plane.								7a	8a
Verbal formation		13b			16b			7b*i*		9a
Mental formation		14b	15b		17b	18b		8b	9b	

The chart above summarises the sequence of paired enquiries from nos. 19 to 78. The iteration loops through three differentiations (types of individual, planes, individuals at planes) using the forward and reverse mode of enquiring. The same sequence reiterates through six time-scaled classifications (present, past, future, present-past, present-future, and past-future), represent by the enneahedral boxes as as shown in the chart. Once you have become familiar with all the answers in the catechisms, it will be useful to revisit this chart as a way to rehearse your knowledge in this particular area.

Chart 6.1 Present, past and future arising of the three formation types

A: arises/ had arisen/ will arise; N: does not arise/ had not arisen/ will not arise

	Present			Past			Future		
	Bodily F.	Verbal F.	Mental F.	Bodily F.	Verbal F.	Mental F.	Bodily F.	Verbal F.	Mental F.
Those at the arising moment of breath-in and breath-out	A	A	A						
Those at the ceasing moment of breath-in and breath-out									
Those at the arising moment of breath-in and breath-out without initial application and sustained application	A	N							
Those at the first *jhāna* attainment, at the arising moment of breath-in and breath-out	A	A							
Those at the first *jhāna* attainment, at the ceasing moment of breath-in and breath-out									
Those at the second and third *jhāna* attainment, at the arising moment of breath-in and breath-out									
Those at the second and third *jhāna* attainment, at the ceasing moment of breath-in and breath-out									
Those at the arising moment of initial application and sustained application		A	A						
Those at the arising moment of initial application and sustained application without breath-in and breath-out	N	A							
Those at the arising moment of *citta* without breath-in and breath-out	N		A						
Those at the arising moment of *citta* without initial application and sustained application		N	A						
Those at the arising moment of *citta* with non-initial application and non-sustained application, without breath-in and breath-out	N	N							
Those at the planes of initial application and sustained application (except those endowed with final-stage *citta*)									
Those at the planes of non-initial application and non-sustained application (except those endowed with final-stage *citta*)									
Those in whose consciousness whereof final-stage *citta* of the sensuous sphere will instantly arise							N	A	A
Those in whose consciousness whereof final-stage *citta* with non-initial application and non-sustained application will instantly arise							N	N	A
Those who are endowed with final-stage *citta*							N	N	N
Those endowed with final-stage *citta* at the planes of initial application and sustained application									
Those endowed with final-stage *citta* at the planes of non-initial application and non-sustained application									
Those endowed with final-stage *citta* with non-initial application and non-sustained application									
Those at the arising moment of final-stage *citta*									
Those at the ceasing moment of final-stage *citta*									
Those at the arising moment of final-stage *citta* with initial application and sustained application									
Those at the ceasing moment of final-stage *citta* with initial application and sustained application									
Those at the ceasing moment of final-stage *citta* at the planes of initial application and sustained application									

	Present			Past			Future		
	Bodily F.	Verbal F.	Mental F.	Bodily F.	Verbal F.	Mental F.	Bodily F.	Verbal F.	Mental F.
Those at the ceasing moment of final-stage *citta* at the planes of non-initial application & non-sustained application									
Those at the arising moment of final-stage *citta* with non-initial application and non-sustained application									
Those at the ceasing moment of final-stage *citta* with non-initial application and non-sustained application									
Those at the first *jhāna* attainment				A	A	A	A	A	A
Those at the first, second, and third *jhāna* attainment				A		A	A		A
Those at the second and third *jhāna* attainment				A	N		A	N	
Those at the second, third, and fourth *jhāna* attainment					N	A		N	A
Those at the fourth *jhāna* attainment				N	N	A	N	N	A
Those at the birth-moment of Pure abode beings				N	N	N			
Those at the birth-moment of Non-percipient beings				N	N	N			
Those at the moment of second *citta* of Pure abode beings				N	N	A			
Sensuous beings				A	A	A	A	A	A
Fine-material beings (except Non-percipients)	N			N	A	A	N	A	A
Immaterial beings	N			N	A	A	N	A	A
Non-percipient beings	N	N	N	N	N	N	N	N	N
Final existence beings							N	A	A
All those at the ceasing moment of *citta*	N	N	N						
Those at Cessation attainment	N	N	N						
At the plane(s) of :	Bodily F.	Verbal F.	Mental F.	Bodily F.	Verbal F.	Mental F.	Bodily F.	Verbal F.	Mental F.
first *jhāna*	A	A	A	A	A	A	A	A	A
first, second and third *jhāna*	A		A	A		A	A		A
second and third *jhāna*	A	N	A	A	N	A	A	N	A
second, third, and fourth *jhāna*		N	A		N	A		N	A
fourth *jhāna*	N	N	A	N	N	A	N	N	A
sensuous sphere	A	A	A	A	A	A	A	A	A
fine-material sphere (except Non-percipience plane)	N	A	A	N	A	A	N	A	A
immaterial sphere	N	A	A	N	A	A	N	A	A
non-percipience	N	N	N	N	N	N	N	N	N

The first 108 pairs (6 x 18) of enquiries and answers with reference to present, past, and future are condensed into Chart 6.1 as shown above. Take note that when certain answers are not presented in regard to either present, past, or future measure, those unavailable answers are not necessarily the same as those available answers from corresponding counterparts. For example, answers are not provided to those sensuous beings, and to those at the different levels of jhānas at present measure of arising. The reason is because their answers are conditional on various factors such as with or without breath-in and breath-out, at the arising or ceasing moment of breath-in and breath-out, or with the presence or absence of initial application and sustained application. In the case of Non-percipient beings, the answers with reference to present, past, and future are invariably the same.

I have put into the chart all the enquiries that are to be dealt with in this Chapter. Some are without answers because they are only to be examined later on. I do so in order that we can know where in other sub-sections they would later only be discussed. However, the same would be unneeded in other charts in the subsequent sections on cessation and arising-cessation. Also, I will not fill up all those blank cells in the chart at this point. All the answers will be summarised into a consolidated chart at the end of this section.

The following clarifies some of the similarities and dissimilarities in the meanings of some of the terms in this and subsequent charts.

1. The term 'birth-moment' refers to not only at the first moment of birth, but also denotes the continual lifespan of the individual. (Death-moment is not mentioned in this section but only in the later two sections with regard to cessation). [5]
2. The term 'planes of *vitakka-vicāra*' (planes of initial application and sustained application) is referring to planes of the sense-sphere.
3. The term 'planes of *avitakka-avicāra*' (non-initial application and non-sustained application) is referring to planes of the fine-material sphere and immaterial sphere.
4. The 'final-stage *citta'* of an individual is not exactly the same meaning as person of '*Arahatta* Path-*citta'*, person of 'final existence', or person of 'Cessation-attainment' as explained earlier on.

At Present

Forward enquiries by Individual

19. *i* (a) Bodily formation arises in this individual. Does verbal formation arise in that individual?
— No. To those at the arising moment of breath-in and breath-out without initial application and sustained application, bodily formation arises; verbal formation does not arise.
— Yes. To those at the first *jhāna* attainment [6] and those of the sensuous sphere, at the arising moment of breath-in and breath-out, bodily formation arises; verbal formation also arises. (The first *jhāna* attainment of the fine-material sphere exists as a result the first *jhāna* at sensuous sphere).

---

[5] *upapajjanta*: (pp. *upapajjati*) the term has a few slightly different shades as 'birth, rebirth, reborn, produced at, came into, emerged, or re-emerged (at somewhere)'. The meaning of 'birth' is considered more appropriate in this chapter. The term *cavanta* (pr. p. of *cavati*) also has a variety of meanings such as 'deceasing, disappearing, vanishing, shifting, falling away'. The meaning of 'dying' or 'death-moment' is chosen for this chapter so that the two terms represent the exact antithesis which are only logical.

[6] Initial application and sustained application are taken as a single *jhāna* factor to be eliminated in the second *jhāna*, and so only the fourth *jhāna* is mentioned instead of the fifth throughout this book.

(b) Or else there is [7] verbal formation arises in this individual. Does bodily formation arise in that individual?
— No. To those at the arising moment of initial application and sustained application without breath-in and breath-out, verbal formation arises; bodily formation does not arise.
— Yes. Refer to the answer in 19 *i* (a) above.

ii (a) Bodily formation arises in this individual. Does mental formation arise in that individual?
— Yes. (Refer to the answer in *ii* (b) below).
— No, such individual does not exist.

(b) Mental formation arises in this individual. Does bodily formation arise in that individual?
— No. To those at the arising moment of *citta* without breath-in and breath-out, mental formation arises; bodily formation does not arise.
— Yes. To those at the arising moment of breath-in and breath-out, both mental formation and bodily formation arise.

20. *i* (a) Verbal formation arises in this individual. Does mental formation arise in that individual?
— Yes. (Refer to the answer in (b) below).
— No such individual verbal formation arises, mental formation therein does not.

(b) Mental formation arises in this individual. Does verbal formation arise in that individual?
— No. To those at the arising moment of *citta* without initial application and sustained application, mental formation arises; verbal formation does not arise.
— Yes. To those at the arising moment of initial application and sustained application, both mental formation and verbal formation arise.

Forward enquiries by Plane

21. *i* (a) Bodily formation arises at this plane. Does verbal formation arise at that plane?
— No. At (the planes of) second and third *jhāna* [8], bodily formation arises; verbal formation does not arise.
— Yes. At (the planes of) first *jhāna*, at sensuous sphere, bodily formation arises;

---

[7] The Pāli term "*Yassa vā pana…*" is used frequently in second enquiries of the pairs of catechisms (translated as "Or else there is…; alternatively"; or equivalent of the computing algorithmic language "Elseif") will be omitted in this and following chapters. The text uses the different singular forms of relative pronouns. The reason for omitting the aforementioned term is because it is easily understood as a reciprocal way of making enquiries, but the inclusion of it would seems somewhat redundant. For the same reason, I have also previously left them out in Volume I.

[8] Planes of *jhāna* (planes of meditative absorption) is distinguished from planes of abode.

verbal formation also arises. (i.e. the arising moment of first *jhāna* lies at sensuous sphere) [9].

(b) Verbal formation arises at this plane. Does bodily formation arise at that plane?
— No. At (the planes of) fine-material sphere and immaterial sphere, verbal formation arises [10] ; bodily formation does not arise.
— Yes. Refer to the answer in 21 *i* (a) above.

ii (a) Bodily formation arises at this plane. Does mental formation arise at that plane?
— Yes. (Refer to the answer in *ii* (b) below).
— No such plane ..... whereat mental formation does not arise.
(b) Mental formation arises at this plane. Does bodily formation arise at that plane?
— No. At (the planes of) fourth *jhāna*, at (the planes of) fine-material and immaterial sphere, mental formation arises; bodily formation does not arise.
— Yes. At (the planes of) first, second, and third *jhāna*, and at (the planes of) sensuous sphere, mental formation arises and bodily formation also arises.

22. *i* (a) Verbal formation arises at this plane. Does mental formation arise at that plane?
— Yes. (Refer to the answer in (b) below).
— No such plane verbal formation arises whereat mental formation does not arise.

(b) Mental formation arises at this plane. Does verbal formation arise at that plane?
— No. At (the planes of) second, third, and fourth *jhāna*, mental formation arises; verbal formation does not arise.
— Yes. At (the planes of) first *jhāna*, at sensuous sphere, at fine-material sphere, and at immaterial sphere [11], both mental formation and verbal formation arise.

Forward enquiries by Individual and Plane

For answers to the following enquiries, refer to those in the preceding 6 pairs in "Forward enquiries on Individual", from 21 *i* (a) to 22 *i* (b).

23. *i* (a) Bodily formation arises in this individual at this plane. Does verbal formation arise in that individual at that plane? (b) Verbal formation arises in this individual at this plane. Does bodily formation arise in that individual at that

---

[9] *Cf.* PañkA, Saṅkhārayamakaṃ, par. 21: *Paṭhamajjhāne kāmāvacareti kāmāvacarabhūmiyaṃ uppanne paṭhamajjhāne.*

[10] *Rūpāvacare arūpāvacare tattha vacīsaṅkhāro uppajjati* .... The above answer is one of the many examples referring to fine-material and immaterial beings at their habitational planes, not at time of *jhāna*. In Chapter Three, it also explains that to immaterial beings, ideation-base (*dhammāyatana*), which includes both verbal formation and mental formation, arises.

[11] Planes of *jhāna* must be distinguished from planes of abode.

plane?

ii (a) Bodily formation arises in this individual at this plane. Does mental formation arise in that individual at that plane? (b) Mental formation arises in this individual at this plane. Does bodily formation arise in that individual at that plane?

iii (a) Verbal formation arises in this individual at this plane. Does mental formation arise in that individual at that plane? (b) Mental formation arises in this individual at this plane. Does verbal formation arise in that individual at that plane?

Opposite enquiries by Individual

24. *i* (a) Bodily formation does not arise in this individual. Does verbal formation not arise in that individual?
— No. To those at the arising moment of initial application and sustained application without breath-in and breath-out, bodily formation does not arise; verbal formation arises.
— Yes. To all those at the ceasing moment of *citta*; those at the arising moment of *citta* with non-initial application and non-sustained application, without breath-in and breath-out; those of Cessation-attainment (*nirodhasamāpannānaṃ*) [12]; and Non-percipient beings, neither bodily formation nor verbal formation arises.

(b) Verbal formation does not arise in this individual. Does bodily formation not arise in that individual?
— No. To those at the arising moment of breath-in and breath-out without initial application and sustained application, verbal formation does not arise; bodily formation arises.
— Yes. Refer to the answer in 24 *i* (a) above.

ii (a) Bodily formation does not arise in this individual. Does mental formation not arise in that individual?
— No. To those at the arising moment of *citta* without breath-in and breath-out, bodily formation does not arise; mental formation arises.
— Yes. To all those at the ceasing moment of *citta*, those of Cessation-attainment (*nirodhasamāpannānaṃ*), and those Non-percipient beings, neither bodily formation nor mental formation arises.

(b) Mental formation does not arise in this individual. Does bodily formation not arise in that individual? — Yes. Refer to the answer in 24 *ii* (a) above.

[12] To those at the moment of entering upon Cessation-attainment, the mental process involving the aggregates of feeling, perception, volitive formation and consciousness, and also the mind-produced matters temporarily cease.

25. *i* (a) Verbal formation does not arise in this individual. Does mental formation not arise in that individual?
— No. To those at the arising moment of *citta* without initial application and sustained application, verbal formation does not arise; but mental formation arises.
— Yes. To all those at the ceasing moment of *citta*, those of Cessation-attainment, and those Non-percipient beings, neither verbal formation nor mental formation arises.

(b) Mental formation does not arise in this individual. Does verbal formation not arise in that individual?
— No such being verbal formation arises; mental formation in whom does not.
— Yes. Refer to the answer in 25 *i* (a) above.

Opposite enquiries by Plane

26. *i* (a) Bodily formation does not arise at this plane. Does verbal formation not arise at that plane?
— No. At (the planes of) fine-material and immaterial sphere, bodily formation does not arise; verbal formation therein arises.
— Yes. At (the planes of) fourth *jhāna*, and at the plane of Non-percipients, neither bodily formation nor verbal formation arise.

(b) Verbal formation does not arise at this plane. Does bodily formation not arise at that plane?
— No. At (the planes of) second and third *jhāna*, verbal formation does not arise; bodily formation therein arises.
— Yes. Refer to the answer in 26 *i* (a) above.

ii (a) Bodily formation does not arise at this plane. Does mental formation not arise at that plane?
— No. At (the planes of) fourth *jhāna*, at (the planes of) fine-material and immaterial sphere, bodily formation does not arise; mental formation arises.
— Yes. At the plane of Non-percipient beings, neither bodily formation nor mental formation arises.

(b) Mental formation does not arise at this plane. Does bodily formation not arise at that plane? — Yes. Refer to the answer in 26 *ii* (a) above.

27. *i* (a) Verbal formation does not arise at this plane. Does mental formation not arise at that plane?
— No. At (the planes of) second, third, and fourth *jhāna*, verbal formation does not arise; mental formation arises.
— Yes. At the plane of Non-percipient beings, neither verbal formation nor mental formation arises.

(b) Mental formation does not arise at this plane. Does verbal formation not arise at that plane? — Yes. Refer to the answer in 27 *i* (a) above.

Opposite enquiries by Individual and Plane

For answers to the following inversive mode of enquiries, refer to the preceding 6 pairs in "Forward enquiries on Individual" from 24 *i* (a) to 25 *i* (b). The only difference is that cessation-attainment (*nirodhasamāpannānaṃ*) herein should not be taken into account as mentioned by the text.

28. *i* (a) Bodily formation does not arise in this individual at this plane. Does verbal formation not arise in that individual to that plane? (b) Verbal formation does not arise in this individual at this plane. Does bodily formation not arise in that individual at that plane?

ii (a) Bodily formation does not arise in this individual at this plane. Does mental formation not arise in that individual at that plane? (b) Mental formation does not arise in this individual at this plane. Does bodily formation not arise in that individual at that plane?

iii (a) Verbal formation does not arise in this individual at this plane. Does mental formation not arise in that individual at that plane? (b) Mental formation does not arise in this individual at this plane. Does verbal formation not arise in that individual at that plane?

In the Past

Forward enquiries by Individual

29. *i* (a) Bodily formation had arisen in this individual. Had verbal formation arisen in that individual?
— Yes. To those at the first *jhāna* attainment, and those of the sensuous sphere, both bodily formation and verbal formation had arisen.
(b) Verbal formation had arisen in this individual. Had bodily formation arisen in that individual?
— Yes. Refer to the answer in 29 *i* (a) above.

ii (a) Bodily formation had arisen in this individual. Had mental formation arisen in that individual?
— Yes. To those at the first, second, and third *jhāna* attainment, and those of the sensuous sphere, both bodily formation and mental formation had arisen.
(b) Mental formation had arisen in this individual. Had bodily formation arisen in that individual?
— Yes. Refer to the answer in 29 *ii* (a) above.

30. *i* (a) Verbal formation had arisen in this individual. Had mental formation arisen in that individual?
— Yes. To those at the first *jhāna* attainment, those of the sensuous sphere, and others of the fine-material sphere and immaterial sphere (except Non-percipients), both verbal formation and mental formation had arisen.
(b) Mental formation had arisen in this individual. Had verbal formation arisen in that individual?
— Yes. Refer to the answer in 30 *i* (a) above.

Forward enquiries by Plane

31. *i* (a) Bodily formation had arisen at this plane. Had verbal formation arisen at that plane? ..... p ..... [13] *ii* (b) Mental formation had arisen at this plane. Had verbal formation arisen at that plane?

The answers in "Forward enquiries on Plane" are the same in all those six time-lagged classifications of enquiries. Refer to the last part in Chart 6.1.

Forward enquiries by Individual and Plane

32. *i* (a) Bodily formation had arisen in this individual at this plane. Had verbal formation arisen in that individual at that plane?
— No. To those at the second and third *jhāna* attainment, bodily formation had arisen; verbal formation had not arisen.
— Yes. To those at the first *jhāna* attainment, and those of the sensuous sphere, both bodily formation and verbal formation had arisen.

(b) Verbal formation had arisen in this individual at this plane. Had bodily formation arisen in that individual at that plane?
— No. To those of the fine-material sphere and immaterial sphere, verbal formation had arisen; bodily formation had not arisen.
— Yes. Refer to the answer in 32 *i* (a) above.

ii (a) Bodily formation had arisen in this individual at this plane. Had mental formation arisen in that individual at that plane?
— There is none in whom bodily formation had arisen, mental formation had not.
— Yes. To those at the first, second and third *jhāna* attainment, and those of the sensuous sphere, both bodily formation and mental formation had arisen.

(b) Mental formation had arisen in this individual at this plane. Had bodily formation arisen in that individual at that plane?
— No. To those at the fourth *jhāna* attainment, at fine-material sphere, and at immaterial sphere, mental formation had arisen; bodily formation had not arisen.

---

[13] .... p .... : designated from the Pāli term *peyyāla* which means 'repetition', a way of indicating that a passage has been omitted which has to be filled up in full".

— Yes. Refer to the answer in 32 *ii* (a) above.

33. *i* (a) Verbal formation had arisen in this individual at this plane. Had mental formation arisen in that individual at that plane?
— There is none in whom verbal formation had arisen, mental formation had not.
— Yes. To those at the first *jhāna* attainment, and those of the sensuous sphere, and others of the fine-material and immaterial sphere (except Non-percipients, and those at the moment of second *citta* of Pure abode beings), both verbal formation and mental formation had arisen.

(b) Mental formation had arisen in this individual at this plane. Had verbal formation arisen in that individual at that plane?
— No. To those at the second, third, and fourth *jhāna* attainment, and to those at the moment of second *citta* of Pure abode beings (*suddhāvāsānaṃ dutiye citte vattamāne tesaṃ*), corresponds to the second *bhavaṅga* when one is reborn in or shifted to an existence of Pure abode) [14], mental formation had arisen; verbal formation had not arisen.
— Yes. Refer to the answer in 33 *i* (a) above.

Opposite enquiries by Individual

34. *i* (a) Bodily formation had not arisen in this individual. Had verbal formation not arisen in that individual?
— *Natthi* [15]. (Bodily formation had not arisen but verbal formation had arisen to those fine-material beings (except Non-percipients) and immaterial beings).

(b) Verbal formation had not arisen in this individual. Had bodily formation not arisen in that individual?
— *Natthi*. (Verbal formation had not arisen but bodily formation had arisen to those at the planes of second and third *jhāna* attainment).

ii (a) Bodily formation had not arisen in this individual. Had mental formation not arisen in that individual?
— *Natthi*. (Bodily formation had not arisen but mental formation had arisen to those at the fourth *jhāna* attainment).

(b) Mental formation had not arisen in this individual. Had bodily formation not arisen in that individual?
— No such being mental formation had arisen but verbal formation had not.

35. *i* (a) Verbal formation had not arisen in this individual. Had mental formation not arisen in that individual?

---

[14] *Cf.* PañkA: 6. Saṅkhārayamakaṃ, par. 37, which mentions "*Suddhāvāsānaṃ dutiye citte vattamāneti paṭisandhito dutiye bhavaṅgacitte*".

[15] *Natthi* in Pāli has the meaning of "none; nothing as such; it is impossible"

— *Natthi.* (Verbal formation had not arisen, but mental formation had arisen to those at the second, third, and fourth *jhāna* attainment at sensuous and fine-material planes, those at fourth *jhāna* attainment in immaterial sphere, and to those at the moment of second *citta* of the Pure abode beings).

(b) Mental formation had not arisen in this individual. Had verbal formation not arisen in that individual?
— No such being mental formation had not arisen but verbal formation had.

Opposite enquiries by Plane

36. *i* (a) Bodily formation had not arisen at this plane. ..... p ..... Had verbal formation not arisen at that plane? ..... p ..... *ii* (b) Mental formation had not arisen at this plane. Had verbal formation not arisen at that plane?

The answers in "Opposite enquiries on Plane" are the same in all those six time-lagged classifications of enquiries. Refer to the last part in Chart 6.1.

Opposite enquiries by Individual and Plane

37. *i* (a) Bodily formation had not arisen in this individual at this plane. Had verbal formation not arisen in that individual at that plane?
— No. To those at the fine-material sphere (except Non-percipience plane) and immaterial sphere, bodily formation had not arisen; verbal formation had arisen.
— Yes. To those at the fourth *jhāna* attainment, those at the moment of second *citta* of Pure abode beings, and those Non-percipient beings, neither bodily formation nor verbal formation had arisen.

(b) Verbal formation had not arisen in this individual at this plane. Had bodily formation not arisen in that individual at that plane?
— No. To those at the second and third *jhāna* attainment, verbal formation had not arisen; but bodily formation had arisen.
— Yes. Refer to the answer in 37 *i* (a) above.

ii (a) Bodily formation had not arisen in this individual at this plane. Had mental formation not arisen in that individual at that plane?
— No. To those at the fourth *jhāna* attainment, and to those at the fine-material planes (except Non-percipients) and immaterial plane, bodily formation had not arisen; mental formation had arisen.
— Yes. To those Pure abode beings and Non-percipient beings at the birth-moment, neither bodily formation nor mental formation had arisen.

(b) Mental formation had not arisen in this individual at this plane. Had bodily formation not arisen in that individual at that plane?
— No such being mental formation had arisen; verbal formation in whom hadn't.
— Yes. Refer to the answer in 37 *ii* (a) above.

38. *i* (a) Verbal formation had not arisen in this individual at this plane. Had mental formation not arisen in that individual at that plane?
— No. To those at the second, third, and fourth *jhāna* attainment, and those at the moment of second *citta* of Pure abode beings, verbal formation had not arisen; mental formation had arisen.
— Yes. To those at the birth-moment of Pure abode beings, and at the birth-moment of Non-percipient beings, neither verbal formation nor mental formation had therein arisen.

(b) Mental formation had not arisen in this individual at this plane. Had verbal formation not arisen in that individual at that plane?
— No such being mental formation had not arisen; verbal formation had arisen.
— Yes. Refer to the answer in 38 *i* (a) above.

In Future

Forward enquiries by Individual

39. *i* (a) Bodily formation will arise in this individual. Will verbal formation arise in that individual?
— No. (To those at the planes of second and third *jhāna* attainment, bodily formation will arise; verbal formation will not arise).
— Yes. (to those at the first *jhāna* attainment, and those of the sensuous sphere).

(b) Verbal formation will arise in this individual. Will bodily formation arise in that individual?
— No. To those in whose consciousness whereof final-stage *citta* [16] of the sensuous sphere will instantly arise, those in the fine-material sphere and immaterial sphere (except Non-percipients), and including those final existence beings [17] of the fine-material and immaterial sphere who, having reborn, will attain *Parinibbāna* at the death-moment [18], verbal formation will arise; bodily formation will not arise.

---

[16] *Pacchimacitta*, I interpret it as "final-stage" state of consciousness instead of "final" state of consciousness, similarly also in Chapter 5. If it is interpreted as 'final consciousness', it will be easily misconceived as the "final dying-moment" of consciousness.

[17] Final existence beings (*Pacchimabhavikā*) : the present existence of those at the planes to which they are born, will be the last in their current lifespans, and will not be subject to reborn again (i.e. attain *parinibbāna* after present life). The detail in Appendix I explains that attainers of *Arahattamagga* and *Anāgāmiphala* (who are reborn for one last time in any of those 7 sensuous planes, of those 15 fine-material planes excluding plane of the Non-percipients), and beings at the immaterial sphere who will attain *parinibbāna* after their current lifespans, are known as "final existence beings".

[18] *Rūpāvacare arūpāvacare pacchimabhavikānaṃ ye ca rūpāvacaraṃ arūpāvacaraṃ upapajjitvā parinibbāyissanti tesaṃ cavantānaṃ tesaṃ.*

— Yes. To those others (those at the first *jhāna* attainment, and those of the sensuous sphere), both verbal formation and bodily formation will arise.

According to the commentarial Pañcappakaraṇa, those endowed with the final-stage state of consciousness (*Pacchimacitta*) [16], by means of all that is final and having no longer subject to the round of rebirths, became the ones known as he who have destroyed all defilement (i.e. *Arahat*). Those final-stage *citta* are said to have come through the dominant power of the second *jhāna* of the fine-material sphere, with non-initial application and non-sustained application at the dying moment of consciousness as the starting point; and through the domination of the fourth *jhāna* of immaterial sphere, but not at the death-moment of consciousness. Those are the origins in regard to individuals endowed with final-stage *citta* [19]. We can hereby conclude that final-stage *citta* does not occur at first *jhāna*. The Yamakapāli text refers to those endowed with final-stage *citta* as persons in whom all the three types of formation will not arise. (See nos. 44-45, 72-73, 77-78). Since it is in future tense, we can not equate synonymy with cessation-attainment (*nirodhasamāpanna*) — a precondition for entering the first stage transcendental cultivation of the 'stream-entry' Path-*citta* (*Sotāpattimaggacitta*).

ii (a) Bodily formation will arise in this individual. Will mental formation arise in that individual?
— No such being bodily formation will arise but mental formation will not.
— Yes. (at the first, second, and third *jhāna* attainment).

(b) Mental formation will arise in this individual. Will bodily formation arise in that individual?
— No. To those in whose consciousness whereof final-stage *citta* of the sensuous sphere will instantly arise, and those of the fine-material and immaterial sphere, including those final existence beings of the fine-material and immaterial sphere who, having reborn, will attain *Parinibbāna* [20] at the death-moment, mental formation will arise; bodily formation will not arise.
— Yes. To those at the first, second, and third *jhāna* attainment, and to others of the sensuous sphere, both mental formation and bodily formation will arise.

40. *i* (a) Verbal formation will arise in this individual. Will mental formation arise in that individual?
— No such being verbal formation will arise but mental formation will not.
— Yes. Refer to the answer in *ii* (b) below.

---

[19] *Cf.* PañkA: Saṅkhārayamakaṃ, par. 44.

[20] *Parinibbāna*: (lit.) full or final *Nibbāna*, the attainment of final liberation not by other kinds of noble persons other than at the death of an *Arahat* (final existence being) after the last life-span, which sets the person completely free from the round of rebirths.

(b) Mental formation will arise in this individual. Will verbal formation arise in that individual?
— No. To those in whose consciousness whereof final-stage *citta* with non-initial application and non-sustained application will instantly arise [21], and those at the planes of second, third, and fourth *jhāna* attainment, mental formation will arise; verbal formation will not arise.
— Yes. To those at the first *jhāna* attainment, those of the sensuous sphere, and others of the fine-material and immaterial sphere (including therein final existence beings), both mental formation and verbal formation will arise.

Forward enquiries by Plane

41. *i* (a) Bodily formation will arise at this plane? Will verbal formation arise at that plane? ..... p ..... *ii* (b) Mental formation will arise at this plane. Will verbal formation arise at that plane?

The answers in "Forward enquiries on Plane" are the same in all those six time-lagged classifications of enquiries. Refer to the last part in Chart 6.1.

Forward enquiries by Individual and Plane

For answers to the following enquiries, refer to those in "Forward enquiries on Individual", from 39 *i* (a) to 40 *i* (b).

42. *i* (a) Bodily formation will arise in this individual at this plane. Will verbal formation arise in that individual at that plane? (b) Verbal formation will arise in this individual at this plane. Will bodily formation arise in that individual at that plane?

ii (a) Bodily formation will arise in this individual at this plane. Will mental formation arise in that individual at that plane? (b) Mental formation will arise in this individual at this plane. Will bodily formation arise in that individual at that plane?

43. *i* (a) Verbal formation will arise in this individual at this plane. Will mental formation arise in that individual at that plane? (b) Mental formation will arise in this individual at this plane. Will verbal formation arise in that individual at that plane?

Opposite enquiries by Individual

44. *i* (a) Bodily formation will not arise in this individual. Will verbal formation not arise in that individual?

---

[21] *Pacchimacittasamaṅgīnaṃ yassa cittassa anantarā avitakkaavicāraṃ pacchimacittaṃ uppajjissati tesaṃ.*

— No. To those in whose consciousness whereof final-stage *citta* of the sensuous sphere will instantly arise; and those of the fine-material and immaterial sphere (except Non-percipients) including those final existence beings of the fine-material and immaterial sphere who, having reborn, will attain *Parinibbāna* at the death-moment, bodily formation will not arise; but verbal formation will arise.
— Yes. To those endowed with final-stage *citta*, those in whose consciousness whereof final-stage *citta* with non-initial application and non-sustained application will instantly arise, and those at the fourth *jhāna* attainment; and to Non-percipient beings, neither bodily formation nor verbal formation will arise.

(b) Verbal formation will not arise in this individual. Will bodily formation not arise in that individual?
— No. To those at the second and third *jhāna* attainment, verbal formation will not arise, but bodily formation will arise.
— Yes. Refer to the answer in 44 *i* (a) above.

ii (a) Bodily formation will not arise in this individual. Will mental formation not arise in that individual?
— No. To those in whose consciousness whereof final-stage *citta* of the sensuous sphere will instantly arise, those of the fine-material and immaterial sphere (except Non-percipients) including final existence beings of the fine-material and immaterial sphere who, having reborn, will attain *Parinibbāna* at the death-moment; and those at the fourth *jhāna* attainment, bodily formation will not arise; but mental formation will arise.
— Yes. To those endowed with final-stage *citta* [22], and to Non-percipient beings, neither bodily formation nor mental formation will arise

(b) Mental formation will not arise in this individual. Will bodily formation not arise in that individual?
— No such being mental formation will not arise but bodily formation will arise.
— Yes. Refer to the answer in 44 *ii* (a) above.

45. *i* (a) Verbal formation will not arise in this individual. Will mental formation arise in that individual?
— No. To those in whose consciousness whereof final-stage *citta* with non-initial application and non-sustained application will instantly arise; and those at the second, third, and fourth *jhāna* attainment, verbal formation will not arise; mental formation will arise.
— Yes. To those endowed with final-stage *citta* [22], and to Non-percipient beings, neither verbal formation nor mental formation will arise.

---

[22] To those endowed with final-stage *citta*, all the three types of formations do not and will not arise at the three mundane spheres, with the only exception as bodily formation which had arisen at the Sense-sphere whilst bodily formation had not arisen at the fine-material and immaterial sphere. (See nos. 72).

(b) Mental formation will not arise in this individual. Will verbal formation arise in that individual?
— No such being mental formation will not arise but verbal formation will arise.
— Yes. Refer to the answer in 45 *i* (a) above.

Opposite enquiries by Plane

46. *i* (a) Bodily formation will not arise at this plane. Will verbal formation not arise at that plane? ..... p ..... *ii* (b) Mental formation will not arise at this plane. Will verbal formation not arise at that plane?

The answers in "Opposite enquiries on Plane" are the same in all those six time-lagged classifications of enquiries. Refer to the last part in Chart 6.1.

Opposite enquiries by Individual and Plane

47. *i* (a) Bodily formation will not arise in this individual at this plane. Will verbal formation not arise in that individual at that plane? (b) Verbal formation will not arise in this individual at this plane. Will bodily formation not arise in that individual at that plane?
ii (a) Bodily formation will not arise in this individual at this plane. Will mental formation not arise in that individual at that plane? (b) Mental formation will not arise in this individual at this plane. Will bodily formation not arise in that individual at that plane?

48. *i* (a) Verbal formation will not arise in this individual at this plane. Will mental formation not arise in that individual at that plane? (b) Mental formation will not arise in this individual at this plane. Will verbal formation not arise in that individual at that plane?

For answers to the above enquiries, refer to those in preceding "Forward enquiries on Individual" from 39 *i* (a) to 40 *i* (b).

Chart 6.2 Present and past arising of the three types of formations

A: arises/ had arisen; N: does not arise/ had not arisen

	Present			Past		
	Bodily F.	Verbal F.	Mental F.	Bodily F.	Verbal F.	Mental F.
Those at the arising moment of breath-in and breath-out	A				A	A
Those at the ceasing moment of breath-in and breath-out						
Those at the arising moment of breath-in and breath-out without initial application and sustained application						
Those at the first *jhāna* attainment, at the arising moment of breath-in and breath-out	A				A	
Those at the first *jhāna* attainment, at the ceasing moment of breath-in and breath-out	N				A	
Those at the second and third *jhāna* attainment, at the arising moment of breath-in and breath-out	A				N	
Those at the second and third *jhāna* attainment, at the ceasing moment of breath-in and breath-out	N				N	
Those at the arising moment of initial application and sustained application		A	A		A	A
Those at the arising moment of initial application and sustained application without breath-in and breath-out						
Those at the arising moment of *citta* without breath-in and breath-out	N				AN	A
Those at the arising moment of *citta* without initial application and sustained application		N				A
Those at the arising moment of *citta* with non-initial application and non-sustained application, without breath-in and breath-out						
Those at the planes of initial application and sustained application (except those endowed with final-stage *citta*)						
Those at the planes of non-initial application and non-sustained application (except those endowed with final-stage *citta*)						
Those in whose consciousness whereof final-stage *citta* of the sensuous sphere will instantly arise						
Those in whose consciousness whereof final-stage *citta* with non-initial application and non-sustained application will instantly arise						
Those who are endowed with final-stage *citta*						
Those who are endowed with final-stage *citta* at the planes of initial application and sustained application						
Those who are endowed with final-stage *citta* at the planes of non-initial application and non-sustained application						
Those endowed with final-stage *citta* with non-initial application and non-sustained application						
Those at the arising moment of final-stage *citta*						
Those at the ceasing moment of final-stage *citta*						
Those at the arising moment of final-stage *citta* with initial application and sustained application						
Those at the ceasing moment of final-stage *citta* with initial application and sustained application						
Those at the ceasing moment of final-stage *citta* at the planes of initial application and sustained application						

	Present			Past		
	Bodily F.	Verbal F.	Mental F.	Bodily F.	Verbal F.	Mental F.
Those at the ceasing moment of final-stage *citta* at the planes of non-initial application and non-sustained application						
Those at the arising moment of final-stage *citta* with non-initial application and non-sustained application						
Those at the ceasing moment of final-stage *citta* with non-initial application and non-sustained application						
Those at the first *jhāna* attainment						
Those at the first, second, and third *jhāna* attainment						
Those at the second and third *jhāna* attainment						
Those at the second, third, and fourth *jhāna* attainment						
Those at the fourth *jhāna* attainment	N				N	
Those at the birth-moment of Pure abode beings	N	N				N
Those at the birth-moment of Non-percipient beings	N	N				N
At the moment of second *citta* of Pure abode beings	N				N	
Sensuous beings						
Fine-material beings (except Non-percipients)	N				A	
Immaterial beings	N				A	
Non-percipient beings	N	N			AN	AN
Fiinal existence beings						
All those at the ceasing moment of *citta*	N	N			A	A
Those at Cessation attainment	N	N			A	A

Present and Past

Forward enquiries by Individual

49. *i* (a) Bodily formation arises in this individual. Had verbal formation arisen in that individual?
— Yes. To those at the arising moment of breath-in and breath-out, bodily formation arises; verbal formation had also arisen.

(b) Verbal formation had arisen in this individual. Does bodily formation arise in that individual?
— No. To all those at the ceasing moment of *citta*, those at the arising moment of *citta* without breath-in and breath-out [23], those of Cessation-attainment, and those Non-percipient beings, verbal formation had arisen but bodily formation does not arise.
— Yes. Refer to the answer in 49 *i* (a) above.

ii (a) Bodily formation arises in this individual. Had mental formation arisen in that individual?
— Yes. (to sensuous beings at the arising moment of breath-in and breath-out).

(b) Mental formation had arisen in this individual. Does bodily formation arise in that individual?
— No. To all those at the ceasing moment of *citta*, those at the arising moment of *citta* without breath-in and breath-out, those of Cessation-attainment, and those Non-percipient beings, mental formation had arisen; bodily formation does not arise.
— Yes. To those at the arising moment of breath-in and breath-out, mental formation had arisen; bodily formation also arises.

50. *i* (a) Verbal formation arises in this individual. Had mental formation arisen in that individual?
— Yes. Refer to the answer in 50 *i* (b) below.

(b) Mental formation had arisen in this individual. Does verbal formation arise in that individual?
— No. To all those at the ceasing moment of *citta*, those at the arising moment of *citta* without initial application and sustained application, those of Cessation-attainment, and those Non-percipient beings, mental formation had arisen; verbal formation does not arise.
— Yes. To those at the arising moment of initial application and sustained application, mental formation had arisen; verbal formation also arises.

Forward enquiries by Plane

51. *i* (a) Bodily formation arises at this plane. Had verbal formation arisen at that plane? ..... p ..... *ii* (b) Mental formation had arisen at this plane. Does verbal formation arise at that plane?

The answers in "Forward enquiries on Plane" are the same in all those six time-lagged classifications of enquiries. Refer to the last part in Chart 6.1.

Forward enquiries by Individual and Plane

52. *i* (a) Bodily formation arises in this individual at this plane. Had verbal formation arisen in that individual at that plane?
— No. To those at the planes of second and third *jhāna* attainment, at the arising moment of breath-in and breath-out, bodily formation arises; verbal formation had not arisen.
— Yes. To those at the first *jhāna* attainment, at the arising moment of breath-in and breath-out of the sensuous sphere, bodily formation arises; verbal formation also had arisen.

(b) Verbal formation had arisen in this individual at this plane. Does bodily formation arise in that individual at that plane?
— No. To those at the first *jhāna* attainment, at the ceasing moment of breath-in and breath-out of the sensuous sphere; those at the arising moment of *citta*

without breath-in and breath-out; and those of the fine-material and immaterial sphere, verbal formation had arisen; bodily formation does not arise.
— Yes. Refer to the answer in 52 *i* (a) above.

ii (a) Bodily formation arises in this individual at this plane. Had mental formation arisen in that individual at that plane?
— Yes. To those at the arising moment of breath-in and breath-out, bodily formation arises; mental formation also had arisen.

(b) Mental formation had arisen in this individual at this plane. Does bodily formation arise in that individual at that plane?
— No. To all those at the ceasing moment of *citta*, and to those at the arising moment of *citta* without breath-in and breath-out, mental formation had arisen; bodily formation does not arise.
— Yes. Refer to the answer in 52 *ii* (a) above.

53. *i* (a) Verbal formation arises in this individual at this plane. Had mental formation arisen in that individual at that plane?
— Yes. To those at the arising moment of initial application and sustained application, verbal formation had arisen; mental formation also arises.

(b) Mental formation had arisen in this individual at this plane. Does verbal formation arise in that individual at that plane?
— No. To all those at the ceasing moment of *citta*, and to those at the arising moment of *citta* without initial application and sustained application, mental formation had arisen; verbal formation does not arise.
— Yes. Refer to the answer in 53 *i* (a) above.

Opposite enquiries by Individual

For answers to the following enquiries, refer to the same in "Opposite enquiries on Individual" from 57 *i* (a) to 58 *i* (b).

54. *i* (a) Bodily formation does not arise in this individual. Had verbal formation not arisen in that individual? (b) Verbal formation had not arisen in this individual. Does bodily formation not arise in that individual?

ii (a) Bodily formation does not arise in this individual. Had mental formation not arisen in that individual? (b) Mental formation had not arisen in this individual. Does bodily formation not arise in that individual?

55. *i* (a) Verbal formation does not arise in this individual. Had mental formation not arisen in that individual? (b) Mental formation had not arisen in this individual. Does verbal formation not arise in that individual?

Opposite enquiries by Plane

56. *i* (a) Bodily formation does not arise at this plane. Had verbal formation not arisen at that plane? ..... p ..... *ii* (b) Mental formation had not arisen at this plane. Does verbal formation not arise at that plane?

The answers in "Opposite enquiries on Plane" are the same in all those six time-lagged classifications of enquiries. Refer to the last part in Chart 6.1.

Opposite enquiries by Individual and Plane

57. *i* (a) Bodily formation does not arise in this individual at this plane. Had verbal formation not arisen in that individual at that plane?
— No. To those at the first *jhāna* attainment, at the ceasing moment of breath-in and breath-out of the sensuous sphere; those at the arising moment of *citta* without breath-in and breath-out [23]; and those of the fine-material and immaterial sphere, bodily formation does not arise; but verbal formation had arisen.
— Yes. To those at the second and third *jhāna* attainment, at the ceasing moment of breath-in and breath-out; those at the arising moment of *citta* without breath-in and breath-out [23]; those at the fourth *jhāna* attainment; those at the moment of second *citta* of Pure abode beings [14] ; and those Non-percipient beings [24], bodily formation does not arise; verbal formation also had not arisen.

(b) Verbal formation had not arisen in this individual at this plane. Does bodily formation not arise in that individual at that plane?
— No. To those at the second and third *jhāna* attainment, at the arising moment of breath-in and breath-out, verbal formation had not arisen; bodily formation therein arises.
— Yes. Refer to the answer in 57 *i* (a) above.

ii (a) Bodily formation does not arise in this individual at this plane. Had mental formation not arisen in that individual at that plane?
— No. To all those at the ceasing moment of *citta*, and those at the arising moment of *citta* without breath-in and breath-out, bodily formation does not arise; mental formation therein had arisen.
— Yes. To those at the birth-moment of Pure abode beings and Non-percipient beings, bodily formation does not arise; mental formation also had not arisen.

---

[23] To those at the arising moment of *citta* without breath-in and breath-out, verbal formation had either arisen or not arisen. The difference is that verbal formation had arisen, and will arise, at the planes of initial application and sustained application; but it had not arisen, and will not arise, at the planes of non-initial application and non-sustained application.

[24] Does not contradict with answers in nos. 49, 50 on account of the peculiarity of Non-percipient beings.

(b) Mental formation had not arisen in this individual at this plane. Does bodily formation not arise in that individual at that plane?
— No such being mental formation had not arisen, but bodily formation arises.
— Yes. Refer to the answer in 57 *ii* (a) above.

58. *i* (a) Verbal formation does not arise in this individual at this plane. Had mental formation not arisen in that individual to that place?
— No. To all those at the ceasing moment of *citta*, and those at the arising moment of *citta* without initial application and sustained application, verbal formation does not arise; but mental formation had arisen.
— Yes. To those at the birth-moment of Pure abode and Non-percipient beings, verbal formation does not arise; mental formation therein also had not arisen.

(b) Mental formation had not arisen in this individual at this plane. Does verbal formation not arise in that individual at that plane?
— No such being mental formation had not arisen, but verbal formation arises.
— Yes. Refer to the answer in 58 *i* (a) above.

Chart 6.3 Present and future arising of the three types of formations

A: arises/ will arise; N: does not arise/ will not arise

	Present			Future		
	Bodily F.	Verbal F.	Mental F.	Bodily F.	Verbal F.	Mental F.
Those at the arising moment of breath-in and breath-out	A					A
Those at the ceasing moment of breath-in and breath-out						
Those at the arising moment of breath-in and breath-out without initial application and sustained application						
Those at the first *jhāna* attainment, at the arising moment of breath-in and breath-out	A				A	
Those at the first *jhāna* attainment, at the ceasing moment of breath-in and breath-out	N				A	
Those at the second and third *jhāna* attainment, at the arising moment of breath-in and breath-out	A				N	
Those at the second and third *jhāna* attainment, at the ceasing moment of breath-in and breath-out	N				N	
Those at the arising moment of initial application and sustained application		A				A
Those at the arising moment of initial application and sustained application without breath-in and breath-out						
Those at the arising moment of *citta* without breath-in and breath-out	N				AN	A
Those at the arising moment of *citta* without initial application and sustained application		N				A
Those at the arising moment of *citta* with non-initial application and non-sustained application, without breath-in and breath-out						
Those at the planes of initial application and sustained application (except those endowed with final-stage *citta*)						
Those at the planes of non-initial application. and non-sustained application (except those endowed with final-stage *citta*)						
Those in whose consciousness whereof final-stage *citta* of the sensuous sphere will instantly arise						
Those in whose consciousness whereof final-stage *citta* with non-initial application and non-sustained application will instantly arise	N				N	
Those who are endowed with final-stage *citta*	N				N	N
Those who are endowed with final-stage *citta* at the planes of initial application and sustained application						
Those who are endowed with final-stage *citta* at the planes of non-initial application and non-sustained application						
Those who are endowed with final-stage *citta* with non-initial application and non-sustained application		N				N
Those at the arising moment of final-stage *citta*						
Those at the ceasing moment of final-stage *citta*						
Those at the arising moment of final-stage *citta* with initial application and sustained application		A				N
Those at the ceasing moment of final-stage *citta* with initial application and sustained application		N				N
Those at the ceasing moment of final-stage *citta* at the planes of initial application and sustained application						

	Present			Future		
	Bodily F.	Verbal F.	Mental F.	Bodily F.	Verbal F.	Mental F.
Those at the ceasing moment of final-stage *citta* at the planes of non-initial application and non-sustained application						
Those at the arising moment of final-stage *citta* with non-initial application and non-sustained application						
Those at the ceasing moment of final-stage *citta* with non-initial application and non-sustained application						
Those at the first *jhāna* attainment						
Those at the first, second, and third *jhāna* attainment						
Those at the second and third *jhāna* attainment						
Those at the second, third, and fourth *jhāna* attainment						
Those at the fourth *jhāna* attainment	N				N	
Those at the birth-moment of Pure abode beings						
Those at the birth-moment of Non-percipient beings						
At the moment of second *citta* of Pure abode beings						
Sensuous beings						
Fine-material beings (except Non-percipients)	N				A	
Immaterial beings	N				A	
Non-percipient beings	N	N			AN	AN
Final existence beings						
All those at the ceasing moment of *citta*	N	N			A	A
Those at Cessation attainment	N	N			A	A

Present and Future

Forward enquiries by Individual

For answers to the following enquiries, refer to the same in "Forward enquiries on Individual and Plane" from 62 *i* (a) to 63 *i* (b).

59. *i* (a) Bodily formation arises in this individual. Will verbal formation arise in that individual? (b) Verbal formation will arise in this individual. Does bodily formation arise in that individual?

ii (a) Bodily formation arises in this individual. Will mental formation arise in that individual? (b) Mental formation will arise in this individual. Does bodily formation arise in that individual?

60. *i* (a) Verbal formation arises in this individual? Will mental formation arise in that individual? (b) Mental formation will arise in this individual. Does verbal formation arise in that individual?

Forward enquiries by Plane

61. *i* (a) Bodily formation arises at this plane. Will verbal formation arise at that plane? ..... p ..... *ii* (b) Mental formation will arise at this plane. Does verbal formation arise at that plane?

The answers in "Forward enquiries on Plane" are the same in all those six time-lagged classifications of enquiries. Refer to the last part in Chart 6.1.

Forward enquiries by Individual and Plane

62. *i* (a) Bodily formation arises in this individual at this plane. Will verbal formation arise in that individual at that plane?
— No. To those at the second and third *jhāna* attainment, at the arising moment of breath-in and breath-out, bodily formation arises; verbal formation therein will not arise.
— Yes. To those at the first *jhāna* attainment, at the arising moment of breath-in and breath-out of the sensuous sphere, bodily formation arises; verbal formation also will arise.

(b) Verbal formation will arise in this individual at this plane. Does bodily formation arise in that individual at that plane?
— No. To those at the first *jhāna* attainment, at the ceasing moment of breath-in and breath-out of the sensuous sphere; those at the arising moment of *citta* without breath-in and breath-out; those of the fine-material and immaterial sphere; those Non-percipient beings (and those of Cessation-attainment, surpassing three mundane spheres), verbal formation will arise; bodily formation does not arise.
— Yes. Refer to the answer in 62*i* (a) above.

ii (a) Bodily formation arises in this individual at this plane. Will mental formation arise in that individual at that plane?
— No such being in whom bodily formation arises, mental formation had not.
— Yes. To those at the arising moment of breath-in and breath-out, bodily formation arises; mental formation also will arise.

(b) Mental formation will arise in this individual at this plane. Does bodily formation arise in that individual at that plane?
— No. To all those at the ceasing moment of *citta*, and those at the arising moment of *citta* without breath-in and breath-out, mental formation will arise; bodily formation therein does not arise.
— Yes. Refer to the answer in 62*i* (a) above.

63. *i* (a) Verbal formation arises in this individual at this plane. Will mental formation arise in that individual at that plane?
— No. To those at the arising moment of final-stage *citta* with initial application

and sustained application, verbal formation arises; mental formation will not arise.
— Yes. To those others at the arising moment of initial application and sustained application, verbal formation arises; mental formation also will arise.

(b) Mental formation will arise in this individual at this plane. Does verbal formation arise in that individual at that plane?
— No. To all those at the ceasing moment of *citta*, those at the arising moment of *citta* without initial application and sustained application, to Non-percipient beings (and those of Cessation-attainment, surpassing mundane spheres), mental formation will arise; verbal formation does not arise.
— Yes. Refer to the answer in 63 *i* (a) above.

Opposite enquiries by Individual

64. *i* (a) Bodily formation does not arise in this individual. Will verbal formation not arise in that individual?
— No. To all those at the ceasing moment of *citta*, those at the arising moment of *citta* without breath-in and breath-out, those of Cessation-attainment, and those Non-percipient beings, bodily formation does not arise; but verbal formation will arise.
— Yes. To those endowed with the final-stage *citta*, and those in whose consciousness whereof final-stage *citta* with non-initial application and non-sustained application will instantly arise, bodily formation does not arise; verbal formation also will not arise.

(b) Verbal formation will not arise in this individual. Does bodily formation not arise in that individual?
— No. (To those at the planes of second and third *jhāna* attainment, at the arising moment of breath-in and breath-out, verbal formation will not arise; but bodily formation arises).
— Yes. Same as the answer in 64 *i* (a) above.

ii (a) Bodily formation does not arise in this individual. Will mental formation not arise in that individual?
— No. Same as the answer in 64 *i* (a) above.
— Yes. To those endowed with the final-stage *citta*, bodily formation does not arise; mental formation also will not arise.

(b) Mental formation will not arise in this individual. Does bodily formation not arise in that individual?
— No such being mental formation will not arise but bodily formation arises.
— Yes. Refer to the answer in 64 *ii* (a) or 64 *i* (a) above.

65. *i* (a) Verbal formation does not arise in this individual. Will mental formation not arise in that individual?

— No. To all those at the ceasing moment of *citta*, those at the arising moment of *citta* without initial application and sustained application, those of Cessation-attainment, and those Non-percipient beings, verbal formation does not arise; but mental formation will arise.
— Yes. To those at the ceasing moment of final-stage *citta* with initial application and sustained application, and those endowed with final-stage *citta* with non-initial application and non-sustained application, verbal formation does not arise; mental formation also will not arise.

(b) Mental formation will not arise in this individual. Does verbal formation not arise in that individual?
— No. To those at the arising moment of final-stage *citta* with initial application and sustained application, mental formation will not arise; but verbal formation arises.
— Yes. Refer to the answer in 65 *i* (a) above.

Opposite enquiries by Plane

66. *i* (a) Bodily formation does not arise at this plane. Will verbal formation not arise at that plane? ..... p ..... *ii* (b) Mental formation will not arise at this plane. Does verbal formation not arise at that plane?

The answers in "Opposite enquiries on Plane" are the same in all those six time-lagged classifications of enquiries. Refer to the last part in Chart 6.1.

Opposite enquiries by Individual and Plane

67. *i* (a) Bodily formation does not arise in this individual at this plane. Will verbal formation not arise in that individual at that plane?
— No. To those at the first *jhāna* attainment, at the ceasing moment of breath-in and breath-out of the sensuous sphere; those at the arising moment of *citta* without breath-in and breath-out [23]; and those of fine-material and immaterial sphere, bodily formation does not arise; verbal formation will arise.
— Yes. To those endowed with the final-stage *citta*; those in whose consciousness whereof final-stage *citta* with non-initial application and non-sustained application will instantly arise; those at the second and third *jhāna* attainment, at the ceasing moment of breath-in and breath-out; those at the arising moment of *citta* without breath-in and breath-out [23]; those at the fourth *jhāna* attainment [25]; and those Non-percipient beings [26], bodily formation does not arise; verbal formation also will not arise.

---

[25] Verbal formation firstly does not arise at the second *jhāna*, with bodily formation only does not arise at the fourth *jhāna*, follows the same lastly by mental formation which then brings about cessation-attainment.

[26] At first it may seem inconsistent with nos. 64 *i* (a) which says that to those Non-percipient beings, bodily formation does not arise; verbal formation will arise. It is not in contradiction because life of a non-percipient being perishes as soon as verbal formation in whom arises.

(b) Verbal formation will not arise in this individual at this plane. Does bodily formation not arise in that individual at that plane?
— No. To those at second and third *jhāna* attainment, at the arising moment of breath-in and breath-out, verbal formation will not arise; bodily formation arises.
— Yes. Refer to the answer in 67 *i* (a) above.

ii (a) Bodily formation does not arise in this individual at this plane. Will mental formation not arise in that individual at that plane?
— No. To all those at the ceasing moment of *citta*, and those at the arising moment of *citta* without breath-in and breath-out, bodily formation does not arise; mental formation will arise.
— Yes. To those endowed with final-stage *citta*, and those Non-percipient beings [27], body formation does not arise; mental formation also will not arise.

(b) Mental formation will not arise in this individual at this plane. Does bodily formation not arise in that individual at that plane?
— No such being mental formation will not arise, but bodily formation arises.
— Yes. Refer to the answer in 67 *ii* (a) above.

68. *i* (a) Verbal formation does not arise in this individual at this plane. Will mental formation not arise in that individual at that plane?
— No. To all those at the ceasing moment of *citta*, and those at the arising moment of *citta* without initial application and sustained application, verbal formation does not arise; mental formation will arise.
— Yes. To those at the ceasing moment of final-stage *citta* with initial application and sustained application, and those endowed with final-stage *citta* with non-initial application and non-sustained application, and to Non-percipient beings, verbal formation does not arise; mental formation also will not arise.

(b) Mental formation will not arise in this individual at this plane. Does verbal formation not arise in that individual at that plane?
— No. To those at the arising moment of final-stage *citta* with initial application and sustained application, mental formation will not arise; but verbal formation arises.
— Yes. Refer to the answer in 68 *i* (a) above.

[27] Does not contradict with nos. 64 *ii* (a) which says that to those non-percipient beings, bodily formation does not arise, but mental formation will arise. To non-percipient beings, life perishes once mental formation in whom arises.

Chart 6.4 Past and future arising of the three types of formations

A: had arisen/ will arise; N: had not arisen/ will not arise

	Present			Past		
	Bodily F.	Verbal F.	Mental F.	Bodily F.	Verbal F.	Mental F.
Those at the arising moment of breath-in and breath-out						
Those at the ceasing moment of breath-in and breath-out						
Those at the arising moment of breath-in and breath-out without initial application and sustained application						
Those at the first *jhāna* attainment, at the arising moment of breath-in and breath-out of the sensuous sphere						
Those at the first *jhāna* attainment, at the ceasing moment of breath-in and breath-out of the sensuous sphere						
Those at the second and third *jhāna* attainment, at the arising moment of breath-in and breath-out						
Those at the second and third *jhāna* attainment, at the ceasing moment of breath-in and breath-out						
Those at the arising moment of initial application and sustained application						
Those at the arising moment of initial application and sustained application without breath-in and breath-out						
Those at the arising moment of *citta* without breath-in and breath-out						
Those at the arising moment of *citta* without initial application and sustained application						
Those at the arising moment of *citta* with non-initial application and non-sustained application, without breath-in and breath-out						
Those at the planes of initial application and sustained application. (except those endowed with final-stage *citta*)		A				A
Those at the planes of non-initial application and non-sustained application (except those endowed with final-stage *citta*)		N				A
Those in whose consciousness whereof final-stage *citta* of the sensuous sphere will instantly arise						
Those in whose consciousness whereof final-stage *citta* with non-initial application and non-sustained application will instantly arise	AN				N	
Those who are endowed with final-stage *citta*	A				N	N
Those who are endowed with final-stage *citta*	N				N	
Those who are endowed with final-stage *citta* at the planes of initial application and sustained application		A				N
Those who are endowed with final-stage *citta* at the planes of non-initial application and non-sustained application		N				N
Those endowed with final-stage *citta* with non-initial application and non-sustained application						
Those at the arising moment of final-stage *citta*						
Those at the ceasing moment of final-stage *citta*						
Those at the arising moment of final-stage *citta* with initial application and sustained application						
Those at the ceasing moment of final-stage *citta* with initial application and sustained application						
Those at the ceasing moment of final-stage *citta* at the planes of initial application and sustained application						

	Present			Past		
	Bodily F.	Verbal F.	Bodily F.	Verbal F.	Bodily F.	Verbal F.
Those at the ceasing moment of final-stage *citta* at the planes of non-initial application and non-sustained application						
Those at the arising moment of final-stage *citta* with non-initial application and non-sustained application						
Those at the ceasing moment of final-stage *citta* with non-initial application and non-sustained application						
Those at the first *jhāna* attainment	A				A	
Those at the first, second, and third *jhāna* attainment	A					A
Those at the second and third *jhāna* attainment	A				N	
Those at the second, third, and fourth *jhāna* attainment						
Those at the fourth *jhāna* attainment	N				N	A
Those at the birth-moment of Pure abode beings						
Those at the birth-moment of Non-percipient beings						
Those at the moment of second *citta* of Pure abode beings						
Sensuous beings	A				A	A
Fine-material beings (except Non-percipients)	N				A	A
Immaterial beings	N				A	A
Non-percipient beings	N	N			N	N
Final existence beings						
All those at the ceasing moment of *citta*						
Those at Cessation attainment						

Past and Future

Forward enquiries by Individual

For answers to the following enquiries, refer to the same in "Forward enquiries on Individual and Plane" from 72 *i* (a) to 73 *i* (b).

69. *i* (a) Bodily formation had arisen in this individual. Will verbal formation arise in that individual? (b) Verbal formation will arise in this individual. Had bodily formation arisen in that individual?

ii (a) Bodily formation had arisen in this individual. Will mental formation arise in that individual? (b) Mental formation will arise in this individual. Had bodily formation arisen in that individual?

70. *i* (a) Verbal formation had arisen in this individual. Will mental formation arise in that individual? (b) Mental formation will arise in this individual. Had verbal formation arisen in that individual?

Forward enquiries by Plane

71. *i* (a) Bodily formation had arisen at this plane. Will verbal formation arise at that plane? ..... p ..... *ii* (b) Mental formation will arise at this plane. Had verbal formation arisen at that plane?

The answers in "Forward enquiries on Plane" are the same in all those six time-lagged classifications of enquiries. Refer to the last part in Chart 6.1.

Forward enquiries by Individual and Plane

72. *i* (a) Bodily formation had arisen in this individual at this plane. Will verbal formation arise in that individual at that plane?
— No. To those endowed with final-stage *citta* at planes of the sensuous sphere; those endowed with final-stage *citta*; those in whose consciousness whereof final-stage *citta* with non-initial application and non-sustained application will instantly arise; and those at the second and third *jhāna* attainment, bodily formation had arisen; verbal formation will not arise.
— Yes. To those at the first *jhāna* attainment, and others of the sensuous sphere, bodily formation had arisen; verbal formation also will arise.

(b) Verbal formation will arise in this individual at this plane. Had bodily formation arisen in that individual at that plane?
— No. To beings of the fine-material and immaterial sphere (except Non-percipients), verbal formation will arise; bodily formation had not arisen.
— Yes. Refer to the answer in 72 *i* (a) above.

ii (a) Bodily formation had arisen in this individual at this plane. Will mental formation arise in that individual at that plane?
— No. To those endowed with final-stage *citta* at planes of the sensuous sphere, bodily formation had arisen; mental formation will not arise.
— Yes. To those at the first, second, and third *jhāna* attainment, and others of the sensuous sphere, bodily formation had arisen; mental formation also will arise.

(b) Mental formation will arise in this individual at this plane. Had bodily formation arisen in that individual at that plane?
— No. To those at the fourth *jhāna* attainment, and those of the fine-material and immaterial sphere (except Non-percipients), mental formation will arise; bodily formation had not arisen.
— Yes. Refer to the answer in 72 *ii* (a) above.

73. *i* (a) Verbal formation had arisen in this individual at this plane. Will mental formation arise in that individual at that plane?

— No. To those endowed with final-stage *citta* at the planes of initial application and sustained application [28], verbal formation had arisen; mental formation will not arise.
— Yes. To others (who are not endowed with final-stage *citta*) at the planes of initial application and sustained application, verbal formation had arisen; mental formation also will arise.

(b) Mental formation will arise in this individual at this plane. Had verbal formation arisen in that individual at that plane?
— No. To those at the planes of non-initial application and non-sustained application (who are not endowed with final-stage *citta*), mental formation will arise; verbal formation had not arisen.
— Yes. Refer to the answer in 73 *i* (a) above.

Opposite enquiries by Individual

For answers to the following enquiries, refer to the same in "Opposite enquiries on Individual and Plane" from 77 *i* (a) to 78 *i* (b).

74. *i* (a) Bodily formation had not arisen in this individual. Will verbal formation not arise in that individual? (b) Verbal formation will not arise in this individual. Had bodily formation not arisen in that individual?

ii (a) Bodily formation had not arisen in this individual. Will mental formation not arise in that individual? (b) Mental formation will not arise in this individual. Had bodily formation not arisen in that individual?

75. *i* (a) Verbal formation had not arisen in this individual. Will mental formation not arisen in that individual? (b) Mental formation will not arise in this individual. Had verbal formation not arisen in that individual?

Opposite enquiries by Plane

76. *i* (a) Bodily formation had not arisen at this plane. Will verbal formation not arise at that plane? ..... p ..... *ii* (b) Mental formation will not arise at this plane. Had verbal formation not arisen at that plane?

The answers in "Opposite enquiries on Plane" are the same in all those six time-lagged classifications of enquiries. Refer to the last part in Chart 6.1.

Opposite enquiries by Individual and Plane

77. *i* (a) Bodily formation had not arisen in this individual at this plane. Will verbal formation not arise in that individual at that plane?

---

[28] *Savitakkasavicārabhūmiyaṃ pacchimacittasamaṅgīnaṃ.* The term *bhūmi* means 'earth, place, area, region', but in this context can also be referred to as 'plane'.

— No. To those at the fine-material and immaterial spheres, bodily formation had not arisen; verbal formation therein will arise.
— Yes. To those endowed with final-stage *citta* at the planes of fine-material and immaterial sphere; those in whose consciousness whereof final-stage *citta* with non-initial application and non-sustained application will instantly arise; those at the fourth *jhāna* attainment; and Non-percipient beings, bodily formation had not arisen; verbal formation also will not arise.

(b) Verbal formation will not arise in this individual at this plane. Had bodily formation not arisen in that individual at that plane?
— No. To those endowed with final-stage *citta* at planes of the sensuous sphere, and those at the second and third *jhāna* attainment, verbal formation will not arise; bodily formation therein had arisen.
— Yes. Refer to the answer in 77 *i* (a) above.

ii (a) Bodily formation had not arisen in this individual at this plane. Will mental formation not arise in that individual at that plane?
— No. To those at the fourth *jhāna* attainment, and those of fine-material and immaterial sphere, bodily formation had not arisen; mental formation will arise.
— Yes. To those endowed with final-stage *citta* at the planes of fine-material and immaterial sphere, and those Non-percipient beings, bodily formation had not arisen; mental formation also will not arise.

(b) Mental formation will not arise in this individual at this plane. Had bodily formation not arisen in that individual at that plane?
— No. To those endowed with final-stage *citta* at planes of the sensuous sphere, mental formation will not arise; but bodily formation had arisen.
— Yes. Refer to the answer in 77 *ii* (a) above.

78. *i* (a) Verbal formation had not arisen in this individual at this plane. Will mental formation not arise in that individual at that plane?
— No. To those at the planes of non-initial application and non-sustained application, verbal formation had not arisen; mental formation therein will arise.
— Yes. To those endowed with final-stage *citta* at the planes of non-initial application and non-sustained application, and those Non-percipient beings, verbal formation had not arisen; mental formation also will not arise.

(b) Mental formation will not arise in this individual at this plane. Had verbal formation not arisen in that individual at that plane?
— No. To those endowed with final-stage *citta* at the planes of initial application and sustained application, mental formation will not arise; verbal formation therein had arisen.
— Yes. Refer to the answer in 78 *i* (a) above.

Consolidated answers from arising of the formations

Chart 6.5 Composition on arising of the three formation types

A: arises/ had arisen/ will arise; N: does not arise/ had not arisen/ will not arise

	Present			Past			Future		
	Bodily F.	Verbal F.	Mental F.	Bodily F.	Verbal F.	Mental F.	Bodily F.	Verbal F.	Mental F.
Those at the arising moment of breath-in and breath-out	A	A	A		A	A			A
Those at the ceasing moment of breath-in and breath-out									
Those at the arising moment of breath-in and breath-out without initial application and sustained application	A	N							
Those at the first *jhāna* attainment, at the arising moment of breath-in and breath-out	A	A			A			A	
Those at the first *jhāna* attainment, at the ceasing moment of breath-in and breath-out	N				A			A	
Those at the second and third *jhāna* attainment, at the arising moment of breath-in and breath-out	A				N			N	
Those at the second and third *jhāna* attainment, at the ceasing moment of breath-in and breath-out	N				N			N	
Those at the arising moment of initial application and sustained application		A	A		A	A			A
Those at the arising moment of initial application and sustained application without breath-in and breath-out	N	A							
Those at the arising moment of *citta* without breath-in and breath-out	N		A		A N	A		A N	A
Those at the arising moment of *citta* without initial application and sustained application		N	A			A			A
Those at the arising moment of *citta* with non-initial application and non-sustained application, without breath-in and breath-out	N	N							
Those at the planes of initial application and sustained application (except those endowed with final-stage *citta*)					A				A
Those at the planes of non-initial application and non-sustained application (except those endowed with final-stage *citta*)					N				A
Those in whose consciousness whereof final-stage *citta* of the sensuous sphere will instantly arise							N	A	A
Those in whose consciousness whereof final-stage *citta* with non-initial application and non-sustained application will instantly arise	N			A N			N	N	A
Those who are endowed with final-stage *citta*	N			A			N	N	N
Those who are endowed with final-stage *citta*	N			N	N		N	N	N
Those endowed with final-stage *citta* at the planes of initial application and sustained application					A				N
Those endowed with final-stage *citta* at the planes of non-initial application and non-sustained application					N				N
Those endowed with final-stage *citta* with non-initial application and non-sustained application		N							N
Those at the arising moment of final-stage *citta*									
Those at the ceasing moment of final-stage *citta*									

	Present			Past			Future		
	Bodily F.	Verbal F.	Mental F.	Bodily F.	Verbal F.	Mental F.	Bodily F.	Verbal F.	Mental F.
Those at the arising moment of final-stage *citta* with initial application and sustained application		**A**							**N**
Those at the ceasing moment of final-stage *citta* with initial application and sustained application		**N**							**N**
Those at the ceasing moment of final-stage *citta* at the planes of initial application and sustained application									
Those at the ceasing moment of final-stage *citta* at the planes of non-initial application and non-sustained application									
Those at the arising moment of final-stage *citta* with non-initial application and non-sustained application									
Those at the ceasing moment of final-stage *citta* with non-initial application and non-sustained application									
Those at the first *jhāna* attainment				***A***	***A***	***A***	*A*	***A***	***A***
Those at the first, second, and third *jhāna* attainment				***A***		*A*	*A*		***A***
Those at the second and third *jhāna* attainment				*A*	***N***		*A*	***N***	
Those at the second, third, and fourth *jhāna* attainment					***N***	***A***		*N*	***A***
Those at the fourth *jhāna* attainment	**N**			***N***	***N***	*A*	*N*	***N***	***A***
Those at the birth-moment of Pure abode beings	**N**	**N**		*N*	*N*	***N***			
Those at the birth-moment of Non-percipient beings	**N**	**N**		*N*	*N*	***N***			
Those at the moment of second *citta* of Pure abode beings	**N**			*N*	***N***	*A*			
Sensuous beings				***A***	*A*	*A*	*A*	***A***	***A***
Fine-material beings (except Non-percipients)	**N**			***N***	***A***	*A*	*N*	***A***	***A***
Immaterial beings	**N**			***N***	***A***	*A*	*N*	***A***	***A***
Non-percipient beings	***N***	***N***	*N*	***N***	**A** ***N***	**A** ***N***	*N*	**A** ***N***	**A** ***N***
Final existence beings							*N*	*A*	*A*
All those at the ceasing moment of *citta*	***N***	***N***	*N*		**A**	**A**		**A**	**A**
Those at Cessation attainment	***N***	***N***	*N*		**A**	**A**		**A**	**A**
At the plane(s) of :									
first *jhāna*	A	A	A	A	A	A	A	A	A
first, second and third *jhāna*	A		A	A		A	A		A
second and third *jhāna*	A	N	A	A	N	A	A	N	A
second, third, and fourth *jhāna*		N	A		N	A		N	A
fourth *jhāna*	N	N	A	N	N	A	N	N	A
sensuous sphere	A	A	A	A	A	A	A	A	A
fine-material sphere (except Non-percipience plane)	N	A	A	N	A	A	N	A	A
immaterial sphere	N	A	A	N	A	A	N	A	A
Non-percipience	N	N	N	N	N	N	N	N	N

Referring to the above chart, the denotation of letters in *italic* are the answers consolidated from the respective first three sub-sections on present, past, and future arising of formations. Those letters in boldface (including *italic* in bold) are the answers to be referred to the other classifications on present-past, present-future, and past-future arising of the formations. As shown in the chart, there are certain types of individuals that have not been examined as of now, but all of those would be discussed in the next sub-section on cessation. This includes individuals not only are distinct at dissimilar ceasing moments of events, but also those at the arising moments of events.

However, there are exceptions. Certain Individual types in regard to 'ceasing moment', are also being examined in the process on Arising—those at the first *jhāna* attainment, second and third *jhāna* attainment, both at the arising and ceasing moment of breath-in and breath-out; and those of final-stage *citta* with initial application and sustained application. With now the big picture in place, inquisitive readers can take this opportunity to fill out those blanks in this chart. As you may be aware, there would be some answers which have to be treated as not applicable, or dependent on varying conditions.

6.2.2 Cessation of formations (with charts)

Chart 6.6 Enquiry sequence on the cessation of formations

		(Respective enquiries below are placed in relation to each of the following formation types accordingly)								
		Does it cease / Does it not cease: i) in that individual? ii) at that plane? iii) in that individual at that plane?			Had it ceased / Had it not ceased : i) in that individual? ii) at that plane? iii) in that individual at that plane?			Will it cease / Will it not cease: i) in that individual? ii) at that plane? iii) in that individual at that plane?		
		Bodily formation	Verbal formation	Mental formation	Bodily formation	Verbal formation	Mental formation	Bodily formation	Verbal formation	Mental formation
Bodily formation	ceases / does not cease : i) in this individual. ii) at this plane. iii) in this individual at this plane.		1a	2a		10a	11a		13a	14a
Verbal formation		1b		3a			12a			15a
Mental formation		2b*i*	3b							
Bodily formation	had ceased / had not ceased : i) in this individual. ii) at this plane. iii) in this individual at this plane.					4a	5a		16a	17a
Verbal formation		10b			4b		6a			18a
Mental formation		11b	12b		5b	6b*i*				
Bodily formation	will cease / will not cease : i) in this individual. ii) at this plane. iii) in this individual at this plane.								7a	8a
Verbal formation		13b			16b			7b*i*		9a
Mental formation		14b	15b		17b	18b		8b	9b	

Like in chart 6.0, the above chart summarises the sequence of enquiries from nos. 79 to 127 in this chapter. The iteration loops through three differentiations (individuals, planes, individuals by planes) by way of forward and reverse mode of enquiries. The same sequence reiterates through six time-scales (present, past, future, present-past, present-future, and past-future), represent by the enneahedral boxes as shown in the chart.

Chart 6.7 Present, past, and future cessation of the formations

C: ceases/ had ceased/ will cease; N: does not cease/ had not ceased/ will not cease

	Present			Past			Future		
	Bodily F.	Verbal F.	Mental F.	Bodily F.	Verbal F.	Mental F.	Bodily F.	Verbal F.	Mental F.
Those at the ceasing moment of breath-in and breath-out	C		C						
Those at the ceasing moment of breath-in and breath-out without initial application and sustained application	C	N							
Those at the first *jhāna* attainment, at the ceasing moment of breath-in and breath-out	C	C							
Those at the ceasing moment of initial application and sustained application		C	C						
Those at the ceasing moment of initial application and sustained application without breath-in and breath-out	N	C							
Those at the ceasing moment of *citta* without breath-in and breath-out	N		C						
Those at the ceasing moment of *citta* without initial application and sustained application		N	C						
Those at the ceasing moment of *citta* with non-initial application and non-sustained application, without breath-in and breath-out	N	N							
Those in whose consciousness whereof final-stage *citta* of the sensuous sphere will instantly arise							N	C	C
Those in whose consciousness whereof final-stage *citta* with non-initial application and non-sustained application will instantly arise							N	N	C
Those endowed with final-stage *citta* with non-initial application and non-sustained application							N	N	
Those at the arising moment of final-stage *citta*							N	C	C
Those at the ceasing moment of final-stage *citta*							N	N	N
Those at the ceasing moment of final-stage *citta* with initial application and sustained application							N	N	
Those at the arising moment of final-stage *citta* with non-initial application and non-sustained application								N	C
Those at the first *jhāna* attainment				C	C	C	C	C	C
Those at the first, second, and third *jhāna* attainment				C		C	C		C
Those at the second and third *jhāna* attainment				C	N		C	N	
Those at the second, third, and fourth *jhāna* attainment					N	C		N	C
Those at the fourth *jhāna* attainment				N	N	C	N	N	C
Those at the birth-moment of Pure abode beings				N	N	N			
Those at the birth-moment of Non-percipient beings				N	N	N			
Those at the moment of second *citta* of Pure abode beings				N	N	C			

	Present			Past			Future		
	Bodily F.	Verbal F.	Mental F.	Bodily F.	Verbal F.	Mental F.	Bodily F.	Verbal F.	Mental F.
Sensuous beings				C	C	C	C	C	C
Fine-material beings (except Non-percipients)				N	C	C	N	C	C
Immaterial beings				N	C	C	N	C	C
Non-percipient beings	N	N	N	N	N	N	N	N	N
Final existence beings							N	C	C
All those at the arising moment of *citta*	N	N	N						
Those at Cessation attainment	N	N	N						
At the plane(s) of :									
first *jhāna*	C	C	C	C	C	C	C	C	C
first, second and third *jhāna*	C		C	C		C	C		C
second and third *jhāna*	C	N	C	C	N	C	C	N	C
second, third, and fourth *jhāna*		N	C		N	C		N	C
fourth *jhāna*	N	N	C	N	N	C	N	N	C
sensuous sphere	C	C	C	C	C	C	C	C	C
fine-material sphere (except Non-percipience plane)	N	C	C	N	C	C	N	C	C
immaterial sphere	N	C	C	N	C	C	N	C	C
Non-percipience	N	N	N	N	N	N	N	N	N

At Present

Forward enquiries by Individual

79. *i* (a) Bodily formation ceases in this individual. Does verbal formation cease in that individual?
— No. To those at the ceasing moment of breath-in and breath-out without initial application and sustained application, bodily formation ceases; verbal formation therein does not cease.
— Yes. To those at the first *jhāna* attainment, at the ceasing moment of breath-in and breath-out of the sensuous sphere, bodily formation ceases; verbal formation also ceases.

(b) Verbal formation ceases in this individual. Does bodily formation cease in that individual?
— No. To those at the ceasing moment of initial application and sustained application without breath-in and breath-out, verbal formation ceases; bodily formation does not cease [29].
— Yes. Refer to the answer in 79 *i* (a) above.

ii (a) Bodily formation ceases in this individual. Does mental formation cease in that individual?

[29] Because bodily formation does not arise in the first place, it hence "does not" cease which is the way of explanation by the Pāli text.

— Yes. (to those at the ceasing moment of breath-in and breath-out).

(b) Mental formation ceases in this individual. Does bodily formation cease in that individual?
— No. To those at the ceasing moment of *citta* without breath-in and breath-out, mental formation ceases; bodily formation does not cease.
— Yes. To those at the ceasing moment of breath-in and breath-out, mental formation ceases; bodily formation also ceases.

80. *i* (a) Verbal formation ceases in this individual. Does mental formation cease in that individual?
— Yes. (at the ceasing moment of initial application and sustained application).

(b) Mental formation ceases in this individual. Does verbal formation cease in that individual?
— No. To those at the ceasing moment of *citta* without initial application and sustained application, mental formation ceases; verbal formation therein does not cease.
— Yes. To those at the ceasing moment of initial application and sustained application, mental formation ceases and verbal formation also ceases.

Forward enquiries by Plane

81. *i* (a) Bodily formation ceases at this plane. Does verbal formation cease at that plane? ..... p ..... *ii* (b) Mental formation ceases at this plane. Does verbal formation cease at that plane?

The answers in "Forward enquiries on Plane" are the same in all six time-lagged classifications of enquiries. Refer to the last part in Chart 6.7 as to plane.

Forward enquiries by Individual and Plane

Answers to the following enquiries are the same as in preceding "Forward enquiries on Individual" from 79 *i* (a) to 80 *i* (b).

82. *i* (a) Bodily formation ceases in this individual at this plane. Does verbal formation cease in that individual at that plane? ..... p ..... *ii* (b) Mental formation ceases in this individual at this plane. Does verbal formation cease in that individual at that plane?

Opposite enquiries by Individual

83. *i* (a) Bodily formation does not cease in this individual. Does verbal formation not cease in that individual?
— No. To those at the ceasing moment of initial application and sustained application without breath-in and breath-out, bodily formation does not cease; but verbal formation therein ceases.

— Yes. To all those at the arising moment of *citta*; those at the ceasing moment of *citta* with non-initial application and non-sustained application, without breath-in and breath-out; those of Cessation-attainment; and those Non-percipient beings, neither bodily formation nor verbal formation ceases.

(b) Verbal formation does not cease in this individual. Does bodily formation not cease in that individual?
— No. To those at the ceasing moment of breath-in and breath-out without initial application and sustained application, verbal formation does not cease; but bodily formation therein ceases.
— Yes. Refer to the answer in 83 *i* (a) above.

ii (a) Bodily formation does not cease in this individual. Does mental formation not cease in that individual?
— No. To those at the ceasing moment of *citta* without breath-in and breath-out, bodily formation does not cease; but mental formation therein ceases.
— Yes. To all those at the arising moment of *citta*, those of Cessation-attainment, and those Non-percipient beings, neither bodily formation nor mental formation ceases.

(b) Mental formation does not cease in this individual. Does bodily formation not cease in that individual? — Yes. Refer to the answer in 83 *ii* (a) above.

84. *i* (a) Verbal formation does not cease in this individual. Does mental formation not cease in that individual?
— No. To those at the ceasing moment of *citta* without initial application and sustained application, verbal formation does not cease; but mental formation ceases.
— Yes. To all those at the arising moment of *citta*, those of Cessation-attainment, and those Non-percipient beings, neither verbal formation nor mental formation ceases.

(b) Mental formation does not cease in this individual. Does verbal formation not cease in that individual? — Yes. Refer to the answer in 84 *i* (a) above.

Opposite enquiries by Plane

85. *i* (a) Bodily formation does not cease at this plane. Does verbal formation not cease at that plane? ..... p ..... *ii* (b) Mental formation will not cease at this plane. Does verbal formation not cease at that plane?

The answers in "Opposite enquiries on Plane" are the same in all six time-lagged classifications of enquiries. Refer to the last part in Chart 6.7 as to plane.

Opposite enquiries by Individual and Plane

86. *i* (a) Bodily formation does not cease in this individual at this plane. Does verbal formation not cease in that individual at that plane? (b) Verbal formation does not cease in this individual at this plane.....p..... Does verbal formation not cease in that individual at that plane?

Answers to the above enquiries are the same as in preceding "Opposite enquiries on Individual", except that those of Cessation-attainment are excluded here for they are supramundane beings who have surpassed the 31 planes.

In the Past

All the catechisms in the section on 'past' are the same as in those similar sections in Origination and Origination-Cessation, except only that for those pairs of enquiries and answers, it requires the tenses of "had arisen" and "had not arisen" to be replaced by "had ceased" and "had not ceased".

Forward enquiries by Individual

87. *i* (a) Bodily formation had ceased in this individual. Had verbal formation ceased in that individual? .....p.....

Forward enquiries by Plane
Forward enquiries by Individual and Plane
Opposite enquiries by Individual
Opposite enquiries by Plane
Opposite enquiries by Individual and Plane

In Future

Forward enquiries by Individual

For answers to the following enquiries, refer to the same in "Forward enquiries on Individual and Plane" from 91 *i* (a) to 92 *i* (b).

88. *i* (a) Bodily formation will cease in this individual. Will verbal formation cease in that individual? (b) Verbal formation will cease in this individual. Will bodily formation cease in that individual?

ii (a) Bodily formation will cease in this individual. Will mental formation cease in that individual? (b) Mental formation will cease in this individual. Will bodily formation cease in that individual?

89. *i* (a) Verbal formation will cease in this individual. Will mental formation cease in that individual? (b) Mental formation will cease in this individual. Will verbal formation cease in that individual?

Forward enquiries by Plane

90. *i* (a) Bodily formation will cease at this plane. Will verbal formation cease at that plane? ..... p ..... Mental formation will cease at this plane. Will verbal formation cease at that plane?

The answers in "Forward enquiries on Plane" are the same in all six time-lagged classifications of enquiries. Refer to the last part in Chart 6.7 as to plane.

Forward enquiries by Individual and Plane

91. *i* (a) Bodily formation will cease in this individual at this plane. Will verbal formation cease in that individual at that plane?
— No. To those at the second and third *jhāna* attainment, bodily formation will cease; verbal formation therein will not cease.
— Yes. Same answer as in *i* (b) below.

(b) Verbal formation will cease in this individual at this plane. Will bodily formation cease in that individual at that plane?
— No. To those at the arising moment of final-stage *citta* of the sensuous sphere; to those in whose consciousness whereof final-stage *citta* of the sensuous sphere will instantly arise; to those of the fine-material and immaterial sphere (except Non-percipients), including those final existence beings in fine-material and immaterial sphere who, having reborn, will attain *Parinibbāna* at the death-moment, verbal formation will cease; bodily formation will not cease.
— Yes. To those at the first *jhāna* attainment, and others of the sensuous sphere, both verbal formation and bodily formation will cease.

ii (a) Bodily formation will cease in this individual at this plane. Will mental formation cease in that individual at that plane?
— Yes. Same answer as in 91 *ii* (b) below.

(b) Mental formation will cease in this individual at this plane. Will bodily formation cease in that individual at that plane?
— No. To those at the arising moment of final-stage *citta* of the sensuous sphere, those in whose consciousness whereof final-stage *citta* of the sensuous sphere will instantly arise, those at the fourth *jhāna* attainment, those of the fine-material and immaterial sphere (except Non-percipients) and including those final existence beings in fine-material and immaterial sphere who, having reborn, will attain *Parinibbāna* at the death-moment, mental formation will cease; bodily formation will not cease.
— Yes. To those at the first, second, and third *jhāna* attainment, and those others of the sensuous sphere, mental formation will cease; bodily formation also will cease.

92. *i* (a) Verbal formation will cease in this individual at this plane. Will mental formation cease in that individual at that plane?
— Yes. Same answer as in 92 *i* (b) below.

(b) Mental formation will cease in this individual at this plane. Will verbal formation cease in this individual at this plane?
— No. To those at the arising moment of final-stage *citta* with non-initial application and non-sustained application, those in whose consciousness whereof final-stage *citta* with non-initial application and non-sustained application will instantly arise; and those at the second, third, and fourth *jhāna* attainment, mental formation will cease; verbal formation will not cease.
— Yes. To those at the first *jhāna* attainment, those of the sensuous sphere, and others of the fine-material and immaterial sphere, both mental formation and verbal formation will cease.

Opposite enquiries by Individual

Answers to the following enquiries are the same as in "Opposite enquiries on Individual and plane" from 96 *i* (a) to 97 *i* (b).

93. *i* (a) Bodily formation will not cease in this individual. Will verbal formation not cease in that individual? (b) Verbal formation will not cease in this individual. Will bodily formation not cease in that individual?

94. *i* (a) Bodily formation will not cease in this individual. Will mental formation not cease in that individual? (b) Mental formation will not cease in this individual. Will bodily formation not cease in that individual?

…..p….. Mental formation will not cease in this individual. Will verbal formation not cease in that individual?

Opposite enquiries by Plane

95. *i* (a) Bodily formation will not cease ..... p ….. *ii* (b) Mental formation will not cease at this plane. Will verbal formation not cease at that plane?

The answers in "Opposite enquiries on Plane" are the same in all six time-lagged classifications of enquiries. Refer to the last part in Chart 6.7 as to plane.

Opposite enquiries by Individual and Plane

96. *i* (a) Bodily formation will not cease in this individual at this plane. Will verbal formation not cease in that individual at that plane?
— No. To those at the arising moment of final-stage *citta* of the sensuous sphere; to those in whose consciousness whereof final-stage *citta* of the sensuous sphere will instantly arise; and to those of the fine-material and immaterial sphere

including final existence beings thereof, bodily formation will not cease; verbal formation therein will cease.
— Yes. To those at the ceasing moment of final-stage *citta* with initial application and sustained application, those endowed with final-stage *citta* with non-initial application and non-sustained application, those in whose consciousness whereof final-stage *citta* with non-initial application and non-sustained application will instantly arise, those at the fourth *jhāna* attainment, and those Non-percipient beings, neither bodily formation nor verbal formation will cease.

(b) Verbal formation will not cease in this individual at this plane. Will bodily formation not cease in that individual at that plane?
— No. To those at the second and third *jhāna* attainment, verbal formation will not cease; bodily formation therein will cease.
— Yes. Refer to the answer in 96 *i* (a) above.

ii (a) Bodily formation will not cease in this individual at this plane. Will mental formation not cease in that individual at that plane?
— No. To those at the arising moment of final-stage *citta* of the sensuous sphere; to those in whose consciousness whereof final-stage *citta* of the sensuous sphere will instantly arise; to those at the fourth *jhāna* attainment, and to those of the fine-material and immaterial sphere including thereof final existence beings, bodily formation will not cease; but mental formation will cease.
— Yes. To those at the ceasing moment of final-stage *citta*, and to Non-percipient beings, neither bodily formation nor mental formation will cease.

(b) Mental formation will not cease in this individual at this plane. Will bodily formation not cease in that individual at that plane?
— Yes. Refer to the answer in 96 *ii* (a) above.

97. *i* (a) Verbal formation will not cease in this individual at this plane. Will mental formation not cease in that individual at that plane?
— No. To those at the arising moment of final-stage *citta* with non-initial application and non-sustained application, those in whose consciousness whereof final-stage *citta* with non-initial application and non-sustained application will instantly arise, and those at the second, third, and fourth *jhāna* attainment, verbal formation will not cease; mental formation will cease.
— Yes. To those at the ceasing moment of final-stage *citta* (of the sensuous sphere), and those Non-percipient beings, neither verbal formation nor mental formation will cease.

(b) Mental formation will not cease in this individuals at this plane. Will verbal formation not cease in that individual at that plane?
— No. No such being.
— Yes. Refer to the answer in 97 *i* (a) above.

Chart 6.8 Present and past cessation of the formation types

A: ceases/ had ceased; N: does not cease/ had not ceased

	Present			Past		
	Bodily F.	Verbal F.	Bodily F.	Verbal F.	Bodily F.	Verbal F.
Those at the arising moment of breath-in and breath-out						
Those at the ceasing moment of breath-in and breath-out	C				C	C
Those at the first *jhāna* attainment, at the arising moment of breath-in and breath-out	N				C	
Those at the first *jhāna* attainment, at the ceasing moment of breath-in and breath-out	C				C	
Those at the second and third *jhāna* attainment, at the arising moment of breath-in and breath-out	N				N	
Those at the second and third *jhāna* attainment, at the ceasing moment of breath-in and breath-out	C				N	
Those at the ceasing moment of initial application and sustained application		C				C
Those at the ceasing moment of *citta* without breath-in and breath-out	N				CN	C
Those at the ceasing moment of *citta* without initial application and sustained application		N				C
Those at the fourth *jhāna* attainment	N				N	
Those at the birth-moment of Pure abode beings	N	N				N
Those at the birth-moment of Non-percipient beings	N	N				N
Those at the moment of second *citta* of Pure abode beings	N	N			N	N
Fine-material beings (except Non-percipients)	N				C	
Immaterial beings	N				C	
Non-percipient beings	N	N			CN	CN
All those at the arising moment of *citta*	N	N			C	C
Those at Cessation attainment	N	N			C	C

Present and Past

Forward enquiries by Individual

For those answers to the following enquiries, refer to the same in "Forward enquiries on Individual and Plane" from 101 *i* (a) to 102 *i* (b).

98. *i* (a) Bodily formation ceases in this individual. Had verbal formation ceased in that individual? (b) Verbal formation had ceased in this individual. Does bodily formation cease in that individual?

ii (a) Bodily formation ceases in this individual. Had mental formation ceased in that individual? (b) Mental formation had ceased in this individual. Does bodily formation cease in that individual?

99. *i* (a) Verbal formation ceases in this individual. Had mental formation ceased in that individual? (b) Mental formation had ceased in this individual. Does verbal formation cease in that individual?

Forward enquiries by Plane

100. *i* (a) Bodily formation ceases at that plane ..... p ..... *ii* (b) Mental formation had ceased at this plane. Does verbal formation cease at that plane?

The answers in "Forward enquiries on Plane" are the same in all those six time-lagged classifications of enquiries. Refer to the last part in Chart 6.7.

Forward enquiries by Individual and Plane

101. *i* (a) Bodily formation ceases in this individual at this plane. Had verbal formation ceased in that individual at that plane?
— No. To those at the second and third *jhāna* attainment, at the ceasing moment of breath-in and breath-out, bodily formation ceases; verbal formation therein had not ceased.
— Yes. To those at the first *jhāna* attainment, at the ceasing moment of breath-in and breath-out of the sensuous sphere, bodily formation ceases; verbal formation also had ceased.

(b) Verbal formation had ceased in this individual at this plane. Does bodily formation cease in that individual at that plane?
— No. To those at the first *jhāna* attainment, at the arising moment of breath-in and breath-out of the sensuous sphere; to all those at the arising moment of *citta*; to those at the ceasing moment of *citta* without breath-in and breath-out; to those of the fine-material and immaterial sphere; also to Non-percipient beings (and those of Cessation-attainment, surpassing the three mundane spheres), verbal formation had ceased; bodily formation therein does not cease.
— Yes. Refer to the answer in 101 *i* (a) above.

ii (a) Bodily formation ceases in this individual at this plane. Had mental formation ceased in that individual at that plane?
— No such being in whom bodily formation ceases, mental formation had not.
— Yes, to those at the ceasing moment of breath-in and breath-out.

(b) Mental formation had ceased in this individual at this plane. Does bodily formation cease in that individual at that plane?
— No. To all those at the arising moment of *citta*, those at the ceasing moment of *citta* without breath-in and breath-out, Non-percipient beings (and those of Cessation-attainment, surpassing mundane spheres), mental formation had ceased; bodily formation does not cease.
— Yes. To those at the ceasing moment of breath-in and breath-out, mental formation had ceased and bodily formation also ceases.

102. *i* (a) Verbal formation ceases in this individual at this plane. Had mental formation ceased in that individual at that plane?
— No such being in whom verbal formation ceases but mental formation had not.
— Yes. Refer to the answer in 102 *i* (b) below.

(b) Mental formation had ceased in this individual at this plane. Does verbal formation cease in that individual at that plane?
— No. To all those at the arising moment of *citta*, those at the ceasing moment of *citta* without initial application and sustained application, those Non-percipient beings (and those of Cessation-attainment, surpassing mundane spheres), mental formation had ceased; verbal formation does not cease.
— Yes. To those at the ceasing moment of initial application and sustained application, mental formation had ceased; verbal formation also ceases.

Opposite enquiries by Individual

For those answers to the following enquiries, refer to the same in "Opposite enquiries on Individual and Plane" from 106 *i* (a) to 107 *i* (b).

103. *i* (a) Bodily formation does not cease in this individual. Had verbal formation not ceased in that individual? (b) Verbal formation had not ceased in this individual. Does bodily formation not cease in that individual?

ii (a) Bodily formation does not cease in this individual. Had mental formation not ceased in that individual? (b) Mental formation had not ceased in this individual. Does bodily formation not cease in that individual?

104. *i* (a) Verbal formation does not cease in this individual. Had mental formation not ceased in that individual? (b) Mental formation had not ceased in this individual. Does verbal formation not cease in that individual?

Opposite enquiries by Plane

105. *i* (a) Bodily formation does not cease ..... p ..... *ii* (b) Mental formation had not ceased at this plane. Does verbal formation not cease at that plane?

The answers in "Forward enquiries on Plane" are the same in all those six time-lagged classifications of enquiries. Refer to the last part in Chart 6.7.

Opposite enquiries by Individual and Plane

106. *i* (a) Bodily formation does not cease in this individual at this plane. Had verbal formation not ceased in that individual at that plane?
— No. To those at the first *jhāna* attainment, at the arising moment of breath-in and breath-out of the sensuous sphere; to those at the ceasing moment of *citta*

without breath-in and breath-out [30]; and to those of the fine-material and immaterial sphere, bodily formation does not cease; verbal formation had ceased.
— Yes. To those at the second and third *jhāna* attainment, at the arising moment of breath-in and breath-out, those at the ceasing moment of *citta* without breath-in and breath-out [30], those at the fourth *jhāna* attainment, those at the moment of second *citta* of Pure abode beings, and Non-percipient beings, bodily formation does not cease; verbal formation also had not ceased.

(b) Verbal formation had not ceased in this individual at this plane. Does bodily formation not cease in that individual at that plane?
— No. To those at the second and third *jhāna* attainment, at the ceasing moment of breath-in and breath-out, verbal formation had not ceased; bodily formation therein ceases.
— Yes. Refer to the answer in 106 *i* (a) above.

ii (a) Bodily formation does not cease in this individual at this plane. Had mental formation not ceased in that individual at that plane?
— No. To all those at the arising moment of *citta*, and those at the ceasing moment of *citta* without breath-in and breath-out, bodily formation does not cease; mental formation had ceased.
— Yes. To those at the birth-moment of Pure abode and Non-percipient beings, bodily formation does not cease; mental formation also had not ceased.

(b) Mental formation had not ceased in this individual at this plane. Does bodily formation not cease in that individual at that plane?
— Yes. Refer to the answer in 106 *ii* (a) above.

107. *i* (a) Verbal formation does not cease in this individual at this plane. Had mental formation not ceased in that individual at that plane?
— No. To all those at the arising moment of *citta*, those at the ceasing moment of *citta* without initial application and sustained application, verbal formation does not cease; mental formation had ceased.
— Yes. To those at the moment of second *citta* of Pure abode beings, and those Non-percipient beings (also those at the birth-moment of Pure abode and Non-percipient beings), verbal formation does not cease; mental formation also had not ceased.

(b) Mental formation had not ceased in this individual at this plane. Does verbal formation not cease in that individual at that plane?
— Yes. Refer to the answer in 107 *i* (a) above.

---

[30] To those at the ceasing moment of *citta* without breath-in and breath-out, verbal formation had ceased, and will cease, at the planes of initial application and sustained application; but it had not ceased, and will not cease, at the planes of non-initial application and non-sustained application.

Chart 6.9 Present and future cessation of the formations types

A: ceases/ will cease; N: does not cease/ will not cease

	Present			Future		
	Bodily F.	Verbal F.	Bodily F.	Verbal F.	Bodily F.	Verbal F.
Those at the ceasing moment of breath-in and breath-out	C					C
Those at the first *jhāna* attainment, at the arising moment of breath-in and breath-out	N				C	
Those at the first *jhāna* attainment, at the ceasing moment of breath-in and breath-out	C				C	
Those at the second and third *jhāna* attainment, at the arising moment of breath-in and breath-out	N				N	
Those at the second and third *jhāna* attainment, at the ceasing moment of breath-in and breath-out	C				N	
Those at the ceasing moment of initial application and sustained application		C				C
Those at the ceasing moment of *citta* without breath-in and breath-out	N				CN	C
Those at the ceasing moment of *citta* without initial application and sustained application		N				C
Those in whose consciousness whereof final-stage *citta* with non-initial application and non-sustained application will instantly arise	N				N	
Those endowed with final-stage *citta* with non-initial application and non-sustained application	N				N	
Those at the ceasing moment of final-stage *citta*	N					N
Those at the ceasing moment of final-stage *citta* with initial application and sustained application	N	C			N	N
Those at the ceasing moment of final-stage *citta* with non-initial application and non-sustained application		N				N
Those at the fourth *jhāna* attainment	N				N	
Fine-material beings (except Non-percipients)	N				C	
Immaterial beings	N				C	
Non-percipient beings	N	N			CN	CN
All those at the arising moment of *citta*	N	N			C	C
Those at Cessation attainment	N	N			C	C

Present and Future

Forward enquiries by Individual

For answers to the following enquiries, refer to the same in "Forward enquiries on Individual and Plane" from nos. 111 *i* (a) to 112 *i* (b).

108. *i* (a) Bodily formation ceases in this individual. Will verbal formation cease in that individual? (b) Verbal formation will cease in this individual. Does bodily formation cease in that individual?

ii (a) Bodily formation ceases in this individual. Will mental formation cease in that individual? (b) Mental formation will cease in this individual. Does bodily formation cease in that individual?

109. *i* (a) Verbal formation ceases in this individual. Will mental formation cease in that individual? (b) Mental formation will cease in this individual. Does verbal formation cease in that individual?

Forward enquiries by Plane

110. *i* (a) Bodily formation ceases at this plane .....p.... *ii* (b) Does verbal formation cease at that plane?

The answers in "Forward enquiries on Plane" are the same in all those six time-lagged classifications of enquiries. Refer to the last part in Chart 6.7.

Forward enquiries by Individual and Plane

111. *i* (a) Bodily formation ceases in this individual at this plane. Will verbal formation cease in that individual at that plane?
— No. To those at the second and third *jhāna* attainment, at the ceasing moment of breath-in and breath-out, bodily formation ceases; verbal formation will not.
— Yes. To those at the first *jhāna* attainment, at the ceasing moment of breath-in and breath-out of the sensuous sphere, bodily formation ceases; verbal formation also will cease.

(b) Verbal formation will cease in this individual at this plane. Does bodily formation cease in that individual at that plane?
— No. To those at the first *jhāna* attainment at the arising moment of breath-in and breath-out of the sensuous sphere; (and all those at the arising moment of *citta*); to those at the ceasing moment of *citta* without breath-in and breath-out; to those of fine-material and immaterial sphere; to Non-percipient beings; (and those of Cessation-attainment, surpassing mundane spheres), verbal formation will cease; bodily formation does not cease.
— Yes. Refer to the answer in *i* (a) above.

ii (a) Bodily formation ceases in this individual at this plane. Will mental formation cease in that individual at that plane?
— Yes. (to those at the ceasing moment of breath-in and breath-out)

(b) Mental formation will cease in this individual at this plane. Does bodily formation cease in that individual at that plane?
— No. To all those at the arising moment of *citta*, those at the ceasing moment of *citta* without breath-in and breath-out, to Non-percipient beings (and those of Cessation-attainment, surpassing mundane spheres), mental formation will cease; bodily formation does not cease.
— Yes. Same answer as in *ii* (a) above.

112. *i* (a) Verbal formation ceases in this individual at this plane. Will mental formation cease in that individual at that plane?
— No. To those at the ceasing moment of final-stage *citta* with initial application and sustained application, verbal formation ceases; mental formation will not cease.
— Yes. To others at the ceasing moment of initial application and sustained application, verbal formation ceases; mental formation also will cease.

(b) Mental formation will cease in this individual at this plane. Does verbal formation cease in that individual at that plane?
— No. To all those at the arising moment of *citta*, those at the ceasing moment of *citta* without initial application and sustained application, those Non-percipient beings (and those of Cessation-attainment, surpassing mundane spheres), mental formation will cease; verbal formation does not cease.
— Yes. To those at the ceasing moment of initial application and sustained application, mental formation will cease; verbal formation also ceases.

Opposite enquiries by Individual

For those answers to the following enquiries, refer to the same in "Opposite enquiries on Individual and Plane" from 116 *i* (a) to 117 *i* (b).

113. *i* (a) Bodily formation does not cease in this individual. Will verbal formation not cease in that individual (b) Verbal formation will not cease in this individual. Does bodily formation not cease in that individual?

ii (a) Bodily formation does not cease in this individual. Will mental formation not cease in that individual? (b) Mental formation will not cease in this individual. Does bodily formation not cease in that individual?

114. *i* (a) Verbal formation does not cease in this individual. Will mental formation not cease in that individual? (b) Mental formation will not cease in this individual. Does verbal formation not cease in that individual?

Opposite enquiries by Plane

115. *i* (a) Bodily formation does not cease at this plane .....p..... Does verbal formation not cease at that plane?

The answers in "Opposite enquiries on Plane" are the same in all those six time-lagged classifications of enquiries. Refer to the last part in Chart 6.7.

Opposite enquiries by Individual and Plane

116. *i* (a) Bodily formation does not cease in this individual at this plane. Will verbal formation not cease in that individual at that plane?

— No. To all those at the arising moment of *citta*; to those at the first *jhāna* attainment, at the arising moment of breath-in and breath-out of the sensuous sphere; to those at the ceasing moment of *citta* without breath-in and breath-out, those of the fine-material and immaterial sphere, those Non-percipient beings, (and those of Cessation-attainment, surpassing mundane spheres), bodily formation does not cease; verbal formation therein will cease.
— Yes. To those at the ceasing moment of final-stage *citta* with initial application and sustained application; those endowed with final-stage *citta* with non-initial application and non-sustained application; those in whose consciousness whereof final-stage *citta* with non-initial application and non-sustained application will instantly arise; those at the second and third *jhāna* attainment, at the arising moment of breath-in and breath-out; those at the ceasing moment of *citta* without breath-in and breath-out; those at the fourth *jhāna* attainment; and those Non-percipient beings, bodily formation does not cease; verbal formation also will not cease.

(b) Verbal formation will not cease in this individual at this plane. Does bodily formation not cease in that individual at that plane?
— No. To those at the second and third *jhāna* attainment, at the ceasing moment of breath-in and breath-out, verbal formation will not cease, but bodily formation therein ceases.
— Yes. Refer to the answer in *i* (a) above.

ii (a) Bodily formation does not cease in this individual at this plane. Will mental formation not cease in that individual at that plane?
— No. To all those at the arising moment of *citta*, those at the ceasing moment of *citta* without breath-in and breath-out, those Non-percipient beings (and those of Cessation-attainment, surpassing mundane spheres), bodily formation does not cease; mental formation will cease [31].
— Yes. To those at the ceasing moment of final-stage *citta*, and to Non-percipient beings, bodily formation does not cease; mental formation also will not cease.

(b) Mental formation will not cease in this individual at this plane. Does bodily formation not cease in that individual at that plane?
— Yes. Refer to the answer in *ii* (a) above.

117. *i* (a) Verbal formation does not cease in this individual at this plane. Will mental formation not cease in that individual at that plane?
— No. To all those at the arising moment of *citta*, those at the ceasing moment of *citta* without initial application and sustained application, Non-percipient beings (and those of Cessation-attainment, surpassing mundane spheres), verbal

[31] To non-percipient beings, bodily formation does not arise and so does not cease; but verbal formation and mental formation will either cease or not cease. Non-percipient being perishes once verbal or mental formation in whom arises.

consciousness does not cease; mental formation will cease.
— Yes. To those at the ceasing moment of final-stage *citta* with non-initial application and non-sustained application, and to Non-percipient beings, verbal formation does not cease; mental formation also will not cease.

(b) Mental formation will not cease in this individual at this plane. Does verbal formation not cease in that individual at that plane?
— No. To those at the ceasing moment of final-stage *citta* with initial application and sustained application, mental formation will not cease; but verbal formation ceases.
— Yes. Refer to the answer in *i* (a) above.

Chart 6.10 Past and future cessation of the formation types

A: had ceased/ will cease; N: had not ceased/ will not cease

	Past			Future		
	Bodily F.	Verbal F.	Bodily F.	Verbal F.	Bodily F.	Verbal F.
Those at the planes of initial application and sustained application (except those endowed with final-stage *citta*)		C				C
Those at the planes of non-initial application and non-sustained application (except those endowed with final-stage *citta*)		N				C
Those in whose consciousness whereof final-stage *citta* with non-initial application and non-sustained application will instantly arise	C				N	
	N				N	
Those endowed with final-stage *citta* with non-initial application and non-sustained application	C				N	
	N				N	
Those at the ceasing moment of final-stage *citta*	C				N	N
	N					N
Those at the ceasing moment of final-stage *citta* with initial application and sustained application	C				N	
	N				N	
Those at the ceasing moment of final-stage *citta* at the planes of initial application and sustained application		C				N
Those at the ceasing moment of final-stage *citta* at the planes of non-initial application and non-sustained application		N				N
Those at the first *jhāna* attainment	C				C	
Those at the first, second, and third *jhāna* attainment	C					C
Those at the second and third *jhāna* attainment	C				N	
Those at the fourth *jhāna* attainment	N				N	C
Sensuous beings	C				C	C
Fine-material beings (except Non-percipients)	N				C	C
Immaterial beings	N				C	C
Non-percipient beings	N	N			N	N

Past and Future

Forward enquiries by Individual

118. *i* (a) Bodily formation had ceased in this individual. Will verbal formation cease in that individual?

— No. To those at the ceasing moment of final-stage *citta* with initial application and sustained application (at sensuous planes), those endowed with final-stage *citta* with non-initial application and non-sustained application (at sensuous planes), and those in whose consciousness whereof final-stage *citta* with non-initial application and non-sustained application will instantly arise (at sensuous planes), bodily formation had ceased; verbal formation will not cease.
— Yes. To others (those at the first *jhāna* attainment, and others of the sensuous sphere), bodily formation had ceased; verbal formation also will cease.

For the rest of the answers, refer to the same in "Forward enquiries on Individual and Plane" from nos. 121 *i* (a) to 122 *i* (b).

(b) Verbal formation will cease in this individual. Had bodily formation ceased in that individual?

ii (a) Bodily formation had ceased in this individual. Will mental formation cease in that individual? (b) Mental formation will cease in this individual. Had bodily formation ceased in that individual?

119. *i* (a) Verbal formation had ceased in this individual. Will mental formation cease in that individual? (b) Mental formation will cease in this individual. Had verbal formation ceased in that individual?

Forward enquiries by Plane

120. *i* (a) Bodily formation had ceased at this plane .....p.... *ii* (b) Mental formation will cease at this plane. Had verbal formation ceased at that plane?

The answers in "Forward enquiries on Plane" are the same in all those six time-lagged classifications of enquiries. Refer to the last part in Chart 6.7.

Forward enquiries by Individual and Plane

121. *i* (a) Bodily formation had ceased in this individual at this plane. Will verbal formation cease in that individual at that plane?
— No. To those at the ceasing moment of final-stage *citta* with initial application and sustained application (at sensuous planes), and those at the second and third *jhāna* attainment, bodily formation had ceased; verbal formation will not cease.
— Yes. To those at the first *jhāna* attainment, and others of the sensuous sphere, bodily formation had ceased; verbal formation also will cease.

(b) Verbal formation will cease in this individual at this plane. Had bodily formation ceased in that individual at that plane?
— No. To those of the fine-material and immaterial sphere, verbal formation will cease; bodily formation had not ceased
— Yes. Refer to the answer in 121 *i* (a) above.

ii (a) Bodily formation had ceased in this individual at this plane. Will mental formation cease in that individual at that plane?
— No. To those at the ceasing moment of final-stage *citta* at sensuous sphere, bodily formation had ceased; mental formation will not cease.
— Yes. To those at the first, second, and third *jhāna* attainment, and others of sensuous sphere, bodily formation had ceased; mental formation also will cease.

(b) Mental formation will cease in this individual at this plane. Had bodily formation ceased in that individual at that plane?
— No. To those at the fourth *jhāna* attainment and those at the fine-material and immaterial sphere, mental formation will cease; bodily formation had not ceased.
— Yes. Refer to the answer in 121 *ii* (a) above.

122. *i* (a) Verbal formation had ceased in this individual at this plane. Will mental formation cease in that individual at that plane?
— No. To those at the ceasing moment of final-stage *citta* at the planes of initial application and sustained application, verbal formation had ceased; mental formation will not cease.
— Yes. To others at the planes of initial application and sustained application [32], verbal formation had ceased; mental formation also will cease.

(b) Mental formation will cease in this individual at this plane. Had verbal formation ceased in that individual at that plane?
— No. To those at the planes of non-initial application and non-sustained application, mental formation will cease; verbal formation had not ceased.
— Yes. Refer to the answer in 122 *i* (a) above.

Opposite enquiries by Individual

For answers to the following enquiries, refer to the same in "Opposite enquiries on Individual and Plane" from nos. 126 *i* (a) to 127 *i* (b).

123. *i* (a) Bodily formation had not ceased in this individual. Will verbal formation not cease in that individual? (b) Verbal formation will not cease in this individual. Had bodily formation not ceased in that individual?

ii (a) Bodily formation had not ceased in this individual. Will mental formation not cease in that individual? (b) Mental formation will not cease in this individual. Had bodily formation not ceased in that individual?

[32] *Cf.* Dhs nos. 1000: *Savitakkasavicārabhūmiyaṃ kāmāvacare, rūpāvacare, apariyāpanne, vitakkavicāre …* The Dhammasaṅgaṇi mentions about the four mentalities at the planes of initial application and sustained application in the world of sense, at fine-material sphere, at place of those known as "unincluded" (free from round of rebirths).

124. *i* (a) Verbal formation had not ceased in this individual. Will mental formation not cease in that individual? (b) Mental formation will not cease in this individual. Had verbal formation not ceased in that individual?

Opposite enquiries by Plane

125. *i* (a) Bodily formation had not ceased at this plane .....p..... Had verbal formation not ceased at that plane?

The answers in "Opposite enquiries on Plane" are the same in all those six time-lagged classifications of enquiries. Refer to the last part in Chart 6.7.

Opposite enquiries by Individual and Plane

126. *i* (a) Bodily formation had not ceased in this individual at this plane. Will verbal formation not cease in that individual at that plane?
— No. To those of the fine-material and immaterial sphere, bodily formation had not ceased; verbal formation will cease.
— Yes. To those at the ceasing moment of final-stage *citta* with initial application and sustained application at fine-material and immaterial sphere, those endowed with final-stage *citta* with non-initial application and non-sustained application [33] (at fine-material and immaterial sphere), those in whose consciousness whereof final-stage *citta* with non-initial application and non-sustained application will instantly arise [33] (at fine-material and immaterial sphere), those at the fourth *jhāna* attainment, and Non-percipient beings, bodily formation had not ceased; verbal formation also will not cease.

(b) Verbal formation will not cease in this individual at this plane. Had bodily formation not ceased in that individual at that plane?
— No. To those at the ceasing moment of final-stage *citta* at planes of the sensuous sphere, and those at the second and third *jhāna* attainment, verbal formation will not cease; but bodily formation had ceased.
— Yes. Refer to the answer in 126 *i* (a) above.

ii (a) Bodily formation had not ceased in this individual at this plane. Will mental formation not cease in that individual at that plane?
— No. To all those at the fourth *jhāna* attainment, those of the fine-material and immaterial sphere, bodily formation had not ceased; mental formation will cease.
— Yes. To those at the ceasing moment of final-stage *citta* at fine-material and immaterial sphere, and to Non-percipient beings, bodily formation had not ceased; mental formation also will not cease.

---

[33] Herein is referring to those at planes of fine-material and immaterial sphere, which then is not contradictory to the same mentioned in 118 *i* (a) which says that "....bodily formation *had ceased*, verbal formation will not cease". It has to be at planes of sensuous sphere in the answers to nos. 118 *i* (a).

(b) Mental formation will not cease in this individual at this plane. Had bodily formation not ceased in that individual at that plane?
— No. To those at the ceasing moment of final-stage *citta* at sensuous sphere, mental formation will not cease; bodily formation had ceased.
— Yes. Refer to the answer in 126 *ii* (a) above.

127. *i* (a) Verbal formation had not ceased in this individual at this plane. Will mental formation not cease in that individual at that plane?
— No. To those at the planes of non-initial application and non-sustained application, verbal formation had not ceased; mental formation will cease.
— Yes. To those at the ceasing moment of final-stage *citta* at the planes of non-initial application and non-sustained application, and to Non-percipient beings, verbal formation had not ceased; mental formation also will not cease.

(b) Mental formation will not cease in this individual at this plane. Had verbal formation not ceased in that individual at that plane?
— No. To those at the ceasing moment of final-stage *citta* at the planes of initial application and sustained application, mental formation will not cease; verbal formation had ceased.
— Yes. Refer to the answer in 127 *i* (a) above.

Consolidated answers from the cessation of formations

Chart 6.11 Composition on cessation of the three formation types

C: ceases/ had ceased/ will cease; N: does not cease/ had not ceased/ will not cease

	Present			Past			Future		
	Bodily F.	Verbal F.	Mental F.	Bodily F.	Verbal F.	Mental F.	Bodily F.	Verbal F.	Mental F.
Those at the ceasing moment of breath-in and breath-out	***C***		*C*		C	C			C
Those at the ceasing moment of breath-in and breath-out without initial application and sustained application	*C*	*N*							
Those at the first *jhāna* attainment, at the arising moment of breath-in and breath-out	N				C			C	
Those at the first *jhāna* attainment, at the ceasing moment of breath-in and breath-out	***C***	*C*			C			C	
Those at the second and third *jhāna* attainment, at the arising moment of breath-in and breath-out	N				N			N	
Those at the second and third *jhāna* attainment, at the ceasing moment of breath-in and breath-out	C				N			N	
Those at the ceasing moment of initial application and sustained application		***C***	*C*			C			C
Those at the ceasing moment of initial application and sustained application without breath-in and breath-out	*N*	*C*							
Those at the ceasing moment of *citta* without breath-in and breath-out	***N***		*C*		C N	C		C N	C
Those at the ceasing moment of *citta* without initial application and sustained application		***N***	*C*			C			C
Those at the ceasing moment of *citta* with non-initial application and non-sustained application, without breath-in and breath-out	*N*	*N*							
Those at the planes of initial application and sustained application (except those endowed with final-stage *citta*)					C				C
Those at the planes of non-initial application and non-sustained application (except those endowed with final-stage *citta*)					N				C
Those in whose consciousness whereof final-stage *citta* of the sensuous sphere will instantly arise							*N*	*C*	*C*
Those in whose consciousness whereof final-stage *citta* with non-initial application and non-sustained application will instantly arise	N			C N			*N*	***N***	*C*
				C				N	
				N				N	
Those endowed with final-stage *citta* with non-initial application and non-sustained application	N						*N*	***N***	
				C				N	
				N				N	
Those at the arising moment of final-stage *citta*							*N*	*C*	*C*
Those at the ceasing moment of final-stage *citta*							*N*	*N*	*N*
Those at the ceasing moment of final-stage *citta*	N								N
				C				N	N
				N					N
Those at the ceasing moment of final-stage *citta* at the planes of initial application and sustained application					C				N

	Present			Past			Future		
	Bodily F.	Verbal F.	Mental F.	Bodily F.	Verbal F.	Mental F.	Bodily F.	Verbal F.	Mental F.
Those at the ceasing moment of final-stage *citta* at the planes of non-initial application and non-sustained application					**N**				**N**
Those at the ceasing moment of final-stage *citta* with initial application and sustained application	**N**	**C**					*N*	***N***	**N**
				C				**N**	
				N				**N**	
Those at the arising moment of final-stage *citta* with non-initial application and non-sustained application								*N*	*C*
Those at the ceasing moment of final-stage *citta* with non-initial application and non-sustained application		**N**							**N**
Those at the first *jhāna* attainment				***C***	*C*	*C*	*C*	***C***	*C*
Those at the first, second, and third *jhāna* attainment				***C***		*C*	*C*		***C***
Those at the second and third *jhāna* attainment				***C***	*N*		*C*	***N***	
Those at the second, third, and fourth *jhāna* attainment					*N*	*C*		*N*	*C*
Those at the fourth *jhāna* attainment	**N**			*N*	***N***	*C*	*N*	***N***	***C***
Those at the birth-moment of Pure abode beings	**N**	**N**		*N*	*N*	***N***			
Those at the birth-moment of Non-percipient beings	**N**	**N**		*N*	*N*	***N***			
Those at the moment of second *citta* of Pure abode beings	**N**	**N**		*N*	***N***	*C*			
Sensuous beings				***C***	*C*	*C*	*C*	***C***	***C***
Fine-material beings (except Non-percipients)	**N**			***N***	***C***	*C*	*N*	***C***	***C***
Immaterial beings	**N**			***N***	***C***	*C*	*N*	***C***	***C***
Non-percipient beings	***N***	***N***	*N*	***N***	**C** ***N***	**C** ***N***	*N*	**C** ***N***	**C** ***N***
Final existence beings							*N*	*C*	*C*
All those at the arising moment of *citta*	***N***	***N***	*N*		**C**	**C**		**C**	**C**
Those at Cessation attainment	***N***	***N***	*N*		**C**	**C**		**C**	**C**
At the plane(s) of :									
first *jhāna*	C	C	C	C	C	C	C	C	C
first, second and third *jhāna*	C		C	C		C	C		C
second and third *jhāna*	C	N	C	C	N	C	C	N	C
second, third, and fourth *jhāna*		N	C		N	C		N	C
fourth *jhāna*	N	N	C	N	N	C	N	N	C
sensuous sphere	C	C	C	C	C	C	C	C	C
fine-material sphere (except Non-percipience plane)	N	C	C	N	C	C	N	C	C
immaterial sphere	N	C	C	N	C	C	N	C	C
Non-percipience	N	N	N	N	N	N	N	N	N

In the above Chart, the denotation of letters in *italic* are the answers consolidated from the respective first three sub-sections on present, past, and future cessation of formations. The denoted letters in boldface, including both as italicised and bold, are the answers to be referred to the other classifications on present-past, present-future, and past-future cessation of the formations.

In this chart, you will notice that individuals at the arising moment of several event types are also being examined in the subject on cessation—those at the first *jhāna* attainment, at the second and third *jhāna* attainment, both at the arising moment and ceasing moment of breath-in and breath-out; and those at the arising moment and ceasing moment of final-stage *citta*. However, I notice that the answers to those at the arising moment and ceasing moment of final-stage *citta* with non-initial application and non-sustained application show incompatibility, and may requires further evaluation, assuming there are no transcriptional error.

6.2.3 Origination and Cessation (with charts)

Chart 6.12 Enquiry sequence on arising and cessation of the three types of formations

		(Respective enquiries below are placed in relation to each of the following formation types accordingly)								
		Does it cease / Does it not cease: i) in that individual? ii) at that plane? iii) in that individual at that plane?			Had it ceased / Had it not ceased i) in that individual? ii) at that plane? iii) in that individual at that plane?			Will it cease / Will it not cease: i) in that individual? ii) at that plane? iii) in that individual at that plane?		
		Bodily F.	Verbal F.	Mental F.	Bodily F.	Verbal F.	Mental F.	Bodily F.	Verbal F.	Mental F.
Bodily formation	arises / does not arise :		1 *i*			7 *i*			9 *i*	
Verbal formation	i) in this individual. ii) at this plane.			2 *i*			8 *i*			10 *i*
Mental formation	iii) in this individual at this plane									
Bodily formation	had arisen / had not arisen :	-	-	-		3 *i*			11 *i*	
Verbal formation	i) in this individual. ii) at this plane.	-	-	-			4 *i*			12 *i*
Mental formation	iii) in this individual at this plane	-	-	-						
Bodily formation	will arise / will not arise :	-	-	-	-	-	-		5 *i*	
Verbal formation	i) in this individual. ii) at this plane.	-	-	-	-	-	-			6 *i*
Mental formation	iii) in this individual at this plane	-	-	-	-	-	-			

		(Respective enquiries below are placed in relation to each of the following formation types accordingly)								
		Does it arise / Does it not arise : i) in that individual? ii) at that plane? iii) in that individual at that plane?			Had it arisen / Had it not arisen : i) in that individual? ii) at that plane? iii) in that individual at that plane?			Will it arise / Will it not arise : i) in that individual? ii) at that plane? iii) in that individual at that plane?		
		Bodily F.	Verbal F.	Mental F.	Bodily F.	Verbal F.	Mental F.	Bodily F.	Verbal F.	Mental F.
Bodily formation	ceases / does not cease :				-	-	-	-	-	-
Verbal formation	i) in this individual. ii) at this plane.	1 *ii*			-	-	-	-	-	-
Mental formation	iii) in this individual at this plane		2 *ii*		-	-	-	-	-	-
Bodily formation	had ceased/ had not ceased :							-	-	-
Verbal formation	i) in this individual. ii) at this plane.	7 *ii*			3 *ii*			-	-	-
Mental formation	iii) in this individual at this plane		8 *ii*			4 *ii*		-	-	-
Bodily formation	will cease / will not cease :									
Verbal formation	i) in this individual. ii) at this plane.	9 *ii*			11 *ii*			5 *ii*		
Mental formation	iii) in this individual at this plane		10 *ii*			12 *ii*			6 *ii*	

Chart 6.13 Present arising and cessation of the formation types

A: arises; C: ceases; N: does not arise, or does not cease

	Arising			Cessation		
	Bodily F.	Verbal F.	Bodily F.	Verbal F.	Bodily F.	Verbal F.
Those at the arising moment of breath-in and breath-out	A				N	N
Those at the arising moment of initial application and sustained application		A				N
Those at the ceasing moment of initial application and sustained application	N				C	
Those at the arising moment of *citta* without breath-in and breath-out	N				N	N
Those at the arising moment of *citta* without initial application and sustained application		N				N
Non-percipient beings	N	N			N	N
Final existence beings						
All those at the ceasing moment of *citta*	N	N			C	C
Those at Cessation attainment	N	N			N	N
At the plane(s) of :						
first *jhāna*	A				C	C
first, second and third *jhāna*	A					C
second and third *jhāna*	A				N	C
second, third, and fourth *jhāna*		N				C
fourth *jhāna*	N				N	C
sensuous sphere	A				C	C
fine-material sphere (except Non-percipience plane)	N				C	C
immaterial sphere	N				C	C
Non-percipience	N				N	N

At Present

For the following enquiries, refer to the answers compiled in Chart 6.13 above.

Forward enquiries by Individual

128. *i* (a) Bodily formation arises in this individual. Does verbal formation cease in that individual? — No. (b) Verbal formation ceases in this individual. Does bodily formation arise in that individual? — No.

ii (a) Bodily formation arises in this individual. Does mental formation cease in that individual? — No. (b) Mental formation ceases in this individual. Does bodily formation arise in that individual? — No.

129. *i* (a) Verbal formation arises in this individual. Does mental formation cease in that individual? — No. (b) Mental formation ceases in this individual. Does verbal formation arise in that individual? — No.

Forward enquiries by Plane

130. *i* (a) Bodily formation arises at this plane. Does verbal formation cease at that plane? .....p..... *ii* (b) Mental formation ceases at this plane. Does verbal formation arise at that plane?

The answers in "Forward enquiries on Plane" are the same in all those six time-lagged classifications of enquiries. Refer to Chart 6.13.

Forward enquiries by Individual and Plane

131. *i* (a) Bodily formation arises in this individual at this plane .....p..... *ii* (b) Mental formation ceases in this individual at this plane. Does verbal formation arise in that individual at that plane?

Opposite enquiries by Individual

132. *i* (a) Bodily formation does not arise in this individual. Does verbal formation not cease in that individual?
— No. To those at the ceasing moment of initial application and sustained application, bodily formation does not arise; verbal formation ceases.
— Yes. To those at the arising moment of *citta* without breath-in and breath-out, those at the ceasing moment of *citta* without initial application and sustained application, those of Cessation-attainment, and those Non-percipient beings, bodily formation does not arise; verbal formation also does not cease.

(b) Verbal formation does not cease in this individual. Does bodily formation not arise in that individual?
— No. To those at the arising moment of breath-in and breath-out, verbal formation does not cease; bodily formation therein arises.
— Yes. Refer to the answer in 132 *i* (a) above.

ii (a) Bodily formation does not arise in this individual. Does mental formation not cease in that individual?
— No. To all those at the ceasing moment of *citta*, bodily formation does not arise; mental formation ceases.
— Yes. To those at the arising moment of *citta* without breath-in and breath-out, those of Cessation-attainment and Non-percipient beings, bodily formation does not arise; mental formation also does not cease.

(b) Mental formation does not cease in this individual. Does bodily formation not cease in that individual?
— No. To those at the arising moment of breath-in and breath-out, mental formation does not cease (does not cease because it arises, as a result of verbal formation arising); bodily formation arises.
— Yes. Refer to the answer in 132 *ii* (a) above.

133. *i* (a) Verbal formation does not arise in this individual. Does mental formation not cease in that individual?
— No. To all those at the ceasing moment of *citta*, verbal formation does not arise; mental formation ceases.
— Yes. To those at the arising moment of *citta* without initial application and sustained application, those of Cessation-attainment and Non-percipient beings, verbal formation does not arise; mental formation also does not cease.

(b) Mental formation does not cease in this individual. Does verbal formation not arise in that individual?
— No. To those at the arising moment of initial application and sustained application, mental formation does not cease (because it arises), verbal formation therein arises.
— Yes. Refer to the answer in 133 *i* (a) above.

Opposite enquiries by Plane

134. *i* (a) Bodily formation does not arise at this plane..... p ..... Does verbal formation not arise at that plane?

Answers in "Opposite enquiries on Plane" are the same in all six time-lagged classifications of enquiries. Refer to Chart 6.13 as to plane.

Opposite enquiries by Individual and Plane

135. *i* (a) Bodily formation does not arise in this individual at this plane .....p.... Does verbal formation not arise in that individual at that plane?

Answers to the above enquiries are the same as in preceding "Opposite enquiries on Individual", except that those of Cessation-attainment are excluded here for they are supramundane beings who have surpassed the 31 planes.

Chart 6.14 Past arising and cessation of the three formation types

A: had arisen; C: had ceased; N: had not arisen, or had not ceased

	Arising			Cessation		
	Bodily F.	Verbal F.	Bodily F.	Verbal F.	Bodily F.	Verbal F.
Those at the first *jhāna* attainment	A	A			C	C
Those at the first, second, and third *jhāna* attainment	A					C
Those at the second and third *jhāna* attainment	A				N	
Those at the second, third, and fourth *jhāna* attainment		N				C
Those at the fourth *jhāna* attainment	N				N	C
Those at the birth-moment of Pure abode beings	N				N	N
Those at the birth-moment of Non-percipient beings	N				N	N
Those at the moment of second *citta* of Pure abode beings	N				N	C
Sensuous beings	A				C	C
Fine-material beings (except Non-percipients)	N				C	C
Immaterial beings	N				C	C
Non-percipient beings	N				N	N
At the plane(s) of :						
first *jhāna* attainment	A				C	C
first, second and third *jhāna* attainment	A					C
second and third *jhāna* attainment	A				N	C
second, third and fourth *jhāna* attainment		N				C
fourth *jhāna* attainment	N				N	C
sensuous sphere	A				C	C
fine-material sphere (except Non-percipience plane)	N				C	C
immaterial sphere	N				C	C
Non-percipience	N				N	N

In the Past

All the catechisms in the section on 'past' are the same as in those similar sections in Origination and Cessation, except for the need to change the appropriate tenses.

Forward enquiries by Individual

136. *i* (a) Bodily formation had arisen in this individual. Had verbal formation ceased in that individual? .....p..... *ii* (b) Mental formation had not ceased in this individual. Had verbal formation not ceased in that individual?

Forward enquiries by Plane
Forward enquiries by Individual and Plane
Opposite enquiries by Individual
Opposite enquiries by Plane
Opposite enquiries by Individual and Plane

Chart 6.15 Future arising and cessation of the three formations

A: will arise; C: will cease; N: will not arise, or will not cease

	Arising			Cessation		
	Bodily F.	Verbal F.	Bodily F.	Verbal F.	Bodily F.	Verbal F.
Those in whose consciousness whereof final-stage *citta* of the sensuous sphere will instantly arise	N				C	C
Those in whose consciousness whereof final-stage *citta* with non-initial application and non-sustained application will instantly arise	N	N			N	C
Those endowed with final-stage *citta* with non-initial application and non-sustained application	N				N	
Those at the arising moment of final-stage *citta*	N				C	C
Those at the ceasing moment of final-stage *citta*				N	N	N
Those at the ceasing moment of final-stage *citta*	N	N				N
	N	N				N
Those at the ceasing moment of final-stage *citta* with initial application and sustained application	N				N	
Those at the first *jhāna* attainment	A	A			C	C
Those at the first, second, and third *jhāna* attainment	A					C
Those at the second and third *jhāna* attainment	A				N	
Those at the second, third, and fourth *jhāna* attainment		N				C
Those at the fourth *jhāna* attainment	N				N	C
Sensuous beings	A	A			C	C
Fine-material beings (except Non-percipients)	N	A			C	C
Immaterial beings	N	A			C	C
Non-percipient beings	N				N	N
Final existence beings	N				C	C
All those at the ceasing moment of *citta*						
At the plane(s) of :						
first *jhāna* attainment	A				C	C
first, second and third *jhāna* attainment	A					C
second and third *jhāna* attainment	A				N	C
second, third and fourth *jhāna* attainment		N				C
fourth *jhāna* attainment	N				N	C
sensuous sphere	A				C	C
fine-material sphere (except Non-percipience plane)	N				C	C
immaterial sphere	N				C	C
Non-percipience	N				N	N

In Future

Forward enquiries by Individual

For answers to the following enquiries, refer to the same in "Forward enquiries on Individual and Plane" from 140 *i* (a) to 141 *i* (b).

137. *i* (a) Bodily formation will arise in this individual. Will verbal formation cease in that individual? (b) Verbal formation will cease in this individual. Will bodily formation arise in that individual?

ii (a) Bodily formation will arise in this individual. Will mental formation cease in that individual? (b) Mental formation will cease in this individual. Will bodily formation arise in that individual?

138. *i* (a) Verbal formation will arise in this individual. Will mental formation cease in that individual? (b) Mental formation will cease in this individual. Will verbal formation arise in that individual?

Forward enquiries by Plane

139. *i* (a) Bodily formation will arise at this plane .....p..... *ii* (b) Mental formation will cease at this plane. Will verbal formation arise at that plane?

The answers in "Forward enquiries on Plane" are the same in all those six time-lagged classifications of enquiries. Refer to Chart 6.15.

Forward enquiries by Individual and Plane

140. *i* (a) Bodily formation will arise in this individual at this plane. Will verbal formation cease in that individual at that plane?
— No. To those at the second and third *jhāna* attainment, bodily formation will arise; verbal formation will not cease.
— Yes. To those at the first *jhāna* attainment, and those of the sensuous sphere, bodily formation will arise; verbal formation also will cease.

(b) Verbal formation will cease in this individual at this plane. Will bodily formation arise in that individual at that plane?
— No. To those at the arising moment of final-stage *citta* of the sensuous sphere, those in whose consciousness whereof final-stage *citta* of the sensuous sphere will instantly arise, and those (including final existence beings) of the fine-material and immaterial sphere, verbal formation will cease; bodily formation will not arise.
— Yes. Refer to the answer in 140 *i* (a) above.

ii (a) Bodily formation will arise in this individual at this plane. Will mental formation cease in that individual at that plane?
— Yes. Refer to the answer in 140 *ii* (b) below.

(b) Mental formation will cease in this individual at this plane. Will bodily formation arise in that individual at that plane?
— No. To those at the arising moment of final-stage *citta* of the sensuous sphere, those in whose consciousness whereof final-stage *citta* of the sensuous sphere

will instantly arise, those at the fourth *jhāna* attainment, and those (including final existence beings) of the fine-material and immaterial sphere, mental formation will cease; bodily formation will not arise.
— Yes. To those at the first, second, and third *jhāna* attainment, and others of the sensuous sphere, mental formation will cease; bodily formation will arise.

141. *i* (a) Verbal formation will arise in this individual at this plane. Will mental formation cease in that individual at that plane?
— Yes. Refer to the answer in 141 *i* (b) below.

(b) Mental formation will cease in this individual at this plane. Will verbal formation arise in that individual at that plane?
— No. To those at the arising moment of final-stage *citta* (with non-initial application and non-sustained application), those in whose consciousness whereof final-stage *citta* with non-initial application and non-sustained application will instantly arise, and those at the second, third, and fourth *jhāna* attainment, mental formation will cease; verbal formation will not arise.
— Yes. To those at the first *jhāna* attainment, those of the sensuous sphere, and others of the fine-material and immaterial sphere, mental formation will cease; verbal formation will arise.

Opposite enquiries by Individual

142. *i* (a) Bodily formation will not arise in this individual. Will verbal formation not cease in that individual?
— No. To those at the arising moment of final-stage *citta* of the sensuous sphere, those in whose consciousness whereof final-stage *citta* of the sensuous sphere will instantly arise, and those final existence beings in the fine-material immaterial sphere, bodily formation will not arise; verbal formation will cease.
— Yes. To those at the ceasing moment of final-stage *citta* with initial application and sustained application, those endowed with final-stage *citta* with non-initial application and non-sustained application, those in whose consciousness whereof final-stage *citta* with non-initial application and non-sustained application will instantly arise, bodily formation will not arise; verbal formation will not cease.

(b) Verbal formation will not cease in this individual. Will bodily formation not cease in that individual? — Yes. Refer to the answer in 142 *i* (a) above.

ii (a) Bodily formation will not arise in this individual. Will mental formation not cease in that individual?
— No. To those at the arising moment of final-stage *citta* of sensuous sphere, those in whose consciousness whereof final-stage *citta* of the sensuous sphere will instantly arise, and those final existence beings at the fine-material immaterial sphere, bodily formation will not arise; mental formation will cease.

— Yes. To those at the ceasing moment of final-stage *citta*, bodily formation will not arise; mental formation also will not cease.

(b) Mental formation will not cease in this individual. Will bodily formation not arise in that individual? — Yes. Refer to the answer in 142 *ii* (a) above.

143. *i* (a) Verbal formation will not arise in this individual. Will mental formation not cease in that individual?
— No. To those at the arising moment of final-stage *citta* (with non-initial application and non-sustained application), and those in whose consciousness whereof final-stage *citta* with non-initial application and non-sustained application will instantly arise, verbal formation will not arise; mental formation will cease.
— Yes. To those at the ceasing moment of final-stage *citta*, verbal formation will not arise; mental formation will not cease.

(b) Mental formation will not cease in this individual. Will verbal formation not arise in that individual? — Yes. Refer to the answer in 143 *i* (a) above.

Opposite enquiries by Plane

144. *i* (a) Bodily formation will not arise at this plane..... p ..... *ii* (b) Mental formation will not cease at this plane. Will verbal formation not arise at that plane?

Answers in "Opposite enquiries on Plane" are the same in all six time-lagged classifications of enquiries. Refer to Chart 6.15.

Opposite enquiries by Individual and Plane

145. *i* (a) Bodily formation will not arise in this individual at this plane. Will verbal formation not cease in that individual at that plane?
— No. To those at the arising moment of final-stage *citta* of sensuous sphere, those in whose consciousness whereof final-stage *citta* of the sensuous sphere will instantly arise, and those at the fine-material and immaterial sphere, bodily formation will not arise; verbal formation will cease.
— Yes. To those at the ceasing moment of final-stage *citta* with initial application and sustained application, those endowed with final-stage *citta* with non-initial application and non-sustained application, those in whose consciousness whereof final-stage *citta* with non-initial application and non-sustained application will instantly arise, those at the planes of fourth *jhāna* attainment, and those Non-percipient beings, bodily formation will not arise; verbal formation will not cease.

(b) Verbal formation will not cease in this individual at this plane. Will bodily formation not arise in that individual at that plane?

— No. To those at the second and third *jhāna* attainment, verbal formation will not cease; bodily formation will arise.
— Yes. Refer to the answer in 145 *i* (a) above.

ii (a) Bodily formation will not arise in this individual at this plane. Will mental formation not cease in that individual at that plane?
— No. To those at the arising moment of final-stage *citta* of the sensuous sphere, those in whose consciousness whereof final-stage *citta* of the sensuous sphere will instantly arise, those at fourth *jhāna* attainment, and those (includes final existence beings) of the fine-material and immaterial sphere, bodily formation will not arise; mental formation will cease.
— Yes. To those at the ceasing moment of final-stage *citta* (in three mundane spheres), and those Non-percipient beings, bodily formation will not arise; mental formation also will not cease.

(b) Mental formation will not cease in this individual at this plane. Will bodily formation not arise in that individual at that plane?
— Yes. Refer to the answer in 145 *ii* (a) above.

146. *i* (a) Verbal formation will not arise in this individual at this plane. Will mental formation not cease in that individual at that plane?
— No. To those at the arising moment of final-stage *citta* (with non-initial application and non-sustained application), those in whose consciousness whereof final-stage *citta* with non-initial application and non-sustained application will instantly arise, and those at second, third, and fourth *jhāna* attainment, verbal formation will not arise; mental formation will cease.
— Yes. To those at the ceasing moment of final-stage *citta*, and Non-percipient beings, verbal formation will not arise and also mental formation will not cease.

(b) Mental formation will not cease in this individual at this plane. Will verbal formation not arise in that individual at that plane?
— Yes. Refer to the answer in 146 *i* (a) above.

Chart 6.16 Present arising and past cessation of the three formation types

A: arises; C: had ceased; N: does not arise, or had not ceased

	Arising			Cessation		
	Bodily F.	Verbal F.	Bodily F.	Verbal F.	Bodily F.	Verbal F.
Those at the arising moment of breath-in and breath-out	A				C	C
Those at the first *jhāna* attainment, at the ceasing moment of breath-in and breath-out	N				C	
Those at the second and third *jhāna* attainment, at the arising moment of breath-in and breath-out	A				N	
Those at the second and third *jhāna* attainment, at the ceasing moment of breath-in and breath-out	N				N	
Those at the arising moment of initial application and sustained application		A				C
Those at the arising moment of *citta* without breath-in and breath-out	N				CN	C
Those at the arising moment of *citta* without initial application and sustained application		N				C
Those at the first *jhāna* attainment		A				C
Those at the fourth *jhāna* attainment	N				N	
Those at the birth-moment of Pure abode beings	N	N				N
Those at the birth-moment of Non-percipient beings	N	N				N
Those at the moment of second *citta* of Pure abode beings	N				N	
Fine-material beings (except Non-percipients)	N				C	
Immaterial beings	N				C	
Non-percipient beings	N	N			CN	CN
All those at the ceasing moment of *citta*	N	N			C	C
Those at Cessation attainment	N	N			C	C

Present and Past

Forward enquiries by Individual

147. *i* (a) Bodily formation arises in this individual. Had verbal formation ceased in that individual? — Yes. Refer to the answer in 147 *i* (b) below.

(b) Verbal formation had ceased in this individual. Does bodily formation arise in that individual?
— No. To all those at the ceasing moment of *citta*, those at the arising moment of *citta* without breath-in and breath-out, those of Cessation-attainment, and Non-percipient beings, verbal formation had ceased; bodily formation does not arise.
— Yes. To those at the arising moment of breath-in and breath-out, verbal formation had ceased; bodily formation arises.

Catechisms on present-past hereafter are not provided by the text. They are to be classified in the same way as in present-past in the section on origination according to the text. I shall compose all of them here. Meanwhile, refer the answers for the next two pairs of questions to those in "Forward enquiries on Individual and Plane", nos. 140 *vi* (a) to *vii* (b).

ii (a) Bodily formation arises in this individual. Had mental formation ceased in that individual? (b) Mental formation had ceased in this individual. Does bodily formation arise in that individual?

iii (a) Verbal formation arises in this individual. Had mental formation ceased in that individual? (b) Mental formation had ceased in this individual. Does verbal formation arise in that individual?

Forward enquiries by Plane

iv (a) Bodily formation arises at this plane ..... p ..... Mental formation had ceased at this plane. Does verbal formation arise at that plane?

The answers in "Forward enquiries on Plane" are the same in all those six time-lagged classifications of enquiries. Refer to Chart 6.16.

Forward enquiries by Individual and Plane

v (a) Bodily formation arises in this individual at this plane. Had verbal formation ceased in that individual at that plane?
— No. To those at the second and third *jhāna* attainment, at the arising moment of breath-in/breath-out, bodily formation arises; verbal formation had not ceased.
— Yes. Refer to the answer in *v* (b) below.

(b) Verbal formation had ceased in this individual at this plane. Does bodily formation arise in that individual at that plane?
—No. To those at the first *jhāna* attainment, at the ceasing moment of breath-in and breath-out of the sensuous sphere; others of the fine-material and immaterial sphere; all those at the ceasing moment of *citta*; those at the arising moment of *citta* without breath-in and breath-out; Non-percipient beings, (and those of Cessation-attainment, transcending mundane spheres), verbal formation had ceased; bodily formation does not arise.
— Yes. To those at the arising moment of breath-in and breath-out out, verbal formation had ceased; bodily formation arises.

vi (a) Bodily formation arises in this individual at this plane. Had mental formation ceased in that individual at that plane?
— Yes. To those at the arising moment of breath-in and breath-out, bodily formation arises; mental formation had ceased.

(b) Mental formation had ceased in this individual at this plane. Does bodily formation arise in that individual at that plane?
— No. To all those at the ceasing moment of *citta*, and to those at the arising moment of *citta* without breath-in and breath-out, those Non-percipient beings (and those of Cessation-attainment, transcending mundane spheres), mental formation had ceased; bodily formation does not arise.
— Yes. Refer to the answer in *vi* (a) above.

vii (a) Verbal formation arises in this individual at this plane. Had mental formation ceased in that individual at that plane?
— Yes. To those at the first *jhāna* attainment, those at the arising moment of initial application and sustained application, verbal formation arises; mental formation had ceased.

(b) Mental formation had ceased in this individual at this plane. Does verbal formation arise in that individual at that plane?
— No. To all those at the ceasing moment of *citta*, those at the arising moment of *citta* without initial application and sustained application, those Non-percipient beings (and those of Cessation-attainment, transcending mundane spheres), mental formation had ceased; verbal formation does not arise.
— Yes. Refer to the answer in *vii* (a) above.

Opposite enquiries by Individual

For those answers to the following enquiries, refer to the same in "Opposite enquiries on Individual and Plane" from *xii* (a) to *xiv* (b).

viii (a) Bodily formation does not arise in this individual. Had verbal formation not ceased in that individual? (b) Verbal formation had not ceased in this individual. Does bodily formation not arise in that individual?

ix (a) Bodily formation does not arise in this individual. Had mental formation not ceased in that individual? (b) Mental formation had not ceased in this individual. Does bodily formation not arise in that individual?

x (a) Verbal formation does not arise in this individual. Had mental formation not ceased in that individual? (b) Mental formation had not ceased in this individual. Does verbal formation not arise in that individual?

Opposite enquiries by Plane

xi (a) Bodily formation does not arise at this plane ..... p ..... Mental formation had not ceased at this plane. Does verbal formation not arise at that plane?

The answers in "Opposite enquiries on Plane" are the same in all those six time-lagged classifications of enquiries. Refer to Chart 6.16.

Opposite enquiries by Individual and Plane

xii (a) Bodily formation does not arise in this individual. Had verbal formation not ceased in that individual at that plane?
— No. To those at the first *jhāna* attainment, at the ceasing moment of breath-in and breath-out of the sensuous sphere; those at the arising moment of *citta* without breath-in and breath-out; and those of the fine-material and immaterial sphere, bodily formation does not arise; verbal formation therein had ceased.
— Yes. To those at the second and third *jhāna* attainment, at the ceasing moment of breath-in and breath-out; those at the arising moment of *citta* without breath-in and breath-out; those at the fourth *jhāna* attainment; those at the moment of second *citta* of the Pure abode beings; and those Non-percipient beings, bodily formation does not arise; verbal formation also had not ceased.

(b) Verbal formation had not ceased in this individual at this plane. Does bodily formation not arise in that individual at that plane?
— No. To those at the second and third *jhāna* attainment, at the arising moment of breath-in and breath-out, verbal formation had not ceased; bodily formation therein arises.
— Yes. Refer to the answer in *xii* (a) above.

xiii (a) Bodily formation does not arise in this individual at this plane. Had mental formation not ceased in that individual at that plane?
— No. To all those at the ceasing moment of *citta*, and those at the arising moment of *citta* without breath-in and breath-out, bodily formation does not arise; mental formation therein had ceased
— Yes. To those at the birth-moment of Pure abode beings and Non-percipient beings, bodily formation does not arise; mental formation also had not ceased.

(b) Mental formation had not ceased in this individual at this plane. Does bodily formation not arise in that individual at that plane?
— No such being mental formation had not ceased, but bodily formation arises.
— Yes. Refer to the answer in *xiii* (a) above.

xiv (a) Verbal formation does not arise in this individual at this plane. Had mental formation not ceased in that individual at that plane?
— No. To all those at the ceasing moment of *citta*, and those at the arising moment of *citta* without initial application and sustained application, verbal formation does not arise; mental formation had ceased.
— Yes. To those at the birth-moment of Pure abode and Non-percipient beings, verbal formation does not arise; mental formation also had not ceased.

(b) Mental formation had not ceased in this individual at this plane. Does verbal formation not arise in that individual at that plane?
— No such being mental formation had not ceased, but verbal formation arises.
— Yes. Refer to the answer in *xiv* (a) above.

Chart 6.17 Present arising and future cessation of the three formation types

A: arises; C: will cease; N: does not arise, or will not cease

	Arising			Cessation		
	Bodily F.	Verbal F.	Bodily F.	Verbal F.	Bodily F.	Verbal F.
Those at the arising moment of breath-in and breath-out	A					C
Those at the first *jhāna* attainment, at the arising moment of breath-in and breath-out	A				C	
Those at the first *jhāna* attainment, at the ceasing moment of breath-in and breath-out	N				C	
Those at the second and third *jhāna* attainment, at the arising moment of breath-in and breath-out	A				N	
Those at the second and third *jhāna* attainment, at the ceasing moment of breath-in and breath-out	N				N	
Those at the arising moment of initial application and sustained application		A				C
Those at the arising moment of *citta* without breath-in and breath-out	N				CN	C
Those at the arising moment of *citta* without initial application and sustained application		N				C
Those in whose consciousness whereof final-stage *citta* with non-initial application and non-sustained application will instantly arise	N				N	
Those endowed with final-stage *citta* with non-initial application and non-sustained application	N				N	
Those at the ceasing moment of final-stage *citta*	N	N				N
Those at the ceasing moment of final-stage *citta* with initial application and sustained application	N				N	
Those at the fourth *jhāna* attainment	N				N	
Fine-material beings (except Non-percipients)	N				C	
Immaterial beings	N				C	
Non-percipient beings	N	N			CN	CN
All those at the ceasing moment of *citta*	N	N			C	C
Those at Cessation attainment	N	N			C	C

Present and Future

Forward enquiries by Individual

For answers to the following enquiries, refer to the same in "Forward enquiries on Individual and Plane" from nos. 151 *i* (a) to 152 *i* (b).

148. *i* (a) Bodily formation arises in this individual. Will verbal formation cease in that individual? (b) Verbal formation will cease in this individual. Does bodily formation arise in that individual?

ii (a) Bodily formation arises in this individual. Will mental formation cease in that individual? (b) Mental formation will cease in this individual. Does bodily formation arise in that individual?

149. *i* (a) Verbal formation arises in this individual. Will mental formation cease in that individual? (b) Mental formation will cease in this individual. Does verbal formation arise in that individual?

Forward enquiries by Plane

150. *i* (a) Bodily formation arises at this plane ....p..... *ii* (b) Mental formation will cease at this plane. Does verbal formation arise at that plane?

The answers in "Forward enquiries on Plane" are the same in all those six time-lagged classifications of enquiries. Refer to Chart 6.17.

Forward enquiries by Individual and Plane

151. *i* (a) Bodily formation arises in this individual at this plane. Will verbal formation cease in that individual at that plane?
— No. To those at the second and third *jhāna* attainment at the arising moment of breath-in and breath-out, bodily formation arises; verbal formation will not cease.
— Yes. To those at the first *jhāna* attainment, at the arising moment of breath-in and breath-out of the sensuous sphere, bodily formation arises; verbal formation will cease.

(b) Verbal formation will cease in this individual at this plane. Does bodily formation arise in that individual at that plane?
— No. To those at the first *jhāna* attainment, at the ceasing moment of breath-in and breath-out of the sensuous sphere; those at the arising moment of *citta* without breath-in and breath-out; all those at the ceasing moment of *citta*; those of the fine-material and immaterial sphere; Non-percipient beings (and those of Cessation-attainment, transcending mundane spheres), verbal formation will cease; bodily formation does not arise.
— Yes. Refer to the answer in 151 *i* (a) above.

ii (a) Bodily formation arises in this individual at this plane. Will mental formation cease in that individual at that plane?
— Yes. To those at the arising moment of breath-in and breath-out, bodily formation arises; mental formation will cease.

(b) Mental formation will cease in this individual at this plane. Does bodily formation arise in that individual at that plane?
— No. To all those at the ceasing moment of *citta*, those at the arising moment of *citta* without breath-in and breath-out, Non-percipient beings (and those of

Cessation-attainment, transcending mundane spheres), mental formation will cease; bodily formation does not arise.
— Yes. Refer to the answer in 151 *ii* (a) above.

152. *i* (a) Verbal formation arises in this individual at this plane. Will mental formation cease in that individual at that plane?
— Yes. To those at the arising moment of initial application and sustained application, verbal formation arises; mental formation will also cease.

(b) Mental formation will cease in this individual at this plane. Does verbal formation arise in that individual at that plane?
— No. To all those at the ceasing moment of *citta*, those at the arising moment of *citta* without initial application and sustained application, Non-percipient beings (and those of Cessation-attainment, transcending the three mundane spheres), mental formation will cease; verbal formation does not arise.
— Yes. Refer to the answer in 152 *i* (a) above.

Opposite enquiries by Individual

For those answers to the following enquiries, refer to the same in "Opposite enquiries on Individual and Plane" from 156 *i* (a) to 157 *i* (b).

153. *i* (a) Bodily formation does not arise in this individual. Will verbal formation not cease in that individual? (b) Verbal formation will not cease in this individual. Does bodily formation not arise in that individual?

ii (a) Bodily formation does not arise in this individual. Will mental formation not cease in that individual? (b) Mental formation will not cease in this individual. Does bodily formation not arise in that individual?

154. *i* (a) Verbal formation does not arise in this individual. Will mental formation not cease in that individual? (b) Mental formation will not cease in this individual. Does verbal formation not arise in that individual?

Opposite enquiries by Plane

155. *i* (a) Bodily formation does not arise at this plane.....p.... *ii* (b) Mental formation will not cease at this plane. Does verbal formation not arise at that plane?

The answers in "Opposite enquiries on Plane" are the same in all those six time-lagged classifications of enquiries. Refer to Chart 6.17.

Opposite enquiries by Individual and Plane

156. *i* (a) Bodily formation does not arise in this individual at this plane. Will verbal formation not cease in that individual at that plane?

— No. To those at the first *jhāna* attainment, at the ceasing moment of breath-in and breath-out of the sensuous sphere, those at the arising moment of *citta* without breath-in and breath-out, those of the fine-material and immaterial sphere, all those at the ceasing moment of *citta*, Non-percipient beings (and those of Cessation-attainment, transcending the three mundane spheres), bodily formation does not arise; verbal formation will cease.

— Yes. To those at the ceasing moment of final-stage *citta* with initial application and sustained application, those endowed with final-stage *citta* with non-initial application and non-sustained application, those in whose consciousness whereof final-stage *citta* with non-initial application and non-sustained application will instantly arise, those at the fourth *jhāna* attainment, those at the second and third *jhāna* attainment at the ceasing moment of breath-in and breath-out, those at the arising moment of *citta* without breath-in and breath-out, and Non-percipient beings, bodily formation does not arise; verbal formation also will not cease.

(b) Verbal formation will not cease in this individual at this plane. Does bodily formation not arise in that individual at that plane?
— No. To those at the second and third *jhāna* attainment, at the arising moment of breath-in/breath-out, verbal formation will not cease; bodily formation arises.
— Yes. Refer to the answer in 156 *i* (a) above.

ii (a) Bodily formation does not arise in this individual at this plane. Will mental formation not cease in that individual at that plane?
— No. To all those at the ceasing moment of *citta*, those at the arising moment of *citta* without breath-in and breath-out, those Non-percipient beings (and those of Cessation-attainment, transcending the three mundane spheres), bodily formation does not arise; mental formation will cease.
— Yes. To those at the ceasing moment of final-stage *citta*, and those Non-percipient beings, bodily formation does not arise; mental formation also will not cease.

(b) Mental formation will not cease in this individual at this plane. Does bodily formation not arise in that individual at that plane?
— Yes. Refer to the answer in 156 *ii* (a) above.

157. *i* (a) Verbal formation does not arise in this individual at that plane. Will mental formation not cease in that individual at that plane?
— No. To all those at the ceasing moment of *citta*, those at the arising moment of *citta* without initial application and sustained application, Non-percipient beings (and those of Cessation-attainment, transcending the three mundane spheres), verbal formation does not arise; mental formation will cease.

— Yes. To those at the ceasing moment of final-stage *citta*, and to Non-percipient beings, verbal formation does not arise; mental formation therein will not cease.

(b) Mental formation will not cease in this individual at this plane. Does verbal formation not arise in that individual at that plane?
— Yes. Refer to the answer in 157 *i* (a) above.

Chart 6.18 Past origination and future cessation of the three formation types

A: had arisen; C: will cease; N: had not arisen, or will not cease

	Arising			Cessation		
	Bodily F.	Verbal F.	Bodily F.	Verbal F.	Bodily F.	Verbal F.
Those at the planes of initial application and sustained application (except those endowed with final-stage *citta*)		A				C
Those at the planes of non-initial application and non-sustained application (except those endowed with final-stage *citta*)		N				C
Those in whose consciousness whereof final-stage *citta* with non-initial application and non-sustained application will instantly arise	A N				N N	
Those endowed with final-stage *citta* with non-initial application and non-sustained application	A N				N N	
Those at the ceasing moment of final-stage *citta*	A N				N	N N
Those at the ceasing moment of final-stage *citta* with initial application and sustained application	A N				N N	
Those at the ceasing moment of final-stage *citta* at the planes of initial application and sustained application		A				N
Those at the ceasing moment of final-stage *citta* at the planes of non-initial application and non-sustained application		N				N
Those at the first *jhāna* attainment	A				C	
Those at the first, second, and third *jhāna* attainment	A					C
Those at the second and third *jhāna* attainment	A				N	
Those at the fourth *jhāna* attainment	N				N	C
Sensuous beings	A				C	C
Fine-material beings (except Non-percipients)	N				C	C
Immaterial beings	N				C	C
Non-percipient beings	N	N			N	N

Past and Future

Forward enquiries by Individual

158. *i* (a) Bodily formation had arisen in this individual. Will verbal formation cease in that individual?

— No. To those at the ceasing moment of final-stage *citta* with initial application and sustained application (at sensuous sphere), those endowed with final-stage *citta* with non-initial application and non-sustained application (at sensuous sphere), those in whose consciousness whereof final-stage *citta* with non-initial application and non-sustained application will instantly arise (at sensuous sphere), and those at the second and third *jhāna* attainment, bodily formation had arisen; verbal formation will not cease.
— Yes. To those others (those at the first *jhāna* attainment, and others of the sensuous sphere), bodily formation had arisen; verbal formation will cease.

(b) Verbal formation will cease in this individual. Had bodily formation arisen in that individual?
— Yes. Refer to the answer in 158 *i* (a) above.
— No. To those of the fine-material and immaterial sphere, verbal formation will cease; bodily formation had not arisen.

ii (a) Bodily formation had arisen in this individual. Will mental formation cease in that individual?
— No. To those at the ceasing moment of final-stage *citta* (at sensuous sphere), bodily formation had arisen; mental formation will not cease.
— Yes. To those others (those at the first, second, and third *jhāna* attainment and others of the sensuous sphere), bodily formation had arisen; mental formation will cease.

(b) Mental formation will cease in this individual. Had bodily formation arisen in that individual?
— Yes. Refer to the answer in 158 *ii* (a) above.
— No. To those at the fourth *jhāna* attainment, and those at fine-material and immaterial sphere, mental formation will cease; bodily formation had not arisen.

The remaining catechisms on Past-Future of Origination-Cessation are not provided by the text. They are to be classified similarly with those in the section on Cessation. I composed them nonetheless and have put together all the answers in Chart 6.17 above.

iii (a) Verbal formation had arisen in this individual. Will mental formation cease in that individual? (b) Mental formation will cease in this individual. Had verbal formation arisen in that individual? — Refer to the answers in 158 *vi* below.

Forward enquiries by Plane

Refer to the answers in Chart 6.18.

Forward enquiries by Individual and Plane

iv (a) Bodily formation had arisen in this individual at this plane. Will verbal formation cease in that individual at that plane? (b) Verbal formation will cease in this individual at this plane. Had bodily formation arisen in that individual at that plane? —Refer to the answers in 158 *i* above.

v (a) Bodily formation had arisen in this individual at this plane. Will mental formation cease in that individual at that plane? (b) Mental formation will cease in this individual at this plane. Had bodily formation arisen in that individual at that plane? — Refer to the answers in 158 *ii* above.

vi (a) Verbal formation had arisen in this individual at this plane. Will mental formation cease in that individual at that plane?
— No. To those at the ceasing moment of final-stage *citta* at the planes of initial application and sustained application, verbal formation had arisen; mental formation will not cease.
— Yes. To others at the planes of initial application and sustained application, verbal formation had arisen; mental formation will cease.

(b) Mental formation will cease in this individual at this plane. Had verbal formation arisen in that individual at that plane?
— No. To those at the planes of non-initial application and non-sustained application, mental formation will cease; verbal formation had not arisen.
— Yes. Refer to the answer in *vi* (a) above.

Opposite enquiries by Individual

vii (a) Bodily formation had not arisen in this individual .....p..... Had verbal formation not arisen in that individual?

For answers to the enquiries above, refer to the same in "Opposite enquiries on Individual and Plane" below, from *viii* (a) to *x* (b).

Opposite enquiries by Plane

Refer to the answers in Chart 6.18.

Opposite enquiries by Individual and Plane

viii (a) Bodily formation had not arisen in this individual at this plane. Will verbal formation not cease in that individual at that plane?
— No. To those of the fine-material and immaterial sphere, bodily formation had not arisen; but verbal formation will cease.
— Yes. To those at the ceasing moment of final-stage *citta* with initial application and sustained application at planes of fine-material and immaterial sphere, those endowed with final-stage *citta* with non-initial application and non-

sustained application (at fine-material and immaterial sphere), those in whose consciousness whereof final-stage *citta* with non-initial application and non-sustained application will instantly arise (at fine-material and immaterial sphere), those at the fourth *jhāna* attainment, and Non-percipient beings, bodily formation had not arisen; verbal formation will not cease.

(b) Verbal formation will not cease in this individual at this plane. Had bodily formation not arisen in that individual at that plane?
— No. To those at the ceasing moment of final-stage *citta* at the sensuous sphere, and those at the second and third *jhāna* attainment, verbal formation will not cease; but bodily formation had arisen.
— Yes. Refer to the answer in *viii* (a) above.

ix (a) Bodily formation had not arisen in this individual at this plane. Will mental formation not cease in that individual at that plane?
— No. To all those at the fourth *jhāna* attainment, those of the fine-material and immaterial sphere, bodily formation had not ceased; mental formation will cease.
— Yes. To those at the ceasing moment of final-stage *citta* at the fine-material and immaterial sphere, and to Non-percipient beings, bodily formation had not arisen; mental formation also will not cease.

(b) Mental formation will not cease in this individual at this plane. Had bodily formation not arisen in that individual at that plane?
— No. To those at the ceasing moment of final-stage *citta* at the sensuous sphere, mental formation will not cease; bodily formation had arisen.
— Yes. Refer to the answer in *ix* (a) above.

x (a) Verbal formation had not arisen in this individual at this plane. Will mental formation not cease in that individual at that plane?
— No. To those at the planes of non-initial application and non-sustained application, verbal formation had not arisen; mental formation will cease.
— Yes. To those at the ceasing moment of final-stage *citta* at the planes of non-initial application and non-sustained application, and to Non-percipient beings, verbal formation had not arisen; mental formation also will not cease.

(b) Mental formation will not cease in this individual at this plane. Had verbal formation not arisen in that individual at that plane?
— No. To those at the ceasing moment of final-stage *citta* at the planes of initial application and sustained application, mental formation will not cease; verbal formation had arisen.
— Yes. Refer to the answer in *x* (a) above.

Consolidated answers from the arising-cessation of formations

Chart 6.19 Composition on the arising and cessation of the three formation types

A: arises/ had arisen/ will arise; C: ceases/ had ceased/ will cease;
N_a: does not arise/ had not arisen/ will not arise,
N_c: does not cease/ had not ceased/ will not cease

	Present			Past			Future		
	Bodily F.	Verbal F.	Mental F.	Bodily F.	Verbal F.	Mental F.	Bodily F.	Verbal F.	Mental F.
Those at the arising moment of breath-in and breath-out	***A***	*N_c*	*N_c*		C	C			C
Those at the first *jhāna* attainment, at the arising moment of breath-in and breath-out	A							C	
Those at the first *jhāna* attainment, at the ceasing moment of breath-in and breath-out	N_a				C			C	
Those at the second and third *jhāna* attainment, at the arising moment of breath-in and breath-out	A				N_c			N_c	
Those at the second and third *jhāna* attainment, at the ceasing moment of breath-in and breath-out	N_a				N_c			N_c	
Those at the arising moment of initial application and sustained application		***A***	*N_c*			C			C
Those at the ceasing moment of initial application and sustained application	N_a	C							
Those at the arising moment of *citta* without breath-in and breath-out	***N_a***	*N_c*	*N_c*		CN_c	C		CN_c	C
Those at the arising moment of *citta* without initial application and sustained application		***N_a***	*N_c*			C			C
Those at the planes of initial application and sustained application (except those endowed with final-stage *citta*)					A				C
Those at the planes of non-initial appl.and non-sustained appl. (except those endowed with final-stage *citta*)					N_a				C
Those in whose consciousness whereof final-stage *citta* of the sensuous sphere will instantly arise							*N_a*	*C*	*C*
Those in whose consciousness whereof final-stage *citta* with non-initial application and non-sustained application will instantly arise	N_a			A N_a			*N_a*	***N_c*** *N_a*	*C*
				A				N_c	
				N_a				N_c	
Those endowed with final-stage *citta* with non-initial application and non-sustained application	N_a						*N_a*	***N_c***	
				A				N_c	
				N_a				N_c	
Those at the arising moment of final-stage *citta*							*N_a*	*C*	*C*
Those at the ceasing moment of final-stage *citta*							*N_a*	*N_a*	*N_c*
Those at the ceasing moment of final-stage *citta*	N_a	N_a							N_c
				A				N_c	N_c
				N_a					N_c

	Present			Past			Future		
	Bodily F.	Verbal F.	Mental F.	Bodily F.	Verbal F.	Mental F.	Bodily F.	Verbal F.	Mental F.
Those at the arising moment of final-stage *citta* with initial application and sustained application	-	-	-	-	-	-	-	-	-
Those at the ceasing moment of final-stage *citta* with initial application and sustained application	**Na**						*Na*	***Nc***	
				A				**Nc**	
				Na				**Nc**	
Those at the ceasing moment of final-stage *citta* at the planes of initial application and sustained application					**A**				**Nc**
Those at the ceasing moment of final-stage *citta* at the planes of non-initial application and non-sustained application					**Na**				**Nc**
Those at the first *jhāna* attainment				***A***	*C* *A*	***C***	***A***	***C*** *A*	*C*
Those at the first, second, and third *jhāna* attainment				***A***		*C*	***A***		***C***
Those at the second and third *jhāna* attainment				***A***	*Nc*		*A*	***Nc***	
Those at the second, third, and fourth *jhāna* attainment					*Na*	*C*		*Na*	*C*
Those at the fourth *jhāna* attainment	**Na**			***Na***	***Nc***	*C*	*Na*	***Nc***	***C***
Those at the birth-moment of Pure abode beings	**Na**	**Na**		*Na*	*Nc*	***Nc***			
Those at the birth-moment of Non-percipient beings	**Na**	**Na**		*Na*	*Nc*	***Nc***			
Those at the moment of second *citta* of Pure abode beings	**Na**			*Na*	***Nc***	*C*			
Sensuous beings				***A***	*C*	*C*	*A*	***C*** ***A***	***C***
Fine-material beings (except Non-percipients)	**Na**			***Na***	***C***	*C*	*Na*	***C*** *A*	***C***
Immaterial beings	**Na**			***Na***	***C***	*C*	*Na*	***C*** *A*	***C***
Non-percipient beings	***Na***	*Nc* ***Na***	*Nc*	***Na***	**CNc** ***Na***	C*Nc*	***Na***	**CNc**	**CNc**
Final existence beings							*Na*	*C*	*C*
All those at the ceasing moment of *citta*	***Na***	*C* ***Na***	*C*		**C**	**C**		**C**	**C**
Those at Cessation attainment	***Na***	*Nc* ***Na***	*Nc*		**C**	**C**		**C**	**C**

Referring to the above Chart, the denotation of letters in *italic* are the answers consolidated from the respective first three sub-sections on present, past, and future arising of formations. Those boldfaced letters, including whether in *italic* or not, are the answers to be referred to the other classifications on present-past, present-future, and past-future arising of the formations.

A better picture with regrouped consolidation

Chart 6.20 Regrouped consolidation of Arising, Cessation, Arising-and-Cessation of the three formation types

A: arises/ had arisen/ will arise; C: ceases/ had ceased/ will cease;
N_a: does not arise/ had not arisen/ will not arise,
N_c: does not cease/ had not ceased/ will not cease

	Present			Past			Future		
	Bodily F.	Verbal F.	Mental F.	Bodily F.	Verbal F.	Mental F.	Bodily F.	Verbal F.	Mental F.
Those at the arising and ceasing moment of breath-in and breath-out	*A*	*A*	*A*		A	A			A
	C		*C*		C	C			C
	A	*N_c*	*N_c*		C	C			C
Those at the arising and ceasing moment of breath-in and breath-out without initial application and sustained application	*A*	*N_a*							
	C	*N*							
	-	-	-	-	-	-	-	-	-
Those at the first *jhāna* attainment, at the arising moment of breath-in and breath-out	*A*	*A*			A			A	
	N_c				C			C	
	A							C	
Those at the first *jhāna* attainment, at the ceasing moment of breath-in and breath-out	N_a				A			A	
	C	*C*			C			C	
	N_a				C			C	
Those at the second and third *jhāna* attainment, at the arising moment of breath-in and breath-out	A				N_a			N_a	
	N_c				N_c			N_c	
	A				N_c			N_c	
Those at the second and third *jhāna* attainment, at the ceasing moment of breath-in and breath-out	N_a				N_a			N_a	
	C				N_c			N_c	
	N_a				N_c			N_c	
Those at the arising and ceasing moment of initial application and sustained application		*A*	*A*		A	A			A
		C	*C*			C			C
		A	*N_c*			C			C
Those at the arising and ceasing moment of initial application and sustained application without breath-in and breath-out	*N_a*	*A*							
	N_c	*C*							
Those at the arising and ceasing moment of *citta* without breath-in and breath-out	*N_a*		*A*		AN_a	A		AN_a	A
	N_c		*C*		CN_c	C		CN_c	C
	N_a	*N_c*	*N_c*		CN_c	C		CN_c	C
Those at the arising and ceasing moment of *citta* without initial application and sustained application		*N_a*	*A*			A			A
		N_c	*C*			C			C
		N_a	*N_c*			C			C
Those at the arising and ceasing moment of *citta* with non-initial application and non-sustained application, without breath-in and breath-out	*N_a*	*N_a*							
	N_c	*N_c*							
Those at the planes of initial application and sustained application (except those with final-stage *citta*)					A				A
					C				C
					A				C

	Present			Past			Future		
	Bodily F.	Verbal F.	Mental F.	Bodily F.	Verbal F.	Mental F.	Bodily F.	Verbal F.	Mental F.
Those at the planes of non-initial application and non-sustained application (except those with final-stage *citta*)					**N_a**				**A**
					N_c				**C**
					N_a				**C**
Those in whose consciousness whereof final-stage *citta* of the sensuous sphere will instantly arise							*N_a*	*A*	*A*
							N_c	*C*	*C*
							N_a	*C*	*C*
Those in whose consciousness whereof final-stage *citta* with non-initial application and non-sustained application will instantly arise	**N_a**			**A** **N_a**			*N_a*	***N_a***	*A*
	N_c			**C** **N_c**			*N_c*	***N_c***	*C*
	N_a			**A** **N_a**			*N_a*	***N_c*** *N_a*	*C*
				A				**N_a**	
				C				**N_c**	
				A				**N_c**	
				N_a				**N_a**	
				N_c				**N_c**	
				N_a				**N_c**	
Those endowed with final-stage *citta*	**N_a**			**A**			*N_a*	***N_a***	***N_a***
Those endowed with final-stage *citta*	**N_a**			**N_a**	**N_a**		*N_a*	***N_a***	***N_a***
Those endowed with final-stage *citta* at the planes of initial application and sustained application					**A**				**N_a**
Those endowed with final-stage *citta* at the planes of non-initial application and non-sustained application					**N_a**				**N_a**
Those who are endowed with final-stage *citta* with non-initial application and non-sustained application		**N_a**							**N_a**
	N_c						*N_c*	***N_c***	
	N_a						*N_a*	***N_c***	
				A				**N_c**	
				C				**N_c**	
				N_a				**N_c**	
				N_c				**N_c**	
Those at the arising moment of final-stage *citta*							*N_c*	*C*	*C*
							N_a	*C*	*C*
Those at the ceasing moment of final-stage *citta*							*N_c*	*N_c*	*N_c*
							N_a	*N_a*	*N_c*
Those at the ceasing moment of final-stage *citta*	**N_c**			**C**				**N_c**	**N_c**
	N_a			**A**				**N_c**	**N_c**
	N_c			**N_c**					**N_c**
	N_a			**N_a**					**N_c**
Those at the arising moment of final-stage *citta* with initial application and sustained application		**A**							**N_a**

	Present			Past			Future		
	Bodily F.	Verbal F.	Mental F.	Bodily F.	Verbal F.	Mental F.	Bodily F.	Verbal F.	Mental F.
Those at the ceasing moment of final-stage *citta* with initial application and sustained application		N_a							N_a
	N_c	C					N_c	N_c	N_c
	N_a						N_a	N_c	
				C				N_c	
				A				N_c	
				N_c				N_c	
				N_a				N_c	
Those at the ceasing moment of final-stage *citta* at the planes of initial application and sustained application					C				N_c
					A				N_c
Those at the ceasing moment of final-stage *citta* at the planes of non-initial application and non-sustained application					N_c				N_c
					N_a				N_c
Those at the arising moment of final-stage *citta* with non-initial application and non-sustained application								N_c	C
Those at the ceasing moment of final-stage *citta* with non-initial application and non-sustained application		N_c							N_c
Those at the first *jhāna* attainment				A	A	A	A	A	A
				C	C	C	C	C	C
Those at the first, second, and third *jhāna* attainment				A		A	A		A
				C		C	C		C
				A		C	A		C
Those at the second and third *jhāna* attainment				A	N_a		A	N_a	
				C	N_c		C	N_c	
				A	N_c		A	N_c	
Those at the second, third, fourth *jhāna* attainment					N_a	A		N_a	A
					N_c	C		N_c	C
					N_a	C		N_a	C
Those at the fourth *jhāna* attainment	N_a			N_a	N_a	A	N_a	N_a	A
	N_c			N_c	N_c	C	N_c	N_c	C
	N_a			N_a	N_c	C	N_a	N_c	C
Those at the birth-moment of Pure abode beings	N_a	N_a		N_a	N_a	N_a			
	N_c	N_c		N_c	N_c	N_c			
	N_a	N_a		N_a	N_c	N_c			
Those at the birth-moment of Non-percipient beings	N_a	N_a		N_a	N_a	N_a			
	N_c	N_c		N_c	N_c	N_c			
	N_a	N_a		N_a	N_c	N_c			
Those at the moment of second *citta* of Pure abode beings	N_a			N_a	N_a	A			
	N_c			N_c	N_c	C			
	N_a			N_a	N_c	C			

	Present			Past			Future		
	Bodily F.	Verbal F.	Mental F.	Bodily F.	Verbal F.	Mental F.	Bodily F.	Verbal F.	Mental F.
Sensuous beings				A	A	A	A	A	A
				C	C	C	C	C	C
				A	C	C	A	C A	C
Fine-material beings and immaterial beings (except those of Non-percipience plane)	Na			Na	A	A	Na	A	A
	Nc			Nc	C	C	Nc	C	C
	Na			Na	C	C	Na	C A	C
Non-percipient beings	Na	Na	Na	Na	A Na	A Na	Na	A Na	A Na
	Nc	Nc	Nc	Nc	C Nc	C Nc	Nc	C Nc	C Nc
Final existence beings							Na	A	A
							N	C	C
All those at the ceasing moment of *citta*	Na	Na	Na		A	A		A	A
	Nc	Nc	Nc		C	C		C	C
Those at Cessation attainment	Na	Na	Na		A	A		A	A
	Nc	Nc	Nc		C	C		C	C

6.3 Comprehension of formation types

159. *i* (a) This person is comprehending bodily formation. Is that person comprehending verbal formation? — Yes.
(b) This person is comprehending verbal formation. Is that person comprehending bodily formation? —Yes.
… p … This person will not comprehend verbal formation. Had that person not comprehend verbal formation?

The above catechisms are to be continued in the same manner as the section on Comprehension at aggregates in Chapter Two is classified. I have formulated the questions and concise answers in Chart below according to their sequence. In this chart, the symbol *y* denotes the answer "Yes", *n* stands for "No".

Chart 6.21. Catechism on Comprehension (*Pariñña*)

	bodily formation?	verbal formation?
Present :		
This person is comprehending bodily formation. Is that person comprehending		1*y*
This person is comprehending verbal formation. Is that person comprehending	2*y*	
This person is not comprehending bodily formation, thereby is not comprehending		3*y*
This person is not comprehending verbal formation, thereby is not comprehending	4*y*	
Past :		
This person had comprehended bodily formation, and thereby had comprehended		5*y*
This person had comprehended verbal formation, and thereby had comprehended	6*y*	
This person had not comprehended bodily formation, thereby had not comprehended		7*y*
This person had not comprehended verbal formation, thereby had not comprehended	8*y*	
Future :		
This person will comprehend bodily formation. Will that person comprehend		9*y*
This person will comprehend verbal formation. Will that person comprehend	10*y*	
This person will not comprehend bodily formation. Will that person not comprehend		11*y*
This person will not comprehend verbal formation. Will that person not comprehend	12*y*	
Present-and-Past :		
This person is comprehending bodily formation. Had that person comprehended		13*n*
This person had comprehended verbal formation. Is that person comprehending	14*n*	
This person is not comprehending bodily formation. Had that person not comprehended		15
This person had not comprehended verbal formation. Is that person comprehending	16	
Present-and-Future :		
This person is comprehending bodily formation. Will that person comprehend		17*n*
This person will comprehend verbal formation. Is that person comprehending	18*n*	
This person is not comprehending bodily formation. Will that person not comprehend		19
This person will not comprehend verbal formation. Is that person not comprehending	20	
Past-and-Future :		
This person had comprehended bodily formation. Will that person comprehend		21*n*
This person will comprehend verbal formation. Had that person comprehended	22*n*	
This person had not comprehended bodily formation. Will that person not comprehend		23
This person will not comprehend verbal formation. Had that person not comprehend	24	

In the first pair of enquiries, it is to be read as "when this person is comprehending bodily formation, this person is also comprehending verbal formation. When the person is not comprehending bodily formation, he similarly is not comprehending verbal formation (as well as mental formation). The same basis is used to explain remaining occurrences at present (3*y* to 4*y*), in the past (5*y* to 8*y*), in future (9*y* to 12*y*), present-past (3*y* to 4*y*), present-future (17*y* to 18*y*), and past-future (21*n* to 22*n*).

In nos. 15, *Arahat* is not comprehending bodily formation, but it is not that he had not comprehended verbal formation (He had). It is only to those common worldlings who *will not attain* the Path, that they are not comprehending bodily formation, and also had not comprehended verbal formation. In nos. 16, *Arahatta*

Path-attainer (*Aggamaggasamaṅgī*) had not comprehended verbal formation (to its entirety) [34], but it is not that he is not comprehending bodily formation (He is). It is only to those common worldlings who *will not attain* the Path, that they had not comprehended verbal formation, and also is not comprehending bodily formation.

In nos. 17, *Arahatta* Path-attainer is comprehending bodily formation, but he will not be comprehending verbal formation. In nos. 18, those common worldlings who *will attain* the Path will comprehend verbal formation, but they are not comprehending bodily formation.

In nos. 19, it is to those common worldlings who *will attain* the Path, that they are not comprehending bodily formation; but it is not that they will not comprehend verbal formation (They will). It is only to Arahats, and to those common worldlings (*puthujjanā*, or *nevasekkhanāsekkhā*) who *will not attain* the Path, that they are not comprehending bodily formation and also will not be comprehending verbal formation.

In nos. 20, *Arahatta* Path-attainer will not be comprehending verbal formation; it is not that he is not comprehending bodily formation (He is comprehending). It is only to Arahats and to those common worldlings who *will not attain* the Path, that they will not be comprehending verbal formation and are also not comprehending bodily formation.

In nos. 21, *Arahat* had comprehended bodily formation, but he will not be comprehending verbal formation. In nos. 22, it is those common worldlings who *will attain* the Path, will comprehend verbal formation; but they had not comprehended bodily formation.

Regarding nos. 23, those common worldlings who *will attain* the Path, they had not comprehended bodily formation; it is not that they will not comprehend verbal formation (They will). It is only to the *Arahatta* Path-attainer, and to those common worldlings who *will not attain* the Path, that they had not comprehended bodily formation and also will not be comprehending verbal formation.

As for nos. 24, an *Arahat* will not be comprehending verbal formation; it is not that he had not comprehended bodily formation (He had). It is only to *Arahatta* Path-attainer, and to those common worldlings who *will not attain* the Path, that they will not be comprehending verbal formation and also had not comprehended bodily formation.

The next chart summarises what have just been described in the aforesaid with regard to *Arahat*, *Arahatta* Path-attainer, and those common worldlings (*puthujjanas*) who will attain the Path and those who will not attain the Path

---

[34] *Aggamaggasamaṅgī*, which means a person who is endowed with the 'highest' Path-*citta*, is herein known as the *Arahatta* Path-attainer. A person with the *Arahatta* Path-*citta* had not comprehended verbal formation, for it is said that to the *Arahatta* Path individuals, the full realisation and attainment thereof is incomplete.

Chart 2.16. Arahats, *Arahatta* Path individuals, and common worldlings on the comprehension of formations

Arahat (*Arahā*)	*Arahatta* Path-attainer (*Aggamaggasamaṅgī*)	Person(s) who will attain the Path	Person(s) who will not attain the Path	
	•			is comprehending bodily formation; he is also comprehending verbal formation
•		•	•	is not comprehending bodily formation; he is also not comprehending verbal formation
•				had comprehended bodily formation; similarly had comprehended verbal formation
	•	•	•	had not comprehended bodily formation; similarly had not comprehended verbal formation
		•		will comprehend bodily formation; and will also comprehend verbal formation
•	•		•	will not be comprehending bodily formation; also will not be comprehending verbal formation
	•			is comprehending bodily formation
•		•	•	is not comprehending bodily formation
•				had comprehended bodily formation
	•	•	•	had not comprehended bodily formation
•				had comprehended verbal formation
	•	•	•	had not comprehended verbal formation
		•		will comprehend verbal formation
•	•		•	will not be comprehending verbal formation

CHAPTER 7

VII. Pairs on Latent Inclination
(*Anusayayamaka*)

The seven states of underlying inclination, or simply latent states, are comprised of seven of the ten fetters of defilement wherein restlessness (*uddhacca*) is subsumed as under the broader spectrum of ignorance (*avijjā*), desire for the existence of fine-materiality and immateriality (*rūparāga, arūparāga*) are taken as under lust for existence (*bhavarāga*), and self-elusive individualistic view, and clinging to practising rites and ceremonies including worship of deities and animism, self-mortification, etc. (*sakkāyadiṭṭhi, sīlabbataparāmāsa*) are treated as a part of wrong views (*diṭṭhi*). In other words, Chapter Seven is in fact also about the ten fetters of defilement.

Chapter Seven uses the same methodology as in preceding chapters, examining by pairs of catechisms, routing through all permutations by means of forward and opposite dichotomised mode of enquiries. The difference here is that instead of a one-to-one pairing, it makes use of mixed pairing, from single base, two bases... up to six bases. Altogether there are six methods of pairing the enquiries. This chapter incorporates eight sections to examine latent states. Among them, the first two topics on 'lying unmanifest' and 'unmanifest with', are only different by the way questions and answers are phrased to ascertain our levels of understanding, but the two sets of results are just the same. The next two topics in respect of latent states as to 'renouncing' and 'comprehending', are also identical in results, except only the questions and answers are differently worded. For examples, it is with full understanding that *Sotāpatti* Path-attainer are renouncing wrong views and skepticism. When latent states of conceit and ignorance, or part thereof remain as unmanifest in *Anāgāmi* Path-attainer, it is simply the lacking of full understanding of them. The other two topics regarding 'elimination' and 'arising' of latent states are antithetical of each other. What latent states have been eliminated in that person, the same in whom does not any longer arise. The last two topics involve, respectively, sets of questions and answers, are dealing with nine groups of persons. The Q&A are designed to examine those states which will remain as latent in a person on conditions of whether or not that person has mentally shifted from an element, and whether or not that person has mentally reemerged in other elements. The answers in the last section would defy our understanding if we conceive those conditions in terms of physical death and reborn in another element or place. It is not the similar case as in the preceding six sections as you would see from the answers in the charts, that lust for the existence of fine-materiality and immateriality does not lie latent to those in the sensuous world, and similarly desire for sensuous pleasures and aversion do not lie latent in fine-material world and immaterial world. In order to make the reading handily, I combined the last two sections into one.

Chapter 7: Pairs on Latent Inclination

1. Definitions.

There are seven latent states or proclivities (*Satta anusayā*) [35], namely the respective latent states of :

- attachment to sensuous pleasures (*kāmarāga*) [36]
- aversion or hatred (*paṭigha*) [37]
- conceit or pride (*māna*) [38]
- wrong views (*diṭṭhi*) [39]
- skeptical doubt (*vicikicchā*) [40]
- lust for existence or becoming (*bhavarāga*) [41]
- ignorance (*avijjā*) [42]

---

[35] These latent states are collectively called 'proclivities' because, owing to their pertinacity, they ever and again tend to become conditions for the arising of new sensuous desires, etc." (Vis.M. XXII, 60). Other closer meanings are 'inclinations, tendencies'. The sources of the seven latent states are: DN33 Saṅgītisutta; DN34 Dasuttarasutta; AN7 Saṃyojanasutta; Vibh 17, Khuddakavatthuvibhaṅgo, nos. 949. The seven are also derived from the ten kinds of fetters (*saṃyojanāni*) in respect of *kāmarāga, paṭigha, māna, diṭṭhi, vicikicchā, sīlabbataparāmāsa, bhavarāga, issā, macchariya, avijjā.* *(*Cnd23 Khaggavisāṇasuttaniddeso, nos. 148 ; Dhs nos. 1118-1128, 1477).

[36] *Kāmarāgānusayo* corresponds to the greed-*cetasika*, arising at the 19 types of plesant feelings (4+4+5+5+1) and 32 types of neither-pleasant-nor-unpleasant feeling (4+6+16+6), at the 11 planes of sensuous sphere. (See the chart in Appendix II).

[37] *Paṭigha* with the rendering as 'aversion' is preferred. The reason is because 'aversion', as repulsion of the mind, is present in all kinds of hate from enragement to annoyance, to even the slightest sense of inconspicuous displeasure, and so that it is differentiated semantically from hatred (*dosa*) which is a more intensified form of aversion. *Paṭighānusayo* in this context is treated as identical to the hatred-*cetasika.*

[38] *Mānānusayo*, corresponds to the conceit-*cetasika*, arising at the 4 greed-rooted unwholesome cittas dissociated from wrong views. Conceit lays latent in *Puthujjana, Sotāpanna, Sakadāgāmi and Anāgāmi*, with the exception of *Arahat*

[39] *Diṭṭhānusayo*, born of the fallacy-*cetasika* and associates with the 4 *diṭṭhigata sampayutta* with cause (*hetu*), is arising at the 19 plesant feelings, 3 unpleasant feelings, and 32 neither-pleasant-nor-unpleasant feelings of the common worldings (See the chart in Appendix II), with the exception of 4 noble persons (*Sotāpanna*, *Sakadāgāmi*, *Anāgāmi* and *Arahat*).

[40] *Vicikicchānusayo*, stems from the conceit-*cetasika*, accompanies the 1 delusion-rooted citta associated with doubt. It is lays latent only in *Puthujjana*, It is absent in *Sotāpanna, Sakadāgāmi, Anāgāmi* and *Arahat.*

[41] *Bbhavarāgānusayo*, born of the greed-*cetasika* and is associated with the 4 *diṭṭhigata vippayutta* with cause (*hetu*), is characteristic of the fine-material and immaterial planes.

[42] *Avijjānusayo*, corresponds to delusion-*cetasika* that arises with the 2 delusion-rooted cittas associated with doubt and restlessness. Delusion (*moha*) can coexist with the 12 unwholesome cittas; can arise without greed and hatred; can become a precursor precipitates into the predominance of greed and hatred. However, the 8 greed-rooted cittas and 2 hatred-rooted cittas can not coexist.

7.1 Arising States (*Uppattiṭṭhāna*)

2. (i) Where is latent state of *kāmarāga* unmanifest? — in two feelings of the worlds of desire (*kāmadhātu*) [43]. (viz. *sukhavedanā* and *upekkhāvedanā*) [44].

(ii) Where is latent state of *paṭigha* unmanifest? — in unpleasant feeling (*dukkhāya vedanāya*) [45].

(iii) Where is latent state of *māna* unmanifest? — in two feelings of the worlds of desire; and in two feelings of the worlds of fine-material and immaterial.

(iv) Where is latent state of *diṭṭhi* unmanifest? — in the *dhamma* [46] of all that is gotten into this existing body. (*sabbasakkāyapariyāpannesu dhammesu*).

(v) Where is latent state of *vicikicchā* unmanifest? — in the *dhamma* of all that is gotten into this existing body.

(vi) Where is latent state of *bhavarāga* unmanifest? — in the fine-material worlds and immaterial worlds.

(vii) Where is latent state of *avijjā* unmanifest? — in the *dhamma* of all that is gotten into this existing body.

The only exception is at the plane of non-percipience wherefrom these latent states do not lie unmanifest. Once any of the latent states arises, life of a non-percipient ends and recur with the cycle of births.

7.2 The Great Division (with charts) (*Mahāvāro*)

The following Chart 7.0 maps out the sequence of enquiries from nos. 3 to 65. The sequence loops through three differentiation types (by person, by plane, by person and plane) using the forward and reverse/opposite mode of enquiries. The enneahedral boxes as shown in the chart represent the six types of pairing methods, are dealt with making enquiries on states of latency. This iteration process from the mono-based to sextuplet-based similarly applies to all the

---

[43] *Dhātu* (element) herein implies the 18 physical and mental elements which condition the five aggregates. *Kāmadhātuyā* in this sense is analogous to the inner, dense 'world' of desires. I would thus prefer to use the meaning of 'world' or 'element-world', so as the rendering for *rūpadhātuyā* (of fine elements) and *arūpadhātuyā* (of ultra fine elements).

[44] The two feelings of the worlds of desire (*sukhavedanā upekkhāvedanā*): pleasant or happy feeling, and feeling which is neither pleasant nor unpleasant

[45] *Dukkha*: this term has shades of meaning by the different authors such as 'unpleasantness, unsatisfactoriness, uncomfortableness, painfulness, suffering'. In this chapter, *dukkhāya vedanāya* remains interpreted as 'unpleasant feeling', or 'feeling of unpleasantness'.

[46] *dhamma*: the term covers various meanings such as 'norm, truth, object, state, phenomenon, the law of nature', and so on. In this chapter I will leave the word *dhamma* as it.

subsequent sets of enquiries, except for the last two sections.

Chart 7.0 Pairing methods of enquiries on latencies lying unmanifest

		(Respective enquiries below are dealt with each of the following latent states accordingly)													
		Does it / Do they lie unmasnifest: Does it not / Do they not lie unmasnifest: i) in that person? ii) at that plane? iii) in that person at that plane?							Does it / Do they lie unmasnifest: Does it not/ Do they not lie unmasnifest: i) in that person? ii) at that plane? iii) in that person at that plane?						
The latent state(s) of:		kāmarāga	paṭigha	māna	diṭṭhi	vicikicchā	bhavarāga	avijjā	kāmarāga	paṭigha	māna	diṭṭhi	vicikicchā	bhavarāga	avijjā
kāmarāga	lie(s) unmasnifest :		1*a*	2*a*	3*a*	4*a*	5*a*	6*a*			1*a*	2*a*	3*a*	4*a*	5*a*
paṭigha	does not/ do not lie	1*b*		7*a*	8*a*	9*a*	10*a*	11*a*							
māna	unmasnifest :	2*b*	7*b*		12*a*	13*a*	14*a*	15*a*	1*b*						
diṭṭhi	i) in this person.	3*b*	8*b*	12*b*		16*a*	17*a*	18*a*	2*b*						
vicikicchā	ii) at this plane.	4*b*	9*b*	13*b*	16*b*		19*a*	20*a*	3*b*						
bhavarāga	iii) in this person	5*b*	10*b*	14*b*	17*b*	19*b*		21*a*	4*b*						
avijjā	at this plane.	6*b*	11*b*	15*b*	18*b*	20*b*	21*b*		5*b*						
kāmarāga	lie(s) unmasnifest :														
paṭigha	does not/ do not lie				1a	2a	3a	4a					1a	2a	3a
māna	unmasnifest :														
diṭṭhi	i) in this person.	1*b*													
vicikicchā	ii) at this plane.	2*b*							1*b*						
bhavarāga	iii) in this person	3*b*							2*b*						
avijjā	at this plane.	4*b*							3*b*						
kāmarāga	lie(s) unmasnifest :														
paṭigha	does not/ do not lie														
māna	unmasnifest :						1a	2a							1a
diṭṭhi	i) in this person.														
vicikicchā	ii) at this plane.														
bhavarāga	iii) in this person	1*b*													
avijjā	at this plane.	2*b*							1*b*						

7.2.1 Latent states (lying unmanifest) (*Anusaya*)

Chart 7.1 below summarises the questions and answers from catechisms nos. 3-13 and from 36-45, taking into account types of person. *Arahat* is only mentioned in the opposite mode of enquiries. As shown in the chart, *Anāgāmi* is the first to root out the latencies of *kāmarāga* and *paṭigha* on account of his eradication of the four greed-rooted cittas dissociated from wrong views, and two hatred-rooted cittas associated with aversion. Because of this, *Anāgāmi* also renounces a part of *māna*, *bhavarāga*, *avijjā*.

Chart 7.1 Latent states lie unmanifest (enquiries by person)

Y: lies unmanifest
N: does not lie unmanifest (either it is inexistent, or has been renounced and eliminated)

	latent state of :						
	kāmarāga	paṭigha	māna	diṭṭhi	vicikicchā	bhavarāga	avijjā
Puthujjana	Y	Y	Y	Y	Y	Y	Y
Sotāpanna	Y	Y	Y	N	N	Y	Y
Sakadāgāmi	Y	Y	Y	N	N	Y	Y
Anāgāmi	N	N	Y	N	N	Y	Y
Arahat	N	N	N	N	N	N	N

Chart 7.2 below summarises the questions and answers from catechisms nos. 14-24 and from 46-55 by taking into account plane-types. *Apariyāpanna* is only mentioned in the opposite mode of enquiries.

Chart 7.2 Latent states lie unmanifest (enquiries by plane)

Y: lies unmanifest
N: does not lie unmanifest (either it is inexistent, or has been renounced and eliminated)

		latent state of :						
		kāmarāga	paṭigha	māna	diṭṭhi	vicikicchā	bhavarāga	avijjā
In unpleasant feeling	in the elemental world of sensuous desire	N	Y	N	Y	Y	N	Y
In pleasant feeling		Y	N	Y	Y	Y	N	Y
In neither pleasant feeling nor unpleasant feeling		Y	N	Y	Y	Y	N	Y
In unpleasant feeling	in the elemental world of fine-material and immaterial	N	N	Y	Y	Y	Y	Y
In pleasant feeling		N	N	Y	Y	Y	Y	Y
In neither pleasant feeling nor unpleasant feeling		N	N	Y	Y	Y	Y	Y
In unpleasant feeling	in *apariyāpanna* (supremundane)	N	N	N	N	N	N	N
In pleasant feeling		N	N	N	N	N	N	N
In neither pleasant feeling nor unpleasant feeling		N	N	N	N	N	N	N

Chart 7.3 Latent states lie unmanifest (enquiries by person and plane)

Y: lies unmanifest; N: does not lie unmanifest (either it is inexistent or it has been eliminated)

Person	Feeling	in elemental worlds of sensuous desire	in elemental worlds of fine-material and immaterial	in *apariyāpanna* (supramundane)	latent state of :						
					kāmarāga	paṭigha	māna	diṭṭhi	vicikicchā	bhavarāga	avijjā
In Puthujjana (including *Gotrabhū* at *apariyāpanna*)	with unpleasant feeling	•			N	Y	N	Y	Y	N	Y
	with pleasant feeling	•			Y	N	Y	Y	Y	N	Y
	with neither pleasant feeling nor unpleasant feeling	•			Y	N	Y	Y	Y	N	Y
	with unpleasant feeling		•		N	N	Y	Y	Y	Y	Y
	with pleasant feeling		•		N	N	Y	Y	Y	Y	Y
	with neither pleasant feeling nor unpleasant feeling		•		N	N	Y	Y	Y	Y	Y
	with unpleasant feeling			•	N	N	N	N	N	N	N
	with pleasant feeling			•	N	N	N	N	N	N	N
	with neither pleasant feeling nor unpleasant feeling			•	N	N	N	N	N	N	N
In Sotāpanna	with unpleasant feeling	•			N	Y	N	N	N	N	Y
	with pleasant feeling	•			Y	N	Y	N	N	N	Y
	with neither pleasant feeling nor unpleasant feeling	•			Y	N	Y	N	N	N	Y
	with unpleasant feeling		•		N	N	Y	N	N	Y	Y
	with pleasant feeling		•		N	N	Y	N	N	Y	Y
	with neither pleasant feeling nor unpleasant feeling		•		N	N	Y	N	N	Y	Y
	with unpleasant feeling			•	N	N	N	N	N	N	N
	with pleasant feeling			•	N	N	N	N	N	N	N
	with neither pleasant feeling nor unpleasant feeling			•	N	N	N	N	N	N	N
In Sakadāgāmi	with unpleasant feeling	•			N	Y	N	N	N	N	Y
	with pleasant feeling	•			Y	N	Y	N	N	N	Y
	with neither pleasant feeling nor unpleasant feeling	•			Y	N	Y	N	N	N	Y
	with unpleasant feeling		•		N	N	Y	N	N	Y	Y
	with pleasant feeling		•		N	N	Y	N	N	Y	Y
	with neither pleasant feeling nor unpleasant feeling		•		N	N	Y	N	N	Y	Y
	with unpleasant feeling			•	N	N	N	N	N	N	N
	with pleasant feeling			•	N	N	N	N	N	N	N
	with neither pleasant feeling nor unpleasant feeling			•	N	N	N	N	N	N	N
In Anāgāmi	with unpleasant feeling	•			N	N	N	N	N	N	Y
	with pleasant feeling	•			N	N	Y	N	N	N	Y
	with neither pleasant feeling nor unpleasant feeling	•			N	N	Y	N	N	N	Y
	with unpleasant feeling		•		N	N	Y	N	N	Y	Y
	with pleasant feeling		•		N	N	Y	N	N	Y	Y
	with neither pleasant feeling nor unpleasant feeling		•		N	N	Y	N	N	Y	Y
	with unpleasant feeling			•	N	N	N	N	N	N	N
	with pleasant feeling			•	N	N	N	N	N	N	N
	with neither pleasant feeling nor unpleasant feeling			•	N	N	N	N	N	N	N
In Arahat	with unpleasant feeling	•			N	N	N	N	N	N	N
	with pleasant feeling	•			N	N	N	N	N	N	N
	with neither pleasant feeling nor unpleasant feeling	•			N	N	N	N	N	N	N
	with unpleasant feeling		•		N	N	N	N	N	N	N
	with pleasant feeling		•		N	N	N	N	N	N	N
	with neither pleasant feeling nor unpleasant feeling		•		N	N	N	N	N	N	N
	with unpleasant feeling			•	N	N	N	N	N	N	N
	with pleasant feeling			•	N	N	N	N	N	N	N
	with neither pleasant feeling nor unpleasant feeling			•	N	N	N	N	N	N	N

Chart 7.3 above summarises the questions and answers from catechisms nos. 25-35 and from 56-65 based on types of person and plane. *Arahat* and the other three fruition-attainers in *apariyāpanna* are only mentioned in the opposite mode of enquiries, in which a special type of common wordling (*Gotrabhū*) is also being included in *apariyāpanna*, although the exact word *Gotrabhū* is not mentioned by the text.

The following mix-types of persons, designated by symbols, would be used in those answers attached to the enquiries by person, and by person-plane.

Two persons ★ (*Sotāpanna, Sakadāgāmi*)
Two persons ☆ (*Anāgāmi, Arahat*)
Three persons ③ (*Puthujjana, Sotāpanna, Sakadāgāmi*)
Three persons ⁝ (*Sotāpanna, Sakadāgāmi, Anāgāmi*)
Four persons ④ (*Puthujjana, Sotāpanna, Sakadāgāmi, Anāgāmi*)

Forward enquiries on person

Mono-based

3. *i* (a) Latent state of *kāmarāga* lies unmanifest in this person. Does latent state of *paṭigha* lie unmanifest in that person?
—Yes. (in *Puthujjana, Sotāpanna, Sakadāgāmi*)
(b) Latent state of *paṭigha* lies unmanifest in this person. Does latent state of *kāmarāga* lie unmanifest in that person? —Yes. (Same as above)

ii (a) Latent state of *kāmarāga* lies unmanifest in this person. Does latent state of *māna* lie unmanifest in that person? —Yes. (*in* three persons ③)
(b) Latent state of *māna* lies unmanifest in this person. Does latent state of *kāmarāga* lie unmanifest in that person?
—In *Anāgāmi* [47], *māna* lies unmanifest; *kāmarāga* does not lie unmanifest. In three persons ③ [48], both *māna* and *kāmarāga* lie unmanifest.

---

[47] *Anāgāmī*: Attainer of the path-*citta* of 'non-returning' (*Anāgāmi-maggacittaṃ*) cut offs five fetters of the lower region (*sakkāyadiṭṭhi*, *vicikicchā*, *sīlabbataparāmāsa*, *kāmacchandā*, *byāpāda*). As he had eliminated fetters of sensuous desire and ill-will, he had effectively eradicated the four greed-rooted unwholesome cittas dissociated from wrong views (hence he renounces some of *māna*, *bhavarāga*, and *avijja*), and had also eradicated 2 hatred-rooted cittas (hence *paṭigha* is totally removed). *Anāgāmī* thus permanently breaks off from rebirth in the sense-sphere. But because *Anāgāmi* had not attained *Arahat*ship, he will instead be born for one last time in the fine-material sphere wherefrom he will attain enlightenment. The Puggalapaññatti mentions five classes of *Anāgāmī* who progress from Avihā abbot to Akaniṭṭha abbot (Pure abodes) to annihilate the upper five fetters. (Vibh nos. 834, Pug nos. 35-40; DN nos. 28, 29)

[48] The three persons ③: *Puthujjana* (common worldlings), *Sotāpanna* (the stream-winner) and *Sakadāgāmi* (the once-returner). *Puthujjana*, or '*nevasekkhanāsekkhā*', refers to worldlings of the three mundane spheres who are not at least free from *sakkāyadiṭṭhi*, *vicikicchā*, *sīlabbataparāmāsa* of the ten fetters. (Pug nos. 9; AN 1.268–276). Attainer of the path-citta

iii (a) Latent state of *kāmarāga* lies unmanifest in this person. Does latent state of *diṭṭhi* lie unmanifest in that person?
—In two persons ★, *kāmarāga* lies unmanifest; *diṭṭhi* does not. In *Puthujjana*, both *kāmarāga* and *diṭṭhi* lie unmanifest.
(b) Latent state of *diṭṭhi* lies unmanifest in this person. Does latent state of *kāmarāga* lie unmanifest in that person? —Yes (in *Puthujjana*).

iv (a) Latent state of *kāmarāga* lies unmanifest in this person. Does latent state of *vicikicchā* lie unmanifest in that person?
—In two persons ★, *kāmarāga* lies unmanifest; *vicikicchā* does not. In *Puthujjana*, both *kāmarāga* and *vicikicchā* lie unmanifest.
(b) Latent state of *vicikicchā* lies unmanifest in this person. Does latent state of *kāmarāga* lie unmanifest in that person? —Yes (in *Puthujjana*).

v (a) Latent state of *kāmarāga* lies unmanifest in this person. Does Latent state of *bhavarāga* lie unmanifest in that person? —Yes. (*Puthujjana, Sotāpanna, Sakadāgāmi*).
(b) Latent state of *bhavarāga* lies unmanifest in this person. Does latent state of *kāmarāga* lie unmanifest in that person?
—In *Anāgāmi, bhavarāga* lies unmanifest; *kāmarāga* does not lie unmanifest. In three persons ③, both *bhavarāga* and *kāmarāga* lie unmanifest.

vi (a) Latent state of *kāmarāga* lies unmanifest in this person. Does latent state of *avijjā* lie unmanifest in that person? —Yes. (the three persons ③).
(b) Latent state of *avijjā* lies unmanifest in this person. Does latent state of *kāmarāga* lie unmanifest in that person?
—In *Anāgāmi, avijjā* lies unmanifest; *kāmarāga* does not. In three persons ③, both *avijjā* and *kāmarāga* lie unmanifest.

4. *i* (a) Latent state of *paṭigha* lies unmanifest in this person. Does latent state of *māna* lie unmanifest in that person? —Yes. (the three persons ③).
(b) Latent state of *māna* lies unmanifest in this person. Does latent state of *paṭigha* lie unmanifest in that person?

---

of 'stream-winning' (*Sotāpatti-maggacittaṃ*) had eliminated the 4 greed-rooted cittas associated with wrong views, and 1 delusion-rooted *citta* associated with skeptical doubt (correspond to the three fetters of defilement as *sakkāyadiṭṭhi*, *vicikicchā*, and *sīlabbataparāmāsa*). By virtue of this, *Sotāpattimaggasamaṅgī* hence renounces a part of *kāmarāga*, *paṭigha*, *māna*, *bhavarāga*, and *avijja*. *Sotāpanna* will be reborn at most seven times on earth or in deva worlds (except *ekabījī* single-seed attainer, the third kind of stream-winner who will be reborn in human existence for one only last time) before his suffering ends. (Pug nos. 31-33; AN 3.87-3.88, 9.12). *Sakadāgāmi* only attenuates his taints of greed (*lobha*, hence *kāmarāga*), hatred (*dosa*, hence *paṭigha*), and delusion (*uddhacca,* hence *avijjā*) in the remaining unwholesome cittas. He is destined to be reborn as deva in sensuous plane only once more to attain enlightenment (Pug nos. 34). Unless otherwise stated, all those answers given as the "three persons" shall be referred to the aforesaid explanation.

—In *Anāgāmi, māna* lies unmanifest; *paṭigha* does not. In three persons ③, both *māna* and *paṭigha* lie unmanifest.

ii (a) Latent state of *paṭigha* lies unmanifest in this person. Does latent state of *diṭṭhi* lie unmanifest in that person?.....p..... Does latent state of *vicikicchā* lie unmanifest in that person?
—In two persons ★, *paṭigha* lies unmanifest; *vicikicchā* (and *diṭṭhi*) does not. In *Puthujjana*, both *paṭigha* and *vicikicchā* (and *diṭṭhi*) lie unmanifest.
(b) Latent state of *vicikicchā* lies unmanifest in this person. Does latent state of *paṭigha* lie unmanifest in that person? —Yes. (*Puthujjana*)

iii (a) Latent state of *paṭigha* lies unmanifest in this person. Does latent state of *bhavarāga* lie unmanifest in that person? .....p..... Does latent state of *avijjā* lie unmanifest in that person? —Yes. (the three persons ③).
(b) Latent state of *avijjā* lies unmanifest in this person. Does latent state of *paṭigha* lie unmanifest in that person?
—In *Anāgāmi, avijjā* lies unmanifest; *paṭigha* does not. In three persons ③, both *avijjā* and *paṭigha* lie unmanifest.

5. *i* (a) Latent state of *māna* lies unmanifest in this person. Does latent state of *diṭṭhi* lie unmanifest in that person? .....p.....Does latent state of *vicikicchā* lie unmanifest in that person?
—In three persons ⁝ , *māna* lies unmanifest; *vicikicchā* (and *diṭṭhi*) does not. In *Puthujjana*, both *māna* and *vicikicchā* (and *diṭṭhi*) lie unmanifest.
(b) Latent state of *vicikicchā* lies unmanifest in this person. Does latent state of *māna* lie unmanifest in that person? —Yes. (*Puthujjana*)

ii (a) Latent state of *māna* lies unmanifest in this person. Does latent state of *bhavarāga* lie unmanifest in that person? ....p....Does latent state of *avijjā* lie unmanifest in that person? —Yes. (in four persons ④)
(b) Latent state of *avijjā* lies unmanifest in this person. Does latent state of *māna* lie unmanifest in that person? —Yes. (in four persons ④)

6. *i* (a) Latent state of *diṭṭhi* lies unmanifest in this person. Does latent state of *vicikicchā* lie unmanifest in that person? —Yes. (in *Puthujjana*)
(b) Latent state of *vicikicchā* lies unmanifest in this person. Does latent state of *diṭṭhi* lie unmanifest in that person? —Yes. (in *Puthujjana*)

ii (a) Latent state of *diṭṭhi* lies unmanifest in this person. Does latent state of *bhavarāga* lie unmanifest in that person? .....p..... Does latent state of *avijjā* lie unmanifest in that person? —Yes. (in *Puthujjana*)
(b) Latent state of *avijjā* lies unmanifest in this person. Does latent state of *diṭṭhi* lie unmanifest in that person?
—In three persons ⁝ , *avijjā* lies unmanifest; *diṭṭhi* (and *bhavarāga*) does not. In *Puthujjana*, the three latent states lie unmanifest.

7. *i* (a) Latent state of *vicikicchā* lies unmanifest in this person. Does latent state of *bhavarāga* lie unmanifest in that person? …..p…..Does latent state of *avijjā* lie unmanifest in that person? —Yes. (in *Puthujjana*)
(b) Latent state of *avijjā* lies unmanifest in this person. Does latent state of *vicikicchā* lie unmanifest in that person?
—In three persons ⋮, *avijjā* (and *bhavarāga*) lies unmanifest; *vicikicchā* does not. In *Puthujjana*, the three latent states lie unmanifest.

8. *i* (a) Latent state of *bhavarāga* lies unmanifest in this person. Does latent state of *avijjā* lie unmanifest in that person? —Yes. (in four persons ④)
(b) Latent state of *avijjā* lies unmanifest in this person. Does latent state of *bhavarāga* lie unmanifest in that person? —Yes.. (in four persons ④)

Couplet-based

9. *i* (a) Latent state of *kāmarāga* and *paṭigha* lie unmanifest in this person. Does latent state of *māna* lie unmanifest in that person? —Yes. (three persons ③)
(b) Latent state of *māna* lies unmanifest in this person. Do latent states of *kāmarāga* and *paṭigha* lie unmanifest in that person?
—In *Anāgāmi, māna* lies unmanifest; *kāmarāga* and *paṭigha* do not. In three persons ③, *māna* lies unmanifest; *kāmarāga* and *paṭigha* too.

ii (a) Latent states of *kāmarāga* and *paṭigha* lie unmanifest in this person. Does latent state of *diṭṭhi* lie unmanifest in that person? …..p…..Does latent state of *vicikicchā* lie unmanifest in that person?
—In two persons ★, *kāmarāga* and *paṭigha* lie unmanifest; *vicikicchā* (and *diṭṭhi*) does not. In *Puthujjana, kāmarāga* and *paṭigha* lie unmanifest; *vicikicchā* (and *diṭṭhi*) too.
(b) Latent state of *vicikicchā* lies unmanifest in this person. Do latent states of *kāmarāga* and *paṭigha* lie unmanifest in that person? —Yes. (in *Puthujjana*)

iii (a) Latent states of *kāmarāga* and *paṭigha* lie unmanifest in this person. Does Latent state of *bhavarāga* lie unmanifest in that person? ......p….. Does latent state of *avijjā* lie unmanifest in that person? —Yes. (In three persons ③).
(b) Latent state of *avijjā* lies unmanifest in this person. Do latent states of *kāmarāga* and lie unmanifest in that person?
—In *Anāgāmi, avijjā* (and *bhavarāga*) lies unmanifest; *kāmarāga* and *paṭigha* do not. In three persons ③, *avijjā* (and *bhavarāga*) lies unmanifest; *kāmarāga* and *paṭigha* too.

Triplet-based

10. *i* (a) Latent states of *kāmarāga*, *paṭigha* and *māna* lie unmanifest in this person. Does latent state of *diṭṭhi* lie unmanifest in that person? …..p…..Does latent state of *vicikicchā* lie unmanifest in that person?

—In two persons ★, *kāmarāga*, *paṭigha* and *māna* lie unmanifest; *diṭṭhi* (and *vicikicchā*) does not. In *Puthujjana*, *kāmarāga*, *paṭigha* and *māna* lie unmanifest, *diṭṭhi* (and *vicikicchā*) too.
(b) Latent state of *vicikicchā* lies unmanifest in this person. Do latent states of *kāmarāga*, *paṭigha* and *māna* lie unmanifest in that person?
—Yes. (in *Puthujjana*)

ii (a) Latent states of *kāmarāga*, *paṭigha* and *paṭigha* lie unmanifest in this person. Does latent state of *bhavarāga* lie unmanifest in that person? .....p.....Does latent state of *avijjā* lie unmanifest in that person? —Yes. (as in *ii* b below)
(b) Latent state of *avijjā* lies unmanifest in this person. Do latent states of *kāmarāga*, *paṭigha* and *māna* lie unmanifest in that person?
—In *Anāgāmi, avijjā* and *māna* (and *bhavarāga*) lie unmanifest; *kāmarāga* and *paṭigha* do not. In three persons ③, *avijjā* lies unmanifest; *kāmarāga*, *paṭigha, māna* (and *bhavarāga*) too.

Quadruplet-based

11. *i* (a) Latent states of *kāmarāga*, *paṭigha*, *māna* and *diṭṭhi* lie unmanifest in this person. Does latent state of *vicikicchā* lie unmanifest in that person? —Yes.
(b) Latent state of *vicikicchā* lies unmanifest in this person. Do latent states of *kāmarāga*, *paṭigha*, *māna* and *diṭṭhi* lie unmanifest in that person? —Yes.

ii (a) Latent states of *kāmarāga*, *paṭigha*, *māna* and *diṭṭhi* lie unmanifest in this person. Does latent state of *bhavarāga* lie unmanifest in that person? .....p..... Does latent state of *avijjā* lie unmanifest in that person? —Yes. (in *Puthujjana*)
(b) Latent state of *avijjā* lies unmanifest in this person. Do latent states of *kāmarāga*, *paṭigha*, *māna* and *diṭṭhi* lie unmanifest in that person?
—In *Anāgāmi, avijjā* and *māna* lie unmanifest; latent states of *kāmarāga*, *paṭigha* and *diṭṭhi* do not. In two persons ★, latent states of *avijjā*, *kāmarāga*, *paṭigha* and *māna* lie unmanifest; *diṭṭhi* does not. In *Puthujjana*, *avijjā* lies unmanifest; latent states of *kāmarāga*, *paṭigha*, *māna* and *diṭṭhi* too.

Quintuplet-based

12. *i* (a) Latent states of *kāmarāga*, *paṭigha*, *māna*, *diṭṭhi* and *vicikicchā* lie unmanifest in this person. Does latent state of *bhavarāga* lie unmanifest in that person? .....p..... Does latent state of *avijjā* lie unmanifest in that person? —Yes.
(b) Latent state of *avijjā* lies unmanifest in this person. Do latent states of *kāmarāga*, *paṭigha*, *māna*, *diṭṭhi* and *vicikicchā* lie unmanifest in that person?
—In *Anāgāmi, avijjā* and *māna* lie unmanifest; latent states of *kāmarāga*, *paṭigha*, *diṭṭhi* and *vicikicchā* do not. In *Puthujjana*, *avijjā* lies unmanifest; latent states of *kāmarāga*, *paṭigha*, *māna*, *diṭṭhi* and *vicikicchā* too. In two persons ★, latent states of *avijjā*, *kāmarāga*, *paṭigha* and *māna* lie unmanifest; *diṭṭhi* and *vicikicchā* do not.

Sextuplet-based

13. *i* (a) Latent states of *kāmarāga*, *paṭigha*, *māna*, *diṭṭhi*, *vicikicchā*, and *bhavarāga* lie unmanifest in this person. Does latent state of *avijjā* lie unmanifest in that person?
—Yes. (*Puthujjana*)
(b) Latent state of *avijjā* lies unmanifest in this person. Do latent states of *kāmarāga*, *paṭigha*, *māna*, *diṭṭhi*, *vicikicchā*, and *bhavarāga* lie unmanifest in that person?
—In *Anāgāmi,* latent states of *avijjā*, *māna* and *bhavarāga* lie unmanifest; *kāmarāga*, *paṭigha*, *diṭṭhi* and *vicikicchā* do not. In two persons ★, latent states of *avijjā*, *kāmarāga*, *paṭigha*, *māna* and *bhavarāga* lie unmanifest; *diṭṭhi* and *vicikicchā* do not. In *Puthujjana*, *avijjā* lies unmanifest; latent states of *kāmarāga*, *paṭigha*, *māna*, *diṭṭhi*, *vicikicchā* and *bhavarāga* too.

Forward enquiries by plane

Mono-based

14. *i* (a) Latent state of *kāmarāga* lies unmanifest at this plane. Does latent state of *paṭigha* lie unmanifest at that plane? —No. (in sensuous element)
(b) Latent state of *paṭigha* lies unmanifest at this plane. Does latent state of *kāmarāga* lie unmanifest at that plane?
—No. (in unpleasant feeling, in sensuous element)

ii (a) Latent state of *kāmarāga* lies unmanifest at this plane. Does latent state of *māna* lie unmanifest at that plane? —Yes. (Same as below)
(b) Latent state of *māna* lies unmanifest at this plane. Does latent state of *kāmarāga* lie unmanifest at that plane?
—In elemental world of fine-material and immaterial, *māna* lies unmanifest; *kāmarāga* does not. In two feelings of the elemental world of sensuous desire, *māna* lies unmanifest; *kāmarāga* too.

iii (a) Latent state of *kāmarāga* lies unmanifest at this plane. Does latent state of *diṭṭhi* ....p.... Does latent state of *vicikicchā* lie unmanifest at that plane?
—Yes. Refer to answer below.
(b) Latent state of *vicikicchā* lies unmanifest at this plane. Does latent state of *kāmarāga* lie unmanifest at that plane?
—In unpleasant feeling, and in the elemental world of fine-material and immaterial, *vicikicchā* lies unmanifest; *kāmarāga* does not. In two feelings of the elemental world of sensuous desire, *vicikicchā* lies unmanifest; *kāmarāga* too.

iv (a) Latent state of *kāmarāga* lies unmanifest at this plane. Does latent state of *bhavarāga* lie unmanifest at that plane?
—No. (in two feelings of the elemental world of sensuous desire)
(b) Latent state of *bhavarāga* lies unmanifest at this plane. Does latent state of *kāmarāga* lie unmanifest at that plane?

—No. (in elemental world of fine-material and immaterial)

v (a) Latent state of *kāmarāga* lies unmanifest at this plane. Does latent state of *avijjā* lie unmanifest at that plane? —Yes. Refer to answer below.
(b) Latent state of *avijjā* lies unmanifest at this plane. Does latent state of *kāmarāga* lie unmanifest at that plane?
—In unpleasant feeling, and in elemental world of fine-material and immaterial, *avijjā* lies unmanifest; *kāmarāga* does not. In two feelings of the elemental world of sensuous desire, *avijjā* lies unmanifest; *kāmarāga* too.

15. *i* (a) Latent state of *paṭigha* lies unmanifest at this plane. Does latent state of *māna* lie unmanifest at that plane?
—No. (in unpleasant feeling, in sensuous element)
(b) Latent state of *māna* lies unmanifest at this plane. Does latent state of *paṭigha* lie unmanifest at that plane?
—No. (in two feelings of the elemental world of sensuous desire, and in elemental world of fine-material and immaterial).

ii (a) Latent state of *paṭigha* lies unmanifest at this plane. Does latent state of *diṭṭhi* lie unmanifest at that plane? .....p..... Does latent state of *vicikicchā* unmanifest at that plane? —Yes.
(b) Latent state of *vicikicchā* lies unmanifest at this plane. Does latent state of *paṭigha* lie unmanifest at that plane?
—In two feelings of the elemental world of sensuous desire, and in elemental world of fine-material and immaterial, *vicikicchā* lies unmanifest; *paṭigha* does not. In unpleasant feeling, *vicikicchā* lies unmanifest; *paṭigha* too.

iii (a) Latent state of *paṭigha* lies unmanifest at this plane. Does latent state of *bhavarāga* lie unmanifest at that plane?
—No. (in unpleasant feeling, in sensuous element)
(b) Latent state of *bhavarāga* lies unmanifest at this plane. Does latent state of *paṭigha* lie unmanifest at that plane?
—No. (in elemental world of fine-material and immaterial)

iv (a) Latent state of *paṭigha* lies unmanifest at this plane. Does latent state of *avijjā* lie unmanifest at that plane? —Yes. Refer to the answer below.
(b) Latent state of *avijjā* lies unmanifest at this plane. Does latent state of *paṭigha* lie unmanifest at that plane?
—In two feelings of the elemental world of sensuous desire, and in the elemental world of fine-material and immaterial, *avijjā* lies unmanifest; *paṭigha* does not. In unpleasant feeling (in sensuous element), *avijjā* lies unmanifest; *paṭigha* too.

16. *i* (a) Latent state of *māna* lies unmanifest at this plane. Does latent state of *diṭṭhi* lie unmanifest at that plane? .....p..... Does latent state of *vicikicchā* lie unmanifest at that plane? —Yes. Refer to the answer below.
(b) Latent state of *vicikicchā* lies unmanifest at this plane. Does latent state of *māna* lie unmanifest at that plane?

—In unpleasant feeling (in sensuous element), *vicikicchā* lies unmanifest; *māna* does not. In two feelings of the elemental world of sensuous desire, and in elemental world of fine-material and immaterial, *vicikicchā* lies unmanifest; *māna* too.

ii (a) Latent state of *māna* lies unmanifest at this plane. Does latent state of *bhavarāga* lie unmanifest at that plane?
—In two feelings of the elemental world of sensuous desire, *māna* lies unmanifest; *bhavarāga* does not. In elemental world of fine-material and immaterial, *māna* lies unmanifest; *bhavarāga* too.
(b) Latent state of *bhavarāga* lies unmanifest at this plane. Does latent state of *māna* lie unmanifest at that plane? —Yes. Refer to aforesaid.

iii (a) Latent state of *māna* lies unmanifest at this plane. Does latent state of *avijjā* lie unmanifest at that plane? —Yes. Refer to the answer below.
(b) Latent state of *avijjā* lies unmanifest at this plane. Does latent state of *māna* lie unmanifest at that plane?
—In unpleasant feeling (in sensuous element), *avijjā* lies unmanifest; *māna* does not. In two feelings of the elemental world of sensuous desire, and in elemental world of fine-material and immaterial, *avijjā* lies unmanifest; *māna* too.

17. *i* (a) Latent state of *diṭṭhi* lies unmanifest at this plane. Does latent state of *vicikicchā* lie unmanifest at that plane? —Yes. (except in *apariyāpanna*)
(b) Latent state of *vicikicchā* lies unmanifest at this plane. Does latent state of *diṭṭhi* lie unmanifest at that plane? —Yes. (except in *apariyāpanna*)

ii (a) Latent state of *diṭṭhi* lies unmanifest at this plane. Does latent state of *bhavarāga* lie unmanifest at that plane?
—In three feelings of the elemental world of sensuous desire, *diṭṭhi* lies unmanifest; *bhavarāga* does not. In elemental world of fine-material and immaterial, *diṭṭhi* lies unmanifest; *bhavarāga* too.
(b) Latent state of *bhavarāga* lies unmanifest at this plane. Does latent state of *diṭṭhi* lie unmanifest at that plane? —Yes. Refer to aforesaid.

ii (a) Latent state of *diṭṭhi* lies unmanifest at this plane. Does latent state of *avijjā* lie unmanifest at the plane? —Yes. (except in *apariyāpanna*)
(b) Latent state of *avijjā* lies unmanifest at this plane. Does latent state of *diṭṭhi* lie unmanifest at that plane? —Yes. (except in *apariyāpanna*)

18. *i* (a) Latent state of *vicikicchā* lies unmanifest at this plane. Does latent state of *bhavarāga* lie unmanifest at that plane?
—In three feelings of the elemental world of sensuous desire, *vicikicchā* lies unmanifest; *bhavarāga* does not. In elemental world of fine-material and immaterial, *vicikicchā* lies unmanifest; *bhavarāga* too.
(b) Latent state of *bhavarāga* lies unmanifest at this plane. Does latent state of *vicikicchā* lie unmanifest at that plane? —Yes. Refer to aforesaid.

ii (a) Latent state of *vicikicchā* lies unmanifest at this plane. Does latent state of *avijjā* lie unmanifest at that plane? —Yes. (except in *apariyāpanna*)
(b) Latent state of *avijjā* lies unmanifest at this plane. Does latent state of *vicikicchā* lie unmanifest at that plane? Yes. (except in *apariyāpanna*)

19. *i* (a) Latent state of *bhavarāga* lies unmanifest at this plane. Does latent state of *avijjā* lie unmanifest at that plane? —Yes. Refer to the answer below.
(b) Latent state of *avijjā* lies unmanifest at this plane. Does latent state of *bhavarāga* lie unmanifest at that plane?
—In three feelings of the elemental world of sensuous desire, *avijjā* lies unmanifest; *bhavarāga* does not. In elemental world of fine-material and immaterial, *avijjā* lies unmanifest; *bhavarāga* too.

Couplet-based

20. *i* (a) Latent states of *kāmarāga* and *paṭigha* lie unmanifest at this plane. Does latent state of *māna* lie unmanifest at that plane? —None.
(b) Latent state of *māna* lies unmanifest at this plane. Do latent states of *kāmarāga* and *paṭigha* lie lie unmanifest at that plane?
—In elemental world of fine-material and immaterial, *māna* lies unmanifest; *kāmarāga* and *paṭigha* do not. In two feelings of the elemental world of sensuous desire, *māna* and *kāmarāga* lie unmanifest; *paṭigha* does not.

ii (a) Latent states of *kāmarāga* and *paṭigha* lie unmanifest at this plane. Does latent state of *diṭṭhi* unmanifest at that plane? .....p..... Does latent state of *vicikicchā* unmanifest at that plane? —No such person.
(b) Latent state of *vicikicchā* lies unmanifest at this plane. Do latent states of *kāmarāga* and *paṭigha* lie unmanifest at that plane?
—In elemental world of fine-material and immaterial, *vicikicchā* lies unmanifest; *kāmarāga* and *paṭigha* do not. In two feelings of the elemental world of sensuous desire, *vicikicchā* and *kāmarāga* (and *diṭṭhi*) lie unmanifest; *paṭigha* does not. In unpleasant feeling (in sensuous element), *vicikicchā* and *paṭigha* (and *diṭṭhi*) lie unmanifest; *kāmarāga* does not.

iii (a) Latent states of *kāmarāga* and *paṭigha* lie unmanifest at this plane. Does latent state of *bhavarāga* lie unmanifest at that plane? —None.
(b) Latent state of *bhavarāga* lies unmanifest at this plane. Do latent states of *kāmarāga* and *paṭigha* lie unmanifest at that plane? —No. (in elemental world of fine-material and immaterial)

iv (a) Latent states of *kāmarāga* and *paṭigha* lie unmanifest at this plane. Does latent state of *avijjā* lie unmanifest at that plane? —None.
(b) Latent state of *avijjā* lies unmanifest at this plane. Do latent states of *kāmarāga* and *paṭigha* lie unmanifest at that plane?
—In elemental world of fine-material and immaterial, *avijjā* lies unmanifest; *kāmarāga* and *paṭigha* do not. In two feelings of the elemental world of sensuous

desire, *avijjā* and *kāmarāga* lie unmanifest; *paṭigha* does not. In unpleasant feeling, *avijjā* and *paṭigha* lie unmanifest; *kāmarāga* does not.

Triplet-based

21. *i* (a) Latent states of *kāmarāga, paṭigha* and *māna* lie unmanifest at this plane. Does latent state of *diṭṭhi* lie unmanifest at that plane? .....p.....Does latent state of *vicikicchā* lie unmanifest at that plane? —None.
(b) Latent state of *vicikicchā* lies unmanifest at this plane. Do latent states of *kāmarāga, paṭigha* and *māna* lie unmanifest at that plane?
—In elemental world of fine-material and immaterial, *vicikicchā* and *māna* (and *diṭṭhi*) lie unmanifest; *kāmarāga* and *paṭigha* do not. In two feelings of the elemental world of sensuous desire, *vicikicchā, kāmarāga* and *māna* (and *diṭṭhi*) lie unmanifest; *paṭigha* does not. In unpleasant feeling, *vicikicchā* and *paṭigha* (and *diṭṭhi*) lie unmanifest; *kāmarāga* and *māna* do not.

ii (a) Latent states of *kāmarāga, paṭigha* and *māna* lie unmanifest at this plane. Does latent state of *bhavarāga* lie unmanifest at that plane? —None.
(b) Latent state of *bhavarāga* lies unmanifest at this plane. Do latent states of *kāmarāga, paṭigha* and *māna* lie unmanifest at that plane?
—In elemental world of fine-material and immaterial, *bhavarāga* and *māna* lie unmanifest; *kāmarāga* and *paṭigha* do not.

iii (a) Latent states of *kāmarāga, paṭigha* and *māna* lie unmanifest at this plane. Does latent state of *avijjā* lie unmanifest at that plane? —None.
(b) Latent state of *avijjā* lies unmanifest at this plane. Do latent states of *kāmarāga, paṭigha* and *māna* lie unmanifest at that plane?
—In elemental world of fine-material and immaterial, *avijjā* and *māna* lie unmanifest; *kāmarāga* and *paṭigha* do not. In two feelings of the elemental world of sensuous desire, *avijjā, kāmarāga* and *māna* lie unmanifest; *paṭigha* does not. In unpleasant feeling (in sensuous element), *avijjā* and *paṭigha* lie unmanifest; *kāmarāga* and *māna* do not.

Quadruplet-based

22. *i* (a) Latent states of *kāmarāga, paṭigha, māna* and *diṭṭhi* lie unmanifest at this plane. Does latent state of *vicikicchā* unmanifest at that plane? —None.
(b) Latent state of *vicikicchā* lies unmanifest at this plane. Do latent states of *kāmarāga, paṭigha, māna* and *diṭṭhi* lie unmanifest at that plane?
—In elemental world of fine-material and immaterial, *vicikicchā, māna* and *diṭṭhi* lie unmanifest; *kāmarāga* and *paṭigha* do not. In two feelings of the elemental world of sensuous desire, *vicikicchā, kāmarāga, māna* and *diṭṭhi* lie unmanifest; *paṭigha* does not. In unpleasant feeling, latent states of *vicikicchā, paṭigha* and *diṭṭhi* lie unmanifest; *kāmarāga* and *māna* do not.

ii (a) Latent states of *kāmarāga, paṭigha, māna* and *diṭṭhi* lie unmanifest at this plane. Does latent state of *bhavarāga* unmanifest at that plane? —None.

(b) Latent state of *bhavarāga* lies unmanifest at this plane. Do latent states of *kāmarāga, paṭigha, māna* and *diṭṭhi* lie unmanifest at that plane?
—In elemental world of fine-material and immaterial, *bhavarāga, māna* and *diṭṭhi* lie unmanifest; *kāmarāga* and *paṭigha* do not.

iii (a) Latent states of *kāmarāga, paṭigha, māna* and *diṭṭhi* lie unmanifest at this plane. Does latent state of *avijjā* lie unmanifest at that plane? —None.
(b) Latent state of *avijjā* lies unmanifest at this plane. Do latent states of *kāmarāga, paṭigha, māna* and *diṭṭhi* lie unmanifest at that plane?
—In elemental world of fine-material and immaterial, *avijjā, māna* and *diṭṭhi* lie unmanifest; *kāmarāga* and *paṭigha* do not. In two feelings of the elemental world of sensuous desire, latent states of *avijjā, kāmarāga, māna* and *diṭṭhi* lie unmanifest; *paṭigha* does not. In unpleasant feeling (in sensuous element), latent states of *avijjā, paṭigha* and *diṭṭhi* lie unmanifest; *kāmarāga* and *māna* do not.

Quintuplet-based

23. *i* (a) Latent states of *kāmarāga, paṭigha, māna, diṭṭhi* and *vicikicchā* lie unmanifest at this plane. Does latent state of *bhavarāga* lie unmanifest at that plane? —None.
(b) Latent state of *bhavarāga* lies unmanifest at this plane. Do latent states of *kāmarāga, paṭigha, māna, diṭṭhi* and *vicikicchā* lie unmanifest at that plane?
—In elemental world of fine-material and immaterial, *bhavarāga, māna, diṭṭhi* and *vicikicchā* lie unmanifest; *kāmarāga* and *paṭigha* do not.

ii (a) Latent states of *kāmarāga, paṭigha, māna, diṭṭhi* and *vicikicchā* lie unmanifest at this plane. Does latent state of *avijjā* lie unmanifest at that plane? —None.
(b) Latent state of *avijjā* lies unmanifest at this plane. Do latent states of *kāmarāga, paṭigha, māna, diṭṭhi* and *vicikicchā* lie unmanifest at that plane?
—In elemental world of fine-material and immaterial, *avijjā, māna, diṭṭhi* and *vicikicchā* lie unmanifest; *kāmarāga* and *paṭigha* do not. In two feelings of the elemental world of sensuous desire, latent states of *avijjā, kāmarāga, māna, diṭṭhi* and *vicikicchā* lie unmanifest; *paṭigha* does not. In unpleasant feeling (in sensuous element), latent states of *avijjā, paṭigha, diṭṭhi* and *vicikicchā* lie unmanifest; *kāmarāga* and *māna* do not.

Sextuplet-based

24. *i* (a) Latent states of *kāmarāga, paṭigha, māna, diṭṭhi, vicikicchā* and *bhavarāga* lie unmanifest at this plane. Does latent state of *avijjā* lie unmanifest at that plane? —None.
(b) Latent state of *avijjā* lies unmanifest at this plane. Do latent states of *kāmarāga, paṭigha, māna, diṭṭhi, vicikicchā* and *bhavarāga* lie unmanifest at that plane?
—In elemental world of fine-material and immaterial, latent states of *avijjā, māna, diṭṭhi, vicikicchā* and *bhavarāga* lie unmanifest; *kāmarāga* and *paṭigha* do

not. In two feelings of the elemental world of sensuous desire, latent states of *avijjā, kāmarāga, māna, diṭṭhi* and *vicikicchā* lie unmanifest; *paṭigha* and *bhavarāga* do not. In unpleasant feeling (in sensuous element), latent states of *avijjā, paṭigha, diṭṭhi* and *vicikicchā* lie unmanifest; *kāmarāga, māna* and *bhavarāga* do not.

Forward enquiries by person and plane

Mono-based

25. *i* (a) Latent state of *kāmarāga* lies unmanifest in this person at this plane. Does latent state of *paṭigha* lie unmanifest in that person at that plane?
—No. (in three persons ③, with two feelings of the elemental world of desire).
(b) Latent state of *paṭigha* lies unmanifest in this person at this plane. Does latent state of *kāmarāga* lie unmanifest in that person at that plane?
—No. (In three persons ③, with unpleasant feeling).

ii (a) Latent state of *kāmarāga* lies unmanifest in this person at this plane. Does latent state of *māna* lie unmanifest in that person at that plane?
—Yes. Refer to the answer in 25 *ii* (b) below.
(b) Latent state of *māna* lies unmanifest in this person at this plane. Does latent state of *kāmarāga* lie unmanifest in that person at that plane?
—No. In *Anāgāmi*, in (or with) two feelings of the elemental world of sensuous desire [49], and in elemental world of fine-material and immaterial; and in three persons ③, in elemental world of fine-material and immaterial—*māna* lies unmanifest, but *kāmarāga* does not lie unmanifest (it is inexistent) [50].
—Yes. In those persons (three persons ③), with two feelings of the elemental world of sensuous desire, both *māna* and *kāmarāga* lie unmanifest.

iii (a) Latent state of *kāmarāga* lies unmanifest in this person at this plane. Does latent state of *diṭṭhi* ....p.... *vicikicchā* lie unmanifest in that person at that plane?
—No. In two persons ★ with two feelings of the elemental world of sensuous desire, *kāmarāga* lies unmanifest, but *vicikicchā* (and *diṭṭhi*) does not.
—Yes. In *Puthujjana*, with two feelings of the elemental world of sensuous desire, both *kāmarāga* and *vicikicchā* (also *diṭṭhi*) lie unmanifest.
(b) Latent state of *vicikicchā* lies unmanifest in this person at this plane. Does latent state of *kāmarāga* lie unmanifest in that person at that plane?

---

[49] ... kāmadhātuyā dvīsu vedanāsu ... (also tīsu vedanāsu, dukkhāya vedanāya), although literally means " ... in the two feelings of ...", but in syntax of English is preferrably to be translated as "... with the feelings of ...".

[50] Does not lie unmanifest: whenever a latent state does not lie latent, it may be conceived differently as it has either become conspicuous, or it is inexistent or is not present. The correct explanation has to be "it is inexistent" as provided in the parenthesis. In other examples, it is because the particular latent state "has been eradicated". For instance, to *Sotāpanna* and *Sakadāgāmi*, latent conceit lies unmanifest, but latent wrong views and skeptical doubt do not, because those two had been eradicated. It is to be interpreted in this manner for other similar answers, but will not all be filled in unless are otherwise needed.

—No. In *Puthujjana*, with unpleasant feeling, and in elemental world of fine-material and immaterial, *vicikicchā* (also *diṭṭhi*) lies latent; *kāmarāga* does not.
—Yes. Refer to the answer in *iii* (a) above.

iv (a) Latent state of *kāmarāga* lies unmanifest in this person at this plane. Does latent state of *bhavarāga* lie unmanifest in that person at that plane?
—No. (in three persons ③, with two feelings of the elemental world of desire).
(b) Latent state of *bhavarāga* lies unmanifest in this person at this plane. Does latent state of *kāmarāga* unmanifest at that person at that plane?
—No. (In four persons ④ in elemental world fine-material and immaterial)

v (a) Latent state of *kāmarāga* lies unmanifest in this person at this plane. Does latent state of *avijjā* lie unmanifest in that person at that plane? —Yes. Refer to answer below.
(b) Latent state of *avijjā* lies unmanifest in this person at this plane. Does latent state of *kāmarāga* lie unmanifest in that person at that plane?
—No. In *Anāgāmi*, with three feelings of the elemental world of sensuous desire, and in the elemental world of fine-material and immaterial; in three persons ③, with unpleasant feeling, and in the elemental world of fine-material and immaterial—*avijjā* lies unmanifest; *kāmarāga* does not.
—Yes. In those persons (three persons ③), with two feelings of the elemental world of sensuous desire, both *avijjā* and *kāmarāga* lie unmanifest.

26. *i* (a) Latent state of *paṭigha* lies unmanifest in this person at this plane. Does latent state of *māna* lie unmanifest in that person at that plane?
—No. (In three persons ③ with unpleasant feeling, in the sensuous element).
(b) Latent state of *māna* lies unmanifest in this person at this plane. Does latent state of *paṭigha* lie unmanifest in that person at that plane?
—No. (In three persons ③, with two feelings of the elemental world of desire, and in the elemental world of fine-material and immaterial; and in *Anāgāmi*).

ii (a) Latent state of *paṭigha* lies unmanifest in this person at this plane. Does latent state of *diṭṭhi* .....p..... *vicikicchā* lie unmanifest in that person at that plane?
—No. In two persons ★ with unpleasant feeling, *paṭigha* lies unmanifest; *vicikicchā* does not (the same to *diṭṭhi*)
—Yes. In *Puthujjana*, with unpleasant feeling, both *paṭigha* and *vicikicchā* lie unmanifest.
(b) Latent state of *vicikicchā* lies unmanifest in this person at this plane. Does latent state of *paṭigha* lie unmanifest in that person at that plane?
—No. In *Puthujjana*, with two feelings of the elemental world of sensuous desire, and in the elemental world of fine-material and immaterial, *vicikicchā* lies unmanifest; *paṭigha* does not.
—Yes, in those persons with unpleasant feeling (Puthujjanas).

iii (a) Latent state of *paṭigha* lies unmanifest in this person at this plane. Does latent state of *bhavarāga* lie unmanifest in that person at that plane?

—No. (In three persons ③ with unpleasant feeling in sensuous element, *paṭigha* lies unmanifest; *bhavarāga* does not).
(b) Latent state of *bhavarāga* lies unmanifest in this person at this plane. Does latent state of *paṭigha* lie unmanifest in that person at that plane?
—No. (in four persons ④, in elemental world of fine-material and immaterial)

iv (a) Latent state of *paṭigha* lies unmanifest in this person at this plane. Does latent state of *avijjā* lie unmanifest in that person at that plane?
—Yes. (in three persons ③ with unpleasant feeling).
(b) Latent state of *avijjā* lies unmanifest in this person at this plane. Does latent state of *paṭigha* lie unmanifest in that person at that plane?
—No. In *Anāgāmi*, with three feelings of the elemental world of sensuous desire, and in the elemental world of fine-material and immaterial; in three persons ③, with two feelings of the elemental world of sensuous desire, and in the elemental world of fine-material and immaterial, *avijjā* lies unmanifest; *paṭigha* does not.
—Yes. In those persons (three persons ③), with unpleasant feeling, both latencies of *avijjā* and *paṭigha* lie unmanifest.

27. *i* (a) Latent state of *māna* lies unmanifest in this person at this plane. Does latent state of *diṭṭhi* …..p….. *vicikicchā* lie unmanifest in that person at that plane?
—No. In three persons ⁝, with two feelings of the elemental world of sensuous desire, and in the elemental world of fine-material and immaterial, *māna* lies unmanifest; *vicikicchā* does not (the same to *diṭṭhi*).
—Yes. In *Puthujjana*, with two feelings of the elemental world of sensuous desire, and in the elemental world of fine-material and immaterial, both *māna* and *vicikicchā* (and *diṭṭhi*) lie unmanifest.
(b) Latent state of *vicikicchā* lies unmanifest in this person at this plane. Does latent state of *māna lie unmanifest in that* person at that plane?
—No. In *Puthujjana*, with unpleasant feeling, *vicikicchā* (and *diṭṭhi*) lies unmanifest; *māna* does not.
—Yes. Refer to the answer in *i* (a) above.

ii (a) Latent state of *māna* lies unmanifest in this person at this plane. Does latent state of *bhavarāga* lie unmanifest in that person at that plane?
—No. In four persons ④ with two feelings of the elemental world of sensuous desire, *māna* lies unmanifest; *bhavarāga* does not [51].
—Yes. In those (same) persons in the elemental world of fine-material and immaterial, both *māna* and *bhavarāga* lie unmanifest.
(b) Latent state of *bhavarāga* lies unmanifest in this person at this plane. Does latent state of *māna* lie unmanifest in that person at that plane?
—Yes. Refer to the answer in *ii* (a) above.

---

[51] Three noble persons of *Anāgāmiphala, Arahattamagga, and Arahattaphala* are also found in sense-sphere and fine-material sphere (except the 4 woeful realms). It is only the person of *Anāgāmimagga* who will be reborn in the five Pure abodes (See Appendix I).

iii (a) Latent state of *māna* lies unmanifest in this person at this plane. Does latent state of *avijjā* lie unmanifest in that person at that plane?
—Yes. Refer to the answer in *iii* (b) below.
(b) Latent state of *avijjā* lies unmanifest in this person at this plane. Does latent state of *māna lie unmanifest in that* person at that plane?
—No. In four persons ④ with unpleasant feeling, *avijjā* lies unmanifest; *māna* does not.
—Yes. In those (same) persons, with two feelings of the elemental world of sensuous desire, and in the elemental world of fine-material and immaterial, both *avijjā* and *māna* lie unmanifest.

28. *i* (a) Latent state of *diṭṭhi* lies unmanifest in this person at this plane. Does latent state of *vicikicchā* lie unmanifest in that person at that plane?
—Yes. (in *Puthujjana*, with three feelings of the elemental world of sensuous desire, and in the elemental world of fine-material and immaterial).
(b) Latent state of *vicikicchā* lies unmanifest in this person at this plane. Does latent state of *diṭṭhi* lie unmanifest in that person at that plane?—Yes, same above.

ii (a) Latent state of *diṭṭhi* .....p..... Latent state of *vicikicchā* lies unmanifest in this person at this plane. Does latent state of *bhavarāga* lie unmanifest in that person at that plane?
—No. In *Puthujjana*, with three feelings of the elemental world of sensuous desire, *vicikicchā* (and *diṭṭhi*) lies unmanifest; *bhavarāga* does not.
—Yes. In those (same) persons in elemental world of fine-material and immaterial, *vicikicchā* and *bhavarāga* (and *diṭṭhi*) lie unmanifest.
(b) Latent state of *bhavarāga* lies unmanifest in this person at this plane. Does latent state of *vicikicchā* lie unmanifest in that person at that plane?
—No. In three persons ⁝, in the elemental world of fine-material and immaterial, *bhavarāga* lies unmanifest; *vicikicchā* does not.
—Yes. In *Puthujjana*, in the elemental world of fine-material and immaterial, both *bhavarāga* and *vicikicchā* lie unmanifest.

29. *i* (a) Latent state of *vicikicchā* lies unmanifest in this person at this plane. Does latent state of *avijjā* lie unmanifest in that person at that plane?
—Yes. Refer to the answer in *i* (b) below.
(b) Latent state of *avijjā* lies unmanifest in this person at this plane. Does latent state of *vicikicchā* lie unmanifest in that person at that plane?
—No. In three persons ⁝ with three feelings of elemental world of sensuous desire, and in elemental world of fine-material and immaterial, *avijjā* lies unmanifest; *vicikicchā* does not.
—Yes. In *Puthujjana*, with three feelings of the elemental world of sensuous desire, and in the elemental world of fine-material and immaterial, both *avijjā* and *vicikicchā* lie unmanifest.

30. *i* (a) Latent state of *bhavarāga* lies unmanifest in this person at this plane. Does latent state of *avijjā* lie unmanifest in that person at that plane?

—Yes. Refer to the answer in *i* (b) below.
(b) Latent state of *avijjā* lies unmanifest in this person at this plane. Does latent state of *bhavarāga* lie unmanifest in that person at that plane?
—No. In four persons ④ with three feelings of the elemental world of sensuous desire, *avijjā* lies unmanifest; *bhavarāga* does not.
—Yes. In those (same) persons, in elemental world of fine-material and immaterial, both *avijjā* and *bhavarāga* lie unmanifest.

Couplet-based

31. *i* (a) Latent states of *kāmarāga* and *paṭigha* lie unmanifest in this person at this plane. Does latent state of *māna lie unmanifest in that* person at that plane?
—None.
(b) Latent *state of māna* lies unmanifest in this person at this plane. Do latent states of *kāmarāga* and *paṭigha* lie unmanifest in that person at that plane?
—No. In *Anāgāmi*, with two feelings of the elemental world of sensuous desire, and in the elemental world of fine-material and immaterial; and in three persons ③, in the elemental world of fine-material and immaterial—*māna* lies unmanifest; *kāmarāga* and *paṭigha* do not. In those persons (three persons ③), with two feelings of the elemental world of sensuous desire, *māna* and *kāmarāga* lie unmanifest; *paṭigha* does not.

ii (a) Latent states of *kāmarāga* and *paṭigha* lie unmanifest in this person at this plane. Does latent state of *diṭṭhi* .....p..... *vicikicchā* lie unmanifest in that person at that plane? —No such person.
(b) Latent state of *vicikicchā* lies unmanifest in this person at this plane. Do latent states of *kāmarāga* and *paṭigha* lie unmanifest in that person at that plane?
—No. In *Puthujjana* in the elemental world of fine-material and immaterial, *vicikicchā* (and *diṭṭhi*) lies unmanifest; *kāmarāga* and *paṭigha* do not. In those (same) persons, with two feelings of the elemental world of sensuous desire, *vicikicchā* and *kāmarāga* lie unmanifest; *paṭigha* does not. In those (same) persons, with unpleasant feeling, *vicikicchā* and *paṭigha* lie unmanifest; *kāmarāga* does not.

iii (a) Latent states of *kāmarāga* and *paṭigha* lie unmanifest in this person at this plane. Does latent state of *bhavarāga* lie unmanifest in that person at that plane?
—None.
(b) Latent state of *bhavarāga* lies unmanifest in this person at this plane. Do latent states of *kāmarāga* and *paṭigha* lie unmanifest in that person at that plane?
—No. (In four persons ④ in the elemental world of fine-material and immaterial).

iv (a) Latent states of *kāmarāga* and *paṭigha* lie unmanifest in this person at this plane. Does latent state of *avijjā* lie unmanifest in that person at that plane?
—None.
(b) Latent state of *avijjā* lies unmanifest in this person at this plane. Do latent states of *kāmarāga* and *paṭigha* lie unmanifest in that person at that plane?

—No. In *Anāgāmi*, with three feelings of the elemental world of sensuous desire, and in elemental world of fine-material and immaterial, *avijjā* lies unmanifest; *kāmarāga* and *paṭigha* don't. In three persons ③, in elemental world of fine-material immaterial, *avijjā* lies unmanifest; *kāmarāga* and *paṭigha* do not. In those persons ③, with two feelings of the elemental world of sensuous desire, *avijjā* and *kāmarāga* lie unmanifest; *paṭigha* does not. In those persons ③, with unpleasant feeling, *avijjā* and *paṭigha* lie unmanifest; *kāmarāga* does not.

Triplet-based

32. *i* (a) Latent states of *kāmarāga*, *paṭigha* and *māna* lie unmanifest in this person at this plane. Does latent state of *diṭṭhi* .....p..... *vicikicchā* lie unmanifest in that person at that plane? —No such person.
(b) Latent state of *vicikicchā* lies unmanifest in this person at this plane. Do latent states of *kāmarāga*, *paṭigha* and *māna* lie unmanifest in that person at that plane?
—No. In *Puthujjana* in elemental world of fine-material and immaterial, *vicikicchā* and *māna* lie unmanifest; *kāmarāga* and *paṭigha* do not. In those (same) persons, with two feelings of the elemental world of sensuous desire, *vicikicchā*, *kāmarāga* and *māna* lie unmanifest; *paṭigha* does not. In those (same) persons, with unpleasant feeling, *vicikicchā* and *paṭigha* lie unmanifest; *kāmarāga* and *māna* do not.

ii (a) Latent states of *kāmarāga*, *paṭigha* and *māna* lie unmanifest in this person at this plane. Does latent state of *bhavarāga* lie unmanifest in that person at that plane? —No such person.
(b) Latent state of *bhavarāga* lies unmanifest in this person at this plane. Do latent states of *kāmarāga*, *paṭigha* and *māna* lie unmanifest in that person at that plane?
—No. In four persons ④ in elemental world of fine-material and immaterial, *bhavarāga* and *māna* lie unmanifest; *kāmarāga* and *paṭigha* do not.

iii (a) Latent states of *kāmarāga*, *paṭigha* and *māna* lie unmanifest in this person at this plane. Does latent state of *avijjā* lie unmanifest in that person at that plane?
—No such person.
(b) Latent state of *avijjā* lies unmanifest in this person at this plane. Do latent states of *kāmarāga*, *paṭigha* and *māna* lie unmanifest in that person at that plane?
—No. In *Anāgāmi*, with unpleasant feeling, *avijjā* lies unmanifest; *kāmarāga*, *paṭigha* and *māna* do not. In those (same) persons, with two feelings of the elemental world of sensuous desire, and in elemental world of fine-material and immaterial, *avijjā* and *māna* lie unmanifest; *kāmarāga* and *paṭigha* do not. In three persons ③, in elemental world of fine-material and immaterial, *avijjā* and *māna* lie unmanifest; *kāmarāga* and *paṭigha* do not. In those persons ③,with two feelings of the elemental world of sensuous desire, *avijjā*, *kāmarāga* and *māna* lie unmanifest; paṭigha does not. In those persons ③, with unpleasant feeling, *avijjā* and *paṭigha* lie unmanifest; *kāmarāga* and *māna* do not.

Quadruplet-based

33. *i* (a) Latent states of *kāmarāga, paṭigha, māna* and *diṭṭhi* lie unmanifest in this person at this plane. Does latent state of *vicikicchā* lie unmanifest in that person at that plane? —No such person.
(b) Latent state of *vicikicchā* lies unmanifest in this person at this plane. Do latent states of *kāmarāga, paṭigha, māna* and *diṭṭhi* lie unmanifest in that person at that plane?
—No. In *Puthujjana* in elemental world of fine-material and immaterial, *vicikicchā, māna* and *diṭṭhi* lie unmanifest; *kāmarāga* and *paṭigha* do not. In those (same) persons, with two feelings of the elemental world of sensuous desire, *vicikicchā, kāmarāga, māna* and *diṭṭhi* lie unmanifest; *paṭigha* does not. In those (same) persons, with unpleasant feeling, *vicikicchā, paṭigha* and *diṭṭhi* lie unmanifest; *kāmarāga* and *māna* do not.

ii (a) Latent states of *kāmarāga, paṭigha, māna* and *diṭṭhi* lie unmanifest in this person at this plane. Does latent state of *bhavarāga* lie unmanifest in that person at that plane? —No such person.
(b) Latent state of *bhavarāga* lies unmanifest in this person at this plane. Do latent states of *kāmarāga, paṭigha, māna* and *diṭṭhi* lie unmanifest in that person at that plane?
—No. In three persons ③, in elemental world of fine-material and immaterial, *bhavarāga* and *māna* lie unmanifest; *kāmarāga, paṭigha* and *diṭṭhi* do not. In *Puthujjana* in elemental world of fine-material and immaterial, *bhavarāga, māna* and *diṭṭhi* lie unmanifest; *kāmarāga* and *paṭigha* do not.

iii (a) Latent states of *kāmarāga, paṭigha, māna* and *diṭṭhi* lie unmanifest in this person at this plane. Does latent state of *avijjā* lie unmanifest in that person at that plane? —No such person.
(b) Latent state of *avijjā* lies unmanifest in this person at this plane. Do latent states of *kāmarāga, paṭigha, māna* and *diṭṭhi* lie unmanifest in that person at that plane?
—No. In *Anāgāmi*, with unpleasant feeling, *avijjā* lies unmanifest; *kāmarāga, paṭigha, māna* and *diṭṭhi* do not. In those (same) persons, with two feelings of the elemental world of sensuous desire, and in the elemental world of fine-material and immaterial, *avijjā* and *māna* lie unmanifest; *kāmarāga, paṭigha* and *diṭṭhi* do not. In two persons ★, in elemental world of fine-material and immaterial, *avijjā* and *māna* lie unmanifest; *kāmarāga, paṭigha* and *diṭṭhi* do not. In those persons ★, with two feelings of the elemental world of sensuous desire, *avijjā, kāmarāga* and *māna* lie unmanifest; *paṭigha* and *diṭṭhi* do not. In *Puthujjana* in elemental world of fine-material and immaterial, *avijjā, māna* and *diṭṭhi* lie unmanifest; *kāmarāga* and *paṭigha* do not. In those (same) persons, with two feelings of elemental world of sensuous desire, *avijjā, kāmarāga, māna* and *diṭṭhi* lie unmanifest; *paṭigha* does not. In those (same) persons, with unpleasant feeling, *avijjā, paṭigha* and *diṭṭhi* lie unmanifest; *kāmarāga* and *māna* do not.

Quintuplet-based

34. *i* (a) Latent states of *kāmarāga, paṭigha, māna, diṭṭhi* and *vicikicchā* lie unmanifest in this person at this plane. Does latent state of *bhavarāga* lie unmanifest in that person at that plane? —No such person.
(b) Latent state of *bhavarāga* lies unmanifest in this person at this plane. Do latent states of *kāmarāga, paṭigha, māna, diṭṭhi* and *vicikicchā* lie unmanifest in that person at that plane?
—No. In three persons :, in elemental world of fine-material and immaterial, *bhavarāga* and *māna* lie unmanifest; *kāmarāga, paṭigha, diṭṭhi* and *vicikicchā* do not. In *Puthujjana* in elemental world of fine-material and immaterial, *bhavarāga, māna, diṭṭhi, vicikicchā* lie unmanifest; *kāmarāga* and *paṭigha* do not.

ii (a) Latent states of *kāmarāga, paṭigha, māna, diṭṭhi* and *vicikicchā* lie unmanifest in this person at this plane. Does latent state of *avijjā* lie unmanifest in that person at that plane? —No such person.
(b) Latent state of *avijjā* lies unmanifest in this person at this plane. Do latent states of *kāmarāga, paṭigha, māna, diṭṭhi* and *vicikicchā* lie unmanifest in that person at that plane?
—No. In *Anāgāmi,* with unpleasant feeling, *avijjā* lies unmanifest; *kāmarāga, paṭigha, māna, diṭṭhi* and *vicikicchā* do not. In those (same) persons, with two feelings of the elemental world of sensuous desire, and in the elemental world of fine-material and immaterial, *avijjā* and *māna* lie unmanifest; *kāmarāga, paṭigha, diṭṭhi* and *vicikicchā* do not. In those two persons ★, in elemental world of fine-material and immaterial, *avijjā* and *māna* lie unmanifest; *kāmarāga, paṭigha, diṭṭhi* and *vicikicchā* do not. In those (same) persons, with two feelings of the elemental world of sensuous desire, *avijjā, kāmarāga* and *māna* lie unmanifest; *paṭigha, diṭṭhi* and *vicikicchā* do not. In those (same) persons, with unpleasant feeling, *avijjā* and *paṭigha* lie unmanifest; *kāmarāga, māna, diṭṭhi* and *vicikicchā* do not. In *Puthujjana* in elemental world of fine-material and immaterial, *avijjā, māna, diṭṭhi* and *vicikicchā* lie unmanifest; *kāmarāga* and *paṭigha* do not. In those (same) persons, with two feelings of the elemental world of sensuous desire, *avijjā, kāmarāga, māna, diṭṭhi* and *vicikicchā* lie unmanifest; *paṭigha* do not. In those (same) persons, with unpleasant feeling, *avijjā, paṭigha, diṭṭhi* and *vicikicchā* lie unmanifest; *kāmarāga* and *māna* do not.

Sextuplet-based

35. *i* (a) Latent states of *kāmarāga, paṭigha, māna, diṭṭhi, vicikicchā* and *bhavarāga* lie unmanifest in this person at this plane. Does latent state of *avijjā* lie unmanifest in that person at that plane? —No such person.

(b) Latent state of *avijjā* lies unmanifest in this person at this plane. Do latent states of *kāmarāga, paṭigha, māna, diṭṭhi, vicikicchā* and *bhavarāga* lie unmanifest in that person at that plane?

—No. In *Anāgāmi*, with unpleasant feeling (of sensuous element), *avijjā* lies unmanifest; *kāmarāga, paṭigha, māna, diṭṭhi, vicikicchā* and *bhavarāga* do not. In those (same) persons, with two feelings of the elemental world of sensuous desire, *avijjā* and *māna* lie unmanifest; *kāmarāga, paṭigha, diṭṭhi, vicikicchā* and *bhavarāga* do not. In those (same) persons in the elemental world of fine-material and immaterial, *avijjā, māna* and *bhavarāga* lie unmanifest; *kāmarāga, paṭigha, diṭṭhi* and *vicikicchā* do not. In two persons ★, in elemental world of fine-material and immaterial, *avijjā, māna* and *bhavarāga* lie unmanifest; *kāmarāga, paṭigha, diṭṭhi* and *vicikicchā*do do not. In those (same) persons, with two feelings of the elemental world of sensuous desire, *avijjā, kāmarāga* and *māna* lie unmanifest; *paṭigha, diṭṭhi, vicikicchā* and *bhavarāga* do not. In those (same) persons, with unpleasant feeling, *avijjā* and *paṭigha* lie unmanifest; *kāmarāga, māna, diṭṭhi, vicikicchā* and *bhavarāga* do not. In *Puthujjana* in elemental world of fine-material and immaterial, *avijjā, māna, diṭṭhi, vicikicchā* and *bhavarāga* lie unmanifest; *kāmarāga* and *paṭigha* do not. In those (same) persons, with two feelings of the elemental world of sensuous desire, *avijjā, kāmarāga, māna, diṭṭhi* and *vicikicchā* lie unmanifest; *paṭigha* and *bhavarāga* do not. In those (same) persons, with unpleasant feeling, *avijjā, paṭigha, diṭṭhi* and *vicikicchā* lie unmanifest; *kāmarāga, māna* and *bhavarāga* do not.

Opposite enquiries by person

Mono-based

36. *i* (a) Latent state of *kāmarāga* does not lie unmanifest in this person. Does latent state of *paṭigha* not lie unmanifest in that person? —Yes. (in *Arahat*)
(b) Latent state of *paṭigha* does not lie unmanifest in this person. Does latent state of *kāmarāga* not lie unmanifest in that person? —Yes. Same answer as above.

ii (a) Latent state of *kāmarāga* does not lie unmanifest in this person. Does latent state of *māna* not lie unmanifest in that person?
—In *Anāgāmi, kāmarāga* does not lie unmanifest; *māna* does. In *Arahat* [52], *kāmarāga* does not lie unmanifest; *māna* too.
(b) Latent state of *māna* does not lie unmanifest in this person. Does latent state of *kāmarāga* not lie unmanifest in that person? —Yes. Refer to aforesaid.

[52] *Arahat*: Attainer of the *Arahatta* path-citta (*Arahatta-maggacittaṃ*) has cut off the remaining five subtle fetters of the upper region (*rūparāga, arūparāga, māna, uddhacca, avijjā*), or herein indicates that he had eradicated all the seven latent states. *Rūparāga* and *arūparāga* are examples of *bhavarāga*. Because *Arahat* had eliminated the delusion-rooted *citta* associated with restlessness (*uddhacca*) and all forms of greed and desire taking object of sensuous, fine-material and immaterial existence (*kāmarāga, bhavarāga*), he had completely uprooted all remaining traces of conceit (*māna*) and ignorance (*avijjā*). The *Arahatta* fruition-*citta* at moment of attainment is a resultant *citta* (*vipākacitta*). *Arahat* at sense-sphere is free from wholesome, unwholesome, and resultant cittas binding to the worlds of desire, except for the 8 functional cittas (*kiriyacittāni*) with cause but without kammic effect—which are two feelings of the sensuous worlds.

iii (a) Latent state of *kāmarāga* does not lie unmanifest in this person. Does latent state of *diṭṭhi* .....p..... *vicikicchā* not lie unmanifest in that person? —Yes.
(b) Latent state of *vicikicchā* does not lie unmanifest in this person. Does latent state of *kāmarāga* not lie unmanifest in that person?
—In two persons ★, *vicikicchā* does not lie unmanifest; *kāmarāga* does. In two persons ☆, *vicikicchā* does not lie unmanifest; *kāmarāga* too.

iv (a) Latent state of *kāmarāga* does not lie unmanifest in this person. Does latent state of *bhavarāga* .....p..... *avijjā* not lie unmanifest in that person?
—In *Anāgāmi, kāmarāga* does not lie unmanifest; *avijjā* does. In *Arahat*, *kāmarāga* does not lie unmanifest; *avijjā* too.
(b) Latent state of *avijjā* does not lie unmanifest in this person. Does latent state of *kāmarāga* not lie unmanifest in that person? —Yes. Refer to aforesaid.

37. *i* (a) Latent state of *paṭigha* does not lie unmanifest in this person. Does latent state of *māna* not lie unmanifest in that person?
—In *Anāgāmi, paṭigha* does not lie unmanifest; *māna* does. In *Arahat*, *paṭigha* does not lie unmanifest; *māna* too.
(b) Latent state of *māna* does not lie unmanifest in this person. Does latent state of *paṭigha* not lie unmanifest in that person? —Yes. Refer to aforesaid.

ii (a) Latent state of *paṭigha* does not lie unmanifest in this person. Does latent state of *diṭṭhi* .....p..... *vicikicchā* not lie unmanifest in that person? —Yes.
(b) Latent state of *vicikicchā* does not lie unmanifest in this person. Does latent state of *paṭigha* not lie unmanifest in that person?
—In two persons ★, *vicikicchā* does not lie unmanifest; *paṭigha* does. In two persons ☆, *vicikicchā* does not lie unmanifest; *paṭigha* too.

iii (a) Latent state of *paṭigha* does not lie unmanifest in this person. Does latent state of *bhavarāga* .....p..... *avijjā* not lie unmanifest in that person?
—In *Anāgāmi, paṭigha* does not lie unmanifest; *avijjā* does. In *Arahat*, *paṭigha* does not lie unmanifest; *avijjā* too.
(b) Latent state of *avijjā* does not lie unmanifest in this person. Does latent state of *paṭigha* not lie unmanifest in that person? —Yes. Refer to aforesaid.

38. *i* (a) Latent state of *māna* does not lie unmanifest in this person. Does latent state of *diṭṭhi* .....p..... *vicikicchā* not lie unmanifest in that person? —Yes.
(b) Latent state of *vicikicchā* does not lie unmanifest in this person. Does latent state of *māna* not lie unmanifest in that person?
—In three persons ⁝ , *vicikicchā* does not lie unmanifest; *māna* does. In *Arahat*, *vicikicchā* does not lie unmanifest; *māna* too.

i (a) Latent state of *māna* does not lie unmanifest in this person. Does latent state of *bhavarāga* .....p..... *avijjā* not lie unmanifest in that person?
—Yes. (in *Arahat*)

(b) Latent state of *avijjā* does not lie unmanifest in this person. Does latent state of *māna* not lie unmanifest in that person? —Yes. (in *Arahat*)

39. *i* (a) Latent state of *diṭṭhi* does not lie unmanifest in this person. Does latent state of *vicikicchā* not lie unmanifest in that person? —Yes. (in *Arahat*)
(b) Latent state of *vicikicchā* does not lie unmanifest in this person. Does latent state of *diṭṭhi* not lie unmanifest in that person? —Yes. (in *Arahat*)

ii (a) Latent state of *diṭṭhi* .....p..... *vicikicchā* does not lie unmanifest in this person. Does latent state of *bhavarāga* .....p..... *avijjā* not lie unmanifest in that person?
—In three persons ⁝ , *vicikicchā* does not lie unmanifest; *avijjā* does. In *Arahat*, *vicikicchā* does not lie unmanifest; *avijjā* too.
(b) Latent state of *avijjā* does not lie unmanifest in this person. Does latent state of *vicikicchā* not lie unmanifest in that person? —Yes. Refer to aforesaid.

40. *i* (a) Latent state of *bhavarāga* does not lie unmanifest in this person. Does latent state of *avijjā* not lie unmanifest in that person? —Yes. (in *Arahat*)
(b) Latent state of *avijjā* does not lie unmanifest in this person. Does latent state of *bhavarāga* not lie unmanifest in that person? —Yes. (in *Arahat*)

Couplet-based

41. *i* (a) Latent states of *kāmarāga* and *paṭigha* do not lie unmanifest in this person. Does latent state of *māna* not lie unmanifest in that person?
—In *Anāgāmi, kāmarāga* and *paṭigha* do not lie unmanifest, but *māna* does. In *Arahat*, *kāmarāga* and *paṭigha* do not lie unmanifest; *māna* too.
(b) Latent state of *māna* does not lie unmanifest in this person. Do latent states of *kāmarāga* and *paṭigha* not lie unmanifest in that person?
—Yes. Refer to aforesaid.

ii (a) Latent states of *kāmarāga* and *paṭigha* do not lie unmanifest in this person. Does latent state of *diṭṭhi* .....p..... *vicikicchā* not lie unmanifest in that person?
—Yes.
(b) Latent state of *vicikicchā* does not lie unmanifest in this person. Do latent states of *kāmarāga* and *paṭigha* not lie unmanifest in that person?
—In two persons ★, *vicikicchā* does not lie unmanifest, but *kāmarāga* and *paṭigha* do. In two persons ☆, *vicikicchā* does not lie unmanifest; *kāmarāga* and *paṭigha* too.

iii (a) Latent states of *kāmarāga* and *paṭigha* do not lie unmanifest in this person. Does latent state of *bhavarāga* .....p..... *avijjā* not lie unmanifest in that person?
—In *Anāgāmi, kāmarāga* and *paṭigha* do not lie unmanifest; *avijjā* (and *bhavarāga*) does.
(b) Latent state of *avijjā* does not lie unmanifest in this person. Do latent states of *kāmarāga* and *paṭigha* not lie unmanifest in that person?
—Yes. Refer to aforesaid.

Triplet-based

42. *i* (a) Latent states of *kāmarāga, paṭigha* and *māna* do not lie unmanifest in this person. Does latent state of *diṭṭhi ....p..... vicikicchā* not lie unmanifest in that person? —Yes.
(b) Latent state of *vicikicchā* does not lie unmanifest in this person. Do latent states of *kāmarāga, paṭigha* and *māna* not lie unmanifest in that person?
—In two persons ★, *vicikicchā* does not lie unmanifest, but *kāmarāga, paṭigha* and *māna* do. In *Anāgāmi, vicikicchā, kāmarāga* and *paṭigha* do not lie unmanifest, but *māna* does. In *Arahat, vicikicchā* does not lie unmanifest; *kāmarāga, paṭigha* and *māna* too.

ii (a) Latent states of *kāmarāga, paṭigha* and *māna* do not lie unmanifest in this person. Does latent state of *bhavarāga* .....p..... *avijjā* not lie unmanifest in that person? —Yes. (in *Arahat*)
(b) Latent state of *avijjā* does not lie unmanifest in this person. Do latent states of *kāmarāga, paṭigha* and *māna* not lie unmanifest in that person?
—Yes. (in *Arahat*)

Quadruplet-based

43. *i* (a) Latent states of *kāmarāga, paṭigha, māna* and *diṭṭhi* do not lie unmanifest in this person. Does latent state of *vicikicchā* not lie unmanifest in that person?
—Yes.
(b) Latent state of *vicikicchā* does not lie unmanifest in this person. Do latent states of *kāmarāga, paṭigha, māna* and *diṭṭhi* not lie unmanifest in that person?
—In two persons ★, *vicikicchā* and *diṭṭhi* do not lie unmanifest, but *kāmarāga, paṭigha* and *māna* do. In *Anāgāmi, vicikicchā, kāmarāga, paṭigha* and *diṭṭhi* do not lie unmanifest, but *māna* does. In *Arahat, vicikicchā* does not lie unmanifest; *kāmarāga, paṭigha, māna* and *diṭṭhi* too .....p.....

Quintuplet-based

44. *i* (a) Latent states of *kāmarāga, paṭigha, māna, diṭṭhi* and *vicikicchā* do not lie unmanifest in this person. Does latent state of *bhavarāga* .....p..... *avijjā* not lie unmanifest in that person? —Yes. (in *Arahat*)
(b) Latent state of *avijjā* does not lie unmanifest in this person. Do latent states of *kāmarāga, paṭigha, māna, diṭṭhi* and *vicikicchā* not lie unmanifest in that person? —Yes.

Sextuplet-based

45. *i* (a) Latent states of *kāmarāga, paṭigha, māna, diṭṭhi, vicikicchā* and *bhavarāga* do not lie unmanifest in this person. Does latent state of *avijjā* not lie unmanifest in that person? —Yes. (in *Arahat*)

Latent state of *avijjā* does not lie unmanifest in this person. Do latent states of *kāmarāga, paṭigha, māna, diṭṭhi, vicikicchā* and *bhavarāga* not lie unmanifest in that person? —Yes.

Opposite enquiries by plane

Mono-based

46. *i* (a) Latent state of *kāmarāga* does not lie unmanifest at this plane. Does latent state of *paṭigha* not lie unmanifest at that plane?
—In unpleasant feeling (in sensuous element), *kāmarāga* does not lie unmanifest, but *paṭigha* does. In elemental world of fine-material and immaterial, and in *apariyāpanna* [53], *kāmarāga* does not lie unmanifest; *paṭigha* too.
(b) Latent state of *paṭigha* does not lie unmanifest at this plane. Does latent state of *kāmarāga* not lie unmanifest at that plane?
—In two feelings of the elemental world of sensuous desire, *paṭigha* does not lie unmanifest, but *kāmarāga* does. In elemental world of fine-material and immaterial, and in *apariyāpanna, paṭigha* does not lie unmanifest; *kāmarāga* too.

ii (a) Latent state of *kāmarāga* does not lie unmanifest at this plane. Does latent state of *māna* not lie unmanifest at that plane?
—In elemental world of fine-material and immaterial, *kāmarāga* does not lie unmanifest, but *māna* does. In unpleasant feeling (in sensuous element), and in *apariyāpanna, kāmarāga* does not lie unmanifest; *māna* too.
(b) Latent state of *māna* does not lie unmanifest at this plane. Does latent state of *kāmarāga* not lie unmanifest at that plane? —Yes. Refer to aforesaid.

iii (a) Latent state of *kāmarāga* does not lie unmanifest at this plane. Does latent state of *diṭṭhi* .....p..... *vicikicchā* not lie unmanifest at that plane?
—In unpleasant feeling (in sensuous element), and in elemental world of fine-material and immaterial, *kāmarāga* does not lie unmanifest, but *vicikicchā* does. In *apariyāpanna, kāmarāga* does not lie unmanifest; *vicikicchā* too.
(b) Latent state of *vicikicchā* does not lie unmanifest at this plane. Does latent state of *kāmarāga* not lie unmanifest in that plane? —Yes. Refer to the aforesaid.

iv (a) Latent state of *kāmarāga* does not lie unmanifest at this plane. Does latent state of *bhavarāga* not lie unmanifest at that plane?
—In elemental world of fine-material and immaterial, *kāmarāga* does not lie unmanifest, but *bhavarāga* does. In unpleasant feeling (in sensuous element), and in *apariyāpanna, kāmarāga* does not lie unmanifest; *bhavarāga* too.
(b) Latent state of *bhavarāga* does not lie unmanifest at this plane. Does latent state of *kāmarāga* not lie unmanifest at that plane?

---

[53] *apariyāpanna*: literally, the "not included", the untainted, in transcendental sphere (*Lokuttarā*) which is made up of the nine supramundane attainments, namely the four supramundane paths, four supramundane fruitions, and the unconditioned element.

—In two feelings of the elemental world of sensuous desire, *bhavarāga* does not lie unmanifest, but *kāmarāga* does. In unpleasant feeling (in sensuous element), and in *apariyāpanna, bhavarāga* does not lie unmanifest; *kāmarāga* too.

v (a) Latent state of *kāmarāga* does not lie unmanifest at this plane. Does latent state of *avijjā* not lie unmanifest at that plane?
—In unpleasant feeling (in sensuous element), and in elemental world of fine-material and immaterial, *kāmarāga* does not lie unmanifest, but *avijjā* does. In *apariyāpanna, kāmarāga* does not lie unmanifest; *avijjā* too.
(b) Latent state of *avijjā* does not lie unmanifest at this plane. Does latent state of *kāmarāga* not lie unmanifest at that plane? —Yes. Refer to the aforesaid.

47. *i* (a) Latent state of *paṭigha* does not lie unmanifest at this plane. Does latent state of *māna* not lie unmanifest at that plane?
—In two feelings of the elemental world of sensuous desire, and in the elemental world of fine-material and immaterial, *paṭigha* does not lie unmanifest, but *māna* does. In *apariyāpanna, paṭigha* does not lie unmanifest; *māna* too.
(b) Latent state of *māna* does not lie unmanifest at this plane. Does latent state of *paṭigha* not lie unmanifest at that plane?
—In unpleasant feeling (in sensuous element), *māna* does not lie unmanifest, but *paṭigha* does. In *apariyāpanna, māna* does not lie unmanifest; *paṭigha* too.

ii (a) Latent state of *paṭigha* does not lie unmanifest at this plane. Does latent state of *diṭṭhi* .....p..... *vicikicchā* not lie unmanifest at that plane?
—In two feelings of the elemental world of sensuous desire, and in the elemental world of fine-material and immaterial, *paṭigha* does not lie unmanifest, but *vicikicchā* (and *diṭṭhi*) does. In *apariyāpanna, paṭigha* does not lie unmanifest; *vicikicchā* (and *diṭṭhi*) too.
(b) Latent state of *vicikicchā* does not lie unmanifest at this plane. Does latent state of *paṭigha* not lie unmanifest at that plane? —Yes. Refer to the aforesaid.

iii (a) Latent state of *paṭigha* does not lie unmanifest at this plane. Does latent states of *bhavarāga* not lie unmanifest at that plane?
—In elemental world of fine-material and immaterial, *paṭigha* does not lie unmanifest, but *bhavarāga* does. In two feelings of the elemental world of sensuous desire, and in *apariyāpanna, paṭigha* does not lie unmanifest; *bhavarāga* too.
(b) Latent state of *bhavarāga* does not lie unmanifest at this plane. Does latent state of *paṭigha* not lie unmanifest at that plane?
—In unpleasant feeling (in sensuous element), *bhavarāga* does not lie unmanifest, but *paṭigha* does. In two feelings of the elemental world of sensuous desire, and in *apariyāpanna, bhavarāga* does not lie unmanifest; *paṭigha* too.

iv (a) Latent state of *paṭigha* does not lie unmanifest at this plane. Does latent state of *avijjā* not lie unmanifest at that plane?

—In two feelings of the elemental world of sensuous desire, and in the elemental world of fine-material and immaterial, *paṭigha* does not lie unmanifest, but *avijjā* does. In *apariyāpanna*, *paṭigha* does not lie unmanifest; *avijjā* too.
(b) Latent state of *avijjā* does not lie unmanifest at this plane. Does latent state of *paṭigha* not lie unmanifest at that plane? —Yes. Refer to the aforesaid.

48. *i* (a) Latent state of *māna* does not lie unmanifest at this plane. Does latent state of *diṭṭhi* .....p..... *vicikicchā* not lie unmanifest at that plane?
—In unpleasant feeling (in sensuous element), *māna* does not lie unmanifest, but *vicikicchā* does. In *apariyāpanna*, *māna* does not lie unmanifest; *vicikicchā* too.
(b) Latent state of *vicikicchā* does not lie unmanifest at this plane. Does latent state of *māna* not lie unmanifest at that plane? —Yes. Refer to the aforesaid.

ii (a) Latent state of *māna* does not lie unmanifest at this plane. Does latent state of *bhavarāga* not lie unmanifest at that plane? —Yes. Refer to answer below.
(b) Latent state of *bhavarāga* does not lie unmanifest at this plane. Does latent state of *māna* not lie unmanifest at that plane?
—In two feelings of the elemental world of sensuous desire, *bhavarāga* does not lie unmanifest, but *māna* does. In unpleasant feeling (in sensuous element), and in *apariyāpanna*, *bhavarāga* does not lie unmanifest; *māna* too.

iii (a) Latent state of *māna* does not lie unmanifest at this plane. Does latent state of *avijjā* not lie unmanifest at that plane?
—In unpleasant feeling (in sensuous element), *māna* does not lie unmanifest, but *avijjā* does. In *apariyāpanna*, *māna* does not lie unmanifest; *avijjā* too.
(b) Latent state of *avijjā* does not lie unmanifest at this plane. Does latent state of *māna* not lie unmanifest at that plane? —Yes. Refer to the aforesaid.

49. *i* (a) Latent state of *diṭṭhi* does not lie unmanifest at this plane. Does latent state of *vicikicchā* not lie unmanifest at that plane? —Yes, in *apariyāpanna*.
(b) Latent state of *vicikicchā* does not lie unmanifest at this plane. Does latent state of *diṭṭhi* not lie unmanifest at that plane? —Yes. (Same as aforesaid)

ii (a) Latent state of *diṭṭhi* .....p..... *vicikicchā* does not lie unmanifest at this plane. Does latent state of *bhavarāga* not lie unmanifest at that plane?
—Yes. See answer below.
(b) Latent state of *bhavarāga* does not lie unmanifest at this plane. Does latent state of *vicikicchā* not lie unmanifest at that plane?
—In three feelings of the elemental world of sensuous desire, *bhavarāga* does not lie unmanifest, but *vicikicchā* does. In *apariyāpanna*, *bhavarāga* does not lie unmanifest; *vicikicchā* too.

iii (a) Latent state of *vicikicchā* does not lie unmanifest at this plane. Does latent state of *avijjā* not lie unmanifest at that plane? — Yes, in *apariyāpanna*.
(b) Latent state of *avijjā* does not lie unmanifest at this plane. Does latent states of *vicikicchā* not lie unmanifest at that plane? —Yes. (Same as aforesaid)

50. *i* (a) Latent state of *bhavarāga* does not lie unmanifest at this plane. Does latent state of *avijjā* not lie unmanifest at that plane?
—In three feelings of the elemental world of sensuous desire, *bhavarāga* does not lie unmanifest, but *avijjā* does. In *apariyāpanna*, *bhavarāga* does not lie unmanifest; *avijjā* too.
(b) Latent state of *avijjā* does not lie unmanifest at this plane. Does latent state of *bhavarāga* not lie unmanifest at that plane? —Yes. Refer to the aforesaid.

Couplet-based

51. *i* (a) Latent states of *kāmarāga* and *paṭigha* do not lie unmanifest at this plane. Does latent state of *māna* not lie unmanifest at that plane?
—In elemental world of fine-material and immaterial, *kāmarāga* and *paṭigha* do not lie unmanifest, but *māna* does. In *apariyāpanna*, *kāmarāga* and *paṭigha* do not lie unmanifest; *māna* too.
(b) Latent state of *māna* does not lie unmanifest at this plane. Do latent states of *kāmarāga* and *paṭigha* not lie unmanifest at that plane?
—In unpleasant feeling (in sensuous element), *māna* and *kāmarāga* do not lie unmanifest, but *paṭigha* does. In *apariyāpanna*, *māna* does not lie unmanifest; *kāmarāga* and *paṭigha* too.

ii (a) Latent states of *kāmarāga* and *paṭigha* do not lie unmanifest at this plane. Does latent state of *diṭṭhi* .....p..... *vicikicchā* not lie unmanifest at that plane?
—In elemental world of fine-material and immaterial, *kāmarāga* and *paṭigha* do not lie unmanifest, but *vicikicchā* does. In *apariyāpanna*, *kāmarāga* and *paṭigha* do not lie unmanifest; *vicikicchā* too.
(b) Latent state of *vicikicchā* does not lie unmanifest at this plane. Do latent states of *kāmarāga* and *paṭigha* not lie unmanifest at that plane?
—Yes. Refer to the aforesaid.

iii (a) Latent states of *kāmarāga* and *paṭigha* do not lie unmanifest at this plane. Does latent state of *bhavarāga* not lie unmanifest at that plane?
—In elemental world of fine-material and immaterial, *kāmarāga* and *paṭigha* do not lie unmanifest; *bhavarāga* does. In *apariyāpanna*, *kāmarāga* and *paṭigha* do not lie unmanifest; *bhavarāga* too.
(b) Latent state of *bhavarāga* does not lie unmanifest at this plane. Do latent states of *kāmarāga* and *paṭigha* not lie unmanifest at that plane?
—In unpleasant feeling (in sensuous element), *bhavarāga* and *kāmarāga* do not lie unmanifest, but *paṭigha* does. In two feelings of the elemental world of desire, *bhavarāga* and *paṭigha* do not lie unmanifest, but *kāmarāga* does. In *apariyāpanna*, *bhavarāga* does not lie unmanifest; *kāmarāga* and *paṭigha* too.

iv (a) Latent states of *kāmarāga* and *paṭigha* do not lie unmanifest at this plane. Does latent state of *avijjā* not lie unmanifest at that plane?
—In elemental world of fine-material and immaterial, *kāmarāga* and *paṭigha* do not lie unmanifest, but *avijjā* does. In *apariyāpanna*, *kāmarāga* and *paṭigha* do not lie unmanifest; *avijjā* too.

(b) Latent state of *avijjā* does not lie unmanifest at this plane. Do latent states of *kāmarāga* and *paṭigha* not lie unmanifest at that plane? —Yes. (in *apariyāpanna*)

Triplet-based

52. *i* (a) Latent states of *kāmarāga*, *paṭigha* and *māna* do not lie unmanifest at this plane. Does latent state of *diṭṭhi* .....p..... *vicikicchā* not lie unmanifest at that plane? —Yes.
(b) Latent state of *vicikicchā* does not lie unmanifest at this plane. Do latent states of *kāmarāga*, *paṭigha* and *māna* not lie unmanifest at that plane?
—Yes. (in *apariyāpanna*)

ii (a) Latent states of *kāmarāga*, *paṭigha* and *māna* do not lie unmanifest at this plane. Does latent state of *bhavarāga* not lie unmanifest at that plane? —Yes.
(b) Latent state of *bhavarāga* does not lie unmanifest at this plane. Do latent states of *kāmarāga*, *paṭigha* and *māna* not lie unmanifest at that plane?
—In unpleasant feeling (in sensuous element), *bhavarāga*, *kāmarāga* and *māna* do not lie unmanifest, but *paṭigha* does. In two feelings of the elemental world of sensuous desire, *bhavarāga* and *paṭigha* do not lie unmanifest, but *kāmarāga* and *māna* do. In *apariyāpanna*, *bhavarāga* does not lie unmanifest, latent states of *kāmarāga*, *paṭigha* and *māna* too.

iii (a) Latent states of *kāmarāga*, *paṭigha* and *diṭṭhi* do not lie unmanifest at this plane. Does latent state of *avijjā* not lie unmanifest at that plane?
—Yes. (in *apariyāpanna*)
(b) Latent state of *avijjā* does not lie unmanifest at this plane. Do latent states of *kāmarāga*, *paṭigha* and *māna* not lie unmanifest at that plane?
—Yes. (in *apariyāpanna*)

Quadruplet-based

52. *i* (a) Latent states of *kāmarāga*, *paṭigha*, *māna* and *diṭṭhi* do not lie unmanifest at this plane. Does latent state of *vicikicchā* not lie unmanifest at that plane? —Yes.
(b) Latent states of *vicikicchā* does not lie unmanifest at this plane. Do latent state of *kāmarāga*, *paṭigha*, *māna* and *diṭṭhi* not lie unmanifest at that plane?
—Yes (in *apariyāpanna*)

Quintuplet-based

54. *i* (a) Latent states of *kāmarāga*, *paṭigha*, *māna*, *diṭṭhi* and *vicikicchā* do not lie unmanifest at this plane. Does latent state of *bhavarāga* not lie unmanifest at that plane? —Yes.
(b) Latent state of *bhavarāga* does not lie unmanifest at this plane. Do latent states of *kāmarāga*, *paṭigha*, *māna*, *diṭṭhi* and *vicikicchā* not lie unmanifest at that plane?

—In unpleasant feeling, states of *bhavarāga*, *kāmarāga* and *māna* do not lie unmanifest; but *paṭigha*, *diṭṭhi* and *vicikicchā* do. In two feelings of elemental world of sensuous desire, *bhavarāga* and *paṭigha* do not lie unmanifest; but *kāmarāga*, *māna*, *diṭṭhi* and *vicikicchā* do. In *apariyāpanna*, *bhavarāga* does not lie unmanifest; latent states of *kāmarāga*, *paṭigha*, *māna*, *diṭṭhi*, *vicikicchā* too.

ii (a) Latent states of *kāmarāga*, *paṭigha*, *māna*, *diṭṭhi* and *vicikicchā* do not lie unmanifest at this plane. Does latent state of *avijjā* not lie unmanifest at that plane? —Yes.
(b) Latent state of *avijjā* does not lie unmanifest at this plane. Do latent states of *kāmarāga*, *paṭigha*, *māna*, *diṭṭhi* and *vicikicchā* not lie unmanifest at that plane? —Yes. (in *apariyāpanna*)

Sextuplet-based

55. *i* (a) Latent states of *kāmarāga*, *paṭigha*, *māna*, *diṭṭhi*, *vicikicchā* and *bhavarāga* do not lie unmanifest at this plane. Does latent state of *avijjā* not lie unmanifest at that plane? —Yes. (in *apariyāpanna*)
(b) Latent state of *avijjā* does not lie unmanifest at this plane. Do latent states of *kāmarāga*, *paṭigha*, *māna*, *diṭṭhi*, *vicikicchā* and *bhavarāga* not lie unmanifest at that plane? —Yes. (in *apariyāpanna*)

Opposite enquiries by person and plane

Mono-based

56. *i* (a) Latent state of *kāmarāga* does not lie unmanifest in this person at this plane. Does latent state of *paṭigha* not lie unmanifest in that person at that plane?
—No. In three persons ③ with unpleasant feeling, *kāmarāga* does not lie unmanifest, but *paṭigha* does.
—Yes In those persons (three persons ③), in elemental world of fine-material and immaterial, and in *apariyāpanna* [54] (*Gotrabhū* and two persons ★); and in two persons ☆, in all places—*kāmarāga* does not lie unmanifest; *paṭigha* too.
(b) Latent state of *paṭigha* does not lie unmanifest in this person at this plane. Does latent state of *kāmarāga* not lie unmanifest in that person at that plane?
—No. In three persons ③ with two feelings of the elemental world of sensuous desire, *paṭigha* does not lie unmanifest, but *kāmarāga* does.
—Yes. Refer to the answer in *i* (a) above.

ii (a) Latent state of *kāmarāga* does not lie unmanifest in this person at this plane. Does latent state of *māna* not lie unmanifest in that person at that plane?
—No. In three persons ③, in elemental world of fine-material and immaterial, *kāmarāga* does not lie unmanifest, but *māna* does.

[54] *Gotrabhū*, is still *puthujjana*, but is now in a fit state to be joining lineage of the Ariyas in *Sotāpattimagga*. As indicated in the answers, a kind of *puthujjana* is included at the *apariyāpanna*, although the word *Gotrabhū* is not mentioned by the text.

—Yes. In those persons, with unpleasant feeling (three persons ③), and in *apariyāpanna* (*Gotrabhū* and two persons ★), *kāmarāga* does not lie unmanifest; *māna* too.
—No. In *Anāgāmi*, with two feelings of the elemental world of sensuous desire, and in the elemental world of fine-material and immaterial, *kāmarāga* does not lie unmanifest; *māna* does.
—Yes. In those persons, with unpleasant feeling, and in *apariyāpanna* (in *Anāgāmi*); in *Arahat*, in all places—both *kāmarāga*, *māna* do not lie unmanifest.
(b) Latent state of *māna* does not lie unmanifest in this person at this plane. Does latent state of *kāmarāga* not lie unmanifest in that person at that plane?
—Yes. Refer to the answer in *ii* (a) above.

iii (a) Latent state of *kāmarāga* does not lie unmanifest in this person at this plane. Does latent state of *diṭṭhi* …..p….. *vicikicchā* not lie unmanifest in that person at that plane?
—No. In *Puthujjana*, with unpleasant feeling, and in elemental world of fine-material and immaterial, *kāmarāga* does not lie unmanifest, but *vicikicchā* does.
—Yes. In those persons, in *apariyāpanna* [54] (*Gotrabhū* and two persons ★); in two persons ☆, in all places—*kāmarāga* does not lie unmanifest; *vicikicchā* (and *diṭṭhi*) also does not lie unmanifest.
(b) Latent state of *vicikicchā* does not lie unmanifest in this person at this plane. Does latent state of *kāmarāga* not lie unmanifest in that person at that plane?
—No. In two persons ★, with two feelings of the elemental world of sensuous desire, *vicikicchā* does not lie unmanifest, but *kāmarāga* does.
—Yes. In those (same) persons, with unpleasant feeling; those in the elemental world of fine-material and immaterial; those in *apariyāpanna* [54] (*Gotrabhū* and two persons ★); and in two persons ☆, in all places—*vicikicchā* does not lie unmanifest; *kāmarāga* too.

iv (a) Latent state of *kāmarāga* does not lie unmanifest in this person at this plane. Does latent state of *bhavarāga* not lie unmanifest in that person at that plane?
—No. In three persons ③, in elemental world of fine-material and immaterial; and in *Anāgāmi,* in the elemental world of fine-material and immaterial—*kāmarāga* does not lie unmanifest, but *bhavarāga* does.
—Yes. In those persons ③, with unpleasant feeling, and in *apariyāpanna* (*Gotrabhū* and two persons ★); in those persons, with three feelings of the elemental world of sensuous desire, and in *apariyāpanna* (*Anāgāmi*); in *Arahat*, in all places—*kāmarāga* does not lie unmanifest; *bhavarāga* too.
(b) Latent state of *bhavarāga* does not lie unmanifest in this person at this plane. Does latent state of *kāmarāga* not lie unmanifest in that person at that plane?
—No. In three persons ③, with two feelings of the elemental world of sensuous desire, *bhavarāga* does not lie unmanifest, but *kāmarāga* does.
—Yes. Refer to the answer in *iv* (a) above.

v (a) Latent state of *kāmarāga* does not lie unmanifest in this person at this plane. Does latent state of *avijjā* not lie unmanifest in that person at that plane?

—No. In three persons ③, with unpleasant feeling, and in elemental world of fine-material and immaterial; in *Anāgāmi*, with three feelings of the elemental world of sensuous desire, and in the elemental world of fine-material and immaterial—*kāmarāga* does not lie unmanifest, but *avijjā* does.
—Yes. In those persons ③, in *apariyāpanna* [54] (*Gotrabhū* and three persons ⁝); and in *Arahat*, in all places—*kāmarāga* does not lie unmanifest; *avijjā* too.
(b) Latent state of *avijjā* does not lie unmanifest in this person at this plane. Does latent state of *kāmarāga* not lie unmanifest in that person at that plane?
—Yes. Refer to the answer in *v* (a) above.

57. *i* (a) Latent state of *paṭigha* does not lie unmanifest in this person at this plane. Does latent state of *māna* not lie unmanifest in that person at that plane?
—No. In three persons ③, with two feelings of the elemental world of sensuous desire, and in the elemental world of fine-material and immaterial; in *Anāgāmi*, with two feelings of the elemental world of desire, and in the elemental world of fine-material and immaterial—*paṭigha* does not lie unmanifest, but *māna* does.
—Yes. In those persons ③, in *apariyāpanna* (*Gotrabhū* and two persons ★); in those persons, with unpleasant feeling, and in *apariyāpanna* (in *Anāgāmi*); and in *Arahat*, in all places—*paṭigha* does not lie unmanifest; *māna* too.
(b) Latent state of *māna* does not lie unmanifest in this person at this plane. Does latent state of *paṭigha* not lie unmanifest in that person at that plane?
—No. In three persons ③, with unpleasant feeling, *māna* does not lie unmanifest, but *paṭigha* does.
—Yes. Refer to the answer in *i* (a) above.

ii (a) Latent state of *paṭigha* does not lie unmanifest in this person at this plane. Does latent state of *diṭṭhi* .....p..... *vicikicchā* not lie unmanifest in that person at that plane?
—No. In *Puthujjana*, with two feelings of the elemental world of sensuous desire, and in the elemental world of fine-material and immaterial, *paṭigha* does not lie unmanifest, but *vicikicchā* (and *diṭṭhi*) does.
—Yes. Refer to answer in (b) below.
(b) Latent state of *vicikicchā* does not lie unmanifest in this person at this plane. Does latent state of *paṭigha* not lie unmanifest in that person at that plane?
—No. In two persons ★, with unpleasant feeling, *vicikicchā* (and *diṭṭhi*) does not lie unmanifest, but *paṭigha* does.
—Yes. In those (same) persons, with two feelings of the elemental world of sensuous desire, in the elemental world of fine-material and immaterial, and in *apariyāpanna*; and in two persons ☆, in all places—*vicikicchā* (and *diṭṭhi*) does not lie unmanifest; *paṭigha* too.

iii (a) Latent state of *paṭigha* does not lie unmanifest in this person at this plane. Does latent state of *bhavarāga* not lie unmanifest in that person at that plane?
—No. In three persons ③, in the elemental world of fine-material and immaterial; and in *Anāgāmi,* in the elemental world of fine-material and immaterial—*paṭigha* does not lie unmanifest; *bhavarāga* does.

—Yes. In those persons ③, with two feelings of the elemental world of sensuous desire, and in *apariyāpanna* [54] (*Gotrabhū* and two persons ★); in those persons, with three feelings of the elemental world of sensuous desire, and in *apariyāpanna* (*Anāgāmi*); and in *Arahat*, in all places—*paṭigha* does not lie unmanifest; *bhavarāga* too.
(b) Latent state of *bhavarāga* does not lie unmanifest in this person at this plane. Does latent state of *paṭigha* not lie unmanifest in that person at that plane?
—No. In three persons ③, with unpleasant feeling, *bhavarāga* does not lie unmanifest, but *paṭigha* does.
—Yes. Refer to the answer in *iii* (a) above.

iv (a) Latent state of *paṭigha* does not lie unmanifest in this person at this plane. Does latent state of *avijjā* not lie unmanifest in that person at that plane?
— No. In three persons ③, with two feelings of the elemental world of sensuous desire, and in the elemental world of fine-material and immaterial; in *Anāgāmi,* with three feelings of the elemental world of sensuous desire, and in the elemental world of fine-material and immaterial—*paṭigha* does not lie unmanifest, but *avijjā* does.
—Yes. In those persons, in *apariyāpanna* (*Gotrabhū* and three persons ⁝); and in *Arahat*, in all states—*paṭigha* does not lie unmanifest; *avijjā* too.
(b) Latent state of *avijjā* does not lie unmanifest in this person at this plane. Does latent state of *paṭigha* not lie unmanifest in that person at that plane?
—Yes. Refer to the answer in *iv* (a) above.

58. *i* (a) Latent state of *māna* does not lie unmanifest in this person at this plane. Does latent state of *diṭṭhi* …..p….. *vicikicchā* not lie unmanifest in that person at that plane?
—No. In *Puthujjana*, with unpleasant feeling, *māna* does not lie unmanifest, but *vicikicchā* (and *diṭṭhi*) does.
—Yes. In those persons, in *apariyāpanna*; and in *Arahat*, in all places—*māna* does not lie unmanifest; *vicikicchā* (and *diṭṭhi*) too.
(b) Latent state of *vicikicchā* does not lie unmanifest in this person at this plane. Does latent state of *māna* not lie unmanifest in that person at that plane?
— No. In three persons ⁝ , with two feelings of the elemental world of sensuous desire, and in the elemental world of fine-material and immaterial, *vicikicchā* (and *diṭṭhi*) does not lie unmanifest, but *māna* does.
—Yes. Refer to the answer in *i* (a) above.

ii (a) Latent state of *māna* does not lie unmanifest in this person at this plane. Does latent state of *bhavarāga* not lie unmanifest in that person at that plane?
—Yes. (See below)
(b) Latent state of *bhavarāga* does not lie unmanifest in this person at this person. Does latent state of *māna* not lie unmanifest in that person at that plane?
—No. In four persons ④, with two feelings of the elemental world of sensuous desire, *bhavarāga* does not lie unmanifest, but *māna* does.

—Yes. In those persons, with unpleasant feeling (four persons ④), and in *apariyāpanna*; and in *Arahat*, in all places—*bhavarāga* does not lie unmanifest; *māna* too.

iii (a) Latent state of *māna* does not lie unmanifest in this person at this plane. Does latent state of *avijjā* not lie unmanifest in that person at that plane?
—No. In four persons ④ with unpleasant feeling, *māna* does not lie unmanifest, but *avijjā* does.
—Yes. In those (same) persons, in *apariyāpanna*; and in *Arahat*, in all places—*māna* does not lie unmanifest; *avijjā* too.
(b) Latent state of *avijjā* does not lie unmanifest in this person at this plane. Does latent state of *māna* not lie unmanifest in that person at that plane?
—Yes. Refer to the answer in *iii* (a) above.

59. *i* (a) Latent state of *diṭṭhi* does not lie unmanifest in this person at this plane. Does latent state of *vicikicchā* not lie unmanifest in that person at that plane?
—Yes (all, except Puthujjanas).
(b) Latent state of *vicikicchā* does not lie unmanifest in this person at this plane. Does latent state of *diṭṭhi* not lie unmanifest in that person at that plane?
—Yes. (Same as aforesaid)

ii (a) Latent state of *diṭṭhi* .....p..... *vicikicchā* does not lie unmanifest in this person at this plane. Does latent state of *bhavarāga* not lie unmanifest in that person at that plane?
—No. In three persons ⁝ , in elemental world of fine-material and immaterial, *vicikicchā* does not lie unmanifest (and *diṭṭhi*), but *bhavarāga* does.
—Yes. In those (same) persons, with three feelings of the elemental world of sensuous desire, and (those four persons) in *apariyāpanna*; and in *Arahat*, in all places—*vicikicchā* (and *diṭṭhi*) does not lie unmanifest; *bhavarāga* too.
(b) Latent state of *bhavarāga* does not lie unmanifest in this person at this plane. Does latent state of *vicikicchā* not lie unmanifest in that person at that plane?
—No. In *Puthujjana*, with three feelings of the elemental world of sensuous desire, *bhavarāga* does not lie unmanifest, but *vicikicchā* (and *diṭṭhi*) does.
—Yes. Refer to the answer in *ii* (a) above.

iii (a) Latent state of *vicikicchā* does not lie unmanifest in this person at this plane. Does latent state of *avijjā* not lie unmanifest in that person at that plane?
—No. In three persons ⁝ , with three feelings of the elemental world of sensuous desire, and in the elemental world of fine-material and immaterial, *vicikicchā* does not lie unmanifest, but *avijjā* does.
—Yes. In those (same) persons, in *apariyāpanna*; and in *Arahat*, in all places—*vicikicchā* does not lie unmanifest; *avijjā* too.
(b) Latent state of *avijjā* does not lie unmanifest in this person at this plane. Does latent state of *vicikicchā* not lie unmanifest in that person at that plane?
—Yes. Refer to the answer in *iii* (a) above.

60. *i* (a) Latent state of *bhavarāga* does not lie unmanifest in this person at this plane. Does latent state of *avijjā* not lie unmanifest in that person at that plane?
—No. In four persons ④ with three feelings of the elemental world of sensuous desire, *bhavarāga* does not lie unmanifest, but *avijjā* does.
—Yes. In those (four) persons, in *apariyāpanna*; and in *Arahat*, in all places—*bhavarāga* does not lie unmanifest; *avijjā* too.
(b) Latent state of *avijjā* does not lie unmanifest in this person at this plane. Does latent state of *bhavarāga* not lie unmanifest in that person at that plane?
—Yes. Refer to aforesaid.

Couplet-based

61. *i* (a) Latent states of *kāmarāga* and *paṭigha* do not lie unmanifest in this person at this plane. Does latent state of *māna* not lie unmanifest in that person at that plane?
—No. In three persons ③, in the elemental world of fine-material and immateria; in *Anāgāmi,* with two feelings of the elemental world of sensuous desire, and in the elemental world of fine-material and immaterial—*kāmarāga* and *paṭigha* do not lie unmanifest, but *māna* does.
—Yes. In those persons, in *apariyāpanna*; in those persons, with unpleasant feeling (*Anāgāmi*), and in *apariyāpanna*; in *Arahat*, in all places—*kāmarāga* and *paṭigha* do not lie unmanifest; *māna* too.
(b) Latent state of *māna* does not lie unmanifest in this person at this plane. Do latent states of *kāmarāga* and *paṭigha* not lie unmanifest in that person at that plane?
—No. In three persons ③ with unpleasant feeling, *māna* and *kāmarāga* do not lie unmanifest, but *paṭigha* does.
—Yes. Refer to aforesaid.

ii (a) Latent states of *kāmarāga* and *paṭigha* do not lie unmanifest in this person at this plane. Does latent state of *diṭṭhi* .....p..... *vicikicchā* not lie unmanifest in that person at that plane?
—No. In *Puthujjana*, in elemental world of fine-material and immaterial, *kāmarāga* and *paṭigha* do not lie unmanifest, but *vicikicchā* (and *diṭṭhi*) does.
—Yes. Refer to the answer in (b) below.
(b) Latent state of *vicikicchā* does not lie unmanifest in this person at this plane. Do latent states of *kāmarāga* and *paṭigha* not lie unmanifest in that person at that plane?
—No. In two persons ★, with unpleasant feeling, *vicikicchā* and *kāmarāga* (and *diṭṭhi*) do not lie unmanifest, but *paṭigha* does. In those (same) persons, with two feelings of the elemental world of sensuous desire, *vicikicchā* and *paṭigha* (and *diṭṭhi*) do not lie unmanifest, but *kāmarāga* does.
—Yes. In those (same) persons, in the elemental world of fine-material and immaterial, and (all those) in *apariyāpanna*; in two persons ☆, in all places—*vicikicchā* (and *diṭṭhi*) does not lie unmanifest; *kāmarāga* and *paṭigha* too.

iii (a) Latent states of *kāmarāga* and *paṭigha* do not lie unmanifest in this person at this plane. Does latent state of *bhavarāga* not lie unmanifest in that person at that plane?
—No. In three persons ③, in elemental world of fine-material and immaterial; and in *Anāgāmi*, in elemental world of fine-material and immaterial—*kāmarāga* and *paṭigha* do not lie unmanifest, but *bhavarāga* does.
—Yes. In those persons (*Anāgāmi*) with three feelings of the elemental world of sensuous desire; those in *apariyāpanna*; and *Arahat*, in all places—*kāmarāga* and *paṭigha* do not lie unmanifest; *bhavarāga* too.
(b) Latent state of *bhavarāga* does not lie unmanifest in this person at this plane. Do latent states of *kāmarāga* and *paṭigha* not lie unmanifest in that person at that plane?
—No. In three persons ③ with unpleasant feeling (in sensuous element), *bhavarāga* and *kāmarāga* do not lie unmanifest, but *paṭigha* does. In those (same) persons with two feelings of the elemental world of sensuous desire, neither *bhavarāga* nor *paṭigha* lies unmanifest, but *kāmarāga* does.
—Yes. Refer to the answer in *iii* (a) above.

iv (a) Neither latent state of *kāmarāga* nor latent state of *paṭigha* lies unmanifest in this person at this plane. Does latent state of *avijjā* not lie unmanifest in that person at that plane?
—No. In three persons ③ in the elemental world of fine-material and immaterial; in *Anāgāmi,* with three feelings of the elemental world of sensuous desire, and in the elemental world of fine-material and immaterial—neither *kāmarāga* nor *paṭigha* lies unmanifest, but *avijjā* does.
—Yes. In those persons. in *apariyāpanna*; and in *Arahat*, in all places—neither *kāmarāga* nor *paṭigha* lies unmanifest; *avijjā* too.
(b) Latent state of *avijjā* does not lie unmanifest in this person at this plane. Do latent states of *kāmarāga* and *paṭigha* not lie unmanifest in that person at that plane? —Yes. Refer to the answer in *iv* (a) above.

Triplet-based

62. *i* (a) Latent states of *kāmarāga*, *paṭigha* and *māna* does not lie unmanifest in this person at this plane. Does latent state of *diṭṭhi* .....p.... *vicikicchā* not lie unmanifest in that person at that plane? —Yes. Refer to the answer below.
(b) Latent state of *vicikicchā* does not lie unmanifest in this person at this plane. Do latent states of *kāmarāga*, *paṭigha* and *māna* not lie unmanifest in that person at that plane?
—No. In two persons ★ with unpleasant feeling, *vicikicchā*, *kāmarāga* and *māna* (and *diṭṭhi*) do not lie unmanifest, but *paṭigha* does. In those (same) persons, with two feelings of the elemental world of sensuous desire, *vicikicchā* and *paṭigha* (and *diṭṭhi*) do not lie unmanifest, but *kāmarāga* and *māna* do. In those (same) persons in the elemental world of fine-material and immaterial; and in *Anāgāmi,* with two feelings of the elemental world of sensuous desire, and in the elemental

world of fine-material and immaterial— *vicikicchā*, *kāmarāga* and *paṭigha* (and *diṭṭhi*) do not lie unmanifest, but *māna* does.
—Yes. In those persons.in *apariyāpanna* (*Gotrabhū* and two persons ★); in those persons, with unpleasant feeling, and in *apariyāpanna* (*Anāgāmi*); and in *Arahat*, in all places—*vicikicchā* (and *diṭṭhi*) does not lie unmanifest; *kāmarāga*, *paṭigha* and *māna* too.

ii (a) Latent states of *kāmarāga*, *paṭigha* and *māna* do not lie unmanifest in this person at this plane. Does latent state of *bhavarāga* not lie unmanifest in that person at that plane?
—Yes. Refer to the answer below.
(b) Latent state of *bhavarāga* does not lie unmanifest in this person at this plane. Do latent states of *kāmarāga*, *paṭigha* and *māna* not lie unmanifest in that person at that plane?
— No. In three persons ③ with unpleasant feeling, *bhavarāga*, *kāmarāga* and *māna* do not lie unmanifest, but *paṭigha* does. In those (same) persons, with two feelings of the elemental world of sensuous desire, *bhavarāga* and *paṭigha* do not lie unmanifest, but *kāmarāga* and *māna* do. In *Anāgāmi*, with two feelings of the elemental world of sensuous desire, *bhavarāga*, *kāmarāga* and *paṭigha* do not lie unmanifest, but *māna* does.
—Yes. In those persons, in *apariyāpanna* (three persons); in those persons, with unpleasant feeling, and in *apariyāpanna* (*Anāgāmi*); and in *Arahat*, in all places—*bhavarāga* does not lie unmanifest; *kāmarāga*, *paṭigha* and *māna* too.

iii (a) Latent states of *kāmarāga*, *paṭigha* and *māna* do not lie unmanifest in this person at this plane. Does latent state of *avijjā* not lie unmanifest in that person at that plane?
— No. In *Anāgāmi*, with unpleasant feeling, *kāmarāga*, *paṭigha* and *māna* do not lie unmanifest, but *avijjā* does.
—Yes. In those persons, in *apariyāpanna*; and in *Arahat*, in all places—*kāmarāga*, *paṭigha* and *māna* do not lie unmanifest; *avijjā* too.
(b) Latent state of *avijjā* does not lie unmanifest in this person at this plane. Do latent states of *kāmarāga*, *paṭigha* and *māna* not lie unmanifest in that person at that plane? —Yes. Refer to the aforesaid.

Quadruplet-based

63. *i* (a) Latent states of *kāmarāga*, *paṭigha*, *māna* and *diṭṭhi* do not lie unmanifest in this person at this plane. Does latent state of *vicikicchā* not lie unmanifest in that person at that plane? —Yes. Refer to the answer below.
(b) Latent state of *vicikicchā* does not lie unmanifest in this person at this plane. Do latent states of *kāmarāga*, *paṭigha*, *māna* and *diṭṭhi* not lie unmanifest in that person at that plane?
—No. In two persons ★, with unpleasant feeling, *vicikicchā*, *kāmarāga*, *māna* and *diṭṭhi* do not lie unmanifest, but *paṭigha* does. In those (same) persons, with two feelings of the elemental world of sensuous desire, *vicikicchā* and *paṭigha*

do not lie unmanifest, but *kāmarāga* and *māna* do. In those (same) persons (in the elemental world of fine-material and immaterial); in *Anāgāmi,* with two feelings of the elemental world of sensuous desire, and in the elemental world of fine-material and immaterial—*vicikicchā*, *kāmarāga*, *paṭigha* and *diṭṭhi* do not lie unmanifest, but *māna* does.
—Yes. In those persons, in *apariyāpanna* (three persons); in those persons, with unpleasant feeling, and in *apariyāpanna* (*Anāgāmi*); in *Arahat*, in all places—*vicikicchā* does not lie unmanifest; *kāmarāga*, *paṭigha*, *māna* and *diṭṭhi* too.

Quintuplet-based

64. *i* (a) Latent states of *kāmarāga*, *paṭigha*, *māna*, *diṭṭhi* and *vicikicchā* do not lie unmanifest in this person at this plane. Does latent state of *bhavarāga* not lie unmanifest in that person at that plane?
—Yes. Refer to the answer below.
(b) Latent state of *bhavarāga* does not lie unmanifest in this person at this plane. Do latent states of *kāmarāga*, *paṭigha*, *māna*, *diṭṭhi* and *vicikicchā* not lie unmanifest in that person at that plane?
—No. In *Puthujjana*, with unpleasant feeling, *bhavarāga*, *kāmarāga* and *māna* do not lie unmanifest, but *paṭigha*, *diṭṭhi* and *vicikicchā* do. In those (same) persons, with two feelings of the elemental world of sensuous desire, *bhavarāga* and *paṭigha* do not lie unmanifest, but *kāmarāga*, *māna*, *diṭṭhi* and *vicikicchā* do. In two persons ★, with unpleasant feeling, *bhavarāga*, *kāmarāga*, *māna*, *diṭṭhi* and *vicikicchā* do not lie unmanifest, but *paṭigha* does. In those (same) persons, with two feelings of the elemental world of sensuous desire, *bhavarāga*, *paṭigha*, *diṭṭhi* and *vicikicchā* do not lie unmanifest, but *kāmarāga* and *māna* do. In *Anāgāmi*, with two feelings of the elemental world of sensuous desire, *bhavarāga*, *kāmarāga*, *paṭigha*, *diṭṭhi* and *vicikicchā* do not lie unmanifest, but *māna* does.
—Yes. In those persons, in *apariyāpanna* (three persons); in those persons, with unpleasant feeling, and in *apariyāpanna* (*Anāgāmi*); in *Arahat*, in all places—*bhavarāga* do not lie unmanifest; *kāmarāga*, *paṭigha*, *māna*, *diṭṭhi*,*vicikicchā* too.

Sextuplet-based

65. *i* (a) Latent states of *kāmarāga*, *paṭigha*, *māna*, *diṭṭhi*, *vicikicchā* and *bhavarāga* do not lie unmanifest in this person at this plane? Does latent state of *avijjā* not lie unmanifest in that person at that plane?
—No. In *Anāgāmi*, with unpleasant feeling, *kāmarāga*, *paṭigha*, *māna*, *diṭṭhi*, *vicikicchā* and *bhavarāga* do not lie unmanifest, but *avijjā* does.
—Yes. In those persons, in *apariyāpanna*; in *Arahat*, in all places—*kāmarāga*, *paṭigha*, *māna*, *diṭṭhi*, *vicikicchā* and *bhavarāga* do not lie unmanifest; *avijjā* too.
(b) Latent state of *avijjā* does not lie unmanifest in this person at this plane. Do latent states of *kāmarāga*, *paṭigha*, *māna*, *diṭṭhi*, *vicikicchā* and *bhavarāga* not lie unmanifest in that person at that plane? —Yes. Refer to the aforesaid.

7.2.2 Unmanifest with latent states (*Sānusaya*)

Chart 7.4 Unmanifest with latent states (enquiries by person)

Y: is unmanifest with
N: is not unmanifest with (either it is inexistent, or has been renounced and eliminated)

	latent state of : kāmarāga	paṭigha	māna	diṭṭhi	vicikicchā	bhavarāga	avijjā
Puthujjana	Y	Y	Y	Y	Y	Y	Y
Sotāpanna	Y	Y	Y	N	N	Y	Y
Sakadāgāmi	Y	Y	Y	N	N	Y	Y
Anāgāmi	N	N	Y	N	N	Y	Y
Arahat	N	N	N	N	N	N	N

Chart 7.4 above summarises the questions and answers from catechisms nos. 66-76 and from 99-109. The answers are the same as those in Chart 7.1.

Chart 7.5 Unmanifest with latent states (enquiries by plane)

Y: is unmanifest with
N: is not unmanifest with (either it is inexistent, or has been renounced and eliminated)

		latent state of : kāmarāga	paṭigha	māna	diṭṭhi	vicikicchā	bhavarāga	avijjā
In unpleasant feeling	in the elemental world of sensuous desire	N	Y	N	Y	Y	N	Y
In pleasant feeling		Y	N	Y	Y	Y	N	Y
In neither pleasant feeling nor unpleasant feeling		Y	N	Y	Y	Y	N	Y
In unpleasant feeling	in the elemental world of fine-material and immaterial	N	N	Y	Y	Y	Y	Y
In pleasant feeling		N	N	Y	Y	Y	Y	Y
In neither pleasant feeling nor unpleasant feeling		N	N	Y	Y	Y	Y	Y
In unpleasant feeling	in *apariyāpanna* (supramundane)	N	N	N	N	N	N	N
In pleasant feeling		N	N	N	N	N	N	N
In neither pleasant feeling nor unpleasant feeling		N	N	N	N	N	N	N

Chart 7.5 above summarises the catechisms nos. 77-87 and from 110-120 with regard to plane. The answers are the same as those in Chart 7.2.

Chart 7.6 Unmanifest with latent states (enquiries by person and plane)

Y : Is unmanifest with; N : is not unmanifest with (either it is inexistent, or has been eliminated)

		in elemental world of sensuous desire	in elemental world of fine-material and immaterial	in *apariyāpanna* (supramundane)	latent state of : kāmarāga	paṭigha	māna	diṭṭhi	vicikicchā	bhavarāga	avijjā
In *Puthujjana* (including *Gotrabhū* at *apariyāpanna*)	with unpleasant feeling	•			N	Y	N	Y	Y	N	Y
	with pleasant feeling	•			Y	N	Y	Y	Y	N	Y
	with neither pleasant feeling nor unpleasant feeling	•			Y	N	Y	Y	Y	N	Y
	with unpleasant feeling		•		N	N	Y	Y	Y	Y	Y
	with pleasant feeling		•		N	N	Y	Y	Y	Y	Y
	with neither pleasant feeling nor unpleasant feeling		•		N	N	Y	Y	Y	Y	Y
	with unpleasant feeling			•	N	N	N	N	N	N	N
	with pleasant feeling			•	N	N	N	N	N	N	N
	with neither pleasant feeling nor unpleasant feeling			•	N	N	N	N	N	N	N
In *Sotāpanna*	with unpleasant feeling	•			N	Y	N	N	N	N	Y
	with pleasant feeling	•			Y	N	Y	N	N	N	Y
	with neither pleasant feeling nor unpleasant feeling	•			Y	N	Y	N	N	N	Y
	with unpleasant feeling		•		N	N	Y	N	N	Y	Y
	with pleasant feeling		•		N	N	Y	N	N	Y	Y
	with neither pleasant feeling nor unpleasant feeling		•		N	N	Y	N	N	Y	Y
	with unpleasant feeling			•	N	N	N	N	N	N	N
	with pleasant feeling			•	N	N	N	N	N	N	N
	with neither pleasant feeling nor unpleasant feeling			•	N	N	N	N	N	N	N
In *Sakadāgāmi*	with unpleasant feeling	•			N	Y	N	N	N	N	Y
	with pleasant feeling	•			Y	N	Y	N	N	N	Y
	with neither pleasant feeling nor unpleasant feeling	•			Y	N	Y	N	N	N	Y
	with unpleasant feeling		•		N	N	Y	N	N	Y	Y
	with pleasant feeling		•		N	N	Y	N	N	Y	Y
	with neither pleasant feeling nor unpleasant feeling		•		N	N	Y	N	N	Y	Y
	with unpleasant feeling			•	N	N	N	N	N	N	N
	with pleasant feeling			•	N	N	N	N	N	N	N
	with neither pleasant feeling nor unpleasant feeling			•	N	N	N	N	N	N	N
In Anāgāmi	with unpleasant feeling	•			N	N	N	N	N	N	Y
	with pleasant feeling	•			N	N	Y	N	N	N	Y
	with neither pleasant feeling nor unpleasant feeling	•			N	N	Y	N	N	N	Y
	with unpleasant feeling		•		N	N	Y	N	N	Y	Y
	with pleasant feeling		•		N	N	Y	N	N	Y	Y
	with neither pleasant feeling nor unpleasant feeling		•		N	N	Y	N	N	Y	Y
	with unpleasant feeling			•	N	N	N	N	N	N	N
	with pleasant feeling			•	N	N	N	N	N	N	N
	with neither pleasant feeling nor unpleasant feeling			•	N	N	N	N	N	N	N
In *Arahat*	with unpleasant feeling	•			N	N	N	N	N	N	N
	with pleasant feeling	•			N	N	N	N	N	N	N
	with neither pleasant feeling nor unpleasant feeling	•			N	N	N	N	N	N	N
	with unpleasant feeling		•		N	N	N	N	N	N	N
	with pleasant feeling		•		N	N	N	N	N	N	N
	with neither pleasant feeling nor unpleasant feeling		•		N	N	N	N	N	N	N
	with unpleasant feeling			•	N	N	N	N	N	N	N
	with pleasant feeling			•	N	N	N	N	N	N	N
	with neither pleasant feeling nor unpleasant feeling			•	N	N	N	N	N	N	N

Chart 7.6 above summarises the questions and answers from catechisms nos. 88-98 and from 121-131, with regard to person and plane. The answers are the same as those in Chart 7.3.

Forward enquiries by person

66. *i* (a) This person is unmanifest with latent state of *kāmarāga*. Is that person unmanifest with latent state of *paṭigha*? —Yes. (three persons ③)
(b) This person is unmanifest with latent state of *paṭigha*. Is that person unmanifest with latent state of *kāmarāga*? —Yes. (Same as above)

ii (a) This person is unmanifest with latent state of *kāmarāga*. Is that person unmanifest with latent state of *māna*? —Yes. (Same as below)
(b) This person is unmanifest with latent state of *māna*. Is that person unmanifest with latent state of *kāmarāga*?
—No. *Anāgāmi* is unmanifest with latent state of *māna*, and not unmanifest with latent state of *kāmarāga*.
—Yes. Three persons ③ (*Puthujjana, Sotāpanna, Sakadāgāmi*) are unmanifest with both latent states of *māna* and *kāmarāga*. ..... p .....

Forward enquiries by plane

77. *i* (a) This plane is unmanifest with latent state of *kāmarāga*. Is that plane unmanifest with latent state of *paṭigha*? —No. (The elemental world of sensuous desire is unmanifest with *kāmarāga*, but not *paṭigha*).
(b) This plane is unmanifest with the latent state of *paṭigha*. Is that plane unmanifest with the latent state of *kāmarāga*? —No. (Unpleasant feeling in elemental world of sensuous desire is unmanifest with latent state of *paṭigha* , but not latent state of *kāmarāga*). ..... p .....

Forward enquiries by person and plane

88. This person is unmanifest with latent state of *kāmarāga* at this plane. Is that person unmanifest with latent state of *paṭigha* at that plane?
—No. (in three persons ③ with two feelings of the elemental world of sensuous desire).
(b) This person is unmanifest with latent state of *paṭigha* at this plane. Is that person unmanifest with latent state of *kāmarāga* at that plane?
—No. (In three persons ③ with unpleasant feeling of the elemental world of sensuous desire) ..... p .....

Opposite enquiries by person
Opposite enquiries by plane
Opposite enquiries by person and plane

The remaining catechisms as shown above should be constructed in the same manner as in the given examples (continue until nos. 131), or by following the same method of iterations as in section 7.2.1. The answers are the same as those.

7.2.3 Renouncing latent states (*Pajahana*)

Chart 7.7 Renouncing latent states (enquiries by person)

Y: yes, is renouncing; R_p: is renouncing a part of it
N: no, is not renouncing (sometimes avoids duplication in individual abandonment of states)
NR_p : is not renouncing completely, except for renouncing a part of it

	the latent state of:						
	kāmarāga	paṭigha	māna	diṭṭhi	vicikicchā	bhavarāga	avijjā
Attainer of the eight Path of 'stream-winning' (*Sotāpattimaggasamaṅgī*)	N R_p	N R_p	N R_p	Y	Y	N R_p	N R_p
Attainer of the 'once-returning' Path (*Sakadāgāmimaggasamaṅgī*)	N	N	N	N	N	N	N
Attainer of the 'non-returning' Path (*Anāgāmimaggasamaṅgī*)	Y	Y	N R_p	N	N	N R_p	N R_p
Attainer of the highest *Arahatta* Path (*Aggamaggasamaṅgī*)	N	N	Y	N	N	Y	Y

Chart 7.7 above summarises the questions and answers from catechisms nos. 132-142 and from 154-164. Attainer of the 'stream-winning' Path eliminated the 4 greed-roted cittas associated with wrong views and 1 delusion-rooted cittas associated with doubt, hence he is renouncing [55] *diṭṭhi* and *vicikicchā*, and only renouncing a part of the remaining latent states. Attainer of the 'once-returning' Path only attenuates *māna*, *diṭṭhi*, *vicikicchā*, *bhavarāga* and *avijjā*. Attainer of the 'non-returning' Path eliminated the 4 greed-roted cittas dissociated from wrong views and 2 hatred-rooted cittas, hence he is renouncing *kāmarāga* (sensuous desires) and *paṭigha* (aversion); *māna* (conceit), *bhavarāga* (desires for existence or becoming) and *avijjā* (ignorance) are renounced only to some degree. Attainer of the *Arahatta* Path eliminated the last remaining delusion-rooted citta associated with restlessness (*uddhacca*), hence he is renouncing altogether the latent states of *māna*, *bhavarāga* and *avijjā*.

Chart 7.8 below summarises the questions and answers from catechisms nos. 143-153 and from 176-186. The data and answers are quite straightforward. There is no more latent state to be renounced in *apariyāpanna*, for they are done in the mundane worlds prior to that.

---

[55] *pajahati*: it is preferable to interpret it in present participle of 'renouncing' instead of 'renounce'.For example, we say that *Sotāpattimaggasamaṅgī* is renouncing *diṭṭhi* and *vicikicchā; Anāgāmimaggasamaṅgī* is renouncing *kāmarāga* and *paṭigha*; thereby *Aggamaggasamaṅgī* is not at the same renouncing any of these four anusayas. Otherwise we may be perceiving wrongly as attainer of the *Arahatta* Path 'does not renounce' at all any of these four anusayas.

Chart 7.8 Renouncing latent states (enquiries by plane)

Y: yes, is thereat renounced; N: no, thereat is not renounced

		latent state of :						
		kāmarāga	paṭigha	māna	diṭṭhi	vicikicchā	bhavarāga	avijjā
In unpleasant feeling	in elemental world of sensuous desire	N	Y	N	Y	Y	N	Y
In pleasant feeling		Y	N	Y	Y	Y	N	Y
In neither pleasant feeling nor unpleasant feeling		Y	N	Y	Y	Y	N	Y
In unpleasant feeling	in elemental world of fine-material and immaterial	N	N	Y	Y	Y	Y	Y
In pleasant feeling		N	N	Y	Y	Y	Y	Y
In neither pleasant feeling nor unpleasant feeling		N	N	Y	Y	Y	Y	Y
In unpleasant feeling	in *apariyāpanna* (supramundane)	N	N	N	N	N	N	N
In pleasant feeling		N	N	N	N	N	N	N
In neither pleasant feeling nor unpleasant feeling		N	N	N	N	N	N	N

The following Chart 7.9 summarises the questions and answers from catechisms nos. 154-164 and from 187-197. The denoted symbol NR_p means that the particular latent state is not renounced completely, because only a part of it is being renounced. For examples, *Sotāpatti* Path-attainer is only renouncing some of *kāmarāga* and *paṭigha*, in the element world of desire; renouncing only some of *māna* in two feelings of the elemental world of sensuous desire, and in the elemental world of fine-materiality and immateriality; renouncing only some of *avijjā* in the elemental world of sensuous desire, fine-materiality and immateriality; and is only renouncing some of *bhavarāga* in the elemental world of fine-materiality and immateriality. *Sakadāgāmi* Path-attainer is not renouncing the remaining latent states, except for only making attenuation of them. In all four persons in *apariyāpanna*, none of them has any remaining underlying latency to be renounced. *Anāgāmi* Path-attainer is renouncing *kāmarāga* and *paṭigha* completely; *māna*, *bhavarāga* and *avijjā* are renounced through *Arahatta* Path-attainer.

The Pāli text in nos. 154-164 and nos. 187-197 has not given any indication that *māna*, *bhavarāga* and *avijjā* are renouncing in part by *Anāgāmi* Path-attainer in the elemental world of fine-materiality and immateriality, except saying that the three latencies are therein not renouncing. It only indicates that *māna* and *avijjā* are renouncing in part in the element world of desire. I have included my comment in the chart (indicated by $\boldsymbol{R_p}$ in boldface) that *māna*, *bhavarāga* and *avijjā* should also be renouncing in part by *Anāgāmi* Path-attainer in the elemental world of fine-materiality and immateriality. I could be wrong.

Chart 7.9 Renouncing latent states (enquiries by person and plane)

Y: yes, is renouncing; R_p: is renouncing a part of it
N: no, is not renouncing (sometimes avoids duplication in individual abandonment of states)
NR_p : is not renouncing completely, except for renouncing a part of it

		in elemental world of sensuous desire	in elemental world of fine-material and immaterial	in *apariyāpanna* (supramundane)	latent state of: kāmarāga	paṭigha	māna	diṭṭhi	vicikicchā	bhavarāga	avijjā
Sotāpatti Path-attainer	with unpleasant feeling	•			N	NR_p	N	Y	Y	N	NR_p
	with pleasant feeling	•			NR_p	N	NR_p	Y	Y	N	NR_p
	with neither pleasant feeling nor unpleasant feeling	•			NR_p	N	NR_p	Y	Y	N	NR_p
	with unpleasant feeling		•		N	N	NR_p	Y	Y	NR_p	NR_p
	with pleasant feeling		•		N	N	NR_p	Y	Y	NR_p	NR_p
	with neither pleasant feeling nor unpleasant feeling		•		N	N	NR_p	Y	Y	NR_p	NR_p
	with unpleasant feeling			•	N	N	N	N	N	N	N
	with pleasant feeling			•	N	N	N	N	N	N	N
	with neither pleasant feeling nor unpleasant feeling			•	N	N	N	N	N	N	N
Sakadāgāmi Path-attainer	with unpleasant feeling	•			N	N	N	N	N	N	N
	with pleasant feeling	•			N	N	N	N	N	N	N
	with neither pleasant feeling nor unpleasant feeling	•			N	N	N	N	N	N	N
	with unpleasant feeling		•		N	N	N	N	N	N	N
	with pleasant feeling		•		N	N	N	N	N	N	N
	with neither pleasant feeling nor unpleasant feeling		•		N	N	N	N	N	N	N
	with unpleasant feeling			•	N	N	N	N	N	N	N
	with pleasant feeling			•	N	N	N	N	N	N	N
	with neither pleasant feeling nor unpleasant feeling			•	N	N	N	N	N	N	N
Anāgāmi Path-attainer	with unpleasant feeling	•			N	Y	N	N	N	N	NR_p
	with pleasant feeling	•			Y	N	NR_p	N	N	N	NR_p
	with neither pleasant feeling nor unpleasant feeling	•			Y	N	NR_p	N	N	N	NR_p
	with unpleasant feeling		•		N	N	N**R_p**	N	N	N**R_p**	N**R_p**
	with pleasant feeling		•		N	N	N**R_p**	N	N	N**R_p**	N**R_p**
	with neither pleasant feeling nor unpleasant feeling		•		N	N	N**R_p**	N	N	N**R_p**	N**R_p**
	with unpleasant feeling			•	N	N	N	N	N	N	N
	with pleasant feeling			•	N	N	N	N	N	N	N
	with neither pleasant feeling nor unpleasant feeling			•	N	N	N	N	N	N	N
Arahatta Path-attainer	with unpleasant feeling	•			N	N	N	N	N	N	Y
	with pleasant feeling	•			N	N	Y	N	N	N	Y
	with neither pleasant feeling nor unpleasant feeling	•			N	N	Y	N	N	N	Y
	with unpleasant feeling		•		N	N	Y	N	N	Y	Y
	with pleasant feeling		•		N	N	Y	N	N	Y	Y
	with neither pleasant feeling nor unpleasant feeling		•		N	N	Y	N	N	Y	Y
	with unpleasant feeling			•	N	N	N	N	N	N	N
	with pleasant feeling			•	N	N	N	N	N	N	N
	with neither pleasant feeling nor unpleasant feeling			•	N	N	N	N	N	N	N

Forward enquiries by person

Mono-based

132. This person is renouncing latent state of *kāmarāga*. Is that person renouncing latent state of *paṭigha*? —Yes. (*Anāgāmi* Path-attainer)
This person is renouncing latent state of *paṭigha*. Is that person renouncing latent state of *kāmarāga*? —Yes. (Same as aforesaid)

This person is renouncing latent state of *kāmarāga*. Is that person renouncing latent state of *māna*?
— (*Anāgāmi* Path-attainer) is renouncing a part of *māna*. (without eradication)
This person is renouncing latent state of *māna*. Is that person renouncing latent state of *kāmarāga*?
—No. (*Arahatta* Path-attainer)

This person is renouncing latent state of *kāmarāga*. Is that person renouncing latent state of *diṭṭhi* …..p….. *vicikicchā*? —No. (*Anāgāmi* Path-attainer)
This person is renouncing latent state of *vicikicchā*. Is that person renouncing latent state of *kāmarāga*?
—(*Sotāpatti* Path-attainer) is renouncing a part of *kāmarāga*.

This person is renouncing latent state of *kāmarāga*. Is that person renouncing latent state of *bhavarāga* …..p….. *avijjā*?
—(*Anāgāmi* Path-attainer) is renouncing a part of *bhavarāga* and *avijjā*.
This person is renouncing latent state of *avijjā*. Is that person renouncing latent state of *kāmarāga*? —No. (*Arahatta* Path-attainer)

133. This person is renouncing latent state of *paṭigha*. Is that person renouncing latent state of *māna*? —(*Anāgāmi* Path-attainer) is renouncing a part of *māna*.
This person is renouncing latent state of *māna*. Is that person renouncing latent state of *paṭigha*? —No. (*Arahatta* Path-attainer)

This person is renouncing latent state of *paṭigha*. Is that person renouncing latent state of *diṭṭhi* …..p….. *vicikicchā*? —No. (*Anāgāmi* Path-attainer)
This person is renouncing latent state of *vicikicchā*. Is that person renouncing latent state of *paṭigha*? —(*Sotāpatti* Path-attainer) renouncing a part of *paṭigha*.

This person is renouncing latent state of *paṭigha*. Is that person renouncing latent state of *bhavarāga* …..p….. *avijjā*?
— (*Anāgāmi* Path-attainer) is renouncing a part of *bhavarāga* (and *avijjā*).
This person is renouncing latent state of *avijjā*. Is that person renouncing latent state of *paṭigha*? —No. (*Arahatta* Path-attainer)

134. This person is renouncing latent state of *māna*. Is that person renouncing latent state of *diṭṭhi* …..p….. *vicikicchā*? —No. (*Arahatta* Path-attainer)

This person is renouncing latent state of *vicikicchā*. Is that person renouncing latent state of *māna*? —(*Sotāpatti* Path-attainer) is renouncing a part of *māna*.

This person is renouncing latent state of *māna*. Is that person renouncing latent state of *bhavarāga* …..p….. a*vijjā*? —Yes. (*Arahatta* Path-attainer)
(This person) is renouncing latent state of *avijjā*. Is that person renouncing latent state of *māna*? —Yes. (*Arahatta* Path-attainer)

135. This person is renouncing latent state of *diṭṭhi*. Is that person renouncing latent state of *vicikicchā*? —Yes. (*Sotāpatti* Path-attainer)
This person is renouncing latent state of *vicikicchā*. Is that person renouncing latent state of *diṭṭhi*? —Yes (*Sotāpatti* Path-attainer) …..p…..

136. This person is renouncing latent state of *vicikicchā*. Is that person renouncing latent state of *bhavarāga* …..p….. *avijjā*?
—(*Sotāpatti* Path-attainer) is renouncing a part of *bhavarāga* (and *avijjā*).
This person is renouncing latent state of *avijjā*. Is that person renouncing latent state of *vicikicchā*? —No. (*Arahatta* Path-attainer)

137. This person is renouncing latent state of *bhavarāga*. Is that person renouncing latent state of *avijjā*? —Yes. (*Arahatta* Path-attainer)
This person is renouncing latent state of *avijjā*. Is that person renouncing latent state of *bhavarāga*? —Yes. (*Arahatta* Path-attainer)

Couplet-based

138. This person is renouncing latent states of *kāmarāga* and *paṭigha*. Is that person renouncing latent state of *māna*?
—(*Anāgāmi* Path-attainer) is renouncing a part of *māna*.
This person is renouncing latent state of *māna*. Is that person renouncing latent states of *kāmarāga* and *paṭigha*? —No. (*Arahatta* Path-attainer)

This person is renouncing latent states of *kāmarāga* and *paṭigha*. Is that person renouncing latent state of *diṭṭhi* …..p….. *vicikicchā*?
—No. (*Anāgāmi* Path-attainer)
This person is renouncing latent state of *vicikicchā*. Is that person renouncing latent states of *kāmarāga* and *paṭigha*?
—(*Sotāpatti* Path-attainer) is renouncing a part of *kāmarāga* and *paṭigha*.

This person is renouncing latent states of *kāmarāga* and *paṭigha*. Is that person renouncing latent state of *bhavarāga* …..p….. *avijjā*?
—(*Anāgāmi* Path-attainer) is renouncing a part of *bhavarāga* (and *avijjā*).
This person is renouncing latent state of *avijjā*. Is that person renouncing latent states of *kāmarāga* and *paṭigha*? —No. (*Arahatta* Path-attainer)

Triplet-based

139. This person is renouncing latent states of *kāmarāga*, *paṭigha* and *māna*. Is that person renouncing latent state of *diṭṭhi* .....p..... *vicikicchā*?
—None. (No such person who is renouncing all of them at the same time)
This person is renouncing latent state of *vicikicchā*. Is that person renouncing latent states of *kāmarāga*, *paṭigha* and *māna*?
— (*Sotāpatti* Path-attainer) is renouncing a part of *kāmarāga*, *paṭigha* and *māna*.

This person is renouncing latent states of *kāmarāga*, *paṭigha* and *māna*. Is that person renouncing latent state of *bhavarāga* .....p..... *avijjā*? —None.
This person is renouncing latent state of *avijjā*. Is that person renouncing latent states of *kāmarāga*, *paṭigha* and *māna*?
—No. (*Arahatta* Path-attainer) renouncing *avijjā*, *māna*, not *kāmarāga*, *paṭigha*

Quadruplet-based

140. This person is renouncing latent states of *kāmarāga*, *paṭigha*, *māna* and *diṭṭhi*. Is that person renouncing latent state of *vicikicchā*? —None.
This person is renouncing latent state of *vicikicchā*. Is that person renouncing latent states of *kāmarāga*, *paṭigha*, *māna* and *diṭṭhi*?
—(*Sotāpatti* Path-attainer) is renouncing *vicikicchā*, and also renouncing a part of *kāmarāga*, *paṭigha* and *māna* ....p....

Quintuplet-based

141. This person is renouncing latent states of *kāmarāga*, *paṭigha*, *māna*, *diṭṭhi* and *vicikicchā*. Is that person renouncing latent state of *bhavarāga* .....p..... *avijjā*? —None.
This person is renouncing latent state of *avijjā*. Is that person renouncing latent states of *kāmarāga*, *paṭigha*, *māna*, *diṭṭhi* and *vicikicchā*?
— (*Arahatta* Path-attainer) is renouncing *avijjā*, and *māna*, not the remaining.

Sextuplet-based

142. This person is renouncing latent state of *kāmarāga*, *paṭigha*, *māna*, *diṭṭhi*, *vicikicchā* and *bhavarāga*. Is that person renouncing latent state of *avijjā*?
—None.
This person is renouncing latent state of *avijjā*. Is that person renouncing latent states of *kāmarāga*, *paṭigha*, *māna*, *diṭṭhi*, *vicikicchā* and *bhavarāga*?
— (*Arahatta* Path-attainer) is renouncing *māna* and *bhavarāga*.

Forward enquiries by plane

Mono-based

143. This plane is renouncing latent state of *kāmarāga*. Is that plane renouncing latent state of *paṭigha*? (or, Latent state of *kāmarāga* is renounced at this plane. Is latent state of *paṭigha* renounced at that plane?
—No. (In two feelings of the elemental world of sensuous desire)

Latent state of *paṭigha* is renounced at this plane. Is Latent state of *kāmarāga* renounced at this plane?
—No. (In unpleasant feeling, in the elemental world of sensuous desire)

Latent state of *kāmarāga* is renounced at this plane. Is latent state of *māna* renounced at that plane? —Yes. Refer to the answer below.
Latent state of *māna* is renounced at this plane. Is latent state of *kāmarāga* renounced at that plane?
—No. In the elemental world of fine-material and immaterial, *māna* is renounced; *kāmarāga* is not.
—Yes. In two feelings of the elemental world of sensuous desire, *māna* is renounced; *kāmarāga* too.

Latent state of *kāmarāga* is renounced at this plane. Is latent state of *diṭṭhi* .....p..... *vicikicchā* renounced at that plane?—Yes. Refer to answer below.
Latent state of *vicikicchā* is renounced at this plane. Is latent state of *kāmarāga* renounced at that plane?
—No. In unpleasant feeling, in the elemental world of fine-material and immaterial *vicikicchā* (and *diṭṭhi*) is renounced; *kāmarāga* is not.
—Yes. In two feelings of the elemental world of sensuous desire, *vicikicchā* (and *diṭṭhi*) is renounced; *kāmarāga* too.

Latent state of *kāmarāga* is renounced at this plane. Is latent state of *bhavarāga* renounced at that plane?
—No. (In two feelings of the elemental world of sensuous desire)
Latent state of *bhavarāga* is renounced at this plane. Is latent state of *kāmarāga* renounced at that plane?
—No. (In the elemental world of fine-material and immaterial)

Latent state of *kāmarāga* is renounced at this plane. Is latent state of *avijjā* renounced at that plane?
—Yes. Refer to the answer below.
Latent state of *avijjā* is renounced at this plane. Is latent state of *kāmarāga* renounced at that plane?
—No. In unpleasant feeling, in the elemental world of fine-material and immaterial, *avijjā* is renounced; *kāmarāga* is not.
—Yes. In two feelings of the elemental world of sensuous desire, both *avijjā*, and *kāmarāga* are renounced.

144. Latent state of *paṭigha* is renounced at this plane. Is latent state of *māna* renounced at that plane? —No. (In unpleasant feeling, in the elemental world of sensuous desire)
Latent state of *māna* is renounced at this plane. Is latent state of *paṭigha* renounced at that plane? —No. (In two feelings of the elemental world of sensuous desire, and in the elemental world of fine-material and immaterial)

Latent state of *paṭigha* is renounced at this plane. Is latent state of *diṭṭhi* …..p….. *vicikicchā* renounced at that plane?
—Yes. Refer to the answer below.
Latent state of *vicikicchā* is renounced at this plane. Is latent state of *paṭigha* renounced at that plane?
—No. In two feelings of the elemental world of sensuous desire, and in elemental world of fine-material and immaterial, *vicikicchā* (and *diṭṭhi*) is renounced; *paṭigha* is not.
—Yes. In unpleasant feeling (in sensuous element), *vicikicchā* and *paṭigha* (and *diṭṭhi*) are renounced .

Latent state of *paṭigha* is renounced at this plane. Is latent state of *bhavarāga* renounced at that plane?
—No. (In unpleasant feeling, in the elemental world of sensuous desire)
Latent state of *bhavarāga* is renounced at this plane. Is latent state of *paṭigha* renounced at that plane?
—No. (In the elemental world of fine-material and immaterial)

Latent state of *paṭigha* is renounced at this plane. Is latent state of *avijjā* renounced at that plane? —Yes.
Latent state of *avijjā* is renounced at this plane. Is latent state of *paṭigha* renounced at that plane?
—No. In two feelings of the elemental world of sensuous desire, and in the elemental world of fine-material and immaterial, *avijjā* is renounced; *paṭigha* is not.
—Yes. In unpleasant feeling (in sensuous element), both *avijjā* and *paṭigha* are renounced.

145. Latent state of *māna* is renounced at this plane. Is latent state of *diṭṭhi* …..p….. *vicikicchā* renounced at that plane? —Yes. See answer below.
Latent state of *vicikicchā* is renounced at this plane. Is *māna* renounced at that plane?
— No. In unpleasant feeling (in sensuous element), *vicikicchā* (and *diṭṭhi*) is renounced; *māna* is not renounced.
—Yes. In two feelings of the elemental world of sensuous desire, and in elemental world of fine-material and immaterial, *vicikicchā* and *māna* (and *diṭṭhi*) are renounced.

Latent state of *māna* is renounced at this plane. Is latent state of *bhavarāga* renounced at that plane?
— No. In two feelings of the elemental world of sensuous desire, *māna* is renounced; but *bhavarāga* is not.
—Yes. In the elemental world of fine-material and immaterial, both *māna* and *bhavarāga* are renounced.
Latent state of *bhavarāga* is renounced at this plane. Is latent state of *māna* renounced at that plane? —Yes. Refer to the aforesaid.

Latent state of *māna* is renounced at this plane. Is latent state of *avijjā* renounced at that plane? —Yes. Refer to the answer below.
Latent state of *avijjā* is renounced at this plane. Is latent state of *māna* renounced at that plane?
— No. In unpleasant feeling, *avijjā* is renounced; *māna* is not.
—Yes. In two feelings of the elemental world of sensuous desire, and in elemental world of fine-material and immaterial, both *avijjā* and *māna* are renounced.

146. Latent state of *diṭṭhi* is renounced at this plane. Is latent state of *vicikicchā* renounced at that plane?
—Yes. (in elemental world of sensuous desire, fine-material and immaterial)
Latent state of *vicikicchā* is renounced at this plane. Is latent state of *diṭṭhi* renounced at that plane? —Yes. (Same as above) .....p.....

147. Latent state of *vicikicchā* is renounced at this plane. Is latent state of *bhavarāga* renounced at that plane?
—No. In three feelings of the elemental world of sensuous desire, *vicikicchā* is renounced; *bhavarāga* is not.
—Yes In the elemental world of fine-material and immaterial, both *vicikicchā* and *bhavarāga* are renounced.
Latent state of *bhavarāga* is renounced at this plane. Is latent state of *vicikicchā* renounced at that plane? —Yes. Refer to the aforesaid.

Latent state of *vicikicchā* is renounced at this plane. Is latent state of *avijjā* renounced at that plane?
—Yes (in elemental world of sensuous desire, fine-material, and immaterial)
Latent state of *avijjā* is renounced at this plane. Is latent state of *vicikicchā* renounced at that plane? —Yes. (Same as above)

148. Latent state of *bhavarāga* is renounced at this plane. Is latent state of *avijjā* renounced at that plane? —Yes. Refer to the answer below.
Latent state of *avijjā* is renounced at this plane. Is latent state of *bhavarāga* renounced at that plane?
—No. In three feelings of the elemental world of sensuous desire, *avijjā* is renounced; but *bhavarāga* is not.
—Yes. In the elemental world of fine-material and immaterial, both *avijjā* and *bhavarāga* are renounced.

Couplet-based

149. Latent states of *kāmarāga* and *paṭigha* are renounced at this plane. Is latent state of *māna* renounced at that plane? —None.
Latent state of *māna* is renounced at this plane. Are latent states of *kāmarāga* and *paṭigha* renounced at that plane?

—No. In the elemental world of fine-material and immaterial, *māna* is renounced; *kāmarāga* and *paṭigha* are not. In two feelings of the elemental world of sensuous desire, *māna* and *kāmarāga* are renounced; *paṭigha* is not.

Latent states of *kāmarāga* and *paṭigha* are renounced at this plane. Is latent state of *diṭṭhi* …..p….. *vicikicchā* renounced at that plane? —None.
Latent state of *vicikicchā* is renounced at this plane. Are latent states of *kāmarāga* and *paṭigha* renounced at that plane?
—No. In the elemental world of fine-material and immaterial, *vicikicchā* (and *diṭṭhi*) is renounced, *kāmarāga* and *paṭigha* are not. In two feelings of the elemental world of sensuous desire, *vicikicchā* and *kāmarāga* (and *diṭṭhi*) are renounced; *paṭigha* is not. In unpleasant feeling, *vicikicchā* and *paṭigha* (and *diṭṭhi*) are renounced; *kāmarāga* is not.

Latent states of *kāmarāga* and *paṭigha* are renounced at this plane. Is latent state of *bhavarāga* renounced at that plane? —None.
Latent state of *bhavarāga* is renounced at this plane. Are latent states of *kāmarāga* and *paṭigha* renounced at that plane?
—No. (In the elemental world of fine-material and immaterial)

Latent states of *kāmarāga* and *paṭigha* are renounced at this plane. Is latent state of *avijjā* renounced at that plane? —None.
Latent state of *avijjā* is renounced at this plane. Are latent states of *kāmarāga* and *paṭigha* renounced at that plane?
—No. In the elemental world of fine-material and immaterial, *avijjā* is renounced; *kāmarāga* and *paṭigha* are not. In two feelings of the elemental world of sensuous desire, *avijjā* and *kāmarāga* are renounced; *paṭigha* is not. In unpleasant feeling, *avijjā* and *paṭigha* are renounced; *kāmarāga* is not.

Triplet-based

150. Latent states of *kāmarāga*, *paṭigha* and *māna* are renounced at this plane. Is latent state of *diṭṭhi* …..p….. *vicikicchā* renounced at that plane? —None.
Latent state of *vicikicchā* is renounced at this plane. Are latent states of *kāmarāga*, *paṭigha* and *māna* renounced at that plane?
—No. In the elemental world of fine-material and immaterial, *vicikicchā* and *māna* (and *diṭṭhi*) are renounced, *kāmarāga* and *paṭigha* are not. In two feelings of the elemental world of sensuous desire, *vicikicchā*, *kāmarāga* and *māna* (and *diṭṭhi*) are renounced; *paṭigha* is not. In unpleasant feeling, *vicikicchā* and *paṭigha* (and *diṭṭhi*) are renounced; *kāmarāga* and *māna* are not.

Latent states of *kāmarāga*, *paṭigha* and *māna* are renounced at this plane. Is latent state of *bhavarāga* renounced at that plane? —None.
Latent state of *bhavarāga* is renounced at this plane. Are latent states of *kāmarāga*, *paṭigha* and *māna* renounced at that plane?
—(At the planes of fine-material and immaterial, *bhavarāga* is renounced, but *kāmarāga* and *paṭigha* are not renounced); *māna* is also renounced.

Latent states of *kāmarāga*, *paṭigha* and *māna* are renounced at this plane. Is latent state of *avijjā* renounced at that plane? —None.
Latent state of *avijjā* is renounced at this plane. Are latent states of *kāmarāga*, *paṭigha* and *māna* renounced at that plane?
—No. In elemental world of fine-material and immaterial, *avijjā* and *māna* are renounced; *kāmarāga* and *paṭigha* are not. In two feelings of the elemental world of sensuous desire, *avijjā*, *kāmarāga* and *māna* are renounced; *paṭigha* is not. In unpleasant feeling, *avijjā* and *paṭigha* are renounced; *kāmarāga* and *māna* are not.

Quadruplet-based

151. Latent states of *kāmarāga*, *paṭigha*, *māna* and *diṭṭhi* are renounced at this plane. Is latent state of *vicikicchā* renounced at that plane? —None.
Latent state of *vicikicchā* is renounced at this plane. Are latent states of *kāmarāga*, *paṭigha*, *māna* and *diṭṭhi* renounced at that plane?
—No. In the elemental world of fine-material and immaterial, *vicikicchā*, *māna* and *diṭṭhi* are renounced; *kāmarāga* and *paṭigha* are not. In two feelings of the elemental world of sensuous desire, *vicikicchā*, *kāmarāga*, *māna* and *diṭṭhi* are renounced; *paṭigha* is not. In unpleasant feeling, *vicikicchā*, *paṭigha* and *diṭṭhi* are renounced; *kāmarāga* and *māna* are not .....p.....

Quintuplet-based

152. Latent states of *kāmarāga*, *paṭigha*, *māna*, *diṭṭhi* and *vicikicchā* are renounced at this plane. Is latent state of *bhavarāga* renounced at that plane? —None.
Latent state of *bhavarāga* is renounced at this plane. Are latent states of *kāmarāga*, *paṭigha*, *māna*, *diṭṭhi* and *vicikicchā* renounced at that plane?
—(At the planes of fine-material and immaterial, *bhavarāga* is renounced; *kāmarāga* and *paṭigha* are not renounced); *māna*, *diṭṭhi* and *vicikicchā* are also renounced.

Latent states of *kāmarāga*, *paṭigha*, *māna*, *diṭṭhi* and *vicikicchā* are renounced at this plane. Is latent state of *avijjā* renounced at that plane? —None.
Latent state of *avijjā* is renounced at this plane. Are latent states of *kāmarāga*, *paṭigha*, *māna*, *diṭṭhi* and *vicikicchā* renounced at that plane?
—No. In the elemental world of fine-material and immaterial, *avijjā*, *māna*, *diṭṭhi* and *vicikicchā* are renounced; *kāmarāga* and *paṭigha* are not. In two feelings of the elemental world of sensuous desire, *avijjā*, *kāmarāga*, *māna*, *diṭṭhi* and *vicikicchā* are renounced; *paṭigha* is not. In unpleasant feeling, *avijjā*, *paṭigha*, *diṭṭhi* and *vicikicchā* are renounced; *kāmarāga* and *māna* are not.

Sextuplet-based

153. Latent states of *kāmarāga*, *paṭigha*, *māna*, *diṭṭhi*, *vicikicchā* and *bhavarāga* are renounced at this plane. Is latent state of *avijjā* renounced at that plane? —None.
Latent state of *avijjā* is renounced at this plane. Are latent states of *kāmarāga*, *paṭigha*, *māna*, *diṭṭhi*, *vicikicchā* and *bhavarāga* renounced at that plane?
—No. In the elemental world of fine-material and immaterial, *avijjā*, *māna*, *diṭṭhi*, *vicikicchā* and *bhavarāga* are renounced; *kāmarāga* and *paṭigha* are not. In two feelings of the elemental world of sensuous desire, *avijjā*, *kāmarāga*, *māna*, *diṭṭhi* and *vicikicchā* are renounced; *paṭigha* and *bhavarāga* are not. In unpleasant feeling, *avijjā*, *paṭigha*, *diṭṭhi* and *vicikicchā* are renounced; *kāmarāga*, *māna* and *bhavarāga* are not.

Forward enquiries by person and plane

Mono-based

154. This person is renouncing latent state of *kāmarāga* at this plane. Is that person renouncing latent state of *paṭigha* at that plane?
—No. (*Anāgāmi* Path-attainer in two feelings of the elemental world of sensuous desire)
This person is renouncing latent state of *paṭigha* at this plane. Is that person renouncing latent state of *kāmarāga* at that plane?
—No. (*Anāgāmi* Path-attainer in unpleasant feeling of the elemental world of sensuous desire)

This person is renouncing latent state of *kāmarāga* at this plane. Is that person renouncing latent state of *māna* at that plane?
—(*Anāgāmi* Path-attainer in two feelings of the elemental world of sensuous desire) is only renouncing a part of *māna*.
This person is renouncing latent state of *māna* at this plane. Is that person renouncing latent state of *kāmarāga* at that plane?
—No. (*Arahatta* Path-attainer, in two feelings of the elemental world of sensuous desire, and in elemental world of fine-material and immaterial)

This person is renouncing latent state of *kāmarāga* at this plane. Is that person renouncing latent state of *diṭṭhi* .....p..... *vicikicchā* at that plane?
—No. (*Anāgāmi* Path-attainer in two feelings of the elemental world of sensuous desire)
This person is renouncing latent state of *vicikicchā* at this plane. Is that person renouncing latent state of *kāmarāga* at that plane?
—*Aṭṭhamako*, namely *Sotāpatti Maggaṭṭhāna* person (*aṭṭhamako*) [56], or *Sotāpatti Path-attainer*, in unpleasant feeling, and in elemental world of fine-material and immaterial, is renouncing *vicikicchā* (and *diṭṭhi*), but not *kāmarāga*. Those (same)

---

[56] *Aṭṭhamako*: (lit) the eight, namely the lowest of the 8 kinds of noble persons—the person who has attained the 'stream-winning' Path.

persons, in two feelings of the elemental world of sensuous desire, are renouncing *vicikicchā* (and *diṭṭhi*), and renouncing a part of *kāmarāga*.

This person is renouncing latent state of *kāmarāga* at this plane. Is that person renouncing latent state of *bhavarāga* at that plane?
—No. (*Anāgāmi* Path-attainer in two feelings of the elemental world of sensuous desire)
This person is renouncing latent state of *bhavarāga* at this plane. Is that person renouncing latent state of *kāmarāga* at that plane?
—No. (*Arahatta* Path-attainer, in elemental world of fine-material and immaterial)

This person is renouncing latent state of *kāmarāga* at this plane. Is that person renouncing latent state of *avijjā* at that plane?
—(*Anāgāmi* Path-attainer in two feelings of the elemental world of sensuous desire) is renouncing a part of *avijjā*.
This person is renouncing latent state of *avijjā* at this plane. Is that person renouncing latent state of *kāmarāga* at that plane?
—No. (*Arahatta* Path-attainer, in three feelings of the elemental world of sensuous desire, and in elemental world of fine-material and immaterial)

155. This person is renouncing latent state of *paṭigha* at this plane. Is that person renouncing latent state of *māna* at that plane?
—No. (*Anāgāmi* Path-attainer in unpleasant feeling)
This person is renouncing latent state of *māna* at this plane. Is that person renouncing latent state of *paṭigha* at that plane?
—No. (*Arahatta* Path-attainer, in two feelings of the elemental world of sensuous desire, and in elemental world of fine-material and immaterial)

This person is renouncing latent state of *paṭigha* at this plane. Is that person renouncing latent state of *diṭṭhi* .....p.... *vicikicchā* at that plane?
—No. *Sotāpatti* Path-attainer, in two feelings of the elemental world of sensuous desire, and in elemental world of fine-material and immaterial, is renouncing *vicikicchā*, but not *paṭigha*.
—Those (same) persons, in unpleasant feeling, are renouncing *vicikicchā*, and are renouncing a part of *paṭigha*.

This person is renouncing latent state of *paṭigha* at this plane. Is that person renouncing latent state of *bhavarāga* at that plane?
—No. (*Anāgāmi* Path-attainer in unpleasant feeling)
This person is renouncing latent state of *bhavarāga* at this plane. Is that person renouncing latent state of *paṭigha* at that plane?
—No. (*Arahatta* Path-attainer in elemental world of fine-material and immaterial)

This person is renouncing latent state of *paṭigha* at this plane. Is that person renouncing latent state of *avijjā* at that plane?

—(*Anāgāmi* Path-attainer in unpleasant feeling) is renouncing a part of *avijjā*.
This person is renouncing latent state of *avijjā* at this plane. Is that person renouncing latent state of *paṭigha* at that plane?
—No. (*Arahatta* Path-attainer, except in *apariyāpanna*)

156. This person is renouncing latent state of *māna* at this plane. Is that person renouncing latent state of *diṭṭhi* …..p….. *vicikicchā* at that plane?
—No. (*Arahatta* Path-attainer, in two feelings of the elemental world of sensuous desire, and in elemental world of fine-material and immaterial)
This person is renouncing latent state of *vicikicchā* at this plane. Is that person renouncing latent state of *māna* at that plane?
—No. *Sotāpatti* Path-attainer in unpleasant feeling, is renouncing *vicikicchā*, but not *māna*.
—Those (same) persons, in two feelings of the elemental world of sensuous desire, and in elemental world of fine-material and immaterial, are renouncing *vicikicchā*, and a part of *māna*.

This person is renouncing latent state of *māna* at this plane. Is that person renouncing latent state of *bhavarāga* at that plane?
—No. *Arahatta* Path-attainer (*Aggamaggasamaṅgī*)[57], or attainer of the highest Path-*citta*, with two feelings of the elemental world of sensuous desire, is renouncing *māna*, but not *bhavarāga*.
—Yes. Those (same) persons, in the elemental world of fine-material and immaterial, are renouncing *māna*, and also *bhavarāga*.
This person is renouncing latent state of *bhavarāga* at this plane. Is that person renouncing latent state of *māna* at that plane? —Yes. Refer to the aforesaid.

This person is renouncing latent state of *māna* at this plane. Is that person renouncing latent state of *avijjā* at that plane?
—Yes. Refer to the answer below.
This person is renouncing latent state of *avijjā* at this plane. Is that person renouncing latent state of *māna* at that plane?
—No. *Arahatta* Path-attainer in unpleasant feeling, is renouncing *avijjā*, but not *māna*.
—Yes. Those (same) persons, in two feelings of the elemental world of sensuous desire, and in elemental world of fine-material and immaterial, are renouncing *avijjā*, and also *māna*.

157. This person is renouncing latent state of *diṭṭhi* at this plane. Is that person renouncing latent state of *vicikicchā* at that plane?
—Yes. (*Sotāpatti* Path-attainer, except in *apariyāpanna*)
This person is renouncing latent state of *vicikicchā* at this plane. Is that person renouncing latent state of *diṭṭhi* at that plane?

[57] *Aggamaggasamaṅgī*: the person who has attained the highest, *Arahatta* Path.

—Yes. (Same as aforesaid) …..p…..

158. This person is renouncing latent state of *vicikicchā* at this plane. Is that person renouncing latent state of *bhavarāga* at that plane?
—No. *Sotāpatti* Path-attainer, in three feelings of the elemental world of sensuous desire, is renouncing *vicikicchā*, but not *bhavarāga*.
—Those (same) persons, in the elemental world of fine-material and immaterial, are renouncing *vicikicchā*, and a part of *bhavarāga*.
This person is renouncing latent state of *bhavarāga* at this plane. Is that person renouncing latent state of *vicikicchā* at that plane?
—No. (*Arahatta* Path-attainer, in elemental world of fine-material and immaterial)

This person is renouncing latent state of *vicikicchā* at this plane. Is that person renouncing latent state of *avijjā* at that plane?
—(*Sotāpatti* Path-attainer, except in *apariyāpanna*) is renouncing a part of *avijjā*.
This person is renouncing latent state of *avijjā* at this plane. Is that person renouncing latent state of *vicikicchā* at that plane?
—No. (*Arahatta* Path-attainer, except in *apariyāpanna*)

159. This person is renouncing latent state of *bhavarāga* at this plane. Is that person renouncing latent state of *avijjā* at that plane?
—Yes. (Same as below)
This person is renouncing latent state of *avijjā* at this plane. Is that person renouncing latent state of *bhavarāga* at that plane?
—No. *Arahatta* Path-attainer, in three feelings of the elemental world of sensuous desire, is renouncing *avijjā*, but not *bhavarāga*.
—Yes. Those (same) persons, in the elemental world of fine-material and immaterial, are renouncing *avijjā*, and also *bhavarāga*.

Couplet-based

160. This person is renouncing latent states of *kāmarāga* and *paṭigha* at this plane. Is that person renouncing latent state of *māna* at that plane?
—None. (No, *Anāgāmi* Path-attainer, in two feelings of the elemental world of sensuous desire, is renouncing *kāmarāga* and *paṭigha*, but not *māna*)
This person is renouncing latent state of *māna* at this plane. Is that person renouncing latent states of *kāmarāga* and *paṭigha* at that plane?
—No. (*Arahatta* Path-attainer, in two feelings of the elemental world of sensuous desire, and in elemental world of fine-material and immaterial)

This person is renouncing latent states of *kāmarāga* and *paṭigha* at this plane. Is that person renouncing latent state of *diṭṭhi* ….p… *vicikicchā* at that plane?
—None.
This person is renouncing latent state of *vicikicchā* at this plane. Is that person renouncing latent states of *kāmarāga* and *paṭigha* at that plane?

—No. *Sotāpatti* Path-attainer, in the elemental world of fine-material and immaterial, is renouncing *vicikicchā*, but not *kāmarāga* and *paṭigha*.
— Those (same) persons, in two feelings of the elemental world of sensuous desire, are renouncing *vicikicchā* and a part of *kāmarāga*, but not *paṭigha*. Those (same) persons, in unpleasant feeling, is renouncing *vicikicchā* and a part of *paṭigha*, but not *kāmarāga*.

This person is renouncing latent states of *kāmarāga* and *paṭigha* at this plane. Is that person renouncing latent state of *bhavarāga* at that plane?
—None. (No, *Anāgāmi* Path-attainer, in two feelings of the elemental world of sensuous desire, is renouncing *kāmarāga* and *paṭigha*, but not *bhavarāga*)
This person is renouncing latent state of *bhavarāga* at this plane. Is that person renouncing latent states of *kāmarāga* and *paṭigha* at that plane?
—No. (*Arahatta* Path-attainer in elemental world of fine-material and immaterial)

This person is renouncing latent states of *kāmarāga* and *paṭigha* at this plane. Is that person renouncing latent state of *avijjā* at that plane?
—None. (No, *Anāgāmi* Path-attainer, in two feelings of the elemental world of sensuous desire, is renouncing *kāmarāga* and *paṭigha*, but not *avijjā*)
This person is renouncing latent state of *avijjā* at this plane. Is that person renouncing latent states of *kāmarāga* and *paṭigha* at that plane?
—No. (*Arahatta* Path-attainer, except in *apariyāpanna*)

Triplet-based

161. This person is renouncing latent states of *kāmarāga*, *paṭigha* and *māna* at this plane. Is that person renouncing latent state of *diṭṭhi* .....p..... *vicikicchā* at that plane? —No such person.
This person is renouncing latent state of *vicikicchā* at this plane. Is that person renouncing latent states of *kāmarāga*, *paṭigha* and *māna* at that plane?
—*Sotāpatti* Path-attainer, in the elemental world of fine-material and immaterial, is renouncing *vicikicchā* and a part of *māna*, but not *kāmarāga* and *paṭigha*. Those (same) persons, in two feelings of the elemental world of sensuous desire, are renouncing *vicikicchā* and a part of *kāmarāga* and *māna*, but not *paṭigha*. Those (same) persons, in unpleasant feeling, are renouncing *vicikicchā* and a part of *paṭigha*, but not *kāmarāga* and *māna*.
This person is renouncing latent states of *kāmarāga*, *paṭigha* and *māna* at this plane. Is that person renouncing latent state of *bhavarāga* at that plane? —None.
This person is renouncing latent state of *bhavarāga* at this plane. Is that person renouncing latent states of *kāmarāga*, *paṭigha* and *māna* at that plane?
—Yes. (*Arahatta* Path-attainer in elemental world of fine-material and immaterial) is renouncing *māna*.

This person is renouncing latent states of *kāmarāga*, *paṭigha* and *māna* at this plane. Is that person renouncing latent state of *avijjā* at that plane? —None.

This person is renouncing latent state of *avijjā* at this plane. Is that person renouncing latent states of *kāmarāga, paṭigha* and *māna* at that plane?
—No. *Arahatta* Path-attainer in unpleasant feeling is renouncing *avijjā*, but not *kāmarāga, paṭigha* and *māna*. Those (same) persons, in two feelings of the elemental world of sensuous desire, and in elemental world of fine-material and immaterial, are renouncing *avijjā* and *māna*, but not *kāmarāga* and *paṭigha*.

Quadruplet-based

162. This person is renouncing latent states of *kāmarāga*, *paṭigha*, *māna* and *diṭṭhi* at this plane. Is that person renouncing latent state of *vicikicchā* at that plane? —None.
This person is renouncing latent state of *vicikicchā* at this plane. Is that person renouncing latent states of *kāmarāga, paṭigha*, *māna* and *diṭṭhi* at that plane?
—*Sotāpatti* Path-attainer, in the elemental world of fine-material and immaterial, are renouncing *vicikicchā* and *diṭṭhi*, and are also renouncing a part of *māna*, but not *kāmarāga* and *paṭigha*. Those (same) persons, in two feelings of the elemental world of sensuous desire, are renouncing *vicikicchā* and *diṭṭhi*, and also renouncing a part of *kāmarāga* and *māna*, but not *paṭigha*. Those (same) persons, in unpleasant feeling, are renouncing *vicikicchā* and *diṭṭhi*, and also renouncing a part of *paṭigha*, but not *kāmarāga* and *māna* .....p.....

Quintuplet-based

163. This person is renouncing latent states of *kāmarāga, paṭigha*, *māna*, *diṭṭhi* and *vicikicchā* at this plane. Is that person renouncing latent state of *bhavarāga* at that plane? —No such person.
This person is renouncing latent state of *bhavarāga* at this plane. Is that person renouncing latent states of *kāmarāga, paṭigha*, *māna*, *diṭṭhi* and *vicikicchā* at that plane?
—(*Arahatta* Path-attainer in elemental world of fine-material and immaterial) is also renouncing *māna* thereat.

This person is renouncing latent states of *kāmarāga*, *paṭigha*, *māna*, *diṭṭhi* and *vicikicchā* at this plane. Is that person renouncing latent state of *avijjā* at that plane? —No such person.
This person is renouncing latent state of *avijjā* at this plane. Is that person renouncing latent states of *kāmarāga, paṭigha*, *māna*, *diṭṭhi* and *vicikicchā* at that plane?
—No. *Arahatta* Path-attainer in unpleasant feeling is renouncing *avijjā*, except for *kāmarāga, paṭigha*, *māna*, *diṭṭhi* and *vicikicchā*. Those (same) persons, in two feelings of the elemental world of sensuous desire, and in elemental world of fine-material and immaterial, are renouncing *avijjā* and *māna*, except for *kāmarāga, paṭigha*, *diṭṭhi* and *vicikicchā*.

Sextuplet-based

164. This person is renouncing latent states of *kāmarāga, paṭigha, māna, diṭṭhi, vicikicchā* and *bhavarāga* at this plane. Is that person renouncing latent state of *avijjā* at that plane? —None.
This person is renouncing latent state of *bhavarāga* at this plane. Is that person renouncing latent states of *kāmarāga, paṭigha, māna, diṭṭhi, vicikicchā* and *bhavarāga* at that plane?
—No. *Arahatta* Path-attainer in unpleasant feeling is renouncing *avijjā*, except for *kāmarāga, paṭigha, māna, diṭṭhi, vicikicchā* and *bhavarāga*. Those (same) persons, in two feelings of the elemental world of sensuous desire, are renouncing *avijjā* and *māna*, except for *kāmarāga, paṭigha, diṭṭhi, vicikicchā* and *bhavarāga*. Those (same) persons, in elemental world of fine-material and immaterial, are renouncing *avijjā, māna* and *bhavarāga*, except for *kāmarāga, paṭigha, diṭṭhi* and *vicikicchā*.

Opposite enquiries by person

Mono-based

165. This person is not renouncing latent state of *kāmarāga*. Is that person not renouncing latent state of *paṭigha*?
—Yes. (*Sotāpatti* Path-attainer, *Sakadāgāmi* Path-attainer, *Arahatta* Path-attainer)
This person is not renouncing latent state of *paṭigha*. Is that person not renouncing latent state of *kāmarāga*?
—Yes. (Same as aforesaid)

This person is not renouncing latent state of *kāmarāga*. Is that person not renouncing latent state of *māna*?
—No. *Arahatta* Path-attainer is not renouncing *kāmarāga* but *māna*.
—Yes. With the exception of two Path-attainers, the remaining persons (*Sotāpatti* Path-attainer, *Sakadāgāmi* Path-attainer) are not renouncing *kāmarāga* and *māna*.
This person is not renouncing latent state of *māna*. Is that person not renouncing latent state of *kāmarāga*?
—No. *Anāgāmi Maggaṭṭhāna* person (*Anāgāmimaggasamaṅgī*) [58], or *Anāgāmi* Path-attainer is not renouncing *māna* but *kāmarāga*.
—Yes. Refer to the aforesaid.

This person is not renouncing latent state of *kāmarāga*. Is that person not renouncing latent state of *diṭṭhi* .....p..... *vicikicchā*?
—No. *Sotāpatti* Path-attainer is not renouncing *kāmarāga*, except for *vicikicchā* (and *diṭṭhi*).
—Yes. With the exception of *Anāgāmi* Path-attainer and *Sotāpatti* Path-attainer, the remaining persons are not renouncing *kāmarāga* and *vicikicchā*.

[58] *Anāgāmimaggasamaṅgī*: the person who has attained the 'non-returning' Path.

This person is not renouncing latent state of *vicikicchā*. Is that person not renouncing latent state of *kāmarāga*?
—No. *Anāgāmi* Path-attainer is not renouncing *vicikicchā* (and *diṭṭhi*), but is renouncing *kāmarāga*.
—Yes. Refer to the aforesaid.

This person is not renouncing latent state of *kāmarāga*. Is that person not renouncing latent state of *bhavarāga* .....p..... *avijjā*?
—No. *Arahatta* Path-attainer is not renouncing *kāmarāga*, but is renouncing *avijjā* (and also *bhavarāga*).
—Yes. With the exception of two Path-attainers, the remaining persons (*Sotāpatti* Path-attainer, *Sakadāgāmi* Path-attainer) are not renouncing both *kāmarāga* and *avijjā*.
This person is not renouncing latent state of *avijjā*. Is that person not renouncing latent state of *kāmarāga*?
—No. *Anāgāmi* Path-attainer is not renouncing *avijjā* (and *bhavarāga*), but renouncing *kāmarāga*.
—Yes. Refer to the aforesaid.

166. This person is not renouncing latent state of *paṭigha*. Is that person not renouncing latent state of *māna*?
—No. *Arahatta* Path-attainer is not renouncing *paṭigha* but *māna*.
—Yes. With the exception of two Path-attainers, remaining persons (*Sotāpatti* Path-attainer, *Sakadāgāmi* Path-attainer) are not renouncing *paṭigha* and *māna*.
This person is not renouncing latent state of *māna*. Is that person not renouncing latent state of *paṭigha*?
—No. *Anāgāmi* Path-attainer is not renouncing *māna* but *paṭigha*.
—Yes. Refer to the aforesaid.

This person is not renouncing latent state of *paṭigha*. Is that person not renouncing latent state of *diṭṭhi* .....p..... *vicikicchā*?
—No. *Sotāpatti* Path-attainer is not renouncing *paṭigha*, but renouncing *vicikicchā* (and *diṭṭhi*) .
—Yes. With the exception of *Anāgāmi* Path-attainer and *Sotāpatti* Path-attainer, the remaining persons are not renouncing both *paṭigha* and *vicikicchā*.
This person is not renouncing latent state of *vicikicchā*. Is that person not renouncing latent state of *paṭigha*?
—No. *Anāgāmi* Path-attainer is not renouncing *vicikicchā* (and *diṭṭhi*), but *paṭigha*.
—Yes. Refer to the aforesaid.

This person is not renouncing latent state of *paṭigha*. Is that person not renouncing latent state of *bhavarāga* .....p..... *avijjā*?
—No. *Arahatta* Path-attainer is not renouncing *paṭigha*, but renouncing *avijjā* (and *bhavarāga*).
—Yes. With the exception of two Path-attainers, the remaining persons

(*Sotāpatti* Path-attainer, *Sakadāgāmi* Path-attainer) are not renouncing both *paṭigha* and *avijjā*.
This person is not renouncing latent state of *avijjā*. Is that person not renouncing latent state of *paṭigha*?
—No. *Anāgāmi* Path-attainer is not renouncing *avijjā* (and *bhavarāga*), but renouncing *paṭigha*.
—Yes. Refer to the aforesaid.

167. This person is not renouncing latent state of *māna*. Is that person not renouncing latent state of *diṭṭhi* …..p….. *vicikicchā*?
—No. *Sotāpatti* Path-attainer is not renouncing *māna* but *vicikicchā* (and *diṭṭhi*).
—Yes. With the exception of *Arahatta* Path-attainer and *Sotāpatti* Path-attainer, the remaining persons are not renouncing both *māna* and *vicikicchā*.
This person is not renouncing latent state of *vicikicchā*. Is that person not renouncing latent state of *māna*?
—No. *Arahatta* Path-attainer is not renouncing *vicikicchā* (and *diṭṭhi*) but *māna*.
—Yes. Refer to the aforesaid.

This person is not renouncing latent state of *māna*. Is that person not renouncing latent state of *bhavarāga* …..p….. *avijjā*?
—Yes. (except *Arahatta* Path-attainer)
This person is not renouncing latent state of *avijjā*. Is that person not renouncing latent state of *māna*? —Yes. (Same as aforesaid)

168. This person is not renouncing latent state of *diṭṭhi*. Is that person not renouncing latent state of *vicikicchā*?
—Yes. (except *Sotāpatti* Path-attainer)
This person is not renouncing latent state of *vicikicchā*. Is that person not renouncing latent state of *diṭṭhi*?
—Yes. (same as aforesaid) ……p…..

169. This person is not renouncing latent state of *vicikicchā*. Is that person not renouncing latent state of *bhavarāga* …..p….. *avijjā*?
—No. *Arahatta* Path-attainer is not renouncing *vicikicchā*, but renouncing *avijjā* (and *bhavarāga*).
—Yes. With the exception of *Arahatta* Path-attainer and *Sotāpatti* Path-attainer, the remaining persons are not renouncing *vicikicchā* and *bhavarāga* (and *avijjā*).
This person is not renouncing latent state of *avijjā*. Is that person not renouncing latent state of *vicikicchā*?
—No. *Sotāpatti* Path-attainer is not renouncing *avijjā* (and *bhavarāga*), but renouncing *vicikicchā*.
—Yes. Refer to the aforesaid.

170. This person is not renouncing latent state of *bhavarāga*. Is that person not renouncing latent state of *avijjā*?
—Yes. (except *Arahatta* Path-attainer)

This person is not renouncing latent state of *avijjā*. Is that person not renouncing latent state of *bhavarāga*?
—Yes. Refer to the aforesaid.

Couplet-based

171. This person is not renouncing latent states of *kāmarāga* and *paṭigha*. Is that person not renouncing latent state of *māna*?
—No. *Arahatta* Path-attainer is not renouncing *kāmarāga* and *paṭigha*, but renouncing *māna*.
—Yes. With the exception of two Path-attainers, the remaining persons are not renouncing *kāmarāga* and *paṭigha*, and also *māna*.
This person is not renouncing latent state of *māna*. Is that person not renouncing latent states of *kāmarāga* and *paṭigha*?
—No. *Anāgāmi* Path-attainer is not renouncing *māna* but *kāmarāga* and *paṭigha*.
—Yes. Refer to the aforesaid.

This person is not renouncing latent states of *kāmarāga* and *paṭigha*. Is that person not renouncing latent state of *diṭṭhi* .....p..... *vicikicchā*?
—No. *Sotāpatti* Path-attainer is not renouncing *kāmarāga* and *paṭigha*, except for *vicikicchā*.
—Yes. With the exception of *Anāgāmi* Path-attainer and *Sotāpatti* Path-attainer, the remaining persons are not renouncing *kāmarāga*, *paṭigha*, and also *vicikicchā*.
This person is not renouncing latent state of *vicikicchā*. Is that person not renouncing latent states of *kāmarāga* and *paṭigha*?
—No. *Anāgāmi* Path-attainer is not renouncing *vicikicchā*, except for *kāmarāga* and *paṭigha*.
—Yes. Refer to the aforesaid.

This person is not renouncing latent states of *kāmarāga* and *paṭigha*. Is that person not renouncing latent state of *bhavarāga* .....p..... *avijjā*?
—No. *Arahatta* Path-attainer is not renouncing *kāmarāga* and *paṭigha*, but renouncing *avijjā*.
—Yes. With the exception of two Path-attainers, the remaining persons are not renouncing *kāmarāga*, *paṭigha,* and also *avijjā*.
This person is not renouncing latent state of *avijjā*. Is that person not renouncing latent states of *kāmarāga* and *paṭigha*?
—No. *Anāgāmi* Path-attainer is not renouncing *avijjā* but *kāmarāga* and *paṭigha*.
—Yes. Refer to the aforesaid.

Triplet-based

172. This person is not renouncing latent states of *kāmarāga*, *paṭigha* and *māna*. Is that person not renouncing latent state of *diṭṭhi* .....p..... *vicikicchā*?
—No. *Sotāpatti* Path-attainer is not renouncing *kāmarāga*, *paṭigha* and *māna*, except for *vicikicchā*.

—Yes. With the exception of two Path-attainers and *Sotāpatti* Path-attainer, the remaining persons (*Sakadāgāmi* Path-attainer) are not renouncing *kāmarāga*, *paṭigha* and *māna*, and also *vicikicchā*.
This person is not renouncing latent state of *vicikicchā*. Is that person not renouncing latent states of *kāmarāga*, *paṭigha* and *māna*?
—No. *Anāgāmi* Path-attainer is not renouncing *vicikicchā* and *māna*, except for *kāmarāga* and *paṭigha*. *Arahatta* Path-attainer is not renouncing *vicikicchā*, *kāmarāga* and *paṭigha*, except for *māna*.
—Yes. Refer to the aforesaid.

This person is not renouncing latent states of *kāmarāga*, *paṭigha* and *māna*. Is that person not renouncing latent state of *bhavarāga* …..p….. *avijjā*?
—Yes. Refer to the answer below.
This person is not renouncing latent state of *avijjā*. Is that person not renouncing latent states of *kāmarāga*, *paṭigha* and *māna*?
—No. *Anāgāmi* Path-attainer is not renouncing *avijjā*, *māna* (and *bhavarāga*), except for *kāmarāga* and *paṭigha*.
—Yes. With the exception of two Path-attainers, the remaining persons (*Sotāpatti* Path-attainer, *Sakadāgāmi* Path-attainer) are not renouncing *avijjā* (and *bhavarāga*), and also *kāmarāga*, *paṭigha* and *māna*.

Quadruplet-based

173. This person is not renouncing latent states of *kāmarāga*, *paṭigha*, *māna* and *diṭṭhi*. Is that person not renouncing latent state of *vicikicchā*?
—Yes. Refer to the answer below.
This person is not renouncing latent state of *vicikicchā*. Is that person not renouncing latent states of *kāmarāga*, *paṭigha*, *māna* and *diṭṭhi*?
—No. *Anāgāmi* Path-attainer is not renouncing *vicikicchā*, *māna* and *diṭṭhi*, except for *kāmarāga* and *paṭigha*. *Arahatta* Path-attainer is not renouncing *vicikicchā*, *kāmarāga*, *paṭigha* and *diṭṭhi*, except for *māna*.
—Yes. With the exception of two Path-attainers and *Sotāpatti* Path-attainer, the remaining persons (*Sakadāgāmi* Path-attainer) are not renouncing *vicikicchā*, and also *kāmarāga*, *paṭigha*, *māna* and *diṭṭhi* …..p…..

Quintuplet-based

174. This person is not renouncing latent states of *kāmarāga*, *paṭigha*, *māna*, *diṭṭhi* and *vicikicchā*. Is that person not renouncing latent state of *bhavarāga* …..p….. *avijjā*?
—Yes. Refer to the answer below.
This person is not renouncing latent state of *avijjā*. Is that person not renouncing latent states of *kāmarāga*, *paṭigha*, *māna*, *diṭṭhi* and *vicikicchā*?
—No. *Sotāpatti* Path-attainer is not renouncing *avijjā*, *kāmarāga*, *paṭigha* and *māna*, except for *diṭṭhi* and *vicikicchā*. *Anāgāmi* Path-attainer is not renouncing *avijjā*, *māna*, *diṭṭhi* and *vicikicchā*, except for *kāmarāga* and *paṭigha*.

—Yes. With the exception of two Path-attainers and *Sotāpatti* Path-attainer, the remaining persons (*Sakadāgāmi* Path-attainer) are not renouncing *avijjā*, and also *kāmarāga*, *paṭigha*, *māna*, *diṭṭhi* and *vicikicchā*.

Sextuplet-based

175. This person is not renouncing latent states of *kāmarāga*, *paṭigha*, *māna*, *diṭṭhi*, *vicikicchā* and *bhavarāga*. Is that person not renouncing latent state *avijjā*?
—Yes. Refer to the answer below.
This person is not renouncing latent state of *avijjā*. Is that person not renouncing latent states of *kāmarāga*, *paṭigha*, *māna*, *diṭṭhi*, *vicikicchā* and *bhavarāga*?
—No. *Sotāpatti* Path-attainer is not renouncing *avijjā*, *kāmarāga*, *paṭigha*, *māna* and *bhavarāga*, except for *diṭṭhi* and *vicikicchā*. *Anāgāmi* Path-attainer is not renouncing *avijjā*, *māna*, *diṭṭhi*, *vicikicchā* and *bhavarāga*, except for *kāmarāga* and *paṭigha*.
—Yes. With the exception of two Path-attainers and *Sotāpatti* Path-attainer, the remaining persons (*Sakadāgāmi* Path-attainer) are not renouncing *avijjā*, and also *kāmarāga*, *paṭigha*, *māna*, *diṭṭhi*, *vicikicchā* and *bhavarāga*.

Opposite enquiries by plane

Mono-based

176. Latent state of *kāmarāga* is not renounced at this plane. Is latent state of *paṭigha* not renounced at that plane?
—No. In unpleasant feeling, *kāmarāga* is not renounced, except for *paṭigha*.
—Yes. In the elemental world of fine-material and immaterial, and in *apariyāpanna*, *kāmarāga* is not renounced; *paṭigha* too.
Latent state of *paṭigha* is not renounced at this plane. Is latent state of *kāmarāga* not renounced at that plane?
—No. In two feelings of the elemental world of sensuous desire, *paṭigha* is not renounced, except for *kāmarāga*.
—Yes. Refer to the aforesaid.

Latent state of *kāmarāga* is not renounced at this plane. Is latent state of *māna* not renounced at that plane?
—No. In the elemental world of fine-material and immaterial, *kāmarāga* is not renounced, except for *māna*.
—Yes. In unpleasant feeling (in sensuous element), and in *apariyāpanna*, *kāmarāga* is not renounced; and also *māna*.
Latent state of *māna* is not renounced at this plane. Is latent state of *kāmarāga* not renounced at that plane? —Yes. Refer to the aforesaid.

Latent state of *kāmarāga* is not renounced at this plane. Is latent state of *diṭṭhi* .....p..... *vicikicchā* not renounced at that plane?

—No. In unpleasant feeling (in sensuous element), and in elemental world of fine-material and immaterial, *kāmarāga* is not renounced, except for *vicikicchā* (*diṭṭhi*).
—Yes. In *apariyāpanna*, both *kāmarāga* and *vicikicchā* (and *diṭṭhi*) are not renounced.
Latent state of *vicikicchā* is not renounced at this plane. Is latent state of *kāmarāga* not renounced at that plane? —Yes. (in *apariyāpanna*)

Latent state of *kāmarāga* is not renounced at this plane. Is latent state of *bhavarāga* not renounced at that plane?
—No. In the elemental world of fine-material and immaterial, *kāmarāga* is not renounced, except for *bhavarāga*.
—Yes. In unpleasant feeling, and in *apariyāpanna*, both *kāmarāga* and *bhavarāga* are not renounced.
Latent state of *bhavarāga* is not renounced at this plane. Is latent state of *kāmarāga* not renounced at that plane?
—No. In two feelings of the elemental world of sensuous desire, *bhavarāga* is not renounced, except for *kāmarāga*.
—Yes. In unpleasant feeling, and in *apariyāpanna*, both *bhavarāga* and *kāmarāga* are not renounced.

Latent state of *kāmarāga* is not renounced at this plane. Is latent state of *avijjā* not renounced at that plane?
—No. In unpleasant feeling, and in elemental world of fine-material and immaterial, *kāmarāga* is not renounced, except for *avijjā*.
—Yes. In *apariyāpanna*, both *kāmarāga* and *avijjā* are not renounced.
Latent state of *avijjā* is not renounced at this plane. Is latent state of *kāmarāga* not renounced at that plane? —Yes. Refer to the aforesaid.

177. Latent state of *paṭigha* is not renounced at this plane. Is latent state of *māna* not renounced at that plane?
—No. In two feelings of the elemental world of sensuous desire, and in elemental world of fine-material and immaterial, *paṭigha* is not renounced, except for *māna*.
—Yes. In *apariyāpanna*, both *paṭigha* and *māna* are not renounced.
Latent state of *māna* is not renounced at this plane. Is latent state of *paṭigha* not renounced at that plane?
—No. In unpleasant feeling, *māna* is not renounced, except for *paṭigha*.
—Yes. Refer to the aforesaid.

Latent state of *paṭigha* is not renounced at this plane. Is latent state of *diṭṭhi* .....p..... *vicikicchā* not renounced at that plane?
—No. In two feelings of the elemental world of sensuous desire, and in elemental world of fine-material and immaterial, *paṭigha* is not renounced, except for *vicikicchā*.
—Yes. In *apariyāpanna*, both *paṭigha* and *vicikicchā* are not renounced.

Latent state of *vicikicchā* is not renounced at this plane. Is latent state of *paṭigha* not renounced at that plane? —Yes. Refer to the aforesaid.

Latent state of *paṭigha* is not renounced at this plane. Is latent state of *bhavarāga* not renounced at that plane?
—No. In the elemental world of fine-material and immaterial, *paṭigha* is not renounced, except for *bhavarāga*.
—Yes. In two feelings of the elemental world of sensuous desire, and in *apariyāpanna*, both *paṭigha* and *bhavarāga* are not renounced.
Latent state of *bhavarāga* is not renounced at this plane. Is latent state of *paṭigha* not renounced at that plane?
—No. In unpleasant feeling, *bhavarāga* is not renounced, except for *paṭigha*.
—Yes. Refer to the aforesaid.

Latent state of *paṭigha* is not renounced at this plane. Is latent state of *avijjā* not renounced at that plane?
—No. In two feelings of the elemental world of sensuous desire, and in elemental world of fine-material and immaterial, *paṭigha* is not renounced, except for *avijjā*.
—Yes. In *apariyāpanna*, both *paṭigha* and *avijjā* are not renounced.
Latent state of *avijjā* is not renounced at this plane. Is latent state of *paṭigha* not renounced at that plane? —Yes. Refer to the aforesaid.

178. Latent state of *māna* is not renounced at this plane. Is latent state of *diṭṭhi* .....p..... *vicikicchā* not renounced at that plane?
—No. In unpleasant feeling, *māna* is not renounced, except for *vicikicchā*.
—Yes. In *apariyāpanna,* both *māna* and *vicikicchā* are not renounced.
Latent state of *vicikicchā* is not renounced at this plane. Is latent state of *māna* not renounced at that plane? —Yes. Refer to the aforesaid.

Latent state of *māna* is not renounced at this plane. Is latent state of *bhavarāga* not renounced at that plane? —Yes. Refer to the answer below.
Latent state of *bhavarāga* is not renounced at this plane. Is latent state of *māna* not renounced at that plane?
—No. In two feelings of the elemental world of sensuous desire, *bhavarāga* is not renounced, except for *māna*.
—Yes. In unpleasant feeling, and in *apariyāpanna*, both *bhavarāga* and *māna* are not renounced.

Latent state of *māna* is not renounced at this plane. Is latent state of *avijjā* not renounced at that plane?
—No. In unpleasant feeling, *māna* is not renounced, except for *avijjā*.
—Yes. In *apariyāpanna*, both *māna* and *avijjā* are not renounced.
Latent state of *avijjā* is not renounced at this plane. Is latent state of *māna* not renounced at that plane? —Yes. Refer to the aforesaid.

179. Latent state of *diṭṭhi* is not renounced at this plane. Is latent state of *vicikicchā* not renounced at that plane? —Yes. (in *apariyāpanna*)
This plane is not renouncing latent state of *vicikicchā*. Is that plane not renouncing latent state of *diṭṭhi*? —Yes (in *apariyāpanna*) …..p…..

180. Latent state of *vicikicchā* is not renounced at this plane. Is latent state of *bhavarāga* not renounced at that plane? —Yes. Refer to the answer below.
Latent state of *bhavarāga* is not renounced at this plane. Is latent state of *vicikicchā* not renounced at that plane?
—No. In three feelings of the elemental world of sensuous desire, *bhavarāga* is not renounced, except for *vicikicchā*.
—Yes. In *apariyāpanna*, both *bhavarāga* and *vicikicchā* are not renounced.

Latent state of *vicikicchā* is not renounced at this plane. Is latent state of *avijjā* not renounced at that plane? —Yes. (in *apariyāpanna*)
Latent state of *avijjā* is not renounced at this plane. Is latent state of *vicikicchā* not renounced at that plane? —Yes. (Same as aforesaid)

181. Latent state of *bhavarāga* is not renounced at this plane. Is latent state of *avijjā* not renounced at that plane?
—No. In three feelings of the elemental world of sensuous desire, *bhavarāga* is not renounced, except for *avijjā*.
—Yes. In *apariyāpanna*, both *bhavarāga* and *avijjā* are not renounced.
Latent state of *avijjā* is not renounced at this plane. Is latent state of *bhavarāga* not renounced at that plane?
—Yes. Refer to the aforesaid.

Couplet-based

182. Latent states of *kāmarāga* and *paṭigha* are not renounced at this plane. Is latent state of *māna* not renounced at that plane?
—No. In the elemental world of fine-material and immaterial, *kāmarāga* and *paṭigha* are not renounced, except for *māna*.
—Yes. In *apariyāpanna*, *kāmarāga* and *paṭigha* are not renounced; *māna* too.
Latent state of *māna* is not renounced at this plane. Are latent states of *kāmarāga* and *paṭigha* not renounced at that plane?
—No. In unpleasant feeling, *māna* and *kāmarāga* are not renounced, except for *paṭigha*.
—Yes. Refer to the aforesaid.

Latent states of *kāmarāga* and *paṭigha* are not renounced at this plane. Is latent state of *diṭṭhi* …..p….. *vicikicchā* not renounced at that plane?
—No. In the elemental world of fine-material and immaterial, *kāmarāga* and *paṭigha* are not renounced, except for *vicikicchā*.
—Yes. In *apariyāpanna*, *kāmarāga* and *paṭigha* are not renounced; *vicikicchā* too.

Latent state of *vicikicchā* is not renounced at this plane. Are latent states of *kāmarāga* and *paṭigha* not renounced at that plane?
—Yes. Refer to the aforesaid.

Latent states of *kāmarāga* and *paṭigha* are not renounced at this plane. Is latent state of *bhavarāga* not renounced at that plane?
—No. In the elemental world of fine-material and immaterial, *kāmarāga* and *paṭigha* are not renounced, except for *bhavarāga.*
—Yes. In *apariyāpanna, kāmarāga, paṭigha* are not renounced; *bhavarāga* too.
Latent state of *bhavarāga* is not renounced at this plane. Are latent states of *kāmarāga* and *paṭigha* not renounced at that plane?
—No. In unpleasant feeling, *bhavarāga* and *kāmarāga* are not renounced, except for *paṭigha.* In two feelings of the elemental world of sensuous desire, *bhavarāga* and *paṭigha* are not renounced, except for *kāmarāga.*
—Yes. Refer to the aforesaid.

Latent states of *kāmarāga* and *paṭigha* are not renounced at this plane. Is latent state of *avijjā* not renounced at that plane?
—No. In the elemental world of fine-material and immaterial, *kāmarāga* and *paṭigha* are not renounced, except for *avijjā.*
—Yes. In *apariyāpanna, kāmarāga* and *paṭigha* are not renounced; *avijjā* too.
Latent state of *avijjā* is not renounced at this plane. Are latent states of *kāmarāga* and *paṭigha* not renounced at that plane?
—Yes. Refer to the aforesaid.

Triplet-based

183. Latent states of *kāmarāga, paṭigha* and *māna* are not renounced at this plane. Is latent state of *diṭṭhi* .....p..... *vicikicchā* not renounced at that plane?
—Yes. (in *apariyāpanna*)
Latent state of *vicikicchā* is not renounced at this plane. Are latent state of *kāmarāga, paṭigha* and *māna* not renounced at that plane?
—Yes. (Same as the aforesaid)

Latent states of *kāmarāga, paṭigha* and *māna* are not renounced at this plane. Is latent state of *bhavarāga* not renounced at that plane?
—Yes. Refer to below.
Latent state of *bhavarāga*is not renounced at this plane. Are latent states of *kāmarāga, paṭigha* and *māna* not renounced at that plane?
—No. In unpleasant feeling, *bhavarāga, kāmarāga* and *māna* are not renounced, except for *paṭigha.* In two feelings of the elemental world of sensuous desire, *bhavarāga* and *paṭigha* are not renounced, except for *kāmarāga* and *māna.*
—Yes. In *apariyāpanna, bhavarāga* is not renounced; *kāmarāga, paṭigha* and *māna* are also not renounced.

Latent states of *kāmarāga, paṭigha* and *diṭṭhi* are not renounced at this plane. Is latent state of *avijjā* not renounced at that plane?

—Yes. (in *apariyāpanna*)
Latent state of *avijjā* is not renounced at this plane. Are latent states of *kāmarāga*, *paṭigha* and *māna* not renounced at that plane?
—Yes. (Same as the aforesaid)

Quadruplet-based

184. Latent states of *kāmarāga*, *paṭigha*, *māna* and *diṭṭhi* are not renounced at this plane. Is latent state of *vicikicchā* not renounced at that plane?
—Yes. (in *apariyāpanna*)
Latent state of *vicikicchā* is not renounced at this plane. Are latent states of *kāmarāga*, *paṭigha*, *māna* and *diṭṭhi* not renounced at that plane?
—Yes (in *apariyāpanna*) ….p…..

Quintuplet-based

185. Latent states of *kāmarāga*, *paṭigha*, *māna*, *diṭṭhi* and *vicikicchā* are not renounced at this plane. Is latent state of *bhavarāga* not renounced at that plane?
—Yes. refer to the answer below.
This plane is not renouncing latent state of *bhavarāga*. Is that plane not renouncing latent states of *kāmarāga*, *paṭigha*, *māna*, *diṭṭhi* and *vicikicchā*?
—No. In unpleasant feeling, *bhavarāga*, *kāmarāga* and *māna* are not renounced, except for *paṭigha*, *diṭṭhi* and *vicikicchā*. In two feelings of the elemental world of sensuous desire, *bhavarāga* and *paṭigha* are not renounced, except for *kāmarāga*, *māna*, *diṭṭhi* and *vicikicchā.*
—Yes. In *apariyāpanna, bhavarāga* is not renounced; similarly for *kāmarāga*, *paṭigha*, *māna*, *diṭṭhi* and *vicikicchā* ….p….

Sextuplet-based

186. Latent states of *kāmarāga*, *paṭigha*, *māna*, *diṭṭhi*, *vicikicchā* and *bhavarāga* are not renounced at this plane. Is latent state of *avijjā* not renounced at that plane?
—Yes. (in *apariyāpanna*)
Latent state of *avijjā* is not renounced at this plane. Is latent states of *kāmarāga*, *paṭigha*, *māna*, *diṭṭhi*, *vicikicchā* and *bhavarāga* not renounced at that plane?
—Yes. (in *apariyāpanna*)

Opposite enquiries by person and plane

Mono-based

187. This person is not renouncing latent state of *kāmarāga* at this plane. Is that person not renouncing latent state of *paṭigha* at that plane?
—No. *Anāgāmi* Path-attainer in unpleasant feeling is not renouncing *kāmarāga*, except for *paṭigha*.
—Yes. Those (same) persons, in the elemental world of fine-material and immaterial, and in *apariyāpanna*; and with the exception of *Anāgāmi* Path-

attainer, those remaining persons in all places—they are renouncing neither *kāmarāga* nor *paṭigha*.

This person is not renouncing latent state of *paṭigha* at this plane. Is that person not renouncing latent state of *kāmarāga* at that plane?
—No. *Anāgāmi* Path-attainer, in two feelings of the elemental world of sensuous desire, is not renouncing *paṭigha*, except for *kāmarāga*.
—Yes. Refer to the aforesaid.

This person is not renouncing latent state of *kāmarāga* at this plane. Is that person not renouncing latent state of *māna* at that plane?
—No. *Arahatta* Path-attainer, in two feelings of the elemental world of sensuous desire, and in the elemental world of fine-material and immaterial, is not renouncing *kāmarāga*, except for *māna*.
—Yes. Those (same) persons, in unpleasant feeling, and in *apariyāpanna*; and with the exception of two Path-attainers, those remaining persons in all places (*Sotāpatti* Path-attainer, *Sakadāgāmi* Path-attainer)—they are renouncing neither *kāmarāga* nor *māna*.
This person is not renouncing latent state of *māna* at this plane. Is that person not renouncing latent state of *kāmarāga* at that plane?
—No. *Anāgāmi* Path-attainer, in two feelings of the elemental world of sensuous desire, is not renouncing *māna*, except for *kāmarāga*.
—Yes. Refer to the aforesaid.

This person is not renouncing latent state of *kāmarāga* at this plane. Is that person not renouncing latent state of *diṭṭhi* .....p.... *vicikicchā* at that plane?
—No. *Sotāpatti* Path-attainer, in three feelings of the elemental world of sensuous desire, and in elemental world of fine-material and immaterial, is not renouncing *kāmarāga*, except for *vicikicchā* (and *diṭṭhi*).
—Yes. Those (same) persons, in *apariyāpanna*; and with the exception of *Anāgāmi* Path-attainer and *Sotāpatti* Path-attainer, those remaining persons in all places; and those persons (*Anāgāmi* Path-attainer), with unpleasant feeling, in the elemental world of fine-material and immaterial, and in *apariyāpanna*—they are renouncing neither *kāmarāga* nor *vicikicchā* (and *diṭṭhi*).
This person is not renouncing latent state of *vicikicchā* at this plane. Is that person not renouncing latent state of *kāmarāga* at that plane?
—No. *Anāgāmi* Path-attainer, in two feelings of the elemental world of sensuous desire, is not renouncing *vicikicchā* (and *diṭṭhi*), except for *kāmarāga*.
—Yes. Refer to the aforesaid.

This person is not renouncing latent state of *kāmarāga* at this plane. Is that person not renouncing latent state of *bhavarāga* at that plane?
—No. *Arahatta* Path-attainer, and in elemental world of fine-material and immaterial, is not renouncing *kāmarāga*, except for *bhavarāga*.
—Yes. Those (same) persons, in three feelings of the elemental world of sensuous desire, and in *apariyāpanna*; with the exception of two Path-attainers,

those remaining persons in all places (*Sotāpatti* Path-attainer, *Sakadāgāmi* Path-attainer); and those persons (*Anāgāmi* Path-attainer), with unpleasant feeling, and in the elemental world of fine-material and immaterial, and in *apariyāpanna*—they are renouncing neither *kāmarāga* nor *bhavarāga*.
This person is not renouncing latent state of *bhavarāga* at this plane. Is that person not renouncing latent state of *kāmarāga* at that plane?
—No. *Anāgāmi* Path-attainer, in two feelings of the elemental world of sensuous desire, is not renouncing *bhavarāga*, except for *kāmarāga*.
—Yes. Refer to the aforesaid.

This person is not renouncing latent state of *kāmarāga* at this plane. Is that person not renouncing latent state of *avijjā* at that plane?
—No. *Arahatta* Path-attainer, in three feelings of the elemental world of sensuous desire, and in the elemental world of fine-material and immaterial, is not renouncing *kāmarāga*, except for *avijjā*.
—Yes. Those (same) persons, in *apariyāpanna*; and with the exception of two Path-attainers, those remaining persons (*Sotāpatti* Path-attainer, *Sakadāgāmi* Path-attainer) in all places; and those persons (*Anāgāmi* Path-attainer), with unpleasant feeling, in the elemental world of fine-material and immaterial, and in *apariyāpanna*—they are renouncing neither *kāmarāga* nor *avijjā*.
This person is not renouncing latent state of *avijjā* at this plane. Is that person not renouncing latent state of *kāmarāga* at that plane?
—No. *Anāgāmi* Path-attainer, in two feelings of the elemental world of sensuous desire, is not renouncing *avijjā*, except for *kāmarāga*.
—Yes. Refer to the aforesaid.

188. This person is not renouncing latent state of *paṭigha* at this plane. Is that person not renouncing latent state of *māna* at that plane?
—No. *Arahatta* Path-attainer, in two feelings of the elemental world of sensuous desire, and in elemental world of fine-material and immaterial, is not renouncing *paṭigha*, except for *māna*.
—Yes. Those (same) persons, in unpleasant feeling, and in *apariyāpanna* (*Arahatta* Path-attainer); with the exception of two Path-attainers, those remaining persons in all places (*Sotāpatti* Path-attainer, *Sakadāgāmi* Path-attainer); and those persons (*Anāgāmi* Path-attainer), with two feelings of the elemental world of sensuous desire, in elemental world of fine-material and immaterial, and in *apariyāpanna*—they are renouncing neither *paṭigha* nor *māna*.
This person is not renouncing latent state of *māna* at this plane. Is that person not renouncing latent state of *paṭigha* at that plane?
—No. *Anāgāmi* Path-attainer in unpleasant feeling is not renouncing *māna*, except for *paṭigha*.
—Yes. Refer to the aforesaid.

This person is not renouncing latent state of *paṭigha* at this plane. Is that person not renouncing latent state of *diṭṭhi* .....p..... *vicikicchā* at that plane?

—No. *Sotāpatti* Path-attainer, in three feelings of the elemental world of sensuous desire, and in elemental world of fine-material and immaterial, is not renouncing *paṭigha*, except for *vicikicchā*.
—Yes. Those (same) persons, in *apariyāpanna*; with the exception of *Anāgāmi* Path-attainer and *Sotāpatti* Path-attainer, those remaining persons in all places; and those persons (*Anāgāmi* Path-attainer), with two feelings of the elemental world of sensuous desire, in elemental world of fine-material and immaterial, and in *apariyāpanna*—are renouncing neither *paṭigha* nor *vicikicchā* (and *diṭṭhi*).
This person is not renouncing latent state of *vicikicchā* at this plane. Is that person not renouncing latent state of *paṭigha* at that plane?
—No. *Anāgāmi* Path-attainer in unpleasant feeling is not renouncing *vicikicchā*, except for *paṭigha*.
—Yes. Refer to the aforesaid.

This person is not renouncing latent state of *paṭigha* at this plane. Is that person not renouncing latent state of *bhavarāga* at that plane?
—No. *Arahatta* Path-attainer, in elemental world of fine-material and immaterial, is not renouncing *paṭigha*, except for *bhavarāga*.
—Yes. Those (same) persons, in three feelings of the elemental world of sensuous desire, and in *apariyāpanna*; with the exception of two Path-attainers, those remaining persons in all places (*Sotāpatti* Path-attainer, *Sakadāgāmi* Path-attainer); and those persons (*Anāgāmi* Path-attainer), with two feelings of the elemental world of sensuous desire, in elemental world of fine-material and immaterial, and in *apariyāpanna* —they are renouncing neither *paṭigha* nor *bhavarāga*.
This person is not renouncing latent state of *bhavarāga* at this plane. Is that person not renouncing latent state of *paṭigha* at that plane?
—No. *Anāgāmi* Path-attainer in unpleasant feeling is not renouncing *bhavarāga*, except for *paṭigha*.
—Yes. Refer to the aforesaid.

This person is not renouncing latent state of *paṭigha* at this plane. Is that person not renouncing latent state of *avijjā* at that plane?
—No. *Arahatta* Path-attainer, in three feelings of the elemental world of sensuous desire, and in elemental world of fine-material and immaterial, is not renouncing *paṭigha*, except for *avijjā*.
—Yes. Those (same) persons, in *apariyāpanna*; with the exception of two Path-attainers, those remaining persons (*Sotāpatti* Path-attainer, *Sakadāgāmi* Path-attainer) in all places; and those persons (*Anāgāmi* Path-attainer), with two feelings of the elemental world of sensuous desire, and in elemental world of fine-material and immaterial—they are renouncing neither *paṭigha* nor *avijjā*.
This person is not renouncing latent state of *avijjā* at this plane. Is that person not renouncing latent state of *paṭigha* at that plane?
—No. *Anāgāmi* Path-attainer in unpleasant feeling is not renouncing *avijjā*, except for *paṭigha*.
—Yes. Refer to the aforesaid.

189. This person is not renouncing latent state of *māna* at this plane. Is that person not renouncing latent state of *diṭṭhi* …..p….. *vicikicchā* at that plane?
—No. *Sotāpatti* Path-attainer, in three feelings of the elemental world of sensuous desire, and in elemental world of fine-material and immaterial, is not renouncing *māna*, except for *vicikicchā*.
—Yes. Those (same) persons, in *apariyāpanna*; with the exception of *Arahatta* Path-attainer and *Sotāpatti* Path-attainer, those remaining persons in all places; those persons (*Arahatta* Path-attainer), with unpleasant feeling, and in *apariyāpanna*—they are renouncing neither *māna* nor *vicikicchā*.
This person is not renouncing latent state of *vicikicchā* at this plane. Is that person not renouncing latent state of *māna* at that plane?
—No. *Arahatta* Path-attainer, in two feelings of the elemental world of sensuous desire, and in elemental world of fine-material and immaterial, is not renouncing *vicikicchā*, except for *māna*.
—Yes. Refer to the aforesaid.

This person is not renouncing latent state of *māna* at this plane. Is that person not renouncing latent state of *bhavarāga* at that plane?
—Yes. Refer to the answer below.
This person is not renouncing latent state of *bhavarāga* at this plane. Is that person not renouncing latent state of *māna* at that plane?
—No. *Arahatta* Path-attainer, in two feelings of the elemental world of sensuous desire, is not renouncing *bhavarāga*, except for *māna*.
—Yes. Those (same) persons, in unpleasant feeling, and in *apariyāpanna*; and with the exception of *Arahatta* Path-attainer, those remaining persons in all places—they are renouncing neither *bhavarāga* nor *māna*.

This person is not renouncing latent state of *māna* at this plane. Is that person not renouncing latent state of *avijjā* at that plane?
—No. *Arahatta* Path-attainer in unpleasant feeling is not renouncing *māna*, except for *avijjā*.
—Yes. Those (same) persons, in *apariyāpanna*; and with the exception of *Arahatta* Path-attainer, those remaining persons in all places—they are renouncing neither *māna* nor *avijjā*.
This person is not renouncing latent state of *avijjā* at this plane. Is that person not renouncing latent state of *māna* at that plane?
—Yes. Refer to the aforesaid.

190. This person is not renouncing latent state of *diṭṭhi* at this plane. Is that person not renouncing latent state of *vicikicchā* at that plane?
—Yes. (those in *apariyāpanna*, and others except *Sotāpatti* Path-attainer)
This person is not renouncing latent state of *vicikicchā* at this plane. Is that person not renouncing latent state of *diṭṭhi* at that plane?
—Yes (Same as aforesaid) …..p…..

191. This person is not renouncing latent state of *vicikicchā* at this plane. Is that person not renouncing latent state of *bhavarāga* at that plane?
—No. *Arahatta* Path-attainer, in elemental world of fine-material and immaterial, is not renouncing *vicikicchā*, except for *bhavarāga*.
—Yes. Those (same) persons, in three feelings of the elemental world of sensuous desire, and in *apariyāpanna*; with the exception of *Arahatta* Path-attainer and *Sotāpatti* Path-attainer, those remaining persons in all places, and those persons (*Sotāpatti* Path-attainer), in *apariyāpanna*—they are renouncing neither *vicikicchā* nor *bhavarāga*.
This person is not renouncing latent state of *bhavarāga* at this plane. Is that person not renouncing latent state of *vicikicchā* at that plane?
—No. *Sotāpatti* Path-attainer, in three feelings of the elemental world of sensuous desire, and in elemental world of fine-material and immaterial, is not renouncing *bhavarāga*, except for *vicikicchā*.
—Yes. Refer to the aforesaid.

This person is not renouncing latent state of *vicikicchā* at this plane. Is that person not renouncing latent state of *avijjā* at that plane?
—No. *Arahatta* Path-attainer, in three feelings of the elemental world of sensuous desire, and in elemental world of fine-material and immaterial, is not renouncing *vicikicchā*, except for *avijjā*.
—Yes. Those (same) persons, in *apariyāpanna*; and with the exception of *Arahatta* Path-attainer and *Sotāpatti* Path-attainer, those remaining persons in all places—they are renouncing neither *vicikicchā* nor *avijjā*.
This person is not renouncing latent state of *avijjā* at this plane. Is that person not renouncing latent state of *vicikicchā* at that plane?
—No. *Sotāpatti* Path-attainer, in three feelings of the elemental world of sensuous desire, and in elemental world of fine-material and immaterial, is not renouncing *avijjā*, except for *vicikicchā*.
—Yes. Refer to the aforesaid.

192. This person is not renouncing latent state of *bhavarāga* at this plane. Is that person not renouncing latent state of *avijjā* at that plane?
—No. *Arahatta* Path-attainer, in three feelings of the elemental world of sensuous desire, is not renouncing *bhavarāga*, except for *avijjā*.
—Yes. Those (same) persons, in *apariyāpanna*; and with the exception of *Arahatta* Path-attainer, these remaining persons in all places—they are renouncing neither *bhavarāga* nor *avijjā*.
This person is not renouncing latent state of *avijjā* at this plane. Is that person not renouncing latent state of *bhavarāga* at that plane?
—Yes. Refer to the aforesaid.

Couplet-based

193. This person is not renouncing latent states of *kāmarāga* and *paṭigha* at this plane. Is that person not renouncing latent state of *māna* at that plane?

—No. *Arahatta* Path-attainer, in two feelings of the elemental world of sensuous desire, and in elemental world of fine-material and immaterial, is not renouncing *kāmarāga* and *paṭigha*, except for *māna*.
—Yes. Those (same) persons, in unpleasant feeling, and in *apariyāpanna*; with the exception of two Path-attainers, those remaining persons in all places (*Sotāpatti* Path-attainer, *Sakadāgāmi* Path-attainer); and those persons (*Anāgāmi* Path-attainer), in the elemental world of fine-material and immaterial, and in *apariyāpanna*—they are not renouncing *kāmarāga*, *paṭigha*, and *māna*.
This person is not renouncing latent state of *māna* at this plane. Is that person not renouncing latent states of *kāmarāga* and *paṭigha* at that plane?
—No. *Anāgāmi* Path-attainer in unpleasant feeling is not renouncing *māna* and *kāmarāga*, except for *paṭigha*. Those (same) persons, in two feelings of the elemental world of sensuous desire, are not renouncing *māna* and *paṭigha*, except for *kāmarāga*.
—Yes. Refer to the aforesaid.

This person is not renouncing latent states of *kāmarāga* and *paṭigha* at this plane. Is that person not renouncing latent state *diṭṭhi* .....p..... *vicikicchā* at that plane?
—No. *Sotāpatti* Path-attainer, in three feelings of the elemental world of sensuous desire, and in elemental world of fine-material and immaterial, is not renouncing *kāmarāga* and *paṭigha*, except for *vicikicchā*.
—Yes. Those (same) persons, in *apariyāpanna*; with the exception of *Anāgāmi* Path-attainer and *Sotāpatti* Path-attainer, those remaining persons in all places; and those persons (*Anāgāmi* Path-attainer), in the elemental world of fine-material and immaterial, and in *apariyāpanna*—they are not renouncing *kāmarāga*, *paṭigha*, and also *vicikicchā*.
This person is not renouncing latent state of *vicikicchā* at this plane. Is that person not renouncing latent states of *kāmarāga* and *paṭigha* at that plane?
—No. *Anāgāmi* Path-attainer in unpleasant feeling is not renouncing *vicikicchā* and *kāmarāga*, except for *paṭigha*. Those (same) persons, in two feelings of the elemental world of sensuous desire, is not renouncing *vicikicchā* and *paṭigha*, except for *kāmarāga*.
—Yes. Refer to the aforesaid.

This person is not renouncing latent states of *kāmarāga* and *paṭigha* at this plane. Is that person not renouncing latent state of *bhavarāga* at that plane?
—No. *Arahatta* Path-attainer, in elemental world of fine-material and immaterial, is not renouncing *kāmarāga* and *paṭigha*, except for *bhavarāga*.
—Yes. Those (same) persons, in three feelings of the elemental world of sensuous desire, and in *apariyāpanna*; with the exception of two Path-attainers, those remaining persons in all places (*Sotāpatti* Path-attainer, *Sakadāgāmi* Path-attainer); and those persons (*Anāgāmi* Path-attainer), in the elemental world of fine-material world and immaterial, and in *apariyāpanna*—they are not renouncing *kāmarāga*, *paṭigha*, and also *bhavarāga*.
This person is not renouncing latent state of *bhavarāga* at this plane. Is that person not renouncing latent states of *kāmarāga* and *paṭigha* at that plane?

—No. *Anāgāmi* Path-attainer in unpleasant feeling is not renouncing *bhavarāga* and *kāmarāga*, except for *paṭigha*. Those (same) person, with two feelings of the elemental world of sensuous desire, are not renouncing *bhavarāga* and *paṭigha*, except for *kāmarāga*.
—Yes. Refer to the aforesaid.

This person is not renouncing latent states of *kāmarāga* and *paṭigha* at this plane. Is that person not renouncing latent state of *avijjā* at that plane?
—No. *Arahatta* Path-attainer, in three feelings of the elemental world of sensuous desire, and in elemental world of fine-material and immaterial, is not renouncing *kāmarāga* and *paṭigha*, except for *avijjā*.
—Yes. Those (same) persons, in *apariyāpanna*; with the exception of two Path-attainers, those remaining persons in all places (*Sotāpatti* Path-attainer and *Sakadāgāmi* Path-attainer); and those persons (*Anāgāmi* Path-attainer), in the elemental world of fine-material and immaterial—they are not renouncing *kāmarāga* and *paṭigha*, and also *avijjā*.
This person is not renouncing latent state of *avijjā* at this plane. Is that person not renouncing latent states of *kāmarāga* and *paṭigha* at that plane?
—No. *Anāgāmi* Path-attainer in unpleasant feeling is not renouncing *avijjā* and *kāmarāga*, except for *paṭigha*. Those (same) persons, in two feelings of the elemental world of sensuous desire, areo not renouncing *avijjā* and *paṭigha*, except for *kāmarāga*.
—Yes. Refer to the aforesaid.

Triplet-based

194. This person is not renouncing latent states of *kāmarāga*, *paṭigha* and *māna* at this plane. Is that person not renouncing latent state of *diṭṭhi* .....p..... *vicikicchā* at that plane?
—No. *Sotāpatti* Path-attainer, in three feelings of the elemental world of sensuous desire, and in elemental world of fine-material and immaterial, is not renouncing *kāmarāga*, *paṭigha* and *māna*, except for *vicikicchā*.
—Yes. Those (same) persons, in *apariyāpanna*; with the exception of two Path-attainers and *Sotāpatti* Path-attainer, those remaining persons in all places (*Sakadāgāmi* Path-attainer); those persons (*Anāgāmi* Path-attainer), in the elemental world of fine-material and immaterial, and in *apariyāpanna*; and *Arahatta* Path-attainer in unpleasant feeling (and in *apariyāpanna*)—they are not renouncing *kāmarāga*, *paṭigha*, *māna*, and also *vicikicchā*.
This person is not renouncing latent state of *vicikicchā* at this plane. Is that person not renouncing latent states of *kāmarāga*, *paṭigha* and *māna* at that plane?
—No. *Anāgāmi* Path-attainer in unpleasant feeling is not renouncing *vicikicchā*, *kāmarāga* and *māna*, except for *paṭigha*. Those (same) persons, in two feelings of the elemental world of sensuous desire, are not renouncing *vicikicchā*, *paṭigha* and *māna*, except for *kāmarāga*. *Arahatta* Path-attainer, in two feelings of the elemental world of sensuous desire, and in elemental world of fine-material and immaterial, is not renouncing *vicikicchā*, *kāmarāga* and *paṭigha*, except for *māna*.

—Yes. Refer to the aforesaid.

This person is not renouncing latent states of *kāmarāga*, *paṭigha* and *māna* at this plane. Is that person not renouncing latent state of *bhavarāga* at that plane?
—Yes. Refer to the answer below.
This person is not renouncing latent state of *bhavarāga* at this plane. Is that person not renouncing latent states of *kāmarāga*, *paṭigha* and *māna* at that plane?
—No. *Anāgāmi* Path-attainer in unpleasant feeling is not renouncing *bhavarāga*, *kāmarāga* and *māna*, except for *paṭigha*. Those (same) persons, in two feelings of the elemental world of sensuous desire, are not renouncing *bhavarāga*, *paṭigha* and *māna*, except for *kāmarāga*. *Arahatta* Path-attainer, in two feelings of the elemental world of sensuous desire, is not renouncing *bhavarāga*, *kāmarāga* and *paṭigha*, except for *māna*.
—Yes. Those persons (*Anāgāmi* Path-attainer), in the elemental world of fine-material and immaterial, and in *apariyāpanna*; those persons (*Arahatta* Path-attainer) in unplesant feeling, and in *apariyāpanna*; and with the exception of two Path-attainers, those remaining persons in all places (*Sotāpatti* Path-attainer, *Sakadāgāmi* Path-attainer)—they are not renouncing *bhavarāga*, and also *kāmarāga*, *paṭigha* and *māna*.

This person is not renouncing latent states of *kāmarāga*, *paṭigha* and *māna* at this plane. Is that person not renouncing latent state of *avijjā* at that plane?
—No. *Arahatta* Path-attainer in unpleasant feeling is not renouncing *kāmarāga*, *paṭigha* and *māna*, except for *avijjā*.
—Yes. Those (same) persons, in *apariyāpanna*; with the exception of two Path-attainers, those remaining persons in all places (*Sotāpatti* Path-attainer, *Sakadāgāmi* Path-attainer); and those persons (*Anāgāmi* Path-attainer), in elemental world of fine-material and immaterial, and in *apariyāpanna*—they are not renouncing *kāmarāga*, *paṭigha*, *māna*, and also *avijjā*.
This person is not renouncing latent state of *avijjā* at this plane. Is that person not renouncing latent states of *kāmarāga*, *paṭigha* and *māna* at that plane?
—No. *Anāgāmi* Path-attainer in unpleasant feeling is not renouncing *avijjā*, *kāmarāga* and *māna*, except for *paṭigha*. Those (same) persons, in two feelings of the elemental world of sensuous desire, is not renouncing *avijjā*, *paṭigha* and *māna*, except for *kāmarāga*.
—Yes. Refer to the aforesaid.

Quadruplet-based

195. This person is not renouncing latent states of *kāmarāga*, *paṭigha*, *māna* and *diṭṭhi* at this plane. Is that person not renouncing latent state of *vicikicchā* at that plane?
—Yes. Refer to the answer below.
This person is not renouncing latent state of *vicikicchā* at this plane. Is that person not renouncing latent states of *kāmarāga*, *paṭigha*, *māna* and *diṭṭhi* at that plane?

—No. *Anāgāmi* Path-attainer in unpleasant feeling is not renouncing *vicikicchā, kāmarāga, māna* and *diṭṭhi*, except for *paṭigha*. Those (same) persons, in two feelings of the elemental world of sensuous desire, are not renouncing *vicikicchā, paṭigha, māna* and *diṭṭhi*, except for *kāmarāga*. *Arahatta* Path-attainer, in two feelings of the elemental world of sensuous desire, and in the elemental world of fine-material and immaterial, is not renouncing *vicikicchā, kāmarāga, paṭigha* and *diṭṭhi*, except for *māna*.
—Yes. Those persons (*Anāgāmi* Path-attainer), in the elemental world of fine-material and immaterial, and in *apariyāpanna*; those persons (*Arahatta* Path-attainer), with unpleasant feeling, and in *apariyāpanna*; and with the exception of two Path-attainers and *Sotāpatti* Path-attainer, those remaining persons in all places (*Sakadāgāmi* Path-attainer)—they are not renouncing *vicikicchā*, and also are not renouncing *kāmarāga, paṭigha, māna* and diṭṭh .....p.....

Quintuplet-based

196. This person is not renouncing latent states of *kāmarāga, paṭigha, māna, diṭṭhi* and *vicikicchā* at this plane. Is that person not renouncing latent state of *bhavarāga* at that plane?
—Yes. Refer to the answer below.
This person is not renouncing latent state of *bhavarāga* at this plane. Is that person not renouncing latent states of *kāmarāga, paṭigha, māna, diṭṭhi* and *vicikicchā* at that plane?
—No. *Sotāpatti* Path-attainer, in three feelings of the elemental world of sensuous desire, and in the elemental world of fine-material and immaterial, is not renouncing *bhavarāga, kāmarāga, paṭigha* and *māna*, except for *diṭṭhi* and *vicikicchā*. *Anāgāmi* Path-attainer in unpleasant feeling is not renouncing *bhavarāga, kāmarāga, māna, diṭṭhi* and *vicikicchā*, except for *paṭigha*. Those (same) persons, in two feelings of the elemental world of sensuous desire, are not renouncing *bhavarāga, paṭigha, māna, diṭṭhi* and *vicikicchā*, except for *kāmarāga*. *Arahatta* Path-attainer, in two feelings of the elemental world of sensuous desire, is not renouncing *bhavarāga, kāmarāga, paṭigha, diṭṭhi* and *vicikicchā*, except for *māna*.
—Yes. Those persons (*Anāgāmi* Path-attainer), in elemental world of fine-material and immaterial, and in *apariyāpanna*; those persons (*Arahatta* Path-attainer), with unpleasant feeling, and in *apariyāpanna*; those (other) persons, in *apariyāpanna* (*Sotāpatti* Path-attainer, *Arahatta* Path-attainer); and with the exception of two Path-attainers and *Sotāpatti* Path-attainer, those remaining persons in all places (*Sakadāgāmi* Path-attainer)—they are not renouncing *bhavarāga*, and also *kāmarāga, paṭigha, māna, diṭṭhi* and *vicikicchā*.

This person is not renouncing latent states of *kāmarāga, paṭigha, māna, diṭṭhi* and *vicikicchā* at this plane. Is that person not renouncing latent state of *avijjā* at that plane?
—No. *Arahatta* Path-attainer in unpleasant feeling is not renouncing *kāmarāga, paṭigha, māna, diṭṭhi* and *vicikicchā*, except for *avijjā*.

—Yes. Those persons (*Sotāpatti* Path-attainer and *Arahatta* Path-attainer), in *apariyāpanna*; with the exception of two Path-attainers and *Sotāpatti* Path-attainer, those remaining persons in all places; and those persons (*Anāgāmi* Path-attainer), in the elemental world of fine-material and immaterial, and in *apariyāpanna*—they are not renouncing *kāmarāga*, *paṭigha*, *māna*, *diṭṭhi*, *vicikicchā*, and also *avijjā*.
This person is not renouncing latent state of *avijjā* at this plane. Is that person not renouncing latent states of *kāmarāga*, *paṭigha*, *māna*, *diṭṭhi* and *vicikicchā* at that plane?
—No. *Sotāpatti* Path-attainer, in three feelings of the elemental world of sensuous desire, and in the elemental world of fine-material and immaterial, is not renouncing *avijjā*, *kāmarāga*, *paṭigha* and *māna*, except for *diṭṭhi* and *vicikicchā*. *Anāgāmi* Path-attainer in unpleasant feeling, is not renouncing *avijjā*, *kāmarāga*, *māna*, *diṭṭhi* and *vicikicchā*, except for *paṭigha*. Those (same) persons, with in feelings of the elemental world of sensuous desire, are not renouncing *avijjā*, *kāmarāga*, *māna*, *diṭṭhi* and *vicikicchā*, except for *kāmarāga*.
—Yes. Refer to the aforesaid.

Sextuplet-based

197. This person is not renouncing latent states of *kāmarāga*, *paṭigha*, *māna*, *diṭṭhi*, *vicikicchā* and *bhavarāga* at this plane. Is that person not renouncing latent state of *avijjā* at that plane?
—No. *Arahatta* Path-attainer in unpleasant feeling is not renouncing *kāmarāga*, *paṭigha*, *māna*, *diṭṭhi*, *vicikicchā* and *bhavarāga*, except for *avijjā*.
—Yes. Those persons (*Sotāpatti* Path-attainer and *Arahatta* Path-attainer), in *apariyāpanna*; those persons (*Anāgāmi* Path-attainer), in the elemental world of fine-material and immaterial, and in *apariyāpanna*; and with the exception of two Path-attainers and *Sotāpatti* Path-attainer, those remaining persons in all places—they are not renouncing *kāmarāga*, *paṭigha*, *māna*, *diṭṭhi*, *vicikicch*, *bhavarāga*, and also *avijjā*.
This person is not renouncing latent state of *avijjā* at this plane. Is that person not renouncing latent states of *kāmarāga*, *paṭigha*, *māna*, *diṭṭhi*, *vicikicchā* and *bhavarāga* at that plane?
—No. *Sotāpatti* Path-attainer, in three feelings of the elemental world of sensuous desire, and in the elemental world of fine-material and immaterial, is not renouncing *avijjā*, *kāmarāga*, *paṭigha*, *māna* and *bhavarāga*, except for *diṭṭhi* and *vicikicchā*. *Anāgāmi* Path-attainer in unpleasant feeling is not renouncing *avijjā*, *kāmarāga*, *māna*, *diṭṭhi*, *vicikicchā* and *bhavarāga*, except for *paṭigha*. Those (same) persons, in two feelings of the elemental world of sensuous desire, are not renouncing *avijjā*, *paṭigha*, *māna*, *diṭṭhi*, *vicikicchā* and *bhavarāga*, except for *kāmarāga*.
—Yes. Refer to the aforesaid.

7.2.4 Comprehending latent states (*Pariññā*)

Chart 7.10 below summarises the questions and answers from catechisms nos. 198-208 and from 231-241. The answers are the same as those in Chart 7.7. When a person is renouncing latent states, it means he or she at the same time fully comprehends them. A person is renouncing some latent states because of comprehending only some. Likewise, when a person is renouncing none, it is because of the lack of full understanding regarding the particular latent states. For example, attainers of stream-winning path and once-returning path comprehend only a part of how the harm caused by attachment to sensuous desires and hatred can bring to them, and hence they do not renounce them. It is only by the non-returning path attainer that those two latent states are renounced.

But why is it that according to the answers in the chart, *Arahatta* Path-attainer is not comprehending latent states of *kāmarāga* and *paṭigha*, and in another case of the three persons except *Sotāpatti* Path-attainer, who are not comprehending latent states of *diṭṭhi* and *vicikicchā*? Herein is the reason why the Pāli word *pajahati* has to be interpreted as 'renouncing' instead of just 'renounce', as well as *parijānāti* has to be construed as 'comprehending' instead of 'comprehends'. If the tenses are not constructed in present participle, for example, we will end up saying that *Arahatta* Path-attainer does not comprehend *kāmarāga* and *paṭigha*, and also mistakenly concluding that the three persons except *Sotāpatti* Path-attainer, do not comprehend latent states of *diṭṭhi* and *vicikicchā*. The results in this chart in terms of comprehension by person, have to be taken as at present time and in line with the aim and purpose of individual development at one particular stage. There is no overlap of roles and functions.

Chart 7.10 Comprehending latent states (enquiries by person)

Y: yes, is fully comprehending; C_p: is comprehending a part of it
N: no, is not comprehending (in some cases is to avoid duplication in individual action)
NC_p : is not comprehending completely, except for comprehending a part of it

	latent state of :						
	kāmarāga	paṭigha	māna	diṭṭhi	vicikicchā	bhavarāga	avijjā
Attainer of the eight Path of 'stream-winning' (*Sotāpattimaggasamaṅgī*)	N C_p	N C_p	N C_p	Y	Y	N C_p	N C_p
Attainer of the 'once-returning' Path (*Sakadāgāmimaggasamaṅgī*)	N	N	N	N	N	N	N
Attainer of the 'non-returning' Path (*Anāgāmimaggasamaṅgī*)	Y	Y	N C_p	N	N	N C_p	N C_p
Attainer of the highest *Arahatta* Path (*Aggamaggasamaṅgī*)	N	N	Y	N	N	Y	Y

Chart 7.11 below summarises the catechisms from nos. 209-219 and from 242-252 with regard to plane. The answers are the same as those in Chart 7.8.

Chart 7.11 Comprehending latent states (enquiries by plane)

Y: Yes, is fully comprehended
N: No, is not fully comprehended

		latent state of : kāmarāga	paṭigha	māna	diṭṭhi	vicikicchā	bhavarāga	avijjā
In unpleasant feeling	in the elemental world of desire	N	Y	N	Y	Y	N	Y
In pleasant feeling		Y	N	Y	Y	Y	N	Y
In neither pleasant feeling nor unpleasant feeling		Y	N	Y	Y	Y	N	Y
In unpleasant feeling	in the elemental world of fine-material and immaterial	N	N	Y	Y	Y	Y	Y
In pleasant feeling		N	N	Y	Y	Y	Y	Y
In neither pleasant feeling nor unpleasant feeling		N	N	Y	Y	Y	Y	Y
In unpleasant feeling	in *apariyāpanna* (supramundane)	N	N	N	N	N	N	N
In pleasant feeling		N	N	N	N	N	N	N
In neither pleasant feeling nor unpleasant feeling		N	N	N	N	N	N	N

Chart 7.12 Comprehending latent states (enquiries by person-plane)

Y: yes, is fully comprehending; C_p: is comprehending a part of it
N: no, is not comprehending (in some cases is to avoid duplication in individual action)
NC_p : is not comprehending completely, except for comprehending a part of it

Person	Feeling	in elemental worlds of desire	in elemental worlds of fine-material and immaterial	in *apariyāpanna* (supramundane)	latent state of: kāmarāga	paṭigha	māna	diṭṭhi	vicikicchā	bhavarāga	avijjā
Sotāpatti Path-attainer	with unpleasant feeling	•			N	NC_p	N	Y	Y	N	NC_p
	with pleasant feeling	•			NC_p	N	NC_a	Y	Y	N	NC_p
	with neither pleasant feeling nor unpleasant feeling	•			NC_p	N	NC_a	Y	Y	N	NC_p
	with unpleasant feeling		•		N	NC_p	NC_a	Y	Y	NC_p	NC_p
	with pleasant feeling		•		N	NC_p	NC_a	Y	Y	NC_p	NC_p
	with neither pleasant feeling nor unpleasant feeling		•		N	NC_p	NC_a	Y	Y	NC_p	NC_p
	with unpleasant feeling			•	N	N	N	N	N	N	N
	with pleasant feeling			•	N	N	N	N	N	N	N
	with neither pleasant feeling nor unpleasant feeling			•	N	N	N	N	N	N	N
Sakadāgāmi Path-attainer	with unpleasant feeling	•			N	N	N	N	N	N	N
	with pleasant feeling	•			N	N	N	N	N	N	N
	with neither pleasant feeling nor unpleasant feeling	•			N	N	N	N	N	N	N
	with unpleasant feeling		•		N	N	N	N	N	N	N
	with pleasant feeling		•		N	N	N	N	N	N	N
	with neither pleasant feeling nor unpleasant feeling		•		N	N	N	N	N	N	N
	with unpleasant feeling			•	N	N	N	N	N	N	N
	with pleasant feeling			•	N	N	N	N	N	N	N
	with neither pleasant feeling nor unpleasant feeling			•	N	N	N	N	N	N	N
Anāgāmi Path-attainer	with unpleasant feeling	•			N	Y	N	N	N	N	NY_a
	with pleasant feeling	•			Y	N	NC_p	N	N	N	NC_p
	with neither pleasant feeling nor unpleasant feeling	•			Y	N	NC_p	N	N	N	NC_p
	with unpleasant feeling		•		N	N	**NC_p**	N	N	**NC_p**	**NC_p**
	with pleasant feeling		•		N	N	**NC_p**	N	N	**NC_p**	**NC_p**
	with neither pleasant feeling nor unpleasant feeling		•		N	N	**NC_p**	N	N	**NC_p**	**NC_p**
	with unpleasant feeling			•	N	N	N	N	N	N	N
	with pleasant feeling			•	N	N	N	N	N	N	N
	with neither pleasant feeling nor unpleasant feeling			•	N	N	N	N	N	N	N
Arahatta Path-attainer	with unpleasant feeling	•			N	N	N	N	N	N	Y
	with pleasant feeling	•			N	N	Y	N	N	N	Y
	with neither pleasant feeling nor unpleasant feeling	•			N	N	Y	N	N	N	Y
	with unpleasant feeling		•		N	N	Y	N	N	Y	Y
	with pleasant feeling		•		N	N	Y	N	N	Y	Y
	with neither pleasant feeling nor unpleasant feeling		•		N	N	Y	N	N	Y	Y
	with unpleasant feeling			•	N	N	N	N	N	N	N
	with pleasant feeling			•	N	N	N	N	N	N	N
	with neither pleasant feeling nor unpleasant feeling			•	N	N	N	N	N	N	N

Chart 7.12 above summarises the questions and answers from catechisms nos. 220-230 and from 253-263. The answers are the same as those in Chart 7.9, for when a person is permanently renouncing latent states at particular Path and

plane, he thereat fully comprehends them. When of particular latent states he comprehends only some parts, he naturally is renouncing only some. Likewise, when he is renouncing none, it is because he does not at the same time fully comprehend them. At this point, there is also a person who is renouncing none although he says he fully comprehends them. But it is only understanding theoretically, for preponderance of his/her bad anusayas and cetasikas outweighs the importance and need for purity of living. They are kinds of puthujjanas, but are not being discussed in the catechisms.

The text does not at all indicate that *Anāgāmi* Path-attainer is comprehending a part of *māna*, *bhavarāga* and *avijjā* in the elemental world of fine-material and immaterial. It only indicates that *Anāgāmi* Path-attainer is comprehending a part of *māna* and *avijjā* in the element world of sensuous desire. I have indicated in the chart that *māna*, *bhavarāga* and *avijjā* should also be renounced in part by *Anāgāmi* Path-attainer in the elemental world of fine-materiality and immateriality. I could be wrong.

Forward enquiries by person

198. This person is fully comprehending latent state of *kāmarāga*. Is that person fully comprehending latent state of *paṭigha*?
—Yes. (*Sotāpatti* Path-attainer, *Sakadāgāmi* Path-attainer, *Arahatta* Path-attainer)
This person is fully comprehending latent state of *paṭigha*. Is that person fully comprehending latent state of *kāmarāga*? —Yes. (Same as above)

This person is fully comprehending latent state of *kāmarāga*. Is that person fully comprehending latent state of *māna*? —Yes. (Same as below)
This person is fully comprehending latent state of *māna*. Is that person fully comprehending latent state of *kāmarāga*?
—No. (*Arahatta* Path-attainer, due to latent states of restlessness and ignorance)
….. p …..

Forward enquiries by plane

209. Latent state of *kāmarāga* is fully comprehended at this plane. Is latent state of *paṭigha* fully comprehended at that plane?
—No. (In two feelings of the elemental world of sensuous desire)
(b) Latent state of *paṭigha* is fully comprehended at this plane. Is latent state of *kāmarāga* fully comprehended at that plane?
—No. (In unpleasant feeling, in the elemental world of sensuous desire)
….. p …..

Forward enquiries by person and plane

220. This person is fully comprehending latent state of *kāmarāga* at this plane. Is that person fully comprehending latent state of *paṭigha* at that plane?
—No. (*Anāgāmi* Path-attainer in two feelings of the world of sensuous desire)

(b) This person is fully comprehending latent state of *paṭigha* at this plane. Is that person fully comprehending latent state of *kāmarāga* at that plane?
—No. (Same as aforesaid) ….. p …..

Opposite enquiries by person
Opposite enquiries by plane
Opposite enquiries by person and plane

The rest of catechisms should be constructed in the same manner as in the above examples (ends at nos. 263).

7.2.5 Elimination of latent states (*Pahīna*)

In this chapter, whole or part of the answer with "neither the said latent state has been eliminated nor has it not been eliminated" is given as explanation in the enquiries by plane and by person-and-plane instead of having "no" as the answers, according to the text. For example, because aversion arises only at unpleasant feeling, and does not arise at the other two feelings of the elemental world of sensuous desire, it therefore is not correct to say that aversion has not been eliminated in the latter. The underlying tendency of aversion can only be eliminated at time of unpleasant feeling. There is no chance of it to be renounced and eliminated at pleasant feeling or at equanimous feeling during meditation. Interestingly, the same way of answering with 'neither and no' is also used in all the interrogation sections in the second book of Vibhaṅgapāli, such as 'sometimes is this …; sometimes is that …; sometimes should not be said to be either, is this … or is that …' (siyā … ceva no ca …, siyā na vattabbā …). But why has the neither-and-no answer not been given in the preceding four sections and in previous chapters of Yamakapāli? The explanation goes back to 'elimination' itself which must be supported by the practicality of it being renounceable. If the latent states in question can not coexist, or be renounced simultaneously, then the answer with 'neither and no' should be applied. Those enquiries by person-only are not bounded by this neither-and-nor rationale, because the answers are not being specific to situation and plane. The term elimination in this section is all expressed in past participle (*pahina*, *pahīno*).

The following mix-types of persons, designated by symbols, would be used in those answers attached to the enquiries by person, and by person-plane.

Two persons ★ (Sotāpanna, Sakadāgāmi)
Two persons ☆ (Anāgāmi, Arahat)
Three persons ③ (Puthujjana, Sotāpanna, Sakadāgāmi)
Three persons ⁝ (Sotāpanna, Sakadāgāmi, Anāgāmi)
Four persons ④ (Puthujjana, Sotāpanna, Sakadāgāmi, Anāgāmi)
Four persons ∷ (Sotāpanna, Sakadāgāmi, Anāgāmi, Arahat)

Chart **7.13 Elimination of latent states (enquiries by person)**

Y: Yes, has eliminated; N: No, has not eliminated

	latent state of:						
	kāmarāga	paṭigha	māna	diṭṭhi	vicikicchā	bhavarāga	avijjā
Puthujjana	N	N	N	N	N	N	N
Sotāpanna	N	N	N	Y	Y	N	N
Sakadāgāmi	N	N	N	Y	Y	N	N
Anāgāmi	Y	Y	N	Y	Y	N	N
Arahat	Y	Y	Y	Y	Y	Y	Y

Chart 7.13 above summarises the catechisms from nos. 264-274 and from nos. 297-307.

Chart 7.14 Elimination of latent states (enquiries by plane)

Y: Yes, has been eliminated; N: No, has not been eliminated
Nn: Neither has been eliminated, nor has not been eliminated should be said

		latent state of:						
		kāmarāga	paṭigha	māna	diṭṭhi	vicikicchā	bhavarāga	avijjā
In unpleasant feeling	in elemental world of sensuous desire	*Nn*	Y N	*Nn*	Y N	Y N	*Nn*	Y N
In pleasant feeling		Y N	*Nn*	Y N	Y N	Y N	*Nn*	Y N
In neither pleasant feeling nor unpleasant feeling		Y N	*Nn*	Y N	Y N	Y N	*Nn*	Y N
In unpleasant feeling	in elemental world of fine-material and immaterial	*Nn*	*Nn*	Y N	Y N	Y N	Y N	Y N
In pleasant feeling		*Nn*	*Nn*	Y N	Y N	Y N	Y N	Y N
In neither pleasant feeling nor unpleasant feeling		*Nn*	*Nn*	Y N	Y N	Y N	Y N	Y N

Chart 7.14 above summarises the catechisms from nos. 275-285 and from nos. 308-318. As seen in the chart, there are both positive and negative answers as to elimination of certain latent states in some situations. This just can not be avoided when making tabulation merely by plane, because the different persons had varying completed results on the very same plane or elemental world.

Chart 7.15 Elimination of latent states (enquiries by person and plane)

Y: Yes, has eliminated; N: No, has not eliminated
Nn: Neither has been eliminated nor has not been eliminated should be said

Person	Feeling	in elemental world of sensuous desire	in elemental world of fine-material and immaterial	latent state of: kāmarāga	paṭigha	māna	diṭṭhi	vicikicchā	bhavarāga	avijjā
Puthujjana	with unpleasant feeling	•		*Nn*	N	*Nn*	N	N	*Nn*	N
	with pleasant feeling	•		N	*Nn*	N	N	N	*Nn*	N
	with neither pleasant feeling nor unpleasant feeling	•		N	*Nn*	N	N	N	*Nn*	N
	with unpleasant feeling		•	*Nn*	*Nn*	N	N	N	N	N
	with pleasant feeling		•	*Nn*	*Nn*	N	N	N	N	N
	with neither pleasant feeling nor unpleasant feeling		•	*Nn*	*Nn*	N	N	N	N	N
Sotāpanna	with unpleasant feeling	•		*Nn*	N	*Nn*	Y	Y	*Nn*	N
	with pleasant feeling	•		N	*Nn*	N	Y	Y	*Nn*	N
	with neither pleasant feeling nor unpleasant feeling	•		N	*Nn*	N	Y	Y	*Nn*	N
	with unpleasant feeling		•	*Nn*	*Nn*	N	Y	Y	N	N
	with pleasant feeling		•	*Nn*	*Nn*	N	Y	Y	N	N
	with neither pleasant feeling nor unpleasant feeling		•	*Nn*	*Nn*	N	Y	Y	N	N
Sakadāgāmi	with unpleasant feeling	•		*Nn*	N	*Nn*	Y	Y	*Nn*	N
	with pleasant feeling	•		N	*Nn*	N	Y	Y	*Nn*	N
	with neither pleasant feeling nor unpleasant feeling	•		N	*Nn*	N	Y	Y	*Nn*	N
	with unpleasant feeling		•	*Nn*	*Nn*	N	Y	Y	N	N
	with pleasant feeling		•	*Nn*	*Nn*	N	Y	Y	N	N
	with neither pleasant feeling nor unpleasant feeling		•	*Nn*	*Nn*	N	Y	Y	N	N
Anāgāmi	with unpleasant feeling	•		*Nn*	Y	*Nn*	Y	Y	*Nn*	N
	with pleasant feeling	•		Y	*Nn*	N	Y	Y	*Nn*	N
	with neither pleasant feeling nor unpleasant feeling	•		Y	*Nn*	N	Y	Y	*Nn*	N
	with unpleasant feeling		•	*Nn*	*Nn*	N	Y	Y	N	N
	with pleasant feeling		•	*Nn*	*Nn*	N	Y	Y	N	N
	with neither pleasant feeling nor unpleasant feeling		•	*Nn*	*Nn*	N	Y	Y	N	N
Arahat	with unpleasant feeling	•		*Nn*	Y	*Nn*	Y	Y	*Nn*	Y
	with pleasant feeling	•		Y	*Nn*	Y	Y	Y	*Nn*	Y
	with neither pleasant feeling nor unpleasant feeling	•		Y	*Nn*	Y	Y	Y	*Nn*	Y
	with unpleasant feeling		•	*Nn*	*Nn*	Y	Y	Y	Y	Y
	with pleasant feeling		•	*Nn*	*Nn*	Y	Y	Y	Y	Y
	with neither pleasant feeling nor unpleasant feeling		•	*Nn*	*Nn*	Y	Y	Y	Y	Y

Chart 7.15 above summarises the catechisms from nos. 286-296 and from nos. 319-329. Unlike in Chart 7.9 regarding renunciation of latent states, the term *apariyāpanna* (supramundane) is not mentioned in the section on elimination. The reason being the underlying latencies do not lie unmanifest in the eight noble persons belonging to the sphere of *apariyāpanna*. All needed to be renounced and eliminated are already done prior to *apariyāpanna*, and thereby no need for making further enquiries on renouncing and eliminating by them. The previous catechisms as revealed in Chart 7.3 and Chart 7.9 are only done to show us this fact, and so it was excluded from re-examining again in the section on

elimination.

I constructed the following chart in order to enable a comparative view on these different classes of defilement components, which many of them largely overlap. Regardless of their synonymity, the purpose is to show the overall status as regard renunciation, attenuation, and elimination of all of these faulty factors by the four noble types of persons. This way it should give us a good opportunity to collectively re-examine and understand their relationship.

Chart 7.16 Anusayas with saṃyojanas, faulty cetasikas, and unwholesome cittas—comparing renunciation and elimination

E : has been eliminated; R_a : renounces a part of it; *A* : only attenuates

7 latencies (*anusayā*)		10 fetters (*saṃyojanānī*)		14 unwholesome mental concomitants	12 unwholesome sensuous cittas	Sotāpanna	Sakadāgāmi	Anāgāmi	Arahat
kāmarāga	all which go into this body is likewise *avijjā*	kāmacchandā	all which go into this body is likewise *avijjā*	greed (*lobha*)	8 greed-rooted cittas	R_a	*A*	E	E
bhavarāga		rūparāga,arūparāga				R_a	*A*	*A*	E
paṭigha		byāpāda		hatred (*dosa*)	2 hatred-rooted cittas	R_a	*A*	E	E
māna		māna		conceit (*māna*)	4 greed-rooted cittas without wrong views (and other kinds)	R_a	*A*	*A*	E
diṭṭhi		sakkāyadiṭṭhi, sīlabbataparāmāsa		wrong view (*diṭṭhi*)	4 greed-rooted cittas with wrong views	E	E	E	E
vicikicchā		vicikicchā		doubt (*vicikicchā*)	1 delusiion-rooted citta with doubt	E	E	E	E
avijjā		uddhacca		restlessness (*uddhacca*)	restlessness. delusion, unashamedness, and unconscionableness arise in ALL 12 unwholesome cittas of the sense-world	R_a	*A*	*A*	E
		avijjā		delusion (*moha*)		R_a	*A*	*A*	E
				unashamedness (*ahirīka*)		R_a	*A*	*A*	E
				fearless or unconscionable of wrongdoing (*anottappa*)		R_a	*A*	*A*	E
				envy (*issā*)	2 hatred-rooted cittas (and other kinds)	R_a	*A*	*A*	E
				avarice (*macchariya*)	2 hatred-rooted cittas (and other kinds)	R_a	*A*	*A*	E
				worry/brooding (*kukkucca*)	2 hatred-rooted cittas (and other kinds)	R_a	*A*	*A*	E
				sloth (*thīna*)	5 akusala cittas, prompted.	R_a	*A*	*A*	E
				torpor (*middha*)	(See the 2+2+1 below)	R_a	*A*	*A*	E

A few points to note from the above chart. The mental concomitants of envy, avarice, and worry/brooding need not necessarily arise with aversion in the 2 hatred-rooted cittas, although the three all show mark of aversion. The latency and fetter of *avijjā* is not only ignorance which cloaks us from understanding the true nature of things, whether they are discernible objects or other less perceptible mental phenomena such as these classes of defilement components. As the text explained at the beginning of this chapter, whatsoever that are the inputs into this body (and so mind) are referred to as *avijjā*. It is the wellspring which perpetuates the loop cycle of dependent origination, is eradicated only through *Arahat*. The symbolic 2+2+1 as denoted in the chart indicates the following unwholesome cittas of the sensuous world:

- 2 greed-rooted cittas accompanied by joy (associated with wrong views, and another dissociated from wrong views, both are prompted).
- 2 greed-rooted cittas accompanied by neither-pleasant-nor-unpleasant feeling (associated with wrong views, and another dissociated from wrong views, both are prompted).
- 1 hatred-rooted citta, accompanied by displeasure and associated with aversion, on premeditated basis.

Forward enquiries by person

Mono-based

264. This person has eliminated latent state of *kāmarāga*. Has that person eliminated latent state of *paṭigha*?
—Yes. (Two persons ☆)
This person has eliminated latent state of *paṭigha*. Has that person eliminated latent state of *kāmarāga*?
—Yes. (Two persons ☆)

This person has eliminated latent state of *kāmarāga*. Has that person eliminated latent state of *māna*?
—No. *Anāgāmi* has eliminated *kāmarāga* but not *māna*.
—Yes. *Arahat* has eliminated *kāmarāga*, and also *māna*.
This person has eliminated latent state of *māna*. Has that person eliminated latent state of *kāmarāga*? —Yes. (*Arahat*)

This person has eliminated latent state of *kāmarāga*. Has that person eliminated latent state of *diṭṭhi* ……p….. *vicikicchā*? —Yes. (Two persons ☆)
This person has eliminated latent state of *vicikicchā*. Has that person eliminated latent state of *kāmarāga*?
—No. Two persons ★ have eliminated *vicikicchā* (and *diṭṭhi*), but not *kāmarāga*.
—Yes. Two persons ☆ have eliminated *vicikicchā* (and *diṭṭhi*) and also *kāmarāga*

This person has eliminated latent state of *kāmarāga*. Has that person eliminated latent state of *bhavarāga* ……p….. *avijjā*?
—No. *Anāgāmi* has eliminated *kāmarāga*, but not *avijjā* (and *bhavarāga*).
—Yes. *Arahat* has eliminated *kāmarāga*, and also *avijjā* (and *bhavarāga*).
This person has eliminated *avijjā*. Has that person eliminated *kāmarāga*?
—Yes. Refer to the aforesaid.

265. This person has eliminated latent state of *paṭigha*. Has that person eliminated latent state of *māna*?

—No. *Anāgāmi* has eliminated *paṭigha*, but not *māna*.
—Yes. *Arahat* has eliminated *paṭigha*, and also *māna*.
This person has eliminated latent state of *māna*. Has that person eliminated latent state of *paṭigha*? —Yes. Refer to the aforesaid.

This person has eliminated latent state of *paṭigha*. Has that person eliminated latent state of *diṭṭhi* ......p..... *vicikicchā*? —Yes. (Two persons ☆)
This person has eliminated latent state of *vicikicchā*. Has that person eliminated latent state of *paṭigha*?
—No. Two persons ★ have eliminated *vicikicchā* (and *diṭṭhi*), but not *paṭigha*.
—Yes. Two persons ☆ have eliminated *vicikicchā* (and *diṭṭhi*), and also *paṭigha*.

This person has eliminated latent state of *paṭigha*. Has that person eliminated latent state of *bhavarāga*......p..... *avijjā*?
—No. *Anāgāmi* has eliminated *paṭigha*, but not *avijjā* (and *bhavarāga*).
—Yes. *Arahat* has eliminated *paṭigha*, and also *avijjā* (and *bhavarāga*).
This person has eliminated *avijjā*. Has that person eliminated *paṭigha*? —Yes.

266. This person has eliminated latent state of *māna*. Has that person eliminated latent state of *diṭṭhi*......p..... *vicikicchā*? —Yes. See below.
This person has eliminated latent state of *vicikicchā*. Has that person eliminated latent state of *māna*?
—No. Three persons ⁝ have eliminated *vicikicchā* (and *diṭṭhi*), but not *māna*.
—Yes. *Arahat* has eliminated *vicikicchā* (and *diṭṭhi*), and also *māna*.

This person has eliminated latent state of *māna*. Has that person eliminated latent state of *bhavarāga* ......p..... *avijjā*? —Yes. (*Arahat*)
This person has eliminated latent state of *avijjā*. Has that person eliminated latent state of *māna*? —Yes. (*Arahat*)

267. This person has eliminated latent state of *diṭṭhi*. Has that person eliminated latent state of *vicikicchā*? —Yes. (four persons ∷)
This person has eliminated latent state of *vicikicchā*. Has that person eliminated latent state of *diṭṭhi*? —Yes, same as above ......p.....

268. This person has eliminated latent state of *vicikicchā*. Has that person eliminated latent state of *bhavarāga* ......p..... *avijjā*?
—No. Three persons ⁝ have eliminated *vicikicchā*, but not *avijjā*.
—Yes. *Arahat* has eliminated *vicikicchā*, and also *avijjā*.
This person has eliminated latent state of *avijjā*. Has that person eliminated latent state of *vicikicchā*? —Yes. (*Arahat*)

269. This person has eliminated latent state of *bhavarāga*. Has that person eliminated latent state of *avijjā*? —Yes. (*Arahat*)
This person has eliminated latent state of *avijjā*. Has that person eliminated latent state of *bhavarāga*? —Yes. (*Arahat*)

Couplet-based

270. This person has eliminated latent states of *kāmarāga* and *paṭigha*. Has that person eliminated latent state of *māna*?
—No. *Anāgāmi* has eliminated *kāmarāga* and *paṭigha*, but not *māna*.
—Yes. *Arahat* has eliminated *kāmarāga* and *paṭigha*, and also *māna*.
This person has eliminated latent state of *māna*. Has that person eliminated latent states of *kāmarāga* and *paṭigha*? —Yes. (*Arahat*)

This person has eliminated latent states of *kāmarāga* and *paṭigha*. Has that person eliminated latent state of *diṭṭhi* ......p..... *vicikicchā*? —Yes. See below.
This person has eliminated latent state of *vicikicchā*. Has that person eliminated latent states of *kāmarāga* and *paṭigha*?
—No. Two persons ★ have eliminated *vicikicchā* (and *diṭṭhi*), but not *kāmarāga* and *paṭigha*.
—Yes. Two persons ☆ have eliminated *vicikicchā* (and *diṭṭhi*), and also have eliminated *kāmarāga* and *paṭigha*.

This person has eliminated latent states of *kāmarāga* and *paṭigha*. Has that person eliminated latent state of *bhavarāga*......p..... *avijjā*?
—No. *Anāgāmi* have eliminated *kāmarāga* and *paṭigha*, but not *avijjā*.
—Yes. *Arahat* has eliminated *kāmarāga* and *paṭigha*, and also *avijjā*.
This person has eliminated latent state of *avijjā*. Has that person eliminated latent states of *kāmarāga* and *paṭigha*? —Yes. (*Arahat*)

Triplet-based

271. This person has eliminated latent states of *kāmarāga*, *paṭigha* and *māna*. Has that person eliminated latent state of *diṭṭhi* ......p..... *vicikicchā*? —Yes.
This person has eliminated latent state of *vicikicchā*. Has that person eliminated latent states of *kāmarāga*, *paṭigha* and *māna*?
—No. Two persons ★ have eliminated *vicikicchā*, but not *kāmarāga*, *paṭigha* and *māna*. *Anāgāmi* has eliminated *vicikicchā*, *kāmarāga* and *paṭigha*, but not *māna*.
—Yes. *Arahat* has eliminated *vicikicchā*, and also *kāmarāga*, *paṭigha* and *māna*.

This person has eliminated latent states of *kāmarāga*, *paṭigha* and *māna*. Has that person eliminated latent state of *bhavarāga* ......p..... *avijjā*? —Yes. (*Arahat*)
This person has eliminated latent state of *avijjā*. Has that person eliminated latent states of *kāmarāga*, *paṭigha* and *māna*? —Yes. (*Arahat*)

Quadruplet-based

272. This person has eliminated latent states of *kāmarāga*, *paṭigha*, *māna* and *diṭṭhi*. Has that person eliminated latent state of *vicikicchā*? —Yes. (*Arahat*)
This person has eliminated latent state of *vicikicchā*. Has that person eliminated latent states of *kāmarāga*, *paṭigha*, *māna* and *diṭṭhi*?

—No. Two persons ★ have eliminated *diṭṭhi* and *vicikicchā*, but not *kāmarāga*, *paṭigha* and *māna*. *Anāgāmi* has eliminated *vicikicchā*, *kāmarāga*, *paṭigha* and *diṭṭhi*, but not *māna*.
—Yes. *Arahat* has eliminated *vicikicchā*, and also *kāmarāga*, *paṭigha*, *māna* and *diṭṭhi* ......p.....

Quintuplet-based

273. This person has eliminated latent states of *kāmarāga*, *paṭigha*, *māna*, *diṭṭhi* and *vicikicchā*. Has that person eliminated latent state of *bhavarāga* ......p..... *avijjā*? —Yes. (*Arahat*)
This person has eliminated latent state of *avijjā*. Has that person eliminated latent states of *kāmarāga*, *paṭigha*, *māna*, *diṭṭhi* and *vicikicchā*? —Yes. (*Arahat*)

Sextuplet-based

274. This person has eliminated latent states of *kāmarāga*, *paṭigha*, *māna*, *diṭṭhi*, *vicikicchā* and *bhavarāga*. Has that person eliminated latent state of *avijjā*?
—Yes. (*Arahat*)
This person has eliminated latent state of *avijjā*. Has that person eliminated latent states of *kāmarāga*, *paṭigha*, *māna*, *diṭṭhi*, *vicikicchā* and *bhavarāga*?
—Yes. (*Arahat*)

Forward enquiries by plane

Mono-based

275. Latent state of *kāmarāga* has been eliminated at this plane (*okāsa* as 'plane, place, appearance, or situation'). Has *paṭigha* been eliminated at that plane?
—(*Kāmarāga* has been eliminated in two feelings of the elemental world of sensuous desire) It should not be said to be either, *paṭigha* has been eliminated or has not been eliminated at that plane and in that situation. In other words, neither and nor [59] should be said of *paṭigha* thereat (i.e. neither *paṭigha* has been eliminated nor has it not been eliminated at that plane and situation).
Latent state of *paṭigha* has been eliminated at this plane. Has *kāmarāga* been eliminated at that plane?
—(*Paṭigha* has been eliminated in unpleasant feeling of the sensuous element) Neither and nor should be said of *kāmarāga* thereat.

Latent state of *kāmarāga* has eliminated at this plane. Has *māna* been eliminated at that plane?
—Yes. Refer to the answer in aforesaid.

---

[59] Neither and nor: "neither the said latent state has been eliminated nor has it not been eliminated" should be the appropriate answer. The "no" answer is not exactly correct. For example, aversion arises only at unpleasant feeling, and does not arise at the other two feelings of the sensuous element. Hence it is not correct to say that aversion has not been eliminated in that situation at that plane, i.e. in the other two feelings of the sensuous element.

Latent state of *māna* has been eliminated at this plane. Has latent state of *kāmarāga* been eliminated at that plane?
—In elemental world of fine-material and immaterial, *māna* has been eliminated; but neither and nor should be said of *kāmarāga* thereat.
—Yes. In two feelings of the elemental world of sensuous desire, *māna* has been eliminated, and also *kāmarāga*.

Latent state of *kāmarāga* has been eliminated at this plane. Has latent state of *diṭṭhi* been eliminated at that plane? .....p.....Has latent state of *vicikicchā* been eliminated at that plane? —Yes. See the answer below.
Latent state of *vicikicchā* has been eliminated at this plane. Has latent state of *kāmarāga* been eliminated at that plane?
—In unpleasant feeling, and in elemental world of fine-material and immaterial, *vicikicchā* has been eliminated; but neither and nor should be said of *kāmarāga* thereat.
—Yes. In two feelings of the elemental world of sensuous desire, *vicikicchā* has been eliminated, and also *kāmarāga*.

Latent state of *kāmarāga* has been eliminated at this plane. Has latent state of *bhavarāga* been eliminated at that plane?
—Neither and nor should be said of *bhavarāga* thereat. (in two feelings of the elemental world of sensuous desire)
Latent state of *bhavarāga* has been eliminated at this plane. Has latent state of *kāmarāga* been eliminated at that plane?
—Neither and nor should be said of *kāmarāga* thereat. (in elemental world of fine-material and immaterial)

Latent state of *kāmarāga* has been eliminated at this plane. Has latent state of *avijjā* been eliminated at that plane? —Yes. See the answer below.
Latent state of *avijjā* has been eliminated at this plane. Has latent state of *kāmarāga* been eliminated at that plane?
—In unpleasant feeling, and in elemental world of fine-material and immaterial, *avijjā* has been eliminated; but neither and nor should be said of *kāmarāga* thereat.
—Yes. In two feelings of the elemental world of sensuous desire, *avijjā* has been eliminated, and also *kāmarāga*.

276. Latent state of *paṭigha* has been eliminated at this plane. Has latent state of *māna* been eliminated at that plane?
—Neither and nor should be said of *māna* thereat. (in unpleasant feeling)
Latent state of *māna* has been eliminated at this plane. Has latent state of *paṭigha* been eliminated at that plane?
—Neither and nor should be said of *paṭigha* thereat. (in two feelings of the elemental world of sensuous desire, and in elemental world of fine-material and immaterial)

Latent state of *paṭigha* has been eliminated at this plane. Has latent state of *diṭṭhi* been eliminated at that plane? .....p..... Has latent state of *vicikicchā* been eliminated at that plane? —Yes. See the answer below.
Latent state of *vicikicchā* has been eliminated at this plane. Has latent state of *paṭigha* been eliminated at that plane?
—In two feelings of the elemental world of sensuous desire, and in elemental world of fine-material and immaterial, *vicikicchā* has been eliminated; but neither and nor should be said of *paṭigha* thereat.
—Yes. In unpleasant feeling (of the sensuous element), *vicikicchā* has been eliminated, and also *paṭigha.*

Latent state of *paṭigha* has been eliminated at this plane. Has latent state of *bhavarāga* been eliminated at that plane?
—Neither and nor should be said of *bhavarāga* thereat. (in unpleasant feeling)
Latent state of *bhavarāga* has been eliminated at this plane. Has latent state of *paṭigha* been eliminated at that plane?
—Neither and nor should be said of *paṭigha* thereat. (in elemental world of fine-material and immaterial)

Latent state of *paṭigha* has been eliminated at this plane. Has latent state of *avijjā* been eliminated at that plane? —Yes. See the answer below.
Latent state of *avijjā* has been eliminated at this plane. Has latent state of *paṭigha* been eliminated at that plane?
—In two feelings of the elemental world of sensuous desire, and in elemental world of fine-material and immaterial, *avijjā* has been eliminated; but neither and nor should be said of *paṭigha* thereat.
—Yes. In unpleasant feeling (in sensuous element), *avijjā* has been eliminated, and also *paṭigha.*

277. Latent state of *māna* has been eliminated at this plane. Has latent state of *diṭṭhi* been eliminated at that plane? .....p..... Has latent state of *vicikicchā* been eliminated at that plane? —Yes. See the answer below.
Latent state of *vicikicchā* has been eliminated at this plane. Has latent state of *māna* been eliminated at that plane?
—In unpleasant feeling (in sensuous element), *vicikicchā* has been eliminated; but neither and nor should be said of *māna* thereat.
—Yes. In two feelings of the elemental world of sensuous desire, and in elemental world of fine-material and immaterial, *vicikicchā* has been eliminated; and also *māna.*

Latent state of *māna* has been eliminated at this plane. Has latent state of *bhavarāga* been eliminated at that plane?
—In two feelings of the elemental world of sensuous desire, *māna* has been eliminated; but neither and nor should be said of *bhavarāga* thereat.
—Yes. In the elemental world of fine-material and immaterial, *māna* has been eliminated, and also *bhavarāga.*

Bhavarāga has been eliminated at this plane. Has *māna* been eliminated at that plane? —Yes. (Same as aforesaid)

Latent state of *māna* has been eliminated at this plane. Has latent state of *avijjā* been eliminated at that plane?
—Yes. See answer below.
Latent state of *avijjā* has been eliminated at this plane. Has latent state of *māna* been eliminated at that plane?
—In unpleasant feeling (in sensuous element), *avijjā* has been eliminated; but neither and nor should be said of *māna* thereat.
—Yes. In two feelings of the elemental world of sensuous desire, and in elemental world of fine-material and immaterial, *avijjā* has been eliminated, and also *māna*

278. Latent state of *diṭṭhi* has been eliminated at this plane. Has latent state of *vicikicchā* been eliminated at that plane? —Yes. (Same as below)
Latent state of *vicikicchā* has been eliminated at this plane. Has latent state of *diṭṭhi* been eliminated at that plane? —Yes. (In the three elemental worlds)

Latent state of *diṭṭhi* has been eliminated at this plane. Has latent state of *bhavarāga* been eliminated at that plane?
—In three feelings of the elemental world of sensuous desire, *diṭṭhi* has been eliminated; but neither and nor should be said of *bhavarāga* thereat.
—Yes. In the elemental world of fine-material and immaterial, *diṭṭhi* has been eliminated, and also *bhavarāga.*
Latent state of *bhavarāga* has been eliminated at this plane. Has latent state of *diṭṭhi* been eliminated at that plane? —Yes. (Same as aforesaid)

Latent state of *diṭṭhi* has been eliminated at this plane. Has latent state of *avijjā* been eliminated at the plane? —Yes. (In the three elemental worlds)
Latent state of *avijjā* has been eliminated at this plane. Has latent state of *diṭṭhi* been eliminated at that plane? —Yes. (In the three elemental worlds)

279. Latent state of *vicikicchā* has been eliminated at this plane. Has latent state of *bhavarāga* been eliminated at that plane?
—In three feelings of the elemental world of sensuous desire, *vicikicchā* has been eliminated; but neither and nor should be said of *bhavarāga* thereat.
—Yes. In the elemental world of fine-material and immaterial, *vicikicchā* has been eliminated, and also *bhavarāga.*
Latent state of *bhavarāga* has been eliminated at this plane. Has latent state of *vicikicchā* been eliminated at that plane? —Yes. (Same as aforesaid)

Latent state of *vicikicchā* has been eliminated at this plane. Has latent state of *avijjā* been eliminated at that plane? —Yes. (In the three elemental worlds)
Latent state of *avijjā* has been eliminated at this plane. Has latent state of *vicikicchā* been eliminated at that plane? —Yes. (In the three elemental worlds)

280. Latent state of *bhavarāga* has been eliminated at this plane. Has latent state of *avijjā* been eliminated at that plane? —Yes. See the answer below.
Latent state of *avijjā* has been eliminated at this plane. Has latent state of *bhavarāga* been eliminated at that plane?
—In three feelings of the elemental world of sensuous desire, *avijjā* has been eliminated; but neither and nor should be said of *bhavarāga* thereat.
—Yes. In the elemental world of fine-material and immaterial, *avijjā* has been eliminated, and also *bhavarāga*.

Couplet-based

281. Latent states of *kāmarāga* and *paṭigha* have been eliminated at this plane. Has latent state of *māna* been eliminated at that plane? —None.
Latent state of *māna* has been eliminated at this plane. Have latent states of *kāmarāga* and *paṭigha* been eliminated at that plane?
—In elemental world of fine-material and immaterial, *māna* has been eliminated; but neither and nor should be said of *kāmarāga* and *paṭigha* thereat.
—Yes. In two feelings of the elemental world of sensuous desire, *māna* and *kāmarāga* has been eliminated; but neither and nor should be said of *paṭigha* thereat.

Latent states of *Kāmarāga* and *paṭigha* have been eliminated at this plane. Has latent state of *diṭṭhi* been eliminated at that plane? …..p….. Has latent state of *vicikicchā* been eliminated at that plane? —None.
Latent state of *vicikicchā* has been eliminated at this plane. Have latent states of *kāmarāga* and *paṭigha* been eliminated at that plane?
—In elemental world of fine-material and immaterial, *vicikicchā* has been eliminated; but neither and nor should be said of *kāmarāga* and *paṭigha* thereat.
—In two feelings of the elemental world of sensuous desire, *vicikicchā* and *kāmarāga* have been eliminated; but neither and nor should be said thereat of *paṭigha* thereat.
—Yes. In unpleasant feeling (of the sensuous element), *vicikicchā* and *paṭigha* have been eliminated; but neither and nor should be said thereat of *kāmarāga*.

Latent states of *kāmarāga* and *paṭigha* have been eliminated at this plane. Has latent state of *bhavarāga* been eliminated at that plane? —None.
Latent state of *bhavarāga* has been eliminated at this plane. Have *kāmarāga* and *paṭigha* been eliminated at that plane?
—Neither and nor should be said of *kāmarāga* and *paṭigha* thereat. (in elemental world of fine-material and immaterial)

Latent states of *kāmarāga* and *paṭigha* have been eliminated at this plane. Has latent state of *avijjā* been eliminated at that plane? —None.
Latent state of *avijjā* has been eliminated at this plane. Have latent states of *kāmarāga* and *paṭigha* been eliminated at that plane?

—In the elemental world of fine-material and immaterial, *avijjā* has been eliminated; but neither and nor should be said of *kāmarāga* and *paṭigha* thereat. In two feelings of the elemental world of sensuous desire, *avijjā* and *kāmarāga* have been eliminated; but neither and nor should be said of *paṭigha* thereat. In unpleasant feeling, *avijjā* and *paṭigha* have been eliminated; but neither and nor should be said of *kāmarāga* thereat.

Triplet-based

282. Latent states of *kāmarāga*, *paṭigha* and *māna* have been eliminated at this plane. Has latent state of *diṭṭhi* been eliminated at that plane? .....p.... Has latent states of *vicikicchā* been eliminated at that plane? —None.
Latent state of *vicikicchā* has been eliminated at this plane. Have latent states of *kāmarāga*, *paṭigha* and *māna* been eliminated at that plane?
—In elemental world of fine-material and immaterial, *vicikicchā* and *māna* have been eliminated; but neither and nor should be said of *kāmarāga* and *paṭigha* thereat.
In two feelings of the elemental world of sensuous desire, *vicikicchā*, *kāmarāga* and *māna* have been eliminated; but neither and nor should be said of *paṭigha* thereat. In unpleasant feeling, *vicikicchā* and *paṭigha* have been eliminated; but neither and nor should be said of *kāmarāga* thereat.

Latent states of *kāmarāga*, *paṭigha* and *māna* have been eliminated at this plane. Has latent state of *bhavarāga* been eliminated at that plane? —None.
Latent state of *bhavarāga* has been eliminated at this plane. Have latent states of *kāmarāga*, *paṭigha* and *māna* been eliminated at that plane?
—In elemental world of fine-material and immaterial, *bhavarāga* and *māna* have been eliminated; but neither and nor should be said of *kāmarāga* and *paṭigha* thereat.

Latent states of *kāmarāga*, *paṭigha* and *māna* have been eliminated at this plane. Has latent state of *avijjā* been eliminated at that plane? —None.
Latent state of *avijjā* has been eliminated at this plane. Have latent states of *kāmarāga*, *paṭigha* and *māna* been eliminated at that plane?
—In elemental world of fine-material and immaterial, *avijjā* and *māna* have been eliminated; but neither and nor should be said of *kāmarāga* and *paṭigha* thereat. In two feelings of the elemental world of sensuous desire, *avijjā*, *kāmarāga* and *māna* have been eliminated; but neither and nor should be said of *paṭigha* thereat. In unpleasant feeling, *avijjā* and *paṭigha* have been eliminated; but neither and nor should be said of *kāmarāga* and *māna* thereat.

Quadruplet-based

283. Latent states of *kāmarāga*, *paṭigha*, *māna* and *diṭṭhi* have been eliminated at this plane. Has latent state of *vicikicchā* been eliminated at that plane? —None.
Latent state of *vicikicchā* has been eliminated at this plane. Have latent states of *kāmarāga*, *paṭigha*, *māna* and *diṭṭhi* been eliminated at that plane?

—In elemental world of fine-material and immaterial, *vicikicchā*, *māna* and *diṭṭhi* have been eliminated; but neither and nor should be said of *kāmarāga* and *paṭigha* thereat. In two feelings of the elemental world of sensuous desire, *vicikicchā*, *kāmarāga*, *māna* and *diṭṭhi* have been eliminated; but neither and nor should be said of *paṭigha* thereat. In unpleasant feeling, *vicikicchā*, *paṭigha* and *diṭṭhi* have been eliminated; but neither and nor should be said of *kāmarāga* and *māna* thereat.

Latent states of *kāmarāga*, *paṭigha*, *māna* and *diṭṭhi* have been eliminated at this plane. Has latent state of *bhavarāga* been eliminated at that plane? —None.
Latent state of *bhavarāga* has been eliminated at this plane. Have latent states of *kāmarāga*, *paṭigha*, *māna* and *diṭṭhi* been eliminated at that plane?
—In elemental world of fine-material and immaterial, *bhavarāga*, *māna* and *diṭṭhi* have been eliminated; but neither and nor should be said of *kāmarāga* and *paṭigha* thereat.

Latent states of *kāmarāga*, *paṭigha*, *māna* and *diṭṭhi* have been eliminated at this plane. Has latent state of *avijjā* been eliminated at that plane? —None.
Latent state of *avijjā* has been eliminated at this plane. Have latent states of *kāmarāga*, *paṭigha*, *māna* and *diṭṭhi* been eliminated at that plane?
—In elemental world of fine-material and immaterial, *avijjā*, *māna* and *diṭṭhi* have been eliminated; but neither and nor should be said of *kāmarāga* and *paṭigha* thereat. In two feelings of the elemental world of sensuous desire, *avijjā*, *kāmarāga*, *māna* and *diṭṭhi* have been eliminated; but neither and nor should be said of *paṭigha* thereat. In unpleasant feeling, *avijjā*, *paṭigha* and *diṭṭhi* have been eliminated; but neither and nor should be said of *kāmarāga* and *māna* thereat.

Quintuplet-based

284. Latent states of *kāmarāga*, *paṭigha*, *māna*, *diṭṭhi* and *vicikicchā* have been eliminated at this plane. Has *bhavarāga* been eliminated at that plane? —None.
Latent state of *bhavarāga* has been eliminated at this plane. Have latent states of *kāmarāga*, *paṭigha*, *māna*, *diṭṭhi* and *vicikicchā* been eliminated at that plane?
—In elemental world of fine-material and immaterial, *bhavarāga*, *māna*, *diṭṭhi* and *vicikicchā* have been eliminated; but neither and nor should be said of *kāmarāga* and *paṭigha* thereat.

Latent states of *kāmarāga*, *paṭigha*, *māna*, *diṭṭhi* and *vicikicchā* have been eliminated at this plane. Has *avijjā* been eliminated at that plane? —None.
Latent state of *avijjā* has been eliminated at this plane. Have latent states of *kāmarāga*, *paṭigha*, *māna*, *diṭṭhi* and *vicikicchā* been eliminated at that plane?
—In elemental world of fine-material and immaterial, *avijjā*, *māna*, *diṭṭhi* and *vicikicchā* have been eliminated; but neither and nor should be said of *kāmarāga* and *paṭigha* thereat. In two feelings of the elemental world of sensuous desire, *avijjā*, *kāmarāga*, *māna*, *diṭṭhi* and *vicikicchā* have been eliminated; but neither and nor should be said of *paṭigha* thereat. In unpleasant feeling, *avijjā*, *paṭigha*,

diṭṭhi and *vicikicchā* have been eliminated; but neither and nor should be said of *kāmarāga* and *māna* thereat.

Sextuplet-based

285. Latent states of *kāmarāga, paṭigha, māna, diṭṭhi, vicikicchā* and *bhavarāga* have been eliminated at this plane. Has latent state of *avijjā* been eliminated at that plane? —None.
Latent state of *avijjā* has been eliminated at this plane. Have latent states of *kāmarāga, paṭigha, māna, diṭṭhi, vicikicchā* and *bhavarāga* been eliminated at that plane?
—In elemental world of fine-material and immaterial, *avijjā, māna, diṭṭhi, vicikicchā* and *bhavarāga* have been eliminated; but neither and nor should be said of *kāmarāga* and *paṭigha* thereat. In two feelings of the elemental world of sensuous desire, *avijjā, kāmarāga, kāmarāga, māna, diṭṭhi* and *vicikicchā* have been eliminated; but neither and nor should be said of *paṭigha* and *bhavarāga* thereat. In unpleasant feeling, *avijjā, paṭigha, diṭṭhi* and *vicikicchā* have been eliminated; but neither and nor should be said of *kāmarāga, māna* and *bhavarāga* thereat.

Forward enquiries by person and plane

Mono-based

286. This person has eliminated latent state of *kāmarāga* at this plane. Has that person eliminated latent state of *paṭigha* at that plane?
—It should not be said to be either, this person has eliminated latent state of *paṭigha* or has not eliminated latent state of *paṭigha* at that plane or situation. In other words, neither and nor should be said of *paṭigha* thereat (*Anāgāmi* and *Arahat*, with two feelings of the elemental world of sensuous desire, have both eliminated *kāmarāga*) neither of whom has eliminated *paṭigha* nor has not eliminated *paṭigha* should be said).
This person has eliminated latent state of *paṭigha* at this plane. Has that person eliminated latent state of *kāmarāga* at that plane?
—(*Anāgāmi* and *Arahat*, with unpleasant feeling of the sensuous element, has eliminated *paṭigha*) neither of whom has eliminated *kāmarāga* nor has not eliminated *kāmarāga* should be said).

This person has eliminated latent state of *kāmarāga* at this plane. Has that person eliminated latent state of *māna* at that plane?
—No. *Anāgāmi,* with two feelings of the elemental world of sensuous desire, has eliminated *kāmarāga*, except for *māna*.
—Yes. *Arahat*, with two feelings of the elemental world of sensuous desire, has eliminated *kāmarāga*, and also *māna*.
This person has eliminated latent state of *māna* at this plane. Has that person eliminated latent state of *kāmarāga* at that plane?

—*Arahat*, in elemental world of fine-material and immaterial, has eliminated *māna*; but neither and nor should be said of *kāmarāga* thereat.
—Yes. Refer to the aforesaid.

This person has eliminated latent state of *kāmarāga* at this plane. Has that person eliminated latent state of *diṭṭhi* at that plane? —Yes. See the answer below.
This person has eliminated latent state of *diṭṭhi* at this plane. Has that person eliminated latent state of *kāmarāga* at that plane?
—Two persons ★, with unpleasant feeling, and in elemental world of fine-material and immaterial, have eliminated *diṭṭhi*; but neither and nor should be said of *kāmarāga* thereat. Two persons ☆ with unpleasant feeling, and in elemental world of fine-material and immaterial, have eliminated *diṭṭhi*; but neither and nor should be said of *kāmarāga* thereat.
—No. Those persons (two persons ★), with two feelings of the elemental world of sensuous desire, have eliminated *diṭṭhi*, but not *kāmarāga.*
—Yes. Those persons (two persons ☆), with two feelings of the elemental world of sensuous desire have eliminated *diṭṭhi*, and also *kāmarāga*.

This person has eliminated latent state of *kāmarāga* at this plane. Has that person eliminated latent state of *vicikicchā* at that plane? —Yes. See the answer below
This person has eliminated latent state of *vicikicchā* at this plane. Has that person eliminated latent state of *kāmarāga* at that plane?
—Two persons ★, with unpleasant feeling, and in elemental world of fine-material and immaterial, have eliminated *vicikicchā*; but neither and nor should be said of *kāmarāga* thereat. Two persons ☆ with unpleasant feeling, in elemental world of fine-material and immaterial, have eliminated *vicikicchā*; but neither and nor should be said of *kāmarāga* thereat.
—No. Those persons (two persons ★), with two feelings of the elemental world of sensuous desire, have eliminated *vicikicchā*, but not *kāmarāga*.
—Yes. Those persons (two persons ☆), with two feelings of the elemental world of sensuous desire, have eliminated *vicikicchā*, and also *kāmarāga*.

This person has eliminated latent state of *kāmarāga* at this plane. Has that person eliminated latent state of *bhavarāga* at that plane?
—Neither and nor should be said of *bhavarāga* thereat. (Two persons ☆, with two feelings of the elemental world of sensuous desire)
This person has eliminated latent state of *bhavarāga* at this plane. Has that person eliminated latent state of *kāmarāga* at that plane?
—Neither and nor should be said of *kāmarāga* thereat. (*Arahat*, in elemental world of fine-material and immaterial)

This person has eliminated latent state of *kāmarāga* at this plane. Has that person eliminated latent state of *avijjā* at that plane?
—No. *Anāgāmi,* with two feelings of the elemental world of sensuous desire, has eliminated *kāmarāga*, but not *avijjā* at those planes.

—Yes. *Arahat*, with two feelings of the elemental world of sensuous desire, has eliminated *kāmarāga*, and also *avijjā*.
This person has eliminated latent state of *avijjā* at this plane. Has that person eliminated latent state of *kāmarāga* at that plane?
—*Arahat* in unpleasant feeling, and in elemental world of fine-material and immaterial, has eliminated *avijjā*; but neither and nor should be said of *kāmarāga* thereat.
—Yes. Refer to the aforesaid.

287. This person has eliminated latent state of *paṭigha* at this plane. Has that person eliminated latent state of *māna* at that plane?
—Neither and nor should be said of *māna* thereat (*Anāgāmi* and *Arahat*, with unpleasant feeling of the sensuous element)
This person has eliminated latent state of *māna* at this plane. Has that person eliminated latent state of *paṭigha* at that plane?
—Neither and nor should be said of *paṭigha* thereat. (*Arahat* in two feelings of the elemental world of sensuous desire, and in elemental world of fine-material and immaterial)

This person has eliminated latent state of *paṭigha* at this plane. Has that person eliminated latent state of *diṭṭhi*.....p.....*vicikicchā* at that plane?—Yes. See below
This person has eliminated latent state of *vicikicchā* at this plane. Has that person eliminated latent state of *paṭigha* at that plane?
—Two persons ★, with two feelings of the elemental world of sensuous desire, and in elemental world of fine-material and immaterial, have eliminated *vicikicchā*; but neither and nor should be said of *paṭigha* thereat. Two persons ☆, with two feelings of the elemental world of sensuous desire, and in elemental world of fine-material and immaterial, have eliminated *vicikicchā*; but neither and nor should be said of *paṭigha* thereat.
—No. Those persons ★, with unpleasant feeling, have eliminated *vicikicchā*, but not *paṭigha*.
—Yes. Those persons ☆, with unpleasant feeling, have eliminated *vicikicchā*, and also *paṭigha*.

This person has eliminated latent state of *paṭigha* at this plane. Has that person eliminated latent state of *bhavarāga* at that plane?
—Neither and nor should be said of *bhavarāga* thereat. (*Anāgāmi* and *Arahat*, with unpleasant feeling of the sensuous element)
This person has eliminated latent state of *bhavarāga* at this plane. Has that person eliminated latent state of *paṭigha* at that plane?
—Neither and nor should be said of *paṭigha* thereat. (*Arahat* in elemental world of fine-material and immaterial)

This person has eliminated latent state of *paṭigha* at this plane. Has that person eliminated latent state of *avijjā* at that plane?
—No. *Anāgāmi*, with unpleasant feeling, has eliminated *paṭigha*, but not *avijjā*.

—Yes. *Arahat*, with unpleasant feeling, has eliminated *paṭigha*, and also *avijjā*. This person has eliminated latent state of *avijjā* at this plane. Has that person eliminated latent state of *paṭigha* at that plane?
—*Arahat*, with two feelings of the elemental world of sensuous desire and in elemental world of fine-material and immaterial, has eliminated *avijjā*; but neither and nor should be said of *paṭigha* thereat.
—Yes. Refer to the aforesaid.

288. This person has eliminated latent state of *māna* at this plane. Has that person eliminated latent state of *diṭṭhi*.....p.....*vicikicchā* at that plane?—Yes. See below This person has eliminated latent state of *vicikicchā* at this plane. Has that person eliminated latent state of *māna* at that plane?
—Three persons :, with unpleasant feeling, have eliminated *vicikicchā*; but neither and nor should be said of *māna* thereat. *Arahat*, with unpleasant feeling, has eliminated *vicikicchā*; but neither and nor should be said of *māna* thereat.
—No. Those persons :, with two feelings of the elemental world of sensuous desire, and in elemental world of fine-material and immaterial, have eliminated *vicikicchā*, but not *māna*.
—Yes. Those persons (*Arahat*) with two feelings of the elemental world of sensuous desire, and in elemental world of fine-material and immaterial, have eliminated *vicikicchā*; also *māna*.

This person has eliminated latent state of *māna* at this plane. Has that person eliminated latent state of *bhavarāga* at that plane?
—*Arahat*, with two feelings of the elemental world of sensuous desire, has eliminated *māna*; but neither and nor should be said of *bhavarāga* thereat.
—Yes. Those (same) persons, in elemental world of fine-material and immaterial, have eliminated *māna*, and also *bhavarāga*.
This person has eliminated latent state of *bhavarāga* at this plane. Has that person eliminated latent state of *māna* at that plane? —Yes. Refer to the aforsaid.

This person has eliminated latent state of *māna* at this plane. Has that person eliminated latent state of *avijjā* at that plane? —Yes. See the answer below.
This person has eliminated latent state of *avijjā* at this plane. Has that person eliminated latent state of *māna* at that plane?
—*Arahat*, with unpleasant feeling, has eliminated *avijjā*; but neither and nor should be said of *māna* thereat.
—Yes. Those (same) persons, with two feelings of the elemental world of sensuous desire, and in elemental world of fine-material and immaterial, have eliminated *avijjā*, and also *māna*.

289. This person has eliminated latent state of *diṭṭhi* at this plane. Has that person eliminated latent state of *vicikicchā* at that plane? —Yes. (except Puthujjanas) This person has eliminated latent state of *vicikicchā* at this plane. Has that person eliminated latent state of *diṭṭhi* at that plane?
—Yes (except Puthujjanas) .....p.....

290. This person has eliminated latent state of *vicikicchā* at this plane. Has that person eliminated latent state of *bhavarāga* at that plane?
—Three persons :, with three feelings of the elemental world of sensuous desire, have eliminated *vicikicchā*; but neither and nor should be said of *bhavarāga* thereat. *Arahat*, with three feelings of the elemental world of sensuous desire, has eliminated *vicikicchā*; but neither and nor should be said of *bhavarāga* thereat.
—No. Those persons :, in elemental world of fine-material and immaterial, have eliminated *vicikicchā*, but not *bhavarāga*.
—Yes. Those persons (*Arahat*), in elemental world of fine-material and immaterial, have eliminated *vicikicchā*, and also *bhavarāga*.
This person has eliminated latent state of *bhavarāga* at this plane. Has that person eliminated latent state of *vicikicchā* at that plane?—Yes. Refer to the aforesaid.

This person has eliminated latent state of *vicikicchā* at this plane. Has that person eliminated latent state of *avijjā* at that plane?
—No. Three persons :, with three feelings of the elemental world of sensuous desire, and in elemental world of fine-material and immaterial, have eliminated *vicikicchā*, but not *avijjā*.
—Yes. *Arahat*, with three feelings of the elemental world of sensuous desire, and in elemental world of fine-material and immaterial, has eliminated *vicikicchā*, and also *avijjā*.
This person has eliminated latent state of *avijjā* at this plane. Has that person eliminated latent state of *vicikicchā* at that plane? —Yes. Refer to the aforesaid.

291. This person has eliminated latent state of *bhavarāga* at this plane. Has that person eliminated latent state of *avijjā* at that plane?—Yes. See the answer below
This person has eliminated latent state of *avijjā* at this plane. Has that person eliminated latent state of *bhavarāga* at that plane?
—*Arahat*, with three feelings of the elemental world of sensuous desire, has eliminated *avijjā*; but neither and nor should be said of *bhavarāga* thereat.
—Yes. Those (same) persons, in the elemental world of fine-material and immaterial, have eliminated *avijjā*, and also *bhavarāga*.

Couplet-based

292. This person has eliminated latent states of *kāmarāga* and *paṭigha* at this plane. Has that person eliminated latent state of *māna* at that plane? —None.
This person has eliminated latent state of *māna* at this plane. Has that person eliminated latent states of *kāmarāga* and *paṭigha* at that plane?
—*Arahat*, in elemental world of fine-material and immaterial, has eliminated *māna*; but neither and nor should be said of *kāmarāga* and *paṭigha* thereat. Those (same) persons, with two feelings of the elemental world of sensuous desire, have eliminated *māna* and *kāmarāga*; but neither and nor should be said of *paṭigha* thereat.

This person has eliminated latent states of *kāmarāga* and *paṭigha* at this plane. Has that person eliminated latent state of *diṭṭhi* …..p….. *vicikicchā* at that plane? —None.
This person has eliminated latent state of *vicikicchā* at this plane. Has that person eliminated latent states of *kāmarāga* and *paṭigha* at that plane?
—Two persons ★, in elemental world of fine-material and immaterial, have eliminated *vicikicchā*; but neither and nor should be said of *kāmarāga* and *paṭigha* thereat. Those (same) persons, with two feelings of the elemental world of sensuous desire, have eliminated *vicikicchā*; have not eliminated *kāmarāga*; and neither and nor should be said of *paṭigha* thereat. Those (same) persons, with unpleasant feeling, have eliminated *vicikicchā*; have not eliminated *paṭigha*; and neither and nor should be said of *kāmarāga* thereat.
—Two persons ☆, in elemental world of fine-material and immaterial, have eliminated *vicikicchā*; but neither and nor should be said of *kāmarāga* and *paṭigha* thereat. Those (same) persons, with two feelings of the elemental world of sensuous desire, have eliminated *vicikicchā* and *kāmarāga*; but neither and nor should be said of *paṭigha* thereat. Those (same) persons, with unpleasant feeling, have eliminated *vicikicchā* and *paṭigha*; but neither and nor should be said of *kāmarāga* thereat.

This person has eliminated latent states of *kāmarāga* and *paṭigha* at this plane. Has that person eliminated latent state of *bhavarāga* at that plane? —None.
This person has eliminated latent state of *bhavarāga* at this plane. Has that person eliminated latent states of *kāmarāga* and *paṭigha* at that plane?
—Neither and nor should be said of *kāmarāga* and *paṭigha* thereat. (*Arahat* in elemental world of fine-material and immaterial)

This person has eliminated latent states of *kāmarāga* and *paṭigha* at this plane. Has that person eliminated latent state of *avijjā* at that plane? —None.
This person has eliminated latent state of *avijjā* at this plane. Has that person eliminated latent states of *kāmarāga* and *paṭigha* at that plane?
—*Arahat*, in elemental world of fine-material and immaterial, has eliminated *avijjā*; but neither and nor should be said of *kāmarāga* and *paṭigha* thereat. Those (same) persons, with two feelings of the elemental world of sensuous desire, have eliminated *avijjā* and *kāmarāga*; but neither and nor should be said of *paṭigha* thereat. Those (same) persons, with unpleasant feeling, have eliminated *avijjā* and *paṭigha*; but neither and nor should be said of *kāmarāga* thereat.

Triplet-based

293. This person has eliminated latent states of *kāmarāga*, *paṭigha* and *māna* at this plane. Has that person eliminated latent state of *diṭṭhi* …..p….. *vicikicchā* at that plane? —None.
This person has eliminated latent state of *vicikicchā* at this plane. Has that person eliminated latent states of *kāmarāga*, *paṭigha* and *māna* at that plane?

—Two persons ★, in elemental world of fine-material and immaterial, have eliminated *vicikicchā*; have not eliminated *māna*; but neither and nor should be said of *kāmarāga* and *paṭigha* thereat. Those (same) persons, with two feelings of the elemental world of sensuous desire, have eliminated *vicikicchā*; have not eliminated *kāmarāga* and *māna*; and neither and nor should be said of *paṭigha* thereat. Those (same) persons, with unpleasant feeling, have eliminated *vicikicchā*; have not eliminated *paṭigha*; and neither and nor should be said of *kāmarāga* and *māna* thereat.
—*Anāgāmi,* in elemental world of fine-material and immaterial, has eliminated *vicikicchā*; has not eliminated *māna*; and neither and nor should be said of *kāmarāga* and *paṭigha* thereat. Those (same) persons, with two feelings of the elemental world of sensuous desire, have eliminated *vicikicchā* and *kāmarāga*; have not eliminated *māna*; and neither and nor should be said of *paṭigha* thereat. Those (same) persons, with unpleasant feeling, have eliminated *vicikicchā* and *paṭigha*; but neither and nor should be said of *kāmarāga* and *māna* thereat.
—*Arahat*, in elemental world of fine-material and immaterial, has eliminated *vicikicchā* and *māna*; but neither and nor should be said of *kāmarāga* and *paṭigha* thereat. Those (same) persons, with two feelings of the elemental world of sensuous desire, have eliminated *vicikicchā*, *kāmarāga*, *māna* but neither and nor should be said of *paṭigha* thereat. Those (same) persons, with unpleasant feeling, have eliminated *vicikicchā* and *paṭigha*; but neither and nor should be said of *kāmarāga* and *māna* thereat.

This person has eliminated latent states of *kāmarāga*, *paṭigha* and *māna* at this plane. Has that person eliminated latent state of *bhavarāga* at that plane? —None.
This person has eliminated latent state of *bhavarāga* at this plane. Has that person eliminated latent states of *kāmarāga*, *paṭigha* and *māna* at that plane?
—(*Arahat* in elemental world of fine-material and immaterial) has eliminated *māna*; but neither and nor should be said of *kāmarāga* and *paṭigha* thereat.

This person has eliminated latent states of *kāmarāga*, *paṭigha* and *māna* at this plane. Has that person eliminated latent state of *avijjā* at that plane? —None.
This person has eliminated latent state of *avijjā* at this plane. Has that person eliminated latent states of *kāmarāga*, *paṭigha* and *māna* at that plane?
—*Arahat*, in elemental world of fine-material and immaterial, has eliminated *avijjā* and *māna*; but neither and nor should be said of *kāmarāga* and *paṭigha* thereat. Those (same) persons, with two feelings of the elemental world of sensuous desire, have eliminated *avijjā*, *kāmarāga* and *māna*; but neither and nor should be said of *paṭigha* thereat. Those (same) persons, with unpleasant feeling, have eliminated *avijjā* and *māna*; but neither and nor should be said of *kāmarāga* and *māna* thereat.

Quadruplet-based

294. This person has eliminated latent states of *kāmarāga*, *paṭigha*, *māna* and *diṭṭhi* at this plane. Has that person eliminated latent state of *vicikicchā* at that

plane? —None.
—This person has eliminated latent state of *vicikicchā* at this plane. Has that person eliminated latent states of *kāmarāga*, *paṭigha*, *māna* and *diṭṭhi* at that plane?
—Two persons ★, in elemental world of fine-material and immaterial, have eliminated *vicikicchā* and *diṭṭhi*; have not eliminated *māna*; and neither and nor should be said of *kāmarāga* and *paṭigha* thereat. Those (same) persons, with two feelings of the elemental world of sensuous desire, have eliminated *vicikicchā* and *diṭṭhi*; have not eliminated *kāmarāga* and *māna*; and neither and nor should be said of *paṭigha* thereat. Those (same) persons, with unpleasant feeling, have eliminated *vicikicchā* and *diṭṭhi*; have not eliminated *paṭigha*; and neither and nor should be said of *kāmarāga* and *māna* thereat.
—*Anāgāmi,* in elemental world of fine-material and immaterial, has eliminated *vicikicchā* and *diṭṭhi*; has not eliminated *māna*; and neither and nor should be said of *kāmarāga* and *paṭigha* thereat. Those (same) persons, with two feelings of the elemental world of sensuous desire, have eliminated *vicikicchā*, *kāmarāga* and *diṭṭhi*; have not eliminated *māna*; and neither and nor should be said of *paṭigha* thereat. Those (same) persons, with unpleasant feeling, have eliminated *vicikicchā*, *paṭigha* and *diṭṭhi*; but neither and nor should be said of *kāmarāga* and *māna* thereat.
—*Arahat*, in elemental world of fine-material and immaterial, has eliminated *vicikicchā*, *māna* and *diṭṭhi*; but neither and nor should be said of *kāmarāga* and *paṭigha* thereat. Those (same) persons, with two feelings of the elemental world of sensuous desire, have eliminated *vicikicchā*, *kāmarāga*, *māna* and *diṭṭhi*; but neither and nor should be said of *paṭigha* thereat. Those (same) persons, with unpleasant feeling, have eliminated *vicikicchā*, *paṭigha* and *diṭṭhi*; but neither and nor should be said of *kāmarāga* and *māna* thereat. …..p…..

Quadruplet-based

295. This person has eliminated latent states of *kāmarāga*, *paṭigha*, *māna*, *diṭṭhi* and *vicikicchā* at this plane. Has that person eliminated latent state of *bhavarāga* at that plane? —None.
This person has eliminated latent state of *bhavarāga* at this plane. Has that person eliminated latent states of *kāmarāga*, *paṭigha*, *māna*, *diṭṭhi* and *vicikicchā* at that plane?
—*Arahat*, in elemental world of fine-material and immaterial, has eliminated *bhavarāga*, *māna*, *diṭṭhi* and *vicikicchā*; but neither and nor should be said of *kāmarāga* and *paṭigha* thereat.

This person has eliminated latent states of *kāmarāga*, *paṭigha*, *māna*, *diṭṭhi* and *vicikicchā* at this plane. Has that person eliminated latent state of *avijjā* at that plane? —None.
This person has eliminated latent state of *avijjā* at this plane. Has that person eliminated latent states of *kāmarāga*, *paṭigha*, *māna*, *diṭṭhi* and *vicikicchā* at that plane?

—*Arahat*, in elemental world of fine-material and immaterial, has eliminated *avijjā*, *māna*, *diṭṭhi* and *vicikicchā*; but neither and nor should be said of *kāmarāga* and *paṭigha* thereat. Those (same) persons, with two feelings of the elemental world of sensuous desire, have eliminated *avijjā*, *kāmarāga*, *māna*, *diṭṭhi* and *vicikicchā*; but neither and nor should be said of *paṭigha* thereat. Those (same) persons, with unpleasant feeling, have eliminated *avijjā*, *paṭigha*, *diṭṭhi* and *vicikicchā*; but neither and nor should be said of *kāmarāga* and *māna* thereat.

Sextuplet-based

296. This person has eliminated latent states of *kāmarāga*, *paṭigha*, *māna*, *diṭṭhi*, *vicikicchā* and *bhavarāga* at this plane. Has that person eliminated latent state of *avijjā* at that plane? —None.
This person has eliminated latent state of *avijjā* at this plane. Has that person eliminated latent states of *kāmarāga*, *paṭigha*, *māna*, *diṭṭhi*, *vicikicchā* and *bhavarāga* at that plane?
—*Arahat*, in elemental world of fine-material and immaterial, has eliminated *avijjā*, *māna*, *diṭṭhi*, *vicikicchā* and *bhavarāga*; but neither and nor should be said of *kāmarāga* and *paṭigha* thereat. Those (same) persons, with two feelings of the elemental world of sensuous desire, have eliminated *avijjā*, *kāmarāga*, *māna*, *diṭṭhi* and *vicikicchā*; but neither and nor should be said of *paṭigha* and *bhavarāga* thereat. Those (same) persons, with unpleasant feeling, have eliminated *avijjā*, *paṭigha*, *diṭṭhi* and *vicikicchā vicikicchā*; but neither and nor should be said of *kāmarāga*, *māna* and *bhavarāga* thereat.

Opposite enquiries by person

Mono-based

297. This person has not eliminated latent state of *kāmarāga*. Has that person not eliminated latent state of *paṭigha*? —Yes. (Three persons ③)
This person has not eliminated latent state of *paṭigha*. Has that person not eliminated latent state of *kāmarāga*? —Yes. (Three persons ③)

This person has not eliminated latent state of *kāmarāga*. Has that person not eliminated latent state of *māna*? —Yes. (Three persons ③)
This person has not eliminated latent state of *māna*. Has that person not eliminated latent state of *kāmarāga*?
—No. *Anāgāmi* has not eliminated *māna*, but has eliminated *kāmarāga*.
—Yes. Three persons ③ have not eliminated *māna*, and also *kāmarāga*.

This person has not eliminated latent state of *kāmarāga*. Has that person not eliminated latent state of *diṭṭhi*.....p.....*vicikicchā*?
—No. Two persons ★ have not eliminated *kāmarāga*, but have eliminated *vicikicchā*.
—Yes. *Puthujjana* has not eliminated *kāmarāga*, and also *vicikicchā*.

This person has not eliminated latent state of *vicikicchā*. Has that person not eliminated latent state of *kāmarāga*? —Yes. (*Puthujjana*)

This person has not eliminated latent state of *kāmarāga*. Has that person not eliminated latent state of *bhavarāga*.....p..... *avijjā*? —Yes. (Three persons ③)
This person has not eliminated latent state of *avijjā*. Has that person not eliminated latent state of *kāmarāga*?
—No. *Anāgāmi* has not eliminated *avijjā*, but has eliminated *kāmarāga*.
—Yes. Three persons ③ have not eliminated *avijjā*, and also *kāmarāga*.

298. This person has not eliminated latent state of *paṭigha*. Has that person not eliminated latent state of *māna*? —Yes. (Three persons ③)
This person has not eliminated latent state of *māna*. Has that person not eliminated latent state of *paṭigha*?
—No. *Anāgāmi* has not eliminated *māna*, but has eliminated *paṭigha*.
—Yes. Three persons ③ have not eliminated *māna*, and also *paṭigha*.

This person has not eliminated latent state of *paṭigha*. Has that person not eliminated latent state of *diṭṭhi*.....p..... *vicikicchā*?
—No. Two persons ★ have not eliminated *paṭigha*, but have eliminated *vicikicchā* (and *diṭṭhi*).
—Yes. *Puthujjana* has not eliminated *paṭigha*, and also *vicikicchā* (and *diṭṭhi*).
This person has not eliminated *vicikicchā*. Has that person not eliminated *paṭigha*?
—Yes. (*Puthujjana*)

This person has not eliminated latent state of *paṭigha*. Has that person not eliminated latent state of *bhavarāga*.....p.....*avijjā*? —Yes. (Three persons ③)
This person has not eliminated latent state of *avijjā*. Has that person not eliminated latent state of *paṭigha*?
—No. *Anāgāmi* has not eliminated *avijjā*, but has eliminated *paṭigha*.
—Yes. Three persons ③ have not eliminated *avijjā*, and also *paṭigha*.

299. This person has not eliminated latent state of *māna*. Has that person not eliminated latent state of *diṭṭhi*.....p.....*vicikicchā*?
—No. Three persons ⁝ have not eliminated *māna*, but have eliminated *vicikicchā*.
—Yes. *Puthujjana* has not eliminated *māna*, and also *vicikicchā*.
This person has not eliminated latent state of *vicikicchā*. Has that person not eliminated latent state of *māna*? —Yes. (*Puthujjana*)

This person has not eliminated latent state of *māna*. Has that person not eliminated latent state of *bhavarāga*.....p.....*avijjā*? —Yes. (Four persons ④)
This person has not eliminated latent state of *avijjā*. Has that person not eliminated latent state of *māna*? —Yes. (Four persons ④)

300. This person has not eliminated latent state of *diṭṭhi*. Has that person not eliminated latent state of *vicikicchā*? —Yes. (*Puthujjana*)

This person has not eliminated latent state of *vicikicchā*. Has that person not eliminated latent state of *diṭṭhi*? —Yes. (*Puthujjana*) .....p.....

301. This person has not eliminated latent state of *vicikicchā*. Has that person not eliminated latent state of *bhavarāga* .....p..... *avijjā*? —Yes. See below.
This person has not eliminated latent state of *avijjā*. Has that person not eliminated latent state of *vicikicchā*?
—No. Three persons : have not eliminated *avijjā*, but have eliminated *vicikicchā*.
—Yes. *Puthujjana* has not eliminated *avijjā*, and also *vicikicchā*.

302. This person has not eliminated latent state of *bhavarāga*. Has that person not eliminated latent state of *avijjā*? —Yes. (Four persons ④)
This person has not eliminated *avijjā*. Has that person not eliminated *bhavarāga*?
—Yes. (Four persons ④)

Couplet-based

303. This person has not eliminated latent state of *kāmarāga*. Has that person not eliminated latent state of *māna*? —Yes. (Three persons ③)
This person has not eliminated latent state of *māna*. Has that person not eliminated latent states of *kāmarāga* and *paṭigha*?
—No. *Anāgāmi* has not eliminated *māna*, except for *kāmarāga* and *paṭigha*.
—Yes. Three persons ③ have not eliminated *māna*, and also *kāmarāga*, *paṭigha*

This person has not eliminated latent states of *kāmarāga* and *paṭigha*. Has that person not eliminated latent state of *diṭṭhi*.....p..... *vicikicchā*?
—No. Two ★ persons have not eliminated *kāmarāga* and *paṭigha*, except for *vicikicchā* (and *diṭṭhi*).
—Yes. *Puthujjana* has not eliminated *kāmarāga* and *paṭigha*, and also *vicikicchā* (and *diṭṭhi*).
This person has not eliminated latent state of *vicikicchā*. Has that person not eliminated latent states of *kāmarāga* and *paṭigha*? —Yes. (*Puthujjana*)

This person has not eliminated latent states of *kāmarāga* and *paṭigha*. Has that person not eliminated latent state of *bhavarāga*.....p..... *avijjā*?
—Yes. (Three persons ③)
This person has not eliminated *avijjā*. Has that person not eliminated *kāmarāga* and *paṭigha*?
—No. *Anāgāmi* has not eliminated *avijjā* (and *bhavarāga*), except for *kāmarāga* and *paṭigha*.
—Yes. Three persons ③ have not eliminated *avijjā* (and *bhavarāga*), and also *kāmarāga* and *paṭigha*.

Triplet-based

304. This person has not eliminated latent states of *kāmarāga*, *paṭigha paṭigha* and *māna*. Has that person not eliminated latent state of *diṭṭhi*.....p..... *vicikicchā*?

—No. Two persons ★ have not eliminated *kāmarāga*, *paṭigha* and *māna*, except for *vicikicchā*.
—Yes. *Puthujjana* has not eliminated *kāmarāga*, *paṭigha* and *māna*, and also *vicikicchā*.
This person has not eliminated latent state of *vicikicchā*. Has that person not eliminated latent states of *kāmarāga*, *paṭigha* and *māna*? —Yes. (*Puthujjana*)

This person has not eliminated latent states of *kāmarāga*, *paṭigha* and *māna*. Has that person not eliminated latent state of *bhavarāga*.....p..... *avijjā*? —Yes.
This person has not eliminated latent state of *avijjā*. Has that person not eliminated latent states of *kāmarāga*, *paṭigha* and *māna*?
—No. *Anāgāmi* has not eliminated *avijjā* and *māna*, except for *kāmarāga* and *paṭigha*.
—Yes. Three persons ③ have not eliminated *avijjā*, and also *kāmarāga*, *paṭigha* and *māna*.

Quadruplet-based

305. This person has not eliminated latent states of *kāmarāga*, *paṭigha*, *māna* and *diṭṭhi*. Has that person not eliminated latent state of *vicikicchā*? —Yes.
This person has not eliminated latent state of *vicikicchā*. Has that person not eliminated latent states of *kāmarāga*, *paṭigha*, *māna* and *diṭṭhi*?
—Yes (*Puthujjana*) .....p.....

Quintuplet-based

306. This person has not eliminated latent states of *kāmarāga*, *paṭigha*, *māna*, *diṭṭhi* and *vicikicchā*. Has that person not eliminated latent state of *bhavarāga* ....p.... *avijjā*? —Yes. (*Puthujjana*)
This person has not eliminated latent state of *avijjā*. Has that person not eliminated latent states of *kāmarāga*, *paṭigha*, *māna*, *diṭṭhi* and *vicikicchā*?
—No. *Anāgāmi* has not eliminated *avijjā* and *māna*, except for *kāmarāga*, *paṭigha*, *diṭṭhi* and *vicikicchā*. Two persons ★ have not eliminated *avijjā*, *kāmarāga*, *paṭigha* and *māna*, except for *diṭṭhi* and *vicikicchā*.
—Yes. *Puthujjana* has not eliminated *avijjā*, and also *kāmarāga*, *paṭigha*, *māna*, *diṭṭhi* and *vicikicchā*.

Sextuplet-based

307. This person has not eliminated latent states of *kāmarāga*, *paṭigha*, *māna*, *diṭṭhi*, *vicikicchā* and *bhavarāga*. Has that person not eliminated *avijjā*? —Yes.
This person has not eliminated latent state of *avijjā*. Has that person not eliminated latent states of *kāmarāga*, *paṭigha*, *māna*, *diṭṭhi*, *vicikicchā* and *bhavarāga*?
—No. *Anāgāmi* has not eliminated *avijjā*, *māna* and *bhavarāga*, except for *kāmarāga*, *paṭigha*, *diṭṭhi* and *vicikicchā*. Two persons ★ have not eliminated *avijjā*, *kāmarāga*, *paṭigha*, *māna* and *bhavarāga*, except for *diṭṭhi* and *vicikicchā*.

—Yes. *Puthujjana* has not eliminated *avijjā*, and also *kāmarāga*, *paṭigha*, *māna*, *diṭṭhi*, *vicikicchā* and *bhavarāga*.

Opposite enquiries by plane

Mono-based

308. Latent state of *kāmarāga* has not been eliminated at this plane. Has latent state of *paṭigha* not been eliminated at that plane?
—Neither and nor should be said of *paṭigha* thereat. (in two feelings of the elemental world of sensuous desire)
Latent state of *paṭigha* has not been eliminated at this plane. Has latent state of *kāmarāga* not been eliminated at that plane?
—Neither and nor should be said of *kāmarāga* thereat. (in unpleasant feeling of the elemental world of sensuous desire)

Latent state of *kāmarāga* has not been eliminated at this plane. Has latent state of *māna* not been eliminated at that plane? —Yes. See the answer below.
Latent state of *māna* has not been eliminated at this plane. Has latent state of *kāmarāga* not been eliminated at that plane?
—In the elemental world of fine-material and immaterial, *māna* has not been eliminated; but neither and nor should be said of *kāmarāga* thereat.
—Yes. In two feelings of the elemental world of sensuous desire, *māna* has not been eliminated, and *kāmarāga* too.

Latent state of *kāmarāga* has not been eliminated at this plane. Has latent state of *diṭṭhi* not been eliminated at that plane? …..p….. Has latent state of *vicikicchā* not been eliminated at that plane? —Yes. See the answer below.
Latent state of *vicikicchā* has not been eliminated at this plane. Has latent state of *kāmarāga* not been eliminated at that plane?
—In unpleasant feeling, and in the elemental world of fine-material and immaterial, *vicikicchā* has not been eliminated; but neither and nor should be said of *kāmarāga* thereat.
—Yes. In two feelings of the elemental world of sensuous desire, *vicikicchā* has not been eliminated, and *kāmarāga* too.

Latent state of *kāmarāga* has not been eliminated at this plane. Has latent state of *bhavarāga* not been eliminated at that plane?
—Neither and nor should be said of *bhavarāga* thereat. (in two feelings of the elemental world of sensuous desire)
Latent state of *bhavarāga* has not been eliminated at this plane. Has latent state of *kāmarāga* not been eliminated at that plane?
—Neither and nor should be said of *kāmarāga* thereat. (in elemental world of fine-material and immaterial)

Latent state of *kāmarāga* has not been eliminated at this plane. Has latent state of *avijjā* not been eliminated at that plane? —Yes. See the answer below.

Latent state of *avijjā* has not been eliminated at this plane. Has latent state of *kāmarāga* not been eliminated at that plane?
—In unpleasant feeling, and in elemental world of fine-material and immaterial, *avijjā* has not been eliminated; but neither and nor should be said of *kāmarāga* thereat.
—Yes. In two feelings of the elemental world of sensuous desire, *avijjā* has not been eliminated, and *kāmarāga* too.

309. Latent state of *paṭigha* has not been eliminated at this plane. Has latent state of *māna* not been eliminated at that plane?
—Neither and nor should be said of *māna* thereat. (in unpleasant feeling of the elemental world of sensuous desire)
Latent state of *māna* lies unmanifest at this plane. Is latent state of *paṭigha* unmanifest at that plane?
—Neither and nor should be said of *paṭigha* thereat. (in two feelings of the elemental world of sensuous desire, and in the elemental world of fine-material and immaterial)

Latent state of *paṭigha* has not been eliminated at this plane. Has latent state of *diṭṭhi* not been eliminated at that plane? .....p..... Has latent state of *vicikicchā* not been eliminated at that plane? —Yes. See the answer below.
Latent state of *vicikicchā* has not been eliminated at this plane. Has latent state of *paṭigha* not been eliminated at that plane?
—In two feelings of the elemental world of sensuous desire, and in elemental world of fine-material and immaterial, *vicikicchā* has not been eliminated; but neither and nor should be said of *paṭigha* thereat.
—Yes. In unpleasant feeling, *vicikicchā* has not been eliminated, and *paṭigha* too.

Latent state of *paṭigha* has not been eliminated at this plane. Has latent state of *bhavarāga* not been eliminated at that plane?
—Neither and nor should be said of *bhavarāga* thereat. (in unpleasant feeling)
Latent state of *bhavarāga* has not been eliminated at this plane. Has latent state of *paṭigha* not been eliminated at that plane?
—Neither and nor should be said of *paṭigha* thereat. (in the elemental world of fine-material and immaterial)

Latent state of *paṭigha* has not been eliminated at this plane. Has latent state of *avijjā* not been eliminated at that plane?
—Yes. See the answer below.
Latent state of *avijjā* has not been eliminated at this plane. Has latent state of *paṭigha* not been eliminated at that plane?
—In two feelings of the elemental world of sensuous desire, and in elemental world of fine-material and immaterial, *avijjā* has not been eliminated; but neither and nor should be said of *paṭigha* thereat.
—Yes. In unpleasant feeling, *avijjā* has not been eliminated, and *paṭigha* too.

310. Latent state of *māna* has not been eliminated at this plane. Has latent state of *diṭṭhi* not been eliminated at that plane? .....p..... Has latent state of *vicikicchā* not been eliminated at that plane? —Yes. See the answer below.
Latent state of *vicikicchā* has not been eliminated at this plane. Has latent state of *māna* not been eliminated at that plane?
—In unpleasant feeling, *vicikicchā* has not been eliminated; but neither and nor should be said of *māna* thereat.
—Yes. In two feelings of the elemental world of sensuous desire, and in elemental world of fine-material and immaterial, *vicikicchā* has not been eliminated, and *māna* too.

Latent state of *māna* has not been eliminated at this plane. Has latent state of *bhavarāga* not been eliminated at that plane?
—In two feelings of the elemental world of sensuous desire, *māna* has not been eliminated; but neither and nor should be said of *bhavarāga* thereat.
—Yes. In elemental world of fine-material and immaterial, *māna* has not been eliminated, and *bhavarāga* too.
Latent state of *bhavarāga* has not been eliminated at this plane. Has latent state of *māna* not been eliminated at that plane? —Yes. Refer to the aforesaid

Latent state of *māna* has not been eliminated at this plane. Has latent state of *avijjā* not been eliminated at that plane? —Yes. See the answer below.
Latent state of *avijjā* has not been eliminated at this plane. Has latent state of *māna* not been eliminated at that plane?
—In unpleasant feeling, *avijjā* has not been eliminated; but neither and nor should be said of *māna* thereat.
—Yes. In two feelings of the elemental world of sensuous desire, and in elemental world of fine-material and immaterial, *avijjā* has not been eliminated, and *māna* too.

311. Latent state of *diṭṭhi* has not been eliminated at this plane. Has latent state of *vicikicchā* not been eliminated at that plane? —Yes. See the answer below.
Latent state of *vicikicchā* has not been eliminated at this plane. Has latent state of *diṭṭhi* not been eliminated at that plane?
—Yes (in the elemental world of sensuous desire, fine-material, and immaterial) ....p.....

312. Latent state of *vicikicchā* has not been eliminated at this plane. Has latent state of *bhavarāga* not been eliminated at that plane?
—In three feelings of the elemental world of sensuous desire, *vicikicchā* has not been eliminated; but neither and nor should be said of *bhavarāga* thereat.
—Yes. In elemental world of fine-material and immaterial, *vicikicchā* has not been eliminated, and *bhavarāga* too.
Latent state of *bhavarāga* has not been eliminated at this plane. Has latent state of *vicikicchā* not been eliminated at that plane? —Yes. Refer to the aforesaid

Latent state of *vicikicchā* has not been eliminated at this plane. Has latent state of *avijjā* not been eliminated at that plane?
—Yes. (in elemental world of sensuous desire, fine-material, and immaterial)
Latent state of *avijjā* has not been eliminated at this plane. Has latent state of *vicikicchā* not been eliminated at that plane? —Yes. (Same as aforesaid)

313. Latent state of *bhavarāga* has not been eliminated at this plane. Has latent state of *avijjā* not been eliminated at that plane? —Yes. See the answer below.
Latent state of *avijjā* has not been eliminated at this plane. Has latent state of *bhavarāga* not been eliminated at that plane?
—In three feelings of the elemental world of sensuous desire, *avijjā* has not been eliminated; but neither and nor should be said of *bhavarāga* thereat.
—Yes. In elemental world of fine-material and immaterial, *avijjā* has not been eliminated, and *bhavarāga* too.

Couplet-based

314. Latent states of *kāmarāga* and *paṭigha* have not been eliminated at this plane. Has latent state of *māna* not been eliminated at that plane? —None.
Latent state of *māna* has not been eliminated at this plane. Have latent states of *kāmarāga* and *paṭigha* not been eliminated at that plane?
—In elemental world of fine-material and immaterial, *māna* has not been eliminated; but neither and nor should be said of *kāmarāga* and *paṭigha* thereat.
—Yes. In two feelings of the elemental world of sensuous desire, *māna* and *kāmarāga* have not been eliminated; but neither and nor should be said of *paṭigha* thereat.

Latent states of *kāmarāga* and *paṭigha* have not been eliminated at this plane. Has latent state of *diṭṭhi* not been eliminated at that plane? .....p..... Has latent state of *vicikicchā* not been eliminated at that plane? —None.
Latent state of *vicikicchā* has not been eliminated at this plane. Have latent states of *kāmarāga* and *paṭigha* not been eliminated at that plane?
—In elemental world of fine-material and immaterial, *vicikicchā* has not been eliminated; but neither and nor should be said of *kāmarāga* and *paṭigha* thereat. In two feelings of the elemental world of sensuous desire, *vicikicchā* and *kāmarāga* have not been eliminated; but neither and nor should be said of *paṭigha* thereat. In unpleasant feeling, *vicikicchā* and *paṭigha* have not been eliminated; but neither and nor should be said of *kāmarāga* thereat.

Latent states of *kāmarāga* and *paṭigha* have not been eliminated at this plane. Has latent state of *bhavarāga* not been eliminated at that plane? —None.
Latent state of *bhavarāga* has not been eliminated at this plane. Have latent states of *kāmarāga* and *paṭigha* not been eliminated at that plane?
—Neither and nor should be said of *kāmarāga* and *paṭigha* thereat. (In elemental world of fine-material and immaterial)

Latent states of *kāmarāga* and *paṭigha* have not been eliminated at this plane. Has latent state of *avijjā* not been eliminated at that plane? —None.
Latent state of *avijjā* has not been eliminated at this plane. Have latent states of *kāmarāga* and *paṭigha* not been eliminated at that plane?
—In elemental world of fine-material and immaterial, *avijjā* has not been eliminated; but neither and nor should be said of *kāmarāga* and *paṭigha* thereat. In two feelings of the elemental world of sensuous desire, *avijjā* and *kāmarāga* have not been eliminated; but neither and nor should be said of *paṭigha* thereat. In unpleasant feeling, *avijjā* and *paṭigha* have not been eliminated; but neither and nor should be said of *kāmarāga* thereat.

Triplet-based

315. Latent states of *kāmarāga, paṭigha* and *māna* have not been eliminated at this plane. Has latent state of *diṭṭhi* not been eliminated at that plane?
…..p….. Has *vicikicchā* not been eliminated at that plane? —None.
Latent state of *vicikicchā* has not been eliminated at this plane. Have latent states of *kāmarāga, paṭigha* and *māna* not been eliminated at that plane?
—In the elemental world of fine-material and immaterial, *vicikicchā* and *māna* have not been eliminated; but neither and nor should be said of *kāmarāga* and *paṭigha* thereat. In two feelings of the elemental world of sensuous desire, *vicikicchā, kāmarāga* and *māna* have not been eliminated; but neither and nor should be said of *paṭigha* thereat. In unpleasant feeling, *vicikicchā* and *paṭigha* have not been eliminated; but neither and nor should be said of *kāmarāga* and *māna* thereat.

Latent states of *kāmarāga, paṭigha* and *māna* have not been eliminated at this plane. Has latent state of *bhavarāga* not been eliminated at that plane? —None.
Latent state of *bhavarāga* has not been eliminated at this plane. Have latent states of *kāmarāga, paṭigha* and *māna* not been eliminated at that plane?
—In elemental world of fine-material and immaterial, *bhavarāga* and *māna* have not been eliminated; but neither and nor should be said of *kāmarāga* and *paṭigha* thereat.

Latent states of *kāmarāga, paṭigha* and *māna* have not been eliminated at this plane. Has latent state of *avijjā* not been eliminated at that plane? —None.
Latent state of *avijjā* has not been eliminated at this plane. Have latent states of *kāmarāga, paṭigha* and *māna* not been eliminated at that plane?
—In elemental world of fine-material and immaterial, *avijjā* and *māna* have not been eliminated; but neither and nor should be said of *kāmarāga* and *paṭigha* thereat. In the two feelings of sensuous element, *avijjā, kāmarāga* and *māna* have not been eliminated; but neither and nor should be said of *paṭigha* thereat. In unpleasant feeling, *avijjā* and *paṭigha* have not been eliminated; but neither and nor should be said of *kāmarāga* and *māna* thereat.

Quadruplet-based

316. Latent states of *kāmarāga*, *paṭigha*, *māna* and *diṭṭhi* have not been eliminated at this plane. Has latent state of *vicikicchā* not been eliminated at that plane? —None.
Latent state of *vicikicchā* has not been eliminated at this plane. Have latent states of *kāmarāga*, *paṭigha*, *māna* and *diṭṭhi* not been eliminated at that plane?
—In elemental world of fine-material and immaterial, *vicikicchā*, *māna* and *diṭṭhi* have not been eliminated; but neither and nor should be said of *kāmarāga* and *paṭigha* thereat. In two feelings of the elemental world of sensuous desire, *vicikicchā*, *kāmarāga*, *māna* and *diṭṭhi* have not been eliminated; but neither and nor should be said of *paṭigha* thereat. In unpleasant feeling, *vicikicchā*, *paṭigha* and *diṭṭhi* have not been eliminated; but neither and nor should be said of *kāmarāga* and *māna* thereat.

Latent states of *kāmarāga*, *paṭigha*, *māna* and *diṭṭhi* have not been eliminated at this plane. Has latent state of *bhavarāga* not been eliminated at that plane? —None.
Latent state of *bhavarāga* has not been eliminated at this plane. Have latent states of *kāmarāga*, *paṭigha*, *māna* and *diṭṭhi* not been eliminated at that plane?
—In elemental world of fine-material and immaterial, *bhavarāga*, *māna* and *diṭṭhi* have not been eliminated; but neither and nor should be said of *kāmarāga* and *paṭigha* thereat.

Latent states of *kāmarāga*, *paṭigha*, *māna* and *diṭṭhi* have not been eliminated at this plane. Has latent state of *avijjā* not been eliminated at that plane? —None.
Latent state of *avijjā* has not been eliminated at this plane. Have latent states of *kāmarāga*, *paṭigha*, *māna* and *diṭṭhi* not been eliminated at that plane?
—In elemental world of fine-material and immaterial, *avijjā*, *māna* and *diṭṭhi* have not been eliminated; but neither and nor should be said of *kāmarāga* and *paṭigha* thereat. In two feelings of the elemental world of sensuous desire, *avijjā*, *kāmarāga*, *māna* and *diṭṭhi* have not been eliminated; but neither and nor should be said of *paṭigha* thereat. In unpleasant feeling, *avijjā*, *paṭigha* and *diṭṭhi* have not been eliminated; but neither and nor should be said of *kāmarāga* and *māna* thereat.

Quintuplet-based

317. Latent states of *kāmarāga*, *paṭigha*, *māna*, *diṭṭhi* and *vicikicchā* have not been eliminated at this plane. Has latent state of *bhavarāga* not been eliminated at that plane? —None.
Latent state of *bhavarāga* has not been eliminated at this plane. Have latent states of *kāmarāga*, *paṭigha*, *māna*, *diṭṭhi*, *vicikicchā* not been eliminated at that plane?
—In elemental world of fine-material and immaterial, *bhavarāga*, *māna*, *diṭṭhi* and *vicikicchā* have not been eliminated; but neither and nor should be said of *kāmarāga* and *paṭigha* thereat.

Latent states of *kāmarāga*, *paṭigha*, *māna*, *diṭṭhi* and *vicikicchā* have not been eliminated at this plane. Has *avijjā* not been eliminated at that plane? —None.
Latent state of *avijjā* has not been eliminated at this plane. Have latent states of *kāmarāga*, *paṭigha*, *māna*, *diṭṭhi* and *vicikicchā* not been eliminated at that plane?
—In elemental world of fine-material and immaterial, *avijjā*, *māna*, *diṭṭhi* and *vicikicchā* have not been eliminated; but neither and nor should be said of *kāmarāga* and *paṭigha* thereat. In two feelings of the elemental world of sensuous desire, *avijjā*, *kāmarāga*, *māna*, *diṭṭhi* and *vicikicchā* have not been eliminated; but neither and nor should be said of *paṭigha* thereat. In unpleasant feeling, *avijjā*, *paṭigha*, *diṭṭhi* and *vicikicchā* have not been eliminated; but neither and nor should be said of *kāmarāga* and *māna* thereat.

Sextuplet-based

318. Latent states of *kāmarāga*, *paṭigha*, *māna*, *diṭṭhi*, *vicikicchā* and *bhavarāga* have not been eliminated at this plane. Has latent state of *avijjā* not been eliminated at that plane? —None.
Avijjā has not been eliminated at this plane. Have *kāmarāga*, *paṭigha*, *māna*, *diṭṭhi*, *vicikicchā* and *bhavarāga* not been eliminated at that plane?
—In elemental world of fine-material and immaterial, *avijjā*, *māna*, *diṭṭhi*, *vicikicchā* and *bhavarāga* have not been eliminated; but neither and nor should be said of *kāmarāga* and *paṭigha* thereat. In two feelings of the elemental world of sensuous desire, *avijjā*, *kāmarāga*, *māna*, *diṭṭhi* and *vicikicchā* have not been eliminated; but neither and nor should be said of *paṭigha* and *bhavarāga* thereat. In unpleasant feeling, *avijjā*, *paṭigha*, *diṭṭhi* and *vicikicchā* have not been eliminated; but neither and nor should be said of *kāmarāga*, *māna* and *bhavarāga* thereat.

Opposite enquiries by person and plane

Mono-based

319. This person has not eliminated latent state of *kāmarāga* at this plane. Has that person not eliminated latent state of *paṭigha* at that plane?
—Neither and nor should be said of *paṭigha* thereat. (three persons ③, with two feelings of the elemental world of sensuous desire)
This person has not eliminated latent state of *paṭigha* at this plane. Has that person not eliminated latent state of *kāmarāga* at that plane?
—Neither and nor should be said of *kāmarāga* thereat. (three persons ③, with unpleasant feelings of the elemental world of sensuous desire)

This person has not eliminated latent state of *kāmarāga* at this plane. Has that person not eliminated latent state of *māna* at that plane?—Yes. See answer below
This person has not eliminated latent state of *māna* at this plane. Has that person not eliminated latent state of *kāmarāga* at that plane?
—*Anāgāmi,* in elemental world of fine-material and immaterial, has not eliminated *māna*; but neither and nor should be said of *kāmarāga* thereat. Three

persons ③, in elemental world of fine-material and immaterial, have not eliminated *māna*; but neither and nor should be said of *kāmarāga* thereat.
—No. Those persons (*Anāgāmi*), with two feelings of the elemental world of sensuous desire, have not eliminated *māna*, except for *kāmarāga*.
—Yes. Those persons (three persons ③), with two feelings of the elemental world of sensuous desire, have not eliminated *māna*, and also have not eliminated *kāmarāga*.

This person has not eliminated latent state of *kāmarāga* at this plane. Has that person not eliminated latent state of *diṭṭhi*......p..... *vicikicchā* at that plane?
—No. Two persons ★, with two feelings of the elemental world of sensuous desire, have not eliminated *kāmarāga*, except for *vicikicchā*.
—Yes. *Puthujjana*, with two feelings of the elemental world of sensuous desire, has not eliminated *kāmarāga*, and also *vicikicchā*.
This person has not eliminated latent state of *vicikicchā* at this plane. Has that person not eliminated latent state of *kāmarāga* at that plane?
—*Puthujjana* in unpleasant feeling, and in elemental world of fine-material and immaterial, has not eliminated *vicikicchā*; but neither and nor should be said of *kāmarāga* thereat.
—Yes. Refer to the aforesaid.

This person has not eliminated latent state of *kāmarāga* at this plane. Has that person not eliminated latent state of *bhavarāga* at that plane?
—Neither and nor should be said of *bhavarāga* thereat. (three persons ③, with two feelings of the elemental world of sensuous desire)
This person has not eliminated latent state of *bhavarāga* at this plane. Has that person not eliminated latent state of *kāmarāga* at that plane?
—Neither and nor should be said of *kāmarāga* thereat. (four persons ④, in elemental world of fine-material and immaterial)

This person has not eliminated latent state of *kāmarāga* at this plane. Has that person not eliminated latent state of *avijjā* at that plane?—Yes. See answer below
This person has not eliminated latent state of *avijjā* at this plane. Has that person not eliminated latent state of *kāmarāga* at that plane?
—*Anāgāmi,* with unpleasant feeling, and in elemental world of fine-material and immaterial, has not eliminated *avijjā*; but neither and nor should be said of *kāmarāga* thereat. Three persons ③, with unpleasant feeling, in elemental world of fine-material and immaterial, have not eliminated *avijjā*; but neither and nor should be said of *kāmarāga* thereat.
—No. Those persons (*Anāgāmi*), with two feelings of the elemental world of sensuous desire, have not eliminated *avijjā*, except for *kāmarāga*.
—Yes. Those persons ③, with two feelings of the elemental world of sensuous desire, have not eliminated *avijjā*, and also *kāmarāga*.

320. This person has not eliminated latent state of *paṭigha* at this plane. Has that person not eliminated latent state of *māna* at that plane?

—Neither and nor should be said of *māna* thereat. (three persons ③, with unpleasant feeling of the sensuous element)
This person has not eliminated latent state of *māna* at this plane. Has that person not eliminated latent state of *paṭigha* at that plane?
—Neither and nor should be said of *paṭigha* thereat. (four persons ④, with two feelings of the elemental world of sensuous desire, and in elemental world of fine-material and immaterial)

This person has not eliminated latent state of *paṭigha* at this plane. Has that person not eliminated latent state of *diṭṭhi*.....p.....*vicikicchā* at that plane?
—No. Two persons ★, with unpleasant feeling, have not eliminated *paṭigha*, except for *vicikicchā*.
—Yes. *Puthujjana*, with unpleasant feeling, has not eliminated *paṭigha*, and also *vicikicchā*.
This person has not eliminated latent state of *vicikicchā* at this plane. Has that person not eliminated latent state of *paṭigha* at that plane?
—*Puthujjana*, with two feelings of the elemental world of sensuous desire, and in elemental world of fine-material and immaterial, has not eliminated *vicikicchā*; but neither and nor should be said of *paṭigha* thereat.
—Yes. Refer to the aforesaid.

This person has not eliminated latent state of *paṭigha* at this plane. Has that person not eliminated latent state of *bhavarāga* at that plane?
—Neither and nor should be said of *bhavarāga* thereat. (three persons ③, with unpleasant feeling of the sensuous element)
This person has not eliminated latent state of *bhavarāga* at this plane. Has that person not eliminated latent state of *paṭigha* at that plane?
—Neither and nor should be said of *paṭigha* thereat. (four persons ④, in elemental world of fine-material and immaterial)

This person has not eliminated latent state of *paṭigha* at this plane. Has that person not eliminated latent state of *avijjā* at that plane?—Yes. See answer below.
This person has not eliminated latent state of *avijjā* at this plane. Has that person not eliminated latent state of *paṭigha* at that plane?
—*Anāgāmi,* with two feelings of the elemental world of sensuous desire, and in elemental world of fine-material and immaterial, has not eliminated *avijjā*; but neither and nor should be said of *paṭigha* thereat. Three persons ③, with two feelings of the elemental world of sensuous desire, and in elemental world of fine-material and immaterial, have not eliminated *avijjā*; but neither and nor should be said of *paṭigha* thereat.
—No. Those persons (*Anāgāmi*), with unpleasant feeling, have not eliminated *avijjā*, except for *paṭigha*.
—Yes. Those persons (three persons ③), with unpleasant feeling, have not eliminated *avijjā*, and also *paṭigha*.

321. This person has not eliminated latent state of *māna* at this plane. Has that person not eliminated latent state of *diṭṭhi*.....p.... *vicikicchā* at that plane?
—No. Three persons ⋮, with two feelings of the elemental world of sensuous desire, and in elemental world of fine-material and immaterial, have not eliminated *māna*, except for *vicikicchā*. —Yes. *Puthujjana*, with two feelings of the elemental world of sensuous desire, and in elemental world of fine-material and immaterial, has not eliminated *māna*, and also *vicikicchā*.
This person has not eliminated latent state of *vicikicchā* at this plane. Has that person not eliminated latent state of *māna* at that plane?
—*Puthujjana*, with unpleasant feeling, has not eliminated *vicikicchā*; but neither and nor should be said of *māna* thereat.
—Yes. Refer to the aforesaid.

This person has not eliminated latent state of *māna* at this plane. Has that person not eliminated latent state of *bhavarāga* at that plane?
—Four persons ④, with two feelings of the elemental world of sensuous desire, have not eliminated *māna*; but neither and nor should be said of *bhavarāga* thereat.
—Yes. Those persons (four persons④), in elemental world of fine-material and immaterial, have not eliminated *māna*, and also *bhavarāga*.
This person has not eliminated latent state of *bhavarāga* at this plane. Has that person not eliminated latent state of *māna* at that plane?—Yes (Same as aforesaid)

This person has not eliminated latent state of *māna* at this plane. Has that person not eliminated latent state of *avijjā* at that plane? —Yes. See the answer below.
This person has not eliminated latent state of *avijjā* at this plane. Has that person not eliminated latent state of *māna* at that plane?
—Four persons ④, with unpleasant feeling, have not eliminated *avijjā*; but neither and nor should be said of *māna* thereat.
—Yes. Those persons (four persons ④), with two feelings of the elemental world of sensuous desire, and in elemental world of fine-material and immaterial, have not eliminated *avijjā*, and also *māna*.

322. This person has not eliminated latent state of *diṭṭhi* at this plane. Has that person not eliminated latent state of *vicikicchā* at that plane?—Yes. (*Puthujjana*)
This person has not eliminated latent state of *vicikicchā* at this plane. Has that person not eliminated latent state of *diṭṭhi* at that plane?
—Yes (*Puthujjana*) .....p.....

323. This person has not eliminated latent state of *vicikicchā* at this plane. Has that person not eliminated latent state of *bhavarāga* at that plane?
—*Puthujjana*, with three feelings of the elemental world of sensuous desire, has not eliminated *vicikicchā*; but neither and nor should be said of *bhavarāga* thereat.
—Yes. Those persons (*Puthujjana*), in elemental world of fine-material and immaterial, have not eliminated *vicikicchā*, and also *bhavarāga*.

This person has not eliminated latent state of *bhavarāga* at this plane. Has that person not eliminated latent state of *vicikicchā* at that plane?
—No. Three persons ⋮, in elemental world of fine-material and immaterial, have not eliminated *bhavarāga*, except for *vicikicchā*.
—Yes. Refer to the aforesaid.

This person has not eliminated latent state of *vicikicchā* at this plane. Has that person not eliminated latent state of *avijjā* at that plane? —Yes. (*Puthujjana*)
This person has not eliminated latent state of *avijjā* at this plane. Has that person not eliminated latent state of *vicikicchā* at that plane?
—No. Three persons ⋮, with three feelings of the elemental world of sensuous desire, and in elemental world of fine-material and immaterial, have not eliminated *avijjā*, except for *vicikicchā*.
—Yes. *Puthujjana*, with three feelings of the elemental world of sensuous desire, and in elemental world of fine-material and immaterial, has not eliminated *avijjā*, and also *vicikicchā*.

324. This person has not eliminated latent state of *bhavarāga* at this plane. Has that person not eliminated latent state of *avijjā* at that plane? —Yes. See below.
This person has not eliminated latent state of *avijjā* at this plane. Has that person not eliminated latent state of *bhavarāga* at that plane?
—Four persons ④, with three feelings of the elemental world of sensuous desire, have not eliminated *avijjā*; but neither and nor should be said of *bhavarāga* thereat.
—Yes. Those (same) persons, in elemental world of fine-material and immaterial, have not eliminated *avijjā*, and also *bhavarāga*.

Couplet-based

325. This person has not eliminated latent states of *kāmarāga* and *paṭigha* at this plane. Has that person not eliminated latent state of *māna* at that plane? —None.
This person has not eliminated latent state of *māna* at this plane. Has that person not eliminated latent states of *kāmarāga* and *paṭigha* at that plane?
—*Anāgāmi,* in elemental world of fine-material and immaterial, has not eliminated *māna*; but neither and nor should be said of *kāmarāga* and *paṭigha* thereat. Those (same) persons, with two feelings of the elemental world of sensuous desire, have not eliminated *māna*; but have eliminated *kāmarāga*; and neither and nor should be said of *paṭigha* thereat.
—Three persons ③, in elemental world of fine-material and immaterial, have not eliminated *māna*; but neither and nor should be said of *kāmarāga* and *paṭigha* thereat. Those (same) persons, with two feelings of the elemental world of sensuous desire, have not eliminated *māna* and *kāmarāga*; but neither and nor should be said of *paṭigha* thereat.

This person has not eliminated latent states of *kāmarāga* and *paṭigha* at this plane. Has that person not eliminated latent state of *diṭṭhi*.....p..... *vicikicchā* at that plane? —None.

This person has not eliminated latent state of *vicikicchā* at this plane. Has that person not eliminated latent states of *kāmarāga* and *paṭigha* at that plane?
—*Puthujjana,* in elemental world of fine-material and immaterial, has not eliminated *vicikicchā*; but neither and nor should be said of *kāmarāga* and *paṭigha* thereat. Those (same) persons, with two feelings of the elemental world of sensuous desire, have not eliminated *vicikicchā* and *kāmarāga*; but neither and nor should be said of *paṭigha* thereat. Those (same) persons, with unpleasant feeling, have not eliminated *vicikicchā* and *paṭigha*; but neither and nor should be said of *kāmarāga* thereat.

This person has not eliminated latent states of *kāmarāga* and *paṭigha* at this plane. Has that person not eliminated latent state of *bhavarāga* at that plane? —None.
This person has not eliminated latent state of *bhavarāga* at this plane. Has that person not eliminated latent states of *kāmarāga* and *paṭigha* at that plane?
—Neither and nor should be said of *kāmarāga* and *paṭigha* thereat. (the four persons ④, in elemental world of fine-material and immaterial)

This person has not eliminated latent states of *kāmarāga* and *paṭigha* at this plane. Has that person not eliminated latent state of *avijjā* at that plane? —None.
This person has not eliminated latent state of *avijjā* at this plane. Has that person not eliminated latent states of *kāmarāga* and *paṭigha* at that plane?
—*Anāgāmi,* in elemental world of fine-material and immaterial, has not eliminated *avijjā*; but neither and nor should be said of *kāmarāga* and *paṭigha* thereat. Those (same) persons, with two feelings of the elemental world of sensuous desire, have not eliminated *avijjā*; but have eliminated *kāmarāga*; and neither and nor should be said of *paṭigha* thereat.. Those (same) persons, with unpleasant feeling, have not eliminated *avijjā*; but have eliminated *paṭigha*; and neither and nor should be said of *kāmarāga* thereat.
—Three persons ③, in elemental world of fine-material and immaterial, have not eliminated *avijjā*; but neither and nor should be said of *kāmarāga* and *paṭigha* thereat. Those (same) persons, with two feelings of the elemental world of sensuous desire, have not eliminated *avijjā* and *kāmarāga*; but neither and nor should be said of *paṭigha* thereat. Those (same) persons, with unpleasant feeling, have not eliminated *avijjā* and *paṭigha*; but neither and nor should be said of *kāmarāga* thereat.

Triplet-based

326. This person has not eliminated latent states of *kāmarāga*, *paṭigha* and *māna* at this plane. Has that person not eliminated latent state of *diṭṭhi*……p….. *vicikicchā* at that plane? —None.
This person has not eliminated latent state of *vicikicchā* at this plane. Has that person not eliminated latent states of *kāmarāga*, *paṭigha* and *māna* at that plane?
—*Puthujjana,* in elemental world of fine-material and immaterial, has not eliminated *vicikicchā* and *māna*; but neither and nor should be said of *kāmarāga* and *paṭigha* thereat. Those (same) persons, with two feelings of the elemental

world of sensuous desire, have not eliminated *vicikicchā*, *kāmarāga* and *māna*; but neither and nor should be said of *paṭigha* thereat. Those (same) persons, with unpleasant feeling, have not eliminated *vicikicchā* and *paṭigha*; but neither and nor should be said of *kāmarāga* and *māna* thereat.

This person has not eliminated latent states of *kāmarāga*, *paṭigha* and *māna* at this plane. Has that person not eliminated latent state of *bhavarāga* at that plane? —None.
This person has not eliminated latent state of *bhavarāga* at this plane. Has that person not eliminated latent states of *kāmarāga*, *paṭigha* and *māna* at that plane?
— (Four persons ④, in elemental world of fine-material and immaterial) has not eliminated *māna*; but neither and nor should be said of *kāmarāga* and *paṭigha* thereat.

This person has not eliminated latent states of *kāmarāga*, *paṭigha* and *māna* at this plane. Has that person not eliminated latent state of *avijjā* at that plane? —None.
This person has not eliminated latent state of *avijjā* at this plane. Has that person not eliminated latent states of *kāmarāga*, *paṭigha* and *māna* at that plane?
—*Anāgāmi,* in elemental world of fine-material and immaterial, has not eliminated *avijjā* and *māna*; but neither and nor should be said of *kāmarāga* and *paṭigha* thereat. Those (same) persons, with two feelings of the elemental world of sensuous desire, have not eliminated *avijjā* and *māna*; but have eliminated *kāmarāga*; and neither and nor should be said of *paṭigha* thereat. Those (same) persons, with unpleasant feeling, have not eliminated *avijjā*; but have eliminated *paṭigha*; and neither and nor should be said of *kāmarāga* and *māna* thereat.
Three persons ③, in elemental world of fine-material and immaterial, have not eliminated *avijjā* and *māna*; but neither and nor should be said of *kāmarāga* and *paṭigha* thereat. Those (same) persons, with two feelings of the elemental world of sensuous desire, have not eliminated *avijjā*, *kāmarāga* and *māna*; but neither and nor should be said of *paṭigha* thereat. Those (same) persons, with unpleasant feeling, have not eliminated *avijjā* and *paṭigha*; but neither and nor should be said of *kāmarāga* and *māna* thereat.

Quadruplet-based

327. This person has not eliminated latent states of *kāmarāga*, *paṭigha*, *māna* and *diṭṭhi* at this plane. Has that person not eliminated latent state of *vicikicchā* at that plane? —None.
This person has not eliminated latent state of *vicikicchā* at this plane. Has that person not eliminated latent states of *kāmarāga*, *paṭigha*, *māna* and *diṭṭhi* at that plane?
—*Puthujjana*, in elemental world of fine-material and immaterial, has not eliminated *vicikicchā*, *māna* and *diṭṭhi*; but neither and nor should be said of *kāmarāga* and *paṭigha* thereat. Those (same) persons, with two feelings of the elemental world of sensuous desire, have not eliminated *vicikicchā*, *kāmarāga*,

māna and *diṭṭhi*; but neither and nor should be said of *paṭigha* thereat. Those (same) persons, with unpleasant feeling, have not eliminated *vicikicchā, paṭigha* and *diṭṭhi*; but neither and nor should be said of *kāmarāga* and *māna* thereat. ….p….

Quintuplet-based

328. This person has not eliminated latent states of *kāmarāga, paṭigha, māna, diṭṭhi* and *vicikicchā* at this plane. Has that person not eliminated latent state of *bhavarāga* at that plane? —None.
This person has not eliminated latent state of *bhavarāga* at this plane. Has that person not eliminated latent states of *kāmarāga, paṭigha, māna, diṭṭhi* and *vicikicchā* at that plane?
—Three persons ⁝ , in elemental world of fine-material and immaterial, have not eliminated *bhavarāga* and *māna*; but have eliminated *diṭṭhi* and *vicikicchā*; and neither and nor should be said of *kāmarāga* and *paṭigha* thereat. *Puthujjana*, in elemental world of fine-material and immaterial, has not eliminated *bhavarāga, māna, diṭṭhi* and *vicikicchā*; but neither and nor should be said of *kāmarāga* and *paṭigha* thereat.

This person has not eliminated latent states of *kāmarāga, paṭigha, māna, diṭṭhi* and *vicikicchā* at this plane. Has that person not eliminated latent state of *avijjā* at that plane? —None.
This person has not eliminated latent state of *avijjā* at this plane. Has that person not eliminated latent states of *kāmarāga, paṭigha, māna, diṭṭhi* and *vicikicchā* at that plane?
—*Anāgāmi,* in elemental world of fine-material and immaterial, has not eliminated *avijjā* and *māna*; but has eliminated *diṭṭhi* and *vicikicchā*; and neither and nor should be said of *kāmarāga* and *paṭigha* thereat. Those (same) persons, with two feelings of the elemental world of sensuous desire, have not eliminated *avijjā* and *māna*; but have eliminated *kāmarāga, diṭṭhi* and *vicikicchā*; and neither and nor should be said of *paṭigha* thereat. Those (same) persons, with unpleasant feeling, have not eliminated *avijjā*; but have eliminated *paṭigha, diṭṭhi* and *vicikicchā*; and neither and nor should be said of *kāmarāga* and *māna* thereat.
—Two persons ★, in elemental world of fine-material and immaterial, have not eliminated *avijjā* and *māna*; but have eliminated *diṭṭhi* and *vicikicchā*; and neither and nor should be said of *kāmarāga* and *paṭigha* thereat. Those (same) persons, with two feelings of the elemental world of sensuous desire, have not eliminated *avijjā, kāmarāga* and *māna*; but have eliminated *diṭṭhi* and *vicikicchā*; and neither and nor should be said of *paṭigha* thereat. Those (same) persons, with unpleasant feeling, have not eliminated *avijjā* and *paṭigha*; but have eliminated *diṭṭhi* and *vicikicchā*; and neither and nor should be said of *kāmarāga* and *māna* thereat.
—*Puthujjana*, in elemental world of fine-material and immaterial, has not eliminated *avijjā, māna, diṭṭhi* and *vicikicchā*; but neither and nor should be said of *kāmarāga* and *paṭigha* thereat. Those (same) persons, with two feelings of the

elemental world of sensuous desire, have not eliminated *avijjā*, *kāmarāga māna*, *diṭṭhi* and *vicikicchā*; but neither and nor should be said of *paṭigha* thereat. Those (same) persons, with unpleasant feeling, have not eliminated *avijjā*, *paṭigha*, *diṭṭhi* and *vicikicchā*; but neither and nor should be said of *kāmarāga* and *māna* thereat.

Sextuplet-based

329. This person has not eliminated latent states of *kāmarāga*, *paṭigha*, *māna*, *diṭṭhi*, *vicikicchā* and *bhavarāga* at this plane. Has that person not eliminated latent state of *avijjā* at that plane? —None.

This person has not eliminated *avijjā* at this plane. Has that person not eliminated *kāmarāga*, *paṭigha*, *māna*, *diṭṭhi*, *vicikicchā* and *bhavarāga* at that plane?

—*Anāgāmi,* in elemental world of fine-material and immaterial, has not eliminated *avijjā*, *māna* and *bhavarāga*, but has eliminated *diṭṭhi* and *vicikicchā*; and neither and nor should be said of *kāmarāga* and *paṭigha* thereat. Those (same) persons, with two feelings of the elemental world of sensuous desire, have not eliminated *avijjā* and *māna*; but have eliminated *kāmarāga*, *diṭṭhi* and *vicikicchā*; and neither and nor should be said of *paṭigha* and *bhavarāga* thereat. Those (same) persons, with unpleasant feeling, have not eliminated *avijjā*; but have eliminated *paṭigha*, *diṭṭhi*, *vicikicchā*; and neither and nor should be said of *kāmarāga*, *māna*, *bhavarāga* thereat.

—Two persons ★, in elemental world of fine-material and immaterial, have not eliminated *avijjā*, *māna* and *bhavarāga*; but have eliminated *diṭṭhi* and *vicikicchā*; and neither and nor should be said of *kāmarāga* and *paṭigha* thereat. Those (same) persons, with two feelings of the elemental world of sensuous desire, have not eliminated *avijjā*, *kāmarāga* and *māna*; but have eliminated *diṭṭhi* and *vicikicchā*; and neither and nor should be said of *paṭigha* and *bhavarāga* thereat. Those (same) persons, with unpleasant feeling, have not eliminated *avijjā* and *paṭigha*; but have eliminated *diṭṭhi* and *vicikicchā*; and neither and nor should be said of *kāmarāga*, *māna* and *bhavarāga* thereat.

—*Puthujjana*, in elemental world of fine-material and immaterial, has not eliminated *avijjā*, *māna*, *diṭṭhi*, *vicikicchā* and *bhavarāga*; but neither and nor should be said of *kāmarāga* and *paṭigha* thereat. Those (same) persons, with two feelings of the elemental world of sensuous desire, have not eliminated *avijjā*, *kāmarāga*, *māna*, *diṭṭhi* and *vicikicchā*; but neither and nor should be said of *paṭigha* and *bhavarāga* thereat. Those (same) persons, with unpleasant feeling, have not eliminated *avijjā*, *paṭigha*, *diṭṭhi* and *vicikicchā*; but neither and nor should be said of *kāmarāga*, *māna* and *bhavarāga* thereat.

7.2.6 Arising of latent states (*Uppajjana*)

Forward enquiries by person

330. Latent state of *kāmarāga* arises in this person. Does latent state of *paṭigha* arise in that person? —Yes. (three persons, except *Anāgāmi* and *Arahat*)
Latent state of *paṭigha* arises in this person. Does latent state of *kāmarāga* in that person? —Yes. (three persons, except *Anāgāmi* and *Arahat*)

Latent state of *kāmarāga* arises in this person. Does latent state of *māna* arise in that person? —Yes. (three persons, except *Anāgāmi* and *Arahat*)
Latent state of *māna* arises in this person. Does latent state of *kāmarāga* arise in that person?
—No. In *Anāgāmi, māna* arises; *kāmarāga* in whom does not arise.
—Yes, in three persons (except *Anāgāmi* and *Arahat*)
….. p …..

Opposite enquiries by person

331. Latent state of *kāmarāga* does not arise in this person. Does latent state of *paṭigha* not arise in that person? —Yes. (*Anāgāmi* and *Arahat*)
Paṭigha does not arise to this person. Does latent state of *kāmarāga* not arise in that person? —Yes. (*Anāgāmi* and *Arahat*)

Latent state of *kāmarāga* does not arise in this person. Does latent state of *māna* not arise in that person?
—Yes. In *Arahat*, *kāmarāga* does not arise, and *māna* also does not arise.
Latent state of *māna* does not arise in this person. Does latent state of *kāmarāga* not arise in that person? —Yes. (in *Arahat*)
….. p …..

Forward enquiries by plane
Opposite enquiries by plane
Forward enquiries by person and plane
Opposite enquiries by person and plane

The remaining catechisms as shown above are not given in the text, but should be constructed in the same manner as in the above examples, or in accordance to the sequence in Chart 7.0. The answers as to arising are tabulated in the following three charts. Those information can be used as a rough self-evaluative guide to practitioners, to ascertain the levels of their insight performance. For instance, if a practitioner by way of his actions, whether physically, mentally, or in oral form, exhibits various degrees of mistaken views and skepticism towards the teaching and true intention of the Buddha, we know the person has a lot yet to overcome before attaining fruition as *Sotāpanna*.

However, if a person had overcome these underlying tendencies, but is habitually getting into displeasure, discomfort, disagreement, discrimination, anger, complaint, contempt, and other constituents of *paṭigha*, we know he is certainly quite some way from attaining fulfilment as *Anāgāmi*. Simply, to these noble persons, the said latent states, under whatsoever circumstances, would no longer arise. Enlightenment is never a temporary feat that is recurrent of the old bad habits, but its positive effect is permanent. Otherwise, the term 'elimination' is not being fully understood. And to the common worldlings, all the seven latent states in whom had arisen, are arising every now and then, and will continue to arise until their eventual and successful elimination.

Chart 7.16 Arising of latent states (enquiries by person)

Y: in whom arises; N: in whom does not arise

Common worldlings and the four noble fruition-attainers :	latent state of :						
	kāmarāga	paṭigha	māna	diṭṭhi	vicikicchā	bhavarāga	avijjā
Puthujjana	Y	Y	Y	Y	Y	Y	Y
Sotāpanna	Y	Y	Y	N	N	Y	Y
Sakadāgāmi	Y	Y	Y	N	N	Y	Y
Anāgāmi	N	N	Y	N	N	Y	Y
Arahat	N	N	N	N	N	N	N

Chart 7.17 Arising of latent states (enquiries by plane)

Y: latent state in whom arises; N: latent state in whom does not arise
Nn: Neither is arising, nor is not arising should be said

		latent state of :						
		kāmarāga	paṭigha	māna	diṭṭhi	vicikicchā	bhavarāga	avijjā
In unpleasant feeling	in the elemental world of sensuous desire	*Nn*	N Y	*Nn*	N Y	N Y	*Nn*	N Y
In pleasant feeling		N Y	*Nn*	*Nn*	N Y	N Y	*Nn*	N Y
In neither pleasant feeling nor unpleasant feeling		N Y	*Nn*	*Nn*	N Y	N Y	*Nn*	N Y
In unpleasant feeling	in the elemental world of fine material and immaterial	*Nn*	*Nn*	N Y	N Y	N Y	N Y	N Y
In pleasant feeling		*Nn*	*Nn*	N Y	N Y	N Y	N Y	N Y
In neither pleasant feeling nor unpleasant feeling		*Nn*	*Nn*	N Y	N Y	N Y	N Y	N Y

Chart 7.18 Arising of latent states (enquiries by person and plane)

Y: latent state in whom arises; N: latent state in whom does not arise
Nn: Neither is arising, nor is not arising should be said

		in elemental world of sensuous desire	in elemental world of fine-material and immaterial	latent state of: kāmarāga	paṭigha	māna	diṭṭhi	vicikicchā	bhavarāga	avijjā
Puthujjana (Common worldlings)	with unpleasant feeling	•		*Nn*	Y	*Nn*	Y	Y	*Nn*	Y
	with pleasant feeling	•		Y	*Nn*	Y	Y	Y	*Nn*	Y
	with neither pleasant feeling nor unpleasant feeling	•		Y	*Nn*	Y	Y	Y	*Nn*	Y
	with unpleasant feeling		•	*Nn*	*Nn*	Y	Y	Y	Y	Y
	with pleasant feeling		•	*Nn*	*Nn*	Y	Y	Y	Y	Y
	with neither pleasant feeling nor unpleasant feeling		•	*Nn*	*Nn*	Y	Y	Y	Y	Y
Sotāpanna fruition-attainer	with unpleasant feeling	•		*Nn*	Y	*Nn*	N	N	*Nn*	Y
	with pleasant feeling	•		Y	*Nn*	Y	N	N	*Nn*	Y
	with neither pleasant feeling nor unpleasant feeling	•		Y	*Nn*	Y	N	N	*Nn*	Y
	with unpleasant feeling		•	*Nn*	*Nn*	Y	N	N	Y	Y
	with pleasant feeling		•	*Nn*	*Nn*	Y	N	N	Y	Y
	with neither pleasant feeling nor unpleasant feeling		•	*Nn*	*Nn*	Y	N	N	Y	Y
Sakadāgāmi fruition-attainer	with unpleasant feeling	•		*Nn*	Y	*Nn*	N	N	*Nn*	Y
	with pleasant feeling	•		Y	*Nn*	Y	N	N	*Nn*	Y
	with neither pleasant feeling nor unpleasant feeling	•		Y	*Nn*	Y	N	N	*Nn*	Y
	with unpleasant feeling		•	*Nn*	*Nn*	Y	N	N	Y	Y
	with pleasant feeling		•	*Nn*	*Nn*	Y	N	N	Y	Y
	with neither pleasant feeling nor unpleasant feeling		•	*Nn*	*Nn*	Y	N	N	Y	Y
Anāgāmi fruition-attainer	with unpleasant feeling	•		*Nn*	N	*Nn*	N	N	*Nn*	Y
	with pleasant feeling	•		N	*Nn*	Y	N	N	*Nn*	Y
	with neither pleasant feeling nor unpleasant feeling	•		N	*Nn*	Y	N	N	*Nn*	Y
	with unpleasant feeling		•	*Nn*	*Nn*	Y	N	N	Y	Y
	with pleasant feeling		•	*Nn*	*Nn*	Y	N	N	Y	Y
	with neither pleasant feeling nor unpleasant feeling		•	*Nn*	*Nn*	Y	N	N	Y	Y
Arahat fruition-attainer	with unpleasant feeling	•		*Nn*	N	*Nn*	N	N	*Nn*	N
	with pleasant feeling	•		N	*Nn*	N	N	N	*Nn*	N
	with neither pleasant feeling nor unpleasant feeling	•		N	*Nn*	N	N	N	*Nn*	N
	with unpleasant feeling		•	*Nn*	*Nn*	N	N	N	N	N
	with pleasant feeling		•	*Nn*	*Nn*	N	N	N	N	N
	with neither pleasant feeling nor unpleasant feeling		•	*Nn*	*Nn*	N	N	N	N	N

7.2.7 Groups of Q&A on elemental world (*dhātupucchā, dhātuvisajjanā*)

Chart 7.19 Groups of Q&A on elemental world

Nn : None

	is reemerged in :	is not reemerged in :	is, neither and nor, reemerged in :	sensuous element	fine-material element	immaterial element	How many latent states remain unmanifest?	How many latent states not remaining unmanifest?	How many latent states can be analysed (or be classified)?
This person, shifted from sensuous element,	→			•			to some persons, 7; to some persons, 5	Nn	Nn
	→				•		to some persons, 5; to some persons, 3	Nn	Nn
	→					•	to some persons, 7; to some persons, 5; to some persons, 3	Nn	Nn
		→		•			to some persons, 7; to some persons, 5; to some persons, 3	Nn	Nn
		→			•		to some persons, 7; to some persons, 5; to some persons, 3	Nn	Nn
		→				•	to some persons, 7; to some persons, 5; to some persons, 3	Nn	Nn
			→	•		•	to some persons, 7; to some persons, 5; to some persons, 3	Nn	Nn
			→		•	•	to some persons, 7; to some persons, 5	Nn	Nn
			→	•	•		to some persons, 7; to some persons, 5; to some persons, 3	Nn	Nn
This person, shifted from fine-material element,	→				•		to some persons, 7; to some persons, 5; to some persons, 3	Nn	Nn
	→			•			to some persons, 7	Nn	Nn
	→					•	to some persons, 3	Nn	Nn
		→		•			to some persons, 7; to some persons, 5; to some persons, 3	Nn	Nn
		→			•		to some persons, 7; to some persons, 5; to some persons, 3	Nn	Nn
		→				•	to some persons, 7; to some persons, 5; to some persons, 3	Nn	Nn
			→	•		•	to some persons, 7; to some persons, 5; to some persons, 3	Nn	Nn
			→		•	•	to some persons, 7	Nn	Nn
			→	•	•		to some persons, 7; to some persons, 5; to some persons, 3	Nn	Nn
This person, shifted from immaterial element,	→					•	to some persons, 7; to some persons, 5; to some persons, 3	Nn	Nn
	→			•			to some persons, 7	Nn	Nn
	→				•		to some persons, 7	Nn	Nn
		→		•			to some persons, 7; to some persons, 5; to some persons, 3	Nn	Nn
		→			•		to some persons, 7; to some persons, 5; to some persons, 3	Nn	Nn
		→				•	to some persons, 7	Nn	Nn
			→	•		•	to those reemerged lower, at sensuous element, 7	Nn	Nn
			→		•	•	to some persons, 7	Nn	Nn
			→	•	•		to some persons, 7; to some persons, 5; to some persons, 3	Nn	Nn

	is reemerged in :	is not reemerged in :	is, neither and nor, reemerged in :	sensuous element	fine-material element	immaterial element	How many latent states can be analysed (and be classified)?	How many latent states remain unmanifest?	How many latent states not remaining unmanifest?
This person, shifted not from sensuous element,	→			•			to some persons, 7	Nn	Nn
	→				•		to some persons, 7; to some persons, 5; to some persons, 3	Nn	Nn
	→					•	to some persons, 7; to some persons, 5; to some persons, 3	Nn	Nn
		→		•			to some persons, 7; to some persons, 5; to some persons, 3	Nn	Nn
		→			•		to some persons, 7; to some persons, 5; to some persons, 3	Nn	Nn
		→				•	to some persons, 7; to some persons, 5; to some persons, 3	Nn	Nn
			→	•		•	to some persons, 7; to some persons, 5; to some persons, 3	Nn	Nn
			→		•	•	to some persons, 7	Nn	Nn
			→	•	•		to some persons, 7; to some persons, 5; to some persons, 3	Nn	Nn
This person, shifted not from fine-material element,	→			•			to some persons, 7; to some persons, 5	Nn	Nn
	→				•		to some persons, 7; to some persons, 5; to some persons, 3	Nn	Nn
	→					•	to some persons, 7; to some persons, 5; to some persons, 3	Nn	Nn
		→		•			to some persons, 7; to some persons, 5; to some persons, 3	Nn	Nn
		→			•		to some persons, 7; to some persons, 5; to some persons, 3	Nn	Nn
		→				•	to some persons, 7; to some persons, 5; to some persons, 3	Nn	Nn
			→	•		•	to some persons, 7; to some persons, 5; to some persons, 3	Nn	Nn
			→		•	•	to some persons, 7; to some persons, 5	Nn	Nn
			→	•	•		to some persons, 7; to some persons, 5; to some persons, 3	Nn	Nn
This person, shifted not from immaterial element,	→			•			to some persons, 7; to some persons, 5	Nn	Nn
	→				•		to some persons, 7; to some persons, 5; to some persons, 3	Nn	Nn
	→					•	to some persons, 7; to some persons, 5; to some persons, 3	Nn	Nn
		→		•			to some persons, 7; to some persons, 5; to some persons, 3	Nn	Nn
		→			•		to some persons, 7; to some persons, 5; to some persons, 3	Nn	Nn
		→				•	to some persons, 7; to some persons, 5; to some persons, 3	Nn	Nn
			→	•		•	to some persons, 7; to some persons, 5; to some persons, 3	Nn	Nn
			→		•	•	to some persons, 7; to some persons, 5	Nn	Nn
			→	•	•		to some persons, 7; to some persons, 5; to some persons, 3	Nn	Nn
This person, shifted neither from sensuous element nor from immaterial element,	→			•			to some persons, 7	Nn	Nn
	→				•		to some persons, 7; to some persons, 5; to some persons, 3	Nn	Nn
	→					•	to some persons, 7; to some persons, 5; to some persons, 3	Nn	Nn
		→		•			to some persons, 7; to some persons, 5; to some persons, 3	Nn	Nn
		→			•		to some persons, 7; to some persons, 5; to some persons, 3	Nn	Nn
		→				•	to some persons, 7; to some persons, 5; to some persons, 3	Nn	Nn
			→	•		•	to some persons, 7; to some persons, 5; to some persons, 3	Nn	Nn
			→		•	•	to some persons, 7	Nn	Nn
			→	•	•		to some persons, 7; to some persons, 5; to some persons, 3	Nn	Nn

	is reemerged in :	is not reemerged in :	is, neither and nor, reemerged in :	sensuous element	fine-material element	immaterial element	How many latent states remain unmanifest?	How many latent states not remaining unmanifest?	How many latent states can be analysed (and be classified)?
This person, shifted neither from fine-material element nor from immaterial element,	→			•			to some persons, 7; to some persons, 5	Nn	Nn
	→				•		to some persons, 7; to some persons, 5; to some persons, 3	Nn	Nn
	→					•	to some persons, 7; to some persons, 5; to some persons, 3	Nn	Nn
		→		•			to some persons, 7; to some persons, 5; to some persons, 3	Nn	Nn
		→			•		to some persons, 7; to some persons, 5; to some persons, 3	Nn	Nn
		→				•	to some persons, 7; to some persons, 5; to some persons, 3	Nn	Nn
			→	•		•	to some persons, 7; to some persons, 5; to some persons, 3	Nn	Nn
			→		•	•	to some persons, 7; to some persons, 5	Nn	Nn
			→	•	•		to some persons, 7; to some persons, 5; to some persons, 3	Nn	Nn
This person, shifted neither from sensuous element nor from fine-material element,	→			•			to some persons, 7	Nn	Nn
	→				•		to those reemerged lower, at sensuous element, 7	Nn	Nn
	→					•	to some persons, 7; to some persons, 5; to some persons, 3	Nn	Nn
		→		•			to some persons, 7; to some persons, 5; to some persons, 3	Nn	Nn
		→			•		to some persons, 7; to some persons, 5; to some persons, 3	Nn	Nn
		→				•	to some persons, 7	Nn	Nn
			→	•		•	to some persons, 7	Nn	Nn
			→		•	•	to some persons, 7	Nn	Nn
			→	•	•		to some persons, 7; to some persons, 5; to some persons, 3	Nn	Nn

The above chart summarises the questions and answers from catechisms nos. 332 to 349. In the above chart, the given number of latent states remaining as unmanifest in certain individuals, can be compared with the information I tabulated in Chat 7.20 below. A few things noteworthy of pointing out regarding the answers compiled in the above chart. The information shows that to some persons (puthujjanas), who shifted from sensuous element and reemerged similarly at the sensuous element, 7 latent states remain as unmanifest (the word 'element' and 'elemental world' herein are used interchangeably). *Bhavarāga* in those puthujjanas has been been excluded, is because there are earthlings who hanker after the existence of fine-materiality and immateriality. Secondly, to some persons who have fallen away from sensuous element and reemerged at immaterial element, there are also 7 states lying latent. Also, to some persons who have fallen away from fine-material element and reemerged at either sensuous element or at fine-material element, in either case there are also 7 states lying latent. But why are there lying latent all the 7 states to those reemerged at the fine-material element? Shouldn't it be just 5 or 3 to those persons, since *kāmarāga* and *paṭigha* do not lie latent in fine-material element? In another case of some persons who have fallen away from immaterial element, and reemerged at either sensuous element or fine-material element, or at the same immaterial element which have ceased, in either of these three repositioning there are similarly amongst them 7 latent states underlying in the persons. The answers with 7 latent states remain underlying in those individuals in aforementioned examples, would elude our understanding if we construe them in terms of deceased of life and reborn after death. If we do not interpret them this way, then answers in the aforementioned cases make sense.

Let's ponder over what happens to those who have shifted from fine-material element and reemerged at sensuous element with *bhavarāga* still lying latent? And what happens to earthlings who have shifted from sensuous element and reemerged at fine-material element with *kāmarāga* and *paṭigha* in them remain underlying? It means to them a lack of thorough understanding of what are taught in the preceding six sections which forms the knowledge bedrock of meditation as well as a moral compass in all other daily practices. Put it another way, for some reasons if an earthling died and is reborn at fine-material plane with sensuous desires and hatred still unmanifest or preponderate over others, the person's life instantly ends in the same way as life of a non-percipient being perishes as soon as feeling or any latent state in whom arises.

Chart 7.20 Unmanifest latent states by person and plane

Y: yes ; N: no

	in fine-material and immaterial element,	in sensuous element,	below latent state lies unmanifest							
			kāmarāga	paṭigha	māna	diṭṭhi	vicikicchā	bhavarāga	avijjā	
to Puthujjana	•		Y	Y	Y	Y	Y	Y	Y	7
to Sotāpanna	•		Y	Y	Y	N	N	Y	Y	5
to Sakadāgāmi	•		Y	Y	Y	N	N	Y	Y	5
to Anāgāmi	•		N	N	Y	N	N	Y	Y	3
to Arahat	•		N	N	N	N	N	N	N	0
to Puthujjana		•	N	N	Y	Y	Y	Y	Y	5
to Sotāpanna		•	N	N	Y	N	N	Y	Y	3
to Sakadāgāmi		•	N	N	Y	N	N	Y	Y	3
to Anāgāmi		•	N	N	Y	N	N	Y	Y	3
to Arahat		•	N	N	N	N	N	N	N	0

The following set of questions and the answers regarding element are in separate sections in the text. I have combined them together instead of keeping as they are. The purpose is to make it easier to read.

At base of sensuous world

332. *i* (a) This person, shifted [60] from sensuous element, is reemerged [61] at sensuous element.
How many latent states remain unmanifest? —to some persons, 7 latent states; to some persons, 5 latent states [62].
How many latent states remain not unmanifest? —none.
How many latent states can be analysed? —not possible. [63]

i (b) This person, shifted from sensuous element, has reemerged at fine-material element.
How many latent states remain unmanifest? —to some persons, 5 latent states; to some persons, 3 latent states.
How many latent states remain not unmanifest? —none.
How many latent states can be analysed? —not possible.

i (c) This person, shifted from sensuous element, has reemerged at immaterial element.
How many latent states remain unmanifest? — to some persons, 7 latent states; to some persons, 5 latent states; to some persons, 3 latent states.
How many latent states remain not unmanifest? —none.
How many latent states can be analysed? —not possible.

ii (a) This person, shifted from sensuous element, has reemerged not at sensuous element.
How many latent states remain unmanifest? —to some persons, 7 latent states; to some persons, 5 latent states; to some persons, 3 latent states.
How many latent states remain not unmanifest? —none.
How many latent states can be analysed? —not possible.

ii (b) This person, shifted from sensuous element, has reemerged not at fine-material element.

---

[60] *cuta*: (pp. of *cavati*) can be interpreted as 'died, left one world and reborn into another, passed from one existence to another, disappeared, vanished, fallen away, shifted'. The rendering as 'shifted (from)' is more preferable in the context of this chapter, so that the questions can be congruent with the given answers.

[61] *upapajjanta*: (pp. *upapajjati*) can be interpreted as 'reborn, produced at, placed at, came to, emerged, reemerged'. The interpreted meaning 'reemerged (at/in)' is chosen for this chapter, so that the sentence 'shifted from…, and reemerged at…' can be formed meaningfully.

[62] It should not be four latent states even though *bhavarāga* does not lie latent in *kāmadhātu*. It is because 'stream-winners' and 'once-returners' are also found among men and deities.

[63] *kati anusayā bhaṅgā*: that means to analyse which states are 'latent and arise', and which are 'not latent and do not arise'. *Natthi* (not possible)—is due to the differential properties such that these states sometimes lie latent (and sometimes arise), but sometimes do not lie latent (and sometimes do not arise), and sometimes they should not be said to be as remaining latent or not remaining latent (neither is arising nor is not arising should be said). Chart 7.18 tells you exactly what this is about.

How many latent states remain unmanifest? —to some persons, 7 latent states; to some persons, 5 latent states; to some persons, 3 latent states.
How many latent states remain not unmanifest? —none.
How many latent states can be analysed? —not possible.

ii (c) This person, shifted from sensuous element, has reemerged not at immaterial element.
How many latent states remain unmanifest? —to some persons, 7 latent states; to some persons, 5 latent states; to some persons, 3 latent states.
How many latent states remain not unmanifest? —none.
How many latent states can be analysed? —not possible.

iii (a) This person, shifted from sensuous element, has reemerged neither at sensuous element nor at immaterial element.
How many latent states remain unmanifest? —to some persons, 5 latent states; to some persons, 3 latent states.
How many latent states remain not unmanifest? —none.
How many latent states can be analysed? —not possible.

iii (b) This person, shifted from sensuous element, has reemerged neither at fine-material element nor at immaterial element.
How many latent states remain unmanifest? —to some persons, 7 latent states; to some persons, 5 latent states; to some persons, 3 latent states.
How many latent states remain not unmanifest? —none.
How many latent states can be analysed? —not possible.

iii (c) This person, shifted from sensuous element, has reemerged neither at sensuous element nor at fine-material element.
How many latent states remain unmanifest? —to some persons, 7 latent states; to some persons, 5 latent states; to some persons, 3 latent states.
How many latent states remain not unmanifest? —none.
How many latent states can be analysed? —not possible.

At base of fine-material element

333. *i* (a) This person, shifted from fine-material element, has reemerged at fine-material element.
How many latent states remain unmanifest? —to some persons, 7 latent states; to some persons, 5 latent states; to some persons, 3 latent states.
How many latent states remain not unmanifest? —none.
How many latent states can be analysed? —not possible.

i (b) This person, shifted from fine-material element, has reemerged at sensuous element. [64]
How many latent states remain unmanifest? —to some persons, 7 latent states.
How many latent states remain not unmanifest? —none.
How many latent states can be analysed? —not possible.

i (c) This person, shifted from fine-material element, has reemerged at immaterial element.
How many latent states remain unmanifest? —to some persons, 7 latent states; to some persons, 5 latent states; to some persons, 3 latent states.
How many latent states remain not unmanifest? —none.
How many latent states can be analysed? —not possible.

ii (a) This person, shifted from fine-material element, has reemerged not at sensuous element.
How many latent states remain unmanifest? How many latent states remain not unmanifest? How many latent states can be analysed? —same answer as in *i* (c)

ii (b) This person, shifted from fine-material element, has reemerged not at fine-material element.
How many latent states remain unmanifest? How many latent states remain not unmanifest? How many latent states can be analysed? —same answer as in *i* (c)

ii (c) This being, shifted from fine-material element, has reemerged not at immaterial element.
How many latent states remain unmanifest? How many latent states remain not unmanifest? How many latent states can be analysed? —same answer as in *i* (c)

iii (a) This person, shifted from fine-material element, has reemerged neither at sensuous element nor at immaterial element.
How many latent states remain unmanifest? How many latent states remain not unmanifest? How many latent states can be analysed? —same answer as in *i* (c)

iii (b) This person, shifted from fine-material element, has reemerged neither at fine-material element nor at immaterial element.
How many latent states remain unmanifest? —to some persons, 7 latent states.

---

[64] In the context of transmigratory process, those non-percipient beings, if they had not attained enlightenment at end of life, will be born at the sensuous plane of Manussaloka, Cātummahārājika-devaloka, or some in Asaññasattāvāsa. Pure abode beings, and beings of the four Immaterial planes, if they are doomed to be reborn again, would not be found in any other planes, and certainly not in sensuous planes. The 'stream-winner' will be born at most seven times at the 7 two-rooted sensuous planes and at the 10 three-rooted fine-material planes before attaining final enlightenment. The 'once-returner' will be born in human world only once more to attain final enlightenment. The 'non-returner' will not be born in the sensuous planes but in the pure abodes, to eliminate the upper five fetters of defilement. (See also in Appendix I).

How many latent states remain not unmanifest? —none.
How many latent states can be analysed? —not possible.

iii (c) This person, shifted from fine-material element, has reemerged neither at sensuous element nor at fine-material element.
How many latent states remain unmanifest? How many latent states remain not unmanifest? How many latent states can be analysed? —same answer as in *i* (c)

At base of immaterial element

334. *i* (a) This person, shifted from immaterial element, has reemerged at immaterial element.
How many latent states remain unmanifest? —to some persons, 7 latent states; to some persons, 5 latent states; to some persons, 3 latent states.
How many latent states remain not unmanifest? —none.
How many latent states can be analysed? —not possible.

i (b) This person, shifted from immaterial element, has reemerged at sensuous element.
How many latent states remain unmanifest? —to some persons, 7 latent states.
How many latent states remain not unmanifest? —none.
How many latent states can be analysed? —not possible.

i (c) This person, shifted from immaterial element, has reemerged at fine-material element.
How many latent states remain unmanifest? —to some persons, 7 latent states.
How many latent states remain not unmanifest? —none.
How many latent states can be analysed? —not possible.

ii (a) This person, shifted from immaterial element, has reemerged not at sensuous element.
How many latent states remain unmanifest? How many latent states remain not unmanifest? How many latent states can be analysed? —same answer as in *i* (a)

ii (b) This person, shifted from immaterial element, has reemerged not at fine-material element.
How many latent states remain unmanifest? How many latent states remain not unmanifest? How many latent states can be analysed? —same answer as in *i* (a)

ii (c) This person, shifted from immaterial element, has reemerged not at immaterial element.
How many latent states remain unmanifest? How many latent states remain not unmanifest? How many latent states can be analysed? —same answer as in *i* (b)

iii (a) This person, shifted from immaterial element, has reemerged neither at sensuous element nor at immaterial element.

How many latent states remain unmanifest? —to some reemerged at lower planes, which are only the sensuous planes, are 7 states remain as latent.
How many latent states remain not unmanifest? —none.
How many latent states can be analysed? —not possible.

iii (b) This person, shifted from immaterial element, has reemerged neither at fine-material element nor at immaterial element.
How many latent states remain unmanifest? How many latent states remain not unmanifest? How many latent states can be analysed? —same answer as in *i* (b)

iii (c) This person, shifted from immaterial element, has reemerged neither at sensuous element nor at fine-material element.
How many latent states remain unmanifest? How many latent states remain not unmanifest? How many latent states can be analysed? —same answer as in *i* (a)

Not at base of sensuous element

335. *i* (a) This person, shifted not from sensuous element, has reemerged at sensuous element.
How many latent states remain unmanifest? —to some persons, 7.
How many latent states remain not unmanifest? —none.
How many latent states can be analysed? —not possible.
i (b) This person, shifted not from sensuous element, has reemerged at fine-material element.
How many latent states remain unmanifest? —to some 7; to some, 5; to some, 3
How many latent states remain not unmanifest? —none.
How many latent states can be analysed? —not possible.
i (c) This person, shifted not from sensuous element, has reemerged at immaterial element. How many latent states remain unmanifest? —to some 7; to some, 5; to some, 3
How many latent states remain not unmanifest? —none.
How many latent states can be analysed? —not possible.

ii (a) This person, shifted not from sensuous element, has reemerged not at sensuous element.
How many latent states remain unmanifest?

.....p.....

Not at base of fine-material element
Not at base of immaterial element
Neither at base of sensuous element nor at base of immaterial element
Neither at base of fine-material element nor at base of immaterial element
Neither at base of sensuous element nor at base of fine-material element

340. *i* (a) This person, shifted neither from sensuous element nor from fine-material element, has reemerged at sensuous element. …..p…..

iii (c) This person, shifted neither from sensuous element nor from fine-material element, has reemerged neither at sensuous element nor at fine-material element.
How many latent states remain unmanifest? —to some 7; to some, 5; to some, 3
How many latent states remain not unmanifest? —none.
How many latent states can be analysed? —not possible.

I have not written the remaining catechisms as shown above. Those questions and answers can be followed fairly easily according to the step sequence as displayed in Chart 7.19.

CHAPTER 8

VIII. Pairs on State of Consciousness
(*Cittayamaka*)

This Chapter discusses the general aspects of mental phenomena as 'pure' state of consciousness in three sections. The first section analyses phenomena based on person, *dhamma* (phenomenon, law of nature, etc), person and *dhamma*. It varies slightly from previous chapters in a way it does not adhere rigidly to the standard methodology of enquiring the relationship of conditions in question in the full cycle of iterations. Instead this chapter provides analysis with selectively chosen verbal conditions in fourteen pairs, making enquiries by means of a mix of direct mode and regressive mode of questions. There are ten verbal conditions to be dealt with — arise, is arising, will arise, had arisen, cease, is ceasing, will cease, had ceased, appear, and disappear. Subsequent charts below which show all the given answers, reveal its incompleteness because the analysis is only based on a mix selection. Anyway, the content in this chapter will undoubtedly be overly lengthy if it had used the full iterative method of making enquiries.

The last two sections provide a few examples of the Suttanta method and Abhidhamma method of explaining the arising moment of consciousness.

8.1 Conformity of Pure Citta (*Suddhacittasāmañña*)

The first division consisting of summary of questions, are all repeated in the second division on descriptive exposition. I therefore will omit the first one, which means nos. 1 to 62 will not be included in this written work. Chart 8.1 below summarises the questions and answers from nos. 63 to 113.

Chart 8.1 Designation of pure *citta* based on person

Y: Yes ; N : No	*citta* in whom :											
(Based on person)	arises	is arising	had arisen	will arise	ceases	is ceasing	had ceased	will cease	appears	disappears	has elapsed past arising moment	has elapsed past ceasing moment
To those :												
at the arising moment of consciousness	Y	Y	Y	Y	N	N	Y	Y	Y			
at the ceasing moment of consciousness	N	N	Y	Y	Y	Y	Y	Y	Y	N	Y	N
at the arising moment of final-stage *citta*	Y	Y		N	N	N		Y	Y			
at the ceasing moment of final-stage *citta*	N	N	Y	N	Y	Y	Y	N	Y			
at past state of consciousness		N				N			N	Y	Y	Y
at future state of consciousness		N							N			
at arising moment of future state of consciousness						N	N			N	Y	Y
with *citta* (not the final-stage *citta*)			Y	Y					Y			
endowed with final-stage *citta*			Y	N					Y			
with Cessation-attainment	N	N	Y	Y	N	N	Y	Y	N			
Non-percipient beings	N	N	Y	Y	N	N	Y	Y	N			

Chart 8.2 Designation of pure *citta* based on *dhamma*

Y: Yes ; N : No

(Based on *dhamma*)	*citta* : arises	is arising	had arisen	will arise	ceases	is ceasing	had ceased	will cease	appears	disappears	has elapsed past arising moment	has elapsed past ceasing moment
At the arising moment of consciousness.	Y	Y	N	N	N	N	N	Y	Y			
At the ceasing moment of consciousness.	N	N	N	N	Y	Y	N	N	Y	N	Y	N
At present state of consciousness.			N	N	N				Y			
At past state of consciousness.	N	N	Y	N	N	N	Y	N	N	Y	Y	Y
At future state of consciousness.	N	N	N	Y	N	N	N	Y	N			
At arising moment of past state of consciousness												
At ceasing moment of past state of consciousness	N			N				Y				
At arising moment of future state of consciousness			N		N	N	N	Y		N	N	N
At ceasing moment of future state of consciousness	N		N				N					

Chart 8.2 above summarises the catechisms from nos. 84 to 104. The answers in the dark cells in the above two charts reveal the differences between the two, given the same questions asked and with available answers.

Chart 8.3 Designation of pure *citta* based on person and *dhamma*

Y: Yes ; N : No

(Based on person and *dhamma*)	*citta* in whom : arises	is arising	had arisen	will arise	ceases	is ceasing	had ceased	will cease	appears	disappears	has elapsed past arising moment	has elapsed past ceasing moment
To those :												
at the arising moment of consciousness.	Y	Y	N	N	N	N	N	Y	Y			
at the ceasing moment of consciousness.	N	N	N	N	Y	Y	N	N	Y	N	Y	N
at present state of consciousness.			N	N	N				Y			
at past state of consciousness.	N	N	Y	N	N	N	Y	N	N	Y	Y	Y
at future state of consciousness.	N	N	N	Y	N	N	N	Y	N			
at arising moment of past state of consciousness												
at ceasing moment of past state of consciousness	N			N				Y				
at arising moment of future state of consciousness			N		N	N	N	Y		N	N	N
at ceasing moment of future state of consciousness	N		N				N					

The catechisms on person and *dhamma* are not given in full in the text. However, the results are the same as in those answers in Chart 8.2.

8.1.1 Based on Person (*puggala*)

A minor composite on Arise and Cease (*Uppādanirodhakālasaṁbheda*)

63. *i* (a) *Citta* arises, and does not cease, in this person. Will *citta* cease, and will not arise, in that person?
—Yes. To those at arising moment of final-stage state of consciousness (*pacchimacitta*) [16], *citta* in whom arises and does not cease, will cease and will not arise.
—No. To others at the arising moment of consciousness, *citta* in whom arises and does not cease, will cease and will also arise.
(b) *Citta* will cease, and will not arise, in this person. Will *citta* arise, and does not cease, in that person?
—Yes. (to those at the arising moment of final-stage *citta*)

ii (a) *Citta* does not arise, and (it) ceases, in this person. Will *citta* not cease, and will arise, in that person?
—No. (to those at the ceasing moment of final-stage *citta* … *citta* will not cease and will not arise)
(b) *Citta* will not cease, and will arise, in this person. Does *citta* not arise, and (it) ceases, in that person? —None.

Arise and Appear (*Uppāduppanna*)

64. *i* (a) *Citta* arises in this person. Does *citta* appear in that person?
—Yes. (at the arising moment of consciousness)
(b) *Citta* appears in this person. Does *citta* arise in that person?
—No. To those at the ceasing moment of consciousness, *citta* in whom appears but does not arise.
—Yes. Refer to the aforesaid.

ii (a) *Citta* does not arise in this person. Does *citta* not appear in that person?
—No. To those at the ceasing moment of consciousness, *citta* in whom does not arise, but it appears.
—Yes. To those with Cessation-attainment, and non-percipient beings, *citta* in whom does not arise, and also does not appear.
(b) *Citta* does not appear in this person. Does *citta* not arise in that person?
—Yes. Refer to the aforesaid.

Cease and Appear (*Nirodhuppanna*)

65. *i* (a) *Citta* ceases in this person. Does *citta* appear in that person?
—Yes. (at the ceasing moment of consciousness)
(b) *Citta* appears in this person. Does *citta* cease in that person?
—No. To those at the arising moment of consciousness, *citta* in whom appears, and does not cease.

—Yes. Refer to the aforesaid.

ii (a) *Citta* does not cease in this person. Does *citta* not appear in that person?
—No. To those at the arising moment of consciousness, *citta* in whom does not cease, but it appears.
—Yes. To those with Cessation-attainment, and non-percipient beings, *citta* in whom does not cease, and also does not appear.
(b) Citta does not appear in this person. Does *citta* not cease in that person?
—Yes. Refer to the aforesaid.

Arise (*Uppāda*)

66. *i* (a) *Citta* arises in this person. Had *citta* arisen in that person?
—Yes. (Same as below)
(b) *Citta* had arisen in this person. Does *citta* arise in that person?
—No. To those at the ceasing moment of consciousness, those with Cessation-attainment, and those non-percipient beings, *citta* in whom had arisen; but it does not arise.
—Yes. To those at the arising moment of consciousness, *citta* in whom had arisen, and it also arises.

ii (a) *Citta* does not arise in this person. Had *citta* not arisen in that person?
—No. *Citta* had arisen. (at the ceasing moment of consciousness; those with Cessation-attainment; and non-percipient beings)
(b) *Citta* had not arisen in this person. Does *citta* not arise in that person?
—None.

67. *i* (a) *Citta* arises in this person. Will *citta* arise in that person?
—No. At the arising moment of final-stage state of consciousness, *citta* in whom arises; but will not arise.
—Yes. To others at the arising moment of consciousness, *citta* in whom arises, and also will arise.
(b) *Citta* will arise in this person. Does *citta* arise in that person?
—No. To those at ceasing moment of consciousness, those with Cessation-attainment, and non-percipient beings, *citta* in whom will arise; but does not arise.
—Yes. (Refer to the aforesaid)

ii (a) *Citta* does not arise in this person. Will *citta* not arise in that person?
—No. To those at ceasing moment of consciousness, those with Cessation-attainment, and non-percipient beings, *citta* in whom does not arise; but will arise.
—Yes. To those at the ceasing moment of final-stage state of consciousness, *citta* in whom does not arise, and also will not arise.
(b) *Citta* will not arise in this person. Does *citta* not arise in that person?
—No. To those at the arising moment of final-stage state of consciousness, *citta* in whom will not arise; but *citta* in whom arises.
—Yes. Refer to the aforesaid.

68. *i* (a) *Citta* had arisen in this person. Will *citta* arise in that person?
—No. In those endowed with the final-stage state of consciousness, *citta* had arisen, but in whom *citta* will not arise.
—Yes. In others (at both the arising and ceasing moment of consciousness; those with Cessation-attainment; Non-percipient beings).
(b) *Citta* will arise in this person. Had *citta* arisen in that person?
—Yes. Refer to the aforesaid.

ii (a) *Citta* had not arisen in this person. Will *citta* not arise in that person? None
(b) *Citta* will not arise in this person. Had *citta* not arisen in that person?
—No, it had in whom arisen (at past state of consciousness).

Cease (*Nirodha*)

69. *i* (a) *Citta* ceases in this person. Had *citta* ceased in that person?
—Yes. (Same as the answer below)
(b) *Citta* had ceased in this person. Does *citta* cease in that person?
—No. To those at the arising moment of consciousness, those with Cessation-attainment, and non-percipient beings, *citta* in whom had ceased; but in whom it does not cease.
—Yes. To those at the ceasing moment of consciousness, *citta* in whom had ceased, and also ceases.

ii (a) *Citta* does not cease in this person. Had *citta* not ceased in that person?
—No. It had ceased. (at arising moment of consciousness; those with Cessation-attainment; and non-percipient beings)
(b) *Citta* had not ceased in this person. Does *citta* not cease in that person?
—No such person in whom *citta* both had not ceased and does not cease.

70. *i* (a) *Citta* ceases in this person. Will *citta* cease in that person?
—No. At the ceasing moment of final-stage state of consciousness, *citta* in whom ceases, but will not cease.
—Yes. To others at ceasing moment, *citta* in whom ceases, and will also cease.
(b) *Citta* will cease in this person. Does *citta* cease in that person?
—No. To those at arising moment of consciousness, those with Cessation-attainment, and non-percipients, *citta* in whom will cease; but it does not cease.
—Yes. Refer to the aforesaid.

ii (a) *Citta* does not cease in this person. Will *citta* not cease in that person?
—No. It will cease. (at both arising and ceasing moment of consciousness; at the arising moment of final-stage state of consciousness; to those with Cessation-attainment; and Non-percipient beings)
(b) *Citta* will not cease in this person. Does *citta* not cease in that person?
—No. It ceases. (at the ceasing moment of final-stage state of consciousness)

71. *i* (a) *Citta* had ceased in this person. Will *citta* cease in that person?
—No. To those at the ceasing moment of final-stage state of consciousness, *citta* in whom had ceased, but it will not cease.
—Yes. In others (see answer below), *citta* had ceased, and also will cease.
(b) *Citta* will cease in this person. Had *citta* ceased in that person?
—Yes. (at the arising and ceasing moment of consciousness; those with Cessation-attainment; and non-percipient beings)

ii (a) *Citta* had not ceased in this person. Will *citta* not cease in that person? None.
(b) *Citta* will not cease in this person. Had *citta* not ceased in that person?
—No. It had ceased. (at the ceasing moment of final-stage state of consciousness)

Arise and Cease (*Uppādanirodha*)

72. *i* (a) *Citta* arises in this person. Had *citta* ceased in that person?
—Yes. Refer to the answer below.
(b) *Citta* had ceased in this person. Does *citta* arise in that person?
—No. To those at ceasing moment of consciousness, those with Cessation-attainment, and non-percipients, *citta* in whom had ceased; but it does not arise.
—Yes. To those at the arising moment of consciousness, *citta* in whom had ceased, and also arises.

ii (a) *Citta* does not arise in this person. Had *citta* not ceased in that person?
—No. It had ceased. (at ceasing moment of consciousness; those with Cessation-attainment; and non-percipient beings)
(b) *Citta* had not ceased in this person. Does *citta* not arise in that person? None.

73. *i* (a) *Citta* arises in this person. Will *citta* cease in that person?
—Yes. Refer to the answer below.
(b) *Citta* will cease in this person. Does *citta* arise in that person?
—No. To those at the ceasing moment of consciousness, those with Cessation-attainment, and non-percipient beings, *citta* in whom will cease; but in whom it does not arise.
—Yes. To those at the arising moment of consciousness, *citta* in whom will cease, and it also arises.

ii (a) *Citta* does not arise in this person. Will *citta* not cease in that person?
—No. To those at the ceasing moment of consciousness, those with Cessation-attainment, and those non-percipient beings, *citta* in whom does not arise; but it will cease.
—Yes. To those at the ceasing moment of final-stage state of consciousness, *citta* in whom does not arise, and will also not cease.
(b) *Citta* will not cease in this person. Does *citta* not arise in that person?
—Yes. Refer to the aforesaid.

74. *i* (a) *Citta* had arisen in this person. Will *citta* cease in that person?

—No. To those at the ceasing moment of final-stage state of consciousness, *citta* in whom had ceased, but will not arise.
—Yes. In others, *citta* had arisen, and will also cease. (See the answer below)
(b) *Citta* will cease in this person. Had *citta* arisen in that person?
—Yes. (those at both the arising and ceasing moment of consciousness; those with Cessation-attainment; and non-percipient beings)

ii (a) *Citta* had not arisen in this person. Will *citta* not cease in that person? None.
(b) *Citta* will not cease in this person. Had *citta* not arisen in that person?
—No. It had arisen. (at the ceasing moment of final-stage state of consciousness)

Arising and Not Cease (*Uppajjamānananirodha*)

75. *i* (a) *Citta* arises in this person. Does *citta* not cease in that person?
—Yes. Refer to the answer below.
(b) *Citta* does not cease in this person. Does *citta* arise in that person?
—No. To those with Cessation-attainment, and those non-percipient beings, *citta* in whom does not cease, and it also does not arise.
—Yes. To those at the arising moment of consciousness, *citta* in whom does not cease, but it arises.

ii (a) *Citta* does not arise in this person. Does *citta* cease in that person?
—No. To those with Cessation-attainment, and non-percipient beings, *citta* in whom does not arise; and it does not cease.
—Yes. To those at the ceasing moment of consciousness, *citta* in whom does not arise, but it ceases.
(b) *Citta* ceases in this person. Does *citta* not arise in that person?
—Yes. Refer to the aforesaid.

Arising and Appear (*Uppajjamānuppanna*)

76. *i* (a) *Citta* is arising in this person. Does *citta* appear in that person?
—Yes. Refer to the answer below.
(b) *Citta* appears in this person. Is *citta* arising in that person?
—No. To those at the ceasing moment of final-stage state of consciousness, *citta* in whom appears; but it is not arising.
—Yes. To those at the arising moment of consciousness, *citta* in whom appears; it is also arising.

ii (a) *Citta* is not disappear in this person. Does *citta* not appear in that person?
—No. To those at the ceasing moment of consciousness, *citta* is not arising; but it appears.
—Yes. To those with Cessation-attainment, and those non-percipient beings, *citta* is not arising, and it also does not appear.
(b) *Citta* does not appear in this person. Is *citta* not arising in that person?
—Yes. Refer to the aforesaid.

Ceasing and Appear (*Nirujjhamānuppanna*)

77. *i* (a) *Citta* is ceasing in this person. Does *citta* appear in that person?
—Yes. Refer to the answer below.
(b) *Citta* appears in this person. Is *citta* ceasing in that person?
—No. To those at the arising moment of consciousness, *citta* in whom appears; and also is not ceasing.
—Yes. To those at the ceasing moment of consciousness, *citta* in whom appears, and is also ceasing.

ii (a) *Citta* is not ceasing in this person. Does *citta* not appear in that person?
—No. (Same answer as in 77 *i* (a) above)
—Yes. To those with Cessation-attainment and those non-percipient beings, *citta* in whom is not ceasing; it also does not appear.
(b) *Citta* does not appear in this person. Is *citta* not ceasing in that person?
—Yes. (in those with Cessation-attainment; in non-percipient beings)

Appear and Arise (*Uppannuppāda*)

78. *i* (a) *Citta* appears in this person. Had *citta* arisen in that person?
—Yes. Refer to the answer below.
(b) *Citta* had arisen in this person. Does *citta* appear in that person?
—No. To those with Cessation-attainment, and those non-percipient beings, *citta* in whom had arisen; it does not appear.
—Yes. To (all) those with consciousness (including at both arising and ceasing moment), *citta* in whom had arisen, and it also appears.

ii (a) *Citta* does not appear in this person. Had *citta* not arisen in that person?
—No. It had arisen. (in those with Cessation-attainment; in non-percipient beings)
(b) *Citta* had not arisen in this person. Does *citta* not appear in that person? None.

79. *i* (a) *Citta* appears in this person. Will *citta* arise in that person?
—No. To those endowed with final-stage state of consciousness, *citta* in whom appears; it will not arise (again).
—Yes. To others with consciousness (except final-stage state of consciousness), *citta* in whom appears, and also will arise.
(b) *Citta* will arise in this person. Does *citta* appear in that person?
—No. To those with Cessation-attainment, and those non-percipient beings, *citta* in whom will arise; but it does not appear.
—Yes. Refer to the aforesaid.

ii (a) *Citta* does not appear in this person. Will *citta* not arise in that person?
—No. It will arise. (in those of Cessation-attainment, and non-percipient beings)
(b) *Citta* will not arise in this person. Does *citta* not appear in that person?
—No. *Citta* appears. (in those endowed with final-stage state of consciousness, including at its arising and ceasing moment)

Past and Future (*Atītānāgata*)

80. *i* (a) *Citta* had arisen, and does not appear, in this person. Will *citta* arise in that person?
—Yes. (in those with Cessation-attainment; and non-percipient beings)
(b) *Citta* will arise, and does not appear, in this person. Had *citta* arisen in that person? —Yes. (Same as aforesaid answer)

ii (a) *Citta* had not arisen, and it appears, in this person. Will *citta* not arise in that person? —None.
(b) *Citta* will not arise, and it appears, in this person. Had *citta* not arisen in that person?
—No. It had arisen (in those endowed with final-stage state of consciousness, including at its arising and ceasing moment)

Appear and Arising (*Uppannuppajjamāna*)

81. *i* (a) This *citta* appears. Is that *citta* arising?
—No. At the ceasing moment, *citta* in whom appears, but is not arising.
—Yes. At the arising moment, *citta* in whom appears, and is also arising.
(b) This *citta* is arising. Does that *citta* appear? —Yes. Refer to the aforesaid.

ii (a) This *citta* does not appear. Is that *citta* not arising?
Yes. (at past and future *citta*s; to those with Cessation-attainment; and in non-percipient beings)
(b) This *citta* is not arising. Does that *citta* not appear?
—No. At the ceasing moment, *citta* in whom is not arising, but it appears.
—Yes. At past and future state of consciousness, *citta* in whom is not arising, and it also does not appear.

Disappear and Ceasing (*Niruddhanirujjhamāna*) [65]

82. *i* (a) (*Citta*) disappears (in this person). (*Citta*) is ceasing (in that person)?
—No. (at past state of consciousness)
(b) *Citta* is ceasing in this person. Does *citta* disappear in that person?
—No. (at ceasing moment)

ii (a) *Citta* does not disappear in this person. Is *citta* not ceasing in that person?
—No. At the ceasing moment, *citta* in whom does not disappear; but is ceasing.
—Yes. At the arising moment of future state of consciousness, *citta* in whom does not disappear, and also is not ceasing.
(b) *Citta* is not ceasing in this person. Does *citta* not disappear in that person?

---

[65] *Niruddha*: in nos. 82 *i* (a), for example, "*niruddhaṃ nirujjhamānanti*?", the word *niruddha* is not interpreted as 'ceased, stopped, brought to an end', but meaning 'disappear' (of any of the three moments—as at arising, stationary, ceasing). If the meaning is taken as 'ceased', the answer in 82 *ii* (a) would be contradicting the answers in nos. 69 i(b), 71 i(a), 72 i(b), 74 i(a) which say that 'citta therein had ceased'.

—No. At past state of consciousness, *citta* in whom is not ceasing; it disappears.
—Yes. Refer to the aforesaid.

Time-transgressing (*Atikkantakāla*)

83. *i* (a) *Citta*, in moment-passing, has elapsed past the arising moment in this person. Has *citta*, in moment-passing, elapsed past the ceasing moment in that person?
—No. At the ceasing moment, *citta* in whom has elapsed past arising moment, but has not elapsed past ceasing moment.
—Yes. At past state of consciousness, *citta* in whom has elapsed past arising moment, and also has elapsed past ceasing moment
(b) *Citta*, in moment-passing, has elapsed past the ceasing moment in this person. Has *citta*, in moment-passing, elapsed past the arising moment in that person?
—Yes. Refer to the aforesaid.

ii (a) *Citta*, in moment-passing, has not elapsed past the arising moment in this person. Has *citta*, in moment-passing, not elapsed past the ceasing moment in that person?
—Yes. At the arising moment of future state of consciousness.
(b) *Citta*, in moment-passing, has not elapsed past the ceasing moment in this person. Has *citta*, in moment-passing, not elapsed past the arising moment in that person?
—No. At the ceasing moment, it has elapsed past the arising moment.
—Yes. At the arising moment of future state of consciousness.

8.1.2 Based on Dhamma [46] (*puggala*)

A minor composite on Arise and Cease (*Uppādanirodhakālasaṁbheda*)

84. *i* (a) This *citta* arises, and does not cease. Will that *citta* cease, and will not arise? —Yes. (at the arising moment of consciousness)
(b) This *citta* will cease, and will not arise. Does that *citta* arise, and not cease?
—Yes. (Same as above)

ii (a) This *citta* does not arise, and it ceases. Will that *citta* not cease, and will arise?
—No. (At ceasing moment of consciousness, it will not cease, and will not arise)
(b) This *citta* will not cease, and will arise. Does that *citta* not arise, and it ceases?
—None.

Arise and Appear (*Uppāduppanna*)

85. *i* (a) This *citta* arises. Does that *citta* appear?
—Yes. (at the arising moment of consciousness)
(b) This *citta* appears. Does that *citta* arise?

—No. At the ceasing moment, *citta* appears; but it does not arise.
—Yes. At the arising moment, *citta* appears, and also arises.

ii (a) This *citta* does not arise. Does that *citta* not appear?
—No. At the ceasing moment, *citta* does not arise; and it appears
—Yes. At past and future state of consciousness, *citta* does not arise, it also does not appear.
(b) This *citta* does not appear. Does that *citta* not arise?
—Yes. Refer to the aforesaid.

Cease and Appear (*Nirodhuppanna*)

86. *i* (a) This *citta* ceases. Does that *citta* appear?
—Yes. Refer to the answer below.
(b) This *citta* appears. Does that *citta* cease?
—No. At the arising moment, *citta* appears; it does not cease.
—Yes. At the ceasing moment, *citta* appears; it also ceases.

ii (a) This *citta* does not cease. Does that *citta* not appear?
—No. At the arising moment, *citta* does not cease; and it appear.
—Yes. At past and future consciousness, it does not cease; also does not appear.
(b) This *citta* does not appear. Does that *citta* not cease?
—Yes. Refer to the aforesaid answer.

Arise (*Uppāda*)

87. *i* (a) This *citta* arises. Had that *citta* arisen?
—No. (at the arising moment of consciousness)
(b) This *citta* had arisen. Does that *citta* arise?
—No. (at past state of consciousness)

ii (a) This *citta* does not arise. Had that *citta* not arisen?
—No. Past state of consciousness does not arise; it had arisen.
—Yes. At the ceasing moment of future state of consciousness, *citta* does not arise; it also had not arisen.
(b) This *citta* had not arisen. Does that *citta* not arise?
—No. At the arising moment, *citta* had not arisen; and it arises.
—Yes. Refer to the aforesaid answer.

88. *i* (a) This *citta* arises. Will that *citta* arise?
—No. (at the arising moment of consciousness)
(b) This *citta* will arise. Does that *citta* arise?
—No. (at future state of consciousness)

ii (a) This *citta* does not arise. Will that *citta* not arise?
—No. At future state of consciousness *citta* does not arise; but it will arise.

—Yes. At the ceasing moment of past consciousness, *citta* does not arise, and also will not arise.
(b) This *citta* will not arise. Does that *citta* not arise?
—No. At the arising moment, *citta* will not arise; but it arises.
—Yes. Refer to the aforesaid answer.

89. *i* (a) This *citta* had arisen. Will that *citta* arise?
—No. (at past state of consciousness)
(b) This *citta* will arise. Had that *citta* arisen?
—No. (at future state of consciousness)

ii (a) This *citta* had not arisen. Will that *citta* not arise?
—No. At future state of consciousness, *citta* had not arisen; and it will arise.
—Yes. At present state of consciousness, *citta* had not arisen, and *citta* also will not arise.

(b) This *citta* will not arise. Had that *citta* not arisen?
—No. At past state of consciousness, *citta* will not arise; and it had arisen.
—Yes. Refer to the aforesaid answer.

Cease (*Nirodha*)

90. *i* (a) This *citta* ceases. Had that *citta* ceased? —No. (at the ceasing moment)
(b) This *citta* had ceased. Does that *citta* cease? —No. (at past consciousness)

ii (a) This *citta* does not cease. Had that *citta* not ceased?
—No. Past state of consciousness does not cease; but it had ceased.
—Yes. At the arising moment of future state of consciousness.
(b) This *citta* had not ceased. Does that *citta* not cease?
—No. At the ceasing moment, *citta* had not ceased; but it ceases.
—Yes. Refer to the aforesaid answer.

91. *i* (a) This *citta* ceases. Will that *citta* cease? —No. (at the ceasing moment)
(b) This *citta* will cease. Does that *citta* cease? —No. (at the arising moment)

ii (a) This *citta* does not cease. Will that *citta* not cease?
—No. At the arising moment of future state of consciousness, it will cease.
—Yes. Past state of consciousness does not cease; it also will not cease.
(b) This *citta* will not cease. Does that *citta* not cease?
—No. At the ceasing moment, *citta* will not cease; but it ceases.
—Yes. Refer to the aforesaid answer.

92. *i* (a) This *citta* had ceased. Will that *citta* cease? —No. (past consciousness)
(b) This *citta* will cease. Had that *citta* ceased?
—No. (at the arising moment of future state of consciousness)

ii (a) This *citta* had not ceased. Will that *citta* not cease?

—No. At the arising moment of future state of consciousness, *citta* will cease.
—Yes. At the ceasing moment, *citta* had not ceased, and also will not cease.
(b) This *citta* will not cease. Had that *citta* not ceased?
—No. Past state of consciousness will not cease; and it had ceased.
—Yes. Refer to the aforesaid answer.

Arise and Cease (*Uppādanirodha*)

93. *i* (a) This *citta* arises. Had that *citta* ceased? —No. (at the arising moment)
(b) This *citta* had ceased. Does that *citta* arise? —No. (at past consciousness)

ii (a) This *citta* does not arise. Had that *citta* not ceased?
—No. Past state of consciousness does not arise; and it had ceased.
—Yes. At the ceasing moment of future state of consciousness, it had not ceased.
(b) This *citta* had not ceased. Does that *citta* not arise?
—No. At the arising moment, *citta* had not ceased; and it arises.
—Yes. Refer to the aforesaid.

94. *i* (a) This *citta* arises. Will that *citta* cease? —Yes. Refer to the answer below.
(b) This *citta* will cease. Does that *citta* arise?
—No. Future state of consciousness will cease; and it does not arise.
—Yes. At the arising moment, *citta* will cease, and it also arises.

ii (a) This *citta* does not arise. Will that *citta* not cease?
—No. Future state of consciousness does not arise; and it will cease.
—Yes. At the ceasing moment of past state of consciousness, it will not cease.
(b) This *citta* will not cease. Does that *citta* not arise?
—Yes. Refer to the aforesaid.

95. *i* (a) This *citta* had arisen. Will that *citta* cease? —No. (at past consciousness)
(b) This *citta* will cease. Had that *citta* arisen?
—No. (at the arising moment, and at future state of consciousness)

ii (a) This *citta* had not arisen. Will that *citta* not cease?
—No. At the arising moment future state of consciousness, and it will cease.
—Yes. At the ceasing moment, *citta* had not arisen, and also will not cease.
(b) This *citta* will not cease. Had that *citta* not arisen?
—No. Past state of consciousness will not cease; and it had arisen.
—Yes. Refer to the aforesaid.

Arising and Not Cease (*Uppajjamānananirodha*)

96. *i* (a) This *citta* arises. Does that *citta* not cease?
—Yes. (at the arising moment)
(b) This *citta* does not cease. Does that *citta* arise?
—No. Past and future state of consciousness do not cease; and also do not arise.
—Yes. At the arising moment, *citta* does not cease, and it arises.

ii (a) This *citta* does not arise. Does that *citta* cease?
—No. Past and future state of consciousness do not arise; and also do not cease.
—Yes. At the ceasing moment, *citta* does not arise, and it ceases.
(b) This *citta* ceases. Does that *citta* not arise? —Yes. (Same as above)

Arising and Appear (*Uppajjamānuppanna*)

97. *i* (a) This *citta* is arising. Does that *citta* appear? —Yes. (at arising moment)
(b) This *citta* appears. Is that *citta* arising?
—No. At the ceasing moment, *citta* appears; and it is not arising.
—Yes. At the arising moment, *citta* appears; it is also arising.

ii (a) This *citta* is not arising. Does that *citta* not appear?
—No. At the ceasing moment, *citta* is not arising; but it appears.
(b) This *citta* does not appear. Is that *citta* not arising?
—Yes. (at past and future state of consciousness)

Ceasing and Appear (*Nirujjhamānuppanna*)

98. *i* (a) This *citta* is ceasing. Does that *citta* appear? —Yes. (at ceasing moment)
(b) This *citta appears*. Is that *citta* ceasing?
—No. At the arising moment, *citta* appears; and *citta* is not ceasing.
—Yes. At the ceasing moment, *citta* appears, and it is also ceasing.

ii (a) This *citta* is not ceasing. Does that *citta* not appear?
—No. At the arising moment, *citta* is not ceasing; but it appears.
—Yes. Past and future state of consciousness are not ceasing; also do not appear.
(b) This *citta* does not appear. Is that *citta* not ceasing?
—Yes. Refer to the aforesaid.

Appear and Arise (*Uppannuppāda*)

99. *i* (a) This *citta* appears. Had that *citta* arisen?
—No. (at both arising and ceasing moment of consciousness; at present state of consciousness)
(b) This *citta* had arisen. Does that *citta* appear?
—No. (at past state of consciousness)

ii (a) This *citta* does not appear. Had that *citta* not arisen?
—No. Past state of consciousness does not appear; it had arisen.
—Yes. Future state of consciousness does not appear, and also had not arisen.
(b) This *citta* had not arisen. Does that *citta* not appear?
—No. Present state of consciousness had not arisen; and it appears.
—Yes. Refer to the aforesaid.

100. *i* (a) This *citta* appears. Will that *citta* arise?
—No. (at arising and ceasing moment of consciousness; at present consciousness)
(b) This *citta* will arise. Does that *citta* appear?

—No. (at future state of consciousness)

ii (a) This *citta* does not appear. Will that *citta* not arise?
—No. Future state of consciousness does not appear; and it will arise.
—Yes. Past state of consciousness does not appear, and it also will not arise.
(b) This *citta* will not arise. Does that *citta* not appear?
—No. Present state of consciousness will not arise; and it appears
—Yes. Refer to the aforesaid.

Past and Future (*Atītānāgata*)

101. *i* (a) This *citta* had arisen, and does not appear, in this person. Will that *citta* arise? —No. (It will not arise at past state of consciousness)
(b) This *citta will* arise, and does not appear, in this person. Had that *citta* arisen? —No. (it had not arisen at future state of consciousness)

ii (a) This *citta* had not arisen, and it appears. Will that *citta* not arise?
—Yes. (at the ceasing moment of consciousness)
(b) This *citta* will not arise, and it appears. Had that *citta* not arisen?
—Yes. (Same as aforesaid)

Appear and Arising (*Uppannuppajjamāna*)

102. *i* (a) This *citta* appears. Is that *citta* arising?
—No. At the ceasing moment, *citta* appears, and it is not arising.
—Yes. At the arising moment, *citta* appears, and it is also arising.
(b) This *citta* is arising. Does that *citta* appear?
—Yes. Refer to the aforesaid.

ii (a) This *citta* does not appear. Is that *citta* not arising? —Yes. (Same as below)
(b) This *citta* is not arising. Does that *citta* not appear?
—No. At the ceasing moment, *citta* is not arising; it appears.
—Yes. At past and future state of consciousness, *citta* is not arising; it also does not appear.

Disappear and Ceasing (*Niruddhanirujjhamāna*)

103. *i* (a) This *citta* disappears. Is that *citta* ceasing? —No. (at past consciousness)
(b) This *citta* is ceasing. Does that *citta* disappear? —No. (at the ceasing moment)

ii (a) This *citta* does not disappear. Is that *citta* not ceasing?
—No. At the ceasing moment, *citta* does not disappear, and it is ceasing.
—Yes. At the arising moment of future state of consciousness, *citta* does not disappear, and is also not ceasing.
(b) This *citta* is not ceasing.Does that *citta* not disappear?
—No. Past state of consciousness is not ceasing, and it disappears.
—Yes. Refer to the aforesaid.

Time-transgressing (*Atikkantakāla*)

104. *i* (a) This *citta*, in moment-passing, has elapsed past the arising moment. Has that *citta*, in moment-passing, elapsed past the ceasing moment?
—No. At the ceasing moment, *citta* has elapsed past the arising moment, but has not elapsed past the ceasing moment.
—Yes. At past state of consciousness, *citta* has elapsed past the arising moment, and has also elapsed past the ceasing moment.
(b) This *citta*, in moment-passing, has elapsed past the ceasing moment. Has that *citta*, in moment-passing, elapsed past the arising moment?
—Yes. Refer to the aforesaid.

ii (a) This *citta*, in moment-passing, has not elapsed past the arising moment. Has that *citta*, in moment-passing, not elapsed past the ceasing moment?
—Yes. At the arising moment of future state of consciousness.
(b) This *citta*, in moment-passing, has not elapsed past the ceasing moment. Has that *citta*, in moment-passing, not elapsed past the arising moment?
—No. At the ceasing moment, *citta* has elapsed past the arising moment.
—Yes. At the arising moment of future state of consciousness.

8.1.3 Based on Person and *Dhamma* (*puggaladhamma*)

A minor composite on Arise and Cease (*Uppādanirodhakālasaṁbheda*)

105. *i* (a) This *citta* arises, and does not cease, in this person. Will that *citta* cease, and will not arise, in that person? —Yes. (at the arising moment)
(b) This *citta* will cease, and will not arise, in this person. Does that *citta* arise, and does not cease, in that person? —Yes. (Same as the aforesaid)

ii (a) This *citta* does not arise, and ceases, in this person. Will that *citta* not cease, and will arise, in that person?
—No. (at the ceasing moment of consciousness)
(b) This *citta* will not cease, and will arise, in this person. Does that *citta* not arise, and ceases, in that person? —None.

Arise and Appear (*Uppāduppanna*)

106. *i* (a) This *citta* arises in this person. Does that *citta* appear in that person?
—Yes. Refer to the answer below.
(b) This citta appears in this person. Does that *citta* arise in that person?
—No. To those at the ceasing moment, *citta* in whom appears; it does not arise.
—Yes. To those at the arising moment, *citta* in whom appears, and it also arises.

ii (a) This *citta* does not arise in this person. Does that *citta* not appear in that person?
……p……

The remaining questions are to be constructed in the same manner as the above examples. The answers are the same as those in 8.1.2.

8.2 Distinction in the specificity of *citta* by Suttanta method

114. The mind with desire arises, and does not cease in this person. Will the mind with desire, both arise and not cease in that person?
—No. To those at the arising moment of final-stage *citta* with desire [66], mind with desire in whom arises, does not cease, will cease, and will not arise. —Yes. To others, at the arising moment of mind with desire, ...p.....

8.3 Distinction in specificity of *citta* by Abhidhamma method

115. Wholesome *citta* arises, and does not cease in this person. Will wholesome *citta* cease, and will not arise in that person?
—No. To those at the arising moment of final-stage wholesome consciousness, wholesome *citta* in whom arises, does not cease, will cease, and will not arise. To others, at the arising moment of wholesome consciousness, ...p.....

116. Unwholesome *citta* arises, and does not cease in this person ..... Indeterminate *citta* arises, and does not cease .....p.....

Y: Yes ; N : No

(An example of Suttanta method)	arises	is arising	had arisen	will arise	ceases	is ceasing	had ceased	will cease
To those at the arising moment of final-stage *citta* with desire,	Y				N			
mind with desire	N							Y
(An example of Abhidhamma method)								
To those at the arising moment of final-stage unwholesome	Y				N			
citta, unwholesome citta	N							Y

[66] *Sarāgapacchimacitta*: final-stage state of consciousness with desire (*rāga*). In Chapter 5, we come across those endowed with final-stage *citta* as person different from the "final existence being". In Chapter 6, it mentions those with final-stage *citta* as persons in whom the three types of formation will not arise. In Chapter 8, it mentions to those with final-stage *citta*, *citta* in whom had arisen, it appears, but it will not again arise.

CHAPTER 9

IX. Pairs on *Dhamma*

(*Dhammayamaka*)

The Pāli term '*dhamma'* has different shades of meaning dependent on the context in which it is being used. It can be interpreted as 'norm, truth, object, state, phenomenon, concepts, the law of nature', and so on. The rendering as 'phenomenal state, or nature' would seem to be a better fit for use in this chapter, but I will just leave the word *dhamma* as it.

Chapter 9 follows the same methodology as in the preceding chapters. The chapter examines pairs of enquiries through three main parts. In the first part, it clarifies the terms of wholesome *dhamma* (*kusalā dhammā*), unwholesome *dhamma* (*akusalā dhammā*), and indeterminate *dhamma* (*abyākatā dhammā*). The second part examines process by way of origination, cessation, origination-and-cessation of *dhammā*. The last part examines meditative development of individuals by measure of developing (*bhāveti*) and renouncing (*pajahatī*), and also in negative formulation, in respect of the three types of *dhammā*.

9.1 Clarification of Terms (*Paṇṇatti*)

I leave out the first section on the summary of questions which are already included in the exposition section.

9.1.1 Clarifying word by word

Forward expression

17. *i* (a) That which is wholesome, is it wholesome *dhamma* [67] ? —Yes.
(b) That which is wholesome *dhamma*, is it wholesome? —Yes.
ii (a) That which is unwholesome, is it unwholesome *dhamma* [68] ? —Yes.
(b) That which is unwholesome *dhamma*, is it wholesome? —Yes.
iii (a) That which is indeterminate, is it indeterminate *dhamma* [69] ? —Yes.
(b) That which is indeterminate *dhamma*, is it indeterminate? —Yes.

Opposite expression

18. *i* (a) That which is not wholesome, is it not wholesome *dhamma*?
—Yes. (12 unwholesome states, 56 indeterminate states, designations)

---

[67] *kusalā dhammā* (Dhs nos. 985, 1384): consists of 21 mundane wholesome cittas, 38 cetasikas (13 common non-beautiful factors and 25 beautiful factors). See Appendix III, IV.

[68] *akusalā dhammā* (Dhs nos. 986, 1385): consists of 12 unwholesome cittas, 27 cetasikas (13 common nonbeautiful factors and 14 unwholesome factors). See Appendix III, IV.

[69] *abyākatā dhammā* (Dhs nos. 987, 1386): consists of 36 resultant cittas, 20 functional cittas, 38 cetasikas, 28 matters, and *Nibbāna*. See Appendix III, IV.

(b) That which is not wholesome *dhamma*, is it not wholesome? —Yes.
ii (a) That which is not unwholesome, is it not unwholesome *dhamma*?
—Yes. (21 wholesome states, 56 indeterminate states, designations)
(b) That which is not unwholesome *dhamma*, is it not unwholesome? —Yes.
iii (a) That which is not indeterminate, is it not indeterminate *dhamma*?
—Yes. (21 wholesome states, 12 unwholesome states, designations)
(b) That which is not indeterminate *dhamma*, is it not indeterminate? —Yes.

9.1.2 Wheel based on word-by-word clarification

Forward expression

19. *i* (a) That which is wholesome, is it wholesome *dhamma*? —Yes.
(b) That which is *dhamma*, is it unwholesome *dhamma*? —Yes.
—No. Remainders are *dhamma* (wholesome and indeterminate *dhamma*; designations), but are not unwholesome *dhamma*.
ii (a) That which is wholesome, is it wholesome *dhamma*? —Yes.
(b) That which is *dhamma*, is it indeterminate *dhamma*? —Yes.
—No. Remainders are *dhamma* (wholesome *dhamma*; unwholesome *dhamma*; designations), but are not indeterminate *dhamma*.

20. *i* (a) That which is unwholesome, is it unwholesome *dhamma*? —Yes.
(b) That which is *dhamma*, is it wholesome *dhamma*? —Yes.
—No. Remainders are *dhamma* (unwholesome and indeterminate *dhamma*; designations) but not wholesome *dhamma*.
ii (a) That which is unwholesome, is it unwholesome *dhamma*? —Yes.
(b) That which is *dhamma*, is it indeterminate *dhamma*? —Yes.
—No. Remainders are *dhamma* (wholesome and unwholesome *dhamma*; designations), but are not indeterminate *dhamma*.

21. *i* (a) That which is indeterminate, is it indeterminate *dhamma*? —Yes.
(b) That which is *dhamma*, is it wholesome *dhamma*? —Yes.
—No. Remainders are *dhamma* (unwholesome and indeterminate *dhamma*; designations), but are not wholesome *dhamma*.
ii (a) That which is indeterminate, is it indeterminate *dhamma*? —Yes.
(b) That which is *dhamma*, is it unwholesome *dhamma*? —Yes.
—No. Remainders are *dhamma*, but are not unwholesome *dhamma*.

Opposite expression

22. *i* (a) That which is not wholesome, is it not wholesome *dhamma*? —Yes.
(b) That which is not *dhamma* [70], is it not unwholesome *dhamma*? —Yes.
ii (a) That which is not wholesome, is it not wholesome *dhamma*? —Yes.
(b) That which is not *dhamma*, is it not indeterminate *dhamma*? —Yes.

---

[70] not *dhamma*: other good causes as part of designations are not *dhamma*, and are not unwholesome *dhamma*; wholesome *dhamma* is both *dhamma* and wholesome *dhamma*

23. *i* (a) That which is not unwholesome, is not unwholesome *dhamma*? —Yes.
(b) That which is not *dhamma*, is it not wholesome *dhamma*? —Yes.
ii (a) That which is not unwholesome, is it not unwholesome *dhamma*? —Yes.
(b) That which is not *dhamma*, is it not indeterminate *dhamma*? —Yes.

24. *i* (a) That which is not indeterminate, is not indeterminate *dhamma*? —Yes.
(b) That which is not *dhamma*, is it not wholesome *dhamma*? —Yes.
ii (a) That which is not indeterminate, is it not indeterminate *dhamma*? —Yes.
(b) That which is not *dhamma*, is it not unwholesome *dhamma*? —Yes.

9.1.3 Pure Dhamma

Forward expression

25. *i* (a) That which is wholesome, is it *dhamma*? —Yes.
(b) That which is *dhamma*, is wholesome?
—Yes. Wholesome *dhamma*s are both of which.
—No. The remainders (of the pure *dhamma*, excluding designations) are *dhamma*, but are not wholesome *dhamma*.
ii (a) That which is unwholesome, is it.*dhamma*? —Yes.
(b) That which is *dhamma*, is it unwholesome?
—Yes. Unwholesome *dhamma*s are both of which.
—No. The remainders (wholesome and indeterminate *dhamma*) are *dhamma*, but are not unwholesome *dhamma*.
iii (a) That which is indeterminate, is it *dhamma*? —Yes.
(b) That which is *dhamma*, is it indeterminate? —Yes.
—No. Remainders (wholesome and unwholesome *dhamma*) are *dhamma*, but are not indeterminate *dhamma*.

Opposite expression

26. *i* (a) That which is not wholesome, is it not *dhamma*?
—No. Except wholesome *dhamma*, remainders (of the pure *dhamma*, excluding designations) are *dhamma*, but are not wholesome *dhamma*.
(b) That which is not *dhamma*, is it not wholesome? —Yes.
ii (a) That which is not unwholesome, is it not *dhamma*?
—No. Remainders (of the pure *dhamma*, excluding designations) are *dhamma*, but are not unwholesome *dhamma*.
(b) That which is not *dhamma*, is it not unwholesome? —Yes.
iii (a) That which is not indeterminate, is it not *dhamma*?
—No. Remainders (of the pure *dhamma*, excluding designations) are *dhamma*, but are not indeterminate *dhamma*.
(b) That which is not *dhamma*, is it not indeterminate? —Yes.

9.1.4 Wheel based on pure *dhamma*

Forward expression

27. *i* (a) That which is wholesome, is it *dhamma*? —Yes.
(b) That which is *dhamma*, is it unwholesome *dhamma*?
—No. Except unwholesome *dhamma*, remainders are *dhamma*, but are not unwholesome *dhamma*.
ii (a) That which is wholesome, is it *dhamma*? —Yes.
(b) That which is *dhamma*, is it indeterminate *dhamma*?
—No. Except indeterminate *dhamma*, remainders are *dhamma*, but are not indeterminate *dhamma*.

28. *i* (a) That which is unwholesome, is it *dhamma*? —Yes.
(b) That which is *dhamma*, is it wholesome *dhamma*?
—No. Except wholesome *dhamma*, remainders are *dhamma*, but are not wholesome *dhamma*.
ii (a) That which is unwholesome, is it *dhamma*? —Yes.
(b) That which is *dhamma*, is it indeterminate *dhamma*?
—No. Except indeterminate *dhamma*, remainders are *dhamma*, but are not indeterminate *dhamma*.

29. *i* (a) That which is indeterminate, is it *dhamma*? —Yes.
(b) That which is *dhamma*, is it wholesome *dhamma*?
—No. Except wholesome *dhamma*, remainders are *dhamma*, but are not wholesome *dhamma*.
(b) That which is indeterminate, is it *dhamma*? —Yes.
ii (a) That which is *dhamma*, is it unwholesome *dhamma*?
—No. Except unwholesome *dhamma*, remainders are *dhamma*, but are not unwholesome *dhamma*.

Opposite expression

30. *i* (a) That which is not wholesome, is it not *dhamma*?
—No. Except wholesome, remainders are *dhamma*, not wholesome *dhamma*.
—Yes. Except wholesome and *dhamma*, remainders are not wholesome, and are also not *dhamma*.
(b) That which is not *dhamma*, is it not unwholesome *dhamma*? —Yes.
ii (a) That which is not wholesome, is it not *dhamma*?
—No. Same answer as in 30 *i* (a).
—Yes. Same answer as in 30 *i* (a).
(b) That which is not *dhamma*, is it not indeterminate *dhamma*? —Yes.

31. *i* (a) That which is not unwholesome, is it not *dhamma*?
—No. Except unwholesome, remainders are *dhamma*, but are not unwholesome *dhamma*.
—Yes. Except unwholesome and *dhamma*, remainders are not unwholesome, and are also not *dhamma*.
(b) That which is not *dhamma*, is it not wholesome *dhamma*? —Yes.
ii (a) That which is not unwholesome, is it not *dhamma*?
—No. Same answer as in 31 *i* (a).
—Yes. Same answer as in 31 *i* (a).
(b) That which is not *dhamma*, is it not indeterminate *dhamma*? —Yes.

32. *i* (a) That which is not indeterminate, is it not *dhamma*?
—No. Except indeterminate, remainders are *dhamma*, but are not indeterminate *dhamma*.
—Yes. Except indeterminate and *dhamma*, remainders are not indeterminate and are also not *dhamma*.
(b) That which is not *dhamma*, is it not wholesome *dhamma*? —Yes.
ii (a) That which is not indeterminate, is it not *dhamma*?
—No. Same answer as in 32 *i* (a).
—Yes. Same answer as in 32 *i* (a).
(b) That which is not *dhamma*, is it not unwholesome *dhamma*? —Yes.

Tabulated pairs-sequence of the four methods on 'terms'

The following four charts demonstrate the flow sequence of how those questions in the preceding four methods are being asked.

Chart 9.1 Pairs sequence based on clarification of words

	is it *dhamma*?	is it wholesome?	is it unwholesome?	is it indeterminate?	is it not *dhamma*?	is it not wholesome?	is it not unwholesome?	is it not indeterminate?
That which is wholesome,	1a							
That which is unwholesome,	2a							
That which is indeterminate,	3a							
That which is *dhamma*,		1b	2b	3b				
That which is not wholesome,					4a			
That which is not unwholesome,					5a			
That which is not indeterminate,					6a			
That which is not *dhamma*,						4b	5b	6b

Chart 9.2 Pairs sequence in the subject of wheel based on clarification of words

	is it wholesome *dhamma*?	is it unwholesome *dhamma*?	is it indeterminate *dhamma*?	is it not wholesome *dhamma*?	is it not unwholesome *dhamma*?	is it not indeterminate *dhamma*?
That which is wholesome,	1a, 2a					
That which is unwholesome,		3a, 4a				
That which is indeterminate,			5a, 6a			
That which is not wholesome,				7a, 8a		
That which is not unwholesome,					9a, 10a	
That which is not indeterminate,						11a,12a
That which is *dhamma*,	3b, 5b	1b, 6b	2b, 4b			
That which is not *dhamma*,				9b, 11b	7b, 12b	8b, 10b

Chart 9.3 Pairs sequence based on pure *dhamma*

	is it *dhamma*?	is it wholesome?	is it unwholesome?	is it indeterminate?	is it not *dhamma*?	is it not wholesome?	is it not unwholesome?	is it not indeterminate?
That which is wholesome,	1a							
That which is unwholesome,	2a							
That which is indeterminate,	3a							
That which is *dhamma*,		1b	2b	3b				
That which is not wholesome,					4a			
That which is not unwholesome,					5a			
That which is not indeterminate,					6a			
That which is not *dhamma*,						4b	5b	6b

Chart 9.4 Pairs sequence in the subject of wheel based on pure *dhamma*

	is it *dhamma*?	is it wholesome *dhamma*?	is it unwholesome *dhamma*?	is it indeterminate *dhamma*?	is it not *dhamma*?	is it not wholesome *dhamma*?	is it not unwholesome *dhamma*?	is it not indeterminate *dhamma*?
That which is wholesome,	1a, 2a							
That which is unwholesome,	3a, 4a							
That which is indeterminate,	5a, 6a							
That which is *dhamma*,		3b, 5b	1b, 6b	2b, 4b				
That which is not wholesome,					7a, 8a			
That which is not unwholesome,					9a, 10a			
That which is not indeterminate,					11a,12a			
That which is not *dhamma*,						9b, 11b	7b, 12b	8b, 10b

9.2 Process (*Pavatti*)

9.2.1 Origination of *dhammā* (with charts)

Chart 9.5 Enquiry sequence on origination of *dhammā*

		(With respect to each following *dhammā* type) Do they arise / Do they not arise : i) in that person? ii) at that plane? iii) in that person at that plane?			Had they arisen / Had they not arisen: i) in that person? ii) at that plane? iii) in that person at that plane?			Will they arise / Will they not arise : i) in that person? ii) at that plane? iii) in that person at that plane?		
		Wholesome *dhammā*	Unwholesome *dhammā*	Indeterminate *dhammā*	Wholesome *dhammā*	Unwholesome *dhammā*	Indeterminate *dhammā*	Wholesome *dhammā*	Unwholesome *dhammā*	Indeterminate *dhammā*
Wholesome *dhammā*	arise / do not arise : i) in this person. ii) at this plane. iii) in this person at this plane.		1a	2a		10a	11a		13a	14a
Unwholesome *dhammā*		1b		3a			12a			15a
Indeterminate *dhammā*		2bi	3b							
Wholesome *dhammā*	had arisen/ had not arisen i) in this person. ii) at this plane. iii) in this person at this plane.					4a	5a		16a	17a
Unwholesome *dhammā*		10b			4b		6a			18a
Indeterminate *dhammā*		11b	12b		5b	6bi				
Wholesome *dhammā*	will arise / will not arise : i) in this person. ii) at this plane. iii) in this person at this plane.								7a	8a
Unwholesome *dhammā*		13b			16b			7bi		9a
Indeterminate *dhammā*		14b	15b		17b	18b		8b	9b	

The above chart summarises the sequence of paired enquiries from nos. 33 to 98. The iteration loops through three differentiations (by persons, by planes, by persons at planes) using the regular and reverse mode of enquiring. The same sequence reiterates through six time-scaled classifications (present, past, future, present-past, present-future, and past-future), represent by the enneahedral boxes as shown in the chart.

Chart 9.6 Origination of *dhammā* (by present, past, and future)

A: arise/ had arisen/ will arise; N: does not arise/ had not arisen/ will not arise

	Present			Past			Future		
	wholesome *dhammā*	unwholesome *dhammā*	indeterminate *dhammā*	wholesome *dhammā*	unwholesome *dhammā*	indeterminate *dhammā*	wholesome *dhammā*	unwholesome *dhammā*	indeterminate *dhammā*
To those at the arising moment of :									
consciousness dissociated from goodness	N		A						
consciousness dissociated from badness		N	A						
consciousness dissociated from goodness and badness	N	N							
the highest (*Arahatta*) Path-*citta*									
the final-stage *citta*									
good state	A	N							
good state at five-aggregate plane	A		A						
good state at immaterial plane	A	N	N						
bad state	N	A							
bad state at Immaterial plane	N	A	N						
bad state at five-aggregate plane		A	A						
To those at the ceasing moment of :									
citta (state of consciousness)	N	N	N						
the highest (*Arahatta*) Path-*citta*									
To those :									
all beings at the birth-moment	N	N	A						
all beings at the death-moment	N	N	N						
engaged in Cessation-attainment	N	N							
at the birth-moment at pure abodes				N	N	N			
at the occurrence of second *citta* of the pure abode beings				N	N	A			
at occurrence of second unwholesome *citta* of pure abode beings				N	A				
at immaterial plane (four-aggregate)				A	A	A	A	A	A
at the non-percipience plane	N	N		N	N	A	N	N	A
at the four- and five-aggregate planes				A	A	A	A	A	A
Arahat							N	N	A
endowed with the highest (*Arahatta*) Path							N	N	A
right after this *citta* who will directly attain the highest Path							A	N	A
endowed with the final-stage *citta*							N	N	N
At the plane(s) of :									
non-percipience	N	N	A	N	N	A	N	N	A
five-aggregates	A	A	A	A	A	A	A	A	A
immateriality (or four-aggregates)	A	A	A	A	A	A	A	A	A

Chart 9.6 above displays the condensation of the first 66 pairs of enquiries and answers (nos. 33-98) with reference to present, past, and future. You will notice from the chart that there are some types of individuals without answers

given. This is because some of those are only to be examined in the subsequent sub-sections. The other reason is because enquiries on them are not dealt with. I do not remove them so that you will know where and when they will later be discussed. At the end of this sub-section on origination, a final chart consolidating all the answers will be constructed.

At Present

Forward enquiries by Individual

33. *i* (a) Wholesome *dhammā* arise in this person. Do unwholesome *dhammā* arise in that person? —No (at the arising moment of good state).
(b) Unwholesome *dhammā* arise in this person. Do wholesome *dhammā* arise in that person? —No (at the arising moment of bad state).

ii (a) Wholesome *dhammā* arise in this person. Do indeterminate *dhammā* arise in that person?
—No. To those at the arising moment of good state at immaterial plane, wholesome *dhammā* in whom arise; indeterminate *dhammā* in whom do not arise.
—Yes. To those at the arising moment of good state at five-aggregate plane [71], both wholesome *dhammā* and indeterminate *dhammā* in whom arise.
(b) Indeterminate *dhammā* arise in this person. Do wholesome *dhammā* arise in that person?
—No. To all those at birth-moment [72], and those at the arising moment of *citta* dissociated from good state, indeterminate *dhammā* in whom arise; wholesome *dhammā* in whom do not arise.
—Yes. (Refer to the aforesaid)

Note :

In all the answers for the rest of this chapter, the closing part of the sentence will be omitted. Instead only the subjects (persons, at plane or situation) will be indicated following the Yes or No answer. However, all those answers should be understood to mean entailing the same way of concluding each sentence as shown in the above example nos. 33.

34. *i* (a) Unwholesome *dhammā* arise in this person. Do indeterminate *dhammā* arise in that person?
—No. To those at the arising moment of bad state at immaterial plane …
—Yes. To those at the arising moment of bad state at five-aggregate plane …
(b) Indeterminate *dhammā* arise in this person. Do unwholesome *dhammā* arise in that person?

---

[71] Five-aggregate planes: the 26 planes of existence, excluding non-percipience plane and immaterial planes.
[72] (lit.) at the time of rebirth of all (beings).

—No. To all those at birth-moment, and at the arising moment of *citta* dissociated from badness …
—Yes. (Same as the aforesaid)

Forward enquiries by Plane

35. *i* (a) Wholesome *dhammā* arise at this plane. Do unwholesome *dhammā* arise at that plane? —Yes (at the planes of four aggregates and five aggregates).
(b) Unwholesome *dhammā* arise at this plane. Do wholesome *dhammā* arise at that plane? —Yes. (Same as the aforesaid)

ii (a) Wholesome *dhammā* arise at this plane. Do indeterminate *dhammā* arise at that plane? —Yes. (Same as below)
(b) Indeterminate *dhammā* arise at this plane. Do wholesome *dhammā* arise at that plane?
—No. At the plane of non-percipience.
—Yes. At the planes of four aggregates [73] and five aggregates.

36. *i* (a) Unwholesome *dhammā* arise at this plane. Do indeterminate *dhammā* arise at that plane? —Yes. (Same as below)
(b) Indeterminate *dhammā* arise at this plane. Do unwholesome *dhammā* arise at that plane?
—No. At the plane of non-percipience.
—Yes. At the planes of four- and five-aggregates.

Forward enquiries by Individual and Plane

37. *i* (a) Wholesome *dhammā* arise in this person at this plane. Do unwholesome *dhammā* arise in that person at that plane?
—No. (To those at the arising moment of good state at immaterial plane …)
(b) Unwholesome *dhammā* arise in this person at this plane. Do wholesome *dhammā* arise in that person at that plane?
—No. (To those at the arising moment of bad state at immaterial plane …)

ii (a) Wholesome *dhammā* arise in this person at that plane. Do indeterminate *dhammā* arise in that person at that plane?
—No. To those at the arising moment of good state at immaterial plane …
—Yes. To those at the arising moment of good state at five-aggregate plane …
(b) Indeterminate *dhammā* arise in this person at this plane. Do wholesome *dhammā* arise in that person at that plane?
—No. To all those at birth-moment, and those at the arising moment of *citta* dissociated from goodness ...
—Yes. (Same as the aforesaid)

[73] Four-aggregate planes: namely the four Immaterial planes.

38. *i* (a) Unwholesome *dhammā* arise in this person at that plane. Do indeterminate *dhammā* arise in that person at that plane?
—No. To those at the arising moment of bad state at immaterial plane ...
—Yes. To those at the arising moment of bad state at five-aggregate plane ...
(b) Indeterminate *dhammā* arise in this person at this plane. Do unwholesome *dhammā* arise in that person at that plane?
—No. To all those at birth-moment, and those at the arising moment of *citta* dissociated from badness ....
—Yes. (Same as the aforesaid)

Opposite enquiries by Individual

39. *i* (a) Wholesome *dhammā* do not arise in this person. Do unwholesome *dhammā* not arise in that person?
—No. To those at the arising moment of bad state (in consciousness) ...
—Yes. To all those at the ceasing moment of *citta*, those at the arising moment of *citta* dissociated from both goodness and badness, those engaged in Cessation-attainment, and individuals of non-percipience ....
(b) Unwholesome *dhammā* do not arise in this person. Do wholesome *dhammā* not arise in that person?
—No. To those at the arising moment of good state ....
—Yes. (Same as the aforesaid)

ii (a) Wholesome *dhammā* do not arise in this person. Do indeterminate *dhammā* not arise in that person?
—No. To all those at birth-moment, and those at the arising moment of *citta* dissociated from goodness ....
—Yes. To all those at death-moment, those at the ceasing moment of *citta*, and those at the arising moment of bad state at immaterial plane… (b) Indeterminate *dhammā* do not arise in this person. Do wholesome *dhammā* not arise in that person?
—No. To those at the arising moment of good state at immaterial plane ....
—Yes. (Same as the aforesaid)

40. *i* (a) Unwholesome *dhammā* do not arise in this person. Do indeterminate *dhammā* not arise in that person?
—No. To all those at birth-moment, and those at the arising moment of *citta* dissociated from badness ....
—Yes. To all those at death-moment, those at the ceasing moment of *citta*, and those at the arising moment of good state at immaterial plane ...
(b) Indeterminate *dhammā* do not arise in this person. Do unwholesome *dhammā* not arise in that person?
—No. To those at the arising moment of bad state at immaterial plane ….
—Yes. (Same as the aforesaid)

Opposite enquiries by Plane

41. *i* (a) Wholesome *dhammā* do not arise at this plane. Do unwholesome *dhammā* not arise at that plane? —Yes (at the plane of non-percipience).
(b) Unwholesome *dhammā* do not arise at this plane. Do wholesome *dhammā* not arise at that plane? —Yes. (Same as the aforesaid)

ii (a) Wholesome *dhammā* do not arise at this plane. Do indeterminate *dhammā* not arise at that plane?
—No. Indeterminate *dhammā* arise (at the plane of non-percipience).
(b) Indeterminate *dhammā* do not arise at this plane. Do wholesome *dhammā* not arise at that plane? —No such plane.

42. *i* (a) Unwholesome *dhammā* do not arise at this plane. Do indeterminate *dhammā* not arise at that plane? —No. They arise (at non-percipience plane).
(b) Indeterminate *dhammā* do not arise at this plane. Do unwholesome *dhammā* not arise at that plane? —No such plane.

Opposite enquiries by Individual and Plane

43. *i* (a) Wholesome *dhammā* do not arise in this person at this plane. Do unwholesome *dhammā* not arise in that person at that plane?
—No. To those at the arising moment of bad state …
—Yes. To all those at the ceasing moment of *citta*, those at the arising moment of *citta* dissociated from both goodness and badness, and individuals at non-percipience plane ....
(b) Unwholesome *dhammā* do not arise in this person at this plane. Do wholesome *dhammā* not arise in that person at that plane?
—No. To those at the arising moment of good state...
—Yes. (Same as the aforesaid)

ii (a) Wholesome *dhammā* do not arise in this person at this plane. Do indeterminate *dhammā* not arise in that person at that plane?
—No. To all those at birth-moment, and those at the arising moment of *citta* dissociated from goodness ....
—Yes. To all those at death-moment, those at the ceasing moment of *citta*, and those at arising moment of bad state at immaterial plane ...
(b) Indeterminate *dhammā* do not arise in this person at this plane. Do wholesome *dhammā* not arise in that person at that plane?
—No. To those at the arising moment of good state at immaterial plane ....
—Yes. (Same as the aforesaid)

44. *i* (a) Unwholesome *dhammā* do not arise in this person at this plane. Do indeterminate *dhammā* not arise in that person at that plane?
—No. To all those at birth-moment, and those at the arising moment of *citta* dissociated from badness.

—Yes. To all those at death-moment, those at the ceasing moment of *citta*, and at the arising moment of good state at immaterial plane.
(b) Indeterminate *dhammā* do not arise in this person at this plane. Do unwholesome *dhammā* not arise in that person at that plane?
—No. To those at the arising moment of bad state at immaterial plane ....
—Yes. (Same as the aforesaid)

In the Past

Forward enquiries by Individual

45. *i* (a) Wholesome *dhammā* had arisen in this person. Had unwholesome *dhammā* arisen in that person?
—Yes. (To those at the planes of four aggregates and five aggregates ....)
(b) Unwholesome *dhammā* had arisen in this person. Had wholesome *dhammā* arisen in that person? —Yes. (Same as the aforesaid)
ii (a) Wholesome *dhammā* had arisen in this person. Had indeterminate *dhammā* arisen in that person?
—Yes. (To those at the planes of four aggregates and five aggregates ....)
(b) Indeterminate *dhammā* had arisen in this person. Had wholesome *dhammā* arisen in that person? —Yes. (Same as the aforesaid)

46. *i* (a) Unwholesome *dhammā* had arisen in this person. Had indeterminate *dhammā* arisen in that person?
—Yes. (To those at the planes of four aggregates and five aggregates ....)
(b) Indeterminate *dhammā* had arisen in this person. Had unwholesome *dhammā* arisen in that person? —Yes. (Same as the aforesaid)

Forward enquiries by Plane

47. *i* (a) Wholesome *dhammā* had arisen at this plane. Had unwholesome *dhammā* arisen at that plane?
—Yes. (At four- and five-aggregate planes)
(b) Unwholesome *dhammā* had arisen at this plane. Had wholesome *dhammā* arisen at that plane? —Yes. (Same as the aforesaid)

ii (a) Wholesome *dhammā* had arisen at this plane. Had indeterminate *dhammā* arisen at that plane? —Yes. (Same as below)
(b) Indeterminate *dhammā* had arisen at this plane. Had wholesome *dhammā* arisen at that plane?
—No. At the plane of non-percipience.
—Yes. At the planes of four aggregates and five aggregates.

48. *i* (a) Unwholesome *dhammā* had arisen at this plane. Had indeterminate *dhammā* arisen at that plane? —Yes. (Same as below)
(b) Indeterminate *dhammā* had arisen at this plane. Had unwholesome *dhammā* arisen at that plane?

—No. At the plane of non-percipience.
—Yes. At the planes of four aggregates and five aggregates.

Forward enquiries by Individual and Plane

49. *i* (a) Wholesome *dhammā* had arisen in this person at this plane. Had unwholesome *dhammā* arisen in that person at that plane?
—Yes. (Same as below)
(b) Unwholesome *dhammā* had arisen in this person at this plane. Had wholesome *dhammā* arisen in that person at that plane?
—No. To those at the occurrence of second unwholesome consciousness [74] of the pure abodes ....
—Yes. To others at the four- and five-aggregate planes ....

ii (a) Wholesome *dhammā* had arisen in this person at this plane. Had indeterminate *dhammā* arisen in that person at that plane?
—Yes. (Same as below)
(b) Indeterminate *dhammā* had arisen in this person at this plane. Had wholesome *dhammā* arisen in that person at that plane?
—No. To those at the occurrence of second *citta* of the pure abode beings, and individuals at non-percipience plane ....
—Yes. To others at the four- and five-aggregate planes ....

50. *i* (a) Unwholesome *dhammā* had arisen in this person at this plane. Had indeterminate *dhammā* arisen in that person at that plane?
—Yes. (Same as below)
(b) Indeterminate *dhammā* had arisen in this person at this plane. Had unwholesome *dhammā* arisen in that person at that plane?
—No. To those at the occurrence of second *citta* of the pure abode beings, and individuals at non-percipience plane ....
—Yes. To others at the four- and five-aggregate planes ....

Opposite enquiries by Individual

51. *i* (a) Wholesome *dhammā* had not arisen in this person. Had unwholesome *dhammā* not arisen in that person?
— Natthi. (To those at the occurrence of second *citta* of the pure abode beings, and individuals of non-percipience, unwholesome *dhammā* had in whom also not arisen)
(b) Unwholesome *dhammā* had not arisen in this person. Had wholesome *dhammā* not arisen in that person?
— Natthi (Same as aforesaid)

ii (a) Wholesome *dhammā* had not arisen in this person. Had indeterminate *dhammā* not arisen in that person? —No such person.

---

[74] at one of the 7 javanas (impulsions).

(b) Indeterminate *dhammā* had not arisen in this person. Had wholesome *dhammā* not arisen in that person? —No such person.

52. *i* (a) Unwholesome *dhammā* had not arisen in this person. Had indeterminate *dhammā* not arisen in that person? —No such person.
Indeterminate *dhammā* had not arisen in this person. Had unwholesome *dhammā* not arisen in that person? —No such person.

Opposite enquiries by Plane

53. *i* (a) Wholesome *dhammā* had not arisen at this plane. Had unwholesome *dhammā* not arisen at that plane? —Yes. (At non-percipience plane)
(b) Unwholesome *dhammā* had not arisen at this plane. Had wholesome *dhammā* not arisen at that plane? —Yes. (Same as aforesaid)

ii (a) Wholesome *dhammā* had not arisen at this plane. Had indeterminate *dhammā* not arisen at that plane?
—No. Indeterminate *dhammā* in whom had arisen.
(b) Indeterminate *dhammā* had not arisen at this plane. Had wholesome *dhammā* not arisen at that plane?
—No such person.

54. *i* (a) Unwholesome *dhammā* had not arisen at this plane. Had indeterminate *dhammā* not arisen at that plane?
—No. Indeterminate *dhammā* in whom had arisen.
(b) Indeterminate *dhammā* had not arisen at this plane. Had unwholesome *dhammā* not arisen at that plane?
—No such person.

Opposite enquiries by Individual and Plane

55. *i* (a) Wholesome *dhammā* had not arisen in this person at this plane. Had unwholesome *dhammā* not arisen in that person at that plane?
—No. To those at the occurrence of second unwholesome consciousness of the pure abodes ....
—Yes. To those at the occurrence of second *citta* of the pure abode beings, and individuals at non-percipience plane ....
(b) Unwholesome *dhammā* had not arisen in this person at this plane. Had wholesome *dhammā* not arisen in that person at that plane?
—Yes. (Same as the aforesaid)

ii (a) Wholesome *dhammā* had not arisen in this person at this plane. Had indeterminate *dhammā* not arisen in that person at that plane?
—No. To those at the occurrence of second *citta* of the pure abode beings, and individuals at non-percipience plane ....
—Yes. To those at the birth-moment at pure abodes ....

(b) Indeterminate *dhammā* had not arisen in this person at this plane. Had wholesome *dhammā* not arisen in that person at that plane?
—Yes. (Same as the aforesaid)

56. *i* (a) Unwholesome *dhammā* had not arisen in this person at this plane. Had indeterminate *dhammā* not arisen in that person at that plane?
—No. To those at the occurrence of second *citta* of the pure abode beings, and individuals at non-percipience plane ....
—Yes. To those at the birth-moment at pure abodes ....
(b) Indeterminate *dhammā* had not arisen in this person at this plane. Had unwholesome *dhammā* not arisen in that person at that plane?
—Yes. (Same as the aforesaid)

In Future

Forward enquiries by Individual

57. *i* (a) Wholesome *dhammā* will arise in this person. Will unwholesome *dhammā* arise in that person?
—No. To those right after this state of consciousness who will directly attain the highest (*Arahatta*) Path [75] ....
—Yes. To others (at the four- and five-aggregate planes ....)
(b) Unwholesome *dhammā* will arise in this person. Will indeterminate *dhammā* arise in that person?
—Yes. (Same as the aforesaid)

ii (a) Wholesome *dhammā* will arise in this person. Will indeterminate *dhammā* arise in that person?
—Yes. (Same as below)
(b) Indeterminate *dhammā* will arise in this person. Will wholesome *dhammā* arise in that person?
—No. To those endowed with the highest Path, and to *Arahat* ....
—Yes. To others (those at the four- and five-aggregate planes, and to those right after this state of consciousness who will directly attain *Arahatta* Path at the arising moment of that (*Arahatta* Path) *citta* ...)

58. *i* (a) Unwholesome *dhammā* will arise in this person. Will indeterminate *dhammā* arise in that person? —Yes. (Same as below)
(b) Indeterminate *dhammā* will arise in this person. Will unwholesome *dhammā* arise in that person?
—No. To those endowed with the highest Path, to *Arahat*, and to those right after this state of consciousness who will directly attain the highest Path ....
—Yes. To others. (Same as the answer in 57 *i* b)

[75] *aggamagga*: the highest (of the four supramundane Paths) being the *Arahatta* Path

Forward enquiries by Plane

59. *i* (a) Wholesome *dhammā* will arise at this plane. Will unwholesome *dhammā* arise at that plane?
—Yes. (To those at the four- and five-aggregate planes …)
(b) Unwholesome *dhammā* will arise at this plane. Will wholesome *dhammā* arise at that plane? — Yes. (Same as the aforesaid)

ii (a) Wholesome *dhammā* will arise at this plane. Will indeterminate *dhammā* arise at that plane? —Yes. (Same as below)
(b) Indeterminate *dhammā* will arise at this plane. Will wholesome *dhammā* arise at that plane?
—No. At the plane of non-percipience.
—Yes. At the planes of four- and five-aggregates.

60. *i* (a) Unwholesome *dhammā* will arise at this plane. Will indeterminate *dhammā* arise at that plane? —Yes. (Same as below)
(b) Indeterminate *dhammā* will arise at this plane. Will unwholesome *dhammā* arise at that plane?
—No. At the plane of non-percipience.
—Yes. At the planes of four- and five-aggregates.

Forward enquiries by Individual and Plane

61. *i* (a) Wholesome *dhammā* will arise in this person at this plane. Will unwholesome *dhammā* arise in that person at this plane?
—No. To those right after this state of consciousness who will directly attain the highest Path ....
—Yes. To others at the four- and five-aggregate planes ....
(b) Unwholesome *dhammā* will arise in this person at this plane. Will indeterminate *dhammā* arise in that person at that plane?
—Yes. (Same as the aforesaid)

ii (a) Wholesome *dhammā* will arise in this person at this plane. Will indeterminate *dhammā* arise in that person at that plane? —Yes. (Same as below)
(b) Indeterminate *dhammā* will arise in this person at this plane. Will wholesome *dhammā* arise in that person at that plane?
—No. To those endowed with the highest Path, to *Arahat*, and individuals at non-percipience plane ....
—Yes. To others at the four- and five-aggregate planes ....

62. *i* (a) Unwholesome *dhammā* will arise in this person at this plane. Will indeterminate *dhammā* arise in that person at that plane?
—Yes. (Same as below)
(b) Indeterminate *dhammā* will arise in this person at this plane. Will unwholesome *dhammā* arise in that person at that plane?

—No. To those endowed with the highest Path, to *Arahat*, to those right after this state of consciousness who will directly attain the highest Path, and individuals at non-percipience plane ....
—Yes. To others at the four- and five-aggregate planes ....

Opposite enquiries by Individual

63. *i* (a) Wholesome *dhammā* will not arise in this person. Will unwholesome *dhammā* not arise in that person? —Yes. (Same as below)
(b) Unwholesome *dhammā* will not arise in this person. Will wholesome *dhammā* not arise in that person?
—No. To those right after this state of consciousness who will directly attain the highest Path ....
—Yes. To those endowed with the highest Path, and to *Arahat* ....

ii (a) Wholesome *dhammā* will not arise in this person. Will indeterminate *dhammā* not arise in that person?
—No. To those endowed with the highest Path, and to *Arahat* ....
—Yes. To those endowed with the final-stage state of consciousness ....
(b) Indeterminate *dhammā* will not arise in this person. Will wholesome *dhammā* not arise in that person? —Yes. (Same as the aforesaid)

64. *i* (a) Unwholesome *dhammā* will not arise in this person. Will indeterminate *dhammā* not arise in that person?
—No. To those endowed with the highest Path, to *Arahat*, to those right after this state of consciousness who will directly attain the highest Path ....
—Yes. To those endowed with the final-stage state of consciousness ....
(b) Indeterminate *dhammā* will not arise in this person. Will unwholesome *dhammā* not arise in that person? —Yes. (Same as the aforesaid)

Opposite enquiries by Plane

65. *i* (a) Wholesome *dhammā* will not arise at this plane. Will unwholesome *dhammā* not arise at that plane?
—Yes (at non-percipience plane).
(b) Unwholesome *dhammā* will not arise at this plane. Will wholesome *dhammā* not arise at that plane? — Yes. (Same as the aforesaid)

ii (a) Wholesome *dhammā* will not arise at this plane. Will indeterminate *dhammā* not arise at that plane?
—No. (At non-percipience plane), indeterminate *dhammā* will arise.
(b) Indeterminate *dhammā* will not arise at this plane. Will wholesome *dhammā* not arise at that plane? —No such plane.

66. *i* (a) Unwholesome *dhammā* will not arise at this plane. Will indeterminate *dhammā* not arise at that plane?
—No. (At non-percipience plane), indeterminate *dhammā* will arise.

(b) Indeterminate *dhammā* will not arise at this plane. Will unwholesome *dhammā* not arise at that plane? —No such plane.

Opposite enquiries by Individual and Plane

67. *i* (a) Wholesome *dhammā* will not arise in this person at this plane. Will unwholesome *dhammā* not arise in that person at that plane?
—Yes. (Same as below)
(b) Unwholesome *dhammā* will not arise in this person at this plane. Will wholesome *dhammā* not arise in that person at that plane?
—No. To those right after this state of consciousness who will directly attain the highest Path ....
—Yes. To those endowed with the highest Path, to *Arahat*, and individuals at non-percipience plane ....

ii (a) Wholesome *dhammā* will not arise in this person at this plane. Will indeterminate *dhammā* not arise in that person at that plane?
—No. To those endowed with the highest Path, to *Arahat*, and individuals at non-percipience plane ....
—Yes. To those endowed with the final-stage state of consciousness ....
(b) Indeterminate *dhammā* will not arise in this person at this plane. Will wholesome *dhammā* not arise in that person at that plane? —Yes. (Same as above)

68. *i* (a) Unwholesome *dhammā* will not arise in this person at this plane. Will indeterminate *dhammā* not arise in that person at that plane?
—No. To those endowed with the highest Path, to *Arahat*, to those right after this state of consciousness who will directly attain the highest Path, and individuals at non-percipience plane ....
—Yes. To those endowed with the final-stage state of consciousness.
(b) Indeterminate *dhammā* will not arise in this person at this plane. Will unwholesome *dhammā* not arise in that person at that plane?
—Yes. (Same as the aforesaid)

Chart 9.7 Origination of *dhammā* (by present and past)

A: arise/ had arisen; N: do not arise/ had not arisen

	Present			Past		
	wholesome *dhammā*	unwholesome *dhammā*	indeterminate *dhammā*	wholesome *dhammā*	unwholesome *dhammā*	indeterminate *dhammā*
To those at the arising moment of :						
consciousness dissociated from goodness	N				A	A
consciousness dissociated from badness		N				A
consciousness dissociated from goodness and badness						
the highest (*Arahatta*) Path-*citta*						
the final-stage *citta*						
good state	A				A	A
good state at five-aggregate plane						
good state at immaterial plane						
bad state		A				A
bad state at Immaterial plane						
bad state at five-aggregate plane						
To those at the ceasing moment of :						
citta (state of consciousness)	N	N			A	A
the highest (*Arahatta*) Path-*citta*						
To those :						
all beings at the birth-moment						
all beings at the death-moment						
engaged in Cessation-attainment	N	N			A	A
at the birth-moment at pure abodes	N	N				N
at the occurrence of second *citta* of the pure abode beings	N				N	
at occurrence of second unwholesome *citta* of pure abode beings						
at immaterial plane (four-aggregate)						
at the non-percipience plane	N	N			AN	A
at the four- and five-aggregate planes						
Arahat						
endowed with the highest (*Arahatta*) Path						
right after this *citta* who will directly attain the highest (*Arahatta*) Path						
endowed with the final-stage *citta*						
At the plane(s) of :						
non-percipience	N	N	A	N	N	A
five-aggregates	A	A	A	A	A	A
immateriality (or four-aggregates)	A	A	A	A	A	A

Present and Past

Forward enquiries by Individual

69. *i* (a) Wholesome *dhammā* arise in this person. Had unwholesome *dhammā* arisen in that person? —Yes. (Same as below)
(b) Unwholesome *dhammā* had arisen in this person. Do wholesome *dhammā* arise in that person?
—No. To all those at the ceasing moment of *citta*; those at the arising moment of *citta* dissociated from goodness; those engaged in Cessation-attainment; and individuals of non-percipience ....
—Yes, at the arising moment of good state ....

ii (a) Wholesome *dhammā* arise in this person. Had indeterminate *dhammā* arisen in that person? —Yes. (Same as below)
(b) Indeterminate *dhammā* had arisen in this person. Do wholesome *dhammā* arise in that person?
—No. To all those at the ceasing moment of *citta*, those at the arising moment of *citta* dissociated from goodness, those engaged in Cessation-attainment, and individuals of non-percipience ....
—Yes. To those at the arising moment of good state....

70. *i* (a) Unwholesome *dhammā* arise in this person. Had indeterminate *dhammā* arisen in that person? —Yes. (Same as below)
(b) Indeterminate *dhammā* had arisen in this person. Do unwholesome *dhammā* arise in that person?
—No. To all those at the ceasing moment of *citta*, those at the arising moment of *citta* dissociated from badness, those engaged in Cessation-attainment, and individuals of non-percipience ....
—Yes. To those at the arising moment of bad state ....

Forward enquiries by Plane

71. *i* (a) Wholesome *dhammā* arise at this plane. Had unwholesome *dhammā* arisen at that plane? .....p.....

Forward enquiries by Individual and Plane

72. *i* (a) Wholesome *dhammā* arise in this person at this plane. Had unwholesome *dhammā* arisen in that person at that plane?
—Yes. (Same as below)
(b) Unwholesome *dhammā* had arisen in this person at this plane. Do wholesome *dhammā* arise in that person at that plane?
—No. To all those at the ceasing moment of *citta*, those at the arising moment of *citta* dissociated from goodness ....
—Yes. To those at the arising moment of good state ....

ii (a) Wholesome *dhammā* arise in this person at this plane. Had indeterminate *dhammā* arisen in that person at that plane? —Yes. (Same as below)
(b) Indeterminate *dhammā* had arisen in this person at this plane. Do wholesome *dhammā* arise in that person at that plane?
—No. To all those at the ceasing moment of *citta*, those at the arising moment of *citta* dissociated from goodness, and individuals at non-percipience plane ....
—Yes. To those at the arising moment of good state ....

73. *i* (a) Unwholesome *dhammā* arise in this person at this plane. Had indeterminate *dhammā* arisen in that person at that plane? —Yes. (Same as below)
(b) Indeterminate *dhammā* had arisen in this person at this plane. Do unwholesome *dhammā* arise in that person at that plane?
—No. To all those at the ceasing moment of *citta*, those at the arising moment of *citta* dissociated from badness, and individuals at non-percipience plane ....
—Yes. To those at the arising moment of bad state ....

Opposite enquiries by Individual

74. *i* (a) Wholesome *dhammā* do not arise in this person. Had unwholesome *dhammā* not arisen in that person?
—No. Unwholesome *dhammā* had arisen. (To those at the ceasing moment of *citta,* those at the arising moment of *citta* dissociated from goodness, those engaged in Cessation-attainment ....)
(b) Unwholesome *dhammā* had not arisen in this person. Do wholesome *dhammā* not arise in that person? — Natthi

ii (a) Wholesome *dhammā* do not arise in this person. Had indeterminate *dhammā* not arisen in that person?
—No. Indeterminate *dhammā* had arisen. (to all those at the ceasing moment of *citta,* those at the arising moment of *citta* dissociated from goodness, those engaged in Cessation-attainment, and individuals of non-percipience ....)
(b) Indeterminate *dhammā* had not arisen in this person. Do wholesome *dhammā* not arise in that person? —Natthi

75. *i* (a) Unwholesome *dhammā* do not arise in this person. Had indeterminate *dhammā* not arisen in that person?
—No. Indeterminate *dhammā* had arisen. (to all those at the ceasing moment of *citta,* those at the arising moment of *citta* dissociated from badness, those engaged in Cessation-attainment, and individuals of non-percipience ....)
(b) Indeterminate *dhammā* had not arisen in this person. Do unwholesome *dhammā* not arise in that person? —Natthi

Opposite enquiries by Plane

76. *i* (a) Wholesome *dhammā* do not arise at this plane. Had unwholesome *dhammā* not arisen at that plane? .....p.....

Opposite enquiries by Individual and Plane

77. *i* (a) Wholesome *dhammā* do not arise in this person at this plane. Had unwholesome *dhammā* not arisen in that person at that plane?
—No. To all those at the ceasing moment of *citta*, and those at the arising moment of *citta* dissociated from goodness ....
—Yes. To those at the occurrence of second *citta* of the pure abode beings, and individuals at non-percipience plane [76] ....
(b) Unwholesome *dhammā* had not arisen in this person at this plane. Do wholesome *dhammā* not arise in that person at that plane?
—Yes. (Same as the aforesaid)

ii (a) Wholesome *dhammā* do not arise in this person at this plane. Had indeterminate *dhammā* not arisen in that person at that plane?
—No. To all those at the ceasing moment of *citta*, those at the arising moment of *citta* dissociated from goodness, and individuals at non-percipience plane ....
—Yes. To those at the birth-moment at pure abodes ....
(b) Indeterminate *dhammā* had not arisen in this person at this plane. Do wholesome *dhammā* not arise in that person at that plane?
—Yes. (Same as the aforesaid)

78. *i* (a) Unwholesome *dhammā* do not arise in this person at this plane. Had indeterminate *dhammā* not arisen in that person at that plane?
—No. To all those at the ceasing moment of *citta*, those at the arising moment of *citta* dissociated from badness, and individuals at non-percipience plane ....
—Yes. To those at the birth-moment at pure abodes ....
(b) Indeterminate *dhammā* had not arisen in this person at this plane. Do unwholesome *dhammā* not arise in that person at that plane?
—Yes. (Same as the aforesaid)

[76] To individuals at non-percipience plane, unwholesome *dhammā* had in whom either arisen or not arisen. See 69 *i* (b).

Chart 9.8 Origination of *dhammā* (by present and future)

A: arise/ will arise; N: do not arise/ will not arise

	Present			Future		
	wholesome *dhammā*	unwholesome *dhammā*	indeterminate *dhammā*	wholesome *dhammā*	unwholesome *dhammā*	indeterminate *dhammā*
To those at the arising moment of :						
consciousness dissociated from goodness	N				A	A
consciousness dissociated from badness		N				A
consciousness dissociated from goodness and badness						
the highest (*Arahatta*) Path-*citta*	A				N	
the final-stage *citta*						
good state	A				A	A
good state at five-aggregate plane						
good state at immaterial plane						
bad state		A				A
bad state at Immaterial plane						
bad state at five-aggregate plane						
To those at the ceasing moment of :						
citta (state of consciousness)	N	N			A	A
the highest (*Arahatta*) Path-*citta*	N				N	
To those :						
all beings at the birth-moment						
all beings at the death-moment						
engaged in Cessation-attainment	N	N			A	A
at the birth-moment at pure abodes						
at the occurrence of second *citta* of the pure abode beings						
at occurrence of second unwholesome *citta* of pure abode beings						
at immaterial plane (four-aggregate)						
at the non-percipience plane	N	N			AN	A
at the four- and five-aggregate planes						
Arahat	N				N	
endowed with the highest (*Arahatta*) Path						
right after this *citta* who will directly attain the highest (*Arahatta*) Path						
right after this *citta* who will directly attain the highest (*Arahatta*) Path at the arising moment of that (*Arahatta* Path) *citta*	A				N	
right after this *citta* who will directly attain the highest (*Arahatta*) Path at the ceasing moment of that (*Arahatta* Path) *citta*	N				N	
endowed with the final-stage *citta*	N	N				N
At the plane(s) of :						
non-percipience	N	N	A	N	N	A
five-aggregates	A	A	A	A	A	A
immateriality (or four-aggregates)	A	A	A	A	A	A

Present and Future

Forward enquiries by Individual

79. *i* (a) Wholesome *dhammā* arise in this person. Will unwholesome *dhammā* arise in that person?
—No. To those at the arising moment of the highest Path-*citta*, and to those right after this state of consciousness who will directly attain the highest Path at the arising moment of that (*Arahatta* Path) *citta* ....
—Yes. To others at the arising moment of good state ....
(b) Unwholesome *dhammā* will arise in this person. Do wholesome *dhammā* arise in that person?
—No. To all those at the ceasing moment of *citta*, those at the arising moment of *citta* dissociated from goodness, those engaged in Cessation-attainment, and individuals of non-percipience ....
—Yes. (Same as the aforesaid)

ii (a) Wholesome *dhammā* arise in this person. Will indeterminate *dhammā* arise in that person? —Yes. (Same as below)
(b) Indeterminate *dhammā* will arise in this person. Do wholesome *dhammā* arise in that person?
—No. To all those at the ceasing moment of *citta*, those at the arising moment of *citta* dissociated from goodness, those engaged in Cessation-attainment, and individuals of non-percipience ....
—Yes. To those at the arising moment of good state ....

80. *i* (a) Unwholesome *dhammā* arise in this person. Will indeterminate *dhammā* arise in that person? —Yes. (Same as below)
(b) Indeterminate *dhammā* will arise in this person. Do unwholesome *dhammā* arise in that person?
—No. To all those at the ceasing moment of *citta*, those at the arising moment of *citta* dissociated from badness, those engaged in Cessation-attainment, and individuals of non-percipience ....
—Yes. To those at the arising moment of bad state ....

Forward enquiries by Plane

81. *i* (a) Wholesome *dhammā* arise at this plane. Will unwholesome *dhammā* arise at that plane? .....p.....

Forward enquiries by Individual and Plane

82. *i* (a) Wholesome *dhammā* arise in this person at this plane. Will unwholesome *dhammā* arise in that person at that plane?
—No. To those at the arising moment of the highest Path-*citta*, and to those right after this state of consciousness who will directly attain the highest Path at the arising moment of that (*Arahatta* Path) *citta* ....

—Yes. To others at the arising moment of good state ....
(b) Unwholesome *dhammā* will arise in this person at this plane. Do wholesome *dhammā* arise in that person at that plane?
—No. To all those at the ceasing moment of *citta*, and those at the arising moment of *citta* dissociated from goodness ....
—Yes. To those at the arising moment of good state ....

ii (a) Wholesome *dhammā* arise in this person at this plane. Will indeterminate *dhammā* arise in that person at that plane?
—Yes. (Same as below)
(b) Indeterminate *dhammā* will arise in this person at this plane. Do wholesome *dhammā* arise in that person at that plane?
—No. To all those at the ceasing moment of *citta*, those at the arising moment of *citta* dissociated from goodness, and individuals at non-percipience plane ....
—Yes. To those at the arising moment of good state ...

83. *i* (a) Unwholesome *dhammā* arise in this person at this plane. Will indeterminate *dhammā* arise in that person at that plane?
—Yes. (Same as below)
(b) Indeterminate *dhammā* will arise in this person at this plane. Do unwholesome *dhammā* arise in that person at that plane?
—No. To all those at the ceasing moment of *citta*, those at the arising moment of *citta* dissociated from badness, and individuals at non-percipience plane ....
—Yes. To those at the arising moment of bad state ....

Opposite enquiries by Individual

84. *i* (a) Wholesome *dhammā* do not arise in this person. Will unwholesome *dhammā* not arise in that person?
—No. To all those at the ceasing moment of *citta*, those at the arising moment of *citta* dissociated from goodness, those engaged in Cessation-attainment, and individuals of non-percipience ....
—Yes. To those at the ceasing moment of the highest Path-*citta*, to *Arahat*, to those right after this state of consciousness who will directly attain the highest Path at the ceasing moment of that (*Arahatta* Path) *citta* ....
(b) Unwholesome *dhammā* will not arise in this person. Do wholesome *dhammā* not arise in that person?
—No. To those at the arising moment of the highest Path-*citta*, and to those right after this state of consciousness who will directly attain the highest Path at the arising moment of that (*Arahatta* Path) *citta* ....
—Yes. (Same as the aforesaid)

ii (a) Wholesome *dhammā* do not arise in this person. Will indeterminate *dhammā* not arise in that person?
—No. To all those at the ceasing moment of *citta*, those at the arising moment of *citta* dissociated from goodness, those engaged in Cessation-attainment, and individuals of non-percipience ....
—Yes. To those endowed with the final-stage state of consciousness ....
(b) Indeterminate *dhammā* will not arise in this person. Do wholesome *dhammā* not arise in that person? —Yes. (Same as the aforesaid)

85. *i* (a) Unwholesome *dhammā* do not arise in this person. Will indeterminate *dhammā* not arise in that person?
—No. To all those at the ceasing moment of *citta*, those at the arising moment of *citta* dissociated from badness, those engaged in Cessation-attainment, and individuals of non-percipience ....
—Yes. To those endowed with the final-stage state of consciousness ....
(b) Indeterminate *dhammā* will not arise in this person. Do unwholesome *dhammā* not arise in that person? —Yes. (Same as the aforesaid)

Opposite enquiries by Plane

86. *i* (a) Wholesome *dhammā* do not arise at this plane. Will unwholesome *dhammā* not arise at that plane? .....p.....

Opposite enquiries by Individual and Plane

87. *i* (a) Wholesome *dhammā* do not arise in this person at this plane. Will unwholesome *dhammā* not arise in that person at that plane?
—No. To all those at the ceasing moment of *citta*, and those at the arising moment of *citta* dissociated from goodness ....
—Yes. To those at the ceasing moment of the highest Path-*citta*, to *Arahat*, to those right after this state of consciousness who will directly attain the highest Path at the ceasing moment of that (*Arahatta* Path) *citta*, and to individuals at non-percipience plane [77]....
(b) Unwholesome *dhammā* will not arise in this person at this plane. Do wholesome *dhammā* not arise in that person at that plane?
—No. To those at the arising moment of the highest Path-*citta*, and to those right after this state of consciousness who will directly attain the highest Path at the arising moment of that (*Arahatta* Path) *citta* ....
—Yes. (Same as the aforesaid)

[77] To individuals at non-percipience plane, unwholesome *dhammā* in whom will either arise or not arise. See 84 *i* (a).

ii (a) Wholesome *dhammā* do not arise in this person at this plane. Will indeterminate *dhammā* not arise in that person at that plane?
—No. To all those at the ceasing moment of *citta*, those at the arising moment of *citta* dissociated from goodness, and individuals at non-percipience plane ....
—Yes. To those endowed with the final-stage state of consciousness ....
(b) Indeterminate *dhammā* will not arise in this person at this plane. Do wholesome *dhammā* not arise in that person at that plane?
—Yes. (Same as the aforesaid)

88. *i* (a) Unwholesome *dhammā* do not arise in this person at this plane. Will indeterminate *dhammā* not arise in that person at that plane?
—No. To all those at the ceasing moment of *citta*, those at the arising moment of *citta* dissociated from badness, and individuals at non-percipience plane ....
—Yes. To those endowed with the final-stage state of consciousness ....
(b) Indeterminate *dhammā* will not arise in this person at this plane. Do unwholesome *dhammā* not arise in that person at that plane?
—Yes. (Same as the aforesaid)

Chart 9.9 Origination of *dhammā* (by past and future)

A: had arisen/ will arise; N: had not arisen/ will not arise

	Past			Future		
	wholesome *dhammā*	unwholesome *dhammā*	indeterminate *dhammā*	wholesome *dhammā*	unwholesome *dhammā*	indeterminate *dhammā*
To those at the arising moment of :						
consciousness dissociated from goodness						
consciousness dissociated from badness						
consciousness dissociated from goodness and badness						
the highest (*Arahatta*) Path-*citta*						
the final-stage *citta*						
good state						
good state at five-aggregate plane						
good state at immaterial plane						
bad state						
bad state at Immaterial plane						
bad state at five-aggregate plane						
To those at the ceasing moment of :						
citta (state of consciousness)						
the highest (*Arahatta*) Path-*citta*						
To those :						
all beings at the birth-moment						
all beings at the death-moment						
engaged in Cessation-attainment						
at the birth-moment at pure abodes						
at the occurrence of second *citta* of the pure abode beings						
at occurrence of second unwholesome *citta* of pure abode beings	N	N			A	A
at immaterial plane (four-aggregate)						
at the non-percipience plane	N	N			N	A
at the four- and five-aggregate planes	A	A			A	A
who are born at the woeful planes						
Arahat	A				N	
endowed with the highest (*Arahatta*) Path	A				N	
right after this *citta* who will directly attain the highest (*Arahatta*) Path	A				N	
right after this *citta* who will directly attain the highest (*Arahatta*) Path at the arising moment of that (*Arahatta*)Path) *citta*						
right after this *citta* who will directly attain the highest (*Arahatta*) Path at the ceasing moment of that (*Arahatta*)Path) *citta*						
endowed with the final-stage *citta*	A	A				N
At the plane(s) of :						
non-percipience	N	N	A	N	N	A
five-aggregates	A	A	A	A	A	A
immateriality (or four-aggregates)	A	A	A	A	A	A

Past and Future

Forward enquiries by Individual

89. *i* (a) Wholesome *dhammā* had arisen in this person. Will unwholesome *dhammā* arise in that person?
—No. To those endowed with the highest Path, to *Arahat*, and to those right after this state of consciousness who will directly attain the highest Path ....
—Yes. In others (at the four- and five-aggregate planes) ....
(b) Unwholesome *dhammā* will arise in this person. Had wholesome *dhammā* arisen in that person? —Yes. (Same as the aforesaid)

ii (a) Wholesome *dhammā* had arisen in this person. Will indeterminate *dhammā* arise in that person?
—No. To those endowed with the final-stage state of consciousness ....
—Yes. To others (at the four- and five-aggregate planes and non-percipience plane) ....
(b) Indeterminate *dhammā* will arise in this person. Had wholesome *dhammā* arisen in that person? —Yes. (Same as the aforesaid)

90. *i* (a) Unwholesome *dhammā* had arisen in this person. Will indeterminate *dhammā* arise in that person?
—No. To those endowed with the final-stage state of consciousness ....
—Yes. To others (at the four- and five-aggregate planes) ....
(b) Indeterminate *dhammā* will arise in this person. Had wholesome *dhammā* arisen in that person? —Yes. (Same as the aforesaid)

Forward enquiries by Plane

91. *i* (a) Wholesome *dhammā* had arisen at this plane. Will unwholesome arise at that plane? .....p.....

Forward enquiries by Individual and Plane

92. *i* (a) Wholesome *dhammā* had arisen in this person at this plane. Will unwholesome *dhammā* arise in that person at that plane?
—No. To those endowed with the highest Path, to *Arahat*, and to those right after this state of consciousness who will directly attain the highest Path ....
—Yes. To others at the four- and five-aggregate planes ....
(b) Unwholesome *dhammā* will arise in this person at this plane. Had wholesome *dhammā* arisen in that person at that plane?
—No. To those at the occurrence of second *citta* of the pure abode beings....
—Yes. (Same as the aforesaid)

ii (a) Wholesome *dhammā* had arisen in this person at this plane. Will indeterminate *dhammā* arise in that person at that plane?
—No. To those endowed with the final-stage state of consciousness ....
—Yes. To others at the four- and five-aggregate planes ....

(b) Indeterminate *dhammā* will arise in this person at this plane. Had wholesome *dhammā* arisen in that person at that plane?
—No. To those at the occurrence of second *citta* of the pure abode beings, and individuals at non-percipience plane ....
—Yes. (Same as the aforesaid)

93. *i* (a) Unwholesome *dhammā* had arisen in this person at this plane. Will indeterminate *dhammā* arise in that person at that plane?
—No. To those endowed with the final-stage state of consciousness ....
—Yes. To others at the four- and five-aggregate planes ....
(b) Indeterminate *dhammā* will arise in this person at this plane. Had unwholesome *dhammā* arisen in that person at that plane?
—No. To those at the occurrence of second *citta* of the pure abode beings, and individuals at non-percipience plane ....
—Yes. (Same as the aforesaid)

Opposite enquiries by Individual

94. *i* (a) Wholesome *dhammā* had not arisen in this person. Will unwholesome *dhammā* not arise in that person? —No such person.
(b) Unwholesome *dhammā* will not arise in this person. Had wholesome *dhammā* not arisen in that person?
—No. Wholesome *dhammā* in whom had arisen (those right after this state of consciousness who will directly attain the highest Path; those endowed with the highest Path; and *Arahat*).

ii (a) Wholesome *dhammā* had not arisen in this person. Will indeterminate *dhammā* not arise in that person? —No such person.
(b) Indeterminate *dhammā* will not arise in this person. Had wholesome *dhammā* not arisen in that person?
—No. Wholesome *dhammā* in whom had arisen (those endowed with the final-state of consciousness).

95. *i* (a) Unwholesome *dhammā* had not arisen in this person. Will indeterminate *dhammā* not arise in that person? —No such person.
(b) Indeterminate *dhammā* will not arise in this person. Had unwholesome *dhammā* not arisen in that person?
—No. Unwholesome *dhammā* in whom had arisen (those endowed with the final-stage state of consciousness).

Opposite enquiries by Plane

96. *i* (a) Wholesome *dhammā* had not arisen at this plane. Will unwholesome *dhammā* not arise at that plane? .....p.....

Opposite enquiries by Individual and Plane

97. *i* (a) Wholesome *dhammā* had not arisen in this person at this plane. Will unwholesome *dhammā* not arise in that person at that plane?
—No. To those at the occurrence of second unwholesome consciousness of the pure abodes ....
—Yes. To individuals at non-percipience plane ....
(b) Unwholesome *dhammā* will not arise in this person at this plane. Had wholesome *dhammā* not arisen in that person at that plane?
—No. To those endowed with the highest Path, to *Arahat*, and to those right after this state of consciousness who will directly attain the highest Path ....
—Yes. (Same as the aforesaid)

ii (a) Wholesome *dhammā* had not arisen in this person at this plane. Will indeterminate *dhammā* not arise in that person at that plane?
—No. Indeterminate *dhammā* in whom will arise (those at the occurrence of second *citta* of the pure abode beings, and individuals at non-percipience plane).
(b) Indeterminate *dhammā* will not arise in this person at this plane. Had wholesome *dhammā* not arisen in that person at that plane?
—No. Wholesome *dhammā* in whom had arisen (those with the final-stage state of consciousness).

98. *i* (a) Unwholesome *dhammā* had not arisen in this person at this plane. Will indeterminate *dhammā* not arise in that person at that plane?
—No. Indeterminate *dhammā* in whom will arise (those at the occurrence of second *citta* of the pure abode beings, and individuals at non-percipience plane).
(b) Indeterminate *dhammā* will not arise in this person at this plane. Had unwholesome *dhammā* not arisen in that person at that plane?
—No. Unwholesome *dhammā* in whom had arisen (those endowed with the final-stage state of consciousness).

With reference to Chart 9.10 below, the denotation letters in *italic* are the answers consolidated from the respective first three sub-sections on present, past, and future origination of *dhammā*. Those boldfaced and at the same time italicised letters are the answers to be referred to the other sub-sections of present with past, present with future, past with future origination. You will notice from the chart there is quite a few of the cause-conditions the sub-section of origination has not enquired and examined. Some of them are simply because of their inapplicable situation.

Consolidated answers on origination of *dhammā*

Chart 9.10 Consolidated answers (origination of *dhammā*)

A: arise/ had arisen/ will arise; N: does not arise/ had not arisen/ will not arise

	Present			Past			Future		
	wholesome *dhammā*	unwholesome *dhammā*	indeterminate *dhammā*	wholesome *dhammā*	unwholesome *dhammā*	indeterminate *dhammā*	wholesome *dhammā*	unwholesome *dhammā*	indeterminate *dhammā*
To those at the arising moment of :									
citta dissociated from goodness	N		A		A	A		A	A
citta dissociated from badness		N	A			A			A
citta dissociated from goodness and badness	N	N							
the highest (*Arahatta*) Path-*citta*	A							N	
the final-stage *citta*									
good state	A	N			A	A		A	A
good state at five-aggregate plane	A		A						
good state at immaterial plane	A	N	N						
bad state	N	A				A			A
bad state at Immaterial plane	N	A	N						
bad state at five-aggregate plane		A	A						
To those at the ceasing moment of :									
citta (state of consciousness)	N	N	N		A	A		A	A
the highest (*Arahatta*) Path-*citta*	N							N	
To those :									
all beings at the birth-moment	N	N	A						
all beings at the death-moment	N	N	N						
engaged in Cessation-attainment	N	N			A	A		A	A
at the birth-moment at pure abodes	N	N		N	N	N			
at the occurrence of second *citta* of the pure abode beings	N			N	N	A		A	A
at occurrence of second unwholesome *citta* of pure abode beings				N	A				
at immaterial plane (four-aggregate)				A	A	A			
at the non-percipience plane	N	N		N	AN	A	N	AN	A
at the four- and five-aggregate planes				A	A	A	A	A	A
Arahat	N			A			N	N	A
endowed with the highest (*Arahatta*) Path				A			N	N	A
right after this *citta* who will directly attain the highest Path	A			A			A	N	A
right after this *citta* who will directly attain the highest (*Arahatta*) Path at the arising moment of that (*Arahatta* Path) *citta*	A							N	
right after this *citta* who will directly attain the highest (*Arahatta*) Path at the ceasing moment of that (*Arahatta* Path) *citta*	N							N	
endowed with the final-stage *citta*	N	N		A	A		N	N	N
At the plane(s) of :									
non-percipience	N	N	A	N	N	A	N	N	A
five-aggregates	A	A	A	A	A	A	A	A	A
immateriality (or four-aggregates)	A	A	A	A	A	A	A	A	A

9.2.2 Cessation of *dhammā* (with charts)

Chart 9.11 Enquiry sequence on cessation of *dhammā*

		(With respect to each following *dhammā* type)								
		Do they cease / Do they not cease : i) in that person? ii) at that plane? iii) in that person at that plane?			Had they ceased / Had they not ceased: i) in that person? ii) at that plane? iii) in that person at that plane?			Will they cease / Will they not cease : i) in that person? ii) at that plane? iii) in that person at that plane?		
		Wholesome *dhammā*	Unwholesome *dhammā*	Indeterminate *dhammā*	Wholesome *dhammā*	Unwholesome *dhammā*	Indeterminate *dhammā*	Wholesome *dhammā*	Unwholesome *dhammā*	Indeterminate *dhammā*
Wholesome *dhammā*	cease / do not cease: i) in this person. ii) at this plane. iii) in this person at this plane.		1a	2a		10a	11a		13a	14a
Unwholesome *dhammā*		1b		3a			12a			15a
Indeterminate *dhammā*		2bi	3b							
Wholesome *dhammā*	had ceased/ had not ceased i) in this person. ii) at this plane. iii) in this person at this plane.					4a	5a		16a	17a
Unwholesome *dhammā*		10b			4b		6a			18a
Indeterminate *dhammā*		11b	12b		5b	6bi				
Wholesome *dhammā*	will cease / will not cease: i) in this person. ii) at this plane. iii) in this person at this plane.								7a	8a
Unwholesome *dhammā*		13b			16b			7bi		9a
Indeterminate *dhammā*		14b	15b		17b	18b		8b	9b	

The above chart summarises the sequence of paired enquiries from nos. 99 to 162. The iteration loops through three differentiations (by persons, by planes, by persons at planes) using the regular and reverse mode of enquiring. The same sequence reiterates through six time-scaled classifications (present, past, future, present-past, present-future, and past-future), represent by the enneahedral boxes as shown in the chart.

Chart 9.12 Cessation of *dhammā* (by present, past, and future)

C: cease / had ceased / will cease; N: do not cease / had not ceased / will not cease

	Present			Past			Future		
	wholesome *dhammā*	unwholesome *dhammā*	indeterminate *dhammā*	wholesome *dhammā*	unwholesome *dhammā*	indeterminate *dhammā*	wholesome *dhammā*	unwholesome *dhammā*	indeterminate *dhammā*
To those at the ceasing moment of :									
consciousness dissociated from goodness	N		C						
consciousness dissociated from badness		N	C						
consciousness dissociated from goodness and badness	N	N							
the highest (*Arahatta*) Path-*citta*							N	N	C
the final-stage *citta*									
good state	C	N							
good state at five-aggregate plane	C		C						
good state at immaterial plane	C	N	N						
bad state	N	C							
bad state at Immaterial plane	N	C	N						
bad state at five-aggregate plane		C	C						
To those at the arising moment of :									
citta (state of consciousness)	N	N	N						
the highest (*Arahatta*) Path-*citta*							C	N	
To those :									
all beings at the birth-moment	N	N	N						
all beings at the death-moment	N	N	C						
engaged in Cessation-attainment	N	N							
at the birth-moment at pure abodes				N	N	N			
at the occurrence of second *citta* of the pure abode beings				N	N	C			
at occurrence of second unwholesome *citta* of pure abode beings				N	C				
at immaterial plane (four-aggregate)				C	C	C			
at the non-percipience plane	N	N		N	N	C	N	N	C
at the four- and five-aggregate planes				C	C	C	C	C	C
Arahat							N	N	C
endowed with the highest (*Arahatta*) Path							N	N	C
right after this *citta* who will directly attain the highest Path							C	N	C
endowed with the final-stage *citta*							N	N	N
At the plane(s) of :									
non-percipience	N	N	C	N	N	C	N	N	C
five-aggregates	C	C	C	C	C	C	C	C	C
immateriality (or four-aggregates)	C	C	C	C	C	C	C	C	C

At Present

Forward enquiries by Individual

99. *i* (a) Wholesome *dhammā* cease in this person. Do unwholesome *dhammā* cease in that person?
—No. (Those at the ceasing moment of good state …)
(b) Unwholesome *dhammā* cease in this person. Do wholesome *dhammā* cease in that person?
—No. (Same as the aforesaid)

ii (a) Wholesome *dhammā* cease in this person. Do indeterminate *dhammā* cease in that person?
—No. To those at the ceasing moment of good state at immaterial plane ....
—Yes. To those at the ceasing moment of good state at five-aggregate plane ...
(b) Indeterminate *dhammā* cease in this person. Do wholesome *dhammā* cease in that person?
—No. To all those at death-moment, and at the ceasing moment of *citta* dissociated from goodness ....
—Yes. (Same as the aforesaid)

100. *i* (a) Unwholesome *dhammā* cease in this person. Do indeterminate *dhammā* cease in that person?
—No. To those at the ceasing moment of bad state at immaterial plane ....
—Yes. To those at the ceasing moment of bad state at five-aggregate plane ....
(b) Indeterminate *dhammā* cease in this person. Do unwholesome *dhammā* cease in that person?
—No. To all those at death-moment, and those at the ceasing moment of *citta* dissociated from badness ....
—Yes. (Same as the aforesaid)

Forward enquiries by Plane

101. *i* (a) Wholesome *dhammā* cease at this plane. Do unwholesome *dhammā* cease at that plane?
—Yes. (at the four- and five-aggregate planes)
(b) Unwholesome *dhammā* cease at this plane. Do wholesome *dhammā* cease at that plane? —Yes. (Same as the aforesaid)

ii (a) Wholesome *dhammā* cease at this plane. Do indeterminate *dhammā* cease at that plane? —Yes. (Same as below)
(b) Indeterminate *dhammā* cease at this plane. Do wholesome *dhammā* cease at that plane?
—No. At the plane of non-percipience ....
—Yes. At the planes of four- and five-aggregates ...

102. *i* (a) Unwholesome *dhammā* cease at this plane. Do indeterminate *dhammā* cease at that plane? —Yes. (Same as below)
(b) Indeterminate *dhammā* cease at this plane. Do unwholesome *dhammā* cease at that plane?
—No. At the plane of non-percipience ....
—Yes. At the planes of four- and five-aggregates ....

Forward enquiries by Individual and Plane

103. *i* (a) Wholesome *dhammā* cease in this person at this plane. Do unwholesome *dhammā* cease in that person at that plane?
—No. (those at the ceasing moment of good state)
(b) Unwholesome *dhammā* cease in this person at this plane. Do wholesome *dhammā* cease in that person at that plane?
—No. (Same as the aforesaid)

ii (a) Wholesome *dhammā* cease in this person at that plane. Do indeterminate *dhammā* cease in that person at that plane?
—No. To those at the ceasing moment of good state at Immaterial plane ....
—Yes. To those at the ceasing moment of good state at five-aggregate plane ...
(b) Indeterminate *dhammā* cease in this person at this plane. Do wholesome *dhammā* cease in that person at that plane?
—No. To all those at death-moment, and those at the ceasing moment of *citta* dissociated from goodness ....
—Yes. (Same as the aforesaid)

104. *i* (a) Unwholesome *dhammā* cease in this person at that plane. Do indeterminate *dhammā* cease in that person at that plane?
—No. To those at the ceasing moment of bad state at immaterial plane ....
—Yes. To those at the ceasing moment of bad state at five-aggregate plane ....
(b) Indeterminate *dhammā* cease in this person at this plane. Do unwholesome *dhammā* cease in that person at that plane?
—No. To all those at death-moment, and those at the ceasing moment of *citta* dissociated from badness ....
—Yes. (Same as the aforesaid)

Opposite enquiries by Individual

105. *i* (a) Wholesome *dhammā* do not cease in this person. Do unwholesome *dhammā* not cease in that person?
—No. To those at the ceasing moment of bad state ....
—Yes. To all those at the arising moment of *citta*, those at the ceasing moment of *citta* dissociated from both goodness and badness, those engaged in Cessation-attainment, and individuals of non-percipience ....
(b) Unwholesome *dhammā* do not cease in this person. Do wholesome *dhammā* not cease in that person?
—No. To those at the ceasing moment of good state....

—Yes. (Same as the aforesaid)

ii (a) Wholesome *dhammā* do not cease in this person. Do indeterminate *dhammā* not cease in that person?
—No. To all those at death-moment, and those at the ceasing moment of *citta* dissociated from goodness ....
—Yes. To all those at birth-moment, those at the arising moment of *citta*, and those at the ceasing moment of bad state at immaterial plane ....
(b) Indeterminate *dhammā* do not cease in this person. Do wholesome *dhammā* not cease in that person?
—No. At the ceasing moment of good state at immaterial plane ....
—Yes. (Same as the aforesaid)

106. *i* (a) Unwholesome *dhammā* do not cease in this person. Do indeterminate *dhammā* not cease in that person?
—No. To all those at death-moment, and those at the ceasing moment of *citta* dissociated from badness ....
—Yes. To all those at birth-moment, those at the arising moment of *citta*, and at the ceasing moment of good state at immaterial plane ....
(b) Indeterminate *dhammā* do not cease in this person. Do unwholesome *dhammā* not cease in that person?
—No. At the ceasing moment of bad state at immaterial plane ....
—Yes. (Same as the aforesaid)

Opposite enquiries by Plane

107. *i* (a) Wholesome *dhammā* do not cease at this plane. Do unwholesome *dhammā* not cease at that plane?
—Yes. (at the non-percipience plane)
(b) Unwholesome *dhammā* do not cease at this plane. Do wholesome *dhammā* not cease at that plane?
—Yes. (Same as the aforesaid)

ii (a) Wholesome *dhammā* do not cease at this plane. Do indeterminate *dhammā* not cease at that plane?
—No. Indeterminate *dhammā* cease. (at the non-percipience plane)
(b) Indeterminate *dhammā* do not cease at this plane. Do wholesome *dhammā* not cease at that plane? —No such person.

108. *i* (a) Unwholesome *dhammā* do not cease at this plane. Do indeterminate *dhammā* not cease at that plane?
—No. Indeterminate *dhammā* cease. (at the non-percipience plane)
(b) Indeterminate *dhammā* do not cease at this plane. Do unwholesome *dhammā* not cease at that plane?
—No such person.

Opposite enquiries by Individual and Plane

109. *i* (a) Wholesome *dhammā* do not cease in this person at this plane. Do unwholesome *dhammā* not cease in that person at that plane?
—No. To those at the ceasing moment of bad state ....
—Yes. To all those at the arising moment of *citta*, those at the ceasing moment of *citta* dissociated from both goodness and badness, and those individuals at non-percipience plane ....
(b) Unwholesome *dhammā* do not cease in this person at this plane. Do wholesome *dhammā* not cease in that person at that plane?
—No. To those at the ceasing moment of good state....
—Yes. (Same as the aforesaid)

ii (a) Wholesome *dhammā* do not cease in this person at this plane. Do indeterminate *dhammā* not cease in that person at that plane?
—No. To all those at death-moment, and those at the ceasing moment of *citta* dissociated from goodness ....
—Yes. To all those at birth-moment, those at the arising moment of *citta*, and those at the ceasing moment of bad state at immaterial plane ....
(b) Indeterminate *dhammā* do not cease in this person at this plane. Do wholesome *dhammā* not cease in that person at that plane?
—No. To those at the ceasing moment of good state at immaterial plane ....
—Yes. (Same as the aforesaid)

110. *i* (a) Unwholesome *dhammā* do not cease in this person at this plane. Do indeterminate *dhammā* not cease in that person at that plane?
—No. To all those at death-moment, and those at the ceasing moment of *citta* dissociated from badness ....
—Yes. To all those at birth-moment, those at the arising moment of *citta*, and at the ceasing moment of good state at immaterial plane ....
(b) Indeterminate *dhammā* do not cease in this person at this plane. Do unwholesome *dhammā* not cease in that person at that plane?
—No. To those at the ceasing moment of bad state at immaterial plane ....
—Yes. (Same as the aforesaid)

In the Past

Forward enquiries by Individual

111. *i* (a) Wholesome *dhammā* had ceased in this person. Had unwholesome *dhammā* ceased in that person?
—Yes. (those at the four- and five-aggregate planes)
(b) Unwholesome *dhammā* had ceased in this person. Had wholesome *dhammā* ceased in that person? —Yes. (Same as the aforesaid)

ii (a) Wholesome *dhammā* had ceased in this person. Had indeterminate *dhammā* ceased in that person? —Yes. (those at the four- and five-aggregate planes)

(b) Indeterminate *dhammā* had ceased in this person. Had wholesome *dhammā* ceased in that person? —Yes. (Same as the aforesaid)

112. *i* (a) Unwholesome *dhammā* had ceased in this person. Had indeterminate *dhammā* ceased in that person?
—Yes. (those at the four- and five-aggregate planes).
(b) Indeterminate *dhammā* had ceased in this person. Had unwholesome *dhammā* ceased in that person? —Yes. (Same as the aforesaid)

Forward enquiries by Plane

113. *i* (a) Wholesome *dhammā* had ceased at this plane. Had unwholesome *dhammā* ceased at that plane? —Yes. (at the four- and five-aggregate planes)
(b) Unwholesome *dhammā* had ceased at this plane. Had wholesome *dhammā* ceased at that plane? —Yes. (Same as the aforesaid)

ii (a) Wholesome *dhammā* had ceased at this plane. Had indeterminate *dhammā* ceased at that plane? —Yes. (at the four- and five-aggregate planes)
(b) Indeterminate *dhammā* had ceased at this plane. Had wholesome *dhammā* ceased at that plane?
—No. At the plane of non-percipience ....
—Yes. At the planes of four- and five-aggregates ...

114. *i* (a) Unwholesome *dhammā* had ceased at this plane. Had indeterminate *dhammā* ceased at that plane? —Yes. (Same as below)
(b) Indeterminate *dhammā* had ceased at this plane. Had unwholesome *dhammā* ceased at that plane?
—No. At the plane of non-percipience ....
—Yes. At the planes of four- and five-aggregates ....

Forward enquiries by Individual and Plane

115. *i* (a) Wholesome *dhammā* had ceased in this person at this plane. Had unwholesome *dhammā* ceased in that person at that plane?—Yes (Same as below)
(b) Unwholesome *dhammā* had ceased in this person at this plane. Had wholesome *dhammā* ceased in that person at that plane?
—No. To those at the occurrence of second unwholesome consciousness of the pure abodes ....
—Yes. To others at the four- and five-aggregate planes ....

ii (a) Wholesome *dhammā* had ceased in this person at this plane. Had indeterminate *dhammā* ceased in that person at that plane?
—Yes. (Same as below)
(b) Indeterminate *dhammā* had ceased in this person at this plane. Had wholesome *dhammā* ceased in that person at that plane?
—No. To those at the occurrence of second *citta* of the pure abode beings, and individuals at non-percipience plane ....

—Yes. To others at the four- and five-aggregate planes ....

116. *i* (a) Unwholesome *dhammā* had ceased in this person at this plane. Had indeterminate *dhammā* ceased in that person at that plane?
—Yes. (Same as below)
(b) Indeterminate *dhammā* had ceased in this person at this plane. Had unwholesome *dhammā* ceased in that person at that plane?
—No. To those at the occurrence of second *citta* of the pure abode beings, and individuals at non-percipience plane ....
—Yes. To others at the four- and five-aggregate planes ....

Opposite enquiries by Individual

117. *i* (a) Wholesome *dhammā* had not ceased in this person. Had unwholesome *dhammā* not ceased in that person?
—Natthi. (those at the birth-moment at pure abodes, and those at the occurrence of second *citta* of the pure abode beings)
(b) Unwholesome *dhammā* had not ceased in this person. Had wholesome *dhammā* not ceased in that person?
—Natthi. (See above)

ii (a) Wholesome *dhammā* had not ceased in this person. Had indeterminate *dhammā* not ceased in that person?
—Natthi. (those at the birth-moment at pure abodes)
(b) Indeterminate *dhammā* had not ceased in this person. Had wholesome *dhammā* not ceased in that person?
—Natthi. (See above)

118. *i* (a) Unwholesome *dhammā* had not ceased in this person. Had indeterminate *dhammā* not ceased in that person?
—Natthi. (those at the birth-moment at pure abodes)
(b) Indeterminate *dhammā* had not ceased in this person. Had unwholesome *dhammā* not ceased in that person?
—Natthi. (See above)

Opposite enquiries by Plane

119. *i* (a) Wholesome *dhammā* had not ceased at this plane. Had unwholesome *dhammā* not ceased at that plane? —Yes. (at the non-percipience plane)
(b) Unwholesome *dhammā* had not ceased at this plane. Had wholesome *dhammā* not ceased at that plane? —Yes. (Same as the aforesaid)

ii (a) Wholesome *dhammā* had not ceased at this plane. Had indeterminate *dhammā* not ceased at that plane?
—No. Indeterminate *dhammā* had ceased. (at the non-percipience plane)
(b) Indeterminate *dhammā* had not ceased at this plane. Had wholesome *dhammā* not ceased at that plane? —No such plane.

120. *i* (a) Unwholesome *dhammā* had not ceased at this plane. Had indeterminate *dhammā* not ceased at that plane?
—No. Indeterminate *dhammā* had ceased. (at the non-percipience plane)
(b) Indeterminate *dhammā* had not ceased at this plane. Had unwholesome *dhammā* not ceased at that plane? —No such plane.

Opposite enquiries by Individual and Plane

121. *i* (a) Wholesome *dhammā* had not ceased in this person at this plane. Had unwholesome *dhammā* not ceased in that person at that plane?
—No. To those at the occurrence of second unwholesome consciousness of the pure abodes ....
—Yes. To those at the occurrence of second *citta* of the pure abode beings, and individuals at non-percipience plane ....
(b) Unwholesome *dhammā* had not ceased in this person at this plane. Had wholesome *dhammā* not ceased in that person at that plane?
—Yes. (Same as the aforesaid)

ii (a) Wholesome *dhammā* had not ceased in this person at this plane. Had indeterminate *dhammā* not ceased in that person at that plane?
—No. To those at the occurrence of second *citta* of the pure abode beings, and individuals at non-percipience plane ....
—Yes. To those at the birth-moment at pure abodes ....
(b) Indeterminate *dhammā* had not ceased in this person at this plane. Had wholesome *dhammā* not ceased in that person at that plane?
—Yes. (Same as the aforesaid)

122. *i* (a) Unwholesome *dhammā* had not ceased in this person at this plane. Had indeterminate *dhammā* not ceased in that person at that plane?
—No. To those at the occurrence of second *citta* of the pure abode beings, and individuals at non-percipience plane ....
—Yes. To those at the birth-moment at pure abodes ....
(b) Indeterminate *dhammā* had not ceased in this person at this plane. Had unwholesome *dhammā* not ceased in that person at that plane?
—Yes. (Same as the aforesaid)

In Future

Forward enquiries by Individual

123. *i* (a) Wholesome *dhammā* will cease in this person. Will unwholesome *dhammā* cease in that person?
—No. To those at the arising moment of the highest Path-*citta*, and to those right after this state of consciousness who will directly attain the highest Path ....
—Yes. To others (at the four- and five-aggregate planes) ….
(b) Unwholesome *dhammā* will cease in this person. Will indeterminate *dhammā* cease in that person? —Yes. (Same as the aforesaid)

ii (a) Wholesome *dhammā* will cease in this person. Will indeterminate *dhammā* cease in that person? —Yes. (Same as below)
(b) Indeterminate *dhammā* will cease in this person. Will wholesome *dhammā* cease in that person?
—No. To those at the ceasing moment of the highest Path-*citta*, and to *Arahat* ....
—Yes. To others (at the four- and five-aggregate planes, and those right after this state of consciousness who will directly attain the highest Path) ….

124. *i* (a) Unwholesome *dhammā* will cease in this person. Will indeterminate *dhammā* cease in that person? —Yes. (Same as below)
(b) Indeterminate *dhammā* will cease in this person. Will unwholesome *dhammā* cease in that person?
—No. To those endowed with the highest Path, to *Arahat*, and to those right after this state of consciousness who will directly attain the highest Path ...
—Yes. To others (at the four- and five-aggregate planes) ….

Forward enquiries by Plane

125. *i* (a) Wholesome *dhammā* will cease at this plane. Will unwholesome *dhammā* cease at that plane? .....p.....

Forward enquiries by Individual and Plane

126. *i* (a) Wholesome *dhammā* will cease in this person at this plane. Will unwholesome *dhammā* cease in that person at this plane?
—No. To those at the arising moment of the highest Path-*citta*, and to those right after this state of consciousness who will directly attain the highest Path ....
—Yes. To others at the four- and five-aggregate planes ....
Unwholesome *dhammā* will cease in this person at this plane. Will indeterminate *dhammā* cease in that person at that plane? —Yes. (Same as the aforesaid)

ii (a) Wholesome *dhammā* will cease in this person at this plane. Will indeterminate *dhammā* cease in that person at that plane?
—Yes. (Same as below)
(b) Indeterminate *dhammā* will cease in this person at this plane. Will wholesome *dhammā* cease in that person at that plane?
—No. To those at the ceasing moment of the highest Path-*citta*, to *Arahat*, and to individuals at non-percipience plane ....
—Yes. To others at the four- and five-aggregate planes ....

127. *i* (a) Unwholesome *dhammā* will cease in this person at this plane. Will indeterminate *dhammā* cease in that person at that plane?
—Yes. (Same as below)
(b) Indeterminate *dhammā* will cease in this person at this plane. Will unwholesome *dhammā* cease in that person at that plane?

—No. To those endowed with the highest Path, to *Arahat*, to those right after this state of consciousness who will directly attain the highest Path, and individuals at non-percipience plane ....
—Yes. To others at the four- and five-aggregate planes ....

Opposite enquiries by Individual

128. *i* (a) Wholesome *dhammā* will not cease in this person. Will unwholesome *dhammā* not cease in that person? —Yes. (Same as below)
(b) Unwholesome *dhammā* will not cease in this person. Will wholesome *dhammā* not cease in that person?
—No. To those at the arising moment of the highest Path-*citta*, and to those right after this state of consciousness who will directly attain the highest Path ....
—Yes. To those at the ceasing moment of the highest Path-*citta*, and to *Arahat* ....

ii (a) Wholesome *dhammā* will not cease in this person. Will indeterminate *dhammā* not cease in that person?
—No. To those at the ceasing moment of the highest Path-*citta*, and to *Arahat* ....
—Yes. To those endowed with the final-stage state of consciousness ....
(b) Indeterminate *dhammā* will not cease in this person. Will wholesome *dhammā* not cease in that person?
—Yes. (Same as the aforesaid)

129. *i* (a) Unwholesome *dhammā* will not cease in this person. Will indeterminate *dhammā* not cease in that person?
—No. To those endowed with the highest Path, to *Arahat*, and those right after this state of consciousness who will directly attain the highest Path ....
—Yes. To those endowed with the final-stage state of consciousness ....
(b) Indeterminate *dhammā* will not cease in this person. Will unwholesome *dhammā* not cease at that person?
—Yes. (Same as the aforesaid)

Opposite enquiries by Plane

130. *i* (a) Wholesome *dhammā* will not cease at this plane. Will unwholesome *dhammā* not cease at that plane? .....p.....

Opposite enquiries by Individual and Plane

131. *i* (a) Wholesome *dhammā* will not cease in this person at this plane. Will unwholesome *dhammā* not cease in that person at that plane?
—Yes. (Same as below)
(b) Unwholesome *dhammā* will not cease in this person at this plane. Will wholesome *dhammā* not cease in that person at that plane?
—No. To those at the arising moment of the highest Path-*citta*, and those right after this state of consciousness who will directly attain the highest Path ....
—Yes. To those at the ceasing moment of the highest Path-*citta*, to *Arahat*, and to individuals at non-percipience plane ....

ii (a) Wholesome *dhammā* will not cease in this person at this plane. Will indeterminate *dhammā* not cease in that person at that plane?
—No. To those at the ceasing moment of the highest Path-*citta*, to *Arahat*, and individuals at non-percipience plane ....
—Yes. To those endowed with the final-stage state of consciousness ....
(b) Indeterminate *dhammā* will not cease in this person at this plane. Will wholesome *dhammā* not cease in that person at that plane?
—Yes. (Same as the aforesaid)

132. *i* (a) Unwholesome *dhammā* will not cease in this person at this plane. Will indeterminate *dhammā* not cease in that person at that plane?
—No. To those endowed with the highest Path, to *Arahat*, to those right after this state of consciousness who will directly attain the highest Path at the arising moment of that (*Arahatta* Path) *citta*, and to individuals at non-percipience plane ....
—Yes. To those endowed with the final-stage state of consciousness ....
Indeterminate *dhammā* will not cease in this person at this plane. Will unwholesome *dhammā* not cease in that person at that plane?
—Yes. (Same as the aforesaid)

Chart 9.13 Cessation of *dhammā* (by present and past)

C: cease / had ceased; N: do not cease / had not ceased

	Present			Past		
	wholesome *dhammā*	unwholesome *dhammā*	indeterminate *dhammā*	wholesome *dhammā*	unwholesome *dhammā*	indeterminate *dhammā*
To those at the ceasing moment of :						
consciousness dissociated from goodness	N				C	C
consciousness dissociated from badness		N				C
consciousness dissociated from goodness and badness						
the highest (*Arahatta*) Path-*citta*						
the final-stage *citta*						
good state	C				C	C
good state at five-aggregate plane						
good state at immaterial plane						
bad state		C				C
bad state at Immaterial plane						
bad state at five-aggregate plane						
To those at the arising moment of :						
citta (state of consciousness)	N	N			C	C
the highest (*Arahatta*) Path-*citta*						
To those :						
all beings at the birth-moment						
all beings at the death-moment						
engaged in Cessation-attainment	N	N			C	C
at the birth-moment at pure abodes	N	N				N
at the occurrence of second *citta* of the pure abode beings	N				N	
at occurrence of second unwholesome *citta* of pure abode beings						
at immaterial plane (four-aggregate)						
at the non-percipience plane	N	N			CN	C
at the four- and five-aggregate planes						
Arahat						
endowed with the highest (*Arahatta*) Path						
right after this *citta* who will directly attain the highest (*Arahatta*) Path						
endowed with the final-stage *citta*						
At the plane(s) of :						
non-percipience	N	N	C	N	N	C
five-aggregates	C	C	C	C	C	C
immateriality (or four-aggregates)	C	C	C	C	C	C

Present and Past

Forward enquiries by Individual

133. *i* (a) Wholesome *dhammā* cease in this person. Had unwholesome *dhammā* ceased in that person? —Yes. (Same as below)
(b) Unwholesome *dhammā* had ceased in this person. Do wholesome *dhammā* cease in that person?
—No. To all those at the arising moment of *citta*, at the ceasing moment of *citta* dissociated from goodness, those engaged in Cessation-attainment, and individuals of non-percipience ....
—Yes. To those at the ceasing moment of good state ....

ii (a) Wholesome *dhammā* cease in this person. Had indeterminate *dhammā* ceased in that person? —Yes. (Same as below)
(b) Indeterminate *dhammā* had ceased in this person. Do wholesome *dhammā* cease in that person?
—No. To all those at the arising moment of *citta*, at the ceasing moment of *citta* dissociated from goodness, those engaged in Cessation-attainment, and individuals of non-percipience ....
—Yes. To those at the ceasing moment of good state ....

134. *i* (a) Unwholesome *dhammā* cease in this person. Had indeterminate *dhammā* ceased in that person? —Yes. (Same as below)
(b) Indeterminate *dhammā* had ceased in this person. Do unwholesome *dhammā* cease in that person?
—No. To all those at the arising moment of *citta*, at the ceasing moment of *citta* dissociated from badness, those engaged in Cessation-attainment, and individuals of non-percipience ....
—Yes. To those at the ceasing moment of bad state ....

Forward enquiries by Plane

135. *i* (a) Wholesome *dhammā* cease at this plane. Had unwholesome *dhammā* ceased at that plane? .....p.....

Forward enquiries by Individual and Plane

136. *i* (a) Wholesome *dhammā* cease in this person at this plane. Had unwholesome *dhammā* ceased in that person at that plane?
—Yes. (Same as below)
(b) Unwholesome *dhammā* had ceased in this person at this plane. Do wholesome *dhammā* cease in that person at that plane?
—No. To all those at the arising moment of *citta*, and those at the ceasing moment of *citta* dissociated from goodness ....
—Yes. To those at the ceasing moment of good state ....

ii (a) Wholesome *dhammā* cease in this person at this plane. Had indeterminate *dhammā* ceased in that person at that plane?
—Yes. (Same as below)
(b) Indeterminate *dhammā* had ceased in this person at this plane. Do wholesome *dhammā* cease in that person at that plane?
—No. To all those at the arising moment of *citta*, at the ceasing moment of *citta* dissociated from goodness, and individuals at non-percipience plane ....
—Yes. To those at the ceasing moment of good state ....

137. *i* (a) Unwholesome *dhammā* cease in this person at this plane. Had indeterminate *dhammā* ceased in that person at that plane?
—Yes. (Same as below)
(b) Indeterminate *dhammā* had ceased in this person at this plane. Do unwholesome *dhammā* cease in that person at that plane?
—No. To all those at the arising moment of *citta*, at the ceasing moment of *citta* dissociated from badness, and individuals at non-percipience plane ....
—Yes. To those at the ceasing moment of bad state ....

Opposite enquiries by Individual

138. *i* (a) Wholesome *dhammā* do not cease in this person. Had unwholesome *dhammā* not ceased in that person?
—No. Unwholesome *dhammā* had ceased. (all those at the arising moment of *citta*, those at the ceasing moment of *citta* dissociated from goodness, those engaged in Cessation-attainment, and individuals of non-percipience)
(b) Unwholesome *dhammā* had not ceased in this person. Do wholesome *dhammā* not cease in that person?
—(To those at the occurrence of second *citta* of pure abodes … wholesome *dhammā* in whom do not cease)

ii (a) Wholesome *dhammā* do not cease in this person. Had indeterminate *dhammā* not ceased in that person?
—No. Indeterminate *dhammā* had ceased. (all those at the arising moment of *citta*, those at the ceasing moment of *citta* dissociated from goodness, those engaged in Cessation-attainment, and individuals of non-percipience)
(b) Indeterminate *dhammā* had not ceased in this person. Do wholesome *dhammā* not cease in that person?
—(To those at the birth-moment at pure abodes …. wholesome *dhammā* in whom do not cease)

139. *i* (a) Unwholesome *dhammā* do not cease in this person. Had indeterminate *dhammā* not ceased in that person?
—No. Indeterminate *dhammā* had ceased (all those at the arising moment of *citta*, those at the ceasing moment of *citta* dissociated from badness, those engaged in Cessation-attainment, and individuals of non-percipience)

(b) Indeterminate *dhammā* had not ceased in this person. Do unwholesome *dhammā* not cease in that person?
—(To those at the birth-moment at pure abodes .... unwholesome *dhammā* in whom do not cease)

Opposite enquiries by Plane

140. *i* (a) Wholesome *dhammā* do not cease at this plane. Had unwholesome *dhammā* not ceased at that plane? .....p.....

Opposite enquiries by Individual and Plane

141. *i* (a) Wholesome *dhammā* do not cease in this person at this plane. Had unwholesome *dhammā* not ceased in that person at that plane?
—No. To all those at the arising moment of *citta*, and those at the ceasing moment of *citta* dissociated from goodness ....
—Yes. To those at the occurrence of second *citta* of the pure abodes, and individuals at non-percipience plane ....
(b) Unwholesome *dhammā* had not ceased in this person at this plane. Do wholesome *dhammā* not cease in that person at that plane?
—Yes. (Same as the aforesaid)

ii (a) Wholesome *dhammā* do not cease in this person at this plane. Had indeterminate *dhammā* not ceased in that person at that plane?
—No. To all those at the arising moment of *citta*, at the ceasing moment of *citta* dissociated from goodness, and individuals at non-percipience plane ....
—Yes. To those at the birth-moment at pure abodes ....
(b) Indeterminate *dhammā* had not ceased in this person at this plane. Do wholesome *dhammā* not cease in that person at that plane?
—Yes. (Same as the aforesaid)

142. *i* (a) Unwholesome *dhammā* do not cease in this person at this plane. Had indeterminate *dhammā* not ceased in that person at that plane?
—No. To all those at the arising moment of *citta*, those at the ceasing moment of *citta* dissociated from badness, and individuals at non-percipience plane ....
—Yes. To those at the birth-moment at pure abodes ....
(b) Indeterminate *dhammā* had not ceased in this person at this plane. Do unwholesome *dhammā* not cease in that person at that plane?
—Yes. (Same as the aforesaid)

Chart 9.14 Cessation of *dhammā* (by present and future)

C: cease / will cease; N: do not cease / will not ceased

	Present			Future		
	wholesome *dhammā*	unwholesome *dhammā*	indeterminate *dhammā*	wholesome *dhammā*	unwholesome *dhammā*	indeterminate *dhammā*
To those at the ceasing moment of :						
consciousness dissociated from goodness	N				C	C
consciousness dissociated from badness		N				C
consciousness dissociated from goodness and badness						
the highest (*Arahatta*) Path-*citta*	C				N	
the final-stage *citta*	N	N				N
good state	C				C	C
good state at five-aggregate plane						
good state at immaterial plane						
bad state		C				C
bad state at Immaterial plane						
bad state at five-aggregate plane						
To those at the arising moment of :						
citta (state of consciousness)	N	N			C	C
the highest (*Arahatta*) Path-*citta*	N				N	
To those :						
all beings at the birth-moment						
all beings at the death-moment						
engaged in Cessation-attainment	N	N			C	C
at the birth-moment at pure abodes						
at the occurrence of second *citta* of the pure abode beings						
at occurrence of second unwholesome *citta* of pure abode beings						
at immaterial plane (four-aggregate)						
at the non-percipience plane	N	N			CN	C
at the four- and five-aggregate planes						
Arahat	N				N	
endowed with the highest (*Arahatta*) Path						
right after this *citta* who will directly attain the highest (*Arahatta*) Path						
right after this *citta* who will directly attain the highest (*Arahatta*) Path at the arising moment of that (*Arahatta* Path) *citta*	N				N	
right after this *citta* who will directly attain the highest (*Arahatta*) Path at the ceasing moment of that (*Arahatta* Path) *citta*	C				N	
endowed with the final-stage *citta*						
At the plane(s) of :						
non-percipience	C	C	C	C	C	C
five-aggregates	C	C	C	C	C	C
immateriality (or four-aggregates)	C	C	C	C	C	C

Present and Future

Forward enquiries by Individual

143. *i* (a) Wholesome *dhammā* cease in this person. Will unwholesome *dhammā* cease in that person?
—No. To those at the ceasing moment of the highest Path-*citta*, those right after this state of consciousness who will directly attain the highest Path at the ceasing moment of that (*Arahatta* Path) *citta* ....
—Yes. To others at the ceasing moment of good state ....
(b) Unwholesome *dhammā* will cease in this person. Do wholesome *dhammā* cease in that person?
—No. To all those at the arising moment of *citta*, those at the ceasing moment of *citta* dissociated from goodness, those engaged in Cessation-attainment, and individuals of non-percipience ....
—Yes. To those at the ceasing moment of good state ....

ii (a) Wholesome *dhammā* cease in this person. Will indeterminate *dhammā* cease in that person? —Yes. (Same as below)
(b) Indeterminate *dhammā* will cease in this person. Do wholesome *dhammā* cease in that person?
—No. To all those at the arising moment of *citta*, those at the ceasing moment of *citta* dissociated from goodness, those engaged in Cessation-attainment, and individuals of non-percipience ....
—Yes. To those at the ceasing moment of good state ....

144. *i* (a) Unwholesome *dhammā* cease in this person. Will indeterminate *dhammā* cease in that person? —Yes. (Same as below)
(b) Indeterminate *dhammā* will cease in this person. Do unwholesome *dhammā* cease in that person?
—No. To all those at the arising moment of *citta*, those at the ceasing moment of *citta* dissociated from badness, those engaged in Cessation-attainment, and individuals of non-percipience ....
—Yes. To those at the ceasing moment of bad state ....

Forward enquiries by Plane

145. *i* (a) Wholesome *dhammā* cease at this plane. Will unwholesome *dhammā* cease at that plane? .....p.....

Forward enquiries by Individual and Plane

146. *i* (a) Wholesome *dhammā* cease in this person at this plane. Will unwholesome *dhammā* cease in that person at that plane?
—No. To those at the ceasing moment of the highest Path-*citta*, to those right after this state of consciousness who will directly attain the highest Path at the ceasing moment of that (*Arahatta* Path) *citta* ....

—Yes. To others at the ceasing moment of good state ...
(b) Unwholesome *dhammā* will cease in this person at this plane. Do wholesome *dhammā* cease in that person at that plane?
—No. To all those at the arising moment of *citta*, and at the ceasing moment of *citta* dissociated from goodness ....
—Yes. (Same as the aforesaid)

ii (a) Wholesome *dhammā* cease in this person at this plane. Will indeterminate *dhammā* cease in that person at that plane?
—Yes. (Same as below)
(b) Indeterminate *dhammā* will cease in this person at this plane. Do wholesome *dhammā* cease in that person at that plane?
—No. To all those at the arising moment of *citta*, those at the ceasing moment of *citta* dissociated from goodness, and individuals at non-percipience plane ....
—Yes. To those at the ceasing moment of good state ....

147. *i* (a) Unwholesome *dhammā* cease in this person at this plane. Will indeterminate *dhammā* cease in that person at that plane?
—Yes. (Same as below)
(b) Indeterminate *dhammā* will cease in this person at this plane. Do unwholesome *dhammā* cease in that person at that plane?
—No. To all those at the arising moment of *citta*, those at the ceasing moment of *citta* dissociated from badness, and individuals at non-percipience plane ....
—Yes. To those at the ceasing moment of bad state ....

Opposite enquiries by Individual

148. *i* (a) Wholesome *dhammā* do not cease in this person. Will unwholesome *dhammā* not cease in that person?
—No. To all those at the arising moment of *citta*, those at the ceasing moment of *citta* dissociated from goodness, those engaged in Cessation-attainment, and individuals of non-percipience ....
—Yes. To those at the arising moment of the highest Path-*citta*, to *Arahat*, and those right after this state of consciousness who will directly attain the highest Path at the arising moment of that (*Arahatta* Path) *citta* ....
(b) Unwholesome *dhammā* will not cease in this person. Do wholesome *dhammā* not cease in that person?
—No. To those at the ceasing moment of the highest Path-*citta*, and those right after this state of consciousness who will directly attain the highest Path at the ceasing moment of that (*Arahatta* Path) *citta* ....
—Yes. (Same as the aforesaid)

ii (a) Wholesome *dhammā* do not cease in this person. Will indeterminate *dhammā* not cease in that person?
—No. To all those at the arising moment of *citta*, those at the ceasing moment of *citta* dissociated from goodness, those engaged in Cessation-attainment, and individuals of non-percipience ....
—Yes. To those at the ceasing moment of final-stage state of consciousness ...
(b) Indeterminate *dhammā* will not cease in this person. Do wholesome *dhammā* not cease in that person?
—Yes. (Same as the aforesaid)

149. *i* (a) Unwholesome *dhammā* do not cease in this person. Will indeterminate *dhammā* not cease in that person?
—No. To all those at the arising moment of *citta*, at the ceasing moment of *citta* dissociated from badness, those engaged in Cessation-attainment, and individuals of non-percipience ....
—Yes. To those at the ceasing moment of final-stage *citta*....
(b) Indeterminate *dhammā* will not cease in this person. Do unwholesome *dhammā* not cease in that person?
—Yes. (Same as the aforesaid)

Opposite enquiries by Plane

150. Wholesome *dhammā* do not cease at this plane. Will unwholesome *dhammā* not cease at that plane? .....p.....

Opposite enquiries by Individual and Plane

151. *i* (a) Wholesome *dhammā* do not cease in this person at this plane. Will unwholesome *dhammā* not cease in that person at that plane?
—No. To all those at the arising moment of *citta*, and those at the ceasing moment of *citta* dissociated from goodness ....
—Yes. To those at the arising moment of the highest Path-*citta*, to *Arahat*, and those right after this state of consciousness who will directly attain the highest Path at the arising moment of that (*Arahatta* Path) *citta*, and individuals at the non-percipience plane ....
(b) Unwholesome *dhammā* will not cease in this person at this plane. Do wholesome *dhammā* not cease in that person at that plane?
—No. To those at the ceasing moment of the highest Path-*citta*, and those right after this state of consciousness who will directly attain the highest Path at the ceasing moment of that (*Arahatta* Path) *citta* ....
—Yes. (Same as the aforesaid)

ii (a) Wholesome *dhammā* do not cease in this person at this plane. Will indeterminate *dhammā* not cease in that person at that plane?
—No. To all those at the arising moment of *citta*, at the ceasing moment of *citta* dissociated from goodness, and individuals at non-percipience plane ....
—Yes. To those at the ceasing moment of final-stage state of consciousness ....

(b) Indeterminate *dhammā* will not cease in this person at this plane. Do wholesome *dhammā* not cease in that person at that plane?
—Yes. (Same as the aforesaid)

152. *i* (a) Unwholesome *dhammā* do not cease in this person at this plane. Will indeterminate *dhammā* not cease in that person at that plane?
—No. To all those at the arising moment of *citta*, those at the ceasing moment of *citta* dissociated from badness, and individuals at non-percipience plane ....
—Yes. To those at the ceasing moment of final-stage state of consciousness ....
(b) Indeterminate *dhammā* will not cease in this person at this plane. Do unwholesome *dhammā* not cease in that person at that plane?
—Yes. (Same as the aforesaid)

Chart 9.15 Cessation of *dhammā* (by past and future)

C: had ceased / will cease; N: had not ceased / will not cease

	Past			Future		
	wholesome *dhammā*	unwholesome *dhammā*	indeterminate *dhammā*	wholesome *dhammā*	unwholesome *dhammā*	indeterminate *dhammā*
To those at the ceasing moment of :						
consciousness dissociated from goodness						
consciousness dissociated from badness						
consciousness dissociated from goodness and badness						
the highest (*Arahatta*) Path-*citta*						
the final-stage *citta*	C	C				N
good state						
good state at five-aggregate plane						
good state at immaterial plane						
bad state						
bad state at Immaterial plane						
bad state at five-aggregate plane						
To those at the arising moment of :						
citta (state of consciousness)						
the highest (*Arahatta*) Path-*citta*						
To those :						
all beings at the birth-moment						
all beings at the death-moment						
engaged in Cessation-attainment						
at the birth-moment at pure abodes						
at the occurrence of second *citta* of the pure abode beings	N	N			C	C
at occurrence of second unwholesome *citta* of pure abode beings						
at immaterial plane (four-aggregate)						
at the non-percipience plane	N	N			N	C
at the four- and five-aggregate planes	C	C			C	C
Arahat	C				N	
endowed with the highest (*Arahatta*) Path	C				N	
right after this *citta* who will directly attain the highest (*Arahatta*) Path	C				N	
right after this *citta* who will directly attain the highest (*Arahatta*) Path at the arising moment of that (*Arahatta* Path) *citta*						
right after this *citta* who will directly attain the highest (*Arahatta*) Path at the ceasing moment of that (*Arahatta* Path) *citta*						
endowed with the final-stage *citta*						
At the plane(s) of :						
non-percipience	N	N	C	N	N	C
five-aggregates	C	C	C	C	C	C
immateriality (or four-aggregates)	C	C	C	C	C	C

Past and Future

Forward enquiries by Individual

153. *i* (a) Wholesome *dhammā* had ceased in this person. Will unwholesome *dhammā* cease in that person?
—No. To those endowed with the highest Path, to *Arahat*, and to those right after this state of consciousness who will directly attain the highest Path ....
—Yes. To others (at the four- and five-aggregate planes) ....
Unwholesome *dhammā* will cease in this person. Had wholesome *dhammā* ceased in that person? —Yes. (Same as the aforesaid)

ii (a) Wholesome *dhammā* had ceased in this person. Will indeterminate *dhammā* cease in that person?
—No. To those at the ceasing moment of the final-stage state of consciousness ....
—Yes. To others (at the four- and five-aggregate planes) ....
(b) Indeterminate *dhammā* will cease in this person. Had wholesome *dhammā* ceased in that person? —Yes. (Same as the aforesaid)

154. *i* (a) Unwholesome *dhammā* had ceased in this person. Will indeterminate *dhammā* cease in that person?
—No. To those at the ceasing moment of the final-stage state of consciousness ....
—Yes. To others (at the four- and five-aggregate planes) ....
Indeterminate *dhammā* will cease in this person. Had wholesome *dhammā* ceased in that person? —Yes. (Same as the aforesaid)

Forward enquiries by Plane

155. Wholesome *dhammā* had ceased at this plane. Will unwholesome cease at that plane? .....p.....

Forward enquiries by Individual and Plane

156. *i* (a) Wholesome *dhammā* had ceased in this person at this plane. Will unwholesome *dhammā* cease in that person at that plane?
—No. To those endowed with the highest Path, to *Arahat*, and to those right after this state of consciousness who will directly attain the highest Path ....
—Yes. To others at the four- and five-aggregate planes ....
(b) Unwholesome *dhammā* will cease in this person at this plane. Had wholesome *dhammā* ceased in that person at that plane?
—No. To those at the occurrence of second *citta* of the pure abode beings ....
—Yes. (Same as the aforesaid)

ii (a) Wholesome *dhammā* had ceased in this person at this plane. Will indeterminate *dhammā* cease in that person at that plane?
—No. To those at the ceasing moment of final-stage state of consciousness ...
—Yes. To others at the four- and five-aggregate planes ....

(b) Indeterminate *dhammā* will cease in this person at this plane. Had wholesome *dhammā* ceased in that person at that plane?
—No. To those at the occurrence of second *citta* of the pure abode beings, and individuals at non-percipience plane ....
—Yes. (Same as the aforesaid)

157. *i* (a) Unwholesome *dhammā* had ceased in this person at this plane. Will indeterminate *dhammā* cease in that person at that plane?
—No. To those at the ceasing moment of final-stage state of consciousness ...
—Yes. To others at the four- and five-aggregate planes ....
(b) Indeterminate *dhammā* will cease in this person at this plane. Had unwholesome *dhammā* ceased in that person at that plane?
—No. To those at the occurrence of second *citta* of the pure abode beings, and individuals at non-percipience plane ....
—Yes. (Same as the aforesaid)

Opposite enquiries by Individual

158. *i* (a) Wholesome *dhammā* had not ceased in this person. Will unwholesome *dhammā* not cease in that person? —No such person.
(b) Unwholesome *dhammā* will not cease in this person. Had wholesome *dhammā* not ceased in that person?
—No. They had ceased (in those endowed with the highest Path, *Arahat*, and those right after this state of consciousness who will directly attain the highest Path).

ii (a) Wholesome *dhammā* had not ceased in this person. Will indeterminate *dhammā* not cease in that person? —No such person.
(b) Indeterminate *dhammā* will not cease in this person. Had wholesome *dhammā* not ceased in that person?
—No. Wholesome *dhammā* had ceased (in those at the ceasing moment of final-stage state of consciousness).

159. *i* (a) Unwholesome *dhammā* had not ceased in this person. Will indeterminate *dhammā* not cease in that person? —No such person.
(b) Indeterminate *dhammā* will not cease in this person. Had unwholesome *dhammā* not ceased in that person?
—No. Unwholesome *dhammā* had ceased (in those at the ceasing moment of final-stage state of consciousness).

Opposite enquiries by Plane

160. *i* (a) Wholesome *dhammā* had not ceased at this plane. Will unwholesome *dhammā* not cease at that plane? .....p.....

Opposite enquiries by Individual and Plane

161. *i* (a) Wholesome *dhammā* had not ceased in this person at this plane. Will unwholesome *dhammā* not cease in that person at that plane?
—No. To those at the occurrence of second *citta* of the pure abode beings ....
—Yes. To individuals at the non-percipience plane ....
(b) Unwholesome *dhammā* will not cease in this person at this plane. Had wholesome *dhammā* not ceased in that person at that plane?
—No. To those endowed with the highest Path, to *Arahat*, and to those right after this state of consciousness who will directly attain the highest Path ....
—Yes. (Same as the aforesaid)

ii (a) Wholesome *dhammā* had not ceased in this person at this plane. Will indeterminate *dhammā* not cease in that person at that plane?
—No. Indeterminate *dhammā* will cease (in those at the occurrence of second *citta* of the pure abode beings, and individuals at the non-percipience plane)
(b) Indeterminate *dhammā* will not cease in this person at this plane. Had wholesome *dhammā* not ceased in that person at that plane?
—No. Wholesome *dhammā* had ceased (in those at the ceasing moment of final-stage state of consciousness).

162. *i* (a) Unwholesome *dhammā* had not ceased in this person at this plane. Will indeterminate *dhammā* not cease in that person at that plane?
—No. Indeterminate *dhammā* will cease. (in those at the occurrence of second *citta* of the pure abode beings, and individuals at the non-percipience plane).
(b) Indeterminate *dhammā* will not cease in this person at this plane. Had unwholesome *dhammā* not ceased in that person at that plane?
—No. Unwholesome *dhammā* had ceased (in those at the ceasing moment of final-stage state of consciousness).

Consolidated answers on cessation of *dhammā*

Chart 9.16 Consolidated answers (cessation of *dhammā*)

C: cease / had ceased / will cease; N: do not cease / had not ceased / will not cease

	Present			Past			Future		
	wholesome *dhammā*	unwholesome *dhammā*	indeterminate *dhammā*	wholesome *dhammā*	unwholesome *dhammā*	indeterminate *dhammā*	wholesome *dhammā*	unwholesome *dhammā*	indeterminate *dhammā*
To those at the ceasing moment of :									
citta dissociated from goodness	N		C		C	C		C	C
citta dissociated from badness		N	C			C			C
citta dissociated from goodness and badness	N	N							
the highest (*Arahatta*) Path-*citta*	C						N	N	C
the final-stage *citta*	N	N		C	C				N
good state	C	N			C	C		C	C
good state at five-aggregate plane	C		C						
good state at immaterial plane	C	N	N						
bad state	N	C				C			C
bad state at Immaterial plane	N	C	N						
bad state at five-aggregate plane		C	C						
To those at the arising moment of :									
citta (state of consciousness)	N	N	N		C	C		C	C
the highest (*Arahatta*) Path-*citta*	N						C	N	
To those :									
all beings at the birth-moment	N	N	N						
all beings at the death-moment	N	N	C						
engaged in Cessation-attainment	N	N			C	C		C	C
at the birth-moment at pure abodes	N	N		N	N	N			
at the occurrence of second *citta* of the pure abode beings	N			N	N	C		C	C
at occurrence of second unwholesome *citta* of pure abode beings				N	C				
at immaterial plane (four-aggregate)				C	C	C			
at the non-percipience plane	N	N		N	CN	C	N	CN	C
at the four- and five-aggregate planes				C	C	C	C	C	C
Arahat	N			C			N	N	C
endowed with the highest (*Arahatta*) Path				C			N	N	C
right after this *citta* who will directly attain the highest Path				C			C	N	C
right after this *citta* who will directly attain the highest (*Arahatta*) Path at the arising moment of that (*Arahatta* Path) *citta*	N							N	
right after this *citta* who will directly attain the highest (*Arahatta*) Path at the ceasing moment of that (*Arahatta* Path) *citta*	C							N	
endowed with the final-stage *citta*							N	N	N
At the plane(s) of :									
non-percipience	N	N	C	N	N	C	N	N	C
five-aggregates	C	C	C	C	C	C	C	C	C
immateriality (or four-aggregates)	C	C	C	C	C	C	C	C	C

Chart 9.16 above shows the consolidation of answers obtained from the preceding charts on the classification of cessation. In the chart, those denotation letters in *italic* indicate that they are the answers consolidated from the respective first three sub-sections on present, past, and future origination of *dhammā*. Those boldfaced and at the same time italicised letters are the answers consolidated from the other classifications of present-and-past, present-and-future, past-and-future origination of *dhammā*. You will notice from the chart that there are some incomplete answers. It is because no enquiries are dealt with them.

9.2.3 Origination and Cessation of *dhammā* (with charts)

Chart 9.17 Enquiry sequence on arising and cessation of *dhammā*

		(Respective enquiries below are dealt with in relation to each of the following *dhammā* constituents accordingly)								
		Do they cease / Do they not cease : i) in that person? ii) at that plane? iii) in that person at that plane?			Had they ceased / Had they not ceased: i) in that person? ii) at that plane? iii) in that person at that plane?			Will they cease / Will they not cease : i) in that person? ii) at that plane? iii) in that person at that plane?		
		Wholesome *dhammā*	Unwholesome *dhammā*	Indeterminate *dhammā*	Wholesome *dhammā*	Unwholesome *dhammā*	Indeterminate *dhammā*	Wholesome *dhammā*	Unwholesome *dhammā*	Indeterminate *dhammā*
Wholesome *dhammā*	arise / do not arise :		1a	2a		10a	11a		13a	14a
Unwholesome *dhammā*	i) in this person. ii) at this plane.			3a			12a			15a
Indeterminate *dhammā*	iii) in this person at this plane.									
Wholesome *dhammā*	had arisen/ had not arisen	-	-	-		4a	5a		16a	17a
Unwholesome *dhammā*	i) in this person. ii) at this plane.	-	-	-			6a			18a
Indeterminate *dhammā*	iii) in this person at this plane.	-	-	-						
Wholesome *dhammā*	will arise / will not arise :	-	-	-	-	-	-		7a	8a
Unwholesome *dhammā*	i) in this person. ii) at this plane.	-	-	-	-	-	-			9a
Indeterminate *dhammā*	iii) in this person at this plane.	-	-	-	-	-	-			

		(Respective enquiries below are dealt with in relation to each of the following *dhammā* constituents accordingly)								
		Do they arise / Do they not arise : i) in that person? ii) at that plane? iii) in that person at that plane?			Had they arisen / Had they not arisen: i) in that person? ii) at that plane? iii) in that person at that plane?			Will they arise / Will they not arise : i) in that person? ii) at that plane? iii) in that person at that plane?		
		Wholesome *dhammā*	Unwholesome *dhammā*	Indeterminate *dhammā*	Wholesome *dhammā*	Unwholesome *dhammā*	Indeterminate *dhammā*	Wholesome *dhammā*	Unwholesome *dhammā*	Indeterminate *dhammā*
Wholesome *dhammā*	cease / do not cease: i) in this person. ii) at this plane. iii) in this person at this plane.				-	-	-	-	-	-
Unwholesome *dhammā*		1_b			-	-	-	-	-	-
Indeterminate *dhammā*		2_{bi}	3_b		-	-	-	-	-	-
Wholesome *dhammā*	had ceased / had not ceased i) in this person. ii) at this plane. iii) in this person at this plane.							-	-	-
Unwholesome *dhammā*		10_b			4_b			-	-	-
Indeterminate *dhammā*		11_b	12_b		5_b	6_{bi}		-	-	-
Wholesome *dhammā*	will cease / will not cease: i) in this person. ii) at this plane. iii) in this person at this plane.									
Unwholesome *dhammā*		13_b			16_b			7_{bi}		
Indeterminate *dhammā*		14_b	15_b		17_b	18_b		8_b	9_b	

Chart 9.17 above summarises the sequence of paired enquiries based on combining the origination and cessation of *dhāmmā*. The loop goes through three differentiation types (by persons, by planes, by persons and planes) using forward and reverse mode of enquiring, and further iterates through six time-scaled classifications, represent by the enneahedral boxes as shown in the chart above.

Chart 9.18 Present origination and cessation of *dhammā*

A: arise; C: cease; N: do not arise / do not cease

	Origination			Cessation		
	wholesome *dhammā*	unwholesome *dhammā*	indeterminate *dhammā*	wholesome *dhammā*	unwholesome *dhammā*	indeterminate *dhammā*
To those at the arising moment of :						
citta dissociated from goodness	N				N	N
citta dissociated from badness		N				N
good state	A				N	N
bad state		A				N
To those at the ceasing moment of :						
citta (state of consciousness)	N	N				C
citta dissociated from badness	N				N	
good state at immaterial plane	N	N				N
bad state	N				C	
bad state at Immaterial plane	N	N				N
To those :						
all beings at the birth-moment	N	N				N
all beings at the death-moment	N	N				C
engaged in Cessation-attainment	N				N	
at the non-percipience plane	N				N	

At Present

Forward enquiries by Individual

163. *i* (a) Wholesome *dhammā* arise in this person. Do unwholesome *dhammā* cease in that person? —No. (To those at the arising moment of good state ....)
(b) Unwholesome *dhammā* cease in this person. Do wholesome *dhammā* arise in that person? —No. (To those at the ceasing moment of bad state ....)

ii (a) Wholesome *dhammā* arise in this person. Do indeterminate *dhammā* cease in that person? — No. (To those at the arising moment of good state ....)
(b) Indeterminate *dhammā* cease in this person. Do wholesome *dhammā* arise in that person? — No. (To all those at the death-moment, and at the ceasing moment of *citta*)

164. *i* (a) Unwholesome *dhammā* arise in this person. Do indeterminate *dhammā* cease in that person? — No. (To those at the arising moment of bad state ....)

(b) Indeterminate *dhammā* cease in this person. Do unwholesome *dhammā* arise in that person? —No. (To all those at the death-moment, and at the ceasing moment of *citta*)

Forward enquiries by Plane

165. *i* (a) Wholesome *dhammā* arise at this plane. Do unwholesome *dhammā* cease at that plane?
—Yes. (At the planes of four- and five-aggregates ....)
(b) Unwholesome *dhammā* cease at this plane. Do wholesome *dhammā* arise at that plane? —Yes. (At the planes of four- and five-aggregates ....)

ii (a) Wholesome *dhammā* arise at this plane. Do indeterminate *dhammā* cease at that plane? —Yes. (At the planes of four- and five-aggregates ....)
(b) Indeterminate *dhammā* cease at this plane. Do wholesome *dhammā* arise at that plane?
—No. At the plane of non-percipience ....
—Yes. At the planes of four- and five-aggregates ....

166. *i* (a) Unwholesome *dhammā* arise at this plane. Do indeterminate *dhammā* cease at that plane? —Yes. (At the planes of four- and five-aggregates ....)
(b) Indeterminate *dhammā* cease at this plane. Do unwholesome *dhammā* arise at that plane?
—No. At the plane of non-percipience ...
—Yes. At the planes of four- and five-aggregates ....

Forward enquiries by Individual and Plane

167. *i* (a) Wholesome *dhammā* arise in this person at this plane. Do unwholesome *dhammā* cease in that person at that plane?
—No. (To those at the arising moment of good state ....)
(b) Unwholesome *dhammā* cease in this person at this plane. Do wholesome *dhammā* arise in that person at that plane?
—No. (To those at the ceasing moment of bad state ....)

ii (a) Wholesome *dhammā* arise in this person at this plane. Do indeterminate *dhammā* cease in that person at that plane?
—No. (To those at the arising moment of good state ....)
(b) Indeterminate *dhammā* cease in this person at this plane. Do wholesome *dhammā* arise in that person at that plane?
—No. (To all those at the death-moment, and at the ceasing moment of *citta*)

168. *i* (a) Unwholesome *dhammā* arise in this person at this plane. Do indeterminate *dhammā* cease in that person at that plane?
—No. (To those at the arising moment of bad state ....)

(b) Indeterminate *dhammā* cease in this person at this plane. Do unwholesome *dhammā* arise in that person at that plane?
—No. (To all those at the death-moment, and at the ceasing moment of *citta*)

Opposite enquiries by Individual

169. *i* (a) Wholesome *dhammā* do not arise in this person. Do unwholesome *dhammā* not cease in that person?
—No. To those at the ceasing moment of bad state ....
—Yes. To those at the arising moment of *citta* dissociated from goodness, those at the ceasing moment of *citta* dissociated from badness, those engaged in Cessation-attainment, and individuals of non-percipience ...
(b) Unwholesome *dhammā* do not cease in this person. Do wholesome *dhammā* not arise in that person?
—No. To those at the arising moment of good state ....
—Yes. (Same as the aforesaid)

ii (a) Wholesome *dhammā* do not arise in this person. Do indeterminate *dhammā* not cease in that person?
—No. To all those at death-moment, and at the ceasing moment of *citta*....
—Yes. To all those at birth-moment, those at the arising moment of *citta* dissociated from goodness, and those at the ceasing moment of both good state and bad state at immaterial plane ....
(b) Indeterminate *dhammā* do not cease in this person. Do wholesome *dhammā* not arise in that person?
—No. To those at the arising moment of good state ....
—Yes. (Same as the aforesaid)

170. *i* (a) Unwholesome *dhammā* do not arise in this person. Do indeterminate *dhammā* not cease in that person?
—No. To all those at death-moment, and at the ceasing moment of *citta*....
—Yes. To all those at birth-moment, and at the arising moment of *citta* dissociated from badness, and at the ceasing moment of both good state and bad state at immaterial plane ....
(b) Indeterminate *dhammā* do not cease in this person. Do unwholesome *dhammā* not arise in that person?
—No. To those at the arising moment of bad state ....
—Yes. (Same as the aforesaid)

Opposite enquiries by Plane

171. *i* (a) Wholesome *dhammā* do not arise at this plane. Do unwholesome *dhammā* not cease at that plane? —Yes. (At the plane of non-percipience ....)
(b) Unwholesome *dhammā* do not cease at this plane. Do wholesome *dhammā* not arise at that plane? —Yes. (At the plane of non-percipience ....)

ii (a) Wholesome *dhammā* do not arise at this plane. Do indeterminate *dhammā* not cease at that plane?
—No. Indeterminate *dhammā* cease (at the plane of non-percipience).
(b) Indeterminate *dhammā* do not cease at this plane. Do wholesome *dhammā* not arise at that plane? —No such plane.

172. *i* (a) Unwholesome *dhammā* do not arise at this plane. Do indeterminate *dhammā* not cease at that plane?
—No. Indeterminate *dhammā* cease (at the plane of non-percipience).
(b) Indeterminate *dhammā* do not cease at this plane. Do unwholesome *dhammā* not arise at that plane? —No such plane.

Opposite enquiries by Individual and Plane

173. *i* (a) Wholesome *dhammā* do not arise in this person at this plane. Do unwholesome *dhammā* not cease in that person at that plane?
—No. To those at the ceasing moment of bad state ....
—Yes. To those at the arising moment of *citta* dissociated from goodness, those at the ceasing moment of *citta* dissociated from badness, and individuals at non-percipience plane ....
(b) Unwholesome *dhammā* do not cease in this person at this plane. Do wholesome *dhammā* not arise in that person at that plane?
—No. To those at the arising moment of good state ....
—Yes. (Same as the aforesaid)

ii (a) Wholesome *dhammā* do not arise in this person at this plane. Do indeterminate *dhammā* not cease in that person at that plane?
—No. To all those at death-moment, and at the ceasing moment of *citta*....
—Yes. To all those at birth-moment, at the arising moment of *citta* dissociated from goodness, and at the ceasing moment of good state and bad state at immaterial plane ....
(b) Indeterminate *dhammā* do not cease in this person at this plane. Do wholesome *dhammā* not arise in that person at that plane?
—No. To those at the arising moment of good state ....
—Yes. (Same as the aforesaid)

174. *i* (a) Unwholesome *dhammā* do not arise in this person at this plane. Do indeterminate *dhammā* not cease in that person at that plane?
—No. To all those at death-moment, and at the ceasing moment of *citta* ....
—Yes. To all those at birth-moment, and at the arising moment of *citta* dissociated from badness, and at the ceasing moment of both good state and bad state at immaterial plane ....
(b) Indeterminate *dhammā* do not cease in this person at this plane. Do wholesome *dhammā* not arise in that person at that plane?
—No. To those at the arising moment of bad state ....
—Yes. (Same as the aforesaid)

Chart 9.19 Past origination and cessation of *dhammā*

A: had arisen; C: had ceased; N: had not arisen / had not ceased

	Origination			Cessation		
To those :	wholesome *dhammā*	unwholesome *dhammā*	indeterminate *dhammā*	wholesome *dhammā*	unwholesome *dhammā*	indeterminate *dhammā*
at the birth-moment at pure abodes	N	N				N
at the occurrence of second *citta* of the pure abode beings	N	N			N	C
at occurrence of second unwholesome *citta* of pure abode beings	N				C	
at immaterial plane (four-aggregate)	A	A			C	C
at the non-percipience plane	N	N				C
at the four- and five-aggregate planes	A	A			C	C

In the Past

Forward enquiries by Individual

175. *i* (a) Wholesome *dhammā* had arisen in this person. Had unwholesome *dhammā* ceased in that person?
—Yes. (To those at the four- and five-aggregate planes ....)
(b) Unwholesome *dhammā* had ceased in this person. Had wholesome *dhammā* arisen in that person? —Yes. (Same as the aforesaid)

ii (a) Wholesome *dhammā* had arisen in this person. Had indeterminate *dhammā* ceased in that person? —Yes. (To those at the four- and five-aggregate planes ....)
(b) Indeterminate *dhammā* had ceased in this person. Had wholesome *dhammā* arisen in that person? —Yes. (Same as the aforesaid)

176. *i* (a) Unwholesome *dhammā* had arisen in this person. Had indeterminate *dhammā* ceased in that person?
—Yes. (To those at the four- and five-aggregate planes ....)
(b) Indeterminate *dhammā* had ceased in this person. Had unwholesome *dhammā* arisen in that person? —Yes. (Same as the aforesaid)

Forward enquiries by Plane

177. *i* (a) Wholesome *dhammā* had arisen at this plane. Had unwholesome *dhammā* ceased at that plane? —Yes. (At the four- and five-aggregate planes ....)
(b) Unwholesome *dhammā* had ceased at this plane. Had wholesome *dhammā* arisen at that plane? —Yes. (Same as the aforesaid)

ii (a) Wholesome *dhammā* had arisen at this plane. Had indeterminate *dhammā* ceased at that plane? —Yes. (At the four- and five-aggregate planes ....)
(b) Indeterminate *dhammā* had ceased at this plane. Had wholesome *dhammā* arisen at that plane?
—No. At the plane of non-percipience ...
—Yes. At the planes of four- and five-aggregates ....

178. *i* (a) Unwholesome *dhammā* had arisen at this plane. Had indeterminate *dhammā* ceased at that plane? —Yes. (Same as below)
(b) Indeterminate *dhammā* had ceased at this plane. Had unwholesome *dhammā* arisen at that plane?
—No. At the plane of non-percipience ....
—Yes. At the planes of four- and five-aggregates ....

Forward enquiries by Individual and Plane

179. *i* (a) Wholesome *dhammā* had arisen in this person at this plane. Had unwholesome *dhammā* ceased in that person at that plane? —Yes. Same as below.
(b) Unwholesome *dhammā* had ceased in this person at this plane. Had wholesome *dhammā* arisen in that person at that plane?
—No. To those at the occurrence of second unwholesome consciousness of the pure abodes ....
—Yes. To others at the four- and five-aggregate planes ....

ii (a) Wholesome *dhammā* had arisen in this person at this plane. Had indeterminate *dhammā* ceased in that person at that plane?
—Yes. (Same as below)
(b) Indeterminate *dhammā* had ceased in this person at this plane. Had wholesome *dhammā* arisen in that person at that plane?
—No. To those at the occurrence of second *citta* of the pure abode beings, and individuals at non-percipience plane ....
—Yes. To others at the four- and five-aggregate planes ....

180. *i* (a) Unwholesome *dhammā* had arisen in this person at this plane. Had indeterminate *dhammā* ceased in that person at that plane?
—Yes. (Same as below)
(b) Indeterminate *dhammā* had ceased in this person at this plane. Had unwholesome *dhammā* arisen in that person at that plane?
—No. To those at the occurrence of second *citta* of the pure abode beings, and individuals at non-percipience plane ....
—Yes. To others at the four- and five-aggregate planes ....

Opposite enquiries by Individual

181. *i* (a) Wholesome *dhammā* had not arisen in this person. Had unwholesome *dhammā* not ceased in that person?
—Natthi. (no, those at the occurrence of second *citta* of the pure abode beings ....)

(b) Unwholesome *dhammā* had not arisen in this person. Had wholesome *dhammā* not ceased in that person? [78]
—Natthi. (no, same as aforesaid)

ii (a) Wholesome *dhammā* had not arisen in this person. Had indeterminate *dhammā* not ceased in that person? —no such person.
(b) Indeterminate *dhammā* had not arisen in this person. Had wholesome *dhammā* not ceased in that person? [78] —Same as aforesaid

182. *i* (a) Unwholesome *dhammā* had not arisen in this person. Had indeterminate *dhammā* not ceased in that person? —no such person.
(b) Indeterminate *dhammā* had not arisen in this person. Had unwholesome *dhammā* not ceased in that person? [78] —Same as aforesaid

Opposite enquiries by Plane

183. *i* (a) Wholesome *dhammā* had not arisen at this plane. Had unwholesome *dhammā* not ceased at that plane? —Yes. (At the plane of non-percipience ...)
(b) Unwholesome *dhammā* had not arisen at this plane. Had wholesome *dhammā* not ceased at that plane? —Yes. (At the plane of non-percipience ...)

"*akusalā dhammā na nirujjhittha tattha kusalā dhammā na uppajjitthāti*?" is what is asked according to the text. Herein the way the question (b) is phrased deviates from the flow of Abhidhamma method of making enquiries. The question should have been phrased in the reverse way).

ii (a) Wholesome *dhammā* had not arisen at this plane. Had indeterminate *dhammā* not ceased at that plane?
—No. Indeterminate *dhammā* had ceased (at the plane of non-percipience)
(b) Indeterminate *dhammā* had not arisen at this plane. Had wholesome *dhammā* not ceased at that plane? [78]
—None. (no such plane whereat indeterminate *dhammā* had not ceased, and wholesome *dhammā* had not arisen)

184. *i* (a) Unwholesome *dhammā* had not arisen at this plane. Had indeterminate *dhammā* not ceased at that plane?
—No. Indeterminate *dhammā* had ceased (at the plane of non-percipience)
(b) Indeterminate *dhammā* had not arisen at this plane. Had unwholesome *dhammā* not ceased at that plane? [78]
—None. (no such plane whereat indeterminate *dhammā* had not ceased, and unwholesome *dhammā* had not arisen)

---

[78] In the same case as in 183 *i* (b), it looks like the transcriptional error in CTS4 on the way question is constructed. The question should be asked the other way round by following the usual Abhidhamma method.

Opposite enquiries by Individual and Plane

185. *i* (a) Wholesome *dhammā* had not arisen in this person at this plane. Had unwholesome *dhammā* not ceased in that person at that plane?
—No. To those at the occurrence of second unwholesome consciousness of the pure abodes ....
—Yes. To those at the occurrence of second *citta* of the pure abode beings, and individuals at non-percipience plane ....
(b) Unwholesome *dhammā* had not ceased in this person at this plane. Had wholesome *dhammā* not arisen in that person at that plane?
—Yes. (Same as the aforesaid)

ii (a) Wholesome *dhammā* had not arisen in this person at this plane. Had indeterminate *dhammā* not ceased in that person at that plane?
—No. To those at the occurrence of second *citta* of the pure abode beings, and individuals at non-percipience plane ....
—Yes. To those at the birth-moment at pure abodes ....
(b) Indeterminate *dhammā* had not ceased in this person at this plane. Had wholesome *dhammā* not arisen in that person at that plane?
—Yes. (Same as the aforesaid)

186. *i* (a) Unwholesome *dhammā* had not arisen in this person at this plane. Had indeterminate *dhammā* not ceased in that person at that plane?
—No. To those at the occurrence of second *citta* of the pure abode beings, and individuals at non-percipience plane ....
—Yes. To those at the birth-moment at pure abodes ....
(b) Indeterminate *dhammā* had not ceased in this person at this plane. Had wholesome *dhammā* not arisen in that person at that plane?
—Yes. (Same as the aforesaid)

Chart 9.20 Future origination and cessation of *dhammā*

A: will arise; C: will cease; N: will not arise / will not cease

	Origination			Cessation		
	wholesome *dhammā*	unwholesome *dhammā*	indeterminate *dhammā*	wholesome *dhammā*	unwholesome *dhammā*	indeterminate *dhammā*
To those at the ceasing moment of :						
the final-stage *citta*	N	N				N
To those :						
at immaterial plane (four-aggregate)	A	A			C	C
at the non-percipience plane	N	N			N	C
at the four- and five-aggregate planes	A	A			C	C
Arahat	N	N			N	C
endowed with the highest (*Arahatta*) Path	N	N			N	C
right after this *citta* who will directly attain the highest (*Arahatta*) Path	A	N			N	C

In Future

Forward enquiries by Individual

187. *i* (a) Wholesome *dhammā* will arise in this person. Will unwholesome *dhammā* cease in that person?
—No. To those right after this state of consciousness who will directly attain the highest Path ....
—Yes. To others (those at the four- and five-aggregate planes) ....
(b) Unwholesome *dhammā* will cease in this person. Will wholesome *dhammā* arise in that person? —Yes. (Same as the aforesaid)

ii (a) Wholesome *dhammā* will arise in this person. Will indeterminate *dhammā* cease in that person? —Yes. (Same as below)
(b) Indeterminate *dhammā* will cease in this person. Will wholesome *dhammā* arise in that person?
—No. To those endowed with the highest Path, and to *Arahat* ....
—Yes. To others (those at the four- and five-aggregate planes, and those right after this state of consciousness who will directly attain the highest Path) ....

188. *i* (a) Unwholesome *dhammā* will arise in this person. Will indeterminate *dhammā* cease in that person? —Yes. (Same as below)
(b) Indeterminate *dhammā* will cease in this person. Will unwholesome *dhammā* arise in that person?

—No. To those who are endowed the highest Path, to *Arahat*, and to those right after this state of consciousness who will directly attain the highest Path ....
—Yes. To others (those at the four- and five-aggregate planes) ....

Forward enquiries by Plane

189. *i* (a) Wholesome *dhammā* will arise at this plane. Will unwholesome *dhammā* cease at that plane? —Yes. (At four- and five-aggregate planes ....)
(b) Unwholesome *dhammā* will cease at this plane. Will wholesome *dhammā* arise at that plane? —Yes. (At four- and five-aggregate planes ....)

ii (a) Wholesome *dhammā* will arise at this plane. Will indeterminate *dhammā* cease at that plane? —Yes. (Same as below)
(b) Indeterminate *dhammā* will cease at this plane. Will wholesome *dhammā* arise at that plane?
—No. At non-percipience plane ....
—Yes. At four- and five-aggregate planes ....

190. *i* (a) Unwholesome *dhammā* will arise at this plane. Will indeterminate *dhammā* cease at that plane? —Yes. (Same as below)
(b) Indeterminate *dhammā* will cease at this plane. Will unwholesome *dhammā* arise at that plane?
—No. At non-percipience plane ....
—Yes. At four- and five-aggregate planes ....

Forward enquiries by Individual and Plane

191. *i* (a) Wholesome *dhammā* will arise in this person at this plane. Will unwholesome *dhammā* cease in that person at that plane?
—No. To those right after this state of consciousness who will directly attain the highest Path ....
—Yes. To others at the four- and five-aggregate planes ....
(b) Unwholesome *dhammā* will cease in this person at this plane. Will wholesome *dhammā* arise at that person at that plane?
—Yes. (Same as the aforesaid)

ii (a) Wholesome *dhammā* will arise in this person at this plane. Will indeterminate *dhammā* cease in that person at that plane? —Yes. (Same as below)
(b) Indeterminate *dhammā* will cease in this person at this plane. Will wholesome *dhammā* arise in that person at that plane?
—No. To those endowed with the highest Path, to *Arahat*, and individuals at non-percipience plane ....
—Yes. To others at the four- and five-aggregate planes ....

192. *i* (a) Unwholesome *dhammā* will arise in this person at this plane. Will indeterminate *dhammā* cease in that person at that plane? —Yes. (Same as below)

(b) Indeterminate *dhammā* will cease in this person at this plane. Will unwholesome *dhammā* arise in that person at that plane?
—No. To those endowed with the highest Path, to *Arahat*, to those right after this state of consciousness who will directly attain the highest Path, and individuals at non-percipience plane ....
—Yes. To others at the four- and five-aggregate planes ....

Opposite enquiries by Individual

193. *i* (a) Wholesome *dhammā* will not arise in this person. Will unwholesome *dhammā* not cease in that person? —Yes. (Same as below)
(b) Unwholesome *dhammā* will not cease in this person. Will wholesome *dhammā* not arise in that person?
—No. To those right after this state of consciousness who will directly attain the highest Path ....
—Yes. To those endowed with the highest Path, and to *Arahat* ....

ii (a) Wholesome *dhammā* will not arise in this person. Will indeterminate *dhammā* not cease in that person?
—No. To those endowed with the highest Path, and to *Arahat* ....
—Yes. At the ceasing moment of final-stage state of consciousness ....
(b) Indeterminate *dhammā* will not cease in this person. Will wholesome *dhammā* not arise in that person? —Yes. (Same as the aforesaid)

194. *i* (a) Unwholesome *dhammā* will not arise in this person. Will indeterminate *dhammā* not cease in that person?
—No. To those endowed with the highest Path, to *Arahat*, and to those right after this state of consciousness who will directly attain the highest Path ....
—Yes. To those at the ceasing moment of final-stage state of consciousness ....
(b) Indeterminate *dhammā* will not cease in this person. Will unwholesome *dhammā* not arise in that person? —Yes. (Same as the aforesaid)

Opposite enquiries by Plane

195. *i* (a) Wholesome *dhammā* will not arise at this plane. Will unwholesome *dhammā* not cease at that plane? —Yes. (at non-percipience plane ....)
(b) Unwholesome *dhammā* will not cease at this plane. Will wholesome *dhammā* not arise at that plane? —Yes. (Same as aforesaid)

ii (a) Wholesome *dhammā* will not arise at this plane. Will indeterminate *dhammā* not cease at that plane?
—No. Indeterminate *dhammā* will cease. (at non-percipience plane)
(b) Indeterminate *dhammā* will not cease at this plane. Will wholesome *dhammā* not arise at that plane? —No such person.

196. *i* (a) Unwholesome *dhammā* will not arise at this plane. Will indeterminate *dhammā* not cease at that plane?
—No. Indeterminate *dhammā* will cease. (at non-percipience plane)

(b) Indeterminate *dhammā* will not cease at this plane. Will unwholesome *dhammā* not arise at that plane? —No such person.

Opposite enquiries by Individual and Plane

197. *i* (a) Wholesome *dhammā* will not arise in this person at this plane. Will unwholesome *dhammā* not cease in that person at that plane?
—Yes. (Same as below)
(b) Unwholesome *dhammā* will not cease in this person at this plane. Will wholesome *dhammā* not arise in that person at that plane?
—No. To those right after this state of consciousness who will directly attain the highest Path ....
—Yes. To those endowed with the highest Path, to *Arahat*, and individuals at non-percipience plane ....

ii (a) Wholesome *dhammā* will not arise in this person at this plane. Will indeterminate *dhammā* not cease in that person at that plane?
—No. To those endowed with the highest Path, to *Arahat*, and individuals at non-percipience plane ....
—Yes. To those at the ceasing moment of final-stage state of consciousness ....
(b) Indeterminate *dhammā* will not cease in this person at this plane. Will wholesome *dhammā* not arise in that person at that plane?
—Yes. (Same as the aforesaid)

198. *i* (a) Unwholesome *dhammā* will not arise in this person at this plane. Will indeterminate *dhammā* not cease in that person at that plane?
—No. To those endowed with the highest Path, to *Arahat*, to those right after this state of consciousness who will directly attain the highest Path, and individuals at non-percipience plane ....
—Yes. To those at the ceasing moment of final-stage state of consciousness ....
(b) Indeterminate *dhammā* will not cease in this person at this plane. Will unwholesome *dhammā* not arise in that person at that plane?
—Yes. (Same as the aforesaid)

Chart 9.21 Present-and-past origination and cessation of *dhammā*

A: arise; C: cease; N: had not arisen / had not ceased

	Present Origination			Past Cessation		
	wholesome *dhammā*	unwholesome *dhammā*	indeterminate *dhammā*	wholesome *dhammā*	unwholesome *dhammā*	indeterminate *dhammā*
To those at the arising moment of :						
citta dissociated from goodness	N				C	C
citta dissociated from badness		N				C
good state	A				C	C
bad state		A				C
To those at the ceasing moment of :						
consciousness	N	N			C	C
To those :						
engaged in Cessation-attainment	N	N			C	C
at the birth-moment at pure abodes	N	N				N
right after this *citta* who will directly attain the highest (*Arahatta*) Path	N				N	
at the non-percipience plane	N	N			CN	C

Present and Past

Forward enquiries by Individual

199. *i* (a) Wholesome *dhammā* arise in this person. Had unwholesome *dhammā* ceased in that person? —Yes. (Same as below)
(b) Unwholesome *dhammā* had ceased in this person. Do wholesome *dhammā* arise in that person?
—No. To all those at the ceasing moment of *citta*, at the arising moment of *citta* dissociated from goodness, those engaged in Cessation-attainment, and individuals of non-percipience ....
—Yes. To those at the arising moment of good state, unwholesome *dhammā* had ceased, and wholesome *dhammā* also arise in those persons.

ii (a) Wholesome *dhammā* arise in this person. Had indeterminate *dhammā* ceased in that person? —Yes. (Same as below)
(b) Indeterminate *dhammā* had ceased in this person. Do wholesome *dhammā* arise in that person?
—No. To all those at the ceasing moment of *citta*, at the arising moment of *citta* dissociated from goodness, those engaged in Cessation-attainment, and individuals of non-percipience ....
—Yes. To those at the arising moment of good state ....

200. *i* (a) Unwholesome *dhammā* arise in this person. Had indeterminate *dhammā* ceased in that person? —Yes. (Same as below)
(b) Indeterminate *dhammā* had ceased in this person. Do unwholesome *dhammā* arise in that person?
—No. To all those at the ceasing moment of *citta*, at the arising moment of *citta* dissociated from badness, those engaged in Cessation-attainment, and individuals of non-percipience ....
—Yes. To those at the arising moment of bad state ....

Forward enquiries by Plane

201. *i* (a) Wholesome *dhammā* arise at this plane. Had unwholesome *dhammā* ceased at that plane? .....p.....

Forward enquiries by Individual and Plane

202. *i* (a) Wholesome *dhammā* arise in this person at this plane. Had unwholesome *dhammā* ceased in that person at that plane?
—Yes. (Same as below)
(b) Unwholesome *dhammā* had ceased in this person at this plane. Do wholesome *dhammā* arise in that person at that plane?
—No. To all those at the ceasing moment of *citta*, and at the arising moment of *citta* dissociated from goodness ....
—Yes. To those at the arising moment of good state ....

ii (a) Wholesome *dhammā* arise in this person at this plane. Had indeterminate *dhammā* ceased in that person at that plane? —Yes. (Same as below)
(b) Indeterminate *dhammā* had ceased in this person at this plane. Do wholesome *dhammā* arise in that person at that plane?
—No. To all those at the ceasing moment of *citta*, at the arising moment of *citta* dissociated from goodness, and individuals at non-percipience plane ....
—Yes. To those at the arising moment of good state ....

203. *i* (a) Unwholesome *dhammā* arise in this person at this plane. Had indeterminate *dhammā* ceased in that person at that plane? —Yes. Same as below.
(b) Indeterminate *dhammā* had ceased in this person at this plane. Do unwholesome *dhammā* arise in that person at that plane?
—No. To all those at the ceasing moment of *citta*, at the arising moment of *citta* dissociated from badness, and individuals at non-percipience plane ....
—Yes. To those at the arising moment of bad state ....

Opposite enquiries by Individual

204. *i* (a) Wholesome *dhammā* do not arise in this person. Had unwholesome *dhammā* not ceased in that person?
—No. Unwholesome *dhammā* had ceased. (All those at the ceasing moment of *citta*, at the arising moment of *citta* dissociated from goodness, those of Cessation-attainment, and individuals of non-percipience)

(b) Unwholesome *dhammā* had not ceased in this person. Do wholesome *dhammā* not arise in that person?
—Natthi (yes, to those at the occurrence of second *citta* of the pure-abodes, and individuals at non-percipience plane ....)

ii (a) Wholesome *dhammā* do not arise in this person. Had indeterminate *dhammā* not ceased in that person?
—No. They had ceased. (Same as in 204 *i* (a) above).
(b) Indeterminate *dhammā* had not ceased in this person. Do wholesome *dhammā* not arise in that person?
—Natthi (yes, to those at the birth-moment at pure abodes ....)

205. *i* (a) Unwholesome *dhammā* do not arise in this person. Had indeterminate *dhammā* not ceased in that person?
—No. They had ceased. (All those at the ceasing moment of *citta*, at the arising moment of *citta* dissociated from badness, those engaged in Cessation-attainment, and individuals of non-percipience plane)
(b) Indeterminate *dhammā* had not ceased in this person. Do unwholesome *dhammā* not arise in that person?
—Natthi (yes, to those at the birth-moment at pure abodes ....)

Opposite enquiries by Plane

206. *i* (a) Wholesome *dhammā* do not arise at this plane. Had unwholesome *dhammā* not ceased at that plane? .....p.....

Opposite enquiries by Individual and Plane

207. *i* (a) Wholesome *dhammā* do not arise in this person at this plane. Had unwholesome *dhammā* not ceased in that person at that plane?
—No. To all those at the ceasing moment of *citta*, and at the arising moment of *citta* dissociated from goodness ....
—Yes. To those at the occurrence of second *citta* of the pure abode beings, and individuals at non-percipience plane ....
(b) Unwholesome *dhammā* had not ceased in this person at this plane. Do wholesome *dhammā* not arise in that person at that plane?
—Yes. (Same as the aforesaid)

ii (a) Wholesome *dhammā* do not arise in this person at this plane. Had indeterminate *dhammā* not ceased in that person at that plane?
—No. To all those at the ceasing moment of *citta*, at the arising moment of *citta* dissociated from goodness, and individuals at non-percipience plane ....
—Yes. To those at the birth-moment at pure abodes ....
(b) Indeterminate *dhammā* had not ceased in this person at this plane. Do wholesome *dhammā* not arise in that person at that plane?
—Yes. (Same as the aforesaid)

208. *i* (a) Unwholesome *dhammā* do not arise in this person at this plane. Had indeterminate *dhammā* not ceased in that person at that plane?
—No. To all those at the ceasing moment of *citta*, at the arising moment of *citta* dissociated from badness, and individuals at non-percipience plane ....
—Yes. To those at the birth-moment at pure abodes ....
(b) Indeterminate *dhammā* had not ceased in this person at this plane. Do unwholesome *dhammā* not arise in that person at that plane?
—Yes. (Same as the aforesaid)

Chart 9.22 Present-and-future origination and cessation of *dhammā*

A: arise; C: cease; N: will not arise / will not cease

	Present			Future		
	Origination			Cessation		
	wholesome *dhammā*	unwholesome *dhammā*	indeterminate *dhammā*	wholesome *dhammā*	unwholesome *dhammā*	indeterminate *dhammā*
To those at the arising moment of :						
citta dissociated from goodness	N				C	C
citta dissociated from badness		N				C
the highest (*Arahatta*) Path-*citta*	A				N	
good state	A				C	C
bad state		A				C
To those at the ceasing moment of :						
citta (state of consciousness)	N	N			C	C
the highest (*Arahatta*) Path-*citta*	N				N	
the final-stage *citta*	N	N				N
To those :						
engaged in Cessation-attainment	N	N			C	C
at the non-percipience plane	N	N			CN	C
Arahat	N				N	
right after this *citta* who will directly attain the highest (*Arahatta*) Path at the arising moment of that (*Arahatta* Path) *citta*	A				N	
right after this *citta* who will directly attain the highest (*Arahatta*) Path at the ceasing moment of that (*Arahatta* Path) *citta*	N				N	

Present and Future

Forward enquiries by Individual

209. *i* (a) Wholesome *dhammā* arise in this person. Will unwholesome *dhammā* cease in that person?

—No. To those at the arising moment of the highest Path-*citta*, to those right after this state of consciousness who will directly attain the highest Path at the arising moment of that (*Arahatta* Path) *citta* ....
—Yes. To those at the arising moment of good state ....
(b) Unwholesome *dhammā* will cease in this person. Do wholesome *dhammā* arise in that person?
—No. To all those at the ceasing moment of *citta*, at the arising moment of *citta* dissociated from goodness, those engaged in Cessation-attainment, and individuals of non-percipience ....
—Yes. (Same as the aforesaid)

ii (a) Wholesome *dhammā* arise in this person. Will indeterminate *dhammā* cease in that person? —Yes. (Same as below)
(b) Indeterminate *dhammā* will cease in this person. Do wholesome *dhammā* arise in that person?
—No. To all those at the ceasing moment of *citta*, at the arising moment of *citta* dissociated from goodness, those engaged in Cessation-attainment, and individuals of non-percipience ....
—Yes. To those at the arising moment of good state ....

210. *i* (a) Unwholesome *dhammā* arise in this person. Will indeterminate *dhammā* cease in that person? —Yes. (Same as below)
(b) Indeterminate *dhammā* will cease in this person. Do unwholesome *dhammā* arise in that person?
—No. To all those at the ceasing moment of *citta*, at the arising moment of *citta* dissociated from badness, those engaged in Cessation-attainment, and individuals of non-percipience ...
—Yes. To those at the arising moment of bad state ....

Forward enquiries by Plane

211. *i* (a) Wholesome *dhammā* arise at this plane. Will unwholesome *dhammā* cease at that plane? .....p.....

Forward enquiries by Individual and Plane

212. *i* (a) Wholesome *dhammā* arise in this person at this plane. Will unwholesome *dhammā* cease in that person at that plane?
—No. To those at the arising moment of the highest Path-*citta*, and those right after this state of consciousness who will directly attain the highest Path at the arising moment of that (*Arahatta* Path) *citta* ....
—Yes. To others at the arising moment of good state ....
(b) Unwholesome *dhammā* will cease in this person at this plane. Do wholesome *dhammā* arise in that person at that plane?
—No. To all those at the ceasing moment of *citta*, and at the arising moment of *citta* dissociated from goodness ....
—Yes. To those at the arising moment of good state ....

ii (a) Wholesome *dhammā* arise in this person at this plane. Will indeterminate *dhammā* cease in that person at that plane? —Yes. (Same as below)
(b) Indeterminate *dhammā* will cease in this person at this plane. Do wholesome *dhammā* arise in that person at that plane?
—No. To all those at the ceasing moment of *citta*, at the arising moment of *citta* dissociated from goodness, and individuals at non-percipience plane ....
—Yes. At the arising moment of good state ....

213. *i* (a) Unwholesome *dhammā* arise in this person at this plane. Will indeterminate *dhammā* cease in that person at that plane?
—Yes. (Same as below)
(b) Indeterminate *dhammā* will cease in this person at this plane. Do unwholesome *dhammā* arise in that person at that plane?
—No. To all those at the ceasing moment of *citta*, at the arising moment of *citta* dissociated from badness, and individuals at non-percipience plane ...
—Yes. To those at the arising moment of bad state ....

Opposite enquiries by Individual

214. *i* (a) Wholesome *dhammā* do not arise in this person. Will unwholesome *dhammā* not cease in that person?
—No. To all those at the ceasing moment of *citta*, at the arising moment of *citta* dissociated from goodness, those engaged in Cessation-attainment, and individuals of non-percipience ....
—Yes. To those at the ceasing moment of the highest Path-*citta*, to *Arahat*, and to those right after this state of consciousness who will directly attain the highest Path at the ceasing moment of that (*Arahatta* Path) *citta* ....
(b) Unwholesome *dhammā* will not cease in this person. Do wholesome *dhammā* not arise in that person?
—No. To those at the arising moment of the highest Path-*citta*, and to those right after this state of consciousness who will directly attain the highest Path at the arising moment of that (*Arahatta* Path) *citta* ....
—Yes. (Same as the aforesaid)

ii (a) Wholesome *dhammā* do not arise in this person. Will indeterminate *dhammā* not cease in that person?
—No. To all those at the ceasing moment of *citta*, at the arising moment of *citta* dissociated from goodness, those engaged in Cessation-attainment, and individuals of non-percipience ....
—Yes. To those at the ceasing moment of final-stage state of consciousness ....
(b) Indeterminate *dhammā* will not cease in this person. Do wholesome *dhammā* not arise in that person? —Yes. (Same as the aforesaid)

215. *i* (a) Unwholesome *dhammā* do not arise in this person. Will indeterminate *dhammā* not cease in that person?

—No. To all those at the ceasing moment of *citta*, at the arising moment of *citta* dissociated from badness, those engaged in Cessation-attainment, and individuals of non-percipience ....
—Yes. To those at the ceasing moment of final-stage state of consciousness .... Indeterminate *dhammā* will not cease in this person. Do unwholesome *dhammā* not arise in that person? —Yes. (Same as the aforesaid)

Opposite enquiries by Plane

216. *i* (a) Wholesome *dhammā* do not cease at this plane. Will unwholesome *dhammā* not cease at that plane? .....p.....

Opposite enquiries by Individual and Plane

217. *i* (a) Wholesome *dhammā* do not arise in this person at this plane. Will unwholesome *dhammā* not cease in that person at that plane?
—No. To all those at the ceasing moment of *citta*, and at the arising moment of *citta* dissociated from goodness ....
—Yes. To those at the ceasing moment of the highest Path-*citta*, to *Arahat*, and to those right after this state of consciousness who will directly attain the highest Path at the ceasing moment of that (*Arahatta* Path) *citta*, and individuals at non-percipience plane ....

(b) Unwholesome *dhammā* will not cease in this person at this plane. Do wholesome *dhammā* not arise in that person at that plane?
—No. To those at the arising moment of the highest Path-*citta*, and to those right after this state of consciousness who will directly attain the highest Path at the arising moment of that (*Arahatta* Path) *citta* ....
—Yes. To those at the ceasing moment of the highest Path-*citta*, to *Arahat*, and to those right after this state of consciousness who will directly attain the highest Path at the ceasing moment of that (*Arahatta* Path) *citta*, and individuals at non-percipience plane ....

ii (a) Wholesome *dhammā* do not arise in this person at this plane. Will indeterminate *dhammā* not cease in that person at that plane?
—No. To all those at the ceasing moment of *citta*, at the arising moment of *citta* dissociated from goodness, and individuals at non-percipience plane ....
—Yes. To those at the ceasing moment of final-stage state of consciousness ....
(b) Indeterminate *dhammā* will not cease in this person at this plane. Do wholesome *dhammā* not arise in that person at that plane?
—Yes. (Same as the aforesaid)

218. *i* (a) Unwholesome *dhammā* do not arise in this person at this plane. Will indeterminate *dhammā* not cease in that person at that plane?
—No. To all those at the ceasing moment of *citta*, at the arising moment of *citta* dissociated from badness, and individuals at non-percipience plane ....
—Yes. To those at the ceasing moment of final-stage state of consciousness ....

(b) Indeterminate *dhammā* will not cease in this person at this plane. Do unwholesome *dhammā* not arise in that person at that plane?
—Yes. (Same as the aforesaid)

Chart 9.23 Past-and-future origination and cessation of *dhammā*

A: had arisen; C: had ceased; N: will not arise / will not cease

	Past			Future		
	Origination			Cessation		
	wholesome *dhammā*	unwholesome *dhammā*	indeterminate *dhammā*	wholesome *dhammā*	unwholesome *dhammā*	indeterminate *dhammā*
To those at the ceasing moment of :						
the final-stage *citta*	A	A				N
To those :						
at the occurrence of second *citta* of the pure abode beings	N	N			C	C
at immaterial plane (four-aggregate)	A	A			C	C
at the non-percipience plane	N	N			CN	C
at the four- and five-aggregate planes	A	A			C	C
Arahat	A				N	
endowed with the highest (*Arahatta*) Path	A				N	
right after this *citta* who will directly attain the highest (*Arahatta*) Path	A				N	

Past and Future

Forward enquiries by Individual

219. *i* (a) Wholesome *dhammā* had arisen in this person. Will unwholesome *dhammā* cease in that person?
—No. To those endowed with the highest Path, to *Arahat*, and to those right after this state of consciousness who will directly attain the highest Path ....
—Yes. To others (those at the four- and five-aggregate planes) ....
(b) Unwholesome *dhammā* will cease in this person. Had wholesome *dhammā* arisen in that person? —Yes. (Same as the aforesaid)

ii (a) Wholesome *dhammā* had arisen in this person. Will indeterminate *dhammā* cease in that person?
—No. To those at the ceasing moment of final-stage state of consciousness ...
—Yes. To others (those at the four- and five-aggregate planes) ....

(b) Indeterminate *dhammā* will cease in this person. Had wholesome *dhammā* arisen in that person? —Yes. (Same as the aforesaid)

220. *i* (a) Unwholesome *dhammā* had arisen in this person. Will indeterminate *dhammā* cease in that person?
—No. To those at the ceasing moment of final-stage state of consciousness ....
—Yes. To others (those at the four- and five-aggregate planes) ….
(b) Indeterminate *dhammā* will cease in this person. Had wholesome *dhammā* arisen in that person? —Yes. (Same as the aforesaid)

Forward enquiries by Plane

221. *i* (a) Wholesome *dhammā* had arisen at this plane. Will unwholesome cease at that plane? .....p.....

Forward enquiries by Individual and Plane

222. *i* (a) Wholesome *dhammā* had arisen in this person at this plane. Will unwholesome *dhammā* cease in that person at that plane?
—No. To those endowed with the highest Path, to *Arahat*, and to those right after this state of consciousness who will directly attain the highest Path ....
—Yes. To others at the four- and five-aggregate planes ....
(b) Unwholesome *dhammā* will cease in this person at this plane. Had wholesome *dhammā* arisen in that person at that plane?
—No. To those at the occurrence of second *citta* of the pure abode beings ....
—Yes. To others at the four- and five-aggregate planes ....

ii (a) Wholesome *dhammā* had arisen in this person at this plane. Will indeterminate *dhammā* cease in that person at that plane?
—No. To those at the ceasing moment of final-stage state of consciousness ....
—Yes. To others at the four- and five-aggregate planes ....
(b) Indeterminate *dhammā* will cease in this person at this plane. Had wholesome *dhammā* arisen in that person at that plane?
—No. To those at the occurrence of second *citta* of the pure abode beings, and individuals at non-percipience plane ....
—Yes. To others at the four- and five-aggregate planes ....

223. *i* (a) Unwholesome *dhammā* had arisen in this person at this plane. Will indeterminate *dhammā* cease in that person at that plane?
—No. To those at the ceasing moment of final-stage state of consciousness ....
—Yes. To others at the four- and five-aggregate planes ....
(b) Indeterminate *dhammā* will cease in this person at this plane. Had unwholesome *dhammā* arisen in that person at that plane?
—No. To those at the occurrence of second *citta* of the pure abode beings, and individuals at non-percipience plane ....
—Yes. To others at the four- and five-aggregate planes ....

Opposite enquiries by Individual

224. *i* (a) Wholesome *dhammā* had not arisen in this person. Will unwholesome *dhammā* not cease in that person? —None.
(b) Unwholesome *dhammā* will not cease in this person. Had wholesome *dhammā* not arisen in that person?
—No. They had arisen (in those endowed with the highest Path, *Arahat*, and those right after this state of consciousness who will directly attain the highest Path).

ii (a) Wholesome *dhammā* had not arisen in this person. Will indeterminate *dhammā* not cease in that person? —None.
(b) Indeterminate *dhammā* will not cease in this person. Had wholesome *dhammā* not arisen in that person?
—No. Wholesome *dhammā* had arisen (in those at the ceasing moment of final-stage state of consciousness).

225. *i* (a) Unwholesome *dhammā* had not arisen in this person. Will indeterminate *dhammā* not cease in that person? —None.
(b) Indeterminate *dhammā* will not cease in this person. Had unwholesome *dhammā* not arisen in that person?
—No. Unwholesome *dhammā* had arisen. (in those at the ceasing moment of final-stage state of consciousness).

Opposite enquiries by Plane

226. *i* (a) Wholesome *dhammā* had not arisen at this plane. Will unwholesome *dhammā* not cease at that plane? .....p.....

Opposite enquiries by Individual and Plane

227. *i* (a) Wholesome *dhammā* had not arisen in this person at this plane. Will unwholesome *dhammā* not cease in that person at that plane?
—No. To those at the occurrence of second onsciousness of the pure abodes ....
—Yes. To individuals at non-percipience plane ....
(b) Unwholesome *dhammā* will not cease in this person at this plane. Had wholesome *dhammā* not arisen in that person at that plane?
—No. To those endowed with the highest Path, to *Arahat*, and to those right after this state of consciousness who will directly attain the highest Path ....
—Yes. To individuals at non-percipience plane ....

ii (a) Wholesome *dhammā* had not arisen in this person at this plane. Will indeterminate *dhammā* not cease in that person at that plane?
—No. Indeterminate *dhammā* will cease (in those at the occurrence of second *citta* of the pure abode beings, and individuals at non-percipience plane).
(b) Indeterminate *dhammā* will not cease in this person at this plane. Had wholesome *dhammā* not arisen in that person at that plane?

—No. Wholesome *dhammā* had arisen (in those at the ceasing moment of final-stage state of consciousness).

228. *i* (a) Unwholesome *dhammā* had not arisen in this person at this plane. Will indeterminate *dhammā* not cease in that person at that plane?
—No. Indeterminate *dhammā* will cease (in those at the occurrence of second *citta* of the pure abode beings, and individuals at non-percipience plane).
(b) Indeterminate *dhammā* will not cease in this person at this plane. Had unwholesome *dhammā* not arisen in that person at that plane?
—No. Unwholesome *dhammā* had arisen (in those at the ceasing moment of final-stage state of consciousness).

Consolidated answers on origination-cessation of *dhammā*

Chart 9.24 Consolidated answers (origination and cessation)

A: arises/ had arisen/ will arise; C: ceases/ had ceased/ will cease
N_a: does not arise/ had not arisen/ will not arise
N_c: does not cease/ had not ceased/ will not cease

	Present			Past			Future		
To those at the arising moment of :	wholesome *dhammā*	unwholesome *dhammā*	indeterminate *dhammā*	wholesome *dhammā*	unwholesome *dhammā*	indeterminate *dhammā*	wholesome *dhammā*	unwholesome *dhammā*	indeterminate *dhammā*
citta dissociated from goodness	N_a	N_c	N_c		C	C		C	C
citta dissociated from badness		N_a	N_c			C			C
citta dissociated from goodness and badness									
the highest (*Arahatta*) Path-*citta*	A							N_c	
the final-stage *citta*									
good state	*A*	N_c	N_c		C	C		C	C
good state at five-aggregate plane									
good state at immaterial plane									
bad state		*A*	N_c			C			C
bad state at Immaterial plane									
bad state at five-aggregate plane									

Continue from above.

	Present			Past			Future		
	wholesome *dhammā*	unwholesome *dhammā*	indeterminate *dhammā*	wholesome *dhammā*	unwholesome *dhammā*	indeterminate *dhammā*	wholesome *dhammā*	unwholesome *dhammā*	indeterminate *dhammā*
To those at the ceasing moment of :									
citta (state of consciousness)	N_a	N_a	C		C	C		C	C
citta dissociated from goodness									
citta dissociated from badness	N_a	N_c							
citta dissociated from goodness and badness									
the highest (*Arahatta*) Path-*citta*	N_a							N_c	
the final-stage *citta*	N_a	N_a		A	A		N_a	N_a	N_c
good state									
good state at five-aggregate plane									
good state at immaterial plane	N_a	N_a	N_c						
bad state	N_a	C							
bad state at Immaterial plane	N_a	N_a	N_c						
bad state at five-aggregate plane									
To those at the ceasing moment of :									
all beings at the birth-moment	N_a	N_a	N_c						
all beings at the death-moment	N_a	N_a	C						
engaging in Cessation-attainment	N_a	N_c N_a			C	C		C	C
at the birth-moment at pure abodes	N_a	N_a		N_a	N_a	N_c			
at the occurrence of second *citta* of the pure abode beings	N_a			N_a	N_a N_c	C		C	C
at occurrence of second unwholesome *citta* of pure abode beings				N_a	C				
at immaterial plane (four-aggregate)				A	A C	C	A	A C	C
at the non-percipience plane	N_a	N_c N_a		N_a	N_a CN_c	C	N_a	N_a CN_c	C
at the four- and five-aggregate planes				A	A C	C	A	A C	C
Arahat	N_a			A			N_a	N_a N_c	C
endowed with the highest (*Arahatta*) Path				A			N_a	N_a N_c	C
right after this *citta* who will directly attain the highest Path				A			A	N_a N_c	C
right after this *citta* who will directly attain the highest (*Arahatta*) Path at the arising moment of that (*Arahatta* Path) *citta*	A							N_c	
right after this *citta* who will directly attain the highest (*Arahatta*) Path at the ceasing moment of that (*Arahatta* Path) *citta*	N_a							N_c	
endowed with the final-stage *citta*									

In Chart 9.24 above, those denoted letters in *italic* are answers consolidated from the first three sub-sections on present, past, and future classifications. Those boldfaced and at the same time italicised letters are the answers based on the last three sub-sections on present-and-past, present-and-future, past-and-future classifications. Like in the earlier sections on origination and cessation, this section similarly does not make enquiries on all the types of persons as shown in the chart.

9.3 Meditative Development (*Bhāvanā*)

Chart 9.25 On meditative development

	He/she renounces unwholesome *dhammā*?	He/she renounces wholesome *dhammā*?	He/she renounces indeterminate *dhammā*?		He/she develops wholesome *dhammā*?	He/she develops unwholesome *dhammā*?	He/she develops indeterminate *dhammā*?
This person:develops wholesome *dhammā*.	Y	-	Y	This person: renounces unwholesome *dhammā*.	Y	-	Y
This person develops unwholesome *dhammā*.	-	Y	Y	This person renounces wholesome *dhammā*.	-	Y	Y
This person develops indeterminate *dhammā*.	Y	Y	-	This person renounces indeterminate *dhammā*.	Y	Y	-
	He/she not renounce unwholesome *dhammā*?	He/she not renounce wholesome *dhammā*?	He/she not renounce indeterminate *dhammā*?		He/she not develop wholesome *dhammā*?	He/she not develop unwholesome *dhammā*?	He/she not develop indeterminate *dhammā*?
This person does not:develop wholesome *dhammā*.	Y	-	Y	This person:does not renounce unwholesome *dhammā*.	Y	-	Y
does not:develop unwholesome *dhammā*.	-	Y	Y	This person:does not renounce wholesome *dhammā*.	-	Y	Y
does not:develop indeterminate *dhammā*	Y	Y	-	This person:does not renounce indeterminate *dhammā*.	Y	Y	-

229. *i* (a) This person develops wholesome *dhammā*. Does that person renounce unwholesome *dhammā*? —Yes.

(b) This person renounces unwholesome *dhammā*. Does that person develop wholesome *dhammā*? —Yes.

ii (a) This person does not develop wholesome *dhammā*. Does that person not renounce unwholesome *dhammā*? —Yes.
(b) This person does not renounce unwholesome *dhammā*. Does that person not develop wholesome *dhammā*? —Yes.

The following are adjoined to complete the loop of catechisms although they are not shown in the text.

iii (a) This person develops unwholesome *dhammā*. Does that person renounce wholesome *dhammā*? —Yes.
(b) This person renounces wholesome *dhammā*. Does that person develop unwholesome *dhammā*? —Yes.

iv (a) This person does not develop unwholesome *dhammā*. Does that person not renounce wholesome *dhammā*? —Yes.
(b) This person does not renounce wholesome *dhammā*. Does that person not develop unwholesome *dhammā*? —Yes.

v (a) This person develops wholesome *dhammā*. Does that person renounce indeterminate *dhammā*? —Yes.
(b) This person renounces indeterminate *dhammā*. Does that person develop wholesome *dhammā*? —Yes.

vi (a) This person does not develop wholesome *dhammā*. Does that person not renounce indeterminate *dhammā*? —Yes. (No, if that person does not develop wholesome *dhammā* but at the same time develops unwholesome *dhammā*)
(b) This person does not renounce indeterminate *dhammā*. Does that person not develop wholesome *dhammā*? —Yes.

vii (a) This person develops unwholesome *dhammā*. Does that person renounce indeterminate *dhammā*? —Yes.
(b) This person renounces indeterminate *dhammā*. Does that person develop unwholesome *dhammā*? —Yes.

viii (a) This person does not develop unwholesome *dhammā*. Does that person not renounce indeterminate *dhammā*?—Yes. (No, if that person does not develop unwholesome *dhammā* but at the same time develops wholesome *dhammā*)
(b) This person does not renounce indeterminate *dhammā*. Does that person not develop unwholesome *dhammā*? —Yes.

When a person develops either wholesome *dhammā* or unwholesome *dhammā*, those are not indeterminate *dhammā*. When a person develops meditatively not predicated upon what states should be cultivated nor those others which should be renounced, those are indeterminate *dhammā*. In the latter, the person is said to have not renounced indeterminate *dhammā*.

ix (a) This person develops indeterminate *dhammā*. Does that person renounce wholesome *dhammā*? —Yes.
(b) This person renounces wholesome *dhammā*. Does that person develop indeterminate *dhammā*? —Yes.

x (a) This person does not develop indeterminate *dhammā*. Does that person not renounce wholesome *dhammā*? —Yes.
(b) This person does not renounce wholesome *dhammā*. Does that person not develop indeterminate *dhammā*? —Yes.

xi (a) This person develops indeterminate *dhammā*. Does that person renounce unwholesome *dhammā*? —Yes.

(b) This person renounces unwholesome *dhammā*. Does that person develop indeterminate *dhammā*? —Yes.

xii (a) This person does not develop indeterminate *dhammā*. Does that person not renounce unwholesome *dhammā*? —Yes.
(b) This person does not renounce unwholesome *dhammā*. Does that person not develop indeterminate *dhammā*? —Yes.

CHAPTER 10

X. Pairs on Controlling Faculties
(*Indriyayamaka*)

The Pāli term '*indriyaya'* means 'faculty, function of sense-perceptibility'. It should not be interpreted merely as 'sense-organs' because the fabric of indriyas contains stations and mechanisms of both physical and mental governing functionality. Each of them interconnect with one another, working interdependently. Because of the directive and governing nature of indriyas, I give it a more explicit meaning as 'controlling faculties'.

Indriyas have been expounded in more detail in Chapter five in the second book of Vibhaṅga, including examining their relationships with the enumerations of the Abhidhammamātikā. The subject in this chapter is confined to scrutinising their basic terms and meanings, specifics on their arising, and a time-based analysis on a selected list of six faculties at the end, designed to ensure our comprehension. Because of the long list of faculties, the text reduces exposition of the catechisms to only the arising of the faculties. Cessation with reference to the faculties are not dealt with by the text.

The 22 controlling faculties are enumerated as below.

Sense-based:

1. eye-faculty (*cakkhundriya*)
2. ear-faculty (*sotindriya*)
3. nose-faculty (*ghānindriya*)
4. tongue-faculty (*jivhindriya*)
5. body-faculty (*kāyindriya*)

} physical

6. mind-faculty (*manindriya*) } mental

bodily-based:

7. femininity-faculty (*itthindriya*)
8. masculinity-faculty (*purisindriya*)

} physical

Physical-Mental duality:

9. vitality- or life-faculty (*jīvitindriya*)

Feeling-based:

10. pleasure-faculty (*sukhindriya*)
11. displeasure-faculty (*dukkhindriya*)
12. joy-faculty (*somanassindriya*)
13. melancholy-faculty (*domanassindriya*)
14. equanimity-faculty (*upekkhindriya*)

} mental

<u>Spiritual-based</u>:

15. faith-faculty (*saddhā*)
16. effort-faculty (*vīriyindriya*)
17. mindfulness-faculty (*satindriya*)
18. concentration-faculty (*samādhindriya*)
19. understanding-faculty (*paññindriya*)

<u>Supramundane knowledge-based</u>:

20. I-shall-comprehend-the-unknown faculty (*anaññātaññassāmītindriya*)
21. final-knowledge faculty (*aññindriya*)
22. final-knower faculty (*aññātāvindriya*)

(15–22: mental)

The first five sensitive faculties are the five internal *pasāda rūpā*. Although they are considered "physical", those are matters too fine to be visible to us. The femininity- and masculinity-faculty are referred to the two types of subtle matters called *bhāva rūpā*. After death at the rebirth-linking moment of consciousness (*paṭisandhi viññāna*), the five sensitive faculties began to form from the five *pasāda rūpā* decads, and the two *bhāva rūpā* determining the gender are originated from the two *bhava* decads. Those decads are part of the 'life-forming' basic units of the kamma-produced matter (*kammaja rūpā*) of a new life.

Life-faculty has the function of either physical or mental. For example, gross and subtle matters, non-materiality of mental factors and mind. The faculties of pleasure and displeasure are bodily-based, whereas the faculties of joy and melancholy are mental. Equanimity-faculty has the function of maintaining neutrality of neither being joyful nor in grief while keeping composed and controlled. Faith is established in a person in accordance with the wholesome root cause and good understanding,

Faith, effort, mindfulness, concentration, and understanding are the five requisite conditions for pursuing productive meditation of the higher stage consciousness as prescribed collectively by the name 'Five Faculties' (*Pañc' indriyāni*), from which yhe 'Five Powers' (*Pañca balāni*) are achieved. Concentration-faculty is also the objective of volitive striving to be obtained through practicing the 'Four means to accomplishments' in order to be able to engage in the access absorption of the higher stages of jhānas. The faculties of mindfulness (*sati*), effort (*vīriya*), and concentration (*samādhi*) are also the three constituents of the 'Seven factors of enlightenment' (*Satta bojjhangā*).

The faculty of 'I-shall-comprehend-the-unknown' works at the stream-winning path of consciousness (*Sotāpattimaggacitta*). The faculty of 'final-knowledge' is present in the six noble persons, with the exception of *Sotāpatti*-path person and *Arahat*. However, the difference is that only the *Sakadāgāmi*-path person, *Anāgāmi*-path person, and *Arahatta*-path person are cultivating final knowledge of the dissimilar kinds for removal of their respective regions of mental taint. The final-knower faculty is only experienced by the *Arahat*.

10.1 Clarification of Terms (*Paṇṇatti*)

I omit the first section on the summary of questions because the content has already been included in the subsequent exposition section. There is no need to repeat it all over.

Chart 10.1 below summarises the questions and answers from sub-sections 10.1.1 and 10.1.2. In the charts, I have filled out all the remaining negative answers, even though no enquiries are dealt with them. The denotation Y meaning 'Yes', N meaning "No'. You would notice in the chart that there are both yes and no answers given to some of the questions. Below are some explanations regarding the variations in some of those controlling faculties.

- Divine eye and wisdom eye are the figurative sense of eye, are also called eye, but they are not eye faculty. Eye faculty is both eye and eye faculty.
- Divine ear and 'craved' ear, are also called eye, but they are not ear faculty. Ear faculty is both ear and ear faculty.
- Internal organs, flesh, and so on are a part of body, but they are not body faculty. The body faculty is both the physical body and body faculty.
- The term 'female' is referred to a gender, a designation, an individual, which can not be called femininity faculty. The same is also used to distinguish the term 'male' from masculinity faculty.
- Pleasure, and displeasure (implicit of painful feeling, or suffering) are experienced in the form of bodily contact, not mentally.
- Joy and melancholy (or grief, sorrow) are experienced mentally.
- Equanimity faculty functions based on mental contact. Hence the state of neither pleasure nor displeasure which is the (bodily) equanimity, can not be called equanimity faculty which is mentally based.
- Other than these 22 controlling faculties, the rest are not faculties.

Chart 10.1 Consolidated answers on the clarification of terms of the 22 controlling faculties

	is it faculty?	is it eye faculty?	is it ear faculty?	is it nose faculty?	is it tongue faculty?	is it body faculty?	is it mind faculty?	is it femininity faculty?	is it masculinity faculty?	is it life faculty?	is it pleasure-faculty?	is it displeasure-faculty?	is it joy-faculty?	is it melancholy-faculty?	is it equanimity faculty?	is it faith faculty?	is it effort faculty?	is it mindfulness faculty?	is it concentration faculty?	is it understanding-faculty?	is it I-shall-comprehend-the-unknown faculty?	is it final-knowledge faculty?	is it final-knower faculty?
It is eye,	Y	NY	N	N	N	N	N	N	N	N	N	N	N	N	N	N	N	N	N	N	N	N	N
It is ear,	Y	N	NY	N	N	N	N	N	N	N	N	N	N	N	N	N	N	N	N	N	N	N	N
It is nose,	Y	N	N	Y	N	N	N	N	N	N	N	N	N	N	N	N	N	N	N	N	N	N	N
It is tongue,	Y	N	N	N	Y	N	N	N	N	N	N	N	N	N	N	N	N	N	N	N	N	N	N
It is body,	Y	N	N	N	N	NY	N	N	N	N	N	N	N	N	N	N	N	N	N	N	N	N	N
It is mind,	Y	N	N	N	N	N	Y	N	N	N	N	N	N	N	N	N	N	N	N	N	N	N	N
It is female,	Y	N	N	N	N	N	N	N	N	N	N	N	N	N	N	N	N	N	N	N	N	N	N
It is male,	Y	N	N	N	N	N	N	N	N	N	N	N	N	N	N	N	N	N	N	N	N	N	N
It is life,	Y	N	N	N	N	N	N	N	N	Y	N	N	N	N	N	N	N	N	N	N	N	N	N
It is pleasure,	Y	N	N	N	N	N	N	N	N	N	Y	N	N	N	N	N	N	N	N	N	N	N	N
It is displeasure,	Y	N	N	N	N	N	N	N	N	N	N	Y	N	N	N	N	N	N	N	N	N	N	N
It is joy,	Y	N	N	N	N	N	N	N	N	N	N	N	Y	N	N	N	N	N	N	N	N	N	N
It is melancholy,	Y	N	N	N	N	N	N	N	N	N	N	N	N	Y	N	N	N	N	N	N	N	N	N
It is equanimity,	Y	N	N	N	N	N	N	N	N	N	N	N	N	N	NY	N	N	N	N	N	N	N	N
It is faith,	Y	N	N	N	N	N	N	N	N	N	N	N	N	N	N	Y	N	N	N	N	N	N	N
It is effort,	Y	N	N	N	N	N	N	N	N	N	N	N	N	N	N	N	Y	N	N	N	N	N	N
It is mindfulness,	Y	N	N	N	N	N	N	N	N	N	N	N	N	N	N	N	N	Y	N	N	N	N	N
It is concentration,	Y	N	N	N	N	N	N	N	N	N	N	N	N	N	N	N	N	N	Y	N	N	N	N
It is understanding,	Y	N	N	N	N	N	N	N	N	N	N	N	N	N	N	N	N	N	N	Y	N	N	N
It is I-shall-comprehend-the-unknown,	Y	N	N	N	N	N	N	N	N	N	N	N	N	N	N	N	N	N	N	N	Y	N	N
It is final-knowledge,	Y	N	N	N	N	N	N	N	N	N	N	N	N	N	N	N	N	N	N	N	N	Y	N
It is final-knower,	Y	N	N	N	N	N	N	N	N	N	N	N	N	N	N	N	N	N	N	N	N	N	Y
		are they eye faculty?	are they ear faculty?	are they nose faculty?	are they tongue faculty?	are they body faculty?	are they mind faculty?	are they femininity faculty?	are they masculinity faculty?	are they life faculty?	are they pleasure-faculty?	are they displeasure-faculty?	are they joy-faculty?	are they melancholy-faculty?	are they equanimity faculty?	are they faith faculty?	are they effort faculty?	are they mindfulness faculty?	are they concentration faculty?	are they understanding-faculty?	are they I-shall-comprehend-the-unknown faculty?	are they final-knowledge faculty?	are they final-knower faculty?
These are faculties,		NY	NY	NY	NY	NY	NY	NY	NY	NY	NY	NY	NY	NY	NY	NY	NY	NY	NY	NY	NY	NY	NY

	is it eye?	is it ear?	is it nose?	is it tongue?	is it body?	is it mind?	is it femininity?	is it masculinity?	is it life?	is it pleasure?	is it displeasure?	is it joy?	is it melancholy?	is it equanimity?	is it faith?	is it effort?	is it mindfulness?	is it concentration?	is it understanding?	is it I-shall-comprehend-the-unknown?	is it final-knowledge?	is it final-knower?
It is eye faculty,	Y	N	N	N	N	N	N	N	N	N	N	N	N	N	N	N	N	N	N	N	N	N
It is ear faculty,	N	Y	N	N	N	N	N	N	N	N	N	N	N	N	N	N	N	N	N	N	N	N
It is nose faculty,	N	N	Y	N	N	N	N	N	N	N	N	N	N	N	N	N	N	N	N	N	N	N
It is tongue faculty,	N	N	N	Y	N	N	N	N	N	N	N	N	N	N	N	N	N	N	N	N	N	N
It is body faculty,	N	N	N	N	Y	N	N	N	N	N	N	N	N	N	N	N	N	N	N	N	N	N
It is mind faculty,	N	N	N	N	N	Y	N	N	N	N	N	N	N	N	N	N	N	N	N	N	N	N
It is femininity faculty,	N	N	N	N	N	N	N	N	N	N	N	N	N	N	N	N	N	N	N	N	N	N
It is masculinity faculty,	N	N	N	N	N	N	N	N	N	N	N	N	N	N	N	N	N	N	N	N	N	N
It is life faculty,	N	N	N	N	N	N	N	N	Y	N	N	N	N	N	N	N	N	N	N	N	N	N
It is pleasure faculty,	N	N	N	N	N	N	N	N	N	Y	N	N	N	N	N	N	N	N	N	N	N	N
It is displeasure faculty,	N	N	N	N	N	N	N	N	N	N	Y	N	N	N	N	N	N	N	N	N	N	N
It is joy faculty,	N	N	N	N	N	N	N	N	N	N	N	Y	N	N	N	N	N	N	N	N	N	N
It is melancholy faculty,	N	N	N	N	N	N	N	N	N	N	N	N	Y	N	N	N	N	N	N	N	N	N
It is equanimity faculty,	N	N	N	N	N	N	N	N	N	N	N	N	N	Y	N	N	N	N	N	N	N	N
It is faith faculty,	N	N	N	N	N	N	N	N	N	N	N	N	N	N	Y	N	N	N	N	N	N	N
It is effort faculty,	N	N	N	N	N	N	N	N	N	N	N	N	N	N	N	Y	N	N	N	N	N	N
It is mindfulness faculty,	N	N	N	N	N	N	N	N	N	N	N	N	N	N	N	N	Y	N	N	N	N	N
It is concentration faculty,	N	N	N	N	N	N	N	N	N	N	N	N	N	N	N	N	N	Y	N	N	N	N
It is understanding faculty,	N	N	N	N	N	N	N	N	N	N	N	N	N	N	N	N	N	N	Y	N	N	N
It is I-shall-comprehend-the-unknown faculty,	N	N	N	N	N	N	N	N	N	N	N	N	N	N	N	N	N	N	N	Y	N	N
It is final-knowledge faculty,	N	N	N	N	N	N	N	N	N	N	N	N	N	N	N	N	N	N	N	N	Y	N
It is final-knower faculty,	N	N	N	N	N	N	N	N	N	N	N	N	N	N	N	N	N	N	N	N	N	Y

	is it not faculty?	is it not eye faculty?	is it not ear faculty?	is it not nose faculty?	is it not tongue faculty?	is it not body faculty?	is it not mind faculty?	is it not femininity faculty?	is it not masculinity faculty?	is it not life faculty?	is it not pleasure-faculty?	is it not displeasure-faculty?	is it not joy-faculty?	is it not melancholy-faculty?	is it not equanimity faculty?	is it not faith faculty?	is it not effort faculty?	is it not mindfulness faculty?	is it not concentration faculty?	is it not understanding-faculty?	is it not I-shall-comprehend-the-unknown faculty?	is it not final-knowledge faculty?	is it not final-knower faculty?
It is not eye,	NY	Y	N	N	N	N	N	N	N	N	N	N	N	N	N	N	N	N	N	N	N	N	N
It is not ear,	NY	N	Y	N	N	N	N	N	N	N	N	N	N	N	N	N	N	N	N	N	N	N	N
It is not nose,	NY	N	N	Y	N	N	N	N	N	N	N	N	N	N	N	N	N	N	N	N	N	N	N
It is not tongue,	NY	N	N	N	Y	N	N	N	N	N	N	N	N	N	N	N	N	N	N	N	N	N	N
It is not body,	NY	N	N	N	N	Y	N	N	N	N	N	N	N	N	N	N	N	N	N	N	N	N	N
It is not mind,	NY	N	N	N	N	N	Y	N	N	N	N	N	N	N	N	N	N	N	N	N	N	N	N
It is not female,	NY	N	N	N	N	N	N	NY	N	N	N	N	N	N	N	N	N	N	N	N	N	N	N
It is not male,	NY	N	N	N	N	N	N	N	NY	N	N	N	N	N	N	N	N	N	N	N	N	N	N
It is not life,	NY	N	N	N	N	N	N	N	N	Y	N	N	N	N	N	N	N	N	N	N	N	N	N
It is not pleasure,	NY	N	N	N	N	N	N	N	N	N	Y	N	N	N	N	N	N	N	N	N	N	N	N
It is not displeasure,	NY	N	N	N	N	N	N	N	N	N	N	Y	N	N	N	N	N	N	N	N	N	N	N
It is not joy,	NY	N	N	N	N	N	N	N	N	N	N	N	Y	N	N	N	N	N	N	N	N	N	N
It is not melancholy,	NY	N	N	N	N	N	N	N	N	N	N	N	N	Y	N	N	N	N	N	N	N	N	N

Chapter 10: Pairs on Controlling Faculties

It is not equanimity,	NY	N	N	N	N	N	N	N	N	N	N	N	N	N	NY	N	N	N	N	N	N	N	N
It is not faith,	NY	N	N	N	N	N	N	N	N	N	N	N	N	N	N	Y	N	N	N	N	N	N	N
It is not effort,	NY	N	N	N	N	N	N	N	N	N	N	N	N	N	N	N	Y	N	N	N	N	N	N
It is not mindfulness,	NY	N	N	N	N	N	N	N	N	N	N	N	N	N	N	N	N	Y	N	N	N	N	N
It is not concentration,	NY	N	N	N	N	N	N	N	N	N	N	N	N	N	N	N	N	N	Y	N	N	N	N
It is not understanding,	NY	N	N	N	N	N	N	N	N	N	N	N	N	N	N	N	N	N	N	Y	N	N	N
It is not I-shall-comprehend-the-unknown,	NY	N	N	N	N	N	N	N	N	N	N	N	N	N	N	N	N	N	N	N	Y	N	N
It is not final-knowledge,	NY	N	N	N	N	N	N	N	N	N	N	N	N	N	N	N	N	N	N	N	N	Y	N
It is not final-knower,	NY	N	N	N	N	N	N	N	N	N	N	N	N	N	N	N	N	N	N	N	N	N	Y
		are they not eye?	are they not ear?	are they not nose?	are they not tongue?	are they not body?	are they not mind?	are they not femininity?	are they not masculinity?	are they not life?	are they not pleasure?	are they not displeasure?	are they not joy?	are they not melancholy?	are they not equanimity?	are they not faith?	are they not effort?	are they not mindfulness?	are they not concentration?	are they not understanding?	are they not I-shall-comprehend-the-unknown?	are they not final-knowledge?	are they not final-knower?
These are not faculties,		Y	Y	Y	Y	Y	Y	Y	Y	Y	Y	Y	Y	Y	Y	Y	Y	Y	Y	Y	Y	Y	Y
	is it not faculty?	is it not eye?	is it not ear?	is it not nose?	is it not tongue?	is it not body?	is it not mind?	is it not femininity?	is it not masculinity?	is it not life?	is it not pleasure-?	is it not displeasure-?	is it not joy-?	is it not melancholy-?	is it not equanimity?	is it not faith?	is it not effort?	is it not mindfulness?	is it not concentration?	is it not understanding-?	is it not I-shall-comprehend-the-unknown?	is it not final-knowledge?	is it not final-knower?
It is not eye faculty,	NY	NY	N	N	N	N	N	N	N	N	N	N	N	N	N	N	N	N	N	N	N	N	N
It is not ear faculty,	NY	N	NY	N	N	N	N	N	N	N	N	N	N	N	N	N	N	N	N	N	N	N	N
It is not nose faculty,	NY	N	N	Y	N	N	N	N	N	N	N	N	N	N	N	N	N	N	N	N	N	N	N
It is not tongue faculty,	NY	N	N	N	Y	N	N	N	N	N	N	N	N	N	N	N	N	N	N	N	N	N	N
It is not body faculty,	NY	N	N	N	N	NY	N	N	N	N	N	N	N	N	N	N	N	N	N	N	N	N	N
It is not mind faculty,	NY	N	N	N	N	N	Y	N	N	N	N	N	N	N	N	N	N	N	N	N	N	N	N
It is not femininity faculty,	NY	N	N	N	N	N	N	Y	N	N	N	N	N	N	N	N	N	N	N	N	N	N	N
It is not masculinity faculty,	NY	N	N	N	N	N	N	N	Y	N	N	N	N	N	N	N	N	N	N	N	N	N	N
It is not life faculty,	NY	N	N	N	N	N	N	N	N	Y	N	N	N	N	N	N	N	N	N	N	N	N	N
It is not pleasure faculty,	NY	N	N	N	N	N	N	N	N	N	Y	N	N	N	N	N	N	N	N	N	N	N	N
It is not displeasure faculty,	NY	N	N	N	N	N	N	N	N	N	N	Y	N	N	N	N	N	N	N	N	N	N	N
It is not joy faculty,	NY	N	N	N	N	N	N	N	N	N	N	N	Y	N	N	N	N	N	N	N	N	N	N
It is not melancholy faculty,	NY	N	N	N	N	N	N	N	N	N	N	N	N	Y	N	N	N	N	N	N	N	N	N
It is not equanimity faculty,	NY	N	N	N	N	N	N	N	N	N	N	N	N	N	Y	N	N	N	N	N	N	N	N
It is not faith faculty,	NY	N	N	N	N	N	N	N	N	N	N	N	N	N	N	Y	N	N	N	N	N	N	N
It is not effort faculty,	NY	N	N	N	N	N	N	N	N	N	N	N	N	N	N	N	Y	N	N	N	N	N	N
It is not mindfulness fac.	NY	N	N	N	N	N	N	N	N	N	N	N	N	N	N	N	N	Y	N	N	N	N	N
It is not concentration fac..	NY	N	N	N	N	N	N	N	N	N	N	N	N	N	N	N	N	N	Y	N	N	N	N
It is not understanding fac.	NY	N	N	N	N	N	N	N	N	N	N	N	N	N	N	N	N	N	N	Y	N	N	N
It is not I-shall-comprehend-the-unknown faculty,	NY	N	N	N	N	N	N	N	N	N	N	N	N	N	N	N	N	N	N	N	Y	N	N
It's not final-knowledge fac.	NY	N	N	N	N	N	N	N	N	N	N	N	N	N	N	N	N	N	N	N	N	Y	N
It is not final-knower fac.	NY	N	N	N	N	N	N	N	N	N	N	N	N	N	N	N	N	N	N	N	N		Y

10.1.1 Clarifying word by word

Forward expression

94. *i* (a) That which is eye, is it eye faculty (*cakkhundriya*)?
—No, divine eye (*dibbacakkhu*) and wisdom eye (*paññācakkhu*) are eyes, but not eye faculty. Yes, eye faculty is both (bodily) eye and eye faculty. [79]
(b) That which is eye faculty, is it eye? —Yes. (Same as aforesaid)

ii (a) That which is ear, is it ear faculty (*sotindriya*)?
—No. Divine ear (*dibbasota*) and 'craved ear' (*taṇhāsota*), for examples, are the figurative sense of ear which can not be called ear faculty.
—Yes. Ear faculty is both the physical ear and ear faculty.
(b) That which is ear faculty, is it ear? —Yes. (either way)

iii (a) That which is nose, is it nose faculty (*ghānindriya*)?
—Yes. (bodily nose is also nose faculty).
(b) That which is nose faculty, is it nose? —Yes. (either way)

iv (a) That which is tongue, is it tongue faculty (*jivhindriya*)?
—Yes. (bodily tongue is also tongue faculty)
(b) That which is tongue faculty, is it tongue? —Yes. (either way)

v (a) That which is body, is it body faculty (*kāyindriya*)?
—Yes. Physical body (*kāya*) is both body and body faculty.
—No. Except body (*kāya*), the remaining (internal organs, etc.) are body, but not body faculty.
(b) That which is body faculty, is it body? —Yes. (either way)

vi (a) That which is mind, is it mind faculty (*manindriya*)? —Yes. (either way)
(b) That which is mind faculty, is it mind? —Yes. (either way)

vii (a) That which is female, is it femininity faculty (*itthindriya*)?
—No. (female refers to a gender, a person, able to have pregnancy; femininity faculty refers to the appearance and characteristics of being feminine by nature)
(b) That which is femininity faculty, is it female? —No. (Same as aforesaid)

viii (a) That which is male, is it masculinity faculty (*purisindriya*)?
—No. (male refers to the masculine gender; masculinity faculty refers to the appearance, deportment, characteristics, and everything of a male by nature)
(b) That which is masculinity faculty, is it male? —No. (Same as aforesaid)

---

[79] Three kinds of eye: bodily eye (*maṃsacakkhu*), (divine eye (*dibbacakkhu*), wisdom eye (*paññācakkhu*). *Cf.* DN 10: Saṅgītisutta.

ix (a) That which is life (or vitality), is it life faculty (*jīvitindriya*) [80] ? —Yes.
(b) That which is life faculty, is it life? —Yes. (either way)

x (a) That which is pleasure, is it pleasure-faculty (*sukhindriya*) [81] ? —Yes.
(b) That which is pleasure-faculty, is it pleasure? —Yes. (either way)

xi (a) That which is displeasure, is it displeasure-faculty (*dukkhindriya*) [82] ?
—Yes.
(b) That which is displeasure-faculty, is it pain? —Yes. (either way)

xii (a) That which is joy, is it joy-faculty (*somanassindriya*)?
—Yes. (It experiences delighted or joyful feeling born of mental contact)
(b) That which is joy-faculty, is it joy? —Yes. (either way)

xiii (a) That which is melancholy, is it melancholy-faculty (*domanassindriya*)?
—Yes. (It experiences sorrowful or grievous feeling born of mental contact)
(b) That which is melancholy-faculty, is it melancholy? —Yes. (either way)

xiv (a) That which is equanimity, is it equanimity faculty (*upekkhindriya*)?
—Yes. Equanimity faculty is both equanimity and equanimity faculty.
—No. Except equanimity faculty, the remaining (e.g. neither pleasure nor displeasure) is equanimity, but not equanimity faculty which operates based on mental contact.
(b) That which is equanimity faculty, is it equanimity? —Yes. (either way)

xv (a) That which is confidence or faith (*saddhā*), is it faith faculty (*saddhindriya*)?
—Yes. (with awareness and full understanding of the truth, giving rise to confidence, faith, devotion, unshakeable conviction in the faith faculty)
(b) That which is faith faculty, is it faith? —Yes. (either way)

xvi (a) That which is effort, is it effort faculty (*vīriyindriya*)?
—Yes. (it possesses an ardent, assiduous, and resolute attribute in practising what is taught, in order to be man of morals and ethics)
(b) That which is effort faculty, is it effort? —Yes. (either way)

xvii (a) That which is mindfulness, is it mindfulness faculty (*satindriya*)? —Yes.
(b) That which is mindfulness faculty. Is it mindfulness? —Yes. (either way)

xviii (a) That which is concentration, is it concentration faculty (*samādhindriya*)?
—Yes. (that which is mental serenity or calmness one can focus concentration)
(b) That which is concentration faculty. Is it concentration? —Yes. (either way)

---

[80] *Jīvitindriya*: life faculty which inherently exercises the binding power, and which governs the collaborative functioning of all bodily and mental activities, providing the vitality, continuance, and preservation of life.

[81] Pleasure-faculty and displeasure-faculty functioning by way of bodily contact, not mental.

[82] Displeasure-faculty: it is the bodily contact (not mental contact) through which it experiences unpleasantness, discomfort, painful feeling, pain or suffering.

xix (a) That which is understanding, is it understanding-faculty (*paññindriya*)? —Yes. (It is through understanding that faith and wisdom build on)
(b) That which is understanding-faculty, is it understanding? —Yes. (either way)

xx (a) That which is "I-shall-comprehend-the-unknown." Is it "I-shall-comprehend-the-unknown" faculty [83] (*anaññātaññassāmītindriya*)? —Yes.
(b) That which is "I-shall- comprehend-the-unknown" faculty, is it "I-shall-comprehend-the-unknown?" —Yes. (either way)

xxi (a) That which is the final (or highest) knowledge, is it final-knowledge faculty [84] (*aññindriya*)? —Yes.
(b) That which is the final-knowledge faculty, is it final knowledge?
—Yes. (either way)

xxii (a) That which is final knower, is it final-knower faculty [85] (*aññātāvindriya*)? —Yes.
(b) That which is final-knower faculty, is it final-knower? —Yes. (either way)

Opposite expression

95. *i* (a) That which is not eye, is it not eye faculty?
—Yes. (ear, nose, etc. are neither eye nor eye faculty).
(b) That which is not eye faculty, is it not eye?
—No. Divine eye and wisdom eye are not eye faculty, although are also eye.
—Yes. With the exception of eye and eye faculty, others are neither eye nor eye faculty.

ii (a) That which is not ear, is it not ear faculty? —Yes.
(b) That which is not ear faculty, is it not ear?
—No. Divine ear and 'craved ear' are not ear faculty, although they ear.
—Yes. Except ear and ear faculty, others are neither ear nor ear faculty.

iii (a) That which is not nose, is it nose faculty? —Yes. (either way)
(b) That which is nose faculty, is it not nose? —Yes. (either way)

iv (a) That which is not tongue, is it not tongue faculty? —Yes. (either way)
(b) That which is not tongue faculty, is it not tongue? —Yes. (either way)

---

[83] The faculty of "I-shall-comprehend-the-unknown.": it is by following the noble eightfold Path that one acquires *sotāpattimaggacitta* and realises the 'initial enlightenment' of *sotāpattiphalacitta* which eliminates the three fetters, that gives the name of this faculty.

[84] Faculty of the final knowledge: it refers to the types of wisdom acquired through the four supramundane persons, namely those of *sakadāgāmimaggacitta*, fruition of *sakadāgāphalacitta*, *anāgāmimaggacitta*, and the fruition of *anāgāmiphalacitta*. This faculty is hence asociated with the 'intermediate enlightenment'.

[85] Faculty of the final-knower: it refers to the final knowledge acquired through *arahattamaggacitta* and the fruition-attainment of *arahattaphalacitta* in which an Arahat eliminates all his defilements.

v (a) That which is not body, is it not body faculty? —Yes.
(b) That which is not body faculty. Is it not body?
—No. Except body faculty, others (internal organs) are not body faculty but body.
—Yes. Except body and body faculty, others (eyes, ears, nose, tongue, cognitive objects) are neither body nor body faculty.

vi (a) That which is not mind, is it not mind faculty? —Yes. (either way)
(b) That which is not mind faculty, is it not mind? —Yes. (either way)

vii (a) That which is not female, is it not femininity faculty?
—No. Femininity faculty is not female, but femininity faculty.
—Yes. Besides female and femininity faculty, the remaining faculties and others are neither female nor femininity faculty)
(b) That which is not femininity faculty, is it not female? —Yes. (either way)

viii (a) That which is not male, is it not masculinity faculty?
—No. Masculinity-faculty is not male, but masculinity faculty.
—Yes. Besides male and masculinity faculty, the remaining faculties and others are neither male nor masculinity faculty)
(b) That which is not masculinity faculty, is it male? —Yes. (either way)

ix (a) That which is not life, is it not life faculty? —Yes.
(b) That which is not life faculty, is it not life? —Yes. (either way)

x (a) That which is not pleasure, is it not bodily-pleasure faculty? —Yes.
(b) That which is not bodily-pleasure faculty, is it not bodily pleasure? Yes.

xi (a) That which is not bodily-displeasure faculty, is it not bodily displeasure?
—Yes.
(b) That which is not bodily displeasure, is it not bodily-displeasure faculty?
—Yes. (either way)

xii (a) That which is not joy, is it not joy faculty? —Yes.
(b) That which is not joy faculty, is it not joy? —Yes. (either way)

xiii (a) That which is not melancholy, is it not melancholy faculty? —Yes.
(b) That which is not melancholy faculty, is it not melancholy?
—Yes. (either way)

xiv (a) That which is not equanimity, is it not equanimity faculty? —Yes.
(b) That which is not equanimity faculty, is it not equanimity?
—Yes. Except equanimity, others (pleasure, displeasure, joy, sorrow, etc.) are neither equanimity nor equanimity faculty.

xv (a) That which is not faith, is it not faith faculty? —Yes.
(b) That which is not faith faculty, is it not faith? —Yes. (either way)

xvi (a) That which is not energy, is it not effort faculty? —Yes.
(b) That which is not effort faculty, is it not energy? —Yes. (either way)

xvii (a) That which is not mindfulness, is it not mindfulness faculty? —Yes.
(b) That which is not mindfulness faculty, is it not mindfulness?
—Yes. (either way)

xviii (a) That which is not concentration, is it not concentration faculty? —Yes.
(b) That which is not concentration faculty, is it not concentration?
—Yes. (either way)

xix (a) That which is not understanding, is it not understanding faculty? —Yes.
(b) That which is not understanding faculty, is it not understanding? —Yes.

xx (a) That which is not I-shall-comprehend-the-unknown, is it not I-shall-comprehend-the-unknown faculty? —Yes.
(b) That which is not I-shall-comprehend-the-unknown faculty, is it not I-shall-comprehend-the-unknown? —Yes. (either way)

xxi (a) That which is not final knowledge, is it not final-knowledge faculty? —Yes
(b) That which is not final-knowledge faculty, is it not final knowledge?
—Yes. (either way)

xxii(a) That which is not final-knower, is it not final-knower faculty? —Yes.
(b) That which is not final-knower faculty, is it not final-knower?
—Yes. (either way)

10.1.2 Wheel based on word-by-word clarification

Forward expression

96. *i* (a) That which is eye, is it eye faculty?
—No. Divine eye and wisdom eye are eyes, but not eye faculty.
—Yes. Eye faculty is both eye and eye faculty.
(b) These are faculties. Are they ear faculty?
—No. Others (eye faculty, nose faculty, etc.) are faculties, but not ear faculty.
—Yes. Ear faculty is both faculty and ear faculty.

ii (a) That which is eye, is it eye faculty? —Same as in 96 *i* (a).
(b) These are faculties. Are they nose faculty?
—No. Others (eye faculty, ear faculty, etc.) are faculties, but not nose faculty.
—Yes. Nose faculty is both faculty and nose faculty.

iii (a) That which is eye, is it eye faculty? —Same as in 96 *i* (a).
(b) These are faculties. Are they tongue faculty?
—No. Others (eye faculty, ear faculty, etc.) are faculties, but not tongue faculty.
—Yes. Tongue faculty is both faculty and tongue faculty.

iv (a) That which is eye, is it eye faculty? —Same as in 96 *i* (a).
(b) These are faculties. Are they body faculty?
—No. Others (eye faculty, ear faculty, etc.) are faculties, but not body faculty.
—Yes. Body faculty is both faculty and body faculty.

v (a) That which is eye, is it eye faculty? —Same as in 96 *i* (a).
(b) These are faculties. Are they mind faculty?
—No. Others (eye faculty, ear faculty, etc.) are faculties, but not mind faculty.
—Yes. Mind faculty is both faculty and mind faculty.

vi (a) That which is eye, is it eye faculty? —Same as in 96 *i* (a).
(b) These are faculties. Are they femininity faculty?
—No. Others (ear faculty, etc.) are faculties, but not femininity faculty.
—Yes. Femininity faculty is both faculty and femininity faculty.

vii (a) That which is eye, is it eye faculty? —Same as in 96 *i* (a).
(b) These are faculties. Are they masculinity faculty?
—No. Others (ear faculty, etc.) are faculties, but not masculinity faculty.
—Yes. Masculinity faculty is both faculty and masculinity faculty.

viii (a) That which is eye, is it eye faculty? —Same as in 96 *i* (a).
(b) These are faculties. Are they life faculty?
—No. Others (eye faculty, ear faculty, etc.) are faculties, but not life faculty.
—Yes. Life faculty is both faculty and life faculty.

ix (a) That which is eye, is it eye faculty? —Same as in 96 *i* (a).
(b) These are faculties. Are they bodily-pleasure faculty?
—No. Others (ear faculty, etc.) are faculties, but not bodily-pleasure faculty.
—Yes. Bodily-pleasure faculty is both faculty and bodily-pleasure faculty.
…..P…..

x (a) That which is eye, is it eye faculty? —Same as in 96 *i* (a).
(b) These are faculties. Are they effort faculty?
—No. Others (eye faculty, ear faculty, etc.) are faculties, but not effort faculty.
—Yes. Effort faculty is both faculty and effort faculty.

x (a) That which is eye, is it eye faculty? —Same as in 96 *i* (a).
(b) These are faculties. Are they mindfulness faculty?
—No. Others (ear faculty, etc.) are faculties, but not mindfulness faculty.
—Yes. Mindfulness faculty is both faculty and mindfulness faculty.

xi (a) That which is eye, is it eye faculty? —Same as in 96 *i* (a).
(b) These are faculties. Are they concentration faculty?
—No. Others (ear faculty, etc.) are faculties, but not concentration faculty.
—Yes. Concentration faculty is both faculty and concentration faculty.

xii (a) That which is eye, is it eye faculty? —Same as in 96 *i* (a).
(b) These are faculties. Are they understanding faculty?
—No. Others (ear faculty, etc.) are faculties, but not understanding faculty.
—Yes. Understanding faculty is both faculty and understanding faculty.

xiii (a) That which is eye, is it eye faculty? —Same as in 96 *i* (a).
(b) These are faculties. Are they "I-shall-comprehend-the-"unknown" faculty?
—No. Others (eye faculty, ear faculty, etc.) are faculties, but not "I-shall-comprehend-the-unknown" faculty.
—Yes. "I-shall-comprehend-the-unknown" faculty is both faculty and "I-shall-comprehend-the-unknown' faculty.

xiv (a) That which is eye, is it eye faculty? —Same as in 96 *i* (a).
(b) These are faculties. Are they final-knowledge faculty?
—No. Others (ear faculty, etc.) are faculties, but not final-knowledge faculty.
—Yes. Final-knowledge faculty is both faculty and final-knowledge faculty.

xv (a) That which is eye, is it eye faculty? —Same as in 96 *i* (a).
(b) These are faculties. Are they final-knower faculty?
—No. Others (ear faculty, etc.) are faculties, but not final-knower faculty.
—Yes. Final-knower faculty is both faculty and final-knower faculty.

97. *i* (a) That which is ear, is it ear faculty?
—No. Divine ear, 'craved' ear are ears, but not ear faculty.
—Yes. Ear faculty is both faculty and ear faculty.
(b) These are faculties. Are they eye faculty?
—No. Others (ear faculty, nose faculty, etc.) are faculties, but not eye faculty.
—Yes. Eye faculty is both faculty and eye faculty. .....P.....

ii (a) That which is ear, is it ear faculty? —Same as in 97 *i* (a).
(b) These are faculties. Are they final-knower faculty?
—No. Others (nose faculty, etc.) are faculties, but not final-knower faculty.
—Yes. Final-knower faculty is both faculty and final-knower faculty.

98. *i* (a) That which is nose, is it nose faculty? —Yes. (either way)
(b) These are faculties. Are they eye faculty? —Same as in 97 *i* (b) .....P.....

ii (a) That which is nose, is it nose faulty? —Yes. (either way)
(b) These are faculties. Are they final-knower faculty?
—Same as in 97 *ii* (b) .....P.....

99. *i* (a) That which is tongue, is it tongue faculty? —Yes. (either way)
(b) These are faculties. Are they eye faculty? —Same as in 97 *i* (b) .....P.....

ii (a) That which is tongue, is it tongue faculty? —Yes. (either way)
(b) These are faculties. Are they final-knower faculty?
—Same as in 97 *ii* (b) .....P.....

100. *i* (a) That which is body, is it body faculty?
—No. Except body faculty, others (internal organs, etc.) are body, but not called body faculty.
—Yes. Body faculty is both body and body faculty.
(b) These are faculties. Are they eye faculty? —Same as in 97 *i* (b) .....P.....

ii (a) That which is body, is it body faculty? —Same as the aforesaid.
(b) These are faculties. Are they final-knower faculty?
—Same as in 97 *ii* (b) .....P.....

101. *i* (a) That which is mind, is it mind faculty? —Yes. (either way)
(b) These are faculties. Are they eye faculty? —Same as in 97 *i* (b) .....P.....

ii (a) That which is mind, is it mind faculty? —Yes. (either way)
(b) These are faculties. Are they final-knower faculty?
—Same as in 97 *ii* (b) .....P.....

102. *i* (a) That which is female, is it femininity faculty? —No. Same as 94 *vii* (a).
(b) These are faculties. Are they eye faculty? —Same as in 97 *i* (b) .....P.....

ii (a) That which is female, is it femininity faculty? —No. Same as no. 94 *vii* (a).
(b) These are faculties. Are they final-knower faculty?
—Same as in 97 *ii* (b) .....P.....

103. *i* (a) That which is male, is it masculinity faculty? —No. Same as 95 *vii* (a).
(b) These are faculties. Are they eye faculty? —Same as in 97 *i* (b) .....P.....

ii (a) That which is male, is it masculinity faculty? —No. Same as no. 95 *vii* (a).
(b) These are faculties. Are they final-knower faculty?
—Same as in 97 *ii* (b) .....P.....

104. *i* (a) That which is life, is it life faculty? Yes.
(b) These are faculties. Are they eye faculty? —Same as in 97 *i* (b) .....P.....

ii (a) That which is life, is it life faculty? Yes.
(b) These are faculties. Are they final-knower faculty?
—Same as in 97 *ii* (b) .....P.....

105. *i* (a) That which is bodily pleasure, is it bodily-pleasure faculty?
—Yes. .....P.....
106. *i* (a) That which is bodily displeasure, is it bodily-displeasure faculty?
—Yes. .....P.....
108. *i* (a) That which is melancholy, is it melancholy faculty?
—Yes. .....P.....

109. *i* (a) That which is equanimity, is it equanimity faculty?
—Same as in no. 94 *xiv* (a)

(b) These are faculties. Are they eye faculty? —Same as in 97 *i* (b) .....P.....

ii (a) That which is equanimity, is it equanimity faculty?
—Same as in no. 94 *xiv* (a)
(b) These are faculties. Are they final-knower faculty?
—Same as in 97 *ii* (b) .....P.....

110. That which is faith, is it faith faculty? Yes. .....P.....
111. That which is energy, is it effort faculty? Yes. .....P.....
112. That which is mindfulness, is it mindfulness faculty? Yes. .....P.....
113. That which is concentration, is it concentration faculty? Yes. .....P.....
114. That which is understanding, is it understanding faculty? Yes. .....P.....
115. That which is "I-shall-comprehend-the-unknown", is it "I-shall-comprehend-the-unknown" faculty? —Yes. .....P.....

116. That which is final knowledge, is it final-knowledge faculty?
—Yes. .....P.....
117. That which is final-knower, is it final-knower faculty? —Yes. (either way)
(b) These are faculties. Are they eye faculty? —Same as in 97 *i* (b) .....P.....

ii (a) That which is final-knower, is it final-knower faculty? —Yes. (either way)
(b) These are faculties. Are they final-knowledge faculty?
—Same as in no. 96 *xiv* (b)......P.....

iii (a) That which is final-knower, is it final-knower faculty? —Yes. (either way)
(b) These are faculties. Are they final-knowledge faculty?
—Same as in no. 96 *xiv* (b)

Opposite expression

118. *i* (a) That which is not eye, is it not eye faculty?
—Yes. (With the exception of eye, the remaining controlling faculties are neither eye nor eye faculty).
(b) These are not faculties. Are they not ear faculty?
—Yes. (With the exception of the 22 controlling faculties, others are neither of the two in abovementioned)

ii (a) That which is not eye, is it not eye faculty? —Yes. (Same as in no. 118 *i* a)
(b) These are not faculties. Are they not nose faculty?—Yes (Same as in 118 *i* b)

iii (a) That which is not eye, is it eye faculty? —Yes. (Same as in no. 118 *i* a)
(b) These are not faculties. Are they not tongue faculty?—Yes. (Same as 118 *i* b)

iv (a) That which is not eye, is it not eye faculty? —Yes. (Same as in no. 118 *i* a)
(b) These are not faculties. Are they not body faculty? —Yes. (Same as 118 *i* b)

v (a) That which is not eye, is it not eye faculty? —Yes. (Same as in no. 118 *i* a)
(b) These are not faculties. Are they not mind faculty?

—Yes. (Same as in no. 118)

vi (a) That which is not eye, is it not eye faculty? —Yes. (Same as in no. 118 *i* a)
(b) These are not faculties. Are they not femininity faculty?
—Yes. (Same as in no. 118 *i* b)

vii (a) That which is not eye, is it not eye faculty? —Yes (Same as in no. 118 *i* a)
(b) These are not faculties. Are they not masculinity faculty?
—Yes. (Same as in no. 118 *i* b)

viii (a) That which is not eye, is it not eye faculty?—Yes (Same as in no. 118 *i* a)
(b) These are not faculties. Are they not bodily-pleasure faculty?
—Yes. (Same as in no. 118 *i* b)

ix (a) That which is not eye, is it not eye faculty? —Yes. (Same as in no. 118 *i* a)
(b) These are not faculties. Are they not bodily-displeasure faculty?
—Yes. (Same as in no. 118 *i* b)

x (a) That which is not eye, is it not eye faculty? —Yes. (Same as in no. 118 *i* a)
(b) These are not faculties. Are they not joy faculty?
—Yes. (Same as in no. 118 *i* b)

xi (a) That which is not eye, is it not eye faculty? —Yes. (Same as in no. 118 *i* a)
(b) These are not faculties. Are they not melancholy faculty?
—Yes. (Same as in no. 118 *i* b)

xii (a) That which is not eye, is it not eye faculty? —Yes (Same as in no. 118 *i* a)
(b) These are not faculties. Are they not equanimity faculty?
—Yes. (Same as in no. 118 *i* b)

xiii (a) That which is not eye, is it not eye faculty?—Yes (Same as in no. 118 *i* a)
(b) These are not faculties. Are they faith faculty?
—Yes. (Same as in no. 118 *i* b)

xiv (a) That which is not eye, is it not eye faculty?—Yes (Same as in no. 118 *i* a)
(b) These are not faculties. Are they not effort faculty?
—Yes. (Same as in no. 118 *i* b)

xv (a) That which is not eye, is it not eye faculty?—Yes. (Same as in no. 118 *i* a)
(b) These are not faculties. Are they not mindfulness faculty?
—Yes. (Same as in no. 118 *i* b)

xvi (a) That which is not eye, is it not eye faculty?—Yes (Same as in no. 118 *i* a)
(b) These are not faculties. Are they not concentration faculty?
—Yes. (Same as in no. 118 *i* b)

xvii (a) That which is not eye, is it not eye faculty? —Yes. (Same as in 118 *i* a)
(b) These are not faculties. Are they not understanding faculty?

—Yes. (Same as in no. 118 *i* b)

xviii (a) That which is not eye, is it not eye faculty? —Yes. (Same as in 118 *i* a)
(b) These are not faculties. Are they not "I-shall-comprehend-the-unknown" faculty? —Yes. (Same as in no. 118 *i* b)

xix (a) That which is not eye, is it not eye faculty?—Yes (Same as in no. 118 *i* a)
(b) These are not faculties. Are they not final-knowledge faculty?
—Yes. (Same as in no. 118 *i* b)

xx (a) That which is not eye, is it not eye faculty?—Yes. (Same as in no. 118 *i* a)
(b) These are not faculties. Are they not final-knower faculty?
—Yes. (Same as in no. 118 *i* b)

119. *i* (a) That which is not ear, is it not ear faculty?
—Yes. (the remaining faculties are neither ear nor ear faculty)
(b) These are not faculties. Are they not faculty? —Yes. (See 118 *i* b) .....P.....

ii (a) That which is not ear, is it not ear faculty? —Yes. (Same as aforesaid)
(b) These are not faculties. Are they final-knower faculty? —Yes. (See 118 *i* b)

120. *i* (a) That which is not nose, is it not nose faculty?
—Yes. (the remaining faculties are neither nose nor nose faculty)
(b) These are not faculties. Are they not eye faculty? —Yes (See 118 *i* b) .....P.....

That which is not nose, is it not nose faculty? —Yes. (Same as aforesaid)
(b) These are not faculties. Are they not final-knower faculty?
—Yes. (Same as in no. 118 *i* b)

122. *i* (a) That which is not body, is it body faculty?
—Yes. (the remaining faculties are neither body nor body faculty)
(b) These are not faculties. Are not eye faculty? —Yes (Same as 118 *i* b) .....P.....

ii (a) That which is not body, is it not body faculty? —Yes. (Same as aforesaid)
(b) These are not faculties. Are they not final-knower faculty?
—Yes. (Same as in no. 118 *i* b)

123. *i* (a) That which is not mind, is it not mind faculty?
—Yes. (the remaining faculties are neither mind nor mind faculty)
(b) These are not faculties. Are they not eye faulty?
—Yes. (Same as in no. 118 *i* b)

ii (a) That which is not mind, is it not mind faculty? —Yes. (Same as aforesaid)
(b) These are not faculties. Are they not final-knower faculty?
—Yes. (Same as in no. 118 *i* b)

124. *i* (a) That which is not female, is it not femininity faculty?

—Same as in no. 95 *vii* (a).
(b) These are not faculties. Are they eye faculty? Yes. …..P…..
ii (a) That which is not female, is it not femininity faculty?
—Same as in no. 95 *vii* (a).
(b) These are not faculties. Are they not final-knower?
—Yes. (Same as in no. 118 *i* b)

125. *i* (a) That which is not masculinity, is it not masculinity faculty?
—Same as in no. 95 *viii* (a).
(b) These are not faculties. Are they not final-knower faculty?
—Yes. (Same as in no. 118 *i* b)

126. *i* (a) That which is not life, is it not life faculty?
—Yes. (the remaining faculties are neither life nor life faculty)
(b) These are not faculties. Are they not eye faculty?
—Yes. (Same as in no. 118 *i* b) …..P…..
ii (a) That which is not life, is it not life faculty? —Yes. (Same as aforesaid)
(b) These are not faculties. Are they not final-knower faculty?
—Yes. (Same as in no. 118 *i* b)

127. *i* (a) That which is not bodily pleasure, is it not bodily-pleasure faculty?
—Yes. (Except bodily pleasure, the remaining faculties are neither bodily pleasure nor bodily-pleasure faculty)
(b) These are not faculties. Are they not eye faculty?
—Yes. (Same as in no. 118 *i* b) …..P…..
ii (a) That which is not bodily pleasure, is it not bodily-pleasure faculty?
—Yes. (Same as aforesaid)
(b) These are not faculties. Are they not final-knower faculty?
—Yes. (Same as in no. 118 *i* b)

128. *i* (a) That which is not bodily displeasure, is it not bodily-displeasure faculty?
—Yes. (Except bodily displeasure, the remaining faculties are neither bodily displeasure nor bodily-displeasure faculty)
(b) These are not faculties. Are they not eye faculty?
—Yes. (Same as in no. 118 *i* b) …..P…..
ii (a) That which is not bodily displeasure, is it not bodily-displeasure faculty?
—Yes. (Same as aforesaid)
(b) These are not faculties. Are they not final-knower faculty? —Yes.

129. *i* (a) That which is not joy, is it not joy faculty? —Yes.
(b) These are not faculties. Are they not eye faculty? —Yes. …..P…..
ii (a) That which is not joy, is it not joy faculty? —Yes.
(b) These are not faculties. Are they not final-knower faculty? —Yes.

130. *i* (a) That which is not melancholy, is it not melancholy faculty? —Yes.
(b) These are not faculties. Are they not eye faculty? —Yes. …..P…..

ii (a) That which is not melancholy, is it not melancholy faculty? —Yes.
(b) These are not faculties. Are they not final-knower faculty? —Yes.

131. *i* (a) That which is not equanimity, is it not equanimity faculty? —Yes.
(b) These are not faculties. Are they not eye faculty? —Yes. .....P.....
ii (a) That which is not equanimity, is it not equanimity faculty? —Yes.
(b) These are not faculties. Are they final-knower faculty? —Yes.

132. *i* (a) That which is not faith, is it not faith faculty? —Yes.
(b) These are not faculties. Are they not eye faculty? —Yes. .....P.....
ii (a) That which is not faith, is it not faith faculty? —Yes.
(b) These are not faculties. Are they final-knower faculty? —Yes.

133. *i* (a) That which is not energy, is it not effort faculty? —Yes.
(b) These are not faculties. Are they not eye faculty? —Yes. .....P.....
ii (a) That which is not energy, is it not effort faculty? —Yes.
(b) These are not faculties. Are they final-knower faculty? —Yes.

134. *i* (a) That which is not mindfulness, is it not mindfulness faculty? —Yes.
(b) These are not faculties. Are they not eye faculty? —Yes. .....P.....
ii (a) That which is not mindfulness, is it not mindfulness faculty? —Yes.
(b) These are not faculties. Are they final-knower faculty? —Yes.

135. *i* (a) That which is not concentration, is it not concentration faculty? —Yes.
(b) These are not faculties. Are they not eye faculty? —Yes. .....P.....
ii (a) That which is not concentration, is it not concentration faculty? —Yes.
(b) These are not faculties. Are they not final-knower faculty? —Yes.

136. *i* (a) That which is not understanding, is it not understanding faculty? —Yes.
(b) These are not faculties. Are they not eye faculties? —Yes. .....P.....
ii (a) That which is not understanding, is it not understanding faculty? —Yes.
(b) These are not faculties. Are they not final-knower faculty? —Yes.

137. *i* (a) That which is not "I-shall-comprehend-the-unknown", is it not "I-shall-comprehend-the-unknown" faculty? —Yes.
(b) These are not faculties. Are they not eye faculty? —Yes. .....P.....
ii (a) That which is not "I-shall-comprehend-the-unknown." Is it not "I-shall-comprehend-the-unknown" faculty? —Yes.
(b) These are not faculties. Are they not final knower faculty? —Yes.

138. *i* (a) That which is not final knowledge, is it not final-knowledge faculty? —Yes.
(b) These are not faculties. Are they not eye faculties? —Yes. .....P.....
ii (a) That which is not final knowledge, is it not final-knowledge faculty?Yes
(b) These are not faculties. Are they not final-knower faculty? —Yes.
139. *i* (a) That which is not final knowledge, is it not final-knower faculty? Yes.
(b) These are not faculties. Are they not eye faculties? —Yes. .....P.....

ii (a) That which is not final-knower, is it not final-knower faculty? —Yes.
(b) These are not faculties. Are they not final-knowledge faculties? —Yes.

10.1.3 Pure *Dhamma*

Forward expression

140. *i* (a) That which is eye, is it faculty?
—Yes. (either way)
—No. Divine eye and wisdom eye are called eye, but they are not faculty.
(b) These are faculties. Are they eye faculties?
—Yes. Eye faculty is both faculty and eye faculty.
—No. Others (ear faculty, nose faculty, etc.) are faculties, but not eye faculty.

ii (a) That which is ear, is it faculty?
—Yes. (either way)
—No. Divine ear and 'craved ear' are called ear, but they are not faculty.
(b) These are faculties. Are they ear faculty?
—Yes. Ear faculty is both faculty and ear faculty.
—No. Others (nose faculty, etc.) are faculties, but are not ear faculty.

iii (a) That which is nose, is it faculty? —Yes. (either way)
(b) These are faculties. Are they nose faculty?
—Yes. Nose faculty is both faculty and nose faculty.
—No. Others (eye faculty, ear faculty, etc.) are faculties, but are not nose faculty.

iv (a) That which is tongue, is it faculty? —Yes. (either way)
(b) These are faculties. Are they tongue faculty?
—Yes. Tongue faculty is both faculty and tongue faculty.
—No. Others (eye faculty, etc.) are faculties, but are not tongue faculty.

v (a) That which is body, is it faculty?
—Yes. (either way)
—No. Others (internal organs, etc.) are a part of body, but are not body faculty.
(b) These are faculties. Are they body faculty?
—Yes. Body faculty is both faculty and body faculty.
—No. Others (eye faculty, etc.) are faculties, but are not body faculty.

vi (a) That which is mind, is it faculty? —Yes. (either way)
(b) These are faculties. Are they mind faulty?
—Yes. Mind faculty is both faculty and mind faculty.
—No. Others (eye faculty, etc.) are faculties, but are not mind faculty.

vii (a) That which is female, is it faculty? —No. (female is person, not a faculty)
(b) These are faculties. Are they femininity faculty?
—Yes. Femininity faculty is both faculty and femininity faculty.
—No. Remaining are the 21 faculties; they are not femininity faculty.

viii (a) That which is male, is it faculty? —No. (male is person, not a faculty)
(b) These are faculties. Are they masculinity faculty?
—Yes. Masculinity faculty is both faculty and masculinity faculty.
—No. Remaining are the 21 faculties; they are not masculinity faculty.

ix (a) That which is life, is it faculty? —Yes. (either way)
(b) These are faculties. Are they life faculty?
—Yes. Life faculty is both faculty and life faculty.
—No. Others (eye faculty, etc.) are faculties, but are not life faculty.

x (a) That which is bodily pleasure, is it faculty? —Yes. (either way)
(b) These are faculties. Are they bodily-pleasure faculty?
—Yes. bodily-pleasure faculty is both faculty and bodily-pleasure faculty.
—No. Others (eye faculty, etc.) are faculties, but are not bodily-pleasure faculty.

xi (a) That which is bodily displeasure, is it faculty? —Yes. (either way)
(b) These are faculties. Are they bodily displeasure faculties?
—Yes. Bodily-displeasure faculty is both faculty and bodily-displeasure faculty.
—No. The remaining are 21 faculties, but are not bodily-displeasure faculty.

xii (a) That which is joy, is it faculty? —Yes. (either way)
(b) These are faculties. Are they joy faculty?
—Yes. Joy faculty is both faculty and joy faulty.
—No. The remaining are 21 faculties, but are not joy faculty.

xiii (a) That which is melancholy, is it faculty? —Yes. (either way)
(b) These are faculties. Are they melancholy faculty?
—Yes. Melancholy faculty is both faculty and melancholy faculty.
—No. The remaining are 21 faculties, but are not melancholy faculty.

xiv (a) That which is equanimity, is it faculty?
—Yes. (either way)
—No. Others (e.g. neither happy nor sad, etc.) are equanimity, but not faculty.
(b) These are faculties. Are they equanimity faculty?
—Yes. Equanimity faculty is both faculty and equanimity faculty.
—No. The remaining are 21 faculties, but are not equanimity faculty.

xv (a) That which is faith, is it faculty? —Yes. (either way)
(b) These are faculties. Are they faith faculty?
—Yes. Faith faculty is both faculty and faith faculty.
—No. The remaining are 21 faculties, but are not faith faculty.

xvi (a) That which is energy, is it faculty? —Yes. (either way)
(b) These are faculties. Are they effort faculty?
—Yes. Effort faculty is both faculty and effort faculty.
—No. The remaining are 21 faculties, but are not effort faculty.

xvii (a) That which is mindfulness, is it faculty? —Yes. (either way)
(b) These are faculties. Are they effort faculty?
—Yes. Effort faculty is both faculty and effort faculty.
—No. The remaining are 21 faculties, but are not effort faculty.

xvii (a) That which is mindfulness, is it faculty? —Yes. (either way)
(b) These are faculties. Are they faculty?
—Yes. Mindfulness faculty is both faculty and mindfulness faculty.
—No. The remaining are 21 faculties, but are not mindfulness faculty.

xix (a) That which is concentration, is it faculty? —Yes. (either way)
(b) These are faculties. Are they concentration faculty?
—Yes. Concentration faculty is both faculty and concentration faculty.
—No. The remaining are 21 faculties, but are not concentration faculty.

xx (a) That which is understanding, is it faculty? —Yes. (either way)
(b) These are faculties. Are they understanding faculties?
—Yes. Understanding faculty is both faculty and understanding faculty.
—No. The remaining are 21 faculties, but are not understanding faculty.

xxi (a) That which is "I-shall-comprehend-the-unknown", is it faculty? —Yes.
(b) These are faculties. Are they "I-shall-comprehend-the-unknown faculty?
—"I-shall-comprehend-the-unknown" faculty is both faculty and "I-shall-comprehend-the-unknown" faculty. The remaining are the 21 faculties, but are not "I-shall-comprehend-the-unknown" faculty.

xxii (a) That which is final knowledge, is it faculty? —Yes. (either way)
(b) These are faculties. Are they final-knowledge faculty?
—Yes. Final-knowledge faculty is both faculty and final-knowledge faculty.
—No. The remaining are 21 faculties, but are not final-knowledge faculty.

xxiii (a) That which is final-knower, is it faculty? —Yes. (either way)
(b) These are faculties. Are they final-knower faculty?
—Yes. Final-knower faculty is both faculty and final-knower faculty.
—No. The remaining are 21 faculties, but are not final-knower faculty.

Opposite expression

141. *i* (a) That which is not eye, is it not faculty?
—No. Except for eye, the remaining 21 faculties are not eye but faculties.
—Yes. Except for eye and 22 faculties, others are neither eye nor faculties.
(b) These are not faculties. Are they not eye faculties?
—Yes. (With the exception of the 22 controlling faculties, others are neither of the two in abovementioned)

ii (a) That which is not ear, is it not faculty?

—No. Except for ear, the remaining 21 faculties are not ear but faculties.
—Yes. Except for ear and 22 faculties, others are neither ear nor faculties.
(b) These are not faculties. Are they not ear faculty? —Yes. (Same as in 141 *i* b)

iii (a) That which is not nose, is it not faculty?
—No. Except for nose, the remaining 21 faculties are not nose but faculties.
—Yes. Except for nose and 22 faculties, others are neither nose nor faculties.
(b) These are not faculties. Are they not nose faculty? —Yes (Refer to 141 *i* b)

iv (a) That which is not tongue, is it not faculty?
—No. Except for tongue, the remaining 21 faculties are not tongue but faculties.
—Yes. Except for tongue and 22 faculties, others are neither tongue nor faculties.
(b) These are not faculties. Are they not tongue faculty? —Yes (Refer to 141 *i* b)

v (a) That which is not body, is it not faculty?
—Yes. Except for body and 22 faculties, others are neither body nor faculties.
(b) These are not faculties. Are they not body faculty? —Yes (Refer to 141 *i* b)

vi (a) That which is not mind, is it not faculty?
—No. Except for mind, the remaining 21 faculties are not mind but faculties.
—Yes. Except for mind and 22 faculties, others are neither mind nor faculties.
(b) These are not faculties. Are they not mind faculty? —Yes. (Refer to 141 *i* b)

vii (a) That which is not female, is it not faculty?
—No. Except for female, the 22 faculties are not female but faculties.
—Yes. Except for female and 22 faculties, others are neither female nor faculties.
(b) These are not faculties. Are they not femininity faculty? —Yes. (See 141 *i* b)

viii (a) That which is not male, is it not faculty?
—No. Except for male, the 22 faculties are not male but faculties.
—Yes. Except for male and 22 faculties, others are neither male nor faculties.
(b) These are not faculties. Are they not masculinity faculty?—Yes (See 141 *i* b)

ix (a) That which is not life, is it not faculty?
—No. Except for life, the remaining 21 faculties are not life but faculties.
—Yes. Except for life and 22 faculties, others are neither life nor faculties.
(b) These are not faculties. Are they not life faculty? —Yes. (Refer to 141 *i* b)

x (a) That which is not bodily pleasure, is it not faculty?
—No. Except for bodily pleasure, the remaining 21 faculties are not bodily pleasure but faculties.
—Yes. Except for bodily pleasure and 22 faculties, others are neither bodily pleasure nor faculties.
(b) These are not faculties. Are they not bodily pleasure faculties?
—Yes. (Refer to 141 *i* b)

xi (a) That which is not bodily displeasure, is it not faculty?

—No. Except for bodily displeasure, the remaining 21 faculties are not bodily displeasure but faculties.
—Yes. Except for bodily displeasure and 22 faculties, others are neither bodily displeasure nor faculties.
(b) These are not faculties. Are they not bodily-displeasure faculty?
—Yes. (Refer to 141 *i* b)

xii (a) That which is not joy, is it not faculty?
—No. Except for joy, the remaining 21 faculties are not joy but faculties.
—Yes. Except for joy and 22 faculties, others are neither joy nor faculties.
(b) These are not faculties. Are they not joy faculty? —Yes. (Refer to 141 *i* b)

xiii (a) That which is not melancholy, is it not faculty?
—No. Except for melancholy, the remaining faculties are not melancholy but faculties.
—Yes. Except for melancholy and 22 faculties, others are neither melancholy nor faculties.
(b) These are not faculties. Are they not melancholy faculty?
—Yes. (Refer to 141 *i* b)

xiv (a) That which is not equanimity, is it not faculty?
—No. Except for equanimity, the remaining are not equanimity but faculties.
—Yes. Except for equanimity and 22 faculties, others are neither equanimity nor faculties.
(b) These are not faculties. Are they not equanimity faculty? —Yes (See 141 *i* b)

xv (a) That which is not faith, is it not faculty?
—No. Except for faith, the remaining 21 faculties are not faith but faculties.
—Yes. Except for faith and 22 faculties, others are neither faith nor faculties.
(b) These are not faculties. Are they not faith faculties? —Yes. (Refer to 141 *i* b)

xvi (a) That which is not effort, is it not faculty?
—No. Except for effort, the remaining 21 faculties are not effort but faculties.
—Yes. Except for effort and 22 faculties, others are neither effort nor faculties.
(b) These are not faculties. Are they not effort faculty? —Yes. (Refer to 141 *i* b)

xvii (a) That which is not mindfulness, is it not faculty?
—No. Except for mindfulness, the remaining are not mindfulness but faculties.
—Yes. Except for mindfulness and 22 faculties, others are neither mindfulness nor faculties.
(b) These are not faculties. Are they not mindfulness faculty?
—Yes. (Refer to 141 *i* b)

xviii (a) That which is not concentration, is it not faculty?
—No. Except for concentration, the remaining 21 faculties are not concentration but faculties.

—Yes. Except for concentration and 22 faculties, others are neither concentration nor faculties.
(b) These are not faculties. Are they not concentration faculty?
—Yes. (Refer to 141 *i* b)

xix (a) That which is not understanding, is it not faculty?
—No. Except for understanding, the remaining 21 faculties are not understanding but faculties.
—Yes. Except for understanding and 22 faculties, others are neither understanding nor faculties.
(b) These are not faculties. Are they not understanding faculty?
—Yes. (Refer to 141 *i* b)

xx (a) That which is not "I-shall-comprehend-the-unknown", is it not faculty? No.
—Yes. Except for joy and 22 faculties, others are neither joy nor faculties.
(b) These are not faculties. Are they not "I-shall-comprehend-the-unknown" faculty? —Yes. (Refer to 141 *i* b)

xxi (a) That which is not final knowledge, is it not faculty?
—No, except for final knowledge, the remaining 21 faculties are not final knowledge but faculties.
—Yes. Except for final knowledge and 22 faculties, others are neither final knowledge nor faculties.
(b) These are not faculties. Are they not final-knowledge faculty?
—Yes. (Refer to 141 *i* b)

xxii (a) That which is not final-knower, is it not faculty?
—No, except for final-knower, the remaining 21 faculties are not final-knower but faculties.
—Yes. Except for final-knower and 22 faculties, others are neither final-knower nor faculties.
(b) These are not faculties. Are they not final-knower faculty?
—Yes. (Refer to 141 *i* b)

10.1.4 Wheel, based on pure *dhamma*

Forward expression

142. *i* (a) That which is eye, is it faculty? —Yes. (either way)
(b) These are faculties. Are they ear faculty?
—Yes. Ear faculty is both faculty and ear faculty.
—No. The remaining are 21 faculties, but not ear faculty.

ii (a) That which is eye, is it faculty? —Yes. (either way)
(b) These are faculties. Are they nose faculty?
—Yes. Nose faculty is both faculty and nose faculty.
—No. The remaining are 21 faculties, but not nose faculty.

iii (a) That which is eye, is it faculty? —Yes. (either way)
(b) These are faculties. Are they tongue faculty?
—Yes. Tongue faculty is both faculty and tongue faculty.
—No. The remaining are 21 faculties, but not tongue faculty.

iv (a) That which is eye, is it faculty? —Yes. (either way)
(b) These are faculties. Are they body faculty?
—Yes. Body faculty is both faculty and body faculty.
—No. The remaining are 21 faculties, but not body faculty.

v (a) That which is eye, is it faculty? —Yes. (either way)
(b) These are faculties. Are they mind faculty?
—Yes. Mind faculty is both faculty and mind faculty.
—No. The remaining are 21 faculties, but not mind faculty.

vi (a) That which is eye, is it faculty? —Yes. (either way)
(b) These are faculties. Are they femininity faculty?
—Yes. Femininity faculty is both faculty and femininity faculty.
—No. The remaining are 21 faculties, but not femininity faculty.

vii (a) That which is eye, is it faculty? —Yes. (either way)
(b) These are faculties. Are they masculinity faculty?
—Yes. Masculinity faculty is both faculty and masculinity faculty.
—No. The remaining are 21 faculties, but not masculinity faculty.

viii (a) That which is eye, is it faculty? —Yes. (either way)
(b) These are faculties. Are they life faculty?
—Yes. Life faculty is both faculty and life faculty.
—No. The remaining are 21 faculties, but not life faculty.

ix (a) That which is eye, is it faculty? —Yes. (either way)
(b) These are faculties. Are they bodily-pleasure faculty?
—Yes. Bodily-pleasure faculty is both faculty and bodily-pleasure faculty.
—No. The remaining are 21 faculties, but not bodily-pleasure faculty.

x (a) That which is eye, is it faculty? —Yes. (either way)
(b) These are faculties. Are they bodily-displeasure faculty?
—Yes. Bodily-displeasure faculty is both faculty and bodily-displeasure faculty.
—No. The remaining are 21 faculties, but not bodily-displeasure faculty.

xi (a) That which is eye, is it faculty? —Yes. (either way)
(b) These are faculties. Are they joy faculty?
—Yes. Joy faculty is both faculty and joy faculty.
—No. The remaining are 21 faculties, but not joy faculty.

xii (a) That which is eye, is it faculty? —Yes. (either way)

(b) These are faculties. Are they melancholy faculty?
—Yes. Melancholy faculty is both faculty and melancholy faculty.
—No. The remaining are 21 faculties, but not melancholy faculty.

xiii (a) That which is eye, is it faculty? —Yes. (either way)
(b) These are faculties. Are they equanimity faculty?
—Yes. Equanimity faculty is both faculty and equanimity faculty.
—No. The remaining are 21 faculties, but not equanimity faculty.

xiv (a) That which is eye, is it faculty? —Yes. (either way)
(b) These are faculties. Are they faith faculty?
—Yes. Faith faculty is both faculty and faith faculty.
—No. The remaining are 21 faculties, but not faith faculty.

xv (a) That which is eye, is it faculty? —Yes. (either way)
(b) These are faculties. Are they effort faculty?
—Yes. Effort faculty is both faculty and effort faculty.
—No. The remaining are 21 faculties, but not effort faculty.

xvi (a) That which is eye, is it eye faculty? —Yes. (either way)
(b) These are faculties. Are they mindfulness faculty?
—Yes. Mindfulness faculty is both faculty and mindfulness faculty.
—No. The remaining are 21 faculties, but not mindfulness faculty.

xvii (a) That which is eye, is it faculty? —Yes. (either way)
(b) These are faculties. Are they concentration faculty?
—Yes. Concentration faculty is both faculty and concentration faculty.
—No. The remaining are 21 faculties, but not concentration faculty.

xviii (a) That which is eye, is it faculty? —Yes. (either way)
(b) These are faculties. Are they understanding faculty?
—Yes. Understanding faculty is both faculty and understanding faculty.
—No. The remaining are 21 faculties, but not understanding faculty.

xix (a) That which is eye, is it faculty? —Yes. (either way)
(b) These are faculties. Are they "I-shall-comprehend-the-unknown" faculty?
—Yes. "I-shall-comprehend-the-unknown" faculty is both a faculty and the "I-shall-comprehend-the-unknown" faculty.
—No. Others are 21 faculties, but not I-shall-comprehend-the-unknown faculty.

xx (a) That which is eye, is it faculty? —Yes. (either way)
(b) These are faculties. Are they final-knowledge faculty?
—Yes. Final-knowledge faculty is both faculty and final-knowledge faculty.
—No. The remaining are 21 faculties, but not final- knowledge faculty.

xxi (a) That which is eye, is it faculty? —Yes. (either way)
(b) These are faculties. Are they final-knower faculty?

—Yes. Final-knower faculty is both faculty and final-knower faculty.
—No. The remaining are 21 faculties, but not final-knower faculty.

143. *i* (a) That which is ear, is it faculty? —Yes. (either way)
The remaining is ear, but not faculty.
(b) These are faculties. Are they eye faculty?
—Yes. Eye faculty is both faculty and eye faculty.
—No. The remaining are 21 faculties, but not eye faculty. ….P….

ii (a) That which is ear, is it faculty?
—Yes. (either way)
—No. Others (divine ear, etc.) is ear, but not faculty.
(b) These are faculties. Are they final-knower faculty? —Same as in 142 *xxi* (a)

144. *i* (a) That which is nose, is it faculty? —Yes. (either way)
(b) These are faculties. Are they eye faculties? —Same as in 143 *i* (a) ….P….

ii (a) That which is nose, is it faculty? —Yes. (either way)
(b) These are faculties. Are they final-knower faculty? —Same as in 142 *xxi* (a)

145. *i* (a) That which is tongue, is it faculty? —Yes. (either way)
(b) These are faculties. Are they eye faculties? —Same as in 143 *i* (a) ….P….

ii (a) That which is tongue, is it faculty? —Yes. (either way)
(b) These are faculties. Are they final-knower faculties? —Same as in 142 *xxi* (a)

146. *i* (a) That which is body, is it faculty?
—Yes. (either way)
—No. Others (internal organs, etc.) are a part of body, but are not faculties.
(b) These are faculties. Are they eye faculty? —Same as in 143 *i* (a) ….P….

ii (a) That which is body, is it faculty? —Same as aforesaid.
(b) These are faculties. Are they final-knower faculty? —Same as in 142 *xxi* (a)

147. *i* (a) That which is mind, is it faculty? —Yes. (either way)
(b) These are faculties. Are they eye faculty? —Same as in 143 *i* (a) ….P….

ii (a) That which is mind, is it faculty? —Yes. (either way)
(b) These are faculties. Are they final-knower faculty? —Same as in 142 *xxi* (a)

148. *i* (a) That which is female, is it faculty? —No (female is person, not a faculty)
(b) These are faculties. Are they eye faculty? —Same as in 143 *i* (a) ….P….

ii (a) That which is female, is it faculty? —No. Same as aforesaid
(b) These are faculties. Are they final-knower faculty? —Same as in 142 *xxi* (a)

149. *i* (a) That which is male, is it faculty? —No (male is person, not a faculty)
(b) These are faculties. Are they eye faculty? —Same as in 143 *i* (a) ….P….

ii (a) That which is male, is it faculty? —No. Same as aforesaid
(b) These are faculties. Are they final-knower faculty? —Same as in 142 *xxi* (a)

150. *i* (a) That which is life, is it faculty? —Yes. (either way)
(b) These are faculties. Are they eye faculty? —Same as in 143 *i* (a) ….P….

ii (a) That which is life. That which is faculty? —Yes. (either way)
(b) These are faculties. Are they final-knower faculty? —Same as in 142 *xxi* (a)

151. *i* (a) That which is bodily pleasure, is it faculty? —Yes. (either way)
(b) These are faculties. Are they eye faculties? —Same as in 143 *i* (a) ….P….

ii (a) That which is bodily pleasure, is it faculty? —Yes. (either way)
(b) These are faculties. Are they final-knower faculty? —Same as in 142 *xxi* (a)

152. *i* (a) That which is bodily displeasure, is it faculty? Yes. ….P….
153. *i* (a) That which is joy, is it faculty? —Yes. ….P….
154. *i* (a) That which is melancholy, is it faculty? —Yes. ….P….
155. *i* (a) That which is equanimity, is it faculty?
—Yes. (either way)
—No. The remaining (e.g. neither happy nor sad) is equanimity, but not faculty.
(b) These are faculties. Are they eye faculties? —Same as in 143 *i* (a) ….P….

ii (a) That which is equanimity, is it faculty? —Same as aforesaid.
(b) These are faculties. Are they final-knower faculty? —Same as in 142 *xxi* (a)

156. *i* (a) That which is faith, is it faculty? —Yes. ….P….
157. *i* (a) That which is energy, is it faculty? —Yes. ….P….
158. *i* (a) That which is mindfulness, is it faculty? —Yes. ….P….
159. *i* (a) That which is concentration, is it faculty? —Yes. ….P….
160. *i* (a) That which is understanding, is it faculty? —Yes. ….P….
161. *i* (a) That which is "I-shall-comprehend-the-unknown?" Is it faculty?
—Yes. ….P….

162. *i* (a) That which is final knowledge, is it faculty?
—Yes. (either way). ….P….

163. *i* (a) That which is final-knower, is it faculty? —Yes. (either way)
(b) These are faculties. Are they eye faculty? —Same as in 143 *i* (a) ….P….

ii (a) That which is final-knower, is it faculty? —Yes. (either way)
(b) These are faculties. Are they final-knowledge faculty? —Same as 142 *xx* (a)

Opposite expression

164. *i* (a) That which is not eye, is it not faculty?
—No. Except eye, the remaining 21 faculties are not eye but faculties.

—Yes. Except eye and remaining 21 faculties, others are neither eye nor faculties.
(b) These are not faculties. Are they not ear faculties? Yes. ….P….

ii (a) That which is not eye, is it not faculty? —Same as aforesaid.
(b) These are not faculties. Are they not final-knower faculty? —Yes.

165. *i* (a) That which is not ear, is it not faculty?
—No. Except ear, the remaining 21 faculties are not ear but faculties.
—Yes. Except ear and remaining 21 faculties, others are neither ear nor faculties.
(b) These are not faculties. Are they not eye faculty? Yes. ….P….

ii (a) That which is not ear, is it not faculty? —Same as aforesaid.
(b) These are not faculties. Are they final-knower faculty? —Yes.
166. *i* (a) That which is not nose, is it not faculty?
—No. Except nose, the remaining 21 faculties are not nose but faculties.
—Yes. Except nose and remaining faculties, others are neither nose nor faculties.
(b) These are not faculties. Are they not eye faculty? Yes. ….P….

ii (a) That which is not nose, is it not faculty? —Same as aforesaid.
(b) These are not faculties. Are they not final-knower faculty? —Yes.

167. *i* (a) That which is not tongue, is it not faculty?
—No. Except tongue, the remaining 21 faculties are not tongue but faculties.
—Yes. Except tongue and remaining 21 faculties, others are neither tongue nor faculties.
(b) These are not faculties. Are they not eye faculties? —Yes. ….P….

ii (a) That which is not tongue, is it not faculty? —Same as aforesaid.
(b) These are not faculties. Are they not final-knower faculty? —Yes.

168. *i* (a) That which is not body, is it not faculty? —Yes.
(b) These are not faculties. Are they not eye faculty? —Yes. ….P….

ii (a) That which is not body, is it not faculty? —Same as aforesaid.
(b) These are not faculties. Are they not final-knower faculty? —Yes.

169. *i* (a) That which is not mind, is it not faculty?
—No. Except mind, the remaining 21 faculties are not mind but faculties.
—Yes. Except mind and the remaining 21 faculties, others are neither mind nor faculties.
(b) These are not faculties. Are they not eye faculty? —Yes.. ….P….

ii (a) That which is not mind, is it not faculty? —Same as aforesaid.
(b) These are not faculties. Are they not final-knower faculty? —Yes.

170. *i* (a) That which is not female, is it not faculty?
—No. Except female, the remaining faculties are not female but faculties.

—Yes. Except female and faculties, others are neither female nor faculties.
(b) These are not faculties. Are they not eye faculties?
—Same as aforesaid. ….P….

ii (a) That which is not female, is it not faculty? —Same as aforesaid.
(b) These are not faculties. Are they not final-knower faculty? —Yes.

171. *i* (a) That which is not male, is it not faculty?
—No. Except male, the remaining faculties are not male but faculties.
—Yes. Except male and faculties, others are neither male nor faculties.
(b) These are not faculties. Are they not eye faculties? Yes. ….P….

ii (a) That which is not male, is it not faculty? —Same as aforesaid.
(b) These are not faculties. Are they not final-knower faculty? —Yes.

172. *i* (a) That which is not life, is it not faculty?
—No. Except life, the remaining 21 faculties are not life but faculties.
—Yes. Except life and remaining 21 faculties, others are neither life nor faculties.
(b) These are not faculties. Are they not eye faculty? —Yes. ….P….

ii (a) That which is not life, is it not faculty? —Same as aforesaid.
(b) These are not faculties. Are they not final-knower faculty? —Yes.

173. *i* (a) That which is not bodily pleasure, is it not faculty?
—No. Except bodily pleasure, the remaining 21 faculties are not bodily pleasure but faculties.
—Yes. Except bodily pleasure and remaining 21 faculties, others are neither bodily pleasure nor faculties.
(b) These are not faculties. Are they not eye faculty? —Yes. ….P….

ii (a) That which is not bodily pleasure, is it not faculty? —Same as aforesaid.
(b) These are not faculties. Are they not final-knower faculty? —Yes.

174. *i* (a) That which is not bodily displeasure, is it not faculty?
—No. Except bodily displeasure, the remaining 21 faculties are not bodily displeasure but faculties.
—Yes. Except bodily displeasure and remaining 21 faculties, others are neither bodily displcasure nor faculties.
(b) These are not faculties. Are they not eye faculty? —Yes. ….P….

ii (a) That which is not bodily displeasure, is it not faculty? —Same as aforesaid.
(b) These are not faculties. Are they not final-knower faculty? —Yes.

175. *i* (a) That which is not joy, is it not faculty?
—No. Except joy, the remaining 21 faculties are not joy but faculties.
—Yes. Except joy and remaining 21 faculties, others are neither joy nor faculties.
(b) These are not faculties. Are they not eye faculty? —Yes. ….P….

That which is not joy, is it not faculty? —Same as aforesaid.
(b) These are not faculties. Are they not final-knower faculty? —Yes.

176. *i* (a) That which is not melancholy, is it not faculty?
—No. Except melancholy, the remaining 21 faculties are not melancholy but faculties.
—Yes. Except melancholy and remaining 21 faculties, others are neither melancholy nor faculties.
(b) These are not faculties. Are they not eye faculty? —Yes. ….P….

ii (a) That which is not melancholy, is it not faculty? —Same as aforesaid.
(b) These are not faculties. Are they not final-knower faculty? —Yes.

177. *i* (a) That which is not equanimity, is it not faculty?
—No. Except equanimity, the remaining 21 faculties are not equanimity but faculties.
—Yes. Except equanimity and remaining 21 faculties, others are neither equanimity nor faculties.
(b) These are not faculties. Are they not eye faculty? —Yes. ….P….

ii (a) That which is not equanimity, is it not faculty? —Same as aforesaid.
(b) These are not faculties. Are they not final-knower faculty? —Yes.

178. *i* (a) That which is not faith, is it not faculty?
—No. Except faith, the remaining 21 faculties are not faith but faculties.
—Yes. Except faith and remaining 21 faculties, others are neither faith nor faculties.
(b) These are not faculties. Are they not eye faculty? —Yes. ….P….

ii (a) That which is not faith, is it not faculty? —Same as aforesaid.
(b) These are not faculties. Are they not final-knower faculty? —Yes.

179. *i* (a) That which is not effort, is it not faculty?
—No. Except effort, the remaining 21 faculties are not effort but faculties.
—Yes. Except effort and remaining 21 faculties, others are neither effort nor faculties.
(b) These are not faculties. Are they not eye faculty? —Yes. ….P….

ii (a) That which is not energy, is it not faculty? —Same as aforesaid.
(b) These are not faculties. Are they not final-knower faculty? —Yes.

180. *i* (a) That which is not mindfulness, is it not faculty?
—No. Except mindfulness, the remaining 21 faculties are not mindfulness but faculties.
—Yes. Except mindfulness and remaining 21 faculties, others are neither mindfulness nor faculties.
(b) These are not faculties. Are they not eye faculty? —Yes. ….P….

ii (a) That which is not mindfulness, is it not faculty? —Same as aforesaid.
(b) These are not faculties. Are they not final-knower faculty? —Yes.

181. *i* (a) That which is not concentration, is it not faculty?
—No. Except concentration, remaining 21 faculties are not concentration but faculties.
—Yes. Except concentration and remaining 21 faculties, others are neither concentration nor faculties.
(b) These are not faculties. Are they not eye faculty? —Yes. ....P....

ii (a) That which is not concentration, is it not faculty? —Same as aforesaid.
(b) These are not faculties. Are they not final-knower faculty? —Yes.

182. *i* (a) That which is not understanding, is it not faculty?
—No. Except understanding, the remaining 21 faculties are not understanding but faculties.
—Yes. Except understanding and remaining 21 faculties, others are neither understanding nor faculties.
(b) These are not faculties. Are they not eye faculty? —Yes. ....P....

ii (a) That which is not understanding, is it not faculty? —Same as aforesaid.
(b) These are not faculties. Are they not final-knower faculty? —Yes.

183. *i* (a) That which is not "I-shall-comprehend-the-unknown", is it not faculty?
—No. With the exception of "I-shall-comprehend-the-unknown", the remaining 21 faculties are not "I-shall-comprehend-the- unknown" but faculties.
—Yes. With the exception of "I-shall-comprehend-the-unknown and faculties and the remaining 21 faculties, others are neither" I-shall-comprehend-the-unknown" nor are faculties.
(b) These are not faculties. Are they not eye faculty? —Yes. ....P....

ii (a) That which is not "I-shall-comprehend-the-unknown", is it not faculty?
—Same as aforesaid.
(b) These are not faculties. Are they not final-knower faculty? Yes.

184. *i* (a) That which is not final knowledge, is it not faculty?
—No. With the exception of final knowledge, the remaining 21 faculties are not final knowledge but faculties.
—Yes. With the exception of final knowledge and the remaining 21 faculties, others are neither final knowledge nor faculties.
(b) These are not faculties. Are they not eye faculty? —Yes. ....P....

ii (a) That which is not final knowledge, is it not faculty? —Same as aforesaid.
(b) These are not faculties. Are they not final-knower faculty? —Yes.

185. *i* (a) That which is not final-knower, is it not faculty?
—No. With the exception of final-knower, the remaining 21 faculties are not

final-knower but faculties.
—Yes. With the exception of final-knower and remaining 21 faculties, others are neither final-knower nor faculties.
(b) These are not faculties. Are they not eye faculty? —Yes. ....P....

ii (a) That which is not final-knower, is it not faculty? —Same as aforesaid.
(b) These are not faculties. Are they not final-knowledge faculty? —Yes.

10.2 Process (*Pavatti*)

10.2.1 Origination of controlling faculties (with charts)

A simple calculation shows that altogether it would requires 756 pairs of enquires in order to deal with the 22 types of controlling faculties. Even with dittoes used by the Pāli text, the remaining number of catechisms after reduction is also extremely huge. Based on this reason, we can understand why the text does not provide catechisms on the cessation and origination-cessation of the controlling faculties. Because of the huge contents in this section, I have decided to leave out the translation of text which otherwise would have taken up about 210 pages by this section alone in this volume. I will instead summarise the answers directly into several charts. The answers also reflect detail of the questions asked.

There are some faculties which are not being examined according to the text. The controlling faculties of tongue and body are not dealt with in this section. The two follow the same answers for nose faculty according to planes. The faculties of bodily pleasure and bodily displeasure are also not dealt with in the text. These two faculties vary in results dependent upon the different conditions and the characteristics of individuals which dictate what constitutes pleasure and displeasure to them. Melancholy faculty and the last three faculties are only examined at the third section on comprehension. Melancholy faculty is enquired in terms of its eradication; I-shall-comprehend-the-unknown faculty and final-knowledge faculty are enquired on their cultivation; and final-knower faculty is enquired with regard to its realisation.

In some of the following charts, you will notice that some of the yes and no answers are in boldface. Those are the relevant additions I have included in order to show a more cohesive relationship of the answers taken from the catechisms, and to make the charts look more comprehensible to readers. For instance, the seven physical faculties of eyes, ears, nose, tongue, body, femininity and masculinity, and life faculty which is both physical and mental vitality which sustain life, should always be examined collectively in spite of the limitation imposed by the prescribed modes of enquiries. Similarly, the non-corporeal group of faculties (in respect of mind, joy, equanimity, faith, and understanding) should also have their answers reflecting interconnectivity in the answers insofar as the logics of formulation permit in those enquiries.

Chart 10.2 Present Origination of Controlling Faculties

To those at the birth-moment who :	eye faculty	ear faculty	nose faculty	tongue faculty	body faculty	mind faculty	femininity faculty	masculinity faculty	life faculty	pleasure faculty	displeasure faculty	joy faculty	melancholy faculty	equanimity faculty	faith faculty	effort faculty	mindfulness faculty	concentration faculty	understanding faculty	I-shall-comprehend-the-unknown faculty	final knowledge faculty	final-knower faculty
	in whom (A: arise; N: does not arise)																					
have eye but are without ear,	A	N																				
have eye and ear,	A	A																				
have ear but without eye,	N	A																				
are without ear and without eye,	N	N																				
have eye but without nose,	A		N																			
have eye and nose,	A		A																			
have nose but without eye,	N		A																			
are without nose and without eye,	N		N																			
have eye but are not female,	A						N															
have eye and are female,	A						A															
are female but are without eye,	N						A															
are not female and are without eye,	N						N															
have eye but are not male,	A							N														
have eye and are male,	A							A														
are male but are without eye,	N							A														
are not male and are without eye,	N							N														
have eye,	A					A			A													
are without eye,	N								A													
have eye but are not blessed with joy,	A											N										
have eye and are blessed with joy,	A											A										
are blessed with joy but without eye,	N											A										
are without eye and without joy,	N											N										
have eye but are not blessed with equanimity,	A													N								
have eye and are blessed with equanimity,	A													A								
are blessed with equanimity but without eye,	N													A								
are without equanimity and without eye,	N													N								
have eye but are without root cause (*ahetuka*),	A														N							
have eye and are with root cause (*sahetuka*),	A														A							
have root cause but are without eye,	N														A							
are without root cause and without eye,	N														N							
have eye but are in dissociation from knowledge (*ñāṇa*)	A																		N			
have eye and are in association with knowledge,	A																		A			
are in association with knowledge but are without eye,	N																		A			
are in dissociation from knowledge and without eye,	N																		N			
have mind but without eye,	N					A																
have nose but are not female,			A				N															
have nose and are female,			A				A															
are female but are without nose,			N				A															
are not female and are without nose,			N				N															
have nose but are not male,			A					N														
have nose and are male,			A					A														
are male but are without nose,			N					A														
are not male and are without nose,			N					N														
have nose,			A			A			A													
are without nose,			N						A													
have nose but are without joy,			A									N										
have nose and are with joy,			A									A										
have joy but are without nose,			N									A										
are without joy and without nose,			N									N										

To those at the birth-moment who :	eye faculty	ear faculty	nose faculty	tongue faculty	body faculty	mind faculty	femininity faculty	masculinity faculty	life faculty	pleasure faculty	displeasure faculty	joy faculty	melancholy faculty	equanimity faculty	faith faculty	effort faculty	mindfulness faculty	concentration faculty	understanding faculty	I-shall-comprehend-the-unknown faculty	final knowledge faculty	final-knower faculty
	in whom (A: arise; N: does not arise)																					
have nose but are not blessed with equanimity,			A											N								
have nose and are blessed with equanimity,			A											A								
have equanimity but are without nose,			N											A								
are without equanimity and without nose,			N											N								
have nose but are not blessed with root cause,			A												N							
have nose and are blessed with root cause,			A												A							
are blessed with root cause but are without nose,			N												A							
are without root cause and without nose,			N												N							
have nose but are in dissociation from knowledge,			A																N			
have nose and are in association with knowledge,			A																A			
are in association with knowledge but are without nose,			N																A			
are dissociated from knowledge and without nose,			N																N			
have mind but are without nose,			N			A																
are female.						A	A	N	A													
are male.						A	N	A	A													
are neither female nor male,							N	N														
are not female.							N		A													
are not male.								N	A													
are female, but are not blessed with joy,							A					N										
are female and are blessed with joy,							A					A										
are blessed with joy, but are not female,							N					A										
are not blessed with joy and are not female,							N					N										
are female, but are not blessed with equanimity,							A							N								
are female and are blessed with equanimity,							A							A								
are blessed with equanimity, but are not female,							N							A								
are without equanimity and are not female,							N							N								
are female, but are not blessed with root cause,							A								N							
are female and are blessed with root cause,							A								A							
are blessed with root cause, but are not female,							N								A							
are without root cause and are not female,							N								N							
are female and are in dissociation from knowledge,							A												N			
are female and are in association with knowledge,							A												A			
are in association with knowledge but are not female,							N												A			
are dissociated from knowledge and are not female,							N												N			
are male and are in dissociation from knowledge,								A											N			
are male and are in association with knowledge,								A											A			
are in association with knowledge but are not male,								N											A			
are dissociated from knowledge and are not male,								N											N			
have mind, but are not female,						A	N	A														
are male, but are not blessed with joy,								A				N										
are male and are blessed with joy,								A				A										
are blessed with joy, but are not male,								N				A										
are without joy and are not male,								N				N										
are male, but are not blessed with equanimity,								A						N								
are male and are blessed with equanimity,								A						A								
are blessed with equanimity, but are not male,								N						A								
are without equanimity and are not male,								N						N								
are male, but are not blessed with root cause,								A							N							
are male and are blessed with root cause,								A							A							
are blessed with root cause, but are not male,								N							A							
are not blessed with root cause and are not male,								N							N							
have mind, but are not male,						A		N														

	eye faculty	ear faculty	nose faculty	tongue faculty	body faculty	mind faculty	femininity faculty	masculinity faculty	life faculty	pleasure faculty	displeasure faculty	joy faculty	melancholy faculty	equanimity faculty	faith faculty	effort faculty	mindfulness faculty	concentration faculty	understanding faculty	I-shall-comprehend-the-unknown faculty	final knowledge faculty	final-knower faculty
To those at the birth-moment who :	in whom (A: arise; N: does not arise)																					
are not blessed with joy,									A			N										
are blessed with joy,						A			A			A		N								
are not blessed with equanimity,									A					N								
are blessed with equanimity,						A			A			N		A								
are not blessed with root cause,									A						N							
are blessed with root cause,						A			A						A							
are dissociated from knowledge,									A										N			
are associated with knowledge,						A			A										A			
are without mind,	N	N	N	N	N	N	N	N	A													
have mind,						A			A													
are not blessed with joy, but with root cause,												N			A							
are blessed with joy, but dissociated from knowledge,												A							N			
are blessed with joy, and associated with knowledge												A							A			
are associated with knowledge but not blessed with joy,												N							A			
are dissociated from knowledge and are without joy												N							A			
have mind, but are not blessed with joy,						A						N										
are blessed with equanimity, but are without root cause,														A	N							
are blessed with equanimity and root cause,														A	A							
are blessed with root cause, but not with equanimity,														N	A							
have equanimity, but are dissociated from knowledge,														A					N			
have equanimity and are associated with knowledge,														A					A			
are associated with knowledge but without equanimity,														N					A			
have mind, but are not blessed with equanimity,						A								N								
have root cause, but are dissociated from knowledge,															A				N			
have root cause and are aissociated with knowledge,															A				A			
have mind, but are without root cause,						A									N							
have mind, but are dissociated from knowledge,						A													N			
To those during life at the arising moment of *citta* :																						
(or at the nascent phase of *citta*)						A			A													
dissociated from joy,						A			A			N										
associated with joy,						A			A			A		N								
dissociated from equanimity,						A			A					N								
associated with equanimity,						A			A			N		A								
dissociated from faith,						A			A						N							
associated with faith,						A			A						A							
dissociated from knowledge,						A			A										N			
associated with knowledge,						A			A										A			
associated with joy but dissociated from faith,												A			N							
associated with joy and associated with faith,												A			A							
associated with faith but dissociated from joy,												N			A							
dissociated from faith and dissociated from joy,												N			N							
associated with joy but dissociated from knowledge,												A							N			
associated with joy and associated with knowledge,												A							A			
associated with knowledge but dissociated from joy,												N							A			
dissociated from knowledge and dissociated from joy,												N							N			
associated with equanimity but dissociated from faith,														A	N							
associated with equanimity and associated with faith,														A	A							
associated with faith but dissociated from equanimity,														N	A							
dissociated from faith and dissociated from equanimity,														N	N							
associated with faith but dissociated from knowledge,															A				N			
associated with faith and knowledge,															A				A			

	eye faculty	ear faculty	nose faculty	tongue faculty	body faculty	mind faculty	femininity faculty	masculinity faculty	life faculty	pleasure faculty	displeasure faculty	joy faculty	melancholy faculty	equanimity faculty	faith faculty	effort faculty	mindfulness faculty	concentration faculty	understanding faculty	I-shall-comprehend-the-unknown faculty	final knowledge faculty	final-knower faculty
To those during life, at the arising moment of *citta*:	in whom (A: arise; N: does not arise)																					
associated with equanimity, dissociated from knowledge														A					N			
associated with equanimity and knowledge,														A					A			
associated with knowledge, dissociated from equanimity														N					A			
dissociated from knowledge and equanimity,														N					N			
dissociated from joy and dissociated from equanimity,												N		N								
dissociated from joy and dissociated from faith,												N			N							
dissociated from joy and dissociated from knowledge,												N							N			
dissociated from equanimity and dissociated from faith,														N	N							
dissociated from equanimity and from knowledge														N					N			
dissociated from faith and dissociated from knowledge,															N				N			
To all those :																						
at the ceasing moment of *citta* (during life),						N			N			N		N	N				N			
at death-moment,	N	N	N			N	N	N	N			N		N	N				N			
To those :																						
at the non-percipience plane,						N			A			N		N	N				N			
who entered upon Cessation-attainment,						N						N		N	N				N			
At the plane(s) of :																						
sensuous desire	A	A	A	**A**	**A**	A	A	A	A	**A**	**A**	A		A	A				A			
fine-materiality (except non-percipience plane)	A	A	N	**N**	**N**	A	N	N	A	**N**	**N**	A		A	A				A			
five-aggregates	A	A				A			A			A		A	A				A			
four- and five-aggregates,						A			A			A		A	A				A			
non-percipience	N	N	N	**N**	**N**	N	N	N	A	**N**	**N**	N		N	N				N			
immateriality	N	N	N	**N**	**N**	A	N	N	A	**N**	**N**	N		A	A				A			

There are few points I would like to draw from the answers in the above chart.

- Except only at the death-moment, there is no such person in whom when either of the faculties of eye, ear, tongue, nose, body, femininity, or masculinity does not arise, life faculty also does not arise.
- When a person is without mind at the birth-moment, the five sensory faculties and mind faculty do not arise except for life faculty. It is like the anesthesia syndrome in which a patient suffers brain damage and a total loss of physical sensations.
- Four-aggregate and five-aggregate planes include persons at the sensuous planes, fine-material planes (except non-percipients) and immaterial planes. Hence there are negligible answers under this situation.

Chart 10.3 Past Origination of Controlling Faculties

	eye faculty	ear faculty	nose faculty	tongue faculty	body faculty	mind faculty	femininity faculty	masculinity faculty	life faculty	pleasure faculty	displeasure faculty	joy faculty	melancholy faculty	equanimity faculty	faith faculty	effort faculty	mindfulness faculty	concentration faculty	understanding faculty	I-shall-comprehend-the-unknown faculty	final knowledge faculty	final-knower faculty
To those :	in whom (A: had arisen; N: had not arisen)																					
at the sensuous planes,	A	A	A			A	A	A	A			A		A	A				A			
at the five-aggregate planes,	A	A				A			A			A		A	A				A			
at the four- and five-aggregate planes,						A			A			A		A	A				A			
at the fine-material planes,	A	A	N			A	N	N	A			A		A	A				A			
at the immaterial planes,	N	N	N			A	N	N	A			N		A	A				A			
at the arising moment of birth *citta* at pure abodes,	N	N	N			N	N	N	N			N		N	N				N			
at the occurrence of second *citta* of the pure abodes,						A			A			N		A	A				A			
at the pure abodes,	N	N	N			N	N	N	N			N		N	N				N			
at the non-percipience plane,	N	N	N			N	N	N	A			N		N	N				N			
who entered upon Cessation-attainment,						N						N		N	N				N			
At the plane(s) of :																						
sensuous desire	A	A	A	**A**	**A**	A	A	A	A	**A**	**A**	A		A	A				A			
fine-materiality (except non-percipience plane)	A	A	N	**N**	**N**	A	N	N	A	**N**	**N**	A		A	A				A			
five-aggregates	A	A				A			A			A		A	A				A			
four- and five-aggregates						A			A			A		A	A				A			
non-percipience	N	N	N	**N**	**N**	N	N	N	A	**N**	**N**	N		N	N				N			
immateriality	N	N	N	**N**	**N**	A	N	N	A	**N**	**N**	N		A	A				A			

The questions on past origination of the controlling faculties do not in any way overlap with those previous questions regarding present origination. The answers as to plane are the same, be it present, past or future.

With the exception of life faculty, all the other answers are the same in terms of those persons dwelling at the non-percipience plane and those persons at the arising moment of birth-consciousness at pure abodes. Life faculty had not arisen in those absorbed at the arising moment of birth-consciousness at the pure abodes and in those pure abode beings. In contrast, life faculty had arisen in those dwelling at the non-percipience plane. The arising of life faculty and the remaining seven physical faculties do not apply to those persons in possession of cessation-attainment, except for only the faculties of mind, joy, equanimity, faith, and understanding which all had not arisen.

Chart 10.4 Future Origination of Controlling Faculties

To those :	eye faculty	ear faculty	nose faculty	tongue faculty	body faculty	mind faculty	femininity faculty	masculinity faculty	life faculty	pleasure faculty	displeasure faculty	joy faculty	melancholy faculty	equanimity faculty	faith faculty	effort faculty	mindfulness faculty	concentration faculty	understanding faculty	I-shall-comprehend-the-	final knowledge faculty	final-knower faculty
	in whom (A: will arise; N: will not arise)																					
final existence persons,	N	**N**	N			N	N	N	N			N		N	N				N			
final existence persons at sensuous planes,	**N**	**N**	N			**N**	N	N	N			**N**		**N**								
final existence persons at five-aggregate planes,	N	**N**	N			**N**	N	N	N			N		**N**								
others (not of final existence) at the sensuous planes,	A	A	A			A	A	A	A			A		A	A				A			
others at the five-aggregate planes,	A	**A**				A			A			A		A	**A**				**A**			
others at the four- and five-aggregate planes,						A			A			A		A	A				A			
others at the fine-material planes,	A	A	N			A	N	N	A			A		A	A				A			
others at the immaterial planes,	N	N	N			A	N	N	A			N		A	A				A			
at the non-percipience plane,	N	**N**	N			N	N	N	A			N		N	N				N			
instantly after whose arising moment of *citta*, the final-stage *citta* associated with equanimity will arise,						A			A			N		A	A				A			
instantly after whose arising moment of *citta*, the final-stage *citta* associated with joy will arise,						A			A			A		N	A				A			
endowed with the final-stage *citta*,						N		N	N			N		N	N				N			
who will be born at the fine-material planes, therefrom will attain final liberation (*Parinibbāna*) upon death	A	A	N			A	N	N	A			A		A	A				A			
who will be born at the immaterial plane, therefrom will attain final liberation (*Parinibbāna*) upon death,	N	N	N			A	N	N	A			N		A	A				A			
who will be born with joy at the fine-material plane, therefrom will attain final liberation (*Parinibbāna*) upon death,			N											N								
who will be born with eye and be blessed with joy, will therewith attain final liberation upon death,	A													N								
who will be born with eye and be blessed with equanimity, will therewith attain final liberation upon death,	A											N										
who will be born with nose and be blessed with joy, will therewith attain final liberation upon death,			A											N								
who will be born with nose and be blessed with equanimity, will therewith attain final liberation upon death,			A									N										
who will be reborn in a few existences as men, will thereafter attain final liberation upon death,	A						N															
men who will be reborn in few existences in manhood, who will thereafter attain final liberation upon death,	A	**A**	A			A	N	A	**A**						A				A			
men who will be reborn in few existences in manhood and be blessed with equanimity, will thereafter attain final liberation,	**A**	**A**	A			**A**	N	A	**A**			N		A								
men who will be reborn in few existences in manhood and be blessed with joy, who will thereafter attain final liberation …,	**A**	**A**	A			**A**	N	A	**A**			A		N	A				A			
who will be reborn in a few existences as women, will thereafter attain final liberation upon death,	A							N														
women who will be reborn in few existences in womenkind, who will thereafter attain final liberation upon death,	A	**A**	A			A	A	N	A						A				A			
women who will be reborn in few existences in womenkind and with equanimity, will thereafter attain final liberation …,	**A**	**A**	A			**A**	A	N	**A**			N		A								
women who will be reborn in few existences in womenkind and with joy, will thereafter attain final liberation upon death,	**A**	**A**	A			A	A	N	A			A		N	A				A			
At the plane(s) of :																						
sensuous desire	A	A	A	**A**	**A**	A	A	A	A	**A**	**A**	A		A	A				A			
fine-materiality (except non-percipience plane)	A	A	N	**N**	**N**	A	N	N	A	**N**	**N**	A		A	A				A			
five-aggregates	A	A				A			A			A		A	A				A			
four- and five-aggregates,						A			A			A		A	A				A			
non-percipience	N	N	N	**N**	**N**	N	N	N	A	**N**	**N**	N		N	N				N			
immateriality	N	N	N	**N**	**N**	A	N	N	A	**N**	**N**	N		A	A				A			

Chart 10.5 Present-Past Origination of Controlling Faculties

	Present											Past										
	eye faculty	ear faculty	nose faculty	mind faculty	femininity faculty	masculinity faculty	life faculty	joy faculty	equanimity faculty	faith faculty	understanding faculty	eye faculty	ear faculty	nose faculty	mind faculty	femininity faculty	masculinity faculty	life faculty	joy faculty	equanimity faculty	faith faculty	understanding faculty
To those at the birth-moment :	in whom (A: arises/ had arisen; N: does not arise/ had not arisen)																					
at sensuous planes with eye,	A												A	A	A	A	A	A	A	A	A	A
at sensuous planes without eye,	N												A	A	A	A	A	A	A	A	A	A
at sensuous planes with nose,			A									**A**	**A**		A	A	A	A	A	A	A	A
at sensuous planes without nose,			N									**A**	**A**		A	A	A	A	A	A	A	A
at sensuous planes who are female,					A							**A**	**A**	**A**	A		A	A	A	A	A	A
at sensuous planes who are not female,					N							**A**	**A**	**A**	A		A	A	A	A	A	A
at sensuous planes who are male,						A						**A**	**A**	**A**	A	**A**		A	A	A	A	A
at sensuous planes who are not male,						N						**A**	**A**	**A**	A	**A**		A	A	A	A	A
who are blessed with joy,								A							A					A	A	A
who are blessed with equanimity,									A						A						A	A
who are blessed with root cause,										A					A							A
who are associated with knowledge,											A				A							
at fine-material planes (except for pure abodes),	A		N	**A**	**N**	**N**	A	**A**	**A**	**A**	**A**		N	**N**	A	N	N	A	A	A	A	A
at pure abodes,	A		N	**A**	**N**	**N**	A	N	A	A	A		N	N	N	**N**	**N**	N	N	N	N	N
at non-percipience plane,							A								N				N	N	N	N
at four- and five-aggregate planes,							A								A				A	A	A	A
To those at the death-moment :																						
at sensuous planes,	N		N		N	N	N						A	A	A	A	A	A	A	A	A	A
at fine-material planes,	N												**A**	N	**A**	N	N	**A**	**A**	**A**	**A**	**A**
at five-aggregate planes,	N												A		A			A	A	A	A	A
at four- and five-aggregate planes,							N								A				A	A	A	A
at non-percipience plane,							N								N				N	N	N	N
To those :																						
fine-material beings (except for those at pure abodes and non-percipience plane),	**A**		N		N	N							**A**	**N**	A	N	N	A	A	A	A	A
immaterial beings,	N		N	**A**	N	N	**A**	**N**	**A**	**A**	**A**		**N**	**N**	A	N	N	A	N	A	A	A
non-percipience beings,	N		N	**N**	N	N	**A**	N	N	N	N		A	N	AN	N	N	**A**	N	AN	AN	AN
pure abode beings,	**A**		N		N	N							**N**	**N**	N	**N**	**N**	N	N	N	N	N
at the arising moment of birth *citta* at pure abode,							A												N			
at the ceasing moment of birth *citta* at pure abode,				**N**			N		N	N	N				N				N	N	N	N
at the moment of *Parinibbāna* at pure abode,	N												N		N			N	N	N	N	N
who entered upon Cessation-attainment,				**N**				N	N	N	N				A					A	A	A
To all those :																						
at the death-moment (except for non-percipients)	N		N		N	N	N						A	A	A	A	A	A	A	A	A	A
at the arising moment of *citta* during life,							A								A				A	A	A	A
at the ceasing moment of *citta*,				**N**				N	N	N	N				A					A	A	A
at the ceasing moment of *citta* during life,				**N**			N	N	N	N	N				A				A	A	A	A
To those at the arising moment of *citta* :																						
dissociated from joy,								N	N	N	N				A					A	A	A
associated with joy during life,								A	A	A	A				A					A	A	A
dissociated from equanimity,									N						A						A	A
associated with equanimity during life,									A						A						A	A
dissociated from faith,										N					A							A
associated with faith during life,										A					A							A
dissociated from knowledge,											N				A							
associated with knowledge during life,											A				A							

Note that joy faculty does not arise at the ceasing moment of *citta* during life; at the birth-moment at pure abode; in those at pure abodes, those at non-percipience plane, those at immaterial plane, and those who entered upon Cessation-attainment.

Chart 10.6 Present-Future Origination of Controlling Faculties

	Present											Future										
	eye faculty	ear faculty	nose faculty	mind faculty	femininity faculty	masculinity faculty	life faculty	joy faculty	equanimity faculty	faith faculty	understanding faculty	eye faculty	ear faculty	nose faculty	mind faculty	femininity faculty	masculinity faculty	life faculty	joy faculty	equanimity faculty	faith faculty	understanding faculty
To those at the birth-moment :	in whom (A: arises/ will arise; N: does not arise/ will not arise)																					
of females born as final existence persons,					A							**N**	**N**	N	N		N	N	N	N	N	N
of males born as final existence persons,						A						**N**	**N**	N	N	**N**		N	N	N	N	N
of final existence persons at sensuous planes,	A		A										**N**	N	N	N	N	N	N	N	N	N
of final existence persons at five-aggregate planes,	A												N	N	N	N	N	N	N	N	N	N
of final existence persons at fine-material planes,	**A**	**A**	N		N	N									N			N	N	N	N	N
of final existence persons at immaterial planes,	N	**N**	N		N	N									N			N		N	N	N
To others at the birth-moment (except for final existence persons) :																						
at sensuous planes with eye,	A												A	A	A	A	A	A	A	A	A	A
at sensuous planes without eye,	N												A	A	A	A	A	A	A	A	A	A
at sensuous planes with nose,			A									**A**	**A**		A	A	A	A	A	A	A	A
at sensuous planes without nose,			N									**A**	**A**		A	A	A	A	A	A	A	A
at sensuous planes who are female,					A							**A**	**A**	**A**	A		A	**A**	**A**	**A**	**A**	**A**
at sensuous planes who are not female,					N							**A**	**A**	**A**	A		A	A	A	A	A	A
at sensuous planes who are male,						A						**A**	**A**	**A**	A	**A**		**A**	**A**	**A**	**A**	**A**
at sensuous planes who are not male,						N						**A**	**A**	**A**	**A**	**A**		A	A	A	A	A
who are blessed with joy,								A							A					A	A	A
who are blessed with equanimity,									A						A				**A**		A	A
who are blessed with root cause,										A					A				**A**	**A**		A
who are associated with knowledge,											A				A				**A**	**A**	**A**	
at fine-material planes,	A						**A**						A	N	A	N	N	A	A	**A**	**A**	**A**
at non-percipience plane,	**N**						A						**N**	**N**	N	**N**	**N**	**A**	N	N	N	N
at immaterial planes,	**N**						**A**						**N**	**N**	**A**	**N**	**N**	**A**	**N**	**A**	**A**	**A**
at four- and five-aggregate planes,							A								A				A	A	A	A
To those :																						
who will be born at fine-material planes, who therefrom will attain final liberation (*Parinibbāna*) upon death,	A												A	N		N	N					
who will be born at immaterial plane, who therefrom will attain final liberation (*Parinibbāna*) upon death,	N												N	N		N	N					
who will be born with eye and be blessed with joy, will therewith attain final liberation (*Parinibbāna*) upon death,	A																			N		
who will be born with eye and be blessed with equanimity, will therewith attain final liberation upon death,	A																		N			
who will be born with nose and be blessed with joy, will therewith attain final liberation upon death,			A																	N		
who will be born with nose and be blessed with equanimity, will therewith attain final liberation upon death,			A																N			
who will be born with eye and be blessed with joy, will therewith attain final liberation upon death,	A																			N		
who will be born with eye and be blessed with equanimity, will therewith attain final liberation upon death,	A																		N			
who will be born with nose and be blessed with joy, will therewith attain final liberation upon death,			A																	N		
who will be born with nose and be blessed with equanimity, will therewith attain final liberation upon death,			A																N			
who will be born as male and be blessed with joy, will therewith attain final liberation upon death,			A			A														N		
who will be born as male and be blessed with equanimity, will therewith attain final liberation upon death,						A													N			

	Present											Future										
	eye faculty	ear faculty	nose faculty	mind faculty	femininity faculty	masculinity faculty	life faculty	joy faculty	equanimity faculty	faith faculty	understanding faculty	eye faculty	ear faculty	nose faculty	mind faculty	femininity faculty	masculinity faculty	life faculty	joy faculty	equanimity faculty	faith faculty	understanding faculty
To those :	in whom (A: arises; A*f* will arise; N: does not arise; N*f* will not arise)																					
who will be born as female and be blessed with joy, will therewith attain final liberation (*Parinibbāna*) upon death,					A															N		
who will be born as female and be blessed with equanimity, will therewith attain *Parinibbāna* upon death,					A														N			
who will be reborn in few existences in womenkind, and will thereafter attain *Parinibbāna* upon death,	A	**A**	A		A												N					
who will be reborn in few existences in manhood, and will thereafter attain *Parinibbāna* upon death,	A	**A**	A			A										N						
at the death-moment who will be reborn at fine-material plane, who therefrom will attain *Parinibbāna* upon death,	N		N		N	N							N	N		N	N					
at the death-moment who will be reborn at immaterial plane, who therefrom will attain *Parinibbāna* upon death,	N		N		N	N							N	N		N	N					
at the death-moment who will be reborn with joy, and will thereafter attain *Parinibbāna* upon death,	N	**N**	N		N	N														N		
at the death-moment who will be reborn with equanimity, and will thereafter attain *Parinibbāna* upon death,	N	**N**	N		N	N													N			
at the death-moment who will be reborn as male and be blessed with joy, who will thereafter attain *Parinibbāna* ...,						N														N		
at the death-moment who will be reborn as male and with equanimity, who will thereafter attain *Parinibbāna* ...,						N													N			
men at the death-moment who will take on few rebirths in manhood, who will thereafter attain *Parinibbāna* ...,	N	**N**	N		N											N	N					
at the death-moment who will be reborn as female and be blessed with joy, who will thereafter attain *Parinibbāna* ...,					N															N		
at the death-moment who will be reborn as female and with equanimity, who will thereafter attain *Parinibbāna* ...,					N														N			
women at the death-moment who will take on few rebirths in womankind, who will thereafter attain *Parinibbāna* ...,	N	**N**	N			N										N	N					
at the death-moment who will be reborn with eye and be blessed with joy, who will thereafter attain *Parinibbāna* ...,	N																			N		
at the death-moment who will be reborn with eye and with equanimity, who will thereafter attain *Parinibbāna* ...,	N																		N			
at the attainment of *Parinibbāna* at sensuous planes,	N		N		N	N							**N**	N	N	N	N	N	N	N	N	N
at the attainment of *Parinibbāna* at fine-material planes,	**N**		N		N	N							**N**	**N**	**N**	**N**	**N**	**N**	**N**	N	**N**	**N**
at the attainment of *Parinibbāna* at immaterial planes,	**N**		N		**N**	**N**							**N**	**N**	**N**	**N**	**N**	**N**	**N**	N	**N**	**N**
at the attainment of *Parinibbāna* at five-aggregate planes	N		**N**		**N**	**N**							N	N	**N**	N	N	N	N	N	N	N
instantly after whose arising moment of *citta*, the final-stage *citta* associated with joy will arise,							A	A												N		
instantly after whose ceasing moment of *citta*, the final-stage *citta* associated with joy will arise,							N	N											N	N		
instantly after whose arising moment of *citta*, the final-stage *citta* associated with equanimity will arise,							A		A										N			
instantly after whose ceasing moment of *citta*, the final-stage *citta* associated with equanimity will arise,							N		N										N	N		
who possess the final-stage *citta* associated with joy,									N						N				**N**		N	N
who possess final-stage *citta* associated with equanimity								N							N					N	N	N
final existence persons.					A												N	N				
final existence persons at sensuous planes,	**A**	**A**	**A**		A												N	N				
final existence persons at fine-material planes,	**A**	**A**	N		N	N	**A**								N	N	N	N	N	N	N	N
final existence persons at immaterial planes,	N		N		N	N	**A**						N	N	N	N	N	N	N	N	N	N
fine-material beings (except for final existence persons),	**A**		N		N	N	**A**						**A**	**N**	A	N	N	A	A	A	A	A
immaterial beings (except for final existence persons),	N		N		N	N	**A**						N	N	A	N	N	A	N	A	A	A
non-percipience beings,	N		N		N	N	A	N	N	N	N		N	N	AN	N	N	**A**	N	AN	AN	AN

	Present											Future										
	eye faculty	ear faculty	nose faculty	mind faculty	femininity faculty	masculinity faculty	life faculty	joy faculty	equanimity faculty	faith faculty	understanding faculty	eye faculty	ear faculty	nose faculty	mind faculty	femininity faculty	masculinity faculty	life faculty	joy faculty	equanimity faculty	faith faculty	understanding faculty
who entered upon Cessation-attainment,				**N**				N	N	N	N				A					A	A	A
To those at the arising moment of:	in whom (A: arises; A*f* will arise; N: does not arise; N*f* will not arise)																					
consciousness dissociated from joy,								N							A					A	A	A
consciousness associated with joy,								A							N					**N**	N	N
consciousness associated with joy during life,								A							A					A	A	A
consciousness dissociated from equanimity,									N						A				**A**		A	A
consciousness associated with equanimity during life,									A						A				**A**		A	A
consciousness dissociated from faith,										N					A				**A**	**A**		A
consciousness associated with faith during life,										A					A				**A**	**A**		A
consciousness dissociated from knowledge,											N				A				**A**	**A**	**A**	
consciousness associated with knowledge during life,											A				A				**A**	**A**	**A**	
final-stage *citta* associated with equanimity,									A						N						N	N
final-stage *citta* associated with joy,								A							N					N	N	N
final-stage *citta* (without joy and equanimity),							A			A	A				N				N	N	N	N
To those at the ceasing moment of:																						
citta dissociated from joy,								N							A					A	A	A
citta associated with joy (without future),								N							N					**N**	N	N
citta dissociated from equanimity,									N						A				**A**		A	A
citta dissociated from faith,										**N**					**A**				**A**	**A**		**A**
citta dissociated from knowledge,											**N**				**A**				**A**	**A**	**A**	
final-stage *citta* associated with equanimity,							**N**	**N**	N	**N**	**N**				N				**N**		N	N
final-stage *citta* associated with joy,							**N**	N	**N**	**N**	**N**				N					N	N	N
final-stage *citta*,							N			N	N				N				N	N	N	N
To those at the death-moment :																						
at sensuous planes,	N		N	N	N	N	N	**N**	**N**	**N**	**N**		**A**	A	A	A	A	A	A	A	A	A
at the fine-material planes (except for non-percipients),	N						**N**						**A**	N	**A**	N	N	**A**	**A**	**A**	**A**	**A**
at five-aggregate planes,	N						**N**						**A**		A			**A**	A	A	A	A
at four- and five-aggregate planes,							N								A			**A**	A	A	**A**	**A**
at non-percipience plane,	**N**						N						N	**N**	N	**N**	**N**	**A**	**N**	N	N	N
To all those :																						
at the death-moment (apply only to sensuous beings),	N		N		N	N	N						A	A	A	A	A	A	A	A	A	A
at the arising moment of *citta* during life,							A								A				A	A	A	A
at the ceasing moment of *citta*,								N	N	N	N				A					A	A	A
at the ceasing moment of *citta* during life,							N	N	N	N	N				A				A	A	A	A

In the above chart from 2nd to 3rd row header, although the two statements seem to differ almost negligibly, the answers are vastly opposite each other in respect of the future arising of mental faculties. That is, according to the text regarding those: (i) at the arising moment of *citta* associated with joy, and (ii) at the arising moment of *citta* associated with joy *during life*. Apparently, it is 'in the course of life' and 'not during life' which determines the future arising.

The text has not enquired on these two phenomena: those at the ceasing moment of (i) *citta* dissociated from faith, and (ii) *citta* dissociated from knowledge. Because these two dissociations have been enquired at the arising moment, I take it as possibly an omission for whatever unknown reasons. Thus, I have included them in the chart together with my answers.

Chart 10.7 Past-Future Origination of Controlling Faculties

	Past											Future										
	eye faculty	ear faculty	nose faculty	mind faculty	femininity faculty	masculinity faculty	life faculty	joy faculty	equanimity faculty	faith faculty	understanding faculty	eye faculty	ear faculty	nose faculty	mind faculty	femininity faculty	masculinity faculty	life faculty	joy faculty	equanimity faculty	faith faculty	understanding faculty
To those :	in whom (A: had arisen/ will arise; N: had not arisen/ will not arise)																					
final existence persons (only at sensuous planes)	A		A										N	N	N	N	N	N	N	N	N	N
final existence persons at the sensuous planes,	A		A		A	A							N	N	N	N	N	N	N	N	N	N
final existence persons at the five-aggregate planes,	A												N		N	N	N	N	N	N	N	N
final existence persons at the fine-material plane,	A		N		N	N									N			N	N	N	N	N
final existence persons at the immaterial planes,	N		N		N	N									N			N	N	N	N	N
others at the sensuous planes,	A		A		A	A							A	A	A	A	A	A	A	A	A	A
others at the five-aggregate planes,	A												A		A			A	A	A	A	A
others at the four- and five-aggregate planes,				**A**			A	A	A	A	A				A				A	A	A	A
others at the fine-material plane,	A		N		N	N							A	N	A	N	N	A	A	A	A	A
others at the immaterial planes,	N		N		N	N							N	N	A	N	N	A	N	A	A	A
non-percipience beings,	N		N	**N**	N	N	A	N	N	N	N		N	N	N	N	N	A	N	N	N	N
pure abode beings,	N			**N**									N	N		N	N	N	N	N	N	N
at the birth-moment of pure abode beings,				N			N	N	N	N	N				A				A	A	A	A
at the occurrence of second *citta* of pure abodes,								N							A					A	A	A
instantly after whose *citta*, the final-stage *citta* associated with equanimity will arise,							A		A										N			
instantly after whose *citta*, the final-stage *citta* associated with joy will arise,							A	A												N		
endowed with the final-stage *citta*,							A	A	A	A	A				N		N	N	N	N	N	N
To those :																						
who will be born at fine-material planes, who therefrom will attain final liberation (*Parinibbāna*) upon death,	A		A		A	A							A	N	A	N	N	A	A	A	A	A
who will be born at the immaterial plane, who therefrom will attain final liberation (*Parinibbāna*) upon death,	A		A		A	A							N	N	A	N	N	A	N	A	A	A
men who will be reborn in few existences in manhood, who will thereafter attain final liberation upon death,	A		A													N						
women who will be reborn in few existences in womankind, who will thereafter attain final liberation upon death,	A		A		A												N					
who will be born with eye and be blessed with joy, therewith will attain final liberation upon death,	A																			N		
who will be born with eye and be blessed with equanimity, therewith will attain final liberation upon death,	A																		N			
who will be born with nose and be blessed with joy, therewith will attain final liberation upon death,	A		A																	N		
who will be born with nose and be blessed with equanimity, therewith will attain final liberation upon death,			A																N			
who will be born as male and be blessed with joy, therewith will attain final liberation upon death,						A														N		
who will be born as male and be blessed with equanimity, therewith will attain final liberation upon death,						A													N			
who will be born as female and be blessed with joy, therewith will attain final liberation upon death,					A															N		
who will be born as female and be blessed with equanimity, therewith will attain final liberation upon death,					A														N			

In the above chart, 'those others' at the sensuous planes, five-aggregate planes, four- and five-aggregate planes, fine-material and immaterial planes, are referring to those who are not final existence beings at those places.

10.3 Comprehension of Controlling Faculties

The pairs of enquiries in this section (nos. 435 to 482) are consolidated into the chart below, for example, 1_y–2_y. 3_n–4_n, etc. In the chart, the subscript *y* denotes the answer as "Yes", and the subscript *n* designates the answer as "No". Answers in the chart that are without subscripts attached to them, mean each of them carry both the affirmative and negative responds. Exposition of those duplex answers would be given after the chart.

Chart 10.8 Comprehension of Controlling Faculties (Present)

Present:	eye faculty?	ear faculty?	melancholy faculty?	I-shall-comprehend-the-unknown faculty (*anaññātaññassāmītindriya*)?	final knowledge faculty (*aññindriya*)?	final-knower faculty (*aññātāvindriya*)?
[435]. This person is comprehending eye faculty. Is that person *comprehending*		1_y				
This person is comprehending eye faculty. Is that person *renouncing*			3_n			
This person is comprehending eye faculty. Is that person *cultivating*				5_n		
This person is comprehending eye faculty. Is that person *cultivating*					7_y	
This person is comprehending eye faculty. Is that person *realising*						9_n
This person is *comprehending* ear faculty. Is that person comprehending	2_y					
This person is *renouncing* melancholy faculty. Is that person comprehending	4_n					
This person is *cultivating anaññātaññassāmītindriya*. Is that person comprehending	6_n					
This person is *cultivating* final knowledge faculty. Is that person comprehending	8					
This person is *realising* final-knower faculty. Is that person comprehending	10_n					
[436] This person is renouncing melancholy faculty. Is that person *cultivating*				11_n		
This person is renouncing melancholy faculty. Is that person *cultivating*					13_y	
This person is renouncing melancholy faculty. Is that person *realising*						15_n
This person is *cultivating anaññātaññassāmītindriya*. Is that person renouncing			12_n			
This person is *cultivating* final knowledge. Is that person renouncing			14			
This person is *realising* final-knower faculty. Is that person renouncing			16_n			
[437] This person is cultivating *anaññātaññassāmītindriya*. Is that person *cultivating*					17_n	
This person is cultivating *anaññātaññassāmītindriya*. Is that person *realising*						19_n
This person is cultivating final knowledge. Is that person *cultivating*				18_n		
This person is realising final-knower faculty. Is that person *cultivating*				20_n		
[438] This person is *cultivating* final knowledge. Is that person *realising*						21_n
This person is *realising* final-knower faculty. Is that person *cultivating*					22_n	

Present :	eye faculty?	ear faculty?	melancholy faculty?	I-shall-comprehend-the-unknown faculty (*anaññātaññassāmītindriya*)?	final knowledge faculty (*aññindriya*)?	final-knower faculty (*aññātāvindriya*)?
[439]. This person is not comprehending eye faculty. Is that person not *renouncing*			23			
This person is not comprehending eye faculty. Is that person not *cultivating*				25		
This person is not comprehending eye faculty. Is that person not *cultivating*					27	
This person is not comprehending eye faculty. Is that person not *realising*						29
This person is not *renouncing* melancholy faculty. Is that person not comprehending	24					
This person is not *cultivating anaññātaññassāmītindriya*. That person not comprehending	26					
This person is not *cultivating* final knowledge. Is that person not comprehending	28*y*					
This person is not *realising* final-knower faculty. Is that person not comprehending	30					
[440]. This person is not renouncing melancholy faculty. Is that person not *cultivating*				31		
This person is not renouncing melancholy faculty. Is that person not *cultivating*					33	
This person is not renouncing melancholy faculty. Is that person not *realising*						35
This person is not *cultivating anaññātaññassāmītindriya*. Is that person not renouncing			32			
This person is not *cultivating* final knowledge. Is that person not renouncing			34*y*			
This person is not *realising* final-knower faculty. Is that person not renouncing			36			
[441] This person is not cultivating *anaññātaññassāmītindriya*. That person not *cultivating*					37	
This person is not cultivating *anaññātaññassāmītindriya*. Is that person not *realising*						39
This person is not *cultivating* final knowledge. Is that person not cultivating				38		
This person is not *realising* final-knower faculty. Is that person not cultivating				40		
[442] This person is not *cultivating* final knowledge. Is that person not *realising*						41
This person is not *realising* final-knower faculty. Is that person not *cultivating*					42	

Nos. <u>Quick Answers.</u>

8. No (*Sakadāgāmi*-path person and *Anāgāmi*-path person).
   Yes (*Arahatta*-path person).
14. No (*Sakadāgāmi*-path person and *Arahatta*-path person).
    Yes (*Anāgāmi*-path person).
23. No (*Anāgāmi*-path person).
    Yes (With the exception of *Anāgāmi*-path person and *Arahatta* path person, the remaining persons).
24. No (*Arahatta*-path person).
    Yes (Same as in nos. 23 above).
25. No (The eighth person, of *Sotāpatti*-path).
    Yes (With the exception of *Sotāpatti*-path person and *Arahatta*-path person, the remaining persons).
26. No (*Arahatta*-path person).
    Yes (Same as in nos. 25 above).
27. No (*Sakadāgāmi*-path person and *Anāgāmi*-path person).
    Yes (With the exception of the three persons of *Sakadāgāmi*-path, *Anāgāmi*-path and *Arahatta*-path, the remaining persons).
29. No (*Aggaphala*, the supreme fruition of Arahatship).
    Yes (Except *Arahatta*-path person and *Arahat*, the remaining persons).

30. No (*Arahatta*-path person).
    Yes (Same as in nos. 29 above).
31. No (*Sotāpatti*-path person).
    Yes (Except *Sotāpatti*-path person and *Anāgāmi*-path person, the remaining).
32. No (*Anāgāmi*-path person).
    Yes (Same as in nos. 31 above).
33. No (*Sakadāgāmi*-path person and *Arahatta*-path person).
    Yes (Same as in nos. 27 above).
35. No (Attainer of *Arahatta*-fruition).
    Yes (Except *Anāgāmi*-path person and *Arahat*, the remaining persons).
36. No (*Anāgāmi*-path person).
    Yes (Same as in nos. 35 above).
37. No (Three persons of *Sakadāgāmi*-path, *Anāgāmi*-path and *Arahatta*-path).
    Yes (With the exception of the four path persons, the remaining persons)
38. No (*Sotāpatti*-path person).
    Yes (Same as in nos. 37 above).
39. No (Attainer of *Arahatta*-fruition).
    Yes (Except *Sotāpatti*-path person and *Arahat*, the remaining persons).
40. No (*Sotāpatti*-path person).
    Yes (Same as in nos. 39 above).
41. No (Attainer of *Arahatta*-fruition).
    Yes (With the exception of the three path persons of *Sakadāgāmi, Anāgāmi* and *Arahatta*, and *Arahat*, the remaining persons).
42. No (Three persons of *Sakadāgāmi* path, *Anāgāmi* path, *Arahatta* path).
    Yes (*Sotāpatti*-path person; and persons of *Sotāpanna*-fruition, *Sakadāgāmi*-fruition and *Anāgāmi*-fruition).

Chart 10.8 above examines common worldling (*Puthujjana*) and the eight types of noble persons. The corporeal faculties of eye, ear, etc. are concerning comprehension, melancholy faculty is about its eradication, the last three intellect faculties are regarding their cultivation or development. The expositions below are given according to the enquiry number series in the chart, to those without the yes and no subscripts, i.e. those questions which have duplex answers.

The Q&A below will be useful in helping reader to better understand that chart.

1. Who is comprehending (*parijānāti*) eye-, ear-, and remaining gross faculties?

Arahatta-path person is comprehending them. When he fully understands these gross sense-faculties, in the same way as he comprehends the 16 gross matters, 12 gross bases, and 10 gross elements, he naturally renounces the higher five fetters of attachment to fine-material and immaterial existences, conceitedness, restlessness, and ignorance which are closely bound up with sense faculties. We can therefore say that *Arahatta*-path person is renouncing all seven sense-faculties.

The remaining seven persons are not comprehending these gross sense-faculties because of the differentiation in their roles and functions, aspiration and purpose at any one given stage. Otherwise we make out to no avail how possibly an *Anāgāmi*-path person does not even comprehend an eye faculty.

2. Who is renouncing (*pajahatī*) melancholy faculty?

Anāgāmi-path person is renouncing melancholy faculty. Melancholy is bound up with unpleasant feeling as a result of the latent tendencies of attachment to sensuous desires, and hate factor. A complete renunciation of melancholy faculty is only partial elimination of the lower region of the five fetters, namely attachment to sensuous desires, ill-will, skepticism, heresy of individuality, and ceremonial observances. There are also pleasant feeling tied to pleasure faculty and joy faculty due to sensuous desires, that also have to be renounced by *Anāgāmi*-path person.

Sotāpatti-path person and *Sakadāgāmi*-path person are only renouncing a part of melancholy faculty, and hence are said to be not completely renouncing it. *Arahatta*-path person is post-*Anāgāmi*, and hence is also not renouncing it.

3. Who is cultivating or developing (*bhāveti*) the "I-shall-comprehend-the-unknown" faculty (*anaññātaññassāmītindriya*)?

Sotāpatti-path person is cultivating this faculty. The 'stream-winner' path person strives ardently to renounce and eliminate the first three fetters of skepticism, heretical views of individualistic identity, and clinging to ceremonies and rites. It is thus being given an epithet of the faculty of 'initial enlightenment'.

4. Who is cultivating the final-knowledge faculty (*aññindriya*)?

The three path persons of *Sakadāgāmimagga*, *Anāgāmimagga*, and *Arahattamagga*. At the stage of 'stream-winning' path, three of the ten fetters of defilement had already been eradicated. The 'once-returner' path person is cultivating but does not renounce further fetters in his development effort, that is, he is only able to attenuate intensity of the remaining seven fetters. The 'non-returner' path person is cultivating to renounce remaining fetters, but had only been able to eradicate the two fetters of attachment to sensuous desires, and ill-will (i.e. the latent proclivities of *kāmarāga* and *paṭigha*). *Arahatta*-path person is cultivating to eliminate the remaining last five subtle fetters. *Arahat* is not cultivating the final-knowledge because he had already 'graduated' from the final cultivation. In this regard, therefore the three persons of *Sakadāgāmi*-fruition, *Anāgāmi*-fruition, and *Arahatta*-fruition are not cultivating the final knowledge for elimination of their areas of fetters. It is only when they were previously at the respective path levels that there were cultivating those knowledges. When asking in terms of who had not cultivated the final-knowledge, it is all those persons including mundane worldlings, with the exception of *Arahat*

It is not correct as what some other sources have written that the six persons (the three path persons of *Sakadāgāmimagga*, *Anāgāmimagga*, *Arahattamagga*; and the three fruition persons of *Sotāpannaphala*, *Sakadāgāmiphala*, *Anāgāmiphala*) are cultivating this final-knowledge faculty, without giving any functional differentiation. Otherwise it runs into contradiction with the answers explained in four catechisms, nos. 439 to 442 in the text. However, it would not be wrong if they are referring to these six types of persons as cultivating the final-knowledge as a whole or a mid-point transition which thereby is giving it the name as faculty of the 'intermediate stage of enlightenment'.

4. Who is realising (*sacchikaroti*) the final-knower faculty (*aññātāvindriya*)?

The *Arahatta*-fruition person is realising the final-knower faculty. Put it in another way, we say that *Arahatta*-fruition person had not previously through his developmental experience realised the final-knower faculty. When he had realised it, it means he also had already eliminated the upper region of the remaining subtle five fetters, which includes ignorance arising from the plethora of mental activities cognisable from sense-objects impinging on the sense-bases. He conquered all the taints of mind, and hence it is given another name as the faculty of 'final enlightenment'.

5. Who is not comprehending eye- and the remaining gross faculties, not renouncing melancholy faculty, not cultivating the "I-shall-comprehend-the-unknown" faculty, not cultivating the final-knowledge faculty, and not realising the final-knower faculty?

With the exception of *Arahatta*-path person, common worldling (*Puthujjana*), remaining three path persons, and the four fruition persons are not comprehending eye-faculty and the remaining gross faculties at any one time.

With the exception of *Anāgāmi*-path person, common worldling, remaining three path persons and four fruition persons are not renouncing melancholy faculty at any one time.

With the exception of *Sotāpatti*-path person, common worldling, remaining three path persons and four fruition persons are not cultivating the "I-shall-comprehend-the-unknown" faculty at any one time.

Common worldling and *Arahatta*-fruition person are not cultivating the final-knowledge faculty.

With the exception of *Arahat*, the remaining seven supramundane persons and common worldling are not realising the final-knower faculty.

The functional differences among these nine types of persons can be easily understood from a summarised chart I would be giving at the end of this chapter, analysing by present, past, and future time-measured formulation.

Chart 10.9 Comprehension of Controlling Faculties (Past)

Past:	eye faculty?	melancholy faculty?	I-shall-comprehend-the-unknown faculty (*anaññātaññassāmītindriya*)?	final knowledge faculty (*aññindriya*)?	final-knower faculty (*aññātāvindriya*)?
[443] This person had comprehended eye faculty. Had that person *renounced*		1_y			
This person had comprehended eye faculty. Had that person *cultivated*			3_y		
This person had comprehended eye faculty. Had that person *cultivated*				5_y	
This person had comprehended eye faculty. Had that person *realised*					7
This person had *renounced* melancholy faculty. Had that person comprehended	2				
This person had *cultivated anaññātaññassāmītindriya*. Had that person comprehended	4				
This person had *cultivated* final knowledge faculty. Had that person comprehended	6_y				
This person had *realised* final-knower faculty. Had that person comprehended	8_y				
[444] This person had renounced melancholy faculty. Had that person *cultivated*			9_y		
This person had renounced melancholy faculty. Had that person *cultivated*				11	
This person had renounced melancholy faculty. Had that person *realised*					13
This person had *cultivated anaññātaññassāmītindriya*. Had that person renounced		10			
This person had *cultivated* final knowledge. Had that person renounced		12_y			
This person had *realised* final-knower faculty. Had that person renounced		14_y			
[445] This person had cultivated *anaññātaññassāmītindriya*. Had that person *cultivated*				15	
This person had cultivated *anaññātaññassāmītindriya*. Had that person *realised*					17
This person had cultivated final knowledge. Had that person *cultivated*			16_y		
This person had realised final-knower faculty. Had that person *cultivated*			18_y		
[446] This person had *cultivated* final knowledge. Had that person *realised*					19
This person had *realised* final-knower faculty. Had that person *cultivated*				20_y	
[447]. This person had not comprehended eye faculty. Had that person not *renounced*		21			
This person had not comprehended eye faculty. Had that person not *cultivated*			23		
This person had not comprehended eye faculty. Had that person not *cultivated*				25_y	
This person had not comprehended eye faculty. Had that person not *realised*					27_y
This person had not *renounced* melancholy faculty. Had that person not comprehended	22_y				
This person had not *cultivated anaññātaññassāmītindriya*.That person not comprehended	24_y				
This person had not *cultivated* final knowledge. Had that person not comprehended	26_y				
This person had not *realised* final-knower faculty. Had that person not comprehended	28				
[448]. This person had not renounced melancholy faculty. Had that person not *cultivated*			29		
This person had not renounced melancholy faculty. Had that person not *cultivated*				31_y	
This person had not renounced melancholy faculty. Had that person not *realised*					33_y
This person had not *cultivated anaññātaññassāmītindriya*. Had that person not renounced		30_y			
This person had not *cultivated* final knowledge. Had that person not renounced		32			
This person had not *realised* final-knower faculty. Had that person not renounced		34			
[449] This person had not cultivated *anaññātaññassāmītindriya*.That person not *cultivated*				35_y	
This person had not cultivated *anaññātaññassāmītindriya*. Had that person not *realised*					37_y
This person had not *cultivated* final knowledge. Had that person not cultivated			36		
This person had not *realised* final-knower faculty. Had that person not cultivated			38		
[450] This person had not *cultivated* final knowledge. Had that person not *realised*					39_y
This person had not *realised* final-knower faculty. Had that person not *cultivated*				40	

Nine types of persons are being examined in the above chart, namely *Puthujjana* (common worldling), four types of noble path persons, and four types of noble fruition persons. The subscript y in the chart denotes the yes answer.

Nos. Quick Answers.

2. No (*Arahatta*-path person and *Anāgāmi*-fruition person).
Yes (*Arahat*).
4. No, Six persons (not including *Sotāpanna*-fruition person and *Arahat*) .
Yes (*Arahat*).
7. No. *Aggaphala* person (whose realisation of the final-knower faculty is not perfect, i.e. is still in the process of realising it).
Yes. *Aggaphala* person (who had completely and perfectly realised the final-knower faculty).
10. No. Four persons (the two path persons of *Sakadāgāmi* and *Anāgāmi*, and the two fruition persons of *Sotāpatti* and *Sakadāgāmi*.
Yes. Three persons. (*Arahatta*-path person, *Anāgāmi*-fruition person, and *Arahatta*-fruition person)
11. No. Two persons. (*Arahatta*-path person and *Anāgāmi*-fruition person)
Yes (*Arahat*).
13. No. Three persons. (*Anāgāmi*-fruition person, *Arahatta*-path person, and *Arahatta*-fruition person)
Yes (*Arahat*).
15. No. Six persons (not including *Puthujjana*, *Sotāpatti*-path person, and *Arahat*)
Yes. (*Arahat*)
17. No. Seven persons (not including *Puthujjana* and *Sotāpatti*-path person).
Yes. (*Arahat*)
19. No (Same as in nos. 7 above).
Yes (Same as in nos. 7 above).
21. No. Two persons. (*Arahatta*-path person and *Anāgāmi*-fruition person)
Yes. Six persons. (excluding *Anāgāmi*-fruition person, *Arahatta*-path person, and *Arahat*)
23. No. Six persons (not including *Puthujjana*, *Sotāpatti*-path person and *Arahat*).
Yes. Two persons. (*Puthujjana* and *Sotāpatti*-path person)
28. No. (Same as in nos. 7 above)
Yes. Eight persons (excluding *Aggaphala* person whose is still realising final-knower faculty).
29. No. Four persons. (The two path persons of *Sakadāgāmi* and *Anāgāmi*, and two fruition persons of *Sotāpatti* and *Sakadāgāmi*).
Yes. Two persons. (*Puthujjana* and *Sotāpatti*-path person)
32. No. Two persons. (*Anāgāmi*-fruition person and *Arahatta*-path person)
Yes. Six persons. (not including *Anāgāmi*-fruition person, *Arahatta*-path person and *Arahat*)
34. No. Three persons (*Anāgāmi*-fruition person, *Arahatta*-path person, and *Arahat*)
Yes. Six persons (not including *Anāgāmi*-fruition person, *Arahatta*-path person, and *Arahat*).
36. No. Six persons (not including *Puthujjana*, *Sotāpatti*-path person, and *Arahat*)
Yes. Two persons. (*Puthujjana* and *Sotāpatti*-path person)
38. No. Seven persons (not including *Puthujjana* and *Sotāpatti*-path person)
Yes. Two persons. (*Puthujjana* and *Sotāpatti*-path person)
40. No. (Same as in nos. 7 above)
Yes. Eight persons (not including *Arhat*)

[451-458] Future
[459-466] Present and Past
[467-474] Present and Future
[475-482] Past and Future

The remaining enquiries nos. 451 to 482 are to be formulated in the same pattern as in the preceding two charts. The answers can all be obtained from the summary detail I constructed in Chart 10.10 below.

Chart 10.10 Summary on comprehension of the faculties (present, past, future, present-past, present-future, past-future)

Y: Yes ; N: No

<table>
<tr><th rowspan="2">Subject :</th><th rowspan="2">Time measure :</th><th colspan="8">Eight types of noble persons</th><th colspan="2">Common worldlings</th></tr>
<tr><th>*Arahatta*-fruition person</th><th>*Arahatta*-path person</th><th>*Anāgāmi*-fruition person</th><th>*Anāgāmi*-path person</th><th>*Sakadāgāmi*-fruition person</th><th>*Sakadāgāmi*-path person</th><th>*Sotāpanna*-fruition person</th><th>*Sotāpatti*-path person</th><th>*Puthujjana* who will attend the Path</th><th>*Puthujjana* who will not attend the Path</th></tr>
<tr><td rowspan="4">Comprehension of the faculties of eye and the remaining sense organs</td><td>Is comprehending</td><td>N</td><td>Y</td><td>N</td><td>N</td><td>N</td><td>N</td><td>N</td><td>N</td><td colspan="2">N</td></tr>
<tr><td>Had comprehended</td><td>Y</td><td>N</td><td>N</td><td>N</td><td>N</td><td>N</td><td>N</td><td>N</td><td colspan="2">N</td></tr>
<tr><td rowspan="2">Will comprehend</td><td rowspan="2">N</td><td rowspan="2">N</td><td rowspan="2">Y</td><td rowspan="2">Y</td><td rowspan="2">Y</td><td rowspan="2">Y</td><td rowspan="2">Y</td><td rowspan="2">Y</td><td>Y</td><td>--</td></tr>
<tr><td>--</td><td>N</td></tr>
<tr><td rowspan="4">Renunciation of the melancholy faculty</td><td>Is renouncing</td><td>N</td><td>N</td><td>N</td><td>Y</td><td>N</td><td>N</td><td>N</td><td>N</td><td colspan="2">N</td></tr>
<tr><td>Had renounced</td><td>Y</td><td>Y</td><td>Y</td><td>N</td><td>N</td><td>N</td><td>N</td><td>N</td><td colspan="2">N</td></tr>
<tr><td rowspan="2">Will renounce</td><td rowspan="2">N</td><td rowspan="2">N</td><td rowspan="2">N</td><td rowspan="2">N</td><td rowspan="2">Y</td><td rowspan="2">Y</td><td rowspan="2">Y</td><td rowspan="2">Y</td><td>Y</td><td>--</td></tr>
<tr><td>--</td><td>N</td></tr>
<tr><td rowspan="4">Cultivation of the I-shall-comprehend-the-unknown faculty</td><td>Is cultivating</td><td>N</td><td>N</td><td>N</td><td>N</td><td>N</td><td>N</td><td>N</td><td>Y</td><td colspan="2">N</td></tr>
<tr><td>Had cultivated</td><td>Y</td><td>Y</td><td>Y</td><td>Y</td><td>Y</td><td>Y</td><td>Y</td><td>N</td><td colspan="2">N</td></tr>
<tr><td rowspan="2">Will cultivate</td><td rowspan="2">N</td><td rowspan="2">N</td><td rowspan="2">N</td><td rowspan="2">N</td><td rowspan="2">N</td><td rowspan="2">N</td><td rowspan="2">N</td><td rowspan="2">N</td><td>Y</td><td>--</td></tr>
<tr><td>--</td><td>N</td></tr>
<tr><td rowspan="4">Cultivation of the final knowledge faculty</td><td>Is cultivating</td><td>N</td><td>Y</td><td>N</td><td>Y</td><td>N</td><td>Y</td><td>N</td><td>N</td><td colspan="2">N</td></tr>
<tr><td>Had cultivated</td><td>Y</td><td>N</td><td>N</td><td>N</td><td>N</td><td>N</td><td>N</td><td>N</td><td colspan="2">N</td></tr>
<tr><td rowspan="2">Will cultivate</td><td rowspan="2">N</td><td rowspan="2">N</td><td rowspan="2">Y</td><td rowspan="2">Y</td><td rowspan="2">Y</td><td rowspan="2">Y</td><td rowspan="2">Y</td><td rowspan="2">Y</td><td>Y</td><td>--</td></tr>
<tr><td>--</td><td>N</td></tr>
<tr><td rowspan="5">Realisation of the final-knower faculty (through cultivation)</td><td>Is realising</td><td>Y</td><td>N</td><td>N</td><td>N</td><td>N</td><td>N</td><td>N</td><td>N</td><td colspan="2">N</td></tr>
<tr><td>Had realised (perfectly)</td><td>Y</td><td rowspan="2">N</td><td rowspan="2">N</td><td rowspan="2">N</td><td rowspan="2">N</td><td rowspan="2">N</td><td rowspan="2">N</td><td rowspan="2">N</td><td colspan="2" rowspan="2">N</td></tr>
<tr><td>Had realised (not in its entirety)</td><td>N</td></tr>
<tr><td rowspan="2">Will realise</td><td rowspan="2">N</td><td rowspan="2">Y</td><td rowspan="2">Y</td><td rowspan="2">Y</td><td rowspan="2">Y</td><td rowspan="2">Y</td><td rowspan="2">Y</td><td rowspan="2">Y</td><td>Y</td><td>--</td></tr>
<tr><td>--</td><td>N</td></tr>
</table>

End of the Yamaka, Volume II

Conclusion

At last I am here, putting some final touches to sum up all of what have been discussed so far. Although the ten chapters of Yamaka represent the theoretical bedrock of the Buddhist doctrines, we don't find in it the familiar dogmatic contents as expounded in the other treatises of the Abhidhamma such as the Abhidhammamātikā, 89 states of consciousness, 52 mental factors, thought moments, 28 matters, and the theory of dependent origination. All the enquiries in the ten chapters are invariably driving at the same measures concerning arising and cessation, with clarification of terminologies in their pure forms being given at the outset, and a small section to ensure our comprehension is given at the end of every chapter. The exception is at Chapter two, three, and four in which the findings are restricted to the types of persons at the birth-moment and death-moment. The reason is because matters and the other mental aggregates, the twelve bases, and eighteen elements are all subsumed under aggregate level. Other exceptions are Chapter seven in which the underlying states of propensity of the types of persons are evaluated according to the different stages of development, and Chapter eight in which *citta* is evaluated based on its fundamental changes in phenomenal existence at the arising moment and ceasing moment of the particular states of consciousness. Others on truths, material and mental formations, *dhammā*, and faculties are evaluated based on person types and mix number of determinants as used in aforementioned chapters. Clearly one universal criterion which is used in the assessment of all subject matters in the Yamaka, is the measurement of arising and cessation in accordance with the three divisions of time as present, past, and future. This reminds us of the concept of tri-temporality of the school of Sarvāstivāda in which substances of all dhammas exist in the three periods of time through present, past, and future. It raises a question whether the Yamaka treatise was in any way influenced by the Sarvāstivādins' theory of tri-temporal existence, although that it had been an acute subject of polemics culminated in the compilation of Kathāvatthu by elders of the Theravadins in rebuttal of the dissident creed. Though having said that, the Buddhist canon only came to be fixed around the end of the first century B.C. as mentioned in the Sinhalese and Pāli Commentaries.

Well, the Yamaka has nothing to do with the tri-temporality of existence. The ten chapters of the Yamaka present to us a most basic manual on insight meditation, not intimating anything notional of nihility or the complex instructions, but was designed to help us in cultivating mindfulness and develop the ability to exercising timely restraint over our thoughts and actions. The purpose of this book aims to set in place our clear understanding and awareness of what transpires in the past, present, and future in regard to our incessant states of consciousness — at the arising moment and birth-moment, and at the ceasing moment and death-moment. The organised information provides a direct, refined, and practical pedagogic training of the mind and body that suits everybody regardless of religion and creed, old and young.

A good understanding of the teaching of the Yamaka is essential for any serious meditation practitioner. The Abhidhamma teachings in the Dhammasaṅgaṇi, Vibhaṅga, and Dhātukathā are fundamentally important for insight practical, but they vary in their medothological approach and suit the different intellectual levels of audience. The Yamaka is written exclusively with *vipassana* in mind, intents on eventually relieving us of our persistent bondage to the physical-psycho preoccupations with phenomenal existences and worldly desires. The Yamaka is not actually as difficult as some of you may have thought, for you can clearly see that the whole contents of the text are centered on examining the dualistic eventualities, namely the arising moment and ceasing moment of our minds in three time measures. It is to those who are not acquainted with the knowledge on the kinds of mental concomitants accompanying the types of cittas, that they will have no clue of how to observe the origination of their consciousness and emotions, needless to say about possessing awareness of the particular states of latent proclivities driving which of their mental obsessions. Consciousness arises and ceases in constant recurrence incredibly faster than we can imagine, like the torrent descending from steep waterfall. For the untrained minds to understand how their minds arise and cease in perpetual succession is like trying to understand how the rapid stream connects its uninterrupted flow. With this book finally made easier for study, it can now be used as our reliable guide in our efforts to guard against our fleeting minds, and become wary of sometimes our bizarre, rude, inharmonious, or unwholesome thoughts and behaviours towards the people around us and with us. With the Yamaka, we can be easily trained to become aware of any of our bad thoughts just as soon as it arises, and knowing precisely when, where and how it ceases.

We need not have to stay away from daily activities in order to engage in contemplative training. With the Yamaka, we can be trained to be mindful and aware of every arising and ceasing moment of our minds as we suit ourselves in any comfortable postures and physical motions in our everyday life. Imagine a person, aspiring to live a virtuous life, who is obliged to work six days in office to support ailing parents, and on the rest day still requires to complete house chores in the morning and doing charitable work in the afternoon. In the reality of life, every thinking moments, gestures, responses, movements, and interactions with others are real and better training opportunities for familiarisating with the arising and cessation of mind. We may know barely one percent of the root causes for all thoughts and decisions made in a day. With persistent training, we will master the adeptness and gaining competency in exercising restraint and moderation in regard to arising thoughts instead of simply letting bad and inappropriate state of mind as a result of our underlying propensities, continues unnoticed ad unattended to. The Yamaka, now in an easier format, and complementary to the thirty-seven factors of awakening, shall gear us up with constant vigilance over all actions of our mind and body, leapfrogging us in the path to end mental suffering, a corollary of our own choice and creation. I hope all of you will be rewarded from reading this book.

Appendix I: Types of individual at their planes of existence

	Supramundane stages (Pāli term)	*English terms*	*Chinese terms*	*Beings*	*Causes of rebirth*
8	☆ *Arahattaphala* [87]	Arhatta noble fruition	阿羅漢果	awakened beings of 8 supramundane stages [86]	The final noble path eliminated 5 fetters of the 'upper region'
7	☆ *Arahattamagga* [87]	Arhatta noble path	阿羅漢道支		
6	☆ *Anāgāmiphala* [87]	Non-Returner's noble fruition	不來果		The third noble path eliminated 5 fetters of the 'lower region'
5	† *Anāgāmimagga* [91]	Non-Returner's noble path	不來道支		
4	† *Sakadāgāmiphala* [91]	Once-Returner's noble fruition	一來果		The second noble path only attenuated remainders of the 10 fetters
3	† *Sakadāgāmimagga* [91]	Once-Returner's noble path	一來道支		
2	† *Sotāpattiphala* [91]	Stream-winner's noble fruition	預流果		The first noble path eliminated the 3 fetters
1	*Sotāpattimagga* [88]	Stream-winner's noble path	預流道支		

---

[86] With regard to the 12 unwholesome cittas, the first noble Path (*Sotāpattimagga*) eliminated the 4 greed-rooted cittas associated with wrong view, and 1 delusion-rooted citta associated with doubt (or the 3 Fetters of *sakkāyadiṭṭhi*, *vicikicchā*, *sīlabbataparāmāsa*). The second noble Path (*Sakadāgāmimagga*) only attenuated the remaining 7 active unwholesome cittas. The third noble Path (*Anāgāmimagga*) eliminated the 2 hatred-rooted cittas associated with aversion. The final noble Path (*Arahattamagga*) eliminated the remaining 4 greed-rooted cittas dissociated from wrong view, and 1 delusion-rooted citta associated with restlessness. In another word, the first noble Path eradicated the 3 Fetters (*sakkāyadiṭṭhi*, *vicikicchā*, *sīlabbataparāmāsa*); the second noble Path only attenuated the remainders of the 10 Fetters; the third noble Path eradicated the Five fetters of the 'Lower region' (*sakkāyadiṭṭhi*, *vicikicchā*, *sīlabbataparāmāsa*, *kāmarāga*, *paṭigha*); the final noble Path eradicated the Five Fetters of the 'upper region' (*rūparāga*, *arūparāga*, *māna*, *uddhacca*, *avijjā*). *Cf.* Pug: nos. 36-40, 209.

[87] Non-returner of the noble fruition, and Arahat of the noble path and fuition (Marked by ☆) are also found in the 7 sensuous planes, and 15 fine-material planes (Balance 24 planes excluding Non-percipience plane, 4 immaterial planes, and the 4 woeful realms). *Cf. Khandhayamaka.*

[88] The 'Stream-Winner' of the noble path (*Sotāpattimaggacitta*) would be reborn for at most 7 times in good places in either of the seven sensuous planes and the 10 of the fine-material planes of the triple-rooted worldlings, before finally attaining *Arahatta* noble fruition. *Cf.* Pug 31-33; AN 3.87-3.88, 9.12.

	Plan of rebirth (Pāli term)	English terms	Chinese terms	Beings	Causes of rebirth here
31	*Nevasaññānāsaññā yatana*	Base of neither perception nor non-perception	非想非非想處	Four-aggregates worldlings of the 4 immaterial planes (literally all here are of the Fourth Jhāna)[89]	Attainment of the Base of neither-perception-nor-nonperception (eighth *jhāna*)
30	*Ākiñcaññāyatana*	Base of nothingness	無所有處		Attainment of the Base of nothingness (seventh *jhāna*)
29	*Viññāṇañcāyatana*	Base of infinite consciousness	識無邊處		Attainment of the Base of infinite consciousness (sixth *jhāna*)
28	*Ākāsānañcāyatana*	Base of infinite space	空無邊處		Attainment of the Base of infinite space (fifth *jhāna*)
27	*Akaniṭṭhā-bhavana*	The supreme abode	色究竟天	worldlings of the Pure abodes[89]	Proficiency in fourth *jhāna* (Vibh 1027)
26	*Sudassī-bhavana*	The clear-sighted abode	善現天		Proficiency in fourth *jhāna* (Vibh 1027)
25	*Sudassā-bhavana*	The beautiful abode	善見天		Proficiency in fourth *jhāna* (Vibh 1027)
24	*Atappā-bhavana*	The serene abode	無熱天		Proficiency in fourth *jhāna* (Vibh 1027)
23	*Avihā-bhavana*	The durable abode	無煩天		Proficiency in fourth *jhāna* (Vibh 1027)
22	* *Asaññasattāvāsa*[90]	Abode of the Non-percipients	無想天	Single-aggregate worldlings[89]	Proficiency in fourth *jhāna* (Vibh 1027)

---

[89] Beings of the five Pure abodes, and beings of the four immaterial planes are not found in any other planes, if they are to be reborn again. Beings of *Akaniṭṭhā* and *Nevasaññānāsaññāyatana*, if they do not triumph over bondage of the fine-material worlds, will not be reborn in another plane other than their current plane.

[90] Happy, rootless worldlings (marked in *): refer to the non-percipients, if they do not attain enlightenment in current lifespan, will be reborn in the respective 5th, 6th, and 22nd plane of *Manussaloka*, *Cātummahārājika-devaloka*, and *Asaññasattāvāsa*, and not in any other planes. *Cf. Khandhayamaka*

Appendix I. Types of individual at planes of existence

	Plan of Rebirth (Pāli term)	*English terms*	*Chinese terms*	*Beings*	*Causes of rebirth here*
21	† *Vehapphala-āvāsa* [91]	Abode of great reward	廣果天	triple-rooted worldlings of the 10 fine-material planes	Proficiency in fourth *jhāna* (Vibh 1027)
20	† *Subhakiṇṇa-devaloka* [91]	Refulgent glory heaven	遍淨天		Proficiency in third *jhāna*, highest degree (Vibh 1026)
19	† *Appamāṇasubha-devaloka* [91]	Unbounded glory heaven	無量淨天		Proficiency in third *jhāna*, medium degree (Vibh 1026)
18	† *Parittasubha-devaloka* [91]	Limited glory heaven	少淨天		Proficiency in third *jhāna*, minor degree (Vibh 1026)
17	† *Ābhassara-devaloka* [91]	Brilliant radiance heaven	光音天		Proficiency in second *jhāna*, highest degree (Vibh 1025)
16	† *Appamāṇābha-devaloka* [91]	Unlimited radiance heaven	無量光天		Proficiency in second *jhāna*, medium degree (Vibh 1025)
15	† *Parittābha-devaloka* [91]	Limited radiance heaven	少光天		Proficiency in second *jhāna*, minor degree (Vibh 1025)
14	† *Mahābrahmā-devaloka* [91]	World of the Great Brahmā	大梵天		proficiency in first *jhāna*, highest degree (Vibh 1024)
13	† *Brahmapurohita-devaloka* [91]	World of the devas who are ministers of Brahma	梵輔天		proficiency in first *jhāna*, medium degree (Vibh 1024)
12	† *Brahmapārisajja-devaloka* [91]	World of the retinue of Brahma	梵眾天		proficiency in first *jhāna*, minor degree (Vibh 1024)

[91] Marked in † are beings from their respective abodes who are also found in the 7 sensuous planes — they are triple-rooted worldlings of the 10 fine-material planes, individuals of Once-returner noble path, Non-returner noble path, Stream-winner noble fruition and Once-returner noble fruition. Note that these 4 types of supramundane individuals are not subject to be reborn in 10 fine-material planes of the triple-rooted worldlings but in the 7 sensuous worlds. *Cf. Khandhayamaka.*

	Plan of Rebirth (Pāli term)	***English terms***	***Chinese terms***	***Beings***	***Causes of rebirth here***
11	*Paranimmitavasavattī*	Heaven of those wielding power over the creations of others	他化自在天	dual-rooted worldlings of the 7 sensuous planes	Keeping with the minimal five precepts (Vibh 942), up to the ten precepts (Vibh 968). Unwholesome actions (MN 41; 129). Virtue and wisdom (AN 10:177).
10	*Nimmānaratī*	Heaven of those delight in creation	化樂天		
9	*Tusita-devaloka*	Heaven of the contented	兜率天		
8	*Yāmā-devaloka*	Heaven of the easeful	夜摩天		
7	*Tāvatiṃsa*	Heaven of the thirty-three realms	忉利天		
6	* *Cātummahārājika-devaloka* [90]	Heaven of the four Great Kings	四天王天		
5	* *Manussaloka* [90]	World of humans	人趣		
4	*Asurakāya/ Asurayoni*	Titan birth	阿修羅趣	woeful, rootless worldlings of the 4 woeful realms	Unwholesome actions (MN 41; 129)
3	*Pettivisaya*	Region of Ghosts	惡鬼趣		Wrong views (AN 10:177); unwholesome actions (MN 41; 129)
2	*Tiracchānayoni*	Animal birth	畜生趣		Wrong views (AN 10:177; MN 57)
1	*Niraya*	Purgatory	地獄趣		The five immediate resultant actions (AN 5:129); unwholesome actions (MN 41; 129)

Appendix II: Classification of cittas by Feeling

Cittas classified by feelng:	Kāmakusala	Kāmākusala	Vipāka	Kriya	First jhāna	Second jhāna	Third jhāna	Fourth jhāna	Fifth jhāna		Composition:
Cittas associated with joy (*somanassa*) as pleasant feeling	4	4	5	5	11	11	11	11		**62**	4 kāma kusalas, 4 *lobhamūla*, 4 resultants (*hetuka sobhana-somanassa*), 4 functionals (*hetuka sobhana-somanassa*), 1 investigating resultant, 1 'smile-producing' functional (*hasituppāda*), 44 of 1st to 4th jhānas (11x4=44 excluded 5th jhānas). (4+4+4+4+1+1+44=62)
Cittas associated with happiness (*sukha*) as pleasant feeling			1							**1**	1 body-consciousness resultant, accompanied by happiness. The 63 cittas have 46 cetasikas.
Cittas associated with displeasure (*domanassa*) as unpleasant feeling		2								**2**	2 *kāma sahetuka-akusala* hatred-rooted (*dosamūla*), follows by 21 cetasikas.
Cittas associated with unsatisfactoriness, or pain, suffering (*dukkha*) as unpleasant feeling			1							**1**	1 body-consciousness resultant with unsatisfactoriness (or pain,suffering), follows by 21 cetasikas.
Cittas associated with equanimity (*upekkhā*) as neither pleasant nor unpleasant feeling	4	6	16	6					23	**55**	4 kāma kusalas, 6 kāma akusalas (4 *lobhamūla*, 2 *mohamūla*), 16 resultants (10 kusalas,6 akussla), 6 functionals (2 rootless, 4 beautiful), 23 Fifth-jhānas (3 of rūpavacara, 12 of rūpavacara, 8 of lokuttara). Total 55 cittas are accompanied by 46 cetasikas.
									Total:	**121**	

Note:

i. cittas accompanied by joy are treated as 63 types as joy (*somanassa*) and pleasure/ happiness (*sukha*) are taken together as a group. (62+1=63).
ii. cittas accompanied by pain are treated as 3 types as displeasure (*domanassa*) and suffering (*dukkha*) are grouped as one. (2+1=3).

Appendix III: Summarised tables of the 89 or 121 cittas

	Active States		Indeterminate States		
	Wholesome States	Unwholesome States	Resultant States	Functional States	
Sensuous Sphere	**8**	**12**	**23**	**11**	**54**
Fine-Material Sphere	**5**		**5**	**5**	**15**
Immaterial Sphere	**4**		**4**	**4**	**12**
	(17)	*(12)*	*(32)*	*(20)*	
Supramundane Sphere	**4**		**4**		**8**
Total:	**21**	**12**	**36**	**20**	**89**

Note: the 81 *Lokiyacittāni* of the three mundane spheres (54+15+12 =81) are 'mundane states'; the 27 *Mahaggatacittāni* of the fine-material and immaterial sphere (15+12=27) are the 'sublime states'.

		Uyyutta		*Abyākata*		
		kusala	*akusala*	*vipāka*	*kiriyā*	
Kāmāvacara	sahetuka sobhana-kusala	8				**54**
	sahetuka *lobhamūla*		8			
	sahetuka *dosamūla*		2			
	sahetuka *mohamūla*		2			
	ahetuka-kusala			8		
	ahetuka-akusala			7		
	sahetuka-sobhana-kusala			8		
	ahetuka				3	
	sahetuka-sobhana				8	
Rūpāvacara	First-jhāna	1		1	1	**15**
	Second-jhāna	1		1	1	
	Third-jhāna	1		1	1	
	Fourth-jhāna	1		1	1	
	Fifth-jhāna	1		1	1	
Arūpāvacara	Ākāsānañca āyatana	1		1	1	**12**
	Viññāṇañca āyatana	1		1	1	
	Ākiñcañña āyatana	1		1	1	
	Nevasaññā-nāsaññā āyatana	1		1	1	
Lokuttara		4 x 5		4 x 5		**40**
Total:		**37**	**12**	**52**	**20**	**121**

Appendix IV: 52 Mental Factors (*Cetasikā*)

THE 52 MENTAL FACTORS (*CETASIKĀ*)	
COMMON NON-BEAUTIFUL FACTORS - 13 (*asobhaṇa sādhāraṇā*) **Universals -7 (*Aññasamāna*)** Contact (*phassa*) Feeling (*vedanā*) Perception (*sañña*) Volition/ Intentive thought (*cetanā*) One-pointedness (*ekaggatā*) Vitality-faculty (*jīvitindriya*) Attention (*manasikāra*) **Occasionals (*Pakiṇṇakā*) - 6** Initial application (*vitakka*) Sustained application (*vicāra*) Decision (*adhimokkha*) Energy/ Effort (*viriya*) Zest (*pīti*) Desire (*chanda*) UNWHOLESOME FACTORS-14 (*Akusala*) **Unwholesome Universals - 4** **(*Akusalasādhāraṇā*)** Delusion (*moha*) Shamelessness (*ahirīka*) Unconscientiousnes (*anottappa*) Restlessness (*uddhacca*) **Unwholesome Occasionals - 10** **(*Akusalapakiṇṇakā*)** Greed (*lobha*) Wrong view (*diṭṭhi*) Conceit (*māna*) Hatred (*dosa*) Envy (*Issā*) Avarice (*macchariya*) Worry/Brooding (*kukkucca*) Sloth (*thīna*) Torpor (*middha*) Doubt (*vicikicchā*)	BEAUTIFUL FACTORS - 25 (*sobhaṇa*) **Beautiful Universals - 19** **(*Sobhanāññasamāna*)** Faith (*saddhā*) Mindfulness (*sati*) Discreet shamefulness (*hirī*) Guilt-conscience (*ottappa*) Non-greed (*alobha*) Non-hatred (*adosa*) Neutrality of mind (*tatramajjhattatā*) Calmness of mental body (*kāyapassaddhi*) Calmness of consciousness (*cittapassaddhi*) Lightness of mental body (*kāyalahutā*) Lightness of consciousness (*cittalahutā*) Malleability of mental body (*kāyamudutā*) Malleability of consciousness (*cittamudutā*) Wieldiness of mental body (*kāyakammaññatā*) Wieldiness of consciousness (*cittakammaññatā*) Proficiency of mental body (*kāyapāguññatā*) Proficiency of consciousness (*cittapāguññatā*) Rectitude of mental body (*kāyujjukatā*) Rectitude of consciousness (*cittujjukatā*) **Abstinences (*Virati*) - 3** Right speech (*vaciduccarita virati*) Right action (*kāyaduccarita virati*) Right livelihood (*ājīvaduccarita virati*) **Illimitables (*Appamaññā*) - 2** Compassion (*karuṇā*) Altruistic or Appreciative joy (*muditā*) **Non-Delusion (*Amoha*) - 1** Wisdom faculty (*paññindriya*)

References

[CTS4] Chaṭṭha Saṅgāyana Tipiṭaka 4

[Dhā] Dhātukathā

[Dhs] Dhammasaṅgaṇi

[Pug] Puggalapaññatti

[YamA] Yamaka-Aṭṭhakathā from Pañcappakaraṇa-Aṭṭhakathā

[Vibh] Vibhaṅga

A.P. Buddhadatta Mahāthera. *Concise Pāli-English Dictionary*. Delhi: Motilal Banarsidass, 1997.

Nyanatiloka Mahāthera, Nyanaponika Thera (ed.). *Buddhist Dictionary: Manual of Buddhist Terms and Doctrines*. Kandy: BPS, 1980.

Nyanatiloka Mahāthera. *Guide Through The Abhidhamma Pitaka: A Synopsis of the Philosophical Collection of the Theravada Buddhist Canon*. Sri Lanka: BPS, 1938.

R.C. Childers. *A Dictionary of Pali Language*. London: Trübner & Co, 1875.

T. W. Rhys Davids and William Stede, eds. *The Pali-English Dictionary*. Oxford: PTS, 1921-1925.

Bhikkhu, Isi Nandamedhā and U Kumārābhivaṁsa Sayadaw. *The Book on Pairs* (*Yamaka*), Volume II. < http://www.abhidhamma.com/>.

About The Author

P.B. Tan (隨藏) has written an analytical series of the first four books of the Theravāda Abhidhamma canon. He received his M.A. degree in Buddhist Philosophy in 2015 from the International Buddhist College (IBC) in Thailand. The author currently lives in Kuching, his birthplace, where he continues with his research into other Abhidhamma literatures. Below are his publications.

An Anatomy of Mind. Being Essence of the Dhammasangani in Abhidhamma. (2015)

Essential Teaching of the Dhammasangani from Abhidhamma. (2017)

An Analysis of Mind from the Vibhanga in Abhidhamma.
(First Edition, Sept. 2016)
(Second Edition, Feb. 2017)

An Analysis of Individual-Types from the Abhidhamma (*Puggalapaññatti*). (2016)

A Perfect Knowledge of Mind-Body from the Abhidhamma (Dhātukathā). (March 2017)

An Analytical Study of the Yamaka from Abhidhamma, Volume I
(Third Edition, July. 2018)

Indexes of English Words

Indexes of Pāli Words

Made in United States
Orlando, FL
01 May 2025

60888949R00243